EDITION
6

Research Methods
FOR THE Behavioral Sciences

© Nathan Jasowiak / Shutterstock

FREDERICK J GRAVETTER
The College at Brockport, State University of New York

LORI-ANN B. FORZANO
The College at Brockport, State University of New York

CENGAGE

Australia • Brazil • Mexico • Singapore • United Kingdom • United States

Research Methods for the Behavioral Sciences, **Sixth Edition**
Frederick J. Gravetter and Lori-Ann B. Forzano

Product Director: Marta Lee-Perriard

Product Manager: Andrew Ginsberg

Project Manager: Jennifer Ziegler

Content Developer: Tangelique Williams-Grayer

Product Assistant: Leah Jenson

Marketing Manager: Heather Thompson

Production Management, and Composition: Lumina Datamatics, Inc.

Manufacturing Planner: Karen Hunt

Senior Art Director: Vernon Boes

Cover Image: clivewa / Shutterstock.com

Intellectual Property
  Analyst: Deanna Ettinger
  Project Manager: Betsy Hathaway

For product information and technology assistance, contact us at **Cengage Customer & Sales Support, 1-800-354-9706.**

For permission to use material from this text or product, submit all requests online at **www.cengage.com/permissions.** Further permissions questions can be e-mailed to **permissionrequest@cengage.com.**

Library of Congress Control Number: 2017950596

Student Edition: ISBN: 978-1-337-61331-6
Loose-leaf Edition: ISBN: 978-1-337-61955-4

Cengage
20 Channel Center Street
Boston, MA 02210
USA

Cengage is a leading provider of customized learning solutions with employees residing in nearly 40 different countries and sales in more than 125 countries around the world. Find your local representative at **www.cengage.com.**

Cengage products are represented in Canada by Nelson Education, Ltd.

To learn more about Cengage platforms and services, register or access your online learning solution, or purchase materials for your course, visit **www.cengage.com.**

Printed in Mexico
Print Number: 03   Print Year: 2018

BRIEF CONTENTS

CONTENTS

Preface xvii

About the Authors xxv

CHAPTER 1
Introduction, Acquiring Knowledge, and the Scientific Method

1

CHAPTER 2
Research Ideas and Hypotheses

29

v

CHAPTER 3 **Defining and Measuring Variables**   51

CHAPTER 4   **Ethics in Research**   **81**

CHAPTER 5   **Selecting Research Participants**   **109**

CHAPTER 6   **Research Strategies and Validity**   127

CHAPTER 7   **The Experimental Research Strategy**   **157**

CHAPTER 8 Experimental Designs: Between-Subjects Design 185

CHAPTER 9 Experimental Designs: Within-Subjects Design 211

CHAPTER 10 **The Nonexperimental and Quasi-Experimental Strategies: Nonequivalent Group, Pre–Post, and Developmental Designs**   237

CHAPTER 11 **Factorial Designs**

CHAPTER 12 **The Correlational Research Strategy**   295

CHAPTER 13 **The Descriptive Research Strategy**   313

CHAPTER 14 **Single-Case Experimental Research Designs**   341

CHAPTER 15 **Statistical Evaluation of Data**   373

For years, we have watched students come into the psychology research methods course with a fundamental fear of science. Somewhere, these students seem to have developed the idea that psychology is interesting and fun, but science is tedious and difficult. Many students even resent the fact that they have to take a research methods course: "After all, I want to be a psychologist, not a scientist."

As the semester progresses, however, most of these students begin to lose their fears, and many of them actually begin to enjoy the course. Much of this change in attitude is based on a realization that science is simply the technique that psychologists use to gather information and to answer questions. As long as the questions are interesting, then the task of answering them should also be interesting.

When people watch a magician do an amazing trick, the common response is to ask, "How was that done?" In the same way, when you learn something interesting about human behavior, you ought to ask, "How do they know that?" The answer is that most of the existing knowledge in the behavioral sciences was gathered using scientific research methods. If you are really curious about human behavior, then you should also be curious about the process of studying human behavior.

This textbook is developed from years of teaching research methods. During that time, we tried various examples or explanations in the classroom and observed student response. Over the years, the course evolved into a less intimidating and more interesting approach that is highly effective in getting students interested in research. Our students have been very helpful in this evolutionary process. Their feedback has directed our progress through the development of the research methods course and the writing of this book. In many respects, they have been our teachers.

Overview of Text

Research Methods for the Behavioral Sciences, sixth edition, is intended for an undergraduate Research Methods course in psychology or any of the behavioral sciences. The overall learning objectives of this book include the following:

1. Describe the scientific method and research process
2. Use research databases to locate and obtain psychology articles relevant to a research topic of interest
3. Analyze and evaluate published research
4. Develop an original research question and hypothesis
5. Define measurement validity and reliability, as well as internal and external validity, and identify the various threats to validity
6. Identify ethical issues pertaining to research in psychology
7. Compare and contrast the various research strategies and designs
8. Identify the descriptive and inferential statistical analyses utilized to interpret and evaluate research
9. Compose an APA-style research report or proposal
10. Critically evaluate secondary sources of scientific information

We have organized the text according to the research process, making it appropriate for use in a lecture-only class or a class with a lab component. The text discusses in detail both experimental and nonexperimental research strategies. We use a rather informal writing style that emphasizes discussion and explanation of topics. For each chapter, pedagogical aids include chapter learning objectives, chapter overview, a list of chapter sections, learning objectives at the beginning of each section, Learning Check questions at the end of each section, a running glossary, a chapter summary and a list of Key Words, and a set of end-of-chapter exercises that are identified by learning objectives.

Organization of Text

Overall, the book is organized around the framework of the research process—from start to finish. This step-by-step approach emphasizes the decisions researchers must make at each stage of the process. The chapters of the text have been organized into five sections. Chapters 1 and 2 focus on the earliest considerations in the research process, presenting an overview of the scientific method and including tips for finding a new idea for research and developing a research hypothesis. Chapters 3–6 focus on the preliminary decisions in the research process, and include information on how to measure variables, maintaining ethical responsibility throughout the research process, selecting participants, and choosing a valid research strategy. Chapters 7–9 introduce the experimental research strategy and provide the details of between-subjects and within-subjects experimental designs. Chapters 10–14 present other (nonexperimental) research strategies and their associated research designs, and single-case experimental designs. Chapters 15 and 16 focus on the ending decisions in the research process and include information on how to evaluate, interpret, and communicate the results of the research process.

Although the chapters are organized in a series that we view as appropriate for a one-semester research methods course, the order of chapters can be varied to meet the requirements of different course instructors. For example, the chapters on statistics and APA style can easily be presented much earlier in the course.

Writing Style

We have attempted to use a rather informal, conversational style of writing that emphasizes discussion and explanation of topics rather than a simple "cookbook" presentation of facts. We have found this style to be very successful in our own classes and in our other coauthored textbooks, *Essentials of Statistics for the Behavioral Sciences Statistics for the Behavioral Sciences*. Students find this style very readable and unintimidating. This style is particularly useful for material that students perceive as being difficult, including the topic of this text, research methodology.

Pedagogical Aids

One item that has received particular attention as we developed this text is the use of a variety of pedagogical aids. Each chapter includes many opportunities for students to interact with the material, rather than simply be passively exposed to the material. In addition, the Learning Checks, and end-of-chapter exercises may be used by the instructor as prepackaged assignments.

Each chapter contains the following pedagogical elements:

1. *Chapter Learning Objectives:* Each chapter starts with a complete list of learning objectives to assist students in recognizing what they should be able to do by the end of the whole chapter.

2. *Chapter Overview:* Each chapter starts with a brief summary of the contents of the chapter, often in the context of an engaging research example, to prepare and alert students to the material to come.

3. *Chapter Outline:* To help students see the organization of the material in the chapter, a list of the section titles is presented at the beginning of each chapter.

4. *Multiple Sections:* Each chapter is divided into multiple sections and subsections that are clearly defined with headings to help break the material down into smaller, more manageable chunks.

5. *Learning Objectives:* At the beginning of each section, learning objectives are identified to assist students in recognizing what they should be able to do by the end of that section.

6. *Definitions:* Each Key Word used in the text is first bolded. At the end of the paragraph that contains a new Key Word, a clearly identified, concise definition is provided.

7. *Examples:* Numerous examples are used to illustrate concepts presented in the text. Some examples are hypothetical, but most are selected from interesting current or classic studies in psychology.

8. *Boxes:* Boxed material, separate from the regular text, is used to offer additional, interesting information to help demonstrate a point.

9. *Figures:* When appropriate, diagrams or graphs are included to illustrate a point made in the text.

10. *Tables:* Occasionally, tables are used to present information that may best be communicated in a list or to summarize material.

11. *Margin Notes:* Where appropriate, brief notes are presented in the text margins. These notes are used to offer reminders or cautions to the students.

12. *Learning Checks:* At the end of major sections within each chapter, we provide a set of multiple-choice questions to help students test how well they have learned the material in each section. Each Learning Check contains at least one question corresponding to each of the learning objectives for that section. Answers are provided.

13. *Chapter Summaries:* At the end of each chapter, a general summary is presented to help students review the main points of the chapter.

14. *Key Words:* At the end of each chapter, a list of the Key Words used in the chapter is presented. We list the Key Words in their order of appearance in the chapter so that related terms are grouped together and so that students can spot parts of the chapter that they may need to review.

15. *Exercises:* At the end of each chapter are questions and activities for students to answer and apply. Each exercise is identified with a specific learning objective. The intent of the exercises is to help students assess how well they have mastered the objectives by having them apply what they have learned. Additionally, the instructor can use the exercises as assignments. Exercise 1 identifies other important terms that are defined in the Glossary.

New to This Edition

Previous edition users should know that we have tried to maintain the hallmark features of our textbook: the organization of the chapters and topics (around the research process), the tone of text (student-friendly, conversational), and the variety of pedagogical aids (chapter overviews, Learning Objects per section, multiple-choice Learning Checks (for each Learning Objective) per section, end-of-chapter exercises linked to Learning Objectives, bold terms, definitions, interesting research examples, end-of-chapter summaries, keyword lists, etc.).

Changes Throughout the Book

As with each new edition, we continue to strive to edit each edition to enhance the clarity of material—making changes to wording, organization, trying to be as clear as possible for students to understand.

To reduce some redundancy between the previous edition's Chapter Previews and Chapter Overviews, these sections have now been combined into the Chapter Overview. The emphasis is on piquing students' interest, often by discussing an interesting research example, and putting them in the "mind-set" for the material to come in the chapter.

Throughout the book, research examples have been updated, not only to clearly illustrate concepts but also always with an eye toward selecting examples that are of particular interest and relevance to college students.

End-of-chapter Exercises and Engagement Activities have been combined into one Exercises section.

Almost all end-of-section Learning Checks and end-of-chapter exercises have been revised or replaced, always with a minimum of one question per learning objective.

To be more socially inclusionary, we have removed and replaced most bivariate gender examples.

This *Research Methods* book has been modified to have the same "look and feel" as our *Essentials of Statistics* book, enabling a more seamless transition between from statistics to research methods courses.

Additional Chapter-by-Chapter Revisions

Chapter 1. Deleted Box 1 to reduce size of the chapter. Greatly streamlined the section on the Rational Method. In Step 1 of the research process, more clearly distinguished between a general topic and a specific research idea.

Chapter 2. As in Chapter 1, we increased the distinction between identifying a *general topic*/idea and *finding* a specific research idea/question. Also, like newly done in Chapter 1, distinguishing between hypothesis and predictions and how steps 3 & 4 (Making the study) are needed for the prediction. Sections 2.1 and 2.2 have been reorganized and rewritten to distinguish between part 1, topic, and 2, reviewing literature for idea, by reframed the *necessity* of reviewing the literature—including a new analogy of "joining the research conversation." A new research example and figure help students to think critically about the primary, empirical journal articles they are reading (with the help of critical thinking column of table also), so that they can extend research and create new research ideas.

Chapter 3. Clarified the concept of an operational definition and its limitations. Simplified the discussion of observer error as a component of measurement. Clarified the distinctions between the different scales of measurement.

Chapter 4. Expanded the description of the three basic principles of the Belmont Report, including examples of violations of each from unethical research, and notes about parallels of these principles with the APA Ethics Code. The sections on ethical guidelines for research with humans and nonhumans were updated in accordance with the APA current 2010 with new 2017 APA ethical standards amendments (section 3.04). Citations and website locations for all updated guidelines throughout the chapter are now included. Added recent, interesting fraud example of Diederick Stapel (with over 30 published papers found to be fraudulent). Added additional safeguard to protect from fraud, that is, APA Ethics Code requirement of sharing of data, and journals and funding agencies requirement of open access to data.

Chapter 5. Clarified the discussion of simple random sampling and the distinction between sampling with and without replacement.

Chapter 6. We better aligned the three data structures (used to organize the research strategies), with parallel material presented in Chapter 15, Section 4. The term "assignment bias," which is not commonly indexed, was removed. Instead clarified discussion of participant variables as personal characteristics that differ from one individual to another, and that individual differences are part of any study. Further clarified that if there are consistent differences between groups, on one or more participant variables, then a between-subjects design is confounded by individual differences.

Chapter 7. Updated terminology from *control group* to *control condition*. Simplified and shortened the discussion of simulation and field studies.

Chapter 8. Consistently with revisions made to Chapter 6, removed the term "assignment bias" and instead discussed confounding by individual differences between groups.

Chapter 9. A new introductory section clarifies the distinction between two types of within-subjects experiments: those in which the treatments are administered sequentially over time and those in which the treatments are mixed together in one experimental session.

Chapter 10. Again, more consistent with phrasing for participant variable and individual differences (again, removing reference to assignment bias).

Chapter 11. The same research example was used repeatedly throughout the chapter to illustrate different concepts instead of introducing new examples each time. The concept of a dependent versus an independent relationship between factors was simplified in the discussion of interactions.

Chapter 12. Minor editing for clarity.

Chapter 13. Revised discussion of case studies to emphasize their strength as a means of introducing new therapies or applications rather than serving as negative counterexamples.

Chapter 14. The chapter has been retitled, *Single-Case Experimental Research Designs,* "single-case" more commonly being used by leaders in the field than "single-subject" (Barlow, Nock, & Hersen, 2009; Kazdin, 2016). Also clarified that this chapter is focused on single-case *experimental* designs. Replaced overview research example with an ABAB design, because that is the design discussed first in the chapter. We also reframed the ABAB design as an example of a reversal design. To reduce the complexity and length of chapter, Section 14.5, on less commonly used designs, has been removed with component analysis relocated with multiple baseline designs. Many new single-case experimental designs have been added throughout the chapter.

Chapter 15. Minor editing for clarity.

Chapter 16. Minor editing for clarity. New updated references in Table 16.2.

MINDTAP For Gravetter and Forzano's Research Methods for the Behavioral Sciences

MindTap for Research Methods for the Behavioral Sciences, sixth edition, engages and empowers students to produce their best work—consistently. By seamlessly integrating course material with videos, activities, apps, and much more, MindTap creates a unique learning path that fosters increased comprehension and efficiency.

For students:

- MindTap delivers real-world relevance with activities and assignments that help students build critical thinking and analytic skills that will transfer to other courses and their professional lives.

- MindTap helps students stay organized and efficient with a single destination that reflects what's important to the instructor, along with the tools students need to master the content.
- MindTap empowers and motivates students with information that shows where they stand at all times—both individually and compared to the highest performers in class.

Additionally, for instructors, MindTap allows you to:

- Control what content students see and when they see it with a learning path that can be used as-is or matched to your syllabus exactly.
- Create a unique learning path of relevant readings and multimedia and activities that move students up the learning taxonomy from basic knowledge and comprehension to analysis, application, and critical thinking.
- Integrate your own content into the MindTap Reader using your own documents or pulling from sources such as RSS feeds, YouTube videos, websites, Googledocs, and more.
- Use powerful analytics and reports that provide a snapshot of class progress, time in course, engagement, and completion.
- In addition to the benefits of the platform, MindTap for Research Methods for the Behavioral Sciences:
  - Includes Research Tutor, a project management tool that helps students stay on task with the research proposal assignment that is often included in the behavioral sciences research methods course. Research Tutor breaks the process down into 10 assignable modules that help manage timelines and turn research ideas into well-constructed research proposals, research papers, or presentations. It's the only interactive tool that helps students evaluate and choose an appropriate topic early in the course and stay on task as they move through their study.

Supplements

For instructors, we offer the following supplements—all available online.

- **Cognero.** Cengage Learning Testing Powered by Cognero is a flexible, online system that allows you to author, edit, and manage test bank content from multiple Cengage Learning solutions, create multiple test versions in an instant, and deliver tests from your LMS, your classroom, or wherever you want.
- **Instructor's Manual.** The Online Instructor's Manual contains helpful information including chapter outlines, learning objectives, lecture outlines with discussion points, keywords, annotated learning objectives, lecture ideas, Internet resources, and annotations for the end-of-chapter exercises.
- **PowerPoint.** The Online PowerPoints feature lecture outlines and important visuals from the text.

Acknowledgments

We appreciate the careful reading and thoughtful suggestions provided by the reviewers of this text:

Karen Y. Holmes   Norfolk State University
Carlos Escoto   Eastern Connecticut University
Maria L. Pacella   Kent State University

Stacy J. Bacigalupi	Mt. San Antonio College
Amber Chenoweth	Hiram College
Dr. Chrysalis L. Wright	University of Central Florida
Erin C. Dupuis	Loyola University
Anna Ingeborg Petursdottir	Texas Christian University
Lesley Hathorn	Metropolitan State University—Denver
Terry F. Pettijohn	Ohio State University—Marion
Charlotte Tate	San Francisco State University
Kyle Smith	Ohio Wesleyan University
Patrick K. Cullen	Kent State University
Veanne N. Anderson	Indiana State University
Robert R. Bubb	Auburn University
Chaelon Myme	Thiel College

We appreciate the hard work provided by the staff at Cengage Learning in the production of this text:

Star M. Burruto, Product Team Manager

Andrew Ginsberg, Product Manager

Jasmin Tokatlian and Tangelique Williams Grayer, Content Developers

Leah Jenson, Product Assistant

Heather Thompson, Marketing Manager

Jennifer Ziegler, Content Project Manager

Vernon Boes, Senior Art Director

Karen Hunt, Manufacturing Planner

Deanna Ettinger, IP Analyst

Betsy Hathaway, Senior IP Project Manager

Sharib Asrar, Production Service/Project Manager (Lumina)

Gary Hespenheide, Text and Cover Designer

Finally, our most heartfelt thanks go out to our spouses and children: Charlie Forzano, Ryan Forzano, Alex Forzano, Debbie Gravetter, Justin Gravetter, Melissa Monachino, and Megan Baker. This book could not have been written without their unwavering support and patience.

To Contact Us

Over the years, our students have given us many helpful suggestions, and we have benefited from their feedback. If you have any suggestions or comments about this book, you can write to us at the Department of Psychology, The College at Brockport, State University of New York, 350 New Campus Drive, Brockport, NY 14420. We can also be reached by e-mail at:

Lori-Ann B. Forzano
lforzano@brockport.edu

Frederick J Gravetter
fgravett@brockport.edu

ABOUT THE AUTHORS

Courtesy of Frederick J Gravetter

FREDERICK J GRAVETTER is professor emeritus of psychology at The College at Brockport, State University of New York. While teaching at Brockport, Dr. Gravetter specialized in statistics, experimental design, and cognitive psychology. He received his bachelor's degree in mathematics from M.I.T. and his Ph.D. in psychology from Duke University. In addition to publishing this textbook and several research articles, Dr. Gravetter coauthored *Statistics for the Behavioral Sciences* and *Essentials of Statistics for the Behavioral Sciences.*

Courtesy of Lori-Ann B. Forzano

LORI-ANN B. FORZANO is professor of psychology at The College at Brockport, State University of New York, where she regularly teaches undergraduate and graduate courses in research methods, statistics, learning, animal behavior, and the psychology of eating. She earned a Ph.D. in experimental psychology from the State University of New York at Stony Brook, where she also received her B.S. in psychology. Dr. Forzano's research examines impulsivity and self-control in adults and children. Her research has been published in the *Journal of the Experimental Analysis of Behavior, Learning and Motivation,* and *The Psychological Record.* Dr. Forzano has also coauthored Essentials of Statistics for the Behavioral Sciences.

Introduction, Acquiring Knowledge, and the Scientific Method

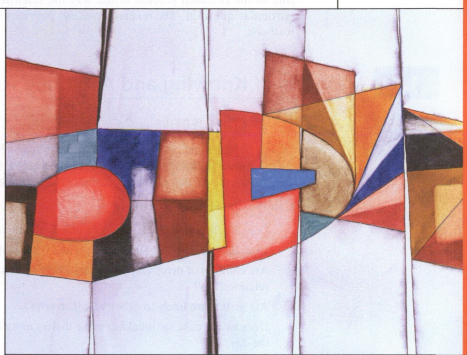

© Nathan Jasowiak / Shutterstock

CHAPTER LEARNING OBJECTIVES

LO1 Compare and contrast the nonscientific methods for knowing or acquiring knowledge (tenacity, intuition, authority, the rational method, and the empirical method). Identify an example and explain the limitations of each method.

LO2 Identify and describe the steps of the scientific method.

LO3 Define *induction* and *deduction* and explain the role of each in the scientific method.

LO4 Distinguish between a hypothesis and a prediction.

LO5 Explain what it means to say that the scientific method is empirical, public, and objective.

LO6 Distinguish between science and pseudoscience.

LO7 Distinguish between qualitative and quantitative research and recognize examples of each.

LO8 Identify and describe the steps in the research process.

CHAPTER OVERVIEW

In this chapter, we introduce the topic of this textbook: research methodology. Research methods are intended to provide scientists with effective procedures for gathering information and answering questions. We begin by discussing the many ways of acquiring knowledge or finding answers to questions, including the scientific method. Next, we provide a thorough discussion of the scientific method. The chapter ends with an outline of the research process or the way the scientific method is applied to answer a particular question. The research process provides the framework for the rest of the textbook.

1.1　Methods of Knowing and Acquiring Knowledge

LEARNING OBJECTIVE

LO1　Compare and contrast the nonscientific methods for knowing or acquiring knowledge (tenacity, intuition, authority, the rational method, and the empirical method). Identify an example and explain the limitations of each method.

Consider the following questions.

Does multitasking make you more efficient with your time?

Does having more friends make you less vulnerable to depression?

Are children of divorced parents less likely to be satisfied with their romantic relationships?

Are girls more likely to cyberbully than boys?

Does eating cake for breakfast make dieters more likely to stick to their diets later in the day?

Are adolescents who play violent video games more aggressive than adolescents who do not play violent video games?

Does playing brain games in adulthood make it less likely you will develop Alzheimer's?

If you find these questions interesting, then you may also be interested in learning how to find the answers. Although there are many different ways to find answers to questions like these, in this book we focus on the method used by behavioral scientists: the scientific method. The scientific method is considered basic, standard practice in the world of science. Students in the behavioral sciences (e.g., psychology, sociology, or criminal justice) should understand how this process works and have some appreciation of its strengths and weaknesses. Before we begin, however, you should realize that the methods used in scientific research are not the only ones available for answering questions, and they are not necessarily the most efficient. There are many different ways of knowing or finding answers to questions. In general, the different ways that people know, or the methods that people use to discover answers, are referred to as **methods of acquiring knowledge**.

Terms printed in boldface are defined in the glossary. Some terms, identified as key words, are also defined in the text.

DEFINITION　**Methods of acquiring knowledge** are ways in which a person can know things or discover answers to questions.

The rest of this chapter examines several established methods of knowing and acquiring knowledge. We begin with five nonscientific approaches: the method of tenacity, the method of intuition, the method of authority, the rational method, and the method of empiricism. We conclude with a more detailed discussion of the scientific method. As you will see, the scientific method combines elements from each of the other methods to produce a general question-answering technique that avoids some of the limitations or pitfalls of other methods. Although the scientific method tends to be more complicated and more time consuming than the other methods, the goal is to obtain better-quality answers or at least a higher level of confidence in the answers. Finally, we warn that the scientific method outlines a general strategy for answering questions; the specific details of applying the scientific method to particular problems form the content of the remainder of the book.

The Method of Tenacity

The **method of tenacity** involves holding on to ideas and beliefs simply because they have been accepted as facts for a long time or because of superstition. Therefore, the method of tenacity is based on habit or superstition. Habit leads us to continue believing something we have always believed. Often this is referred to as belief perseverance. For example, you've probably heard the clichés, "You cannot teach an old dog new tricks" and "Opposites attract." These statements have been presented over and over again, and they have been accepted as true. In general, the more frequently we are exposed to statements, the more we tend to believe them. Advertisers successfully use the method of tenacity, repeating their slogans over and over, hoping consumers will accept them as true (and subsequently buy their products). A very catchy fast-food jingle exclaiming, "I'm lovin' it" hopes we do just that and buy more burgers from them.

DEFINITION

> In the **method of tenacity**, information is accepted as true because it has always been believed or because superstition supports it.

The method of tenacity also involves the persistence of superstitions, which represent beliefs reacted to as fact. For example, everyone "knows" that breaking a mirror will result in 7 years of bad luck and that you should never walk under a ladder or let a black cat cross your path. Many sports figures will only play a game when wearing their lucky socks or jersey, and many students will not take an exam without their lucky pencil or hat. One problem with the method of tenacity is that the information acquired might not be accurate. With regard to the statement about old dogs not being able to learn new tricks, the elderly can and do learn (O'Hara, Brooks, Friedman, Schroder, Morgan, & Kraemer, 2007). With regard to the statement that opposites attract, research shows that people are attracted to people who are like them (Klohnen & Luo, 2003). Another pitfall of the method of tenacity is that there is no method for correcting erroneous ideas. Even in the face of evidence to the contrary, a belief that is widely accepted can be very difficult to change.

The Method of Intuition

In the **method of intuition**, information is accepted as true because it "feels right." With intuition, a person relies on hunches and "instinct" to answer questions. Whenever we say we know something because we have a "gut feeling" about it, we are using the method of intuition. For many questions, this method is the quickest way to obtain answers. When we have no information at all and cannot refer to supporting data or use rational justification, we often resort to intuition. For example, intuition provides answers when we are making personal choices such as: What should I have for dinner? Should I go out tonight or stay in? The ultimate decision is often determined by what I "feel like" doing. Many ethical decisions or moral questions are resolved by the method of intuition. For example, we know that it is wrong to do something because it does not "feel" right. Parents often advise their children to "trust your instincts." Part of intuition is probably based on the subtle cues that we pick up from the people around us. Although we can't explain exactly how we know that a friend is having a bad day, something about the way she moves or speaks tells us that it is true. The predictions and descriptions given by psychics are thought to be intuitive. The problem with the method of intuition is that it has no mechanism for separating accurate from inaccurate knowledge.

> **DEFINITION**
>
> In the **method of intuition**, information is accepted on the basis of a hunch or "gut feeling."

The Method of Authority

In the **method of authority**, a person finds answers by seeking out an authority on the subject. This can mean consulting an expert directly or going to a library or a website to read the works of an expert. In either case, you are relying on the assumed expertise of another person. Whenever you "google it" or consult books, people, television, or the Internet to find answers, you use the method of authority. Some examples of experts are physicians, scientists, psychologists, professors, stockbrokers, and lawyers.

> **DEFINITION**
>
> In the **method of authority**, a person relies on information or answers from an expert in the subject area.

For many questions, the method of authority is an excellent starting point; often, it is the quickest and easiest way to obtain answers. Much of your formal education is based on the notion that answers can be obtained from experts (teachers and textbooks). However, the method of authority has some pitfalls. It does not always provide accurate information. For example, authorities can be biased. We have all seen examples of conflicting testimony by "expert witnesses" in criminal trials. Sources are often biased in favor of a particular point of view or orientation. For example, Democrats and Republicans often have very different answers to the same questions.

Another limitation of the method of authority is that the answers obtained from an expert could represent subjective, personal opinion rather than true expert knowledge. For example, one "expert" reviewer gives a movie a rating of "thumbs up," whereas another expert gives the same movie "thumbs down."

An additional limitation of this method is that we often assume that expertise in one area can be generalized to other topics. For example, advertisers often use the endorsements of well-known personalities to sell their products. When a famous athlete appears on television telling you what soup is more nutritious, should you assume that being an outstanding football player makes him an expert on nutrition? The advertisers would like you to accept his recommendation on authority. Similarly, when Linus Pauling, a chemist who won the Nobel Prize for his work on the chemical bond, claimed that vitamin C could cure the common cold, many people accepted his word on authority. His claim is still widely believed, even though numerous scientific studies have failed to find such an effect.

Another pitfall of the method of authority is that people often accept an expert's statement without question. This acceptance can mean that people do not check the accuracy of their sources or even consider looking for a second opinion. As a result, false information is sometimes taken as truth. In some situations, the authority is accepted without question because the information appears to make sense, so there is no obvious reason to question it. We would all like to believe it when the doctor says, "That mole doesn't look cancerous," but you might be better protected by getting a second opinion.

People sometimes accept the word of an authority because they have complete trust in the authority figure. In this situation, the method of authority is often called the **method of faith** because people accept on faith any information that is given. For instance, young children tend to have absolute faith in the answers they get from their parents. Another example of faith exists within religions. A religion typically has a sacred text and/or individuals (pastors, imams, priests, and rabbis) who present answers that are considered the final word. The problem with the method of faith is that it allows no mechanism to test the accuracy of the information. The method of faith involves accepting another's view of the truth without verification.

DEFINITION

> The **method of faith** is a variant of the method of authority in which people have unquestioning trust in the authority figure and, therefore, accept information from the authority without doubt or challenge.

As a final pitfall of the method of authority, realize that not all "experts" are experts. There are a lot of supposed "experts" out there. Turn on the television to any daytime talk show. During the first 45 minutes of the show, in front of millions of viewers, people haggle with one another: Women complain about their husbands, estranged parents and teenagers reunite, or two women fight over the same boyfriend. Then, in the final 15 minutes, the "expert" comes out to discuss the situations and everyone's feelings. These "experts" are often people who lack the credentials, the experience, or the training to make the claims they are making. Being called an expert does not make someone an expert.

In conclusion, we should point out that there are ways to increase confidence in the information you obtain by the method of authority. First, you can evaluate the source of the information. Is the authority really an expert, and is the information really within the authority's area of expertise? Also, is the information an objective fact, or is it simply a subjective opinion? Second, you can evaluate the information itself. Does the information seem reasonable? Does it agree with other information that you already know? If you have any reason to doubt the information obtained from an authority, the best move is to get a second opinion. If two independent authorities provide the same answer, you can be more confident that the answer is correct. For example, when you obtain information from an Internet site, you should be cautious about accepting the information at face value. Do you have previous experience with the site? Is it known to be reputable? If there is any doubt, it pays to check to see that other sites are providing the same information.

The methods of tenacity, intuition, and authority are satisfactory for answering some questions, especially if you need an answer quickly and there are no serious consequences for accepting a wrong answer. For example, these techniques are usually fine for answering questions about which shoes to wear or what vegetable to have with dinner. However, it should be clear that there are situations for which these uncritical techniques are not going to be sufficient. In particular, if the question concerns a major financial decision or if the answer could significantly change your life, you should not accept information as true unless it passes some critical test or meets some minimum standard of accuracy. The next two methods of acquiring knowledge (and the scientific method) are designed to place more demands on the information and answers they produce.

The Rational Method

The **rational method**, also known as **rationalism**, involves seeking answers by logical reasoning. We begin with a set of known facts or assumptions and use logic to reach a conclusion or get an answer to a question. Suppose a clinical psychologist wants to know whether a client, Amy, is afraid of dogs. A simple example of reasoning that might be used is as follows:

Having a frightening experience with a dog causes fear of dogs in the future.

Amy has a fear of dogs.

Therefore, Amy had a frightening experience with a dog in her past.

In this **argument**, the first two sentences are **premise statements**. That is, they are facts or assumptions that are known (or assumed) to be true. The final sentence is a logical conclusion based on the premises. If the premise statements are, in fact, true and the logic is sound, then the conclusion is guaranteed to be correct. Thus, the answers obtained by the rational method must satisfy the standards established by the rules of logic before they are accepted as true.

Notice that the rational method begins after the premise statements have been presented. In the previous argument, for example, we are not trying to determine whether being frightened by a dog causes fear of dogs; we simply accept this statement as true. Similarly, we are not concerned with proving that Amy is afraid of dogs; we also accept this statement as a fact. Specifically, the rational method does not involve running around making observations and gathering information. Instead, you should think of the rational method as sitting alone, quietly in the dark, mentally manipulating premise statements to determine whether they can be combined to produce a logical conclusion.

DEFINITIONS

> The **rational method**, or **rationalism**, seeks answers by the use of logical reasoning.
>
> In logical reasoning, **premise statements** describe facts or assumptions that are presumed to be true.
>
> An **argument** is a set of premise statements that are logically combined to yield a conclusion.

The preceding example (Amy and the dogs) demonstrates the rational method for answering questions, and it also demonstrates some of the limitations of the rational method. One specific limitation is that the conclusion is not necessarily true unless both of the premise statements are true, even in a valid logical argument. One obvious problem comes from the universal assumption expressed in the first premise statement, "Having a frightening experience with a dog causes fear of dogs in the future." Although this statement might be accurate for many people who have had a bad experience, there is good reason to doubt that it is absolutely true for all people. In general, the truth of any logical conclusion is founded on the truth of the premise statements. If any basic assumption or premise is incorrect, then we cannot have any confidence in the truth of the logical conclusion.

Another limitation of the rational method is that people are not particularly good at logical reasoning. Many people view the argument about Amy and her fear of dogs as an example of sound reasoning. However, it is not a valid argument; specifically, the conclusion is not logically justified by the premise statements. In case you are not convinced that the argument is invalid, consider the following argument, which has exactly the same structure but replaces frightening experiences and fear of dogs with violent contact and concussions:

Violent, head-to-head contact in football games causes concussions.

John has a concussion.

Therefore, John experienced violent, head-to-head contact in a football game.

In this case, it should be clear that the argument is not valid; specifically, the conclusion is not justified by the premise statements. Just because John has a concussion, you cannot conclude that it occurred in a football game. Similarly, you cannot conclude that Amy's fear of dogs was caused by a bad experience with a dog. The simple fact that most people have difficulty judging the validity of a logical argument means they can easily make mistakes using the rational method. Unless the logic is sound, the conclusion might not be correct.

A common application of the rational method occurs when people try to think through a problem before they try out different solutions. Suppose, for example, that you have an exam scheduled, but when you are ready to leave for campus, you discover that your car will not start. One response to this situation is to consider your options logically:

1. You could call American Automobile Association (AAA), but by the time they arrive and fix the car, you probably will have missed the exam.
2. You could take the bus, but you do not have the schedule, so you are not sure if the bus can get you to campus on time.
3. You could ask your neighbor to loan you her car for a few hours.

Notice that instead of actually doing something, you are considering possibilities and consequences to find a logical solution to the problem.

In summary, the rational method is the practice of employing reason as a source of knowledge. Answers obtained using the rational method are not simply accepted as true without verification. Instead, all conclusions are tested by ensuring that they conform to the rules of logic. Because the rational method does not involve directly observing or actively gathering information, it has been said that logic is a way of establishing truth in the absence of evidence. As you will see in Section 1.2, the rational method is a critical component of the scientific method. In the next section, we examine the opposite approach, in which we rely entirely on direct observation to obtain evidence to establish the truth.

The Empirical Method

The empirical method, also known as empiricism, attempts to answer questions by direct observation or personal experience. This method is a product of the empirical viewpoint in philosophy, which holds that all knowledge is acquired through the senses. Note that when we make observations, we use the senses of seeing, hearing, tasting, and so on.

DEFINITION | The **empirical method**, or **empiricism**, uses observation or direct sensory experience to obtain knowledge.

Most of you know, for example, that children tend to be shorter than adults, that it is typically warmer in the summer than in the winter, and that a pound of steak costs more than a pound of hamburger. You know these facts from personal experience and from observations you have made.

Many facts or answers are available simply by observing the world around you: That is, you can use the empirical method. For example, you can check the oil level in your car by simply looking at the dipstick. You could find out the weight of each student in your class just by having each person step on a scale. In many instances, the empirical method provides an easy, direct way to answer questions. However, this method of inquiry also has some limitations.

It is tempting to place great confidence in our own observations. Everyday expressions, such as "I will believe it when I see it with my own eyes," reveal the faith we place in our own experience. However, we cannot necessarily believe everything we see, or hear and feel. Actually, it is fairly common for people to misperceive or misinterpret the world around them. Figure 1.1 illustrates this point with the horizontal-vertical illusion. Most people perceive the vertical line to be longer than the horizontal line. Actually, they are exactly the same length. (You might want to measure them to convince yourself.) This illustration is a classic example of how direct sensory experience can deceive us.

Although direct experience seems to be a simple way to obtain answers, your perceptions can be drastically altered by prior knowledge, expectations, feelings, or beliefs. As a result, two observers can witness exactly the same event and yet "see" two completely different things. For most students, the following example provides a convincing demonstration that sensory experience can be changed by knowledge or beliefs.

Suppose you are presented with two plates of snack food, and you are asked to sample each and then state your preference. One plate contains regular potato chips and the second contains crispy, brown noodles that taste delicious. Based simply on your experience (taste), you have a strong preference for the noodles. Now suppose that you are told that the "noodles" are actually fried worms. Would you still prefer them to the chips? The problem here is that your sensory experience of good taste (the method of empiricism) is in conflict with your long-held beliefs that people do not eat worms (method of tenacity).

It also is possible to make accurate observations but then misinterpret what you see. For years, people watched the day-to-day cycle of the sun rising in the east and setting in the west. These observations led to the obvious conclusion that the sun must travel in a

FIGURE 1.1

The Horizontal-Vertical Illusion

To most people, the vertical line appears to be longer, even though both lines are exactly the same length.

TABLE 1.1

Summary of Nonscientific Methods of Acquiring Knowledge

Method	Way of Knowing or Finding Answer
Tenacity	From habit or superstition
Intuition	From a hunch or feeling
Authority	From an expert
Rationalism	From reasoning; a logical conclusion
Empiricism	From direct sensory observation

huge circle around the earth. Even today, people still speak of the sun "rising" instead of saying that the earth is turning toward the sun.

Finally, the empirical method is usually time consuming and sometimes dangerous. When faced with a problem, for example, you could use the empirical method to try several possible solutions, or you could use the rational method and simply think about each possibility and how it might work. Often, it is faster and easier to think through a problem than to jump in with a trial-and-error approach. Also, it might be safer to use the rational method or the method of authority rather than experience something for yourself. For example, if I wanted to determine whether the mushrooms in my backyard are safe or poisonous, I would rather ask an expert than try the empirical method.

In summary, the empirical method is the practice of employing direct observation as a source of knowledge. In the empirical method, evidence or observations with one's senses are required for verification of information. Note that the observations can be casual and unplanned, such as when you are simply aware of the world around you. At the other end of the continuum, observations can be systematic and purposeful. As you will see in the next section, the planned and systematic application of the empirical method is a critical component of the scientific method.

Summary

As you have seen so far, the scientific method is not the only way to know the answers or find the answers to questions. The methods of tenacity, intuition, authority, rationalism, and empiricism are different ways of acquiring knowledge. Table 1.1 provides a summary of these five methods. We should point out that different people can use different methods to answer the same question and can arrive at different, or sometimes the same, answers. For example, if you wanted to know the weight of one of your classmates, you might have her step on a scale (empirical method), simply ask how much she weighs (method of authority), or compare her physical size to your own and calculate an estimated weight relative to how much you weigh (rational method).

LEARNING CHECK   1. Which method of knowing is being used by a student who believes that his performance on tests is influenced by wearing a lucky hat?

    a. The method of empiricism

    b. The method of faith

    c. The method of tenacity

    d. The method of authority

2. Which method of knowing is used when you find the address and phone number of a restaurant by googling the name of the restaurant?
    a. Method of empiricism
    b. Rational method
    c. Method of authority
    d. Scientific method

3. Last year Tim and his friend Jack were both too short to ride the roller coaster. Jack went to the park this year and was tall enough to ride. Tim knows that he is taller than Jack, so he knows that he will be able to ride the roller coaster as well. Which method of knowing is Tim using?
    a. Method of empiricism
    b. Rational method
    c. Method of authority
    d. Scientific method

4. A restaurant chef tried replacing rice with pasta in one of her recipes to see what would happen. Which method of acquiring knowledge is she using?
    a. Method of empiricism
    b. Rational method
    c. Method of authority
    d. Scientific method

Answers appear at the end of the chapter.

1.2   The Scientific Method

LEARNING OBJECTIVES

LO2   Identify and describe the steps of the scientific method.

LO3   Define *induction* and *deduction* and explain the role of each in the scientific method.

LO4   Distinguish between a hypothesis and a prediction.

LO5   Explain what it means to say that the scientific method is empirical, public, and objective.

LO6   Distinguish between science and pseudoscience.

The **scientific method** is an approach to acquiring knowledge that involves formulating specific questions and then systematically finding answers. The scientific method contains many elements of the methods previously discussed. By combining several different methods of acquiring knowledge, we hope to avoid the pitfalls of any individual method used by itself. The scientific method is a carefully developed system for asking and answering questions so that the answers we discover are as accurate as possible. In the following section, we describe the series of steps that define the scientific method. To help illustrate the steps of the scientific method, we will use a research study investigating the common response of swearing in response to a painful stimulus (Stephens, Atkins, & Kingston, 2009).

The Steps of the Scientific Method

Step 1: Observe Behavior or Other Phenomena

The scientific method often begins with casual or informal observations. Notice that it is not necessary to start with a well-planned, systematic investigation. Instead, simply observe the world around you until some behavior or event catches your attention. For example, the authors of the swearing study observed (themselves or others) swearing in response to pain. Based on their observations, they began to wonder whether swearing has any effect on the experience of pain.

It is also possible that your attention is caught by someone else's observations. For example, you might read a report of someone's research findings (the method of authority), or you might hear others talking about things they have seen or noticed. In any event, the observations catch your attention and begin to raise questions in your mind.

At this stage in the process, people commonly tend to generalize beyond the actual observations. The process of generalization is an almost automatic human response known as **induction**, or **inductive reasoning**. In simple terms, inductive reasoning involves reaching a general conclusion based on a few specific examples. For example, suppose that you taste a green apple and discover that it is sour. A second green apple is also sour and so is the third. Soon, you reach the general conclusion that all green apples are sour. Notice that inductive reasoning reaches far beyond the actual observations. In this example, you tasted only three apples, and yet you reached a conclusion about the millions of other green apples that exist in the world. The researchers in the swearing study probably witnessed only a small number of people swearing but quickly generalized their observations into the conclusion that swearing is a common, almost universal, response to pain.

DEFINITION

> **Induction**, or **inductive reasoning**, involves using a relatively small set of specific observations as the basis for forming a general statement about a larger set of possible observations.

Step 2: Form a Tentative Answer or Explanation (a Hypothesis)

This step in the process usually begins by identifying other factors, or **variables**, that are associated with your observation. For example, what other variables are associated with pain and swearing? The authors of the study began by reviewing other research examining the act of swearing and the experience of pain. (The process of conducting background research is presented in Chapter 2.)

DEFINITION

> **Variables** are characteristics or conditions that change or have different values for different individuals. For example, the weather, the economy, and your state of health can change from day to day. Also, two people can be different in terms of personality, intelligence, age, gender, self-esteem, height, weight, and so on.

The observed relationship between pain and swearing might be related to a variety of other variables. For example, pain can be sharp and temporary like a pinprick or long lasting like holding your hand in ice-cold water, and it can come from different sources (self-inflicted or from outside). Similarly, swearing can depend on the social environment (alone or in a crowded shopping mall) and probably is related to gender and personality. It also is possible that there is nothing unique about using obscenities; it may be that the simple act of yelling is enough to reduce the experience of pain. Any of these variables could influence the relationship between pain and swearing and could be part of an explanation for the relationship. Consider the following possibilities:

1. Swearing in response to pain is more common when the pain is self-inflicted than when it comes from an external source.
2. Swearing in response to pain is more acceptable and, therefore, more common when you are alone than when you are in a social environment.
3. Swearing in response to pain is directly related to the intensity of the pain.

Next, you must select one of the explanations to be evaluated in a scientific research study. Choose the explanation that you consider to be most plausible, or simply pick the one that you find most interesting. Remember, the other explanations are not discarded. If necessary, they can be evaluated in later studies. The researchers in the actual study, however, were simply interested in the effect of swearing on the experience of pain and posed the general explanation:

Swearing is a common response to pain because the act of swearing alters the experience and decreases the perceived intensity of pain.

At this point, you have a **hypothesis**, or a possible explanation, for your observation. Note that your hypothesis is not considered to be a final answer. Instead, the hypothesis is a tentative answer that is intended to be tested and critically evaluated.

DEFINITION	In the context of science, a **hypothesis** is a statement that describes or explains a relationship between or among variables. A hypothesis is not a final answer but rather a proposal to be tested and evaluated. For example, a researcher might hypothesize that there is a relationship between personality characteristics and cigarette smoking. Or another researcher might hypothesize that a dark and dreary environment causes winter depression.

Step 3: Use Your Hypothesis to Generate a Testable Prediction

Usually, this step involves taking the hypothesis and applying it to a specific, observable, real-world situation. For a hypothesis stating that swearing reduces the experience of pain, one specific prediction is that participants should be less responsive to occasional painful stimuli (pinpricks or mild shocks) when they are swearing than when they are not swearing. An alternative prediction is that participants should have an increased tolerance for pain when they are swearing than when they are not swearing.

Note that induction involves an increase from a few to many, and deduction involves a decrease from many to a specific few.
induction = increase
deduction = decrease

Notice that a single hypothesis can lead to several different predictions and that each prediction refers to a specific situation or an event that can be observed and measured. Figure 1.2 shows our original hypothesis and the two predictions that we derived from it. Notice that we are using logic (rational method) to make the prediction. This time, the logical process is known as **deduction** or **deductive reasoning**. We begin with a general (universal) statement and then make specific deductions. In particular, we use our hypothesis as a universal premise statement and then determine the conclusions or predictions that must logically follow if the hypothesis is true.

DEFINITION	**Deduction**, or **deductive reasoning**, uses a general statement as the basis for reaching a conclusion about specific examples.

Induction and deduction are complementary processes. Induction uses specific examples to generate general conclusions or hypotheses, and deduction uses general statements to generate specific predictions. This relationship is depicted in Figure 1.3.

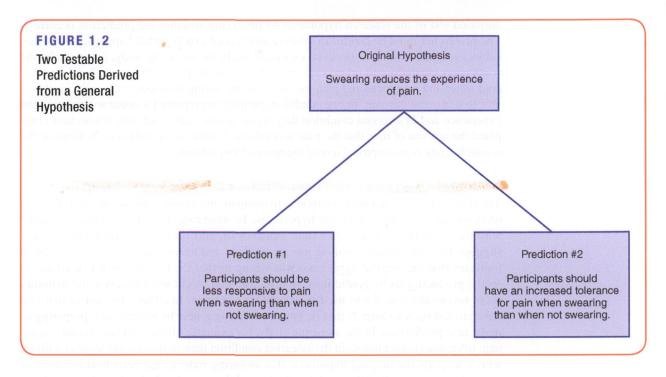

FIGURE 1.2

Two Testable Predictions Derived from a General Hypothesis

Original Hypothesis

Swearing reduces the experience of pain.

Prediction #1

Participants should be less responsive to pain when swearing than when not swearing.

Prediction #2

Participants should have an increased tolerance for pain when swearing than when not swearing.

FIGURE 1.3

Examples of Induction and Deduction

Inductive reasoning uses a few limited observations to generate a general hypothesis. Deductive reasoning uses a general hypothesis or premise to generate a prediction about specific observations.

Set of All Possible Cases

INDUCTION

Generalize from a small set of specific examples to the complete set of all possible examples.

I ate three green apples and all were sour. Therefore, all green apples are sour.

DEDUCTION

Predict a small set of specific examples from a general statement about the complete set of all possible examples.

All green apples are sour. Therefore, if I eat a green apple it will be sour.

A Few Specific Cases

Also notice that the predictions generated from a hypothesis must be testable—that is, it must be possible to demonstrate that the prediction is either correct or incorrect by direct observation. Either the observations will provide support for the hypothesis or they will refute the hypothesis. For a prediction to be truly testable, both outcomes must be possible.

Step 4: Evaluate the Prediction by Making Systematic, Planned Observations

After a specific, testable prediction has been made (the rational method), the next step is to evaluate the prediction using direct observation (the empirical method). This is the actual *research* or *data collection* phase of the scientific method. The goal is to provide a fair and unbiased test of the research hypothesis by observing whether the prediction is correct. The researcher must be careful to observe and record exactly what happens, free of any subjective interpretation or personal expectations. In the swearing study, for example, the researchers created a painful experience by having participants plunge one hand into ice-cold water and then measured pain tolerance by measuring how long each participant was able to withstand the pain. In one condition, participants repeated a swear word during the experience and in a second condition they repeated a neutral word. The researchers compared the amount of time that the pain was tolerated in the two conditions. Notice that the research study is an empirical test of the research hypothesis.

Step 5: Use the Observations to Support, Refute, or Refine the Original Hypothesis

The final step of the scientific method is to compare the actual observations with the predictions that were made from the hypothesis. To what extent do the observations agree with the predictions? Some agreement indicates support for the original hypothesis and suggests that you consider making new predictions and testing them. Lack of agreement indicates that the original hypothesis was wrong or that the hypothesis was used incorrectly, producing faulty predictions. In this case, you might want to revise the hypothesis or reconsider how it was used to generate predictions. In either case, notice that you have circled back to Step 2; that is, you are forming a new hypothesis and preparing to make new predictions. In the swearing study, for example, the researchers found greater pain tolerance (longer times) in the swearing condition than in the neutral-word condition, which supports the original hypothesis that swearing reduces the perceived intensity of pain. However, not all of the participants showed the same level of pain reduction. Some individuals were able to tolerate the ice-cold water for twice as long while swearing than while repeating a neutral word. For others, swearing resulted in little or no increase in pain tolerance. This result indicates that swearing is not the entire answer and other questions must be asked. For example, it is possible that people who swear routinely in their everyday lives do not get the same relief as people for whom swearing is a novel and emotionally stimulating act. Finally, we should note that if the results showed no difference in pain tolerance between the two conditions, then we would have to conclude that swearing does not affect the experience of pain. In this case, other factors must be considered, and other hypotheses must be tested.

Notice that the scientific method repeats the same series of steps over and over again. Observations lead to a hypothesis and a prediction, which lead to more observations, which lead to another hypothesis, and so on. Thus, the scientific method is not a linear process that moves directly from a beginning to an end but rather is a circular process, or a spiral, that repeats over and over, moving higher with each cycle as new knowledge is gained (Figure 1.4).

DEFINITION

The **scientific method** is a method of acquiring knowledge that uses observations to develop a hypothesis, and then uses the hypothesis to make logical predictions that can be empirically tested by making additional, systematic observations. Typically, the new observations lead to a new hypothesis, and the cycle continues.

Other Elements of the Scientific Method

In addition to the basic process that makes up the scientific method, a set of overriding principles governs scientific investigation. Three important principles of the scientific method are as follows: It is empirical, it is public, and it is objective.

FIGURE 1.4

The Process of Scientific Inquiry

The scientific method can be viewed as a circular process or a spiral of steps. Initial observations lead to a hypothesis and a prediction, which leads to more observations and then to a new hypothesis. This never-ending process of using empirical tests (observations) to build and refine our current knowledge (hypothesis) is the basis of the scientific method.

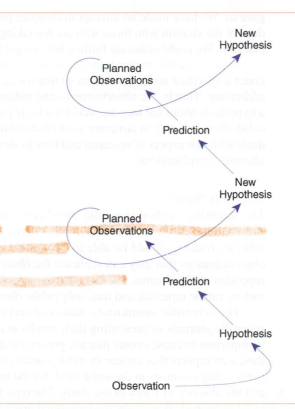

Science Is Empirical

As you know, when we say that science is empirical, we mean that answers are obtained by making observations. Although preliminary answers or hypotheses may be obtained by other means, science requires empirical verification. An answer may be "obvious" by common sense, it might be perfectly logical, and experts in the field might support it, but it is not scientifically accepted until it has been empirically demonstrated.

However, unlike the method of empiricism we previously examined, the scientific method involves structured or systematic observation. The structure of the observations is determined by the procedures and techniques that are used in the research study. More specifically, the purpose of the observations is to provide an empirical test of a hypothesis. Therefore, the observations are structured so that the results either will provide clear support for the hypothesis or will clearly refute the hypothesis. Consider the following question: Do large doses of vitamin C prevent the common cold?

To answer this question, it would not be sufficient simply to ask people if they take vitamin C routinely and how many colds they get in a typical season. These observations are not structured, and no matter what responses are obtained, the results will not necessarily provide an accurate answer to the question. In particular, we have made no attempt to determine the dosage levels of the vitamin C that individuals have taken. No attempt was made to verify that the illnesses reported were, in fact, the common cold and not some type of influenza, pneumonia, or other illness. No attempt was made to take into account the age, general health, or lifestyle of the people questioned (maybe people who take vitamin C tend to lead generally healthy lives). We have made no attempt to reduce the possible biasing effect of people's beliefs about vitamins and colds on the answers they gave us. We have made no attempt to compare people who are receiving a specified daily dose of the vitamin with those who are not taking vitamin C or are getting a phony pill (a placebo). We could elaborate further, but you get the general idea.

In the scientific method, the observations are systematic in that they are performed under a specified set of conditions so that we can accurately answer the question we are addressing. That is, the observations—and indeed the entire study—are structured to test a hypothesis about the way the world works. If you want to know if vitamin C can prevent colds, there is a way to structure your observations to get the answer. Much of this book deals with this aspect of research and how to structure studies to rule out competing and alternative explanations.

Science Is Public

The scientific method is public. By this we mean that the scientific method makes observations available for evaluation by others, especially other scientists. In particular, other individuals should be able to repeat the same step-by-step process that led to the observations so that they can replicate the observations for themselves. **Replication**, or repetition of observation, allows verification of the findings. Note that only public observations can be repeated, and thus only public observations are verifiable.

The scientific community makes observations public by publishing reports in scientific journals or presenting their results at conferences and meetings. This activity is important because events that are private cannot be replicated or evaluated by others. Research reports that appear in most journals have been evaluated by the researcher's peers (other scientists in the same field) for the rigor and appropriateness of methodology and the absence of flaws in the study. The report must meet a variety of standards for it to be published. When you read a journal article, one thing you will note is the level of detail used in describing the methodology of the study. Typically, the report has a separate "method section" that describes in great detail the people or animals that were studied (the participants or subjects of the study, respectively), the instruments and apparatus used to conduct the study, the procedures used in applying treatments and making measurements, and so on. Enough detail should be provided so that anyone can replicate the same study exactly to verify the findings. The notions of replication and verification are important. They provide the checks and balances for research.

As we shall see, there is a multitude of ways—by error or chance—in which a study can result in an erroneous conclusion. Researchers can also commit fraud and deliberately falsify or misrepresent the outcome of research studies. As scientists, it is important that we scrutinize and evaluate research reports carefully and maintain some skepticism about the results until more studies confirm the findings. By replicating studies and subjecting them to peer review, we have checks and balances against errors and fraud.

Science Is Objective

The scientific method is objective. That is, the observations are structured so that the researcher's biases and beliefs do not influence the outcome of the study. Science has been called "a dispassionate search for knowledge," meaning that the researcher does not let personal feelings contaminate the observations. What kind of biases and beliefs are likely to be involved? Often, bias comes from belief in a particular theory. A researcher might try to find evidence to support a specific theory and may have expectations about the outcome of the study. In some cases, expectations can subtly influence the findings.

One way to reduce the likelihood of the influence of experimenter expectation is to keep the people who are making the observations uninformed about the details of the study. In this case, we sometimes say the researcher is *blind* to the details of the study. We discuss this type of procedure in detail later (see Chapter 3, p. 74).

Science versus Pseudoscience

By now it should be clear that science is intended to provide a carefully developed system for answering questions so that the answers we get are as accurate and complete as possible. Note that scientific research is based on gathering evidence from careful, systematic, and objective observations. This is one of the primary features that differentiates science from other, less rigorous disciplines known as **pseudosciences**. Pseudoscience is a system of ideas often presented as science but actually lacking some of the key components that are essential to scientific research. Theories such as aromatherapy, astrology, and intelligent design are examples of pseudoscience that are unsupported by empirical evidence. Pseudoscience is common among popular psychology gurus who write self-help books and appear on TV talk shows presenting novel systems to solve your romantic relationship problems, end your episodes of depression, or help bring a normal life to your autistic child.

Although there is no universally accepted definition of pseudoscience, there is a common set of features that differentiates science and pseudoscience (Herbert et al., 2000; Lilienfeld, Lynn, & Lohr, 2004). The following list presents some of the more important differences.

1. The primary distinction between science and pseudoscience is based on the notion of testable and refutable hypotheses. Specifically, a theory is scientific only if it can specify how it could be refuted. That is, the theory must be able to describe exactly what observable findings would demonstrate that it is wrong. If a research study produces results that do not support a theory, the theory is either abandoned or, more commonly, modified to accommodate the new results. In either case, however, the negative results are acknowledged and accepted. In pseudoscience, on the other hand, the typical response to negative results is to discount them entirely or to explain them away without altering the original theory. For example, if research demonstrates that a particular therapy is not effective, the proponents of the therapy often claim that the failure was caused by a lack of conviction or skill on the part of the therapist—the therapy is fine; it was simply the application that was flawed.

2. Science demands an objective and unbiased evaluation of all the available evidence. Unless a treatment shows consistent success that cannot be explained by other outside factors, the treatment is not considered to be effective. Pseudoscience, on the other hand, tends to rely on subjective evidence such as testimonials and anecdotal reports of success. Pseudoscience also tends to focus on a few selected examples of success and to ignore instances of failure. In clinical practice, nearly any treatment shows occasional success, but handpicking reports that demonstrate success does not provide convincing evidence for an effective treatment.

3. Science actively tests and challenges its own theories and adapts the theories when new evidence appears. As a result, scientific theories are constantly evolving. Pseudoscience, on the other hand, tends to ignore nonsupporting evidence and treats criticism as a personal attack. As a result, pseudoscientific theories tend to be stagnant and remain unchanged year after year.

4. Finally, scientific theories are grounded in past science. A scientific system for teaching communication skills to autistic children is based on established theories of learning and uses principles that have solid empirical support. Pseudoscience tends to create entirely new disciplines and techniques that are unconnected to established theories and empirical evidence. Proponents of such theories often develop their own vaguely scientific jargon or describe links to science that suggest scientific legitimacy without any real substance. Aromatherapy, for example, is sometimes explained by noting that smells activate olfactory nerves, which stimulate the limbic system, which releases endorphins and neurotransmitters. Thus, smells affect your mind and emotions. Note that a similar argument could be used to justify a claim that clinical benefits are produced by looking at colored lights or listening to a bouncing tennis ball.

LEARNING CHECK

1. Which of the following is the best description of the scientific method?
   a. A circular process that leads to a final answer
   b. A linear process that moves directly to a final answer
   c. A circular process that leads to a tentative answer
   d. A linear process that leads to a tentative answer

2. What kind of reasoning uses a few specific observations to produce a general hypothesis?
   a. Inductive reasoning
   b. Deductive reasoning
   c. Scientific reasoning
   d. Predictive reasoning

3. A hypothesis is a _____ statement and a prediction is a _____ statement.
   a. specific; general
   b. specific; specific
   c. general; specific
   d. general; general

4. What is meant by saying that "science is objective"?
   a. Scientific answers are based on direct observation.
   b. Scientific answers are based on logical reasoning.
   c. Scientific answers are obtained without influence by the researcher's biases or beliefs.
   d. Scientific answers are made available for evaluation by others.

5. Which of the following is a distinction between science and pseudoscience?
   a. Pseudoscience tends to dismiss or refuse to accept negative results.
   b. Pseudoscience tends to rely on testimonials and selected results.
   c. Pseudoscience tends to treat criticism as a personal attack.
   d. All of the other options are differences between science and pseudoscience.

Answers appear at the end of the chapter.

1.3   The Research Process

LEARNING OBJECTIVES

LO7   Distinguish between qualitative and quantitative research and recognize examples of each.

LO8   Identify and describe the steps in the research process.

Quantitative and Qualitative Research

The primary purpose for this section is to introduce the steps in the research process. Before we begin that task, however, we should make a distinction between quantitative and qualitative research. Throughout this book, including the remainder of this chapter, we focus on **quantitative research**. The term *quantitative* refers to the fact that this type of research examines variables that typically vary in quantity (size, magnitude, duration, or amount). Part of the research process involves using different methods for measuring variables to determine how much, how big, or how strong they are (Chapter 3). The results, or data, obtained from these measurements are usually numerical scores that can be summarized, analyzed, and interpreted using standard statistical procedures.

There is, however, an alternative approach to gathering, interpreting, and reporting information. The alternative is known as **qualitative research**. The primary distinction between quantitative and qualitative research is the type of data they produce. As noted, quantitative research typically produces numerical scores. The result of qualitative research, however, is typically a narrative report (i.e., a written discussion of the observations). Qualitative research involves careful observation of participants (often including interaction with participants), usually accompanied by extensive note taking. The observations and notes are then summarized in a narrative report that attempts to describe and interpret the phenomenon being studied. A qualitative researcher studying depression in adolescents would simply talk with adolescents, asking questions and listening to answers, and then prepare a written narrative describing the behaviors and attitudes that had been observed. On the other hand, a quantitative researcher would probably develop a test to measure depression for each participant and then compute an average score to describe the amount of depression for different subgroups of adolescents.

DEFINITIONS

> **Quantitative research** is based on measuring variables for individual participants to obtain scores, usually numerical values, which are submitted to statistical analysis for summary and interpretation.
>
> **Qualitative research** is based on making observations that are summarized and interpreted in a narrative report.

Qualitative research is commonly used by social anthropologists, who often immerse themselves in a foreign culture to observe patterns of behavior that help them to understand and describe the social structure and customs of a different civilization. Other examples of qualitative research are Dian Fossey's observations of mountain gorillas (reported in *Gorillas in the Mist,* 1983), Thigpen and Cleckley's detailed description of a woman with multiple-personality disorder (reported in *The Three Faces of Eve,* 1957), and Jean Piaget's observations of his own children, which formed the basis for his theories of child development. None of these researchers measured individual scores but rather made more holistic observations of behavior that resulted in a detailed narrative rather than an average number.

As a final note, we should warn you that the distinction between quantitative and qualitative research is not as simple as numbers versus no numbers. In fact, the scores obtained in quantitative research occasionally are qualitative values. For example, a researcher examining the relationship between education and political orientation could classify participants according to education (college degree, yes/no) and political orientation (conservative/liberal). Notice that these variables do not produce quantitative measurements—both are qualitative. However, the measurements ultimately are transformed into numbers by computing the percentage of college graduates who are conservative and comparing that number with the percentage for those without a college degree. As a result, this study would be classified as quantitative research.

The Steps of the Research Process

The process of planning and conducting a research study involves using the scientific method to address a specific question. During this process, the researcher moves from a general idea to actual data collection and interpretation of the results. Along the way, the researcher is faced with a series of decisions about how to proceed. In this section, we outline the basic steps, or decision points, in the research process. The complete set of steps is also shown in Figure 1.5. Reading this section should give you a better

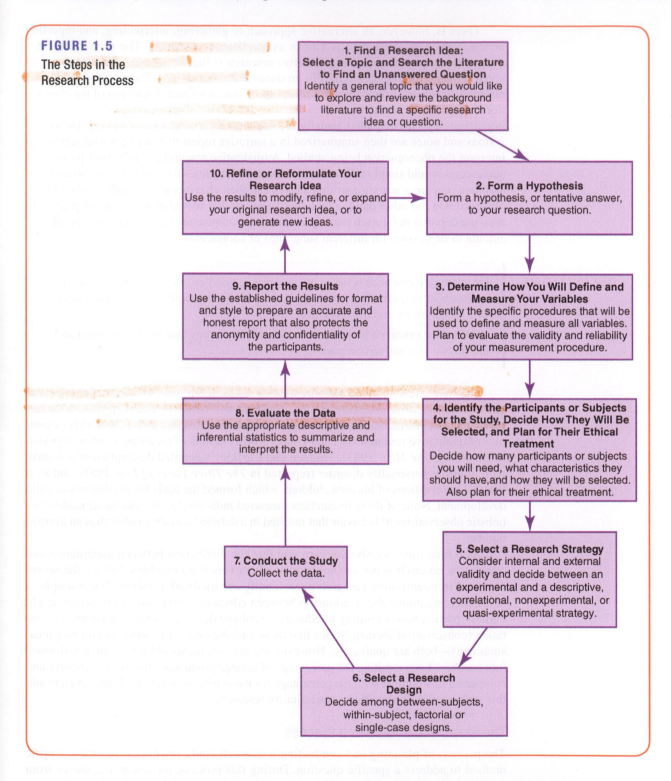

FIGURE 1.5

The Steps in the
Research Process

1. Find a Research Idea:
Select a Topic and Search the Literature
to Find an Unanswered Question
Identify a general topic that you would like
to explore and review the background
literature to find a specific research
idea or question.

10. Refine or Reformulate Your
Research Idea
Use the results to modify, refine, or expand
your original research idea, or to
generate new ideas.

2. Form a Hypothesis
Form a hypothesis, or tentative answer,
to your research question.

9. Report the Results
Use the established guidelines for format
and style to prepare an accurate and
honest report that also protects the
anonymity and confidentiality of
the participants.

3. Determine How You Will Define and
Measure Your Variables
Identify the specific procedures that will be
used to define and measure all variables.
Plan to evaluate the validity and reliability
of your measurement procedure.

8. Evaluate the Data
Use the appropriate descriptive and
inferential statistics to summarize and
interpret the results.

4. Identify the Participants or Subjects
for the Study, Decide How They Will Be
Selected, and Plan for Their Ethical
Treatment
Decide how many participants or subjects
you will need, what characteristics they
should have, and how they will be selected.
Also plan for their ethical treatment.

7. Conduct the Study
Collect the data.

5. Select a Research Strategy
Consider internal and external
validity and decide between an
experimental and a descriptive,
correlational, nonexperimental, or
quasi-experimental strategy.

6. Select a Research
Design
Decide among between-subjects,
within-subject, factorial or
single-case designs.

understanding of the scientific method and how it is used, as well as an overview of the
topics covered in the rest of the book. As a final note, remember that, although research
requires a decision about what to do at each stage in the process, there are no absolutely
right or wrong decisions. Each choice you make along the way has disadvantages as well

as advantages. Much of the material in the remainder of the book focuses on the kinds of decisions that need to be made during the research process and examines the strengths and weaknesses of various choices.

Many people think of research as collecting data in a laboratory, but this is only a small part of the total process. Long before actual data collection begins, most of your research time probably will be devoted to preparation. After data collection, the process continues with evaluation and interpretation of the results, followed by the preparation and public presentation of a research report. We now present the basic steps of the full research process.

Step 1: Find a Research Idea: Select a Topic and Search the Literature to Find an Unanswered Question

The first step in the research process is to find a research idea. This task, discussed in detail in Chapter 2, typically involves two parts:

1. Selecting a general topic area (such as human development, perception, and social interaction).
2. Reviewing the published research reports in that area to identify the relevant variables and find an unanswered question.

You may decide, for example, that you are interested in the topic of obesity and want to examine the variables that contribute to overeating. Ideas for topics can come from a variety of sources including everyday experience, books, journal articles, or class work. It is important that a researcher be honestly interested in the chosen topic. The research process can be a long-term, demanding enterprise. Without intrinsic interest to sustain motivation, it is very easy for a researcher to get tired or bored and give up before the research is completed.

Bear in mind that your general topic is simply a starting point that eventually will evolve into a very specific idea for a research study. Your final research idea will develop as you read through the research literature and discover what other researchers have already learned. Your original topic area will guide you through the literature and help you to decide which research studies are important to you and which are not relevant to your interests. Eventually, you will become familiar with the current state of knowledge and can determine which questions are still unanswered. At this stage, you will be ready to identify your own research question. In Chapter 2, we discuss the task of searching through the research literature to find a question for a research study.

As you become familiar with an area of research, you will learn the different variables that are being investigated and get some ideas about how those variables are related to each other. At this point, you should be looking for an unanswered research question.

Occasionally, finding an unanswered question is very easy. Published research reports often include suggestions for future research or identify limitations of the studies they are reporting. You are welcome to follow the suggestions or try to correct the limitations in your own research. More often, however, the unanswered question is the result of critical reading. As you read a research report, ask yourself why the study was done a certain way. If the study only used participants from middle-class families, perhaps the researchers suspected that family income might influence the results. Ask what might happen if some characteristics of the study were changed. For example, if the study examined eating behavior in restaurants, would the same results apply to eating at home?

In some situations, the research question may simply ask for a description of an individual variable or variables. For example, a researcher might be interested in the sleeping habits of college students. How much sleep do college students typically get? What time do they get up each day? More often, however, the research question concerns a relationship between two or more variables. For example, a researcher may want to know whether there is a relationship between portion size and the amount of food that people eat. Does serving larger portions cause an increase in food consumption?

Step 2: *Form a Hypothesis*

If your unanswered question simply asks for a description of a variable or variables, you can skip this step and go directly to Step 3 of the research process. However, if your question concerns the relationship between variables, the next task is to form a hypothesis, or a tentative answer to the question. In the swearing and pain study, for example, the hypothesis was stated as follows: A painful stimulus will be perceived as less intense if you are cursing than if you are not cursing.

When you are selecting an answer to serve as your hypothesis, you should pick the answer that seems most likely to be correct. Remember, the goal of the research study is to demonstrate that your answer (your hypothesis) is correct. The likelihood of a hypothesis being correct is often based on previous research results. If similar research has demonstrated the importance of one specific variable, it is likely that the same variable will be important in your own study. It is also possible that you can develop a logical argument supporting your hypothesis. If you can make a reasonable argument for your hypothesis, then it is likely that the hypothesis is correct.

Step 3: *Determine How You Will Define and Measure Your Variables*

Later in the research process, the hypothesis will be evaluated in an empirical research study. First, however, you must determine how you will define and measure your variables. In the swearing and pain study, for example, the research hypothesis stated that swearing decreases the perceived intensity of pain. This hypothesis predicts that the same painful stimulus will be perceived as less intense if you are cursing than if you are not cursing. Before they could evaluate this prediction, they had to determine how they could distinguish between *more* pain and *less* pain. Specifically, they had to determine how they would define and measure "the perceived intensity of pain." The researchers chose to use pain tolerance as their definition and measured how long each participant could tolerate the ice-water stimulus. The variables identified in the research hypothesis must be defined in a manner that makes it possible to measure them by some form of empirical observation. These decisions are usually made after reviewing previous research and determining how other researchers have defined and measured their variables.

By defining variables so that they can be observed and measured, researchers can transform the hypothesis (from Step 2 of the research process) into a specific research prediction that can be evaluated with empirical observations in a research study. For the pain and swearing study, the researcher prediction stated that participants would tolerate the ice-water stimulus for a longer time when swearing than when yelling neutral words. Notice that this step is necessary before we can evaluate the hypothesis by actually observing the variables. The key idea is to transform the hypothesis into an empirically testable form.

You should also realize that the task of determining exactly how the variables will be defined and measured often depends on the individuals to be measured. For example, you would certainly measure aggressive behavior for a group of preschool children very differently from aggressive behavior for a group of adults. The task of defining and measuring variables is discussed in Chapter 3.

Step 4: *Identify the Participants or Subjects for the Study, Decide How They Will Be Selected, and Plan for Their Ethical Treatment*

To evaluate a hypothesis scientifically, we first use the hypothesis to produce a specific prediction that can be observed and evaluated in a research study. One part of designing the research study is to decide exactly what individuals will participate, determine how many individuals you will need for your research, and plan where and how to recruit them. If the individuals are human, they are called **participants**. Nonhumans are called **subjects**.

DEFINITIONS

> The individuals who take part in research studies are called **participants** if they are human and **subjects** if they are nonhuman.

At this point, it is the responsibility of the researcher to plan for the safety and well-being of the research participants and to inform them of all relevant aspects of the research, especially any risk or danger that may be involved. Ethical considerations also include determining the procedure that you will use to recruit participants. For example, you may decide to offer some payment or other compensation for participation, but you must be careful that you do not entice or coerce individuals who normally would not participate. Finally, we should note that ethical considerations often interact with your choice of participants. Specifically, ethics may influence your decision about which individuals to select. For example, the pain and swearing study was ethically obliged to use adult participants because it would be unethical to use young children in a study that involved shouting obscenities. On the other hand, the individuals you select may affect your ethical decisions. For example, a research study using young children or other vulnerable groups places a stronger obligation on the researcher than would exist with adult participants who are more capable of caring for their own well-being. The issue of ethical treatment for participants and subjects is discussed in Chapter 4.

In addition, you must decide whether you will place any restrictions on the characteristics of the participants. For example, you may decide to use preschool children. Or you may be more restrictive and use only 4-year-old boys from two-parent, middle-income households who have been diagnosed with a specific learning disability. Be aware, however, that you are also defining limitations for generalizing the results of the study. For example, if you choose to use a sample of 50 college students, then you are justified in generalizing the results to other college students but not to different populations. Different ways to select individuals to participate in research are discussed in Chapter 5.

Notice that when you have completed Steps 3 and 4 you have created a specific research study that will test the original hypothesis from Step 2 of the research process. Specifically, you have specified exactly how the variables will be defined and measured, made a research prediction, and described exactly who will be observed and measured. Ultimately, the research study will test the original hypothesis by actually making the observations.

Step 5: Select a Research Strategy

Choosing a research strategy involves deciding on the general approach you will take to evaluate your research hypothesis. For example, the researchers in the pain and swearing study could have used a survey to determine public opinion about the effect of swearing on the experience of pain rather than using an experiment to measure pain in a laboratory. General research strategies are introduced in Chapter 6 and discussed in Chapters 7, 10, 12, and 13. The choice of a research strategy is usually determined by one of two factors:

1. The type of question asked: Consider, for example, the following two research questions:

   Is there a relationship between sugar consumption and activity level for preschool children?

   Will increasing the level of sugar consumption for preschool children cause an increase in their activity level?

At first glance, it may appear that the two questions are actually the same. In terms of research, however, they are quite different. They will require different research studies and may produce different answers. Consider the following two questions:

Is there a relationship between intelligence and income for 40-year-old men?

Will increasing the salary for 40-year-old men cause an increase in their IQ scores?

In this case, it should be clear that the two questions are not the same and may lead to different conclusions. The type of question that you are asking can dictate the specific research strategy that you must use.

2. Ethics and other constraints: Often, ethical considerations—discussed in Chapter 4—or other factors, such as equipment availability, limit what you can or cannot do in the laboratory. These factors often can force you to choose one research strategy over another. For example, minor degrees of pain, such as putting a hand in ice water, can be administered to individuals in a study if they are informed in advance and agree to participate. More severe injuries, such as repeated concussions, cannot be administered in a laboratory but must be examined in real-world conditions where they exist naturally.

Step 6: Select a Research Design

Selecting a research design involves making decisions about the specific methods and procedures you will use to conduct the research study. Does your research question call for the detailed examination of one individual, or would you find a better answer by looking at the average behavior of a large group? Should you observe one group of individuals as they experience a series of different treatment conditions, or should you observe a different group of individuals for each of the different treatments? Should you make a series of observations of the same individuals over a period of time, or should you compare the behaviors of different individuals at the same time? Answering these questions will help you determine a specific design for the study. Different designs and their individual strengths and weaknesses are discussed in Chapters 8, 9, 10, 11, and 14.

Step 7: Conduct the Study

Finally, you are ready to collect the data. But now you must decide whether the study will be conducted in a laboratory or in the field (in the real world). Will you observe the participants individually or in groups? In addition, you must now implement all your earlier decisions about manipulating, observing, measuring, controlling, and recording the different aspects of your study.

Step 8: Evaluate the Data

Once the data have been collected, you must use various statistical methods to examine and evaluate the data. This involves drawing graphs, computing means or correlations to describe your data, and using inferential statistics to help determine whether the results from your specific participants can be generalized to the rest of the population. Statistical methods are reviewed in Chapter 15.

Step 9: Report the Results

One important aspect of the scientific method is that observations and results must be public. This is accomplished, in part, by a written report describing what was done, what was found, and how the findings were interpreted. In Chapter 16, we review the standard style and procedures for writing research reports. Two reasons to report research results are: (1) the results become part of the general knowledge base that other people can use to answer questions or to generate new research ideas, and (2) the research procedure can be replicated or refuted by other researchers.

Step 10: *Refine or Reformulate Your Research Idea*

Most research studies generate more questions than they answer. If your results support your original hypothesis, it does not mean that you have found a final answer. Instead, the new information from your study simply means that it is now possible to extend your original question into new domains or make the research question more precise. Typically, results that support a hypothesis lead to new questions by one of the following two routes:

1. *Test the boundaries of the result:* Suppose your study demonstrates that higher levels of academic performance are related to higher levels of self-esteem for elementary school children. Will this same result be found for adolescents in middle school? Perhaps adolescents are less concerned about respect from their parents and teachers and are more concerned about respect from peers. If adolescents do not value academic success then you would not expect academic success to be related to their self-esteem. Alternatively, you might want to investigate the relationship between self-esteem and success outside academics. Is there a relationship between success on the athletic field and self-esteem? Notice that the goal is to determine whether your result extends into other areas. How general are the results of your study?

2. *Refine the original research question:* If your results show a relationship between academic success and self-esteem, the next question is, "What causes the relationship?" That is, what is the underlying mechanism by which success in school translates into higher self-esteem? The original question asked, "Does a relationship exist?" Now you are asking, "Why does the relationship exist?"

Results that do not support your hypothesis also generate new questions. One explanation for negative results (results that do not support the hypothesis) is that one of the premises is wrong. Remember, for this example, we assumed that academic success is highly valued and respected. Perhaps this is not true. Your new research question might be, "How important is academic success to parents, to teachers, or to elementary school students?"

Notice that research is not a linear, start-to-finish process. Instead, the process is a spiral or a circle that keeps returning to a new hypothesis to start over again. The never-ending process of asking questions, gathering evidence, and asking new questions is part of the general scientific method. One characteristic of the scientific method is that it always produces tentative answers or tentative explanations. There are no final answers. Consider, for example, the theory of evolution: After years of gathering evidence, evolution is still called a "theory." No matter how much supporting evidence is obtained, the answer to a research question is always open to challenge and eventually may be revised or refuted.

LEARNING CHECK

1. Which of the following is typical of quantitative research?
   a. It involves measuring variables for each individual.
   b. It usually involves numerical scores.
   c. It uses statistical analysis to summarize and interpret results.
   d. All of the above.

2. A researcher conducts a study in which 50 college students are assigned to different treatments and tested. In the study, the students are called
   a. research associates.
   b. research cohorts.
   c. research participants.
   d. research subjects.
3. The first step in the research process is
   a. identifying a topic area and searching the literature to find a research question.
   b. forming a hypothesis.
   c. deciding which individuals should participate in the study.
   d. selecting a research strategy.

Answers appear at the end of the chapter.

CHAPTER SUMMARY

At this point, you should review the learning objectives presented at the beginning of each section and be sure that you have mastered each objective.

Although this textbook is devoted to discussing the scientific method, there are other ways of finding answers to questions. The methods of tenacity, intuition, authority, rationalism, and empiricism are different ways of acquiring knowledge. Each method has its strengths and limitations. The scientific method combines the various methods to achieve a more valid way of answering questions. The scientific method is empirical, public, and objective.

The scientific method consists of five steps: (1) observation of behavior or other phenomena; (2) formation of a tentative answer or explanation, called a hypothesis; (3) utilization of the hypothesis to generate a testable prediction; (4) evaluation of the prediction by making systematic, planned observations; and (5) utilization of the observations to support, refute, or refine the original hypothesis.

The distinction between qualitative and quantitative research is based on the kind of data that they produce. Qualitative studies tend to produce narrative reports and quantitative studies produce numerical data that are evaluated using statistical methods. In this book, we focus on quantitative research. The research process is the way the scientific method is used to answer a particular question. The 10 steps of the research process provide a framework for the remainder of this book.

KEY WORDS

(Defined in the chapter and in the glossary)	method of faith	induction, or inductive reasoning	quantitative research
methods of acquiring knowledge	rational method, or rationalism	variables	qualitative research
method of tenacity	premise statements	hypothesis	participants
method of intuition	argument	deduction, or deductive reasoning	subjects
method of authority	empirical method, or empiricism	scientific method	

EXERCISES

The exercises are identified with specific learning objectives and are intended to assess your mastery of the objectives. You should be aware that exam items are also generated to assess learning objectives.

1. In addition to the key words that were defined in the text, you should be able to define the following terms, which also appear in the glossary:
   replication
   pseudoscience

2. (**LO1**) Describe how some behaviors can be explained by clichés, such as "You can't teach an old dog new tricks" or "You can't make an omelet without breaking eggs."

3. (**LO1**) Describe why you might be cautious about using the Internet to find answers to medical questions.

4. (**LO1**) Suppose that you are debating whether to hitchhike across country or take the bus. Explain how the rational method could help you make a decision.

5. (**LO1**) According to the *gambler's fallacy*, if a coin toss results in heads three times in a row, then the probability of tails increases for the fourth toss. Describe how you would use the empirical method to evaluate this claim.

6. (**LO1**) In this chapter, we identified the method of authority, the rational method, and the empirical method as techniques for acquiring information. For each of the following, choose one of these three methods and describe how you could use it to answer the question. Can you describe an alternative method for finding the answer?
   a. What is the phone number for the psychology department office at your school?

b. What is the current exchange rate for converting Canadian dollars to U.S. dollars?
   c. How tall is your course instructor?
   d. My local pizza shop guarantees "delivery in 30 minutes or your pizza is free." If my pizza arrives 25 minutes after I order it, will it be free?
   e. What is the distance from the floor to the ceiling in your bedroom?

7. (**LO2**) What are the five steps of the scientific method?

8. (**LO3**) Describe the difference between inductive and deductive reasoning and give an example of each.

9. (**LO4**) State a hypothesis that identifies a specific variable that causes some people to choose red as their favorite color. Create a prediction from your hypothesis.

10. (**LO5**) Describe what it means to say that science is empirical, public, and objective, and explain why each of these principles is important.

11. (**LO6**) An expert appears on a shopping network to explain how the different candle fragrances they are selling influence people's moods and behaviors. Explain how you could determine whether the expert's theories are science or pseudoscience.

12. (**LO7**) A social science researcher would like to determine the characteristics of people who live and work in small towns (population less than 2,000).
   a. Explain how this information might be obtained using qualitative research.
   b. Explain how this information might be obtained using quantitative research.

LEARNING CHECK ANSWERS

Section 1.1
1. c, 2. c, 3. b, 4. a

Section 1.2
1. c, 2. a, 3. c, 4. c, 5. d

Section 1.3
1. d, 2. c, 3. a

Research Ideas and Hypotheses

© Nathan Jasowiak / Shutterstock

CHAPTER LEARNING OBJECTIVES

LO1 Identify possible sources and use them to identify a topic area for research.

LO2 Define *applied research* and *basic research* and identify examples of each.

LO3 Define *primary* and *secondary sources*, identify examples of each, and explain the role that each plays in a literature search.

LO4 Describe the process of conducting a literature search, including using an online database such as PsycINFO, and conduct a search to locate current published research related to a specific topic.

LO5 Describe the differences between a full-text database and one that is not full text, and explain the advantages and disadvantages of each in a literature search.

LO6 Identify the basic sections of an APA-style research article, know what to expect in each section, and summarize and critically evaluate the content of each section for an existing article.

LO7 Explain how an idea for a new research study can be obtained from an existing research publication and use existing research publication(s) to find a new research idea.

LO8 Describe the characteristics of a good hypothesis and identify examples of good and bad hypotheses.

CHAPTER OVERVIEW

Research has confirmed what you may have suspected to be true—alcohol consumption increases the attractiveness of opposite-sex individuals (Jones, Jones, Thomas, & Piper, 2003). In the study, college-age participants were recruited from bars and restaurants near a large, city university campus and asked to participate in a "market research" study that was attempting to identify different types of student faces. During the introductory conversation, participants were asked to report their alcohol consumption for the day and were told that moderate consumption would not prevent them from taking part in the study. Participants were then shown a series of photographs of male and female faces and asked to rate the attractiveness of each face on a scale of 1 to 7. At the end of the study, participants were interviewed once again and the researchers excluded any participants who were not heterosexual, or had recognized any of the people in the photographs, or had realized the true purpose of the experiment. For the remaining participants, the results clearly showed that the ratings of female faces were significantly higher for males who had consumed alcohol than for males who had not. Similarly, the ratings for male faces were significantly higher for females who had consumed alcohol than for those who had not. Finally, alcohol consumption had no effect on the ratings for same-sex faces for either group of participants.

The results from this study are reasonable and not particularly surprising. For the purposes of this chapter, however, the question is: How did they find the research idea? All research studies must begin with an idea, and finding a good idea for research is not a trivial task. In this chapter, we discuss in detail the first and second steps of the research process: Step 1—finding a research idea (which involves selecting a topic and searching the literature to find an unanswered question), and Step 2—forming a hypothesis.

As part of Step 1 in the research process, researchers first identify a general topic. Perhaps the topic for Jones et al.'s (2003) study came from observing the behavior of others or even from personal experience of waking up with an unexpected stranger after a night of drinking. This is a common event in movies, television shows, jokes, and occasionally in real life. Or, perhaps the topic arose from an interest in sexual behaviors and more specifically the desire to decrease risky sexual behaviors. Our point is that starting points for research studies can come from a wide variety of sources. To begin this chapter, to help get you started in identifying a general topic area, we discuss various sources of research topics, and we present some general pointers for starting out.

After selecting a topic, previous research in that area must be found and examined to lead you to a new research idea to examine. Much of the chapter is devoted to the topic of a literature search that can help you uncover previous research that investigated similar ideas and may provide background information that contributes to the development of your own idea. In the Jones et al. (2003) study, one possible source for the idea is a logical argument that the authors present at the beginning of their research paper. Based on previous research, they begin with a report that establishes a relationship between risky sexual behavior and alcohol consumption (Cooper, 2002) and then attempt to develop a logical explanation for this relationship. First, they cite research showing that the intention to engage in risky sexual behavior tends to increase as the facial attractiveness of the potential partner increases (Agocha & Cooper, 1999). If the authors can establish that alcohol consumption increases the perceived facial attractiveness of opposite-sex individuals, then the logical argument is complete:

Alcohol increases perceived facial attractiveness.

Increased facial attractiveness increases the likelihood of risky sexual behavior.

Therefore, there is a relationship between alcohol consumption and risky sexual behavior.

Later in this chapter, we discuss different ways to use background literature to find a new research idea, and finally we outline the process of forming a hypothesis and turning an idea into a specific plan for a new research study. The goal for this chapter is to make you familiar with the process of finding ideas for research and to provide you with the skills to make initial plans for your own research study.

2.1   Getting Started: Identifying a Topic Area

LEARNING OBJECTIVES

LO1   Identify possible sources and use them to identify a topic area for research.

LO2   Define *applied research* and *basic research* and identify examples of each.

The first step in the research process is to find an idea for a research study (see Figure 1.5, p. 20). That first step actually consists of two distinct parts. First, you need to identify a general topic area that is interesting to you. Second, you must explore previous research in that topic area to find a specific research idea or question. Therefore, the product of the first part is to come up with a list of words or phrases. In the second part, the previous research in that topic area is examined in a way to identify not only what we know in that area but also to identify what research questions still remain.

For many students, even the first part of Step 1, that is, identifying a general topic area, can seem like an intimidating task. How do you even get started? Unfortunately, many beginning students often believe that coming up with a topic area for research is very difficult, when, in fact, starting points for research are all around us. All that is really necessary is that you see the world around you from an actively curious perspective. Ask yourself why things happen the way they do or what would happen if things were different. Keep your eyes open! Any source can generate topic areas for research.

Common Sources of Research Topics

Personal Interests and Curiosities

Feel free to look for research topics based on your own interests and concerns. What interests you? What makes you curious? One way to find out is to think about the courses you have taken. Which courses were your favorites? Within courses, what were your favorite units or classes? Think about the people and behaviors that interest you. Think about the issues that concern you.

There are several different ways to define an interest area. Here are a few possibilities:

- A particular population or group of individuals; for example, elementary school children, dogs, single-parent families, caretakers, or police officers
- A particular behavior; for example, bullying, adolescent drug use, math anxiety, honesty, overeating, or meditation
- A general topic; for example, autism, depression, workplace stress, child abuse, aging, personality, learning, or motivation

A research project can be about anything, so choose a topic you would like to learn more about.

Casual Observation

Watching the behavior of people or animals you encounter daily can be an excellent source of topics. If you simply watch, you will see people getting angry, laughing at jokes, lying, insulting each other, forming friendships and relationships, eating, sleeping, learning, and forgetting. In addition, you can monitor your own behavior, attitudes, and emotions. Any behavior that attracts your attention and arouses your curiosity can become a good research topic.

Reports of Others' Observations

The reports of observations made by other people are another good source of research ideas. These can include informal sources, such as news reports of current events, reports of recent research results, or even topics introduced in novels and television programs. Research topics do not come exclusively from serious reports. Gossip columns, personal ads, comics, political cartoons, and advertising can stimulate research questions. Keep in mind the fact that published information, especially in nonscientific sources, is not necessarily true and does not always tell the whole story.

You are even more likely to find a good research topic from your academic courses and the associated textbooks and readings. For example, if you enjoyed a developmental psychology class, then get a developmental psychology textbook and read through the list of chapter titles. You probably will find some that you recall as being more interesting than others. Within those chapters, review the topics that are covered and the research studies that are cited. With any luck, you should quickly identify one or two research topics that are of particular interest to you.

Practical Problems or Questions

Occasionally, topics for research will arise from practical problems or questions you encounter in your daily life, such as issues from your job, your family relationships, your schoolwork, or elsewhere in the world around you. For example, you may want to develop a more efficient set of study habits. Should you concentrate your study time in the morning, in the afternoon, or at night? Should you spend a 2-hour block of study time working exclusively on one subject, or should you distribute your time so that each of five different courses gets some attention? Or suppose that you want to simplify the audio controls in your car. What is the best placement of buttons and dials to minimize distraction while driving? Any of these problems could be developed into a research study.

Research that is directed toward solving practical problems is often classified as applied research; in contrast, studies that are intended to solve theoretical issues are classified as basic research. Although these different kinds of research begin with different goals, they are both legitimate sources of research topics and, occasionally, they can overlap. For example, a school board may initiate an applied study to determine whether there is a significant increase in student performance if class size is reduced from 30 students to 25 students. However, the results of the study may have implications for a new theory of learning. In the same way, a scientist who is conducting basic research to test a theory of learning may discover results that can be applied in the classroom.

DEFINITIONS

> **Applied research** is intended to answer practical questions or solve practical problems. Research studies intended to answer theoretical questions or gather knowledge simply for the sake of new knowledge are classified as **basic research**.

Behavioral Theories

Watch for theories that offer explanations for behavior or try to explain why different environmental factors lead to different behaviors. In addition to explaining previous research results, a good theory usually predicts behavior in new situations. Can you think of a way to test the explanations or evaluate the predictions from a theory? Look closely at the different variables that are part of the theory (the factors that cause behavior to change), and ask yourself what might happen if one or more of those variables were manipulated or isolated from the others. Testing the predictions that are part of a theory can be a good topic area for research. Occasionally, you will encounter two different theories that attempt to explain the same behavior. When two opposing theories make different predictions, you have found a good opportunity for research.

LEARNING CHECK

1. While shopping, you observe the behavior of adolescents at the mall and get some ideas about what may be causing the behavior. This is an example of getting research ideas from
   a. theory.
   b. casual observation.
   c. systematic observation.
   d. secondhand information.

2. How would research studies that are intended to answer practical problems be classified?
   a. Basic research
   b. Applied research
   c. Systematic research
   d. Necessary research

3. A researcher is intrigued by an explanation of children's problem-solving strategies found in a journal article and develops a research study to determine whether the article's ideas are correct. How would this study be classified?
   a. Basic research
   b. Applied research
   c. Systematic research
   d. Necessary research

Answers appear at the end of the chapter.

2.2 Searching the Existing Research Literature in a Topic Area

LEARNING OBJECTIVES

LO3 Define *primary* and *secondary sources*, identify examples of each, and explain the role that each plays in a literature search.

LO4 Describe the process of conducting a literature search, including using an online database such as PsycINFO, and conduct a search to locate current published research related to a specific topic.

LO5 Describe the differences between a full-text database and one that is not full text, and explain the advantages and disadvantages of each in a literature search.

Once you have settled on a general topic area for a research study, then the real work begins. The next part of Step 1 in the research process is to review the published research reports in the area to gather background information on the topic you have identified. In particular, your goal is to find a specific research idea or question.

A great analogy for the process of finding a research idea from a review of the existing literature is to consider what happens when you enter a conversation that has already started (Burke, 1974). Imagine for a moment that you are late coming into a party. Many are already paired or in small groups chatting. Upon entering one of these groups, it is in your best interest to listen for a bit and determine what is the topic of conversation, what is currently being discussed, what do you surmise others have already said on these issues, what questions do you have, and what can you contribute to this conversation. Similarly, research ideas do not develop in isolation or simply pop up out of the blue. First we need to get up to speed—We first have to go on a "listening tour." What is the "conversation in the discipline"? What questions have already been asked and answered? Where are the gaps in the "conversation"? What is still unknown? In order to eventually find a research idea, we must start by "getting in on the conversation." In technical jargon this means reviewing the existing literature. There are two purposes to reviewing the literature, to gain general knowledge, that is, get up-to-date (listen), and to find gaps in the literature (identify where you can contribute to the conversation of research!).

Remember that your goal is to "find" an idea or question rather than "make up" or "create" one. Once you are familiar with what is currently known and what is currently being done in a research area, your task is simply to extend the current research one more step. Sometimes, this requires a bit of logic, in which you combine two or more established facts to reach a new conclusion or prediction. Often, the authors of a research report literally give you ideas for new research. It is very common for researchers to include suggestions for future research in the discussion of their results. You are welcome to turn one of these suggestions into a research question. In Section 2.3, we provide additional hints for finding research ideas. For now, do not try to impose your own preconceived idea onto the literature. Instead, let the literature lead you to a new idea.

There are hundreds of research journals and thousands of books devoted just to the field of psychology and thousands more for the rest of the behavioral sciences. This mass of published information is referred to as *the literature*. Your job is to search the literature to find a handful of items that are directly relevant to your research idea. This may, at first, appear to be an overwhelming task; fortunately, however, the literature is filled with useful aids to guide your search. Specifically, all the individual publications are interconnected by cross-referencing, and there are many summary guides providing overviews that can send you directly to specific topic areas. By following the guides and tracing the interconnections, it is possible to conduct a successful literature search without undue pain and suffering.

Tips for Starting a Review of the Literature

The following are a few suggestions that should help make getting oriented for the literature review process a little easier.

Do Your Homework

Once you have identified a research topic, collecting background information is the next essential step. Typically, this involves reading books and journal articles to familiarize yourself with the topic: what is already known, what research has been done, and what questions remain unanswered. No matter what topic you select, it will soon become clear that there are a huge number of books and journal articles containing relevant background information. Do not panic; although the amount of material may appear to be overwhelming, keep these two points in mind:

1. You do not need to know everything about a topic, and you certainly do not need to read everything about a topic before you begin research. You should read enough to gain a solid, basic understanding of the current knowledge in an area, and this is fairly easy to attain. Later in this section, we provide some suggestions for doing library research.

2. You will quickly narrow your research topic from a general area to a very specific idea. For example, when reading a book on developmental psychology, one chapter on social development may capture your attention. Within that chapter, you become interested in the section on play and peer relations, and in that section you find a fascinating paragraph on the role of siblings in the development of a child's social skills. Notice that you have substantially narrowed your interest area from the broad topic of human development to the much more focused topic of siblings and social skills. You have also greatly reduced the amount of relevant background reading.

Keep an Open Mind

As discussed earlier, the best strategy for finding a research idea is to begin with a general topic area and then let your background reading lead you to a more specific idea. As you read or skim through material, look for items that capture your attention; then follow those leads. You need not start with a specific research idea in mind. In fact, beginning with a specific, preconceived research idea can be a mistake; you may find that your specific question has already been answered, or you might have difficulty finding information that is relevant to your preconceived notion. You may find that you do not have the necessary equipment, time, or participants to test your idea. So your best bet is to be flexible and keep an open mind. The existing knowledge in any topic area is filled with unanswered questions that provide the basis for future research.

Also, be critical; ask questions as you read: Why did they do that? Is this result consistent with what I see in my own life? How would this prediction apply to a different situation? Do I really believe this explanation? These questions, expanding or challenging current knowledge, can lead to good research ideas. Other suggestions for critical reading are presented in Section 2.3.

As you move through the project, maintain a degree of flexibility. You may discover a new journal article or get a suggestion from a friend that causes you to revise or refine your original plan. Making adjustments is a normal part of the research process and usually improves the result.

Focus, Focus, Focus

Developing a single, specific research idea is largely a weeding-out process. You probably will find that 1 hour of reading leads you to a dozen legitimate research ideas. It is unlikely that you can answer a dozen questions with one research study, so you will have to throw out most of your ideas (at least temporarily). Your goal is to develop one research question and to find the background information that is directly relevant to that question. Other ideas and other background material may be appropriate for other research, but at this stage, will only complicate the study you are planning. Discard irrelevant items, and focus on one question at a time.

Take One Step at a Time

Like any major project, planning and conducting research can be a long and difficult process. At the beginning, contemplating the very end of a research project may lead you to feel that the task is impossibly large. Remember, you don't need to do the whole thing at once; just take it one step at a time. In this chapter, we move through the beginning steps of the research process. The remainder of the textbook continues that journey, step by step.

Primary and Secondary Sources

Before we discuss the actual process of a literature search, there are a few terms you should know. Individual items in the literature can be classified into two broad categories: primary sources and secondary sources. A **primary source** is a firsthand report in which the authors describe their own observations. Typically, a primary source is a research report, published in a scientific journal or periodical, in which the authors describe their own research study, including why the research was done, how the study was conducted, what results were found, and how those results were interpreted. Some examples of primary sources include (1) empirical journal articles, (2) theses and dissertations, and (3) conference presentations of research results. In contrast, a **secondary source** is a secondhand report in which the authors discuss someone else's observations. Some examples of secondary sources are (1) books and textbooks in which the author describes and summarizes past research, (2) review articles or meta-analyses, (3) the introductory section of research reports, in which previous research is presented as a foundation for the current study, and (4) newspaper and magazine articles that report on previous research.

A meta-analysis is a review and statistical analysis of past research in a specific area that is intended to determine the consistency and robustness of the research results.

DEFINITIONS

A **primary source** is a firsthand report of observations or research results written by the individual(s) who actually conducted the research and made the observations.

A **secondary source** is a description or summary of another person's work. A secondary source is written by someone who did not participate in the research or observations being discussed.

Notice that the principal distinction between a primary source and a secondary source is firsthand versus secondhand reporting of research results. You cannot assume that anything published in a journal or periodical is automatically a primary source and that all other kinds of publications are secondary sources.

Both primary and secondary sources play important roles in the literature search process. Secondary sources can provide concise summaries of past research. A textbook, for example, often summarizes 10 years of research, citing several important studies, in a few paragraphs. A meta-analysis, for example, provides a great overview of an area by combining the results from a number of studies. Individual research reports that fill 10–15 pages in journals are often summarized in one or two sentences in secondary sources. Thus, secondary sources can save you hours of library research. However, you should be aware that secondary sources are always incomplete and can be biased or simply inaccurate. In a secondary source, the author has selected only bits and pieces of the original study; the selected parts might have been taken out of context and reshaped to fit a theme quite different from what the original authors intended. In general, secondary sources tell only part of the truth and can, in fact, distort the truth. To obtain complete and accurate information, it is essential to consult primary sources. Reading primary sources, however, can be a tedious process because they are typically long, detailed reports focusing on a narrowly defined topic. Therefore, plan to use secondary sources to gain an overview and identify a few specific primary sources for more detailed reading. Secondary sources provide a good starting point for a literature search, but you must depend on primary sources for the final answers.

The Purpose of a Literature Search

Research does not exist in isolation. Each research study is part of an existing body of knowledge, building on the foundation of past research and expanding that foundation for future research. Box 2.1 and Figure 2.1 explain how current knowledge grows, with each new piece of information growing out of an existing body of previous knowledge. As you read the literature and develop an idea for a research study, keep in mind that your study should be a logical extension of past research. Throughout the process, remember that a literature search has two basic goals: (1) to gain a general familiarity with the current research in your specific area of interest, and (2) to find a small set of research studies that will serve as the basis for your own research idea.

Ultimately, your goal in conducting a **literature search** is to find a set of published research reports that define the current state of knowledge in an area and to identify an unanswered question—that is, a gap in that knowledge base—that your study will attempt to fill. Eventually, you will complete your research study and write your own research report. The research report begins with an introduction that summarizes past research (from your literature search) and provides a logical justification for your study.

Thus, the purpose of your literature review is to provide the elements needed for an introduction to your own research study. Specifically, you need to find a set of research articles that can be organized into a logical argument supporting and justifying the research you propose to do (see "Characteristics of a Good Hypothesis," p. 45).

Conducting a Literature Search

Up to this point we have concentrated on the purpose for conducting a literature search. Now, we shift our focus to examine how to conduct a literature search.

BOX 2.1 The Growth of Research

Throughout this chapter, we repeat the notion that each research study builds on previous knowledge and attempts to expand that knowledge base. With this thought in mind, it is possible to represent the existing knowledge base (the literature) as a tree-like structure that is continuously growing over time. Figure 2.1 is a graphic representation of this concept, with each point in the figure representing a single research study, and the branches representing the growth and development of the "knowledge tree." When you begin a literature search, you enter this tree and find your way along the branches. Your goal in conducting the search is twofold. First, you must work your way to the very tips of the highest branches and find a cluster of the most recent research studies. Your study will form a new branch coming out of this cluster. Second, you must search backward, down the tree, to identify the historically significant foundations of your work. You probably will find that most of the current research studies in an area cite the same classic studies as their foundations. These classics usually provide a broader perspective for your work and will help you understand and explain the significance of your study as it relates to the more general tree of knowledge.

The tree metaphor is only a conceptual guide to help you visualize the process and the goals of a literature search—the concept of a tree greatly oversimplifies the process. For example, many good research studies involve establishing a connection between two previously unrelated branches of research. Nonetheless, the tree metaphor should help direct your literature search activities. You may, for example, find yourself with a cluster of recent articles that seem to be a dead end, offering no prospect for developing new research. If this happens, you can simply work back down the tree to an earlier branching point and branch off in a new direction without completely abandoning your original research topic.

FIGURE 2.1

How New Research Grows Out of Old

The tree-like structure emphasizes the notion that current research (the tips of the branches) is always based in previous research.

Current Research
(the most recent research studies)

Major Branching Points
(studies that started a new research direction)

Historical Studies
(the foundation of the research area)

It is common to begin your literature search with only a general idea for a research topic. Your purpose, therefore, is to narrow down your general idea to a specific research question and to find all the published information necessary to document and support that question. As you will see, there are many ways to begin a search of the literature. In this section, we identify several different starting points and provide some suggestions to help you find one.

One of the best places to start is with a recently published secondary source, such as a textbook, in a content area appropriate for your idea (perhaps a developmental psychology or social psychology textbook). Use the chapter headings and subheadings in the text to help focus your search on a more narrowly defined area. In addition, make notes of the following items, each of which can serve as an excellent starting point when you begin to search for primary sources (empirical journal articles) relevant to your topic:

- Subject words: Make a list of the correct terms, or **subject words**, used to identify and describe the variables in the study and the characteristics of the participants. Researchers often develop a specific set of terms to describe a topic area, and it is much easier to locate related research articles if you use the correct terms. Most databases have a thesaurus or similar feature that will translate a common term such as *foster homes* into the accepted term *foster care*.
- Author names: Commonly, a small group of individual researchers is responsible for much of the work being done in a specific area. If you repeatedly encounter the same names, make a note of these individuals as the current leading researchers in the area.

As you develop your list of subject words and author names, keep in mind that any single secondary source is necessarily incomplete and probably selective. Thus, it is wise to repeat the list-making process with two or three different sources, and then combine your lists. When you finish, you should have an excellent set of leads to help you move into the primary source literature.

Using Online Databases

Although there are thousands of research articles in psychology published every year, many tools are available to help you search through the publications to find the few that are directly relevant to your research topic. Most of these tools now exist as computer databases. A typical **database** contains about 1 million publications, or records, that are all cross-referenced by subject words and author names. You enter a subject word (or author name) as a search term, and the database searches through all of its records and provides a list of the publications that are related to that subject (or author). Some databases are *full text*, which means that each record is a complete, word-for-word copy of the original publication. Other databases provide only a brief summary of each publication. Typically, the summary includes the title, the authors, the name of the journal or book in which the publication appears, a list of the subject words that describes the publication, and an abstract. The **abstract** is a brief summary of the publication, usually about 100 words.

Because a full-text database requires more space to store each item, it often contains fewer items than other databases. As a result, a database that is not full text tends to provide more complete coverage of a topic area and, therefore, increases the likelihood that you will find publications related to your research topic. If you are still having trouble finding relevant publications, it may be wise to change to a different database in a related area. For example, if you are looking for literature on antioxidants and aging, you might be more successful searching in a medical database rather than one dedicated to psychology. Table 2.1 shows the basic characteristics of four databases commonly available through most college or university libraries.

Table 2.1 also demonstrates the distinction between a full-text database **PsycARTICLES** and the not-full-text database **PsycINFO**. For example, PsycARTICLES contains about 197,000 items selected from 110 journals. By comparison, PsycINFO contains over 4 million items selected from nearly 2,500 periodicals. Clearly, the full-text database contains only a small fraction of the psychology publications that are contained in PsycINFO. If you are conducting a literature search using PsycARTICLES, you probably will not find many relevant publications simply because they are not included in the database. Therefore, we generally recommend that students use a database that is not full text to obtain more complete coverage of a topic area.

The advantage of searching the literature using a database like PsycINFO is that all the references in the database are selected from reputable scientific publications, and most have been edited and reviewed by professional psychologists to ensure that they are legitimate and accurate contributions. This kind of professional screening does not usually exist on the Internet. For example, if you enter the subject word *amnesia* in PsycINFO, you will get a set of reputable scientific references. If you use the same subject word for an Internet search, you could obtain anybody's site with absolutely no guarantees about the quality or validity of the information. (One notable exception at the time of this writing is conducting a search with Google Scholar, which does a good job of screening out the nonscientific items that normally clutter an Internet search.)

Using PsycINFO

The process of conducting a literature search using PsycINFO is presented in short videos prepared by the American Psychological Association (APA) that show samples of a PsycINFO search on several different platforms including APA PsycNET, ProQuest, OvidSP, and EBSCOhost. There is a very good chance that your school uses one of these platforms for PsycINFO. To access the videos, go to www.youtube.com/psycinfo, and select the video that corresponds to the system used by your school library. We should note, however, that the appearance of PsycINFO and the process of accessing the database

TABLE 2.1

Information about Four Databases (Descriptions Provided by the Databases)

PsycINFO® is the American Psychological Association's (APA) renowned resource for abstracts of scholarly journal articles, book chapters, books, and dissertations. It is the largest resource devoted to peer-reviewed literature in behavioral science and mental health, and contains over 4 million citations and summaries dating as far back as the 1600s, with one of the highest DOI matching rates in the publishing industry. Ninety-nine percent of its content is peer-reviewed. Included is information on the psychological aspects of related fields such as medicine, psychiatry, nursing, sociology, education, pharmacology, technology, linguistics, anthropology, business, law and others. Journal coverage, which spans from the 1800s to the present, includes international material selected from around 2,500 periodicals in dozens of languages. PsycINFO is indexed with controlled vocabulary from APA's Thesaurus of Psychological Index Terms®.

PsycARTICLES® from the American Psychological Association (APA), is a definitive source of full-text, peer-reviewed scholarly and scientific articles in psychology. It contains more than 197,000 articles from more than 110 journals published by the American Psychological Association (APA) and from allied organizations including the Canadian Psychological Association and the Hogrefe Publishing Group. It includes all journal articles, book reviews, letters to the editor, and errata from each journal. Coverage spans 1894 to present; nearly all APA journals go back to Volume 1, Issue 1. PsycARTICLES is indexed with controlled vocabulary from APA's Thesaurus of Psychological Index Terms®.

ERIC the Education Resources Information Center, provides access to education literature and resources. The database provides access to information from journals included in the Current Index of Journals in Education and Resources in Education Index. The database contains more than 1.5 million records and links to more than 336,000 full-text documents dating back to 1966.

MEDLINE with Full Text provides the authoritative medical information on medicine, nursing, dentistry, veterinary medicine, the health care system, and pre-clinical sciences found on MEDLINE, plus the database provides full text for more than 1,470 journals indexed in MEDLINE. Of those, nearly 1,450 have cover-to-cover indexing in MEDLINE. And of those, 558 are not found with full text in any version of Academic Search, Health Source or Biomedical Reference Collection.

may differ from one computer system to another. Therefore, we suggest that you ask a professor or a reference librarian to help you get started. Also, if you suspect that your research topic might be outside the field of psychology, you should also check with a librarian to determine whether a database other than PsycINFO would be better for your search.

Screening Articles during a Literature Search

A literature search is likely to uncover hundreds of journal articles. Although each of these articles is related to your topic, most of them probably are not directly related to the research you hope to do. Therefore, as you work through the literature search process, one of your main concerns is to weed out irrelevant material. There are no absolute criteria for determining whether an article is relevant or should be discarded; you must make your own decisions. However, here are some suggestions to help make the selection/weeding process more efficient:

1. Use the title of the article as your first basis for screening. Based only on the titles, you probably can discard about 90% of the articles as not directly relevant or interesting.
2. Use the abstract of the article as your second screening device. If the title sounds interesting, read the abstract to determine whether the article itself is really relevant. Many of the articles that seemed interesting (from the title) get thrown out at this stage. You can find an abstract either in PsycINFO or at the beginning of the article itself.
3. If you are still interested after looking at the title and the abstract, look for a full-text version of the article, or request an interlibrary loan if full text is not available on your

library's system. Once you find the article, first skim it, looking specifically at the introductory paragraphs and the discussion section.

4. If it still looks relevant, then read the article carefully and/or make a copy for your personal use. The process of reading and understanding a research article is discussed in more detail Section 2.3.

5. Use the references from the articles that you have already found to expand your literature search. Although the list of references will contain "old" research studies published years earlier, they may introduce new author names or subject words for your search.

Ending a Literature Search

Theoretically, you should continue a literature search until you reach a point at which you no longer find any new items. Realistically, however, you must decide when to call off the search. At some point, you will realize you are not uncovering new leads and that you should proceed with the items you have found. Throughout the process, keep in mind that the purpose of a literature search is to gain a general familiarity with the current research in your specific area of interest and find a small set of research studies that will serve as the basis for your own research idea. When you feel comfortable with your knowledge about the topic area and have found a few recent research studies that are particularly relevant to your own interests, then you have completed a successful search.

We are deliberately vague about how many articles form a good foundation for developing a new research idea. You may find two or three interrelated articles that all converge on the same idea, or you might find only one research study that appears to be directly relevant to your interests. In any event, the key criterion is that the study (or studies) you find provides some justification for new research. Even if you have only one study, remember that it cites other research studies that form a basis for the current research question. These same studies should be relevant to your research idea, and you are welcome to include them as part of the foundation for your own research.

LEARNING CHECK

1. Which of the following would be a danger of relying upon a primary source?
   a. The author of the primary source may describe or interpret research results incorrectly.
   b. Primary sources typically do not contain the details of methodology that are required for critical evaluation.
   c. The author may describe results incorrectly and the source does not contain details of methodology.
   d. There is no danger because you can rely on primary sources for accurate information.

2. Which of the following is usually the initial factor for determining whether a specific article is relevant to your research question?
   a. Title
   b. Abstract
   c. Discussion section
   d. Results section

3. Which of the following is a brief summary of a psychology article?
   a. Abstract
   b. Synopsis
   c. Key word
   d. Author name

Answers appear at the end of the chapter.

Finding an Idea for a Research Study from a Published Research Article

LEARNING OBJECTIVES

LO6   Identify the basic sections of an APA-style research article, know what to expect in each section, and summarize and critically evaluate the content of each section for an existing article.

LO7   Explain how an idea for a new research study can be obtained from an existing research publication and use existing research publication(s) to find a new research idea.

Once you have located a set of recent and relevant articles, the final part of the Step 1 of the research process is to use these research reports as the foundation for your research idea or research question (see Chapter 1, Step 1 of the research process). Earlier, we called this task "finding a research idea." When you are familiar with the current research in an area (i.e., once you have "listened" in on the research conversation), the idea for the next study simply involves extending the current research one more step. However, discovering this next step might not be as simple as we have implied, and so we list a few suggestions here.

Find Suggestions for Future Research

The easiest way to find new research ideas is to look for them as explicit statements in the journal articles you already have. Near the end of the discussion section of most research reports is a set of suggestions for future research. In most cases, a research study actually generates more questions than it answers. The authors who are reporting their research results usually point out the questions that remain unanswered. You can certainly use these suggestions as ideas for your own research. Instead of specifically making suggestions for future research, authors occasionally point out limitations or problems with their own study. If you can design a new study that fixes the problems, you have found a new research idea.

Combine or Contrast Existing Results

Occasionally, it is possible to find a new research idea by combining two (or more) existing results. For example, several research studies have shown that dietary flavanols, which occur naturally in cocoa, seem to improve cognitive performance. A simple Web search can also produce data on per capita chocolate consumption for several different countries. Combining these two results, Messerti (2012) found and reported a significant correlation between per capita chocolate consumption and the number of Nobel laureates in a total of 23 countries. Another possibility is that two research results seem to contradict each other. In this case, you could look for factors that differentiate the two studies and might be responsible for the different results.

The Components of a Research Article—Critical Reading

Most ideas for new research studies begin with careful reading of past studies. First, you should notice that it is customary for a research article to be arranged into standard, distinct sections. The first column of Table 2.2 lists the sections in order and the content of each section is summarized in the second column. Ideas for new research are most likely to come from the introduction, the discussion, and the references. The **introduction** discusses previous research that forms the foundation for the current research study and presents a clear statement of the problem being investigated. This can help you decide whether the article will be useful in the development of your research idea and may identify previous

TABLE 2.2
Critically Reading a Research Article

This table identifies the major elements that make up a research report and describes the kinds of questions you should ask for a critical evaluation of each element.

Section	Content	Critical Evaluation Questions
Introduction	Literature review	Is the review complete and up to date?
		Are relevant or related topics not covered?
		Is the hypothesis clearly stated?
	Hypothesis or purpose for study	Is the hypothesis directly related to the reviewed literature?
		Does the predicted outcome logically follow from the hypothesis?
	Specific prediction from hypothesis	Can other specific predictions be made?
Method	Participants	Are the participants representative of the population being considered?
		If participants were restricted (e.g., males only), is it justified? Would different participants produce different results?
		Are there alternative ways to define and measure the variables?
	Procedure	Could alternative procedures be used?
Results	Statistics (descriptive and inferential)	Were the appropriate statistics used?
		Exactly what is significant and what is not?
		Are the effects large enough to be meaningful?
Discussion	Results related to hypothesis	Do the results really support (or refute) the hypothesis?
		Are the conclusions justified by the results?
	Justified conclusions	Are alternative conclusions/explanations possible?
	Alternative explanations	Would other variables affect the results?
		Do the results have real-world applications?
	Applications	Is there reason to suspect that the same results would not occur outside the lab?
	Limits to generalization	Would the same results be expected with different participants or under different circumstances?
References	List of items cited	Is the list of references current and complete?

studies that may also be useful. Incidentally, the introduction is not labeled "Introduction." Instead, the text simply begins immediately after the abstract and continues until the next section, which is the **method section**. The method section presents details concerning the participants and the procedures used in the study. Often, a new research study is created by changing the characteristics of the participants or by modifying the procedures. Next is the **results section**, which presents the details of the statistical analysis and usually is not important for generating a new research idea. Immediately following the results is the **discussion section**. The discussion typically begins by summarizing the results of the study, stating the conclusions, and noting any potential applications. Following the discussion is the **reference section**, which lists complete references for all items cited in the report.

If you question each element as you are reading an article, you should finish with a good understanding of the study and you probably will generate some ideas for a new research study. As you read each section, it is wise to take notes for future reference. Be sure to get a complete reference for the article. This includes the author name(s), the year of publication, the title, and the source of the article. If the source is a print journal, get the name of the journal as well as the volume number and the page numbers. If the article is from an electronic source, you also should note the digital object identifier (DOI), which is a unique code that provides continuous access to the article. This information will be necessary for you and others to locate the article in the future and will appear in the list of references that goes in your research report. Second, it is best to summarize and describe the important aspects of the article in your own words. Avoid copying specific phrases or sentences used by the authors. By using your own words during note taking you are less likely to unintentionally plagiarize by incorporating words or ideas from other people into the research report that you write.

If you read critically and question each section of a research report, then you may discover a modification or an extension that will convert the current study into a new research idea. The third column of Table 2.2 lists some questions you can ask while critically reading a research report. For example, would a result that is reported for 8-year-old boys also be obtained if adolescents were used as participants? If a study demonstrates that a treatment is effective under specific circumstances, it is perfectly legitimate to ask whether the treatment would still be effective if the circumstances were changed. Please note that we are not suggesting that you can create good research ideas by simply changing variables randomly. There should be some reason, based on logic or other research results, to expect that changing circumstances might change results. If it is reasonable to modify the characteristics of the participants or use an alternate definition or procedure for measuring the variables, then you have created a modified study for your own research.

If you are considering changing the participants or a variable in an existing study, then it is usually a good idea to expand your literature search to include the new subject terms. Suppose, for example, you used the search terms *competition* and *games* to find an interesting article on competitive behavior for 8-year-old boys. If you are thinking about modifying the study by using *adolescents*, you could add adolescents as a new search term (along with your original two terms) to see if there is additional research that might help you develop your idea.

In general, research is not static. Instead, it is constantly developing and growing as new studies spring from past results. New research ideas usually come from recognizing the direction in which an area of research is moving and then going with the flow.

LEARNING CHECK

1. What is typically included in the introduction section of a research article?
   a. It provides interpretation of the findings.
   b. It describes the overall purpose and rationale of the research.
   c. It includes the results of statistical analyses.
   d. It provides the details of the methodology used in the study.
2. What is typically included in the method section of a research article?
   a. It provides interpretation of the findings.
   b. It describes the overall purpose and rationale of the research.
   c. It includes the results of statistical analyses.
   d. It provides the details of the methodology used in the study.
3. What questions should you ask when reading an introduction to a research article?
   a. Is the literature review up-to-date?
   b. Is the hypothesis related to the literature reviewed?
   c. Does the prediction logically follow the hypothesis?
   d. All of the above.

Answers appear at the end of the chapter.

2.4 Using a Research Idea to Form a Hypothesis and Create a Research Study

LEARNING OBJECTIVE

LO8   Describe the characteristics of a good hypothesis and identify examples of good and bad hypotheses.

The goal of a literature search is to find an idea for a research study. The idea typically involves a general statement about the relationship between two variables. For example:

> Visual imagery is related to human memory.

Often, the research idea is stated as a question, such as:

> Is there a relationship between using visual images and human memory?

The next step in the research process (Step 2; see Chapter 1 research process) is to transform your research idea into a hypothesis. In most cases, the research idea says that there is a relationship between two variables and the hypothesis specifies the nature of the relationship. If the idea is expressed as a research question, then the hypothesis is a tentative answer to the question. For the imagery example, a possible hypothesis is as follows:

> Hypothesis: The use of visual images is related to better memory performance.

Eventually, the results from an empirical research study will either provide support for the hypothesis or will refute the hypothesis. Because the hypothesis identifies the specific variables involved and describes how they are related, it forms the foundation for the research study. Conducting the study provides an empirical test of the hypothesis. The results of the study will either provide support for the hypothesis or will refute the hypothesis.

Characteristics of a Good Hypothesis

Although you will need to make additional decisions about the details of the study, the basic framework is established in the statement of the hypothesis. Therefore, it is essential that you develop a good hypothesis. The following four elements are considered to be important characteristics of a good hypothesis.

Logical

A good hypothesis is usually founded in established theories or developed from the results of previous research. Specifically, a good hypothesis should be the logical conclusion of a logical argument. Consider the following example:

> *Premise 1:* Academic success is highly valued and respected in society (at least by parents and teachers).

> *Premise 2:* Being valued and respected by others contributes to high self-esteem.

> *Conclusion (hypothesis):* For a specific group of students, higher levels of academic success will be related to higher levels of self-esteem.

In this argument, we assume that the two premise statements are *facts* or knowledge that has been demonstrated and reported in the scientific literature. Typically, these facts would be obtained from extensive library research. Library research acquaints you with the relevant knowledge that already exists: What other researchers have already done and what they have found. By knowing the basic facts, theories, predictions, and methods that make up the knowledge base for a specific topic area, you gain a clearer picture of exactly which variables are being studied and exactly which relationships are likely to exist. The logical argument provides a rationale or justification for your hypothesis and establishes a connection between your research and the research results that have been obtained by others.

Testable

In addition to being logical, a good hypothesis must be **testable**; that is, it must be possible to observe and measure all of the variables involved. In particular, the hypothesis must involve real situations, real events, and real individuals. You cannot test a hypothesis that refers to imaginary events or hypothetical situations. For example, you could debate what might have happened if John F. Kennedy had not been assassinated. However, this proposition does not lead to a testable hypothesis. It cannot be observed and, therefore, is inappropriate as scientific hypotheses.

Refutable

One characteristic of a testable hypothesis is that it must be **refutable**; that is, it must be possible to obtain research results that are contrary to the hypothesis. For example, if the hypothesis states that the treatment will cause an increase in scores, it must be possible for the data to show no increase. A refutable hypothesis, often called a falsifiable hypothesis, is a critical component of the research process. Remember, the scientific method requires an objective and public demonstration. A non-refutable hypothesis, one that cannot be demonstrated to be false, is inappropriate for the scientific method. For example, people occasionally claim to have miraculous or magical powers. However, they often add the stipulation that these powers can be seen only in the presence of true believers. When the miracles fail to occur under the watchful eye of scientists, the people simply state that the scientists are nonbelievers. Thus, it is impossible to prove that the claims are false. The result is a claim (or hypothesis) that cannot be refuted.

DEFINITIONS

> A **testable hypothesis** is one for which all of the variables, events, and individuals can be defined and observed.
>
> A **refutable hypothesis** is one that can be demonstrated to be false. That is, it is possible for the outcome to be different from the prediction.

Consider the following hypotheses that are not testable or refutable:

Hypothesis: The more sins a man commits, the less likely he is to get into heaven.

Hypothesis: If old dogs could talk, they would spend most of their time reminiscing about things they had smelled during their lives.

Hypothesis: If people could fly, there would be substantially fewer cases of depression.

Hypothesis: The human mind emits thought waves that influence other people, but that cannot be measured or recorded in any way.

Although you may find these hypotheses interesting, they cannot be tested or shown to be false and, therefore, are unsuitable for scientific research. In general, hypotheses that deal with moral or religious issues, value judgments, or hypothetical situations are untestable or non-refutable. However, this does not mean that religion, morals, or human values are off-limits for scientific research. You could, for example, compare personality characteristics or family backgrounds for religious and nonreligious people, or you could look for behavioral differences between pro-life individuals and pro-choice individuals. Nearly any topic can be studied scientifically if you take care to develop testable and refutable hypotheses.

Positive

A final characteristic of a testable hypothesis is that it must make a positive statement about the existence of something, usually the existence of a relationship, the existence of a difference, or the existence of a treatment effect. The following are examples of such hypotheses:

> Hypothesis 1. For high school students, there is a relationship between intelligence and creativity.
>
> Hypothesis 2. There is a difference between the verbal skills of 3-year-old girls and those of 3-year-old boys.
>
> Hypothesis 3. The new therapy technique will produce significant improvement for severely depressed patients.

On the other hand, a prediction that denies existence is untestable. The following are examples of untestable predictions:

> Hypothesis 4. For adults, there is no relationship between age and memory ability.
>
> Hypothesis 5. There is no difference between the problem-solving strategies used by females and those used by males.
>
> Hypothesis 6. The new training procedure has no effect on students' self-esteem.

The reason that a testable hypothesis must make a positive statement affirming existence is based on the scientific process that is used to test the prediction. Specifically, the basic nature of science is to assume that something does *not* exist until there is enough evidence to demonstrate that it actually does exist. Suppose, for example, that I would like to test the hypothesis that there is a relationship between creativity and intelligence. In this case, I begin with the assumption that a relationship does not exist, and the goal for my research study is to gather enough evidence (data) to provide a convincing demonstration that a relationship does exist. You may recognize this process as the same system used in jury trials: The jury assumes that a defendant is innocent and the prosecution attempts to present enough evidence to prove that the defendant is guilty. The key problem with this system occurs when you fail to obtain convincing evidence. In a jury trial, if the prosecution fails to produce enough evidence, the verdict is *not guilty*. Notice that the defendant has *not* been proved innocent; there simply is not enough evidence to say that the defendant is guilty. Similarly, if we fail to find a relationship in a research study, we cannot conclude that the relationship does not exist; we simply conclude that we failed to find convincing evidence.

Thus, the research process is structured to test for the existence of treatment effects, relationships, and differences; it is not structured to test a prediction that denies existence. For example, suppose I begin with a hypothesis stating that there is no relationship between creativity and IQ. (Note that this hypothesis *denies* existence and, therefore, is not testable.) If I do a research study that fails to find a relationship, have I proved that the hypothesis is correct? It should be clear that I have not proved anything; I have simply failed to find any evidence. Specifically, I cannot conclude that something does not exist simply because I failed to find it. As a result, a hypothesis that denies the existence of a relationship cannot be tested in a research study and, therefore, is not a good foundation for a study.

Using a Hypothesis to Create a Research Study

The next steps in the research process will transform the general hypothesis into a specific research study. Step 3 specifies how the variables will be defined and measured and Step 4 identifies the individuals who will participate in the study, describes how they will be selected, and provides for their ethical treatment. As a result, the hypothesis is converted into a specific research predication that can be verified or refuted by direct observation. For example, a hypothesis may propose that mental imagery improves memory. This general hypothesis can be transformed into several different research studies depending on how the participants and the variables are specified. Two possibilities for specific research predications are as follows:

College students who are instructed to study a list of 40 words by forming a mental image of the object represented by each word will recall more words (on average) than college students who study the same words but are not given instructions to form mental images.

Ten-year-old children who view pictures of 20 items (e.g., a table, a horse, and a tree) will recall more items, on average, than 10-year-old children who view a series of words representing the same 20 items (e.g., *table, horse,* and *tree*).

Note that each research study applies the hypothesis to a concrete situation that can be observed. In general, there are many different ways to convert a hypothesis into a specific research study. The method you select depends on a variety of factors, including the set of individuals you want to study and the measurement techniques that are available. However, each of the many possible research studies should provide a direct test of the basic hypothesis.

As a final note, the fact that several different research studies can be created from the same general hypothesis gives you one more technique for creating a new research study. Specifically, you can take the general hypothesis from an existing study and develop your own new study. For example, we have presented two specific studies based on the general hypothesis that memory is related to images. If you can develop your own study by changing the group of participants, modifying the method for measuring memory, or finding another way to have people use images, then you will have produced your own research study.

LEARNING CHECK

1. For which of the following questions would the scientific method be an appropriate method for seeking an answer.
   a. How many angels can stand on the head of a pin?
   b. Is abortion moral or immoral?
   c. What conditions promote student learning in an elementary classroom?
   d. How would life be different if the computer had never been invented?
2. Which of the following is not a good example of a research hypothesis?
   a. There is no relationship between fatigue and reaction time.
   b. Increased sugar consumption leads to an increased level of activity.
   c. Smaller class size is related to better academic performance.
   d. A person's level of self-esteem is related to how long he or she will persist at a difficult task.

Answers appear at the end of the chapter.

CHAPTER SUMMARY

At this point, you should review the learning objectives presented at the beginning of each section and be sure that you have mastered each objective.

All research begins with a topic area, and, fortunately, there are many places from which topics can come. Feel free to get topics for research from your own personal interests, your own casual observations, reports of others' observations, practical problems, and theories.

Beginning the research process can seem intimidating, but keeping a few points in mind will make the task a little easier. First, pick a topic in which you have some real personal interest to help yourself stay motivated throughout the research process. Second, do your homework on your topic; collect and familiarize yourself with the background information in your area. Third, keep an open mind in settling on a research topic; let your background reading lead you to a specific idea. Fourth, after doing the background reading, focus specifically on one research question. Finally, break down the planning and conducting of your research into manageable steps, and take them one at a time.

Once you settle on a general topic area, you must become familiar with the current research in that area. To find research journal articles in psychology, we recommend PsycINFO because this database provides extensive coverage of psychology literature. Consult your librarian to determine the appropriate databases for other academic disciplines. Based on their titles and abstracts, discard articles that are not directly relevant. As you read selected articles, you will "find" a new research idea. The next step in the research process is to transform your research idea into a hypothesis.

KEY WORDS

applied research

basic research

primary source

secondary source

testable hypothesis

refutable hypothesis

EXERCISES

The exercises are identified with specific learning objectives and are intended to assess your mastery of the objectives. You should be aware that exam items are also generated to assess learning objectives.

1. In addition to the key words, you should be able to define each of the following terms:

   literature search
   subject words
   database
   abstract
   PsycINFO
   PsycARTICLES

   title
   introduction
   method section
   results section
   discussion section
   reference section

2. (**LO1**) Make a list of five ideas for a general research topic that interests you. For each, identify the source of the idea.

3. (**LO2**) Based on the following descriptions of studies, determine whether each of the studies can be classified as basic or applied research.
   a. A researcher conducts a study to determine whether there is a significant increase in job satisfaction if employees can work from home one day a week.
   b. A researcher initiates a study to determine whether students are more likely to complete assigned readings prior to class, if they are given an in-class quiz on the material.
   c. A researcher develops a study to examine personality traits as a predictor of career success.
   d. A researcher conducts a study to determine whether parenting type is an explanation for the development of anxiety in children.

4. (**LO3**) Define *primary* and *secondary sources* and explain how each plays a role in the process of finding a research idea.

5. (**LO4**) Using PsycINFO (or a similar database), find five articles on the topic of preschool daycare and social anxiety. Print out a copy of the Record List page.

6. (**LO4**) Using PsycINFO (or a similar database), find research articles on how background music influences mood. Print out the Detailed Record (including the abstract) for one research article on this topic.

7. (**LO4**) Search in a current newspaper or on a news website and find one news story that is based on the results of a recent research study. Summarize the research result according to the story. Do you have any reason to doubt that this information is accurate?

8. (**LO5**) How does a full-text database differ from other databases?

9. (**LO6**) List the five sections typically found in a research article, and describe briefly what each should contain.

10. (**LO7**) Describe the three ways identified in the text to find or develop a new research idea from existing research report(s).

11. (**LO8**) Is the following hypothesis testable, refutable, and positive? Explain your answer.
    Hypothesis: People who pray regularly are less likely to be injured in an accident.

12. (**LO8**) Determine whether each of the following hypotheses is testable and refutable. If not, explain why.
    a. Young children can see good or evil auras surrounding the people they meet.
    b. A list of three-syllable words is more difficult to memorize than a list of one-syllable words.
    c. The incidence of paranoia is higher among people who claim to have been abducted by aliens than in the general population.
    d. If atomic weapons were never invented, then there would be less anxiety in the world.

LEARNING CHECK ANSWERS

Section 2.1	Section 2.2	Section 2.3	Section 2.4
1. b, 2. b, 3. a	1. d, 2. a, 3. a	1. b, 2. d, 3. d	1. c, 2. a

Defining and Measuring Variables

© Nathan Jasowiak / Shutterstock

CHAPTER LEARNING OBJECTIVES

LO1 Define a *construct* and explain the role that constructs play in theories.

LO2 Define an *operational definition* and explain the purpose and the limitations of operational definitions.

LO3 Define a *positive relationship* and a *negative relationship* and explain how the consistency of positive and negative relationships can be used to establish validity and reliability.

LO4 Define the *validity of measurement* and explain why and how it is measured.

LO5 Define the *reliability of measurement* and explain why and how it is measured.

LO6 Compare and contrast the four scales of measurement (nominal, ordinal, interval, and ratio) and identify examples of each.

LO7 Identify the three modalities of measurement and explain the strengths and weaknesses of each.

CHAPTER OVERVIEW

In this chapter, we consider the procedures used by behavioral scientists to define and measure the variables that they study in their research. We all measure things from time to time and typically view measurement as a simple procedure. However, the process of measurement in research can be complicated and it often involves a number of decisions that have serious consequences for the outcome of a research study. Consider the following example.

Previous research indicates that heterosexual men perceive women as being more attractive when they are wearing red (Elliot & Niesta, 2008). Based on this research, Guéguen and Jacob (2012) reasoned that the color red might influence the way that men react to restaurant waitresses. In their study, waitresses in five different restaurants wore the same T-shirt in six different colors (red, blue, green, yellow, black, and white) on different days during a six-week period. The waitresses were instructed to act normally and to record their perception of each customer's gender and how much was left as a tip. The results show that male customers gave significantly bigger tips to waitresses wearing red but that color had no effect on tipping for female customers.

In this study the variables are objective, concrete, well defined, and easy to measure. There is nothing abstract or uncertain about the color of a T-shirt or the amount of money left as a tip. This clarity is in sharp contrast to the variables that are examined in many behavioral science research studies. Consider, for example, a study by Orth, Robins, and Soto (2010) examining differences in shame, guilt, and pride across ages ranging from 13 years old to 89 years old. Although we all know what is meant by shame, guilt, and pride, these variables are not as easily defined and measured as the color of a T-shirt. However, to determine whether there are changes in shame across the life span, it is first necessary to define exactly what is meant by *shame* and decide how it will be measured.

In this chapter, we examine Step 3 of the research process: How researchers define and measure variables. We begin by considering different types of variables from simple, concrete variables, such as the color of a T-shirt, to more abstract variables, such as guilt or shame. Then we will focus on the process of measurement with particular attention to abstract variables that must be defined and measured using operational definitions. Two criteria used to evaluate the quality of a measurement procedure—validity and reliability—are discussed, and we follow with discussion of the scales of measurement, the modes of measuring, and other aspects of measurement.

3.1 Constructs and Operational Definitions

LEARNING OBJECTIVES

LO1 Define a *construct* and explain the role that constructs play in theories.

LO2 Define an *operational definition* and explain the purpose and the limitations of operational definitions.

The first step in the research process is to find an unanswered question that will serve as a research idea. The second step involves forming a hypothesis, a tentative answer to the question. The next steps in the research process involve using the hypothesis to develop an empirical research study that will either support or refute the hypothesis. We begin by specifying how each of the variables will be measured.

In Chapter 1 (p. 11), we defined variables as characteristics or conditions that change or have different values for different individuals. Usually, researchers are interested in how variables are affected by different conditions or how variables differ from one group of individuals to another. For example, a clinician may be interested in how depression scores change in response to therapy, or a teacher may want to know how much difference there is in the reading scores for third-grade children versus fourth-grade children. To evaluate differences or changes in variables, it is essential that we are able to measure them. Thus, the next step in the research process (Step 3) is determining a method for defining and measuring the variables that are being studied.

Occasionally, a research study involves variables that are well defined, easily observed, and easily measured. For example, a study of physical development might involve the variables of height and weight. Both of these variables are tangible, concrete attributes that can be observed and measured directly. On the other hand, some studies involve intangible, abstract attributes such as motivation or self-esteem. Such variables are not directly observable, and the process of measuring them is more complicated.

Theories and Constructs

In attempting to explain and predict behavior, scientists and philosophers often develop **theories** that contain hypothetical mechanisms and intangible elements. Although these mechanisms and elements cannot be seen and are only assumed to exist, we accept them as real because they seem to describe and explain behaviors that we see. For example, a bright child does poor work in school because she has low "motivation." A kindergarten teacher may hesitate to criticize a lazy child because it may injure the student's "self-esteem." But what is motivation, and how do we know that it is low? What about self-esteem? How do we recognize poor self-esteem or healthy self-esteem when we cannot see it in the first place? Many research variables, particularly variables of interest to behavioral scientists, are in fact hypothetical entities created from theory and speculation. Such variables are called **constructs** or **hypothetical constructs**.

DEFINITIONS

> In the behavioral sciences, a **theory** is a set of statements about the mechanisms underlying a particular behavior. Theories help organize and unify different observations of the behavior and its relationship with other variables. A good theory generates predictions about the behavior.
>
> **Constructs** are hypothetical attributes or mechanisms that help explain and predict behavior in a theory.

Although constructs are hypothetical and intangible, they play very important roles in behavioral theories. In many theories, constructs can be influenced by external stimuli and, in turn, can influence external behaviors.

External Stimulus → Construct → External Behavior

For example, external factors such as rewards or reinforcements can affect motivation (a construct), and motivation can then affect performance. As another example, external factors such as an upcoming exam can affect anxiety (a construct) and anxiety can then affect behavior (worry, nervousness, increased heart rate, and/or lack of concentration). Although researchers may not be able to observe and measure a construct directly, it is possible to examine the factors that influence a construct and the behaviors that are influenced by the construct.

Operational Definitions

Although a construct itself cannot be directly observed or measured, it is possible to observe and measure the external factors and the behaviors that are associated with the construct. Researchers can measure these external, observable events as an indirect method of measuring the construct itself. Typically, researchers identify a behavior or a cluster of behaviors associated with a construct; the behavior is then measured, and the resulting measurements are used as a definition and a measure of the construct. This method of defining and measuring a construct is called an **operational definition**. Researchers often refer to the process of using an operational definition as *operationalizing* a construct.

DEFINITION

> An **operational definition** is a procedure for indirectly measuring and defining a variable that cannot be observed or measured directly. An operational definition specifies a measurement procedure (a set of operations) for measuring an external, observable behavior and uses the resulting measurements as a definition and a measurement of the hypothetical construct.

Although operational definitions are used to measure and define a variety of constructs, such as beauty, hunger, and pain, the most familiar example is probably the IQ test, which is intended to measure intelligence. Notice that "intelligence" is a hypothetical construct; it is an internal attribute that cannot be observed directly. However, intelligence is assumed to influence external behaviors that can be observed and measured. An IQ test actually measures external behavior consisting of responses to questions. The test includes both elements of an operational definition: There are specific procedures for administering and scoring the test, and the resulting scores are used as a definition and a measurement of intelligence. Thus, an IQ score is actually a measure of intelligent behavior but we use the score both to define *intelligence* and to measure it.

In addition to using operational definitions as a basis for measuring variables, they also can be used to define variables to be manipulated. For example, the construct "hunger" can be operationally defined as the number of hours of food deprivation. In a research study, for example, one group could be tested immediately after eating a full meal, a second group could be tested 6 hours after eating, and a third group could be tested 12 hours after eating. In this study, we are comparing three different levels of hunger, which are defined by the number of hours without food. Alternatively, we could measure hunger for a group of rats by recording how much food each animal eats when given free access to a dish of rat chow. The amount that each rat eats defines how hungry it is.

Limitations of Operational Definitions

Although operational definitions are necessary to convert an abstract variable into a concrete entity that can be observed and studied, you should keep in mind that an operational definition is not the same as the construct itself. For example, we can define and measure variables, such as intelligence, motivation, and anxiety, but in fact we are measuring external manifestations that (we hope) provide an indication of the underlying variables. As a result, there are always concerns about the quality of operational definitions and the measurements they produce.

The primary limitation of an operational definition is that there is not a one-to-one relationship between the variable that is being measured and the actual measurements produced by the operational definition. Consider for example, the familiar situation of an instructor evaluating the students in a class. In this situation, the underlying variable is knowledge or mastery of subject matter, and the instructor's goal is to obtain a measure of knowledge for each student. However, *knowledge* is a construct that cannot be directly observed or measured. Therefore, instructors typically give students a task (such as an exam, an essay, or a set of problems), and then measure how well students perform the task. Although it makes sense to expect that performance is a reflection of knowledge, performance and knowledge are not the same thing. For example, physical illness or fatigue may affect performance on an exam, but they probably do not affect knowledge. There is not a one-to-one relationship between the variable that the instructor wants to measure (knowledge) and the actual measurements that are made (performance). The indirect connection between the variable and the measurements can result in two general problems.

First, it is easy for operational definitions to leave out important components of a construct. It is possible, for example, to define *depression* in terms of behavioral symptoms (social withdrawal, insomnia, etc.). However, behavior represents only a part of the total construct. Depression includes cognitive and emotional components that are not included in a totally behavioral definition. One way to reduce this problem is to include two or more different procedures to measure the same variable. Multiple measures for a variable are discussed in more detail at the beginning Section 3.5 on p. 72.

Second, operational definitions often include extra components that are not part of the construct being measured. For example, a self-report of depression in a clinical interview or on a questionnaire is influenced by the participant's verbal skills (ability to understand questions and express feelings and thoughts) as well as the participant's willingness to reveal personal feelings or behaviors that might be perceived as odd or undesirable. A participant who is able and willing to describe personal symptoms may appear to be more depressed than someone who withholds or conceals information.

Using Operational Definitions

Whenever the variables in a research study are hypothetical constructs, you must use operational definitions to define and measure the variables. Usually, however, this does not mean creating your own operational definition. The best method of determining how a variable should be measured is to consult previous research involving the same variable. Research reports typically describe in detail how each variable is defined and measured. By reading several research reports concerning the same variable, you typically can discover that a standard, generally accepted measurement procedure has already been developed. When you plan your own research, the best advice is to use the conventional method of defining and measuring your variables. In this way, your results will be directly comparable to the results obtained in past research. However, keep in mind that any measurement procedure, particularly an operational definition, is simply an attempt to classify the variable being considered. Other measurement procedures are always possible and may provide a better way to define and measure the variable. In general, critically examine any measurement procedure and ask yourself whether a different technique might produce better measurements.

In the following section, we introduce the two general criteria used to evaluate the quality of a measurement procedure, especially an operational definition. In later sections, we examine some specific details of measurement that can influence whether a particular measurement procedure is appropriate for a particular research question. As you read through the following sections, keep in mind that the choice of a measurement procedure

Authors typically describe how variables are defined and measured in the method section of a research report.

involves a number of decisions. Usually, there is no absolutely right or absolutely wrong choice; nonetheless, you should be aware that other researchers had options and choices when they decided how to measure their variables.

LEARNING CHECK

1. What term is used for a variable that cannot be observed or measured directly but is useful for describing and explaining behavior?
   ⓐ Construct
   b. Operational variable
   c. Theoretical variable
   d. Hypothetical variable
2. What is the goal of an operational definition?
   a. Simply to provide a definition of a hypothetical construct
   b. Simply to provide a method for measuring a hypothetical construct
   ⓒ To provide a definition and a method for measuring a hypothetical construct
   d. None of the other options describe the purpose of an operational definition
3. Which of the following is a disadvantage of using an operational definition?
   a. The operational definition may not be an accurate reflection of the construct.
   b. The operational definition may leave out important components of the construct.
   c. The operational definition may include extra components that are not part of the construct.
   ⓓ All of the other options are disadvantages.

Answers appear at the end of the chapter.

3.2 Validity and Reliability of Measurement

LEARNING OBJECTIVES

LO3 Define a *positive relationship* and a *negative relationship* and explain how the consistency of positive and negative relationships can be used to establish validity and reliability.

LO4 Define the *validity of measurement* and explain why and how it is measured.

LO5 Define the *reliability of measurement* and explain why and how it is measured.

In the previous section, we noted that several different methods are usually available for measuring any particular variable. How can we decide which method is best? In addition, whenever the variable is a hypothetical construct, a researcher must use an operational definition as a measurement procedure. In essence, an operational definition is an indirect method of measuring something that cannot be measured directly. How can we be sure that the measurements obtained from an operational definition actually represent the intangible construct? In general, we are asking how good a measurement procedure, or a measurement, is. Researchers have developed two general criteria for evaluating the quality of any measurement procedure: validity and reliability. As you will see, validity and reliability are often defined and measured by the consistency of the relationship between two sets of measurements. Therefore, before we introduce these two topics we will pause to review the definitions and procedures that are used to establish the consistency of a relationship.

Consistency of a Relationship

Often, the validity and reliability of measurements are established by demonstrating the consistency of a relationship between two different measurements. For example, one definition of validity requires that the scores obtained from a new measurement procedure are consistently related to the scores from a well-established technique for measuring the same variable. To show the amount of consistency between two different measurements, the two scores obtained for each person can be presented in a graph called a scatter plot. In a scatter plot, the two scores for each person are represented as a single point, with the horizontal position of the point determined by one score and the vertical position determined by the second score. Figure 3.1(a) shows an example of a consistent **positive relationship** between two measurements. The relationship is described as positive because the two measurements change together in the same direction. Therefore, people who score high on the first measurement (toward the right of the graph) also tend to score high on the second measurement (toward the top of the graph). Similarly, people scoring low on one measurement also score low on the other. On the other hand, Figure 3.1(b) shows an example of a consistent **negative relationship**. This time the two measurements change in opposite directions so that people who score high on one measurement tend to score low on the other. For example, we could measure performance on a math test by counting the number of correct answers or by counting the number of errors. These two measurements should be negatively related. Finally, Figure 3.1(c) shows two measurements that are not consistently related. In this graph, some people who score high on one measurement also

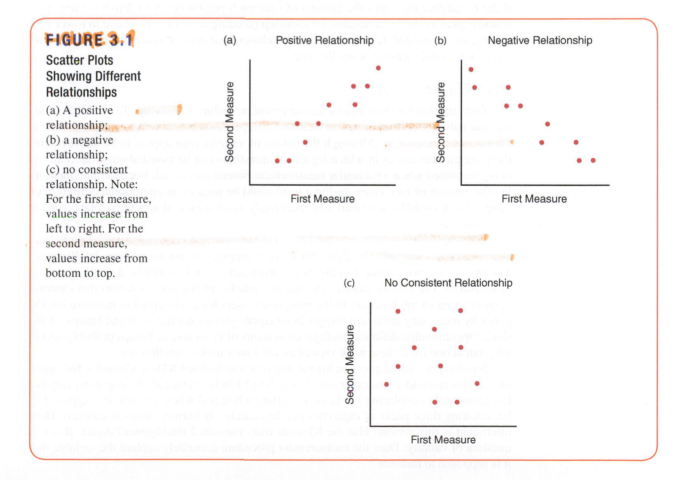

FIGURE 3.1

Scatter Plots Showing Different Relationships

(a) A positive relationship; (b) a negative relationship; (c) no consistent relationship. Note: For the first measure, values increase from left to right. For the second measure, values increase from bottom to top.

(a)   Positive Relationship

(b)   Negative Relationship

(c)   No Consistent Relationship

score high on the second, but others who score high on the first measurement now score low on the second. In this case, there is no consistent, predictable relationship between the two measurements. For example, if you measured shoe size and IQ for each individual in a group of third-grade students, then you should find no relationship between the two variables.

Often, the consistency of a relationship is determined by computing a correlation between the two measurements (see Chapter 15, pp. 384–387). A consistent positive relationship like the one in Figure 3.1(a) produces a correlation near +1.00, a consistent negative relationship like the one in Figure 3.1(b) produces a correlation near −1.00, and an inconsistent relationship like the one in Figure 3.1(c) produces a correlation near zero. The numerical value of the correlation (independent of the sign) describes the consistency of the relationship by measuring the degree to which the data points form a straight line. If the points fit perfectly on a line, the correlation is +1.00 or −1.00. If there is no linear fit whatsoever, the correlation is 0.

Note that the reliability or validity of a measurement procedure is usually established with a consistent positive or a consistent negative relationship, depending on how the variables are defined and measured. Thus, correlations are often used to determine validity and reliability. For example, suppose that a researcher develops a new test to measure intelligence. The validity of the test could be established by demonstrating that the scores from the test are consistently related to traditional IQ scores. Specifically, there should be a consistent positive relationship between the number of items answered correctly on the test and traditional IQ scores (more correct answers go with higher IQs). However, if the researcher measures the amount of time each person needs to finish the test, you would expect a consistent negative relationship (needing more time is related to lower IQ). Finally, an inconsistent relationship, or a correlation near zero, would indicate that the new test is not a valid measure of intelligence.

Validity of Measurement

The first criterion for evaluating a measurement procedure is **validity**. To establish validity, you must demonstrate that the measurement procedure is actually measuring what it claims to be measuring. Although the notion of validity may appear to be self-evident, there are circumstances in which legitimate questions can be asked about what really is being measured when a particular measurement procedure is used. For example, measuring the amount of food eaten during a meal could be used as an operational definition of hunger, but it could be described more accurately as a measure of appetite, metabolism, or even body size.

The question of validity is especially important whenever an operational definition is used to measure a hypothetical construct. For example, how do we measure intelligence? The answer is—we cannot. Intelligence is hypothetical and cannot be directly observed or measured. The best we can do is to measure intelligent behavior or some other external manifestation of intelligence. In the past, researchers have attempted to measure intelligence by measuring brain size (bigger brain equals greater intelligence) and bumps on the skull. Operationally, defining intelligence in terms of brain size or bumps probably seems silly, but at one time, these were viewed as valid measures of intelligence.

Similarly, we could question the validity of a standardized IQ test. Consider, for example, an absent-minded professor who has an IQ of 158 but is incredibly stupid in everyday life (constantly misplacing car keys, forgetting when and where classes are supposed to be, smoking three packs of cigarettes per day, carelessly burning holes in clothes). How intelligent is this person? Has the IQ score truly measured intelligence? Again, this is a question of validity: Does the measurement procedure accurately capture the variable that it is supposed to measure?

DEFINITION	The **validity** of a measurement procedure is the degree to which the measurement process measures the variable that it claims to measure.

Researchers have developed several methods for assessing the validity of measurement. Six of the more commonly used definitions of validity are as follows.

Face Validity

Face validity is the simplest and least scientific definition of validity. Face validity concerns the superficial appearance, or face value, of a measurement procedure. Does the measurement technique look like it measures the variable that it claims to measure? For example, an IQ test ought to include questions that require logic, reasoning, background knowledge, and good memory. Such questions appear to be appropriate for measuring intelligence and, therefore, have high face validity. Face validity is based on subjective judgment and is difficult to quantify. In addition, there are circumstances in which a high level of face validity can create problems. If the purpose of the measurement is obvious, the participants in a research study can see exactly what is being measured and may adjust their answers to produce a better image of themselves. For this reason, researchers often try to disguise the true purpose of measurement devices such as questionnaires, deliberately trying to conceal the variables that they are trying to measure.

Concurrent Validity

Often, the validity of a new measurement is established by demonstrating that the scores obtained from the new measurement technique are directly related to the scores obtained from another, better-established procedure for measuring the same variable. This is called **concurrent validity**. For example, if you had developed a new test to measure intelligence, you could demonstrate that your test really measures intelligence by showing that the scores from your test differentiate individuals in the same way as scores from a standardized IQ test. Basically, concurrent validity establishes consistency between two different procedures for measuring the same variable, suggesting that the two measurement procedures are measuring the same thing. Because one procedure is well established and accepted as being valid, we infer that the second procedure must also be valid. However, the simple fact that the two sets of measurements are related does not necessarily mean that they are identical. For example, we could claim to measure people's height by having them step on a bathroom scale and recording the number that appears. Note that we claim to be measuring *height*, although we are actually measuring *weight*. However, we could provide support for our claim by demonstrating a reasonably strong relationship between our scores and more traditional measurements of height (taller people tend to weigh more; shorter people tend to weigh less). Although we can establish some degree of concurrent validity for our measurements, it should be obvious that a measurement of weight is not really a valid measure of height. In particular, these two measurements behave in different ways and are influenced by different factors. Manipulating diet, for example, influences weight but has little or no effect on height.

Predictive Validity

Most theories make predictions about the constructs they contain. Specifically, theories predict how different values of a construct affect behavior. When the measurements of a construct accurately predict behavior (according to the theory), the measurement procedure is said to have **predictive validity**. For example, school districts often attempt to identify at-risk students so that preventive interventions can be arranged before academic or behavioral problems develop. One technique that is used to identify at-risk students is the Student Risk Screening Scale (SRSS). A recent study (Menzies & Lane, 2012) evaluated the predictive validity of this test by administering it to students three times during a school year. Scores on the test significantly predicted teacher ratings of student self-control and student performance in language arts. Scores also predicted office discipline referrals with higher scores at the beginning of the year associated with more discipline referrals at the year's end. The combination of results provides strong support for the ability of the SRSS to predict future problems, which is a demonstration of predictive validity.

Construct Validity

For most variables that you are likely to encounter, numerous research studies probably already have examined the same variables. Past research has studied each variable in a variety of different situations and has documented which factors influence the variable and how different values of the variable produce different kinds of behavior. In short, past research has demonstrated how the specific variable behaves. If we can demonstrate that measurements of a variable behave in exactly the same way as the variable itself, then we have established the **construct validity** of the measurement procedure.

Suppose, for example, that you are examining a measurement procedure that claims to measure aggression. Past research has demonstrated a relationship between temperature and aggression: In the summer, as temperature rises, people tend to become more aggressive. To help establish construct validity, you would need to demonstrate that the scores you obtain from the measurement procedure also increase as the temperature goes up. Note, however, that this single demonstration is only one small part of construct validity. To completely establish construct validity, you would need to examine all the past research on aggression and show that the measurement procedure produces scores that behave in accordance with everything that is known about the construct "aggression." Because new research results are reported every day, construct validity is never established absolutely. Instead, construct validity is an ideal or a goal that develops gradually from the results of many research studies that examine the measurement procedure in a wide variety of situations.

Earlier, we used the example of attempting to measure height by having people step on a bathroom scale. Because height and weight are related, the measurement that we obtain from the scale would be considered a valid measure of height, at least in terms of concurrent validity. However, the weight measurement is not a valid method of measuring height in terms of construct validity. In particular, height is not influenced by short periods of food deprivation. Weight measurements, on the other hand, are affected by food deprivation. Therefore, measurements of weight do not behave in accordance with what is known about the construct "height," which means that the weight-measurement procedure does not have construct validity as a measure of height.

Convergent and Divergent Validity

Another technique for establishing the validity of a measurement procedure is to demonstrate a combination of convergent and divergent validity (Campbell & Fiske, 1959). In general terms, **convergent validity** involves creating two different methods for measuring the same construct, and then showing that the two methods produce strongly related scores. The goal is to demonstrate that different measurement procedures "converge"—or join—on the same construct. **Divergent validity**, on the other hand, involves demonstrating that we are measuring one specific construct and not combining two different constructs in the same measurement process. The goal is to differentiate between two conceptually distinct constructs by measuring both constructs and then showing that there is little or no relationship between the two measurements. The following scenario illustrates the concepts of convergent and divergent validity.

One variable of concern for researchers interested in couples therapy is the quality of the relationship. Lawrence et al. (2011) have introduced the Relationship Quality Interview (RQI), which is intended to measure relationship quality in five specific domains: (a) emotional intimacy, (b) sexual relationship, (c) support transactions, (d) power sharing, and (e) problem solving. The researchers demonstrated convergent validity by showing strong relationships among the five RQI scale ratings, indicating that the five domains of the RQI are converging on the same construct (relationship quality).

After establishing convergent validity, however, the researchers wanted to demonstrate that the RQI is really measuring relationship quality and not some other variable. For example, the scores may actually reflect the general level of satisfaction with the relationship rather than the quality. It is possible, for example, for couples to be satisfied with a low quality relationship. To resolve this problem, it is necessary to demonstrate that the two constructs, "quality" and "satisfaction," are separate and distinct. The researchers established divergent validity by showing a weak relationship between the RQI quality scores and measures of general satisfaction. Specifically, correlations between the domain-specific measures of quality from the RQI and global relationship satisfaction scores were generally low.

By demonstrating that two or more different methods of measurement produce strongly related scores for the same construct (convergent validity), and by demonstrating a weak relationship between the measurements for two distinct constructs (divergent validity), you can provide very strong and convincing evidence of validity. That is, there is little doubt that you are actually measuring the construct that you intend to measure.

DEFINITIONS

Face validity is an unscientific form of validity demonstrated when a measurement procedure superficially appears to measure what it claims to measure.

Concurrent validity is demonstrated when scores obtained from a new measure are directly related to scores obtained from an established measure of the same variable.

Predictive validity is demonstrated when scores obtained from a measure accurately predict behavior according to a theory.

Construct validity requires that the scores obtained from a measurement procedure behave exactly the same as the variable itself. Construct validity is based on many research studies that use the same measurement procedure and grows gradually as each new study contributes more evidence.

Convergent validity is demonstrated by a strong relationship between the scores obtained from two (or more) different methods of measuring the same construct.

Divergent validity is demonstrated by showing little or no relationship between the measurements of two different constructs.

Reliability of Measurement

The second criterion for evaluating the quality of a measurement procedure is called **reliability**. A measurement procedure is said to have reliability if it produces identical (or nearly identical) results when it is used repeatedly to measure the same individual under the same conditions. For example, if we use an IQ test to measure a person's intelligence today, then use the same test for the same person under similar conditions next week, we should obtain nearly identical IQ scores. In essence, reliability is the stability or the consistency of the measurements produced by a specific measurement procedure.

DEFINITION

> The **reliability** of a measurement procedure is the stability or consistency of the measurement. If the same individuals are measured under the same conditions, a reliable measurement procedure produces identical (or nearly identical) measurements.

The concept of reliability is based on the assumption that the variable being measured is stable or constant. For example, your intelligence does not change dramatically from one day to another but rather stays at a fairly constant level. However, when we measure a variable such as intelligence, the measurement procedure introduces an element of error. Expressed as an equation:

$$\text{Measured Score} = \text{True Score} + \text{Error}$$

For example, if we try to measure your intelligence with an IQ test, the score we get is determined partially by your actual level of intelligence (your true score), but also is influenced by a variety of other factors such as your current mood, your level of fatigue, your general health, how lucky you are at guessing on questions to which you do not know the answers, and so on. These other factors are lumped together as error and are typically a part of any measurement.

It is generally assumed that the error component changes randomly from one measurement to the next, raising your score for some measurements and lowering it for others. Over a series of many measurements, the increases and decreases caused by error should average to zero. For example, your IQ score is likely to be higher when you are well rested and feeling good and lower when you are tired and depressed. Although your actual intelligence has not changed, the error component causes your score to change from one measurement to another.

As long as the error component is relatively small, your scores will be relatively consistent from one measurement to the next, and the measurements are said to be reliable. If you are feeling especially happy and well rested, it may affect your IQ score by a few points, but it is not going to boost your IQ from 110 to 170.

On the other hand, if the error component is relatively large, you will find huge differences from one measurement to the next, and the measurements are, therefore, not reliable. A common example of a measurement with a large error component is reaction time. Suppose, for example, that you are participating in a cognitive skill test. A pair of one-digit numbers is presented on a screen and your task is to press a button as quickly as possible if the two digits add to 10 (Ackerman & Beier, 2007). On some trials, you will be fully alert and focused on the screen, with your finger tensed and ready to move. On other trials, you may be daydreaming or distracted, with your attention elsewhere, so that extra time passes before you can refocus on the numbers, mentally add them, and respond. In general, it is quite common for reaction time on some trials to be twice as long as reaction time on other trials. When scores change dramatically from one trial to another, the measurements are said to be unreliable, and we cannot trust any single measurement to provide an accurate indication of an individual's true score. In the case of reaction time, most researchers solve the problem by measuring reaction times in several trials and computing an average. The average value provides a much more stable, more reliable measure of performance.

The inconsistency in a measurement comes from error. Error can come from a variety of sources. The more common sources of error are as follows:

- *Observer error:* The individual who makes the measurements can introduce simple human error into the measurement process, especially when the measurement involves a degree of human judgment. For example, consider a baseball umpire judging balls and strikes or a college professor grading student essays. The same pitch could be called a ball once and a strike later in the game, or the same essay could receive an A one semester and a B at a different time. In each case, the measurement includes some error introduced by the observer.

- *Environmental changes:* Although the goal is to measure the same individual under identical circumstances, this ideal is difficult to attain. Often, there are small changes in the environment from one measurement to another, and these small changes can influence the measurements. There are so many environmental variables (such as time of day, temperature, weather conditions, and lighting) that it is essentially impossible to obtain two identical environmental conditions.

- *Participant changes:* The participant can change between measurements. As noted earlier, a person's degree of focus and attention can change quickly and can have a dramatic effect on measures of reaction time. Such changes may cause the obtained measurements to differ, producing what appear to be inconsistent or unreliable measurements. For example, hunger probably does not lower intelligence, but it can be a distraction that causes a lower score on an IQ test.

In summary, any measurement procedure involves an element of error and the amount of error determines the reliability of the measurements. When error is large, reliability is low, and when error is small, reliability is high.

Types and Measures of Reliability

We have defined reliability in terms of the consistency between two or more separate measurements. Thus far, the discussion has concentrated on situations involving successive measurements. Although this is one common example of reliability, it is also possible to measure reliability for simultaneous measurements and to measure reliability in terms of the internal consistency among the many items that make up a test or questionnaire.

- *Successive measurements:* The reliability estimate obtained by comparing the scores obtained from two successive measurements is commonly called **test-retest reliability**. A researcher may use exactly the same measurement procedure for the same group of individuals at two different times. Or a researcher may use modified versions of the measurement instrument (such as alternative versions of an IQ test) to obtain two different measurements for the same group of participants. When different versions of the instrument are used for the test and the retest, the reliability measure is often called **parallel-forms reliability**. Typically, reliability is determined by computing a correlation to measure the consistency of the relationship between the two sets of scores (see Figure 3.1).

- *Simultaneous measurements:* When measurements are obtained by direct observation of behaviors, it is common to use two or more separate observers who simultaneously record measurements. For example, two psychologists may watch a group of preschool children and observe social behaviors. Each individual records (measures) what he or she observes, and the degree of agreement between the two observers is called **inter-rater reliability**. This topic is also discussed in Chapter 13. Inter-rater reliability can be measured by computing the correlation between the scores from the two observers (Figure 3.1 and Chapter 13, p. 317) or by computing a percentage of agreement between the two observers (see Chapter 15, pp. 414–417).

- *Internal consistency:* Often, a complex construct such as intelligence or personality is measured using a test or questionnaire consisting of multiple items. The idea is that no single item or question is sufficient to provide a complete measure of the construct. A common example is the use of exams that consist of multiple items (questions or problems) to measure performance in an academic course. The final measurement for each individual is then determined by adding or averaging the responses across the full set of items. A basic assumption in this process is that each item (or group of items) measures a part of the total construct. If this is true, then there should be some consistency between the scores for different items or different groups of items. To measure the degree of consistency, researchers commonly split the set of items in half and compute a separate score for each half. The degree of agreement between the two scores is then evaluated, usually with a correlation (Chapter 15, p. 387). This general process results in a measure of **split-half reliability**. You should note that there are many different ways to divide a set of items in half prior to computing split-half reliability, and the value you obtain depends on the method you use to split the items. However, there are statistical techniques for dealing with this problem, which are discussed in Chapter 15 (pp. 413–414).

DEFINITIONS

> **Test-retest reliability** is established by comparing the scores obtained from two successive measurements of the same individuals and calculating a correlation between the two sets of scores. If alternative versions of the measuring instrument are used for the two measurements, the reliability measure is called **parallel-forms reliability**.
>
> **Inter-rater reliability** is the degree of agreement between two observers who simultaneously record measurements of the behaviors.
>
> **Split-half reliability** is obtained by splitting the items on a questionnaire or test in half, computing a separate score for each half, and then calculating the degree of consistency between the two scores for a group of participants.

The Relationship between Reliability and Validity

Although reliability and validity are both criteria for evaluating the quality of a measurement procedure, these two factors are partially related and partially independent. They are related to each other in that reliability is a prerequisite for validity; that is, a measurement procedure cannot be valid unless it is reliable. If we measure your IQ twice and obtain measurements of 75 and 160, not only are the measurements unreliable but we also have no idea what your IQ actually is. The huge discrepancy between the two measurements is impossible if we are truly measuring intelligence. Therefore, we must conclude that there is so much error in the measurements that the numbers themselves have no meaning.

A measure cannot be valid unless it is reliable, but a measure can be reliable without being valid.

On the other hand, it is not necessary for a measurement to be valid for it to be reliable. For example, we could measure your height and claim that it is a measure of intelligence. Although this is a foolish and invalid method for defining and measuring intelligence, it would be very reliable, producing consistent scores from one measurement to the next. Thus, the consistency of measurement is no guarantee of validity.

In situations in which there is an established standard for measurement units, it is possible to define the **accuracy** of a measurement process. For example, we have standards that define precisely what is meant by an *inch*, a *liter*, a *pound*, and a *second*. The accuracy of a measurement is the degree to which the measurement conforms to the established standard. Occasionally, a measurement procedure produces results that are consistently wrong by a constant amount. The speedometer on a car, for example, may consistently read 10 mph faster than the actual speed. In this case, the speedometer readings are not accurate but they are valid and reliable. When the car is traveling at 40 mph, the speedometer consistently (reliably) reads 50 mph, and when the car is actually going 30 mph, the speedometer reads 40 mph. Note that the speedometer correctly differentiates different speeds, which means that it is producing valid measurements of speed. (Note that a measurement process can be valid and reliable even if it is not accurate.) In the behavioral sciences, it is quite common to measure variables for which there is no established standard. In such cases, it is impossible to define or measure *accuracy*. A test designed to measure depression, for example, cannot be evaluated in terms of accuracy because there is no standard unit of depression that can be used for comparison. For such a test, the question of accuracy is moot, and the only concerns are the validity and the reliability of the measurements.

LEARNING CHECK

1. Research results indicate that the more time individuals spend watching educational television programs as preschool children, the higher their high school grades will be. What kind of relationship exists between educational TV and high school grades?
   a. Cause-and-effect
   b. Coincidental
   c. Positive
   d. Negative

2. A research study reports that participants who scored high on a new test measuring self-esteem made eye contact during an interview, whereas participants who scored low on the test avoided eye contact. Assuming that more eye contact is associated with higher self-esteem, what kind of validity is being demonstrated?
   a. face
   b. concurrent
   c. predictive
   d. convergent

3. Which of the following accurately describes the relationship between validity and reliability?
   a. Measurement cannot be valid unless it is reliable.
   b. Measurement cannot be reliable unless it is valid.
   c. If a measurement is reliable, then it also must be valid.
   d. None of the above is an accurate description.

Answers appear at the end of the chapter.

3.3 Scales of Measurement

LEARNING OBJECTIVE

LO6 Compare and contrast the four scales of measurement (nominal, ordinal, interval, and ratio) and identify examples of each.

In very general terms, measurement is a procedure for classifying individuals into categories. The set of categories is called the **scale of measurement**. Thus, the process of measurement involves two components: a set of categories and a procedure for assigning individuals to categories.

In this section, we focus on scales of measurement. Traditionally, researchers have identified four different types of measurement scales: nominal, ordinal, interval, and ratio. The differences among these four types are based on the relationships that exist among the categories that make up the scales and the information provided by each measurement.

The Nominal Scale

The categories that make up a **nominal scale** simply represent qualitative (not quantitative) differences in the variable measured. The categories have different names but are not related to each other in any systematic way. For example, if you were measuring academic majors for a group of college students, the categories would be art, chemistry, English, history, psychology, and so on. Each student would be placed in a category according to his or her major. Measurements from a nominal scale allow us to determine whether two individuals are the same or different, but they do not permit any quantitative comparison. For example, if two individuals are in different categories, we cannot determine the direction of the difference (is art "more than" English?), and we cannot determine the magnitude of the difference. Other examples of nominal scales are classifying people by race, political affiliation, or occupation.

The Ordinal Scale

The categories that make up an **ordinal scale** have different names and are organized in an ordered series. Often, an ordinal scale consists of a series of ranks (first, second, third, and so on) like the order of finish in a horse race. Occasionally, the categories are identified by verbal labels such as small, medium, and large drink sizes at a fast-food restaurant. In either case, the fact that the categories form an ordered sequence means that there is a directional relationship between the categories. With measurements from an ordinal scale, we can determine whether two individuals are different, and we can determine the direction of difference. However, ordinal measurements do not allow us to determine the magnitude of the difference between the two individuals. For example, a large coffee is bigger than a small coffee but we do not know how much bigger. Other examples of ordinal scales are socioeconomic class (upper, middle, and lower) and T-shirt sizes (small, medium, and large).

Interval and Ratio Scales

The categories on **interval** and **ratio scales** are organized sequentially, and all categories are the same size. Thus, the scale of measurement consists of a series of equal intervals like the inches on a ruler. Other common examples of interval or ratio scales are the measures of time in seconds, weight in pounds, and temperature in degrees Fahrenheit. Notice that in each case, one interval (1 inch, 1 second, 1 pound, and 1 degree) is the same size, no matter where it is located on the scale. The fact that the categories are all the same size makes it possible to determine the distance between two points on the scale. For example, you know that a measurement of 70 degrees Fahrenheit is higher than a measurement of 55 degrees, and you know that it is exactly 15 degrees higher.

The characteristic that differentiates interval and ratio scales is the zero point. The distinguishing characteristic of an interval scale is that it has an arbitrary zero point. That is, the value 0 is assigned to a particular location on the scale simply as a matter of convenience or reference. Specifically, a value of 0 does not indicate the total absence of the variable being measured. For example, a temperature of 0 degrees Fahrenheit does not mean that there is no temperature, and it does not prohibit the temperature from going even lower. Interval scales with an arbitrary zero point are fairly rare. The two most common examples are the Fahrenheit and Celsius temperature scales. Other examples are altitude (above and below sea level), golf scores (above and below par), and other relative measures, such as above and below average rainfall.

A ratio scale, on the other hand, is characterized by a zero point that is not an arbitrary location. Instead, the value 0 on a ratio scale is a meaningful point representing none (a complete absence) of the variable being measured. The existence of an absolute, nonarbitrary zero point means that we can measure the absolute amount of the variable; that is, we can measure the distance from 0. This makes it possible to compare measurements in terms of ratios. For example, a glass with 8 ounces of water (8 more than 0) has twice as much as a glass with 4 ounces (4 more than 0). With a ratio scale, we can measure the direction and magnitude of the difference between measurements and describe differences in terms of ratios. Ratio scales are quite common and include physical measures, such as height and weight, as well as variables, such as reaction time or number of errors on a test.

Remember, the difference between an interval scale and a ratio scale is the definition of the zero point. Thus, measurements of height in inches or weight in pounds could be either interval or ratio depending on how the zero point is defined. For example, with traditional measurements of weight, zero corresponds to none (no weight) and the measurements form a ratio scale. In this case, an 80-pound child (80 pounds above 0) weighs twice as much as a 40-pound child (40 pounds above 0).

Now consider a set of measurements that define the zero point as the average weight for the age group. In this situation, each child is being measured relative to the average, so a child who is 12 pounds above average receives a score of $+12$ pounds. A child who is 4 pounds below average is assigned a score of -4 pounds. Now the measurements make up an interval scale. In particular, a child who is 12 pounds above average ($+12$) does not weigh twice as much as a child who is 6 pounds above average ($+6$). You should note, however, that the ratio and the interval measurements provide the same information about the distance between two scores. For the ratio measurements, 84 pounds is 4 more than 80 pounds. For the interval measurements, a score of +8 pounds is 5 more than a score of +3 pounds. For most applications, the ability to measure distances is far more important than the ability to measure ratios. Therefore, in most situations, the distinction between interval and ratio scales has little practical significance.

Although the distinction between interval and ratio scales has little practical significance, the differences among the other measurement scales can be enormous. Specifically, the amount of information provided by each scale can limit the interpretation of the scores. For example, nominal scales only allow you to determine whether two scores are the same or different. If two scores are different, you cannot measure the size of the difference and you cannot determine whether one score is greater than or less than the other. If your research question is concerned with the direction or the size of differences, nominal measurements cannot be used.

Ordinal scales also allow you to determine whether two scores are the same or different and provide additional information about the direction of the difference. For example, with ordinal measurements you can determine whether one option is preferred over another. However, ordinal scales do not provide information about the magnitude of the difference between the two measurements. Again, this may limit the research questions for which ordinal scales are appropriate.

Finally, interval and ratio scales provide information about differences between individuals, including the direction of the difference (greater than or less than) and the magnitude of the difference. Also, scores from interval or ratio scales are compatible with basic arithmetic, which permits more sophisticated analysis and interpretation. For example, measurements from interval or ratio scales can be used to compute means and variances, and they allow hypothesis testing with *t* tests or analysis of variance. Ordinal measurements, on the other hand, do not produce meaningful values for means and variances and are not appropriate for most commonly used hypothesis tests. As a result, interval or ratio scale data are usually preferred for most research situations.

Dealing with Equivocal Measurements

Although many measurements are clearly classified as either ordinal or interval, there are others that are not obviously in one category or the other. IQ scores, for example, are numerical values that appear to form an interval scale. However, there is some question about the size of one point of IQ. Is the difference between an IQ of 85 and an IQ of 86 exactly the same as the difference between an IQ of 145 and an IQ of 146? If the answer is yes, then IQ scores form an interval scale. However, if you are not sure that one point is exactly the same everywhere on the scale, then IQ scores must be classified as ordinal measurements. It also is common for researchers in the behavioral sciences to measure variables using rating scales. For example, participants are asked to use a scale from 1 to 5 to rate the degree to which they agree (or disagree) with controversial statements. The five numerical values are often labeled, for example:

Strongly Agree	Somewhat Agree	Neutral	Somewhat Disagree	Strongly Disagree
1	2	3	4	5

Although the choices appear to form an interval scale with equal distance between successive numbers, is the distance between *Strongly Agree* and *Somewhat Agree* exactly equal to the distance between *Neutral* and *Somewhat Disagree*? Again, should the scale be treated as ordinal or interval?

Fortunately, the issue of distinguishing between ordinal and interval scales of measurement has been resolved. First, researchers have routinely treated scores from ambiguous scales, such as IQ scores and rating scales, as if they were from an interval scale. By tradition or convention, such scores have been added and averaged and multiplied as if they were regular numerical values. In addition, scientists have argued convincingly for over 50 years that this kind of mathematical treatment is appropriate for these types of ordinal data (Lord, 1953). For a recent review of the history of this issue, see Norman (2010).

Selecting a Scale of Measurement

One obvious factor that differentiates the four types of measurement scales is their ability to compare different measurements. A nominal scale can tell us only that a difference exists. An ordinal scale tells us the direction of the difference (which is more and which is less). With an interval scale, we can determine the direction and the magnitude of a difference. Measurements from a ratio scale allow us to determine the direction, the magnitude, and the ratio of the difference. The ability to compare measurements has a direct effect on the ability to describe relationships between variables. For example, when a research study involves measurements from nominal scales, the results of the study can establish the existence of only a qualitative relationship between variables. With nominal scales, we can determine whether a change in one variable is accompanied by a change in the other variable, but we cannot determine the direction of the change (increase or a decrease), and we cannot determine the magnitude of the change. An interval or a ratio scale, on the other hand, allows a much more sophisticated description of a relationship. For example, we could determine that a 1-point increase in one variable (such as drug dose) results in a 4-point decrease in another variable (such as heart rate).

LEARNING CHECK

1. An elementary school teacher separates students into high, medium, and low reading skill groups. What scale of measurement is being used to create the groups?
    a. Nominal
    b. Ordinal ✓
    c. Interval
    d. Ratio

2. After measuring a set of individuals, a researcher finds that Bob's score is three times greater than Jane's score. What scale of measurement is being used?
    a. Nominal
    b. Ordinal
    c. Interval
    d. Ratio ✓

3. What additional information is obtained by measuring on an interval scale compared to an ordinal scale?
    a. Whether the measurements are the same or different
    b. The direction of the differences
    c. The size of the differences ✓
    d. None of the above

Answers appear at the end of the chapter.

3.4   Modalities of Measurement

LEARNING OBJECTIVE

LO7   Identify the three modalities of measurement and explain the strengths and weaknesses of each.

Earlier in the chapter, variables such as motivation or intelligence were defined as hypothetical constructs because they cannot be directly observed or measured. We also noted that constructs typically influence external responses and behaviors. Researchers observe and measure these external manifestations to develop operational definitions for constructs. However, one major decision for a researcher is to determine which of these external manifestations provide the best indication of the underlying construct. The many different external expressions of a construct are traditionally classified into three categories that also define three different types, or modalities, of measurement. The three categories are self-report, physiological, and behavioral. Consider, for example, the hypothetical construct "fear," and suppose that a researcher would like to evaluate the effectiveness of a therapy program designed to reduce the fear of flying. This researcher must somehow obtain measurements of fear before the therapy begins, then compare them with measurements of fear obtained after therapy. Although fear is an internal construct that cannot be observed directly, it is possible to observe and measure external expressions of fear. For example, an individual may claim to be afraid (self-report), may have an increased heart rate (physiological), or may refuse to travel on an airplane (behavioral). To develop an operational definition for the construct *fear*, researchers must first determine which type of external expression should be used to define and measure fear.

Self-Report Measures

One option for measuring, or operationalizing, the fear of flying is to ask participants to describe or to quantify their own fear. The researcher could simply ask, "Are you afraid to fly?" Or participants could be asked to rate the amount of fear they are experiencing on a scale from 1 to 10. Or they could be given a comprehensive questionnaire about airline travel, and the researcher could use the set of responses to obtain an overall score measuring fear of flying.

The primary advantage of a **self-report measure** is that it is probably the most direct way to assess a construct. Each individual is in a unique position of self-knowledge and self-awareness; presumably, no one knows more about the individual's fear than the individual. Also, a direct question and its answer have more face validity than measuring some other response that theoretically is influenced by fear. On the negative side, however, it is very easy for participants to distort self-report measures. A participant may deliberately lie to create a better self-image, or a response may be influenced subtly by the presence of a researcher, the wording of the questions, or other aspects of the research situation. When a participant distorts self-report responses, the validity of the measurement is undermined.

Self-report measures are discussed in more detail in Section 13.3, in which we present the survey research design.

Physiological Measures

A second option for measuring a construct is to look at the physiological manifestations of the underlying construct. Fear, for example, reveals itself by increased heart rate and perspiration (measured by galvanic skin response, GSR). A researcher measuring "fear of flying" could attach electrodes to participants and monitor heart rates as they board a plane and during the flight. Or a researcher could ask participants to imagine a flight experience while GSR and heart rate are monitored in a laboratory setting.

Other **physiological measures** involve brain-imaging techniques such as positron emission tomography (PET) scanning and magnetic resonance imaging (MRI). These techniques allow researchers to monitor activity levels in specific areas of the brain during different kinds of activity. For example, researchers studying attention have found specific areas of the brain where activity increases as the complexity of a task increases and more attention is required (Posner & Badgaiyan, 1998). Other research has used brain imaging to determine which areas of the brain are involved in different kinds of memory tasks (Wager & Smith, 2003) or in the processing of information about pain (Wager et al., 2004).

One advantage of physiological measures is that they are extremely objective. The equipment provides accurate, reliable, and well-defined measurements that are not dependent on subjective interpretation by either the researcher or the participant. One disadvantage of such measures is that they typically require equipment that may be expensive or unavailable. In addition, the presence of monitoring devices creates an unnatural situation that may cause participants to react differently than they would under normal circumstances. A more important concern with physiological measures is whether they provide a valid measure of the construct. Heart rate, for example, may be related to fear, but heart rate is not the same thing as fear. Increased heart rate may be caused by anxiety, arousal, embarrassment, or exertion as well as by fear. Can we be sure that measurements of heart rate are, in fact, measurements of fear?

Behavioral Measures

Constructs often reveal themselves in overt behaviors that can be observed and measured. The behaviors may be completely natural events such as laughing, playing, eating, sleeping, arguing, or speaking. Or the behaviors may be structured, as when a researcher measures performance on a designated task. In the latter case, a researcher usually develops a specific task in which performance is theoretically dependent on the construct being measured. For example, reaction time could be measured to determine whether a drug affects mental alertness; the number of words recalled from a list provides a measure of memory ability; and performance on an IQ test is a measure of intelligence. To measure the "fear of flying," a researcher could construct a hierarchy of potential behaviors (visiting an airport, walking onto a plane, sitting in a plane while it idles at the gate, riding in a plane while it taxies on a runway, and actually flying) and measuring how far up the hierarchy an individual is willing to go.

Behavioral measures provide researchers with a vast number of options, making it possible to select the behaviors that seem to be best for defining and measuring the construct. For example, the construct "mental alertness" could be operationally defined by behaviors such as reaction time, reading comprehension, logical reasoning ability, or ability to focus attention. Depending on the specific purpose of a research study, one of these measures probably is more appropriate than the others. In clinical situations in which a researcher works with individual clients, a single construct such as depression may reveal itself as a separate, unique behavioral problem for each client. In this case, the clinician can construct a separate, unique behavioral definition of depression that is appropriate for each patient.

In other situations, the behavior may be the actual variable of interest and not just an indicator of some hypothetical construct. For a school psychologist trying to reduce disruptive behavior in the classroom, it is the actual behavior that the psychologist wants to observe and measure. In this case, the psychologist does not use the overt behavior as an operational definition of an intangible construct but rather simply studies the behavior itself.

On the negative side, a behavior may be only a temporary or situational indicator of an underlying construct. A disruptive student may be on good behavior during periods of observation or shift the timing of negative behaviors from the classroom to the school bus on the way home. Usually, it is best to measure a cluster of related behaviors rather than rely on a single indicator. For example, in response to therapy, a disruptive student may stop speaking out of turn in the classroom but replace this specific behavior with another form of disruption. A complete definition of disruptive behavior would require several behavioral indicators.

Behavioral measures are discussed in more detail in Section 13.2, in which we present the observational research design.

LEARNING CHECK

1. Using a PET scan to measure brain activity while participants solve mathematics problems is an example of using what modality of measurement?
    a. Self-report
    b. Survey
    c. Behavioral
    d. Physiological

2. Using an anonymous questionnaire to determine how many times students send or receive text messages during class is an example of using what modality of measurement?
    a. Self-report
    b. Survey
    c. Behavioral
    d. Physiological

3. Counting the number of times a third-grade student leaves his or her seat without permission during a 30-minute observation period is an example of using what modality of measurement?
    a. Self-report
    b. Survey
    c. Behavioral
    d. Physiological

Answers appear at the end of the chapter.

3.5   Other Aspects of Measurement

LEARNING OBJECTIVES

LO8   Define a *ceiling effect* and a floor effect and explain how they can interfere with measurement.

LO9   Define an *artifact* and explain how examples of artifacts (experimenter bias, demand characteristics, and reactivity) can threaten both the validity and reliability of measurement and how they can influence the results of a research study.

Beyond the validity and reliability of measures, the scale of measurement, and the modality of measurement, several other factors should be considered when selecting a measurement procedure. The right decisions about each of these factors can increase the likelihood of success of a research study. In this section, we consider additional issues related to the measurement process: multiple measures, sensitivity of measurement and range effects, artifacts including experimenter bias and participant reactivity, and selection of a measurement procedure.

Multiple Measures

One method of obtaining a more complete measure of a construct is to use two (or more) different procedures to measure the same variable. For example, we could record both heart rate and behavior as measures of fear. The advantage of this multiple-measure technique is that it usually provides more confidence in the validity of the measurements. However, multiple measures can introduce some problems. One problem involves the statistical analysis and interpretation of the results. Although there are statistical techniques for evaluating multivariate data, they are complex and not well understood by many researchers. A more serious problem is that the two measures may not behave in the same way. A therapy program for treating fear, for example, may produce an immediate and large effect on behavior but no effect on heart rate. As a result, participants are willing to approach a feared object after therapy, but their hearts still race. The lack of agreement between two measures can confuse the interpretation of results (did the therapy reduce fear?). The discrepancy between the measurements may be caused by the fact that one measure is more sensitive than the other, or it may indicate that different dimensions of the variable change at different times during treatment (behavior may change quickly, but the physiological aspects of fear take more time). One method for limiting the problems associated with multiple measures is to combine them into a single score for each individual.

Sensitivity and Range Effects

Typically, a researcher begins a study with some expectation of how the variables will behave, specifically the direction and magnitude of changes that are likely to be observed. An important concern for any measurement procedure is that the measurements are sensitive enough to respond to the type and magnitude of the changes that are expected. For example, if a medication is expected to have only a small effect on reaction time, then it is essential that time be measured in units small enough to detect the change. If we measure time in seconds and the magnitude of the effect is 1/100 of a second, then the change will not be noticed. In general, if we expect fairly small, subtle changes in a variable, then the measurement procedure must be sensitive enough to detect the changes, and the scale of measurement must have enough different categories to allow discrimination among individuals.

One particular sensitivity problem occurs when the scores obtained in a research study tend to cluster at one end of the measurement scale. For example, suppose that an educational psychologist intends to evaluate a new teaching program by measuring reading comprehension for a group of students before and after the program is administered. If the students all score around 95% before the program starts, there is essentially no room for improvement. Even if the program does improve reading comprehension, the measurement procedure probably will not detect an increase in scores. In this case, the measurement procedure is insensitive to changes that may occur in one direction. In general, this type of sensitivity problem is called a **range effect**. When the range is restricted at the high end, the problem is called a **ceiling effect** (the measurements bump into a ceiling and can go no higher). Similarly, clustering at the low end of the scale can produce a **floor effect**.

In general, range effects suggest a basic incompatibility between the measurement procedure and the individuals measured. Often, the measurement is based on a task that is too easy (thereby producing high scores) or too difficult (thereby producing low scores) for the participants being tested. Note that it is not the measurement procedure that is at fault but rather the fact that the procedure is used with a particular group of individuals. For example, a measurement that works well for 4-year-old children may produce serious range effects if used with adolescents. For this reason, it is advisable to pretest any measurement procedure for which potential range effects are suspected. Simply measure a small sample of representative individuals to be sure that the obtained values are far enough from the extremes of the scale to allow room to measure changes in either direction.

DEFINITIONS

> A **ceiling effect** is the clustering of scores at the high end of a measurement scale, allowing little or no possibility of increases in value.
>
> A **floor effect** is the clustering of scores at the low end of a measurement scale, allowing little or no possibility of decreases in value.

Artifacts: Experimenter Bias and Participant Reactivity

An **artifact** is a nonnatural feature accidentally introduced into something being observed. In the context of a research study, an artifact is an external factor that may influence or distort the measurements. For example, a doctor who startles you with an ice-cold stethoscope is probably not going to get accurate observations of your heartbeat. An artifact can threaten the validity of the measurements because you are not really measuring what you intended, and it can be a threat to reliability. Although there are many potential artifacts, two deserve special mention: experimenter bias and participant reactivity.

Experimenter Bias

Typically, a researcher knows the predicted outcome of a research study and is in a position to influence the results, either intentionally or unintentionally. For example, an experimenter might be warm, friendly, and encouraging when presenting instructions to a group of participants in a treatment condition expected to produce good performance, and appear cold, aloof, and somewhat stern when presenting the instructions to another group in a comparison treatment for which performance is expected to be relatively poor. The experimenter is manipulating participant motivation, and this manipulation can distort the results. When researchers influence results in this way, the effect is called **experimenter bias**.

DEFINITION

Experimenter bias occurs when the measurements obtained in a study are influenced by the experimenter's expectations or personal beliefs regarding the outcome of the study.

Rosenthal and Fode (1963) identified a variety of ways that an experimenter can influence a participant's behavior:

- By paralinguistic cues (variations in tone of voice) that influence the participants to give the expected or desired responses
- By kinesthetic cues (body posture or facial expressions)
- By verbal reinforcement of expected or desired responses
- By misjudgment of participants' responses in the direction of the expected results
- By not recording participants' responses accurately (errors in recording of data) in the direction of the expected or desired results

In a classic example of experimenter bias, Rosenthal and Fode (1963) had student volunteers act as the experimenters in a learning study. The students were given rats to train in a maze. Half of the students were led to believe that their rats were specially bred to be "maze bright." The remainder were told that their rats were bred to be "maze dull." In reality, both groups of students received the same type of ordinary laboratory rat, neither bright nor dull. Nevertheless, the findings showed differences in the rats' performance between the two groups of experimenters. The "bright" rats were better at learning the maze. The student expectations influenced the outcome of the study. How did their expectations have this effect? Apparently there were differences in how the students in each group handled their rats, and the handling, in turn, altered the rats' behavior.

Note that the existence of experimenter bias means that the researcher is not obtaining valid measurements. Instead, the behaviors or measurements are being distorted by the experimenter. In addition, experimenter bias undermines reliability because the participants may produce very different scores if tested under the same conditions by a different experimenter.

One option for limiting experimenter bias is to standardize or automate the experiment. For example, a researcher could read from a prepared script to ensure that all participants receive exactly the same instructions. Or instructions could be presented on a printed handout or by video. In each case, the goal is to limit the personal contact between the experimenter and the participant. Another strategy for reducing experimenter bias is to use a "blind" experiment. If the research study is conducted by an experimenter (assistant) who does not know the expected results, the experimenter should not be able to influence the participants. This technique is called **single-blind** research. An alternative is to set up a study in which neither the experimenter nor the participant knows the expected result. This procedure is called **double-blind** research and is commonly used in drug studies in which some participants get the real drug (expected to be effective) and others get a placebo (expected to have no effect). The double-blind study is structured so that neither the researcher nor the participants know exactly who is getting which drug until the study is completed.

Finally, we should note that there are many research studies in which the participants do not know the hypothesis. Often participants are deliberately misled about the purpose of the study to minimize the likelihood that their expectations will influence their behaviors. In other studies, the hypothesis simply is never presented to the participants. In these cases, we often describe the participants as being "blind" to the hypothesis or simply as "naïve." However, there is no official term that is used to describe this type of research. In particular, studies in which the participants do not know the hypothesis are not classified as single-blind or double-blind research. These two terms apply to studies in which the hypothesis is unknown to the researcher (single-blind) or is unknown to both the researcher and the participants (double-blind).

DEFINITIONS

A research study is **single-blind** if the researcher does not know the predicted outcome.

A research study is **double-blind** if both the researcher and the participants are unaware of the predicted outcome.

Demand Characteristics and Participant Reactivity

The fact that research studies involve living organisms, particularly humans, introduces another factor that can affect the validity and reliability of the measurements. Specifically, living organisms are active and responsive, and their actions and responses can distort the results. If we observe or measure an inanimate object such as a table or a block of wood, we do not expect the object to have any response, such as, "Whoa! I'm being watched. I had better be on my best behavior." Unfortunately this kind of reactivity can happen with human participants.

Participants who are aware they are being observed and measured may react in unpredictable ways. In addition, the research setting often creates a set of cues or demand characteristics that suggests what kinds of behavior are appropriate or expected. The combination of **demand characteristics** and participant **reactivity** can change participants' normal behavior and thereby influence the measurements they produce.

DEFINITIONS

Demand characteristics refer to any of the potential cues or features of a study that (1) suggest to the participants what the purpose and hypothesis is and (2) influence the participants to respond or behave in a certain way.

Reactivity occurs when participants modify their natural behavior in response to the fact that they are participating in a research study or the knowledge that they are being measured.

Orne (1962) describes participation in a research study as a social experience in which both the researcher and the participant have roles to play. In particular, the researcher is clearly in charge and is expected to give instructions. The participant, on the other hand, is expected to follow instructions. In fact, most participants strive to be a "good subject" and work hard to do a good job for the researcher. Although this may appear to be good for the researcher's study, it can create two serious problems. First, participants often try to figure out the purpose of the study and then modify their responses to fit their perception of the researcher's goals. Second, participants can become so dedicated to performing well that they do things in a research study that they would never do in a normal situation. To demonstrate this phenomenon, Orne (1962) instructed participants to complete a sheet of 224 addition problems. After finishing each sheet, the participant picked up a card with instructions for the next task. Every card contained the same instructions, telling the participants to tear up the sheet they just completed into at least 32 pieces and then go on to the next sheet of problems. The participants continued working problems and tearing them up over and over for hours without any sign of fatigue or frustration.

Clearly, this was a senseless task that no one would do under normal circumstances, yet the research participants were content to do it. Apparently, the act of participating in an experiment "demands" that people cooperate and follow instructions beyond any reasonable limit. However, because the participants are not acting normally, there is reason to question the validity and the reliability of the measurements they produce. When participants hide or distort their true responses, researchers are not measuring what they intended to measure.

Although striving to be a responsible participant is the most common response, individuals may adopt different ways of responding to experimental cues based on whatever they judge to be an appropriate role in the situation. These ways of responding are referred to as **subject roles** or **subject role behaviors**. Four different subject roles have been identified (Weber & Cook, 1972):

1. The **good subject role**. These participants have identified the hypothesis of the study and are trying to produce responses that support the investigator's hypothesis. As good as this may sound, we do not want participants to adopt the good subject role because then we do not know if the results of the study extend to individuals who did not adopt such a role.

2. The **negativistic subject role**. These participants have identified the hypothesis of the study and are trying to act contrary to the investigator's hypothesis. Often these individuals are upset that they must participate and are directing their anger toward sabotaging the study. Clearly, we do not want participants in our study to adopt this role.

3. The **apprehensive subject role**. These participants are overly concerned that their performance in the study will be used to evaluate their abilities or personal characteristics. They try to place themselves in a desirable light by responding in a socially desirable fashion instead of truthfully. Again, we do not want participants to adopt this role because they are not providing truthful responses.

4. The **faithful subject role**. These participants attempt to follow instructions to the letter and avoid acting on any suspicions they have about the purpose of the study. Two types of participants take on this role: those who want to help science and know they should not allow their suspicions to enter into their responses, and those who are simply apathetic and do not give the study much thought. These are the participants we really want in our study.

Reactivity is especially a problem in studies conducted in a **laboratory**, where participants are fully aware that they are participants in a study. Although it is essentially impossible to prevent participants from noticing the demand characteristics of a study and adjusting their behaviors, there are steps to help reduce the effects of reactivity. Often, it is possible to observe and measure individuals without their awareness. For example, in a **field** study, participants are observed in their natural environment and are much less likely to know that they are being investigated, hence they are less reactive. Although this strategy is often possible, some variables are difficult to observe directly (e.g., attitudes), and in some situations, ethical considerations prevent researchers from secretly observing people. An alternative strategy is to disguise or conceal the measurement process. The true purpose of a questionnaire can be masked by embedding a few critical questions in a larger set of irrelevant items or by deliberately using questions with low face validity. Another option is to suggest (subtly or openly) that the participant is performing one task when, in fact, we are observing and measuring something else. In either case, some level of deception is involved, which can raise a question of ethics (see Chapter 4). The most direct strategy for limiting reactivity is to reassure participants that their performance or responses are completely confidential and anonymous, and encourage them to make honest, natural responses. Any attempt to reassure and relax participants helps reduce reactivity.

DEFINITIONS

> A **laboratory** is any setting that is obviously devoted to the discipline of science. It can be any room or any space that the subject or participant perceives as artificial.
>
> A **field** setting is a place that the participant or subject perceives as a natural environment.

Selecting a Measurement Procedure

As seen in the preceding sections, the choice of a measurement procedure involves several decisions. Because each decision has implications for the results of the study, it is important to consider all the options before deciding on a scheme for measurement for your own study or when critically reading a report of results from another research study.

The best starting point for selecting a measurement procedure is to review past research reports involving the variables or constructs to be examined. Most commonly used procedures have been evaluated for reliability and validity. In addition, using an established measurement procedure means that results can be compared directly to the previous literature in the area.

If more than one procedure exists for defining and measuring a particular variable, examine the options and determine which method is best suited for the specific research question. In particular, consider which measure has a level of sensitivity appropriate for detecting the individual differences and group differences that you expect to observe. Also decide whether the scale of measurement (nominal, ordinal, interval, or ratio) is appropriate for the kind of conclusion you would like to make. Simply to establish that differences exist, a nominal scale may be sufficient. On the other hand, to determine the magnitude of a difference, you need either an interval or a ratio scale.

As noted in Chapter 2, critically examining and questioning a published measurement procedure can lead to new research ideas. As you read published research reports, always question the measurement procedures: Why was the variable measured as it was? Would a different scale have been better? Were the results biased by a lack of sensitivity or by range effects? What would happen if the variable(s) were defined and measured in a different way? If you can reasonably predict that a different measurement strategy would change the results, then you have the grounds for a new research study. Keep in mind, however, that if you develop your own operational definition or measurement procedure, you need to demonstrate validity and reliability, a task that is very detailed and time consuming. Some researchers dedicate their entire careers to developing a measure.

LEARNING CHECK

1. Why is the range effect known as a "ceiling effect" a problem for researchers?
   a. The scores are already so high that there is no chance of measuring improvement.
   b. The scores are already so low that there is no chance of measuring a decrease.
   c. There is so much room for improvement that the measurements are almost certain to increase.
   d. There is so much room for lower performance that the measurements are almost certain to decrease.

2. Why is an artifact like experimenter bias a threat to the validity of measurement?
   a. The measurements may be distorted by the artifact.
   b. Different measurements may be obtained under the same conditions if the artifact were not present.
   c. The artifact may provide an alternative explanation for the results.
   d. None of the other options accurately describes the threat.

3. Which of the following describes participants taking on the negativistic subject role?
   a. They are concerned that their performance in the study will be used to evaluate them.
   ⓑ They try to act so that their data are in contrast to the hypothesis.
   c. They try to act so that their data are consistent with the hypothesis.
   d. They try to avoid acting on the basis of their suspicions.

Answers appear at the end of the chapter.

CHAPTER SUMMARY

At this point, you should review the learning objectives presented at the beginning of each section and be sure that you have mastered each objective.

In this chapter, we considered how a researcher defines and measures variables in a study. Because many research variables are intangible hypothetical constructs, operational definitions are developed to define and measure the variables. Many measurement procedures are available for each variable. A researcher decides which procedure to use by evaluating the validity and reliability of the procedure. A valid measure truly measures the variable that it claims to measure. The six most commonly used measures of the validity of measurement are face, concurrent, predictive, construct, convergent, and divergent validity. A measure is reliable if it results in stable and consistent measurements. Three assessments of reliability are test-retest, inter-rater, and split-half reliability.

The process of measurement involves classifying individuals. The set of categories used for classification is called the scale of measurement. Four different types of measurement scales are nominal, ordinal, interval, and ratio. A major decision faced by researchers is which type, or modality, of measurement to use. The three modalities of measurement are self-report, physiological, and behavioral; each has certain advantages and disadvantages. Multiple measures, sensitivity of measurement, artifacts, and selection of a measurement procedure are also considered.

KEY WORDS

theory	construct validity	split-half reliability	reactivity
constructs or hypothetical constructs	convergent validity	ceiling effect	good subject role
	divergent validity	floor effect	negativistic subject role
operational definition	reliability	experimenter bias	apprehensive subject role
validity	test-retest reliability	single-blind research	faithful subject role
face validity	parallel-forms reliability	double-blind research	laboratory
concurrent validity	inter-rater reliability	demand characteristics	field
predictive validity			

EXERCISES

The exercises are identified with specific learning objectives and are intended to assess your mastery of the objectives. You should be aware that exam items are also generated to assess learning objectives.

1. In addition to the key words, you should also be able to define each of the following terms:

positive relationship	ratio scale
negative relationship	self-report measure
accuracy	physiological measure
scale of measurement	behavioral measure
nominal scale	range effect
ordinal scale	artifact
interval scale	subject roles or subject role behaviors

2. (**LO1** and **2**) Hypothetical concepts, such as *honesty*, are variables that cannot be observed or measured directly and, therefore, require operational definitions.
   a. Describe one procedure that might be used to measure honesty.
   b. Use the procedure you described in (a) to explain why there may not be a one-to-one relationship between the actual variable and the measurement produced by the operational definition of the variable.

3. (**LO2**) Briefly explain what an operational definition is and why operational definitions are sometimes necessary.

4. (**LO4**) A researcher evaluates a new cholesterol medication by measuring cholesterol levels for a group of patients before they begin taking the medication and after they have been taking the medication for 8 weeks. A second researcher measures quality of life for a group of 40-year-old men who have been married for at least 5 years and a group of 40-year-old men who are still single. Explain why the first researcher is probably not concerned about the validity of measurement, whereas the second researcher probably is. (Hint: What variable is each researcher measuring and how will it be measured?)

5. (**LO3** and **4**) A clinical researcher has developed a new test for measuring impulsiveness and would like to determine the validity of the test. The new test and an established measure of impulsiveness are both administered to a sample of participants. Describe the pattern of results that would establish concurrent validity for the new test.

6. (**LO5**) Suppose that a social scientist has developed a questionnaire intended to measure the quality of romantic relationships. Describe how you could evaluate the reliability of the questionnaire.

7. (**LO5**) Explain how inter-rater reliability is established.

8. (**LO4** and **5**) A researcher claims that intelligence can be measured by measuring the length of a person's right-hand ring finger. Explain why this procedure is very reliable but probably not valid.

9. (**LO4** and **5**) For each of the following operational definitions, decide whether you consider it to be a valid measure. Explain why or why not. Decide whether you consider it to be a reliable measure. Explain why or why not.
   a. A researcher defines *social anxiety* in terms of the number of minutes before a child begins to interact with adults other than his or her parents.
   b. A professor classifies students as either introverted or extroverted based on the number of questions each individual asks during one week of class.
   c. A sports psychologist measures physical fitness by measuring how high each person can jump.
   d. Reasoning that bigger brains require bigger heads, a researcher measures intelligence by measuring the circumference of each person's head (just above the ears).

10. (**LO6**) In this chapter we identified four scales of measurement: nominal, ordinal, interval, and ratio.
    a. What additional information is obtained from measurements on an ordinal scale compared to measurements from a nominal scale?
    b. What additional information is obtained from measurements on an interval scale compared to measurements from an ordinal scale?
    c. What additional information is obtained from measurements on a ratio scale compared to measurements from an interval scale?

11. Select one construct from the following list:

happiness	hunger
exhaustion	motivation
creativity	fear

   Briefly describe how it might be measured using:
   a. (**LO2** and **7**) an operational definition based on self-report (e.g., a questionnaire).
   b. (**LO2** and **7**) an operational definition based on behavior (e.g., what kinds of behavior would you expect to see from an individual with high self-esteem?)

12. (**LO7**) Describe the relative strengths and weaknesses of self-report measures compared to behavioral measures.

13. (**LO8**) What is a ceiling effect, and how can it be a problem?

14. (**LO9**) Explain how an artifact can limit the validity and reliability of a measurement.

15. (**LO9**) What are demand characteristics, and how do they limit the validity of the measurements obtained in a research study?

16. (**LO9**) Describe how the concept of participant reactivity might explain why a person's behavior in a group of strangers is different from a person's behavior with friends.

LEARNING CHECK ANSWERS

Section 3.1
1. a, 2. c, 3. d

Section 3.2
1. c, 2. c, 3. a

Section 3.3
1. b, 2. d, 3. c

Section 3.4
1. d, 2. a, 3. c

Section 3.5
1. a, 2. a, 3. b

Ethics in Research

© Nathan Jasowiak / Shutterstock

CHAPTER LEARNING OBJECTIVES

LO1 Describe the major historical events that helped shape the current guidelines for the ethical treatment of human participants in research, including the Nuremberg Code, Milgram's obedience study, the National Research Act, and the Belmont Report.

LO2 Describe and apply the three ethical principles of the Belmont Report (i.e., respect, beneficence, and justice) to a research situation.

LO3 Describe the major elements of the APA ethical guidelines concerning human participants in research, including no harm, informed consent, deception, and confidentiality.

LO4 Describe the purpose and responsibilities of the Institutional Review Board (IRB).

LO5 Describe the major elements of the APA ethical guidelines for nonhuman subjects in research.

LO6 Describe the purpose and responsibilities of the Institutional Animal Care and Use Committee (IACUC).

LO7 Define *fraud* and explain the safeguards that exist to prevent it.

LO8 Define *plagiarism* and explain the techniques that can be used to help avoid unintentional plagiarism.

CHAPTER OVERVIEW

Every year multiple criminal convictions are overturned, largely on the basis of new DNA evidence, and innocent people are exonerated and released from prison. Many of those found innocent were originally convicted primarily because they confessed to the crime (Garrett, 2008). Why do innocent people confess? This is a question that has been examined by psychologist Saul Kassin in a series of studies over the past two decades (Kassin & Kiechel, 1996; Perillo & Kassin, 2011). In a typical experiment, participants are told that they are in a reaction time experiment using a computer keyboard to record responses. As a female confederate reads a series of letters, the participant must type each letter as quickly as possible. Before the study begins, however, the participants are warned that there is a glitch in the research software and they should not touch the ALT key because it will cause the computer to crash and destroy the data and the program. About one minute into the experiment, an error message appears on the monitor, and the computer crashes. Immediately, the researcher asks "Did you hit the ALT key?" and participants overwhelmingly deny hitting the key. At this point, the researchers introduce one of several manipulations including the following:

> *False Incriminating Evidence.* In this condition, the researcher asks the confederate who has been reading the series of letters, "Did you see anything?" and she replies that she saw the participant hit the key with the side of his or her finger.

> *Bluff.* In this condition the researcher states that the computer is connected to a server, which stores all of the individual keystrokes and can be checked later in the day.

> *Control.* In the control condition, there is no implication that evidence exists that can be used to show that the participant is guilty.

The researcher, clearly angry, asks the participant several more times if the ALT key was touched and then produces a written confession and asks the participant to sign. Ultimately, only 27% of those in the control condition signed compared to around 80% in the two implied evidence conditions.

Although the results suggest several possible mechanisms that can lead to false confessions and feelings of guilt, our focus in this chapter is on the ethics of the study. First, the researchers clearly lied to the participants about the purpose of the study. More importantly, the researchers took totally innocent people and tried to trick them into feeling guilty and ashamed. Should professional psychologists be doing this? Is it even allowed? Many research studies in the behavioral sciences involve deception or attempt to produce feelings of anger, sadness, embarrassment, or guilt in the participants. You should know, however, that these studies are carefully scrutinized before they are allowed to proceed, and every attempt is made to ensure the safety and dignity of the participants (and animal subjects).

In this chapter, we discuss the ethics of research. Consideration of ethical issues is integral throughout the research process. Researchers have two basic categories of ethical responsibility: (1) responsibility to the individuals, both human and nonhuman, who participate in their research studies, and (2) responsibility to the discipline of science to be accurate and honest in the reporting of their research. We discuss each of these ethical issues in this chapter.

4.1   Introduction

Ethical Concerns Throughout the Research Process

After you have identified a new idea for research, formed a hypothesis, and determined a method for defining and measuring variables, you may think, "Great! Now I'm really ready to begin research." We hope you are beginning to feel the excitement of starting a research project; however, we must now consider the fact that the research process includes an element of serious responsibility.

Up to this point, your research project has been entirely private and personal. You have been working on your own, in the library and on the Internet, gathering information and formulating an idea for a research study. Now, however, you have reached the stage where other individuals become involved with your research: first, the participants or subjects whose behaviors and responses you observe and measure during the course of the study; and second, the people who will see (and, perhaps, be influenced by) your report of the study's results. All these individuals have a right to expect honesty and respect from you, and as you proceed through the following stages of the research process, you must accept the responsibility to behave ethically toward those who will be affected by your research. In general, ethics is the study of proper action (Ray, 2000). This chapter is devoted to the subject of research ethics in particular.

> Caution! Research ethics is not an issue of morality; it concerns the proper conduct of researchers. Researchers have observed their own conduct and reached a consensus regarding acceptable conduct for all researchers.

DEFINITION

> **Research ethics** concerns the responsibility of researchers to be honest and respectful to all individuals who are affected by their research studies or their reports of the studies' results. Researchers are usually governed by a set of ethical guidelines that assist them to make proper decisions and choose proper actions. In psychological research, the American Psychological Association (APA) maintains a set of ethical principles for research (APA, 2002, 2010).

Consider the following examples.

- Suppose that, as a topic for a research study, you are interested in brain injury that may result from repeated blows to the head such as those suffered by boxers and soccer players. For obvious ethical reasons (physical harm), you could not plan a study that involved injuring people's brains to examine the effects. However, you could compare two preexisting groups, for example, a group of college football and ice hockey players and a group of college athletes from noncontact sports (see McAllister et al., 2012, for a sample study).
- Suppose that you are interested in sexual behavior as a research topic. For obvious ethical reasons (privacy), you cannot secretly install video cameras in people's bedrooms. However, you could ask people to complete a questionnaire about their sexual behavior (see Moore, Barr, & Johnson, 2013, for a sample study).

In research, ethical issues must be considered at each step in the research process. Ethical principles dictate (1) what measurement techniques may be used for certain individuals and certain behaviors, (2) how researchers select individuals to participate in studies, (3) which research strategies may be used with certain populations and behaviors, (4) which research designs may be used with certain populations and behaviors, (5) how studies may be carried out with individuals, (6) how data are analyzed, and, finally, (7) how results are reported. The issue of ethics is an overriding one and must be kept in mind at each step of the research process when you make decisions. Scientists' exploration is bounded by ethical constraints.

The Basic Categories of Ethical Responsibility

Researchers have two basic categories of ethical responsibility: (1) responsibility to ensure the welfare and dignity of the individuals, both human and nonhuman, who participate in their research studies; and (2) responsibility to ensure that public reports of their research are accurate and honest.

Any research involving humans or nonhumans immediately introduces questions of ethics. The research situation automatically places the scientist in a position of control over the individuals participating in the study. However, the researcher has no right to abuse this power or to harm the participants or subjects, physically, emotionally, or psychologically. On the contrary, the relative power of the researcher versus the participant or subject means that the researcher has a responsibility to ensure the safety and the dignity of the participants. Committees such as the Institutional Review Board (IRB), which reviews research involving human participants, and the Institutional Animal Care and Use Committee (IACUC), which reviews research with nonhuman subjects, assist researchers in meeting their ethical responsibilities. These committees examine all proposed research with respect to treatment of humans and nonhumans. Details concerning the safe treatment of humans and nonhumans in research are discussed in Sections 4.2 and 4.3, respectively.

Reporting of research also introduces questions of ethics. It is assumed that reports of research are accurate and honest depictions of the procedures used and results obtained in a research study. As we discussed in Chapter 1, the scientific method is intended to be a valid method of acquiring knowledge. Its goal is to obtain answers in which we are confident. Any reporting decision that jeopardizes this confidence is an ethical issue. Two of these issues, fraud and plagiarism, are discussed in Section 4.4.

4.2   Ethical Issues and Human Participants in Research

LEARNING OBJECTIVES

LO1   Describe the major historical events that helped shape the current guidelines for the ethical treatment of human participants in research, including the Nuremberg Code, Milgram's obedience study, the National Research Act, and the Belmont Report.

LO2   Describe and apply the three ethical principles of the Belmont Report (i.e., respect, beneficence, and justice) to a research situation.

LO3   Describe the major elements of the APA ethical guidelines concerning human participants in research, including no harm, informed consent, deception, and confidentiality.

LO4   Describe the purpose and responsibilities of the Institutional Review Board (IRB).

Historical Highlights of Treatment of Human Participants

Until the end of World War II, researchers established their own ethical standards and safeguards for human participants in their research. It was assumed that researchers, guided by their own moral compasses, would protect their participants from harm. However, not all researchers were committed to the ethical treatment of human participants. The major impetus for a shift from individualized ethics to more formalized ethical guidelines was the uncovering of the brutal experiments performed on prisoners in Nazi concentration camps. A variety of sadistic "medical experiments" were conducted on unwilling participants. Some examples are breaking and rebreaking of bones (to see how many times they could be broken before healing failed to occur) and exposure to extremes of high altitude and freezing water (to see how long a person could survive). When these and other atrocities came to light, some of those responsible were tried for their crimes at Nuremberg in 1947. Out of these trials came the **Nuremberg Code**, a set of 10 guidelines for the ethical treatment of human participants in research. It is reprinted here in Table 4.1 (Katz, 1972). The Nuremberg Code laid the groundwork for the ethical standards that are in place today for both psychological and medical research. A similar set of ethical guidelines, known as the Declaration of Helsinki, was adopted by the World Medical Association in 1964 and provides an international set of ethical principles for medical research involving humans (available at www.wma.net).

Tragically, even after the development of the Nuremberg Code, researchers have not always ensured the safety and dignity of human participants. Since the late 1940s, there have been additional examples of maltreatment of human participants in biomedical

TABLE 4.1
Ten Points of the Nuremberg Code

1. The voluntary consent of the human subject is absolutely essential. This means that the person involved should have legal capacity to give consent; should be so situated as to be able to exercise free power of choice, without the intervention of any element of force, fraud, deceit, duress, over-reaching, or other ulterior form of constraint or coercion; and should have sufficient knowledge and comprehension of the elements of the subject matter involved as to enable him to make an understanding and enlightened decision. This latter element requires that before the acceptance of an affirmative decision by the experimental subject there should be known to him the nature, duration, and purpose of the experiment; the method and means by which it is to be conducted; all inconveniences and hazards reasonably to be expected; and the effects upon his health or person which may possibly come from his participation in the experiment. The duty and responsibility for ascertaining the quality of the consent rests upon each individual who initiates, directs, or engages in the experiment. It is a personal duty and responsibility that may not be delegated to another with impunity.

2. The experiment should be such as to yield fruitful results for the good of society, unprocurable by other methods or means of study, and not random and unnecessary in nature.

3. The experiment should be so designed and based on the results of animal experimentation and a knowledge of the natural history of the disease or other problem under study that the anticipated results will justify the performance of the experiment.

4. The experiment should be so conducted as to avoid all unnecessary physical and mental suffering and injury.

5. No experiment should be conducted where there is an a priori reason to believe that death or disabling injury will occur; except, perhaps, in those experiments where the experimental physicians also serve as subjects.

6. The degree of risk to be taken should never exceed that determined by the humanitarian importance of the problem to be solved by the experiment.

7. Proper preparations should be made and adequate facilities provided to protect the experimental subject against even remote possibilities of injury, disability, or death.

8. The experiment should be conducted only by scientifically qualified persons. The highest degree of skill and care should be required through all stages of the experiment of those who conduct or engage in the experiment.

9. During the course of the experiment the human subject should be at liberty to bring the experiment to an end if he has reached the physical or mental state where continuation of the experiment seems to him to be impossible.

10. During the course of the experiment the scientist in charge must be prepared to terminate the experiment at any stage, if he has probable cause to believe, in the exercise of the good faith, superior skill, and careful judgment required of him that a continuation of the experiment is likely to result in injury, disability, or death to the experimental subject.

Source: From Katz, J. (1972). *Experimentation with human beings.* New York: Russell Sage Foundation.

research. In 1963, for example, it was revealed that unsuspecting patients had been injected with live cancer cells (Katz, 1972). In 1972, a newspaper report exposed a Public Health Service study, commonly referred to as the Tuskegee study, in which nearly 400 men had been left to suffer with syphilis long after a cure (penicillin) was available. The study began as a short-term investigation to monitor untreated syphilis but continued for 40 years just so the researchers could examine the final stages of the disease (Jones, 1981).

Similar examples of the questionable treatment of human participants have been found in behavioral research. The most commonly cited example is Milgram's obedience study (Milgram, 1963). Milgram instructed participants to use electric shocks to punish other individuals when they made errors during a learning task. The intensity of the shocks was gradually increased until the participants were administering what appeared to be dangerously strong and obviously painful shocks. In fact, no shocks were used in the study (the "shocked" individuals were pretending); however, the participants (those who administered the shocks) believed that they were inflicting real pain and suffering. Although the participants in Milgram's study sustained no physical harm, they suffered shame and embarrassment for having behaved inhumanely toward their fellow human beings. The participants entered the study thinking that they were normal, considerate human beings, but they left with the knowledge that they could all too easily behave inhumanely.

It is important to note two things about these cases. First, although they constitute a very small percentage of all the research that is conducted, many examples of questionable treatment exist. Second, it is events like these that shaped the guidelines we have in place today. In the late 1960s, the U.S. Surgeon General required all institutions receiving federal funding for research from the Public Health Service to review proposed research to safeguard human participants. Because of the growing concern about research ethics, in 1974 Congress passed the **National Research Act**. The act mandated regulations for the protection of human participants and had the Department of Health, Education, and Welfare create the National Commission for the Protection of Human Subjects of Biomedical and Behavioral Research (Dunn & Chadwick, 1999). In 1979, the National Commission published *The Belmont Report: Ethical Principles and Guideline for the Protection of Human Subjects of Research*. The **Belmont Report** summarizes the basic ethical principles identified by the National Commission, which are used as the foundation upon which the federal regulations for protecting human participants are based, even to this day.

The Belmont Report identifies three basic principles:

1. The **principle of respect for persons** (**autonomy**) requires that individuals should consent to participate in studies (i.e., after learning about the research study, people should be free to decide whether they would like to participate in the study) and those who cannot give their consent, such as children, people with diminished abilities, and prisoners, need special protection. Milgram's study and the Tuskegee study violated the principle of respect. Milgram's participants did not know that they were in an experiment on obedience, and the Tuskegee participants were not informed that there was an effective treatment for their disease.

2. The **principle of beneficence** requires that the researcher does not harm the participants, minimizes risks, and maximizes possible benefits. Clearly both Milgram's study and the Tuskegee study caused harm to the participants. Personal distress resulted in Milgram's study and physical harm in the Tuskegee study. To underscore just how ethically vile the Tuskegee study was, 65 years after the Tuskegee study began, in 1997, then U.S. President, Bill Clinton, apologized to survivors and family members for the U.S. government's role in the research study (CDC, 1997).

3. The **principle of justice** requires fair and nonexploitative procedures for the selection and treatment of participants so that the costs and benefits of participation are distributed equally, such that participants are representative of the people who may benefit from the research (Gillespie, 1999). The Tuskegee study violates the principle of justice as well. Everyone could benefit from understanding syphilis; however, only poor, African–American males were used as participants and therefore unduly bore the burden of risk.

Although the development of ethical guidelines may seem like ancient history to many of you in college today, you should realize that they were put in place just in time to protect your parents, who may have participated in research studies during their years in college. Before the 1970s, formal guidelines and standards were rare and researchers were generally left on their own to decide what procedures were proper and acceptable. The Milgram's study, for example, may seem somewhat bizarre and inhumane, but it was preceded by other psychological research in which human participants actually were shocked for making errors (Crafts & Gilbert, 1934).

American Psychological Association Guidelines

Ethical Guidelines for the Use and Treatment of Human Participants in Research

Around the same time that the federal government began to concern itself with protecting human participants in research, the American Psychological Association (APA) prepared its first set of now widely distributed and accepted guidelines (1973). The first APA committee on ethics was set up in 1952; however, it was not until the mid 1960s, in response to major criticisms of Milgram's now famous obedience study, that APA members began to discuss a formal code of ethics.

You may have noticed the term *guidelines*. Because it is impossible to anticipate every specific research situation, the guidelines are intended to identify general areas in which researchers should be cautious and aware of ethical concerns. The APA guidelines have been updated and expanded several times since they were first developed and are periodically revised. The most recent version was published in 2002, with amendments added in 2010 and 2016 (APA, 2010). The **APA Ethics Code** contains 10 ethical standards, and you should be completely familiar with all of them before beginning any research with human participants. (You can visit http://www.apa.org/ethics/code/ for more information.) The Ethics Code is intended to provide guidance for psychologists and standards of professional conduct that can be applied by the APA and by other bodies that choose to adopt them.

A summary of the most recent ethical guidelines concerning human participants in research (APA, 2010) is presented in Table 4.2. This summary is based on the *APA guidelines in Ethical Principles of Psychologists and Code of Conduct* (APA, 2010) and includes the elements most relevant to the use and treatment of human participants in research (parts of Standards 2, 3, 4, 6, and 8). The APA guidelines are continually reviewed and revised—as are federal, state, and local regulations—so researchers always must check to make sure they are abiding by the current rules.

Major Ethical Issues

Rather than discussing each of the guidelines point by point, we present in detail a few issues that are the most important for new researchers. You should notice that the Belmont principles of respect, beneficence, and justice are paralleled in the APA Ethics Code guidelines of no harm and informed consent.

No Harm (Item 1, Table 4.2)   The researcher is obligated to protect participants from physical or psychological harm. The entire research experience should be evaluated to identify risks of harm, and when possible, such risks should be minimized or removed from the study. Any risk of harm must be justified. The justification may be that the

TABLE 4.2

Selected Elements from the APA Ethical Guidelines Concerning Human Participants in Research

This summary is based on the *APA guidelines in Ethical Principles of Psychologists and Code of Conduct* (APA, 2010) and includes the elements most relevant to the use and treatment of human participants in research. The section numbers correspond to the standards referred to in the *APA Ethical Principles of Psychologists and Code of Conduct.*

1. No Harm (Sections 3.04 and 8.08)
Psychologists take reasonable steps to avoid harming their research participants, and to minimize harm where it is foreseeable and unavoidable.

Psychologists do not engage in torture, which is defined as inflicting severe pain or suffering, either physical or mental, or committing any other cruel, inhuman, or degrading behavior.

When psychologists become aware that research procedures have harmed a participant, they take reasonable steps to minimize the harm.

2. Privacy and Confidentiality (Sections 4.01–4.05)
Psychologists have a primary obligation and take reasonable precautions to protect confidential information.

Psychologists discuss with persons the relevant limits of confidentiality.

Psychologists discuss confidential information only for appropriate scientific or professional purposes, and only with persons clearly concerned with such matters.

Psychologists may disclose confidential information with the appropriate consent of the individual or another legally authorized person on behalf of the participant, unless prohibited by law.

3. Institutional Approval (Section 8.01)
When institutional approval is required, psychologists provide accurate information about their research proposals and obtain approval prior to conducting the research. They conduct research in accordance with the approved research protocol.

4. Competence (Sections 2.01 and 2.05)
Psychologists conduct research with populations and in areas only within the boundaries of their competence.

Psychologists planning to conduct research involving populations, area, techniques, or technologies new to them undertake relevant education, training, supervised experience, consultation, or study.

Psychologists who delegate work to research assistants take reasonable steps to authorize only those responsibilities that such persons can be expected to perform competently on the basis of their education, training, or experience, and see that such persons perform these services competently.

5. Record Keeping (Sections 6.01–6.02)
Psychologists create, and to the extent the records are under their control, maintain, disseminate, store, retain, and dispose of records and data relating to their scientific work in order to allow for replication of research design and analyses and meet institutional requirements.

Psychologists maintain confidentiality in creating, storing, accessing, transferring, and disposing of records under their control, whether these are written, automated, or in any other medium.

6. Informed Consent to Research (Sections 3.10 and 8.02–8.04)
When psychologists conduct research, they obtain informed consent of the individual using language that is reasonably understandable to that person except when conducting such activities without consent.

For persons who are legally incapable of giving informed consent, psychologists nevertheless (1) provide an appropriate explanation, (2) seek the individual's assent, (3) consider such persons' preferences and best interests, and (4) obtain appropriate permission from a legally authorized person, if such substitute consent is permitted or required by law.

When obtaining informed consent, psychologists inform participants about:
a. the purpose of the research, expected duration, and procedures.
b. their right to decline to participate and to withdraw from the research once participation has begun.
c. the foreseeable consequences of declining or withdrawing.
d. reasonable foreseeable factors that may be expected to influence their willingness to participate (such as potential risks, discomfort, or adverse effects).
e. any prospective research benefits.
f. limits of confidentiality.
g. incentives for participation.
h. who to contact for questions about the research and research participants' rights.

They provide opportunity for the prospective participants to ask questions and receive answers.

Psychologists conducting intervention research involving the use of experimental treatments clarify to participants at the onset of the research:

a. the experimental nature of the treatment.
b. the services that will or will not be available to the control group(s) if appropriate.
c. the means by which assignment to treatment and control groups will be made.
d. available treatment alternatives if an individual does not wish to participate in the research or wishes to withdraw once the study has begun.
e. compensation for or monetary costs of participating.

Psychologists obtain informed consent from research participants prior to recording their voices or images for data collection unless: (1) the research consists solely of naturalistic observations in public places, and it is not anticipated that the recording will be used in a manner that could cause personal identification or harm; or (2) the research design includes deception, and consent for the use of the recording is obtained during the debriefing (see also Standard 8.07, Deception in Research).

When psychologists conduct research with students or subordinates as participants, psychologists take steps to protect the prospective participants from adverse consequences of declining or withdrawing from participation.

When research participation is a course requirement or an opportunity for extra credit, the prospective participant is given the choice of equitable alternative activities.

7. Dispensing with Informed Consent (Section 8.05)

Psychologists may dispense with informed consent only (1) where research would not reasonably be assumed to create distress or harm, and involves (a) *the study of normal educational practices, curricula, or classroom management methods conducted in educational settings*; (b) *only anonymous questionnaires, naturalistic observations, or archival research for which disclosure of responses would not place participants at risk of criminal or civil liability or damage their reputation, and confidentiality is protected*; or (c) *the study of factors related to job or organization effectiveness conducted in organizational settings for which there is no risk to participants' employability, and confidentiality is protected* or (2) where otherwise permitted by law or federal or institutional regulations.

8. Offering Inducements for Research Participation (Section 8.06)

Psychologists make reasonable efforts to avoid offering excessive or inappropriate financial or other inducements for research participation when such inducements are likely to coerce participation.

9. Deception in Research (Section 8.07)

Psychologists do not conduct a study involving deception unless they have determined that the use of deceptive techniques is justified by the study's significant prospective scientific, educational, or applied value, and that effective nondeceptive alternative procedures are not feasible.

Psychologists do not deceive prospective participants about research that is reasonably expected to cause physical pain or severe emotional distress.

Psychologists explain any deception that is an integral feature of the design and conduct of an experiment to participants as early as is feasible, preferably at the conclusion of their participation but no later than the conclusion of the data collection, and permit participants to withdraw their data (see also Standard 8.08, Debriefing).

10. Debriefing (Section 8.08)

Psychologists provide a prompt opportunity for participants to obtain appropriate information about the nature, results, and conclusions of the research, and then take reasonable steps to correct any misconceptions that participants may have of which the psychologists are aware.

If scientific or humane values justify delaying or withholding this information, psychologists take reasonable measures to reduce the risk of harm.

scientific benefits of the study far outweigh the small, temporary harm that can result. Or it may be that greater harm is likely to occur unless some minor risk is accepted during the study. (Doctors and their patients face this concern when deciding whether to use a medication that has known side effects.) In any event, participants must be informed of any potential risks, and the researcher must take steps to minimize any harm that can occur. In the behavioral sciences, the risk of physical harm is relatively rare (except in areas in which psychology and medicine overlap). Psychological harm, on the other hand, is a common concern. During or after a study, participants may feel increased anxiety, anger, lower self-esteem, or mild depression, especially in situations in which they feel they have been cheated, tricked, deceived, or insulted. Occasionally researchers deliberately create these situations as an integral part of the study; for example, participants may be given an impossible task so the researcher can observe responses to failure (note that Item 9 in Table 4.2 allows deception). Often, participants generate their own mental distress from imaginative speculation about the purpose of the research. In either case, researchers should reassure participants by explaining before the study exactly what will be done and why (insofar as possible), and by providing a complete explanation and justification for the research as soon as possible after the study is completed. The goal is for participants to leave the study feeling just as well as when they entered. (Deception and how to deal with it are covered in more detail later in this section, pp. 93–95.) Finally, research involving sensitive topics such as physical or sexual abuse and violence against women can produce serious ethical dilemmas for researchers who risk re-traumatizing their participants by reawakening memories of prior traumas (Fontes, 2004).

One area of debate concerning the issue of no harm is the topic of **clinical equipoise** (Young, 2002). The basic concept is that clinicians have an ethical responsibility to provide the best possible treatment for their patients. However, many research studies evaluate and compare different treatment options by randomly assigning patients to different treatments. If the clinician knows (or even believes) that one of the treatment conditions is inferior to the others, then some patients are being denied the best possible treatment and the ethical principle of no harm is being violated. The solution to this dilemma is to conduct studies that only compare equally preferred treatments; this is the principle of clinical equipoise. This means that a researcher can compare treatments when:

a.   there is honest uncertainty about which treatment is best.
b.   there is honest professional disagreement among experts concerning which treatment is best.

Note that universally adopting the principle of equipoise would effectively eliminate many common research studies such as those that involve a no-treatment control group or studies that compare an active drug with a placebo. It is unlikely that equipoise will become common practice in the near future.

In general, the principle of no harm means that a researcher is obligated to anticipate and remove any harmful elements in a research study. During the study, a researcher also must monitor the well-being of the participants and halt the study at any sign of trouble. A classic example of monitoring well-being is a prison simulation study by Haney, Banks, and Zimbardo (1973). In this study, male undergraduates were randomly assigned to play the roles of prisoners and guards for a 1-week period. Except for prohibiting physical abuse, the participants did not receive any specific training. Within a few days, however, the prisoners began to display signs of depression and helplessness, and the guards showed aggressive and dehumanizing behavior toward the prisoners. Half of the prisoners developed severe emotional disturbances and had to be "released" for their own well-being. Ultimately, the entire study was stopped prematurely for the safety of the remaining participants. Although these results are somewhat extreme, they do demonstrate the need for continuous observation during the course of a research study to ensure that the no-harm principle is maintained throughout.

Informed Consent (Item 6, Table 4.2)   The ethical principle of **informed consent** is that human participants should be given complete information about the research and their roles in it before agreeing to participate. They should understand the information and then voluntarily decide whether to participate. This ideal is often difficult to achieve. Here, we consider three components of informed consent and examine the problems that can exist with each.

1. *Information:* Often, it is difficult or impossible to provide participants with complete information about a research study prior to their participation. One common practice is to keep participants "blind" to the purpose of the study. If participants know that one treatment is supposed to produce better performance, they may adjust their own levels of performance in an attempt to satisfy the experimenter. To avoid this problem, researchers often tell participants exactly what will be done in the study but do not explain why. In situations in which the study relies on deception, disguised measurement, concealed observation, and so on, informing the participants would undermine the goals of the research. In clinical research, the outcome of an experimental therapy (risks and benefits) may not be known. In this case, a researcher may not be able to tell the participant exactly what will happen. Although some information may be disguised, concealed, or simply unknown, it is essential that participants be informed of any known potential risks.

2. *Understanding:* Simply telling participants about the research does not necessarily mean they are informed, especially in situations in which the participants may not be competent enough to understand. This problem occurs routinely with special populations such as young children, developmentally disabled people, and psychiatric patients. In these situations, it is customary to provide information to the participant as well as to a parent or guardian who also must approve of the participation. With special populations, researchers occasionally speak of obtaining *assent* from the participants and *consent* from an official guardian. Even with regular populations, there may be some question about true understanding. Researchers must express their explanations in terms that the participants can easily understand and should give the participants ample opportunity to ask questions.

3. *Voluntary Participation:* The goal of informed consent is that participants should decide to participate of their own free will. Often, however, participants may feel coerced to participate or perceive that they have limited choice. For example, a researcher who is a teacher, professor, or clinician may be in a position of power or control over the potential participants who may perceive a threat of retribution if they do not cooperate. Suppose, for example, that your professor asked for volunteers from the class to help with a research project. Would you feel a little extra pressure to volunteer just to avoid jeopardizing your grade in the class? This problem is particularly important with institutionalized populations (prisoners, hospital patients, etc.) who must depend on others in nearly every aspect of their lives. In these cases, it is especially important that the researcher explain to the participants that they are completely free to decline participation or to leave the study at any time without negative consequences.

DEFINITION

> The principle of **informed consent** requires the investigator to provide all available information about a study so that an individual can make a rational, informed decision to participate in the study.

The procedure for obtaining informed consent varies from study to study, depending in part on the complexity of the information presented and the actual degree of risk involved in the study. In most situations, researchers use a written consent form. A **consent form** contains a statement of all the elements of informed consent and a line for the participant's and/or guardian's signature. The form is provided before the study so the potential participants have all the information they need to make an informed decision regarding participation. Consent forms vary according to the specifics of the study but typically contain some common elements. Table 4.3 lists the common components of consent forms (Kazdin, 2003).

Although consent forms are very commonly used, in some situations involving minimal risk, it is possible to obtain verbal consent without a written consent form. And in some situations (such as the administration of anonymous questionnaires), it is permissible to dispense with informed consent entirely (see Item 7 in Table 4.2, and further discussion in the IRB section on page 98).

TABLE 4.3
Components of Informed Consent Forms

Section of the Form	Purpose and Contents
Overview	Presentation of the goals of the study, why this study is being conducted, and who is responsible for the study and its execution.
Description of procedures	Clarification of the experimental conditions, assessment procedures, and requirements of the participants.
Risks and inconveniences	Statement of any physical and psychological risks and an estimate of their likelihood. Inconveniences and demands to be placed on the participants (e.g., how many sessions, requests to do anything, or contact at home).
Benefits	A statement of what the participants can reasonably hope to gain from participation, including psychological, physical, and monetary benefits.
Costs and economic considerations	Charges to the participants (e.g., in treatment) and payment (e.g., for participation or completing various forms).
Confidentiality	Assurances that the information is confidential and will only be seen by people who need to do so for the purposes of research (e.g., scoring and data analyses), procedures to assure confidentiality (e.g., removal of names from forms, storage of data). Also, caveats are included here if it is possible that sensitive information (e.g., psychiatric information, criminal activity) can be subpoenaed.
Alternative treatments	In an intervention study, alternatives available to the client before or during participation are outlined.
Voluntary participation	A statement that the participant is willing to participate and can decline participation now or later without penalty of any kind.
Questions and further information	A statement that the participant is encouraged to ask questions at any time and can contact one or more individuals (listed by name and phone number) who are available for such questions.
Signature lines	A place for the participant and the experimenter to sign.

Source: From Kazdin, A. E., *Research Design in Clinical Psychology.* Copyright 2003 by Allyn & Bacon. Reprinted with permission.

Deception (Item 9, Table 4.2)   Often, the goal of a research study is to examine behavior under "normal" circumstances. To achieve this goal, researchers must sometimes use **deception**.

For example, if participants know the true purpose of a research study, they may modify their natural behaviors to conceal embarrassing secrets or to appear to be better than they really are. To avoid this problem, researchers sometimes do not tell participants the true purpose of the study. One technique is to use **passive deception**, or **omission**, and simply withhold information about the study. Another possibility is to use **active deception**, or **commission**, and deliberately present false or misleading information. In simple terms, passive deception is keeping secrets and active deception is telling lies.

DEFINITIONS

> **Deception** occurs when a researcher purposefully withholds information or misleads participants with regard to information about a study. There are two forms of deception: passive and active.
>
> **Passive deception** (or **omission**) is the withholding or omitting of information; the researcher intentionally does not tell participants some information about the study.
>
> **Active deception** (or **commission**) is the presenting of misinformation about the study to participants. The most common form of active deception is misleading participants about the specific purpose of the study.

In a classic study of human memory, for example, Craik and Lockhart (1972) did not inform the participants that they were involved in a study of memory (passive deception). Instead, the participants viewed words that were presented one at a time and were asked to respond to the words in different ways. Some participants were asked to decide whether the word was printed in uppercase letters or lowercase letters. Others were asked to make judgments about the meaning of each word. After responding to a large number of words, the participants were given a surprise memory test and asked to recall as many of the words as possible. None of the participants were informed that the true purpose of the study was to test memory. In this case, the deception was necessary to prevent the participants from trying to memorize the words as they were presented.

Active deception can take a variety of forms. For example, a researcher can state an explicit lie about the study, give false information about stimulus materials, give false feedback about a participant's performance, or use **confederates** to create a false environment. Although there is some evidence that the use of active deception is declining (Nicks, Korn, & Mainieri, 1997), this technique has been standard practice in many areas of research, particularly in social psychology. For example, Asch (1956) told participants that they were in a perception study and asked each individual in a group of eight to identify the stimulus line that correctly matched the length of a standard line. Seven of the eight individuals were confederates working with Asch. For the first few lines, the confederates selected the correct match, but on later trials, they unanimously picked what was obviously the wrong line. Although the real participants often appeared anxious and confused, nearly one-third of them conformed to the group behavior and also picked the obviously wrong line. Asch was able to demonstrate this level of social conformity by actively deceiving his participants. If individuals are simply asked whether they conform, the vast majority say no (Wolosin, Sherman, & Mynat, 1972).

A more recent example of deception in social psychology is the false-confession research described at the beginning of this chapter (Kassin & Kiechel, 1996; Perillo & Kassin, 2011). The participants in these studies were told that they were in a reaction time experiment but actually were tricked into accepting guilt and confessing to an act that they did not commit. In this study, the researchers used active deception to generate an unusual

Confederates are people who pretend to be participants in a research study but actually work for the researcher.

behavior (false confessions) in a controlled laboratory situation where it could be examined scientifically.

In any study involving deception, the principle of informed consent is compromised because participants are not given complete and accurate information. In these situations, a researcher has a special responsibility to safeguard the participants. The APA guidelines identify three specific areas of responsibility (see Item 9 in Table 4.2):

1. The deception must be justified in terms of some significant benefit that outweighs the risk to the participants. The researcher must consider all alternatives to deception and must justify the rejection of any alternative procedures.
2. The researcher cannot conceal from the prospective participants information about research that is expected to cause physical pain or severe emotional distress.
3. The researcher must debrief the participants by providing a complete explanation as soon as possible after participation is completed.

The first point, justification of the deception, obviously involves weighing the benefits of the study against the rights of the individual participants. Usually, the final decision is not left entirely to the researcher but requires review and approval by a group of individuals charged with the responsibility of ensuring ethical conduct in all human research (e.g., the IRB, which is discussed later). This review group also can suggest alternative procedures not requiring deception, and the researcher must consider and respond to its suggestions (the review process is also discussed later).

The second point is that researchers definitely cannot use deception to withhold information about risk or possible harm. Suppose, for example, that a researcher wants to examine the influence of increased anxiety on performance. To increase anxiety, the researcher informs one group of participants that they may receive relatively mild electric shocks occasionally during the course of the study. No shocks are actually given, so the researcher is deceiving the participants; however, this type of deception involves no harm or risk and probably would be considered acceptable. On the other hand, suppose that the researcher wants to examine how performance is influenced by sudden, unexpected episodes of pain. To create these episodes, the researcher occasionally administers mild shocks during the study without warning the participants. To ensure that the shocks are unexpected, the informed consent process does not include any mention of shocks. In this case, the researcher is withholding information about a potential risk, and this type of deception is not allowed.

The final point is that deceived participants must receive a **debriefing** that provides a full description of the true purpose of the study, including the use and purpose of deception, after the study is completed. The debriefing serves many purposes, such as:

- conveying what the study was really all about, if deception was used.
- counteracting or minimizing any negative effects of the study.
- conveying the educational objective of the research (i.e., explaining the value of the research and the contribution to science of participation in the research).
- explaining the nature of and justification for any deception used.
- answering any questions the participant has.

DEFINITION

A **debriefing** is a post-experimental explanation of the purpose of a study that is given to a participant, especially if deception was used.

Overall, the intent of debriefing is to counteract or minimize harmful effects. Unfortunately, evidence suggests that debriefing may not always achieve its purpose. Although some studies show that debriefing can effectively remove harm and leave no lingering effects (Holmes, 1976a, 1976b; Smith & Richardson, 1983), other studies indicate that debriefing is not effective, is not believed, and may result in increased suspicion (Fisher & Fyrberg, 1994; Ring, Wallston, & Corey, 1970). Most of this work is based on studies in which participants were interviewed immediately after being debriefed. However, some researchers believe that participants may not truthfully reveal their reactions to debriefing, especially when the debriefing informs them of previous deception (Baumrind, 1985; Rubin, 1985). Finally, there is some evidence that debriefing only further annoys or embarrasses participants (Fisher & Fyrberg, 1994); not only were they deceived during the study but also the researcher is forcing them to face that fact. Still, the participants deserve a full and complete explanation, and the researcher has an obligation to safeguard participants as much as possible.

Some things that seem to influence a debriefing's effectiveness include:

- the participants' suspicions (how likely they are to think the debriefing is merely a continuation of the deception).
- the nature of the deception (whether it was passive or active; debriefing is less effective with active deception).
- the sincerity of the experimenter (the last thing a participant needs is a condescending experimenter).
- the time interval between the end of the study and the delivery of the debriefing (the sooner the better).

In some situations, the research design permits a researcher to inform participants that deception may be involved and to ask the participants for consent to be deceived. Drug research, for example, often involves comparison of one group of participants who receive the drug and a second group of participants who are given a **placebo** (an ineffective, inert substitute). At the beginning of the experiment, all participants are informed that a placebo group exists but none know whether they are in the drug group or the placebo group. Thus, before they consent to participate, participants are informed that they may be deceived. This kind of prior disclosure helps minimize the negative effects of deception; that is, participants are less likely to become angry or feel tricked or abused. On the other hand, when participants know that deception is involved, they are likely to become more defensive and suspicious of all aspects of the research. In addition, participants may adopt unusual responses or behaviors that can undermine the goals of the research. For example, in some studies that examined the effectiveness of experimental AIDS medications, groups of participants conspired to divide and share their medications, assuming that this strategy would ensure that everyone got at least some of the real drug (Melton, Levine, Koocher, Rosenthal, & Thompson, 1988).

Deception can also cause participants to become skeptical of experiments in general. Having been deceived, a person may refuse to participate in any future research or may enter future studies with a defensive or hostile attitude. Deceived participants may share their negative attitudes and opinions with their friends, and one deceptive experiment may contaminate an entire pool of potential research participants.

Confidentiality (Item 2, Table 4.2)   The essence of research in the behavioral sciences is the collection of information by researchers from the individuals who participate in their studies. Although the specific information can vary tremendously from one study to another, the different types of information can be categorized as follows:

- attitudes and opinions (e.g., politics and prejudices)
- measures of performance (e.g., manual dexterity, reaction time, and memory)
- demographic characteristics (e.g., age, income, and sexual orientation)

The APA ethical guideline requiring that researchers ensure the confidentiality of their research participants is similar to the Health Insurance Portability and Accountability Act (HIPAA) of 1996 provision that addresses the security and privacy of health information.

Any of these items can be considered private and personal by some people, and it is reasonable that some participants would not want this information to be made public. Therefore, the APA ethical guidelines require that researchers ensure the confidentiality of their research participants (see Item 2 in Table 4.2). Confidentiality ensures that the information obtained from a research participant will be kept secret and private. The enforcement of confidentiality benefits both the participants and the researcher. First, participants are protected from embarrassment or emotional stress that could result from public exposure. Also, researchers are more likely to obtain willing and honest participants. Most individuals demand an assurance of confidentiality before they are willing to disclose personal and private information.

Although there are different techniques for preserving confidentiality, the basic process involves ensuring that participants' records are kept anonymous. Anonymity means that the information and measurements obtained from each participant are not referred to by the participant's name, either during the course of the study or in the written report of the research results.

DEFINITIONS

> **Confidentiality** is the practice of keeping strictly secret and private the information or measurements obtained from an individual during a research study.
>
> **Anonymity** is the practice of ensuring that an individual's name is not directly associated with the information or measurements obtained from that individual.

To ensure the confidentiality of the data, usually, one of the following two strategies is used:

1. No names or other identification appears on data records. This strategy is used in situations in which there is no need whatsoever to link an individual participant to the specific information that the participant provides. For example, a study may involve participants completing a questionnaire concerning their attitudes about racial discrimination in the work place, or individuals may be observed in a campus café to record their recycling behavior. If participants are promised payment or extra credit, researchers often keep a separate list of the participants so that they can receive promised payment or extra credit, and so they can be contacted later if necessary. However, this list is completely separate from the data and is destroyed at the end of the study. There is no way that the researcher or anyone else can connect a specific set of responses to a specific participant.

2. Researchers use a coding system to keep track of which participant names go with which sets of data. This strategy is used in situations in which it is necessary to reconnect specific names with specific data at different times during a research study. For example, a study may involve measuring the same participants at different times under different conditions. In this case, the researcher wants to examine how each participant changes over time. When a participant shows up for the third stage of the study, the researcher must be able to retrieve the same participant's responses from the first two stages. Only the code name or code number identifies the actual data, and the researcher keeps a separate, secured list to connect the participants with the codes. Thus, anyone who has access to the data has only the codes and cannot associate a specific participant with any specific data. The secured list is used only to retrieve previous data from a particular participant, and the list is destroyed at the conclusion of the study.

In most research reports, the results are presented as average values that have been collapsed across a large group of individual participants, and there is no mention of any individual participants, code numbers, or code names. In situations in which a single participant is examined in great detail, researchers must take special care to preserve anonymity. In these situations, only the code name or code number is used to identify the participant, and any description of the participant is edited to eliminate unique characteristics that could lead to individual identification.

The Institutional Review Board

Although the final responsibility for the protection of human participants rests with the researcher, most human-participant research must be reviewed and approved by a group of individuals not directly affiliated with the specific research study. As part of the guidelines for the protection of human participants, the U.S. Department of Health and Human Services (HHS) requires review of all human-participant research conducted by government agencies and institutions receiving government funds. This includes all colleges, universities, hospitals, and clinics, essentially every place where human-participant research takes place. This review is to assure compliance with all requirements of Title 45, Part 46 of the Code of Federal Regulations (45 CFR 46). The **Common Rule**, as it is typically referred to, published in 1991, is based on the principles of the Belmont Report and provides a common set of federal regulations for protecting human participants to be used by review boards (Dunn & Chadwick, 1999).

Each institution or agency is required to establish a committee called an **Institutional Review Board** (**IRB**), which is composed of both scientists and nonscientists. The IRB examines all proposed research involving human participants with respect to seven basic criteria. If the IRB finds that a proposed research study fails to satisfy any one of the criteria, the research project is not approved. In addition, the IRB can require a research proposal be modified to meet its criteria before the research is approved. Following is a listing and brief discussion of the seven basic IRB criteria (Office of Human Research Protection, 1993).

1. *Minimization of Risk to Participants.* The purpose of this criterion is to ensure that research procedures do not unnecessarily expose participants to risk. In addition to evaluating the degree of risk in a proposed study, the IRB reviews the research to ensure that every precaution has been taken to minimize risk. This may involve requiring the researcher to justify any component of the research plan that involves risk, and the IRB may suggest or require alternative procedures.

2. *Reasonable Risk in Relation to Benefits.* The IRB is responsible for evaluating the potential risks to participants as well as the benefits that result from the research. The benefits include immediate benefits to the participants as well as general benefits such as advanced knowledge.

3. *Equitable Selection.* The purpose of this criterion is to ensure that the participant selection process does not discriminate among individuals in the population and does not exploit vulnerable individuals. For example, a researcher who is recruiting volunteers from the general community can inadvertently exclude the Spanish-speaking population if all the publicity used to solicit participants is in English. The issue for the IRB is not to ensure a random sample (although this should benefit the researcher) but rather to ensure equal opportunity for all potential participants. The concern with vulnerability is that some individuals (children and people who are developmentally disabled, psychologically impaired, or institutionalized) might be easily tricked or coerced into "volunteering" without a complete understanding of their actions.

4. *Informed Consent.* The notion of informed consent is one of the basic elements of all ethical codes and is a primary concern for the IRB. The IRB carefully reviews and critiques the procedures used to obtain informed consent, making sure that the researcher

provides complete information about all aspects of the research that might be of interest or concern to a potential participant. In addition, the IRB ensures that the information is presented in a form that participants can easily understand. For example, the information should be in everyday language and presented at a level appropriate for the specific participants (the presentation of information for college students would be different from the presentation for 6-year-old children). In addition, the IRB typically looks for a clear statement informing participants that they have the right to withdraw from the study at any time without penalty. The goal is to ensure that participants receive complete information and understand the information before they decide to participate in the research.

5. *Documentation of Informed Consent.* The IRB determines whether it is necessary to have a written consent form signed by the participant and the researcher.

6. *Data Monitoring.* During the course of the research study, the researcher should make provision for monitoring the data to determine whether any unexpected risks or causes of harm have developed. In some research situations, the researcher should monitor the testing of each individual participant so the procedure can be interrupted or stopped at the first indication of developing harm or danger.

7. *Privacy and Confidentiality.* This criterion is intended to protect participants from the risk that information obtained during a research study could be released to outside individuals (parents, teachers, employers, and peers) where it might have embarrassing or personally damaging consequences. The IRB examines all record keeping within the study: How are participants identified? How are data coded? Who has access to participant names and data? The goal is to guarantee basic rights of privacy and to ensure confidentiality for the participants.

DEFINITION

> The **Institutional Review Board (IRB)** is a committee that examines all proposed research with respect to its treatment of human participants. IRB approval must be obtained before any research is conducted with human participants.

To implement the criteria for approval of human-participant research, the IRB typically requires that researchers submit a written research proposal that addresses each of the seven criteria. Often, the local IRB has forms that a researcher must complete. Research proposals are classified into three categories that determine how each proposal will be reviewed. A proposal fits in Category I (Exempt Review) if the research presents no possible risk to adult participants. Examples of Category I proposals are anonymous, mailed surveys on innocuous topics and anonymous observation of public behavior. This research is exempt from the requirements of informed consent, and the proposal is reviewed by the IRB Chair. A proposal fits in Category II (Expedited Review) if the research presents no more than minimal risk to participants and typically includes research on individual or group behavior of normal adults when there is no psychological intervention or deception. Research under this category does not require written documentation of informed consent, but oral consent is required. Category II proposals are reviewed by several IRB members. Also note that most often, classroom research projects fall into the expedited review category. Category III (Full Review) is used for research proposals that include any questionable elements such as special populations, unusual equipment or procedures, deception, intervention, or invasive measurements. A meeting of all of the IRB members is required, and the researcher must appear in person to discuss, explain, and answer questions about the research. During the discussion of Category III research, the IRB members may become active participants in the development of the research plan, making suggestions or contributions that modify the research proposal. Throughout the process, the primary concern of the IRB is to ensure the protection of human participants.

LEARNING CHECK

1. What kind of research was the focus for most of the early attempts to establish ethical research guidelines?
   a. Psychological research with animal subjects
   b. Psychological research with humans
   c. Medical research with humans
   d. Medical research with animals

2. Which principle of the Belmont Report corresponds to the guideline of "No Harm"?
   a. Respect
   b. Beneficence
   c. Justice
   d. None of the Belmont principles corresponds to "No Harm."

3. If a researcher explains what will happen in a research study using language that potential participants probably cannot understand, then what ethical guideline is being violated?
   a. Confidentiality
   b. Preventing harm
   c. Informed consent
   d. Anonymity

4. Which of the following is a responsibility of the IRB?
   a. They decide whether the process for selecting participants is fair and equitable.
   b. They decide whether it is necessary to have a signed informed consent form for each participant.
   c. They decide whether the privacy and confidentially of participants is protected.
   d. All of the above.

Answers appear at the end of the chapter.

4.3 Ethical Issues and Nonhuman Subjects in Research

LEARNING OBJECTIVES

LO5 Describe the major elements of the APA ethical guidelines for nonhuman subjects in research.

LO6 Describe the purpose and responsibilities of the Institutional Animal Care and Use Committee (IACUC).

Thus far, we have considered ethical issues involving human participants in research. However, much research is conducted with nonhumans—animals—as subjects, and here, too, many ethical issues must be considered. For many people, the first ethical question is whether nonhuman subjects should be used at all in behavioral research. However, nonhuman subjects have been a part of behavioral science research for more than 100 years and probably will continue to be used as research subjects for the foreseeable future. Researchers who use nonhumans as subjects do so for a variety of reasons including: (1) to understand animals for their own sake, (2) to understand humans (many processes can be generalized from nonhumans to humans), and (3) to conduct research that is impossible to conduct using human participants. An excellent summary of the animal research debate is presented in a book chapter by Baker and Serdikoff (2013).

Historical Highlights of Treatment of Nonhuman Subjects

To protect the welfare of nonhumans, various organizations have been formed including the Society for the Prevention of Cruelty to Animals (SPCA) established in the United States in 1866 (Ray, 2000). More recent regulation of the use of nonhumans in research began in 1962, when the federal government first issued guidelines. In 1966, the Animal Welfare Act was enacted; it was most recently amended in 2013. The Animal Welfare Act deals with general standards for animal care and treatment (USDA, 2013; https://www.nal.usda.gov/awic/animal-welfare-act). In addition, the U.S. Government Principles for the Utilization and Care of Vertebrate Animals Used in Testing, Research, and Training were incorporated into the Public Health Service (PHS) Policy on Humane Care and Use of Laboratory Animals in 1986, and continue to provide a framework for conducting research (National Institute of Health: Office of Laboratory Animal Welfare, 2015). Several organizations, including the American Association for Laboratory Animal Science (AALAS) and the American Association for Accreditation of Laboratory Animal Care (AAALAC), encourage monitoring the care of laboratory animals by researchers.

Today, the federal government regulates the use of nonhuman subjects in research. It requires researchers using nonhuman subjects to follow (1) the guidelines of the local IACUC (the review board for animal research, similar to the IRB, to be discussed later), (2) the U.S. Department of Agriculture's guidelines, (3) guidelines of state agencies, and (4) established guidelines within the academic discipline (e.g., the APA guidelines in psychology). The U.S. Department of Agriculture's requirements for use of nonhumans in research can be found in the *Guide for the Care and Use of Laboratory Animals* (National Research Council, 2011). The PHS requires institutions to use the guide for activities involving animals.

American Psychological Association Guidelines

Ethical Guidelines for the Use and Treatment of Nonhuman Subjects in Research

The APA has prepared a set of ethical guidelines for the use and treatment of nonhuman subjects that parallels the guidelines for human participants presented earlier. Table 4.4 lists the basic standards of the APA Ethics Code for the care and use of animal subjects (APA, 2010). In addition, the APA's Committee on Animal Research and Ethics (CARE) has prepared even more detailed guidelines for researchers working with nonhuman subjects (APA, 2012). This document, *Guidelines for Ethical Conduct in the Care and Use of Nonhuman Animals in Research,* can be obtained from the APA website. Anyone who is planning to conduct research with nonhuman subjects should carefully review and abide by these guidelines. As is the case with human participants, the APA guidelines—as well as federal, state, and local regulations—are continually reviewed and revised; researchers should always check to make sure they are abiding by the current rules.

Major Ethical Issues

The list in Table 4.4 includes many of the same elements contained in the human participants' code. In particular, qualified individuals must conduct research, the research must be justified, and the researcher must be responsible for minimizing discomfort or harm. Because most research animals are housed in a laboratory setting before and after their research experience, the code also extends to the general care and maintenance of animal subjects. In particular, the code refers to federal, state, and local regulations that govern housing conditions, food, sanitation, and medical care for research animals.

TABLE 4.4

APA Ethical Principles for the Humane Care and Use of Animals in Research

The following ethical standard is reprinted from the *Ethical Principles of Psychologists and Code of Conduct* (APA, 2010).

8.09 Humane Care and Use of Animals in Research

Psychologists acquire, care for, use, and dispose of all animals in compliance with current federal, state, and local laws and regulations, and with professional standards.

a. Psychologists trained in research methods and experienced in the care of laboratory animals closely supervise all procedures involving animals and are responsible for ensuring appropriate consideration of their comfort, health, and humane treatment.

b. Psychologists ensure that all individuals under their supervision who are using animals have received instruction in research methods and in the care, maintenance, and handling of the species being used, to the extent appropriate for their role.

c. Psychologists make reasonable efforts to minimize discomfort, infection, illness, and pain of animal subjects.

d. Psychologists use a procedure subjecting animals to pain, stress, or privation only when an alternative procedure is unavailable and the goal is justified by its prospective scientific, educational, or applied value.

e. Psychologists perform surgical procedures under appropriate anesthesia and follow techniques to avoid infection and minimize pain during and after surgery.

f. When it is appropriate that an animal's life be terminated, psychologists proceed rapidly, with an effort to minimize pain, and in accordance with accepted procedures.

Source: From *Ethical Principles of Psychologists and Code of Conduct* (APA, 2010). Retrieved from http://www.apa.org/ethics/code/principles.pdf. Copyright 2010 by the American Psychological Association. Reprinted with permission.

The Institutional Animal Care and Use Committee

Institutions that conduct research with animals have an animal research review board called the **Institutional Animal Care and Use Committee (IACUC)**. The IACUC is responsible for reviewing and approving all research using animal subjects in much the same way that the IRB monitors research with humans. The purpose of the IACUC is to protect animal subjects by ensuring that all research meets the criteria established by the code of ethics. Researchers must submit proposals to the committee and obtain approval before beginning any research with animal subjects. According to the *Guide for the Care and Use of Laboratory Animals* (National Research Council, 2011), the committee must consist of a veterinarian, at least one scientist experienced in research involving animals, and one member of the public with no affiliation with the institution where the research is being conducted.

DEFINITION

> The **Institutional Animal Care and Use Committee (IACUC)** is a committee that examines all proposed research with respect to its treatment of nonhuman subjects. The IACUC approval must be obtained prior to conducting any research with nonhuman subjects.

LEARNING CHECK

1. The guidelines for nonhuman subjects in research are similar to the guidelines for human participants but also include extra provisions concerning what additional topic(s)?

   a. Housing
   b. Medical care
   c. Daily maintenance
   d. All of the above

2. Which of the following is a responsibility for the IRB but is not mentioned in the responsibilities for the IACUC?
    a. Review of research proposals
    b. Minimizing risk of harm to those participating in research
    c. Insuring informed consent
    d. Insuring that researchers are qualified

Answers appear at the end of the chapter.

4.4   Ethical Issues and Scientific Integrity

LEARNING OBJECTIVES

LO7   Define *fraud* and explain the safeguards that exist to prevent it.

LO8   Define *plagiarism* and explain the techniques that can be used to help avoid unintentional plagiarism.

Thus far, we have discussed the ethical issues that researchers face when they make decisions about the individuals, both human and nonhuman, that participate in their research. Later in the research process, to make the research public, the investigator prepares a report describing what was done, what was found, and how the findings were interpreted (see Chapter 1, Step 9). Ethical issues can arise at this point as well. Here we consider two such issues: fraud and plagiarism. Two APA ethical standards (2010) relate to these issues:

8.10   Reporting of Research
    a. Psychologists do not fabricate data. (See also Standard 5.01, Avoidance of False or Deceptive Statements—Psychologists do not make false, deceptive, or fraudulent statements concerning their publications or research findings.)
    b. If psychologists discover significant errors in their published data, they take reasonable steps to correct such errors in a correction, retraction, erratum, or other appropriate publication means.

8.11   Plagiarism
    a. Psychologists do not present portions of another's work or data as their own, even if the other work or data source is cited occasionally.

From *Ethical Principles of Psychologists and Code of Conduct* (APA, 2010). Retrieved from http://www.apa.org/ethics/code/principles.pdf. Copyright 2010 by the American Psychological Association. Reprinted with permission.

Fraud in Science

Error versus Fraud

It is important to distinguish between error and fraud. An error is an honest mistake that occurs in the research process. There are, unfortunately, many opportunities for errors to be made in research, for example, in collecting data, scoring measures, entering data into the computer, or in publication typesetting. Researchers are only human, and humans make mistakes. However, it is the investigator's responsibility to check and double-check the data to minimize the risk of errors.

Fraud, on the other hand, is an explicit effort to falsify or misrepresent data. If a researcher makes up (i.e., fabricates) or changes data to make it support the hypothesis, this constitutes fraud. As you know, the essential goal of science is to discover knowledge and reveal truth, which makes fraud the ultimate enemy of the scientific process. In a recent, and unprecedented, extreme case of fraud reported by the APA, a very prominent Dutch social psychologist, Diederick Stapel was found to have fabricated data over many years in at least 30 published peer-reviewed papers (Verfaellie & McGwin, 2011). The interim report from the university investigating committee (Tilburg University, 2011) points to the researcher's power and poor scientific scrutiny as factors contributing to this misconduct. Because his research findings were on contemporary topics such as racial stereotyping and the effects of advertising, they had wide appeal as evidenced by publication in lay-scientific outlets such as newspapers and magazines. As a result, the discovery of fraud not only led to the retracting of several dozen research articles, it also resulted in public criticism of the respectability of psychological research in the *New York Times* (Carey, 2011).

DEFINITION

> **Fraud** is the explicit effort of a researcher to falsify or misrepresent data.

Why Do Researchers Commit Fraud?

Although researchers know that their reputations and their careers will be seriously damaged if they are caught falsifying their data, on rare occasions, some researchers commit fraud. Why? The primary cause of fraud is the competitive nature of an academic career. You have probably heard the saying, "Publish or perish." There is strong pressure on researchers to have their research published. For example, tenure and promotion within academic departments are often based on research productivity. In addition, researchers must obtain significant findings if they hope to publish their research results or receive grants to support their research. Another possible motivator is a researcher's exceedingly high need for success and the admiration that comes along with it. Researchers invest a great deal of time and resources in conducting their studies, and it can be very disappointing to obtain results that cannot be published.

It is important to keep in mind that discussing possible reasons why a researcher may commit fraud in no way implies that we condone such behavior. There is no justification for such actions. We include this information only to make you aware of the forces that might influence someone to commit such an act.

Safeguards against Fraud

Fortunately, several safeguards are built into the process of scientific research reporting to help keep fraud in check. First, researchers know that other scientists are going to read their reports and conduct further studies, including replications. The process of repeating a previous study, step by step, allows a researcher to verify the results. Recall from Chapter 1 that **replication** is one of the primary means of revealing error and uncovering fraud in research. The most common reason to suspect fraud is that a groundbreaking finding cannot be replicated.

DEFINITION

> **Replication** is repetition of a research study using the same basic procedures used in the original. Either the replication supports the original study by duplicating the original results, or it casts doubt on the original study by demonstrating that the original result is not easily repeated.

A second safeguard against fraud is **peer review,** which takes place when a researcher submits a research article for publication. In a typical peer review process, the editor of the journal and a few experts in the field review the paper in extreme detail. The reviewers critically scrutinize every aspect of the research from the justification of the study to the analysis of data. The primary purpose of peer review is to evaluate the quality of the research study and the contribution it makes to scientific knowledge. The reviewers also are likely to detect anything suspect about the research or the findings.

A third safeguard against fraud is the verification of data through the sharing of research data. According to APA Ethics Code 8.14 (APA, 2010), after research results are published psychologists must share their original data with any other researcher who wishes to reanalyze the data to check significant claims. Further many journals and funding agencies now typically require open access to data sets for other researchers.

The consequences of being found guilty of fraud probably keep many researchers honest. If it is concluded that a researcher's data are fraudulent, a number of penalties can result, including suspension or firing from a job, removal of a degree granted, cancellation of funding for research, and forced return of monies paid from grants. In the case of Diederik Stapel, he was fired from his position as professor and he voluntarily returned his doctorate.

Plagiarism

To present someone else's ideas or words as your own is to commit **plagiarism**. Plagiarism, like fraud, is a serious breach of ethics. Reference citations (giving others credit when credit is due) must be included in your paper whenever someone else's ideas or work has influenced your thinking and writing. Whenever you use direct quotations or even paraphrase someone else's work, you need to give that person credit. If an idea or information you include in a paper is not originally yours, you must cite the source. For students, the penalties for plagiarism may include receiving a failing grade on the paper or in the course and expulsion from the institution. For faculty researchers, the penalties for plagiarism are much the same as those for fraud.

DEFINITION   **Plagiarism** is the unethical representation of someone else's ideas or words as one's own.

Plagiarism can occur on a variety of different levels. At one extreme, you can literally copy an entire paper word for word and present it as your own work, or you can copy and paste passages from articles and sites found on the Internet. In these cases, the plagiarism is clearly a deliberate act committed with complete awareness and is usually easy to identify, especially for faculty using Internet-based plagiarism-prevention services such as Turnitin. However, at the other extreme, plagiarism can be much more subtle and even occur without your direct knowledge or intent. For example, while doing the background research for a paper, you may be inspired by someone's ideas or influenced by the phrases someone used to express a concept. After working on a project for an extended time, it can become difficult to separate your own words and ideas from those that come to you from outside sources. As a result, outside ideas and phrases can appear in your paper without appropriate citation, and you have committed plagiarism.

Fortunately, the following guidelines can help prevent you from plagiarizing (Myers & Hansen, 2006).

1. Take complete notes, including complete citation of the source. (For articles, include author's name, year of publication, title of the article, journal name, volume number, and page numbers. For books, also include the publisher's name and city.)

2. Within your paper, identify the source of any ideas, words, or information that are not your own.

3. Identify any direct quotes by quotation marks at the beginning and end of the quotes, and indicate where you got them.

4. Be careful about paraphrasing (restating someone else's words). It is greatly tempting to lift whole phrases or catchy words from another source. Use your own words instead, or use direct quotes. Be sure to give credit to your sources.

5. Include a complete list of references at the end of the paper. References should include all the information listed in Item 1.

6. If in doubt about whether a citation is necessary, cite the source. You will do no harm by being especially cautious.

There are occasions when your work is based directly on the ideas or words of another person and it is necessary to paraphrase or quote that person's work. For example, your research idea may stem from the results or claims made in a previously published article. To present the foundation for your idea, it is necessary to describe the previous work. In this situation, there are several points to keep in mind. First, you should realize that direct quotes are used very infrequently. They should be used only when it is absolutely necessary to capture the true essence of the statement (note that the author's original words are unlikely to be the only way to express the idea). The use of extensive quoting in a paper constitutes lazy writing. Second, when you paraphrase, you still must cite your source, because you always must give credit for presenting someone else's ideas or words. Third, paraphrasing consists of rewording the meaning or content of someone else's work—not simply repeating it. Paraphrasing is more than simply changing a word or two in each sentence. Table 4.5 shows some examples of plagiarism as well as an acceptable form of paraphrasing.

Throughout this book, we often use other people's ideas, figures, and passages (including the guidelines just stated), but note that we always acknowledge and cite the original authors, artists, and publishers.

TABLE 4.5
Examples of Plagiarism

Original text from Quirin, Kazén, and Kuhl (2009):
Are affective experiences like happiness, sadness, or helplessness always amenable to self-report? Whereas many individuals may be able to describe their affective states or traits relatively accurately, others may provide self reports that deviate from their automatic affective reactions.

1. Repeating large sections of text verbatim is clearly plagiarism, even with a citation.
Are people really in touch with their emotional responses? For example, are feelings like happiness, sadness, or helplessness always available for self-report? Whereas many individuals may be able to describe their feelings relatively accurately, others may provide self reports that deviate from their true reactions (Quirin, Kazén, & Kuhl, 2009).

2. Changing a few words is still plagiarism, even with a citation.
Are feelings like happiness, sadness, or helplessness always available for self-report? Whereas many individuals may be able to describe their feelings relatively accurately, others may provide self reports that deviate from their true reactions (Quirin, Kazén, & Kuhl, 2009).

3. Changing most of the wording but keeping the same structure and order of ideas is a step toward paraphrasing but is still plagiarism, even with a citation.
Is it easy for people to report their feelings? Although some people may be able to give accurate reports, others fail to provide accurate descriptions of how they feel (Quirin, Kazén, & Kuhl, 2009).

4. Rephrasing in your own words, using your own structure, and a citation for the original source is an acceptable paraphrase (not plagiarism).
It is difficult for many people to accurately describe their emotional responses (Quirin, Kazén, & Kuhl, 2009).

CHAPTER 4 | Ethics in Research

LEARNING CHECK

1. Which of the following was not mentioned as a safeguard against fraud?
   a. Careful review by the IRB
   b. Potential replication of the research
   c. Peer review of the research report
   d. The consequences of being found guilty of fraud
2. Which of the following is an example of plagiarism?
   a. Copying someone else's words without giving them credit
   b. Paraphrasing someone else's words without giving them credit
   c. Using someone else's ideas without giving them credit
   d. All of the above are examples of plagiarism

Answers appear at the end of the chapter.

CHAPTER SUMMARY

At this point, you should review the learning objectives presented at the beginning of each section and be sure that you have mastered each objective.

Researchers have two basic categories of ethical responsibility: (1) responsibility to the individuals, both human and nonhuman, who participate in their research studies; and (2) responsibility to the discipline of science and to be accurate and honest in the reporting of their research. Researchers are responsible for ensuring the safety and well-being of their research participants and subjects, and they must abide by all the relevant ethical guidelines when conducting research. Researchers are also obligated to present truthful and accurate reports of their results and to give appropriate credit when they report the work or ideas of others.

Any research involving humans or nonhumans immediately introduces questions of ethics. Historical incidents in which human participants were injured or abused as part of a research study shaped the guidelines we have in place today. Psychological research using humans and nonhumans is regulated by the APA Ethics Code and by federal, state, and local guidelines. The primary goal of the APA Ethics Code is the welfare and protection of the individuals and groups with whom the psychologists work. Tables 4.2 and 4.4 provide summaries of the elements of the Ethics Code most relevant to the use and treatment of human participants and nonhuman subjects, respectively. The points that are most important for new researchers include the issues of no harm, informed consent, deception, and confidentiality. To assist researchers in protecting human participants and nonhuman subjects, IRBs and IACUCs examine all proposed research.

Reporting of research also introduces questions of ethics. It is assumed that reports of research are accurate and honest depictions of the procedures used and results obtained. In this chapter, we considered two reporting issues: fraud and plagiarism.

Ethics in research is an enormous topic. In this chapter, we considered the ethical decisions that researchers make when conducting research and when publishing their results. For more on the topic of research ethics, see Rosnow and Rosenthal (1997), Sales and Folkman (2000), and Stanley, Sieber, and Melton (1996). In addition, if you are interested in reading a more detailed history of the development of current ethical standards, we suggest *Encyclopedia of Bioethics* (Reich, 1995).

KEY WORDS

research ethics	active deception (commission)	Institutional Review Board (IRB)	fraud
informed consent			replication
deception	debriefing	Institutional Animal Care and Use Committee (IACUC)	plagiarism
passive deception (omission)	confidentiality		
	anonymity		

EXERCISES

The exercises are identified with specific learning objectives and are intended to assess your mastery of the objectives. You should be aware that exam items are also generated to assess learning objectives.

1. In addition to the key words, you should also be able to define each of the following terms:

   ethics
   Nuremberg Code
   National Research Act
   Belmont Report
   Principle of respect (autonomy)
   Principle of beneficence
   Principle of justice
   APA Ethics Code
   clinical equipoise
   consent form
   confederate
   placebo
   Common Rule
   peer review

2. (**LO2**) For each of the following, identify which of the three basic principles of the Belmont Report is being violated:
   a. A researcher recruits poor minorities to be participants in a risky experiment.
   b. A researcher tricks people into participating by suggesting that they might win a contest.
   c. A researcher knows that people will feel ashamed after one part of the study.

3. (**LO2**) By manipulating the participants' experiences, it is possible to examine how people's performance and attitudes are influenced by success and failure. To do this, researchers can give some participants a feeling of success and others a feeling of failure by giving false feedback about their performance or by rigging a task to make it easy or impossible (Thompson, Webber, & Montgomery, 2002). Describe how this can be done, so that the Belmont Report principles of respect and beneficence are not violated.

4. (**LO3**) Explain the role of voluntary participation in informed consent.

5. (**LO3**) Explain the difference between passive and active deception.

6. (**LO3**) Explain how the enforcement of confidentiality benefits both the participants and the researcher.

7. (**LO3**) Suppose you are planning a research study in which you intend to manipulate the participants' moods; that is, you plan to create a group of happy people and a group of sad people. For example, one group will spend the first 10 minutes of the experiment listening to upbeat, happy music, and the other group will listen to funeral dirges.
   a. Do you consider the manipulation of people's moods to be an ethical violation of the principle of no harm? Explain why or why not.
   b. Would you tell your participants about the mood manipulation as part of the informed consent process before they begin the study? Explain why or why not.
   c. Assuming that you decided to use deception and not tell your participants that their moods are being manipulated, how would you justify this procedure to an IRB? What could you do to minimize the negative effects of manipulating people's moods (especially the negative mood group)?

8. (**LO4**) Describe in your own words the criteria that the IRB uses to evaluate proposed research.

9. (**LO4**) Find your college's IRB guidelines and procedures (you probably will need to search online through your college's website for "IRB"). With a research idea in mind, determine what category or level of review your proposal would fit into.

10. (**LO5** and **6**) Summarize the major APA ethical standards concerning the care and use of animals in research.

11. (**LO7**) Describe how replication protects against fraud being committed in research.

12. (**LO8**) Explain why plagiarism is unethical.

LEARNING CHECK ANSWERS

Section 4.2
1. c, 2. b, 3. c, 4. d

Section 4.3
1. d, 2. c

Section 4.4
1. a, 2. d

Selecting Research Participants

CHAPTER 5 | Selecting Research Participants

© Nathan Jasowiak / Shutterstock

CHAPTER LEARNING OBJECTIVES

LO1 Describe the relationship between a sample and the population (both target and accessible) in a research study and explain the importance of obtaining representative, as opposed to biased, samples.

LO2 Explain the basic distinction between probability sampling methods and nonprobability sampling methods and recognize examples of these two sampling techniques when they appear in research reports.

LO3 Describe the process of simple random sampling, recognize this technique when it appears in a research report, and explain its strengths and weaknesses.

LO4 Describe the four probability sampling methods presented in the book, other than simple random sampling (stratified random, proportionate stratified random, systematic, and cluster), recognize these techniques when they appear in research reports, and explain the strengths and weaknesses of each.

LO5   Describe the process of convenience sampling, recognize examples of this technique in research reports, and explain why it is used and how researchers using this method can limit the risk of a biased sample.

LO6   Describe quota sampling, recognize examples of this technique in research reports, and explain why it is used.

CHAPTER OVERVIEW

Typically, a relatively small group of individuals, known as a *sample*, is selected to participate in a behavioral sciences research study. For example, a researcher may have a general question about adolescents but actually selects only 20 adolescents to take part in the study. In this situation, one concern is whether the 20 adolescents in the sample are really good representatives for the millions of adolescents in the general population. In this chapter we examine the techniques that researchers use to select the samples that will participate in research studies and to help ensure that their samples are truly representative, Step 4 of the research process outlined in Chapter 1. Fortunately, this task is simplified by a basic fact governing samples: Samples tend to be similar to the populations from which they are taken. For example, if you take a sample from a population that consists of 75% psychology majors and only 25% nonpsychology majors, you probably will get a sample that has more psychology majors than nonmajors. Or, if you select a sample from a population for which the average age is 21 years, you probably will get a sample with an average age around 21 years.

Although samples *tend* to be similar to their populations, most researchers would like more assurance that the samples in their research studies really are good representatives of the populations they want to study. Therefore, researchers have developed a variety of techniques for selecting samples that greatly increase the likelihood of obtaining a representative outcome. In this chapter, we discuss the concept of a representative sample and introduce techniques that help ensure representative samples.

5.1   Introduction to Sampling

LEARNING OBJECTIVES

LO1   Describe the relationship between a sample and the population (both target and accessible) in a research study and explain the importance of obtaining representative, as opposed to biased, samples.

LO2   Explain the basic distinction between probability sampling methods and nonprobability sampling methods and recognize examples of these two sampling techniques when they appear in research reports.

Beyond the research idea, the hypothesis, and how you decide to define and measure your variables, one of the most critical issues in planning research is the selection of research participants (see Chapter 1, Step 4 of the research process). Suppose, for example, that you are interested in using a survey to study high school students' attitudes toward unrestricted searches of their lockers. Who will complete your questionnaire? All the high school students in the nation? Not likely—that would be an enormous and expensive undertaking. Instead, you will have to select a relatively small group of students to represent the entire group. Other practical constraints probably mean that you will be limited to selecting students from your own local region. As a result, a researcher who works in Los Angeles will probably select a very different group of students than would be selected by a researcher working in rural Kentucky. Because these two researchers will have very different participants, it also is likely that they will obtain different results. The bottom line in any research study is that not everyone can participate, and the outcome of the study may depend on the way in which participants are selected.

Populations and Samples

In the terminology of research design, the large group of interest to a researcher is called the **population**, and the small set of individuals who participate in the study is called the **sample**. Figure 5.1 illustrates the relationship between a population and a sample. Typically, populations are huge, containing far too many individuals to measure and study. For example, a researcher may be interested in adolescents, preschool children, men, women, or humans. In each of these cases, the population is much too large to permit a researcher to study every individual. Therefore, a researcher must rely on a smaller group, a sample, to provide information about the population. A sample is selected from a population and is intended to represent that population. The goal of the research study is to examine the sample, then generalize the results to the entire population. Although several different researchers may begin with the same research question concerning the same population, each research study is a unique event that involves its own specific group of participants.

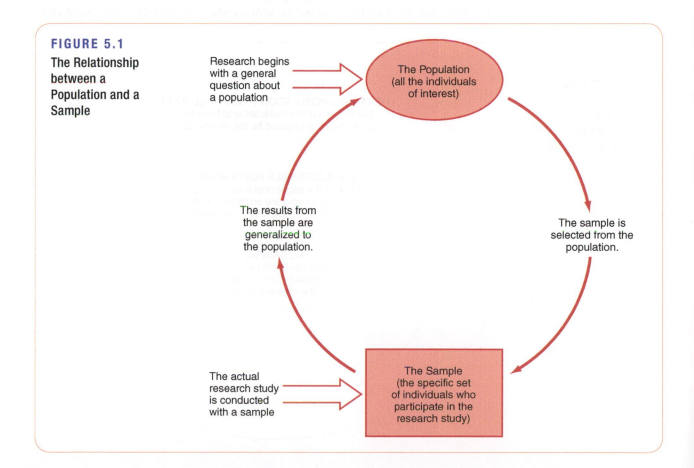

FIGURE 5.1

The Relationship between a Population and a Sample

Research begins with a general question about a population

The Population (all the individuals of interest)

The sample is selected from the population.

The results from the sample are generalized to the population.

The actual research study is conducted with a sample

The Sample (the specific set of individuals who participate in the research study)

DEFINITIONS

A **population** is the entire set of individuals of interest to a researcher. Although the entire population usually does not participate in a research study, the results from the study are generalized to the entire population.

A **sample** is a set of individuals selected from a population and usually is intended to represent the population in a research study.

Before proceeding, we need to distinguish among different types of populations. A **target population** is the group defined by the researcher's specific interests. Individuals in a target population typically share one characteristic. Some examples of target populations are children of divorced parents, elementary-school-aged children, and adolescents diagnosed with bulimia nervosa. Usually, target populations are not easily available. For example, for a researcher interested in the treatment of bulimia nervosa in adolescents, the target population would be all of the adolescents in the world who are diagnosed with this disorder. Clearly, the researcher would not have access to most of these people to recruit as a sample of participants for the research study. However, a researcher would have access to the many local clinics and agencies that treat clients with eating disorders. These local clients (adolescents diagnosed with bulimia nervosa) are the **accessible population** from which the sample is selected. Most researchers select their samples from accessible populations. Therefore, we not only need to be cautious about generalizing the results of a study to the accessible population but we must also always be extremely cautious about generalizing the results of a research study to the target population. Figure 5.2 depicts the relationship among target populations, accessible populations, and samples. For the remainder of the book, we use the term *population* to mean the target population.

FIGURE 5.2

The Relationship among the Target Population, the Accessible Population, and the Sample

THE TARGET POPULATION (THE POPULATION)
The entire set of individuals who have the characteristics required by the researcher

THE ACCESSIBLE POPULATION
A portion of the target population consisting of individuals who are accessible to be recruited as participants in the study

THE SAMPLE
The individuals who are selected to participate in the research study

Representative Samples

We have said that the goal of a research study is to examine a sample and then generalize the results to the population. How accurately we can generalize the results from a given sample to the population depends on the **representativeness** of the sample. The degree of representativeness of a sample refers to how closely the sample mirrors or resembles the population. Thus, one problem that every researcher faces is how to obtain a sample that provides a reasonable representation of the population. To generalize the results of a study to a population, the researcher must select a **representative sample**.

Before even beginning to select a sample, however, you must consider how well the accessible population represents the target population. Specifically, the group of participants who are available for selection may not be completely representative of the more general population. For example, the older adults in the southeastern United States will have a unique cultural background that may differentiate them from other older adults throughout the world. Thus, the ability to generalize the results from a research study may be limited by the specific characteristics of the accessible population. Often, the most a researcher can hope for is to select a sample that is representative of the accessible population.

The major threat to selecting a representative sample is bias. A **biased sample** is one that has characteristics noticeably different from those of the population. If, for example, the individuals in a sample are smarter (or older or faster) than the individuals in the population, then the sample is biased. A biased sample can occur simply by chance; for example, tossing a balanced coin can result in heads 10 times in a row. It is more likely, however, that a biased sample is the result of **selection bias** (also called **sampling bias**), which means that the sampling procedure favors the selection of some individuals over others. For example, if the population we are interested in is adults and we recruit our sample from the students enrolled at a university, we are likely to obtain a sample that is smarter, on average, than the individuals in the entire population. If we recruit from Facebook, our sample is likely to be younger than the population. In general, the likelihood of the sample being representative depends on the procedure that is used to select participants. In this chapter, we consider two basic approaches to sampling, and we examine some of the common strategies or techniques for obtaining samples.

DEFINITIONS

> The **representativeness** of a sample refers to the extent to which the characteristics of the sample accurately reflect the characteristics of the population.
>
> A **representative sample** is a sample with the same characteristics as the population.
>
> A **biased sample** is a sample with different characteristics from those of the population.
>
> **Selection bias** or **sampling bias** occurs when participants or subjects are selected in a manner that increases the probability of obtaining a biased sample.

Sample Size

As we noted, research studies typically use the results from a relatively small sample as the basis for answering questions about a relatively large population. The goal is to obtain a sample that is representative of the population. One fundamental question in reaching this goal is determining how large the sample should be to be representative. Unfortunately, there is no simple answer to this question, but there are some general guidelines that can help you choose a sample size.

The first principle is the simple observation that a large sample is probably more representative than a small sample. In the field of statistics, this principle is known as the **law of large numbers** and states that the larger the sample size, the more likely it is that values obtained from the sample are similar to the actual values for the population. In simple terms, the bigger the sample is, the more accurately it represents the population. However, the accuracy of a sample's representation increases in relation to the square root of the sample size. For example, Figure 5.3 shows how the average difference between a sample mean and the population mean decreases as the sample size increases. Notice that accuracy improves rapidly as the sample size is increased from 4 to 16 to 25, but the improvement in accuracy slows dramatically once the sample size is around 30. Because there is only a limited benefit from increasing sample size beyond 25 or 30, researchers often use this sample size as a goal when planning research.

Although a sample size of 25 or 30 individuals for each group or each treatment condition is a good target, other considerations may make this sample size unreasonably large or small. If, for example, a research study is comparing 10 or 15 different treatment conditions, a separate group of 25 individuals in each condition would require a total sample of 250 to 375 participants. In many situations it could be difficult or impossible to recruit that many individuals, and researchers might have to settle for samples of only 10 or 12 in each condition. At the other extreme, researchers often begin a research study with a specific target for the level of accuracy. For example, a political poll may want a margin of error of 5% in determining voters' preferences between two candidates. In this situation, it can be computed that the sample must have at least 384 individuals to be confident that the preferences observed in the sample are within 5% of the corresponding population preferences.

Another factor influencing sample size is research ethics. Specifically, if a sample is too large, then it is unnecessarily using extra subjects or participants, which can be viewed as unethical. On the other hand, if a sample is too small then it is unlikely that the study will be successful, which is also an unethical waste of resources. If possible, researchers should attempt to anticipate their results and perform some preliminary statistical calculations to determine whether the expected results are likely to be statistically significant. (Statistical significance is discussed in Chapter 15.) The outcome may help determine whether a larger or smaller sample would be appropriate.

In general, there is no simple solution to determining how many individuals should be in a sample. One helpful guide is to review published reports of similar research studies

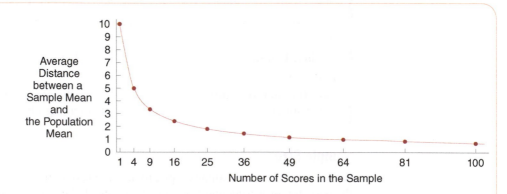

FIGURE 5.3

The Average Distance between a Sample Mean and the Population Mean as a Function of Sample Size

Note that the larger the sample, the more accurately the sample represents the population. However, representativeness increases in relation to the square root of the sample size.

to see how many participants they used, keeping in mind that a larger sample tends to be more representative and increases your chances for a successful study.

Sampling Basics

The process of selecting individuals for a study is called **sampling**. Researchers have developed a variety of different **sampling methods** (also called **sampling techniques** or **sampling procedures**). Sampling methods fall into two basic categories: probability sampling and nonprobability sampling.

In **probability sampling**, the odds of selecting a particular individual are known and can be calculated. For example, if each individual in a population of 100 people is equally likely to be selected, then the probability of selection is 1/100 for each person. Probability sampling has three important conditions:

1. The exact size of the population must be known and it must be possible to list all of the individuals.
2. Each individual in the population must have a specified probability of selection.
3. When a group of individuals are all assigned the same probability, the selection process must be unbiased so that all group members have an equal chance of being selected. Selection must be a **random process**, which simply means that every possible outcome is equally likely. For example, each time you toss a coin, the two possible outcomes (heads and tails) are equally likely.

In **nonprobability sampling**, the odds of selecting a particular individual are not known because the researcher does not know the population size and cannot list the members of the population. In addition, in nonprobability sampling, the researcher does not use an unbiased method of selection. For example, a researcher who wants to study the behavior of preschool children may go to a local childcare center where a group of preschool children is already assembled. Because the researcher is selecting from a restricted group, rather than the entire population of preschool children, this sample has an increased chance of being biased. For example, if the childcare center includes only white, middle-class children, then the sample definitely does not represent the target population of preschool children. In general, nonprobability sampling has a greater risk of producing a biased sample than does probability sampling.

Notice that probability sampling requires extensive knowledge of the population. Specifically, we must be able to list all of the individuals in the population. In most situations, this information is not available to a researcher. As a result, probability sampling is rarely used for research in the behavioral sciences. Nonetheless, this kind of sampling provides a good foundation for introducing the concept of representativeness and demonstrating how different sampling techniques can be used to help ensure a representative sample.

DEFINITIONS

Sampling is the process of selecting individuals to participate in a research study.

In **probability sampling**, the entire population is known, each individual in the population has a specifiable probability of selection, and sampling occurs by a random process based on the probabilities.

A **random process** is a procedure that produces one outcome from a set of possible outcomes. The outcome must be unpredictable each time, and the process must guarantee that each of the possible outcomes is equally likely to occur.

In **nonprobability sampling**, the population is not completely known, individual probabilities cannot be known, and the sampling method is based on factors such as commonsense or ease, with an effort to maintain representativeness and avoid bias.

In the following sections, we discuss five probability sampling methods (simple random, systematic, stratified, proportionate stratified, and cluster sampling) and two nonprobability sampling methods (convenience and quota sampling). For each method, the general goal is to obtain a sample that is representative of the population from which it is taken. For different kinds of research, however, the definition of representative varies; hence, there are several well-defined sampling procedures that attempt to produce a particular kind of representation.

LEARNING CHECK

1. Dr. Near conducts an experiment on memory for individuals who are above the age of 65. Although there are millions of people above the age of 65, she selects a group of 25 to participate in the experiment. What name is given to the group of 25?
   a. A sample
   b. An accessible sample
   c. A population
   d. A subgroup

2. What name is given to the group of individuals from which researchers actually select participants for research studies?
   a. The accessible population
   b. The target population
   c. The representative population
   d. The real population

3. For situations in which the researcher cannot know the complete list of potential participants, what kind of sampling is necessary?
   a. Target sampling
   b. Nontarget sampling
   c. Probability sampling
   d. Nonprobability sampling

Answers appear at the end of the chapter.

5.2 Probability Sampling Methods

LEARNING OBJECTIVES

LO3 Describe the process of simple random sampling, recognize this technique when it appears in a research report, and explain its strengths and weaknesses.

LO4 Describe the four probability sampling methods presented in the book, other than simple random sampling (stratified random, proportionate stratified random, systematic, and cluster), recognize these techniques when they appear in research reports, and explain the strengths and weaknesses of each.

Simple Random Sampling

The starting point for most probability sampling techniques is **simple random sampling**. The basic requirement for random sampling is that each individual in the population has an equal chance of being selected. Equality means that no individual is more likely to be chosen than another. A second requirement that is sometimes added is that each selection is independent of the others. Independence means that the choice of one individual does not influence or bias the probability of choosing another individual.

The process of simple random sampling consists of the following steps:

1. Clearly define the population from which you want to select a sample.
2. List all the members of the population.
3. Use a random process to select individuals from the list.

Often, a simple random sample is obtained by first assigning a number to each individual and then by using a random process to select numbers. For example, suppose a researcher has a population of 100 third-grade children from a local school district, from which a sample of 25 children is to be selected. Each child's name is put on a list, and each child is assigned a number from 1 to 100. Then the numbers 1 to 100 are written on separate pieces of paper and shuffled. Finally, the researcher picks 25 slips of paper and the numbers on the paper determine the 25 participants.

As noted earlier, researchers typically use some random process such as a coin toss or picking numbers from a hat to guide the selection. But what if, in picking the numbers from a hat, the size of the papers is different or the slips of paper are not shuffled adequately? The researcher could select individuals with larger slips of paper or individuals at the end of the list whose slips of paper are at the top of the pile. A more unbiased random process involves assigning each individual a number and then using the random number table for selection of participants. Appendix A contains a table of random numbers and a step-by-step guide for using it.

The obvious goal of a simple random sample is to ensure that the selection procedure cannot discriminate among individuals and thereby result in a nonrepresentative sample. The two principal methods of random sampling are:

1. *Sampling with replacement:* This method requires that an individual selected for the sample be recorded as a sample member and then returned to the population (replaced) before the next selection is made. This procedure ensures that the probability of selection remains constant throughout a series of selections. For example, if we select from a population of 100 individuals, the probability of selecting any particular individual is 1/100. To keep this same probability (1/100) for the second selection, it is necessary to return the first individual to the pool before the next is selected. Because the probabilities stay constant, this technique ensures that the selections are independent.
2. *Sampling without replacement:* As the term indicates, this method removes each selected individual from the population before the next selection is made. This method guarantees that no individual appears more than once in a single sample. However, each time an individual is removed, the probability of selection changes for the remaining individuals. For example, if the population has 100 people, then the probability of being selected starts at 1/100. After the first selection, only 99 people are left and the probability of selection changes to 1/99. Because the probabilities change with each selection, this technique does not produce independent selections.

Sampling with replacement is an assumption of many of the mathematical models that form the foundation of statistical analysis. In most research, however, individuals are not actually replaced because then one individual could appear repeatedly in the same sample. If we conduct a public opinion survey, for example, we would not call the same person 10 times and then claim that we had a sample of 10 individuals. Most populations are so large that the probabilities remain essentially unchanged from one selection to the next, even when we do not replace individuals. For example, the difference between a probability of 1/1,000 and 1/999 is negligible. By using large populations, researchers can sample without replacement, which ensures that individuals are not repeated in one sample, and still satisfy the mathematical assumptions needed for statistical analysis.

Concerns about Simple Random Sampling

The logic behind simple random sampling is that it removes bias from the selection procedure and should result in representative samples. Note that simple random sampling removes bias by leaving each selection to chance. In the long run, this strategy generates a balanced, representative sample. If we toss a coin thousands of times, eventually, the results will be 50% heads and 50% tails. In the short run, however, there are no guarantees. Because chance determines each selection, it is possible (although usually unlikely) to obtain a very distorted sample. We could, for example, toss a balanced coin and get heads 10 times in a row. Similarly, we could get a random sample of 10 males from a population that contains an equal number of men and women. To avoid this kind of nonrepresentative sample, researchers often impose additional restrictions on the random sampling procedure; these are presented later in the sections on stratified and proportionate stratified random sampling.

Systematic Sampling

Systematic sampling is a type of probability sampling that is very similar to simple random sampling. Systematic sampling begins by listing all the individuals in the population, then randomly picking a starting point on the list. The sample is then obtained by moving down the list, selecting every nth name. The size of n is calculated by dividing the population size by the desired sample size. For example, suppose a researcher has a population of 100 third-grade students and would like to select a sample of 25 children. Each child's name is put on a list and assigned a number from 1 to 100. Then, the researcher uses a random process such as a table of random numbers to select the first participant, for example, participant number 11. With a population of 100 children and a desired sample size of 25, the size of n in this example is 100/25 = 4. Therefore, every fourth individual after participant 11 (15, 19, 23, and so on) is selected. Note that systematic sampling is identical to simple random sampling (i.e., follow the three steps) for selection of the first participant; however, after the first individual is selected, the researcher does not continue to use a random process to select the remaining individuals for the sample.

This technique is less random than simple random sampling because the principle of independence is violated. Specifically, if we select participant number 11, we are biased against choosing participants number 12, 13, and 14, and we are biased in favor of choosing participant number 15. However, as a probability sampling method, this method ensures a high degree of representativeness.

Stratified Random Sampling

A population usually consists of a variety of identifiable subgroups. For example, the population of registered voters in California can be subdivided into Republicans and Democrats, different ethnic groups, different age groups, and so on. The different subgroups can be viewed as different layers or strata like the layers of rock on a cliff face (Figure 5.4). Often, a researcher's goal for a *representative sample* is to ensure that each of the different subgroups is adequately represented. One technique for accomplishing this goal is to use **stratified random sampling**. To obtain this kind of sample, we first identify the specific subgroups (or strata) to be included in the sample. Then we select equal-sized random samples from each of the pre-identified subgroups, using the same steps as in simple random sampling. Finally, we combine the subgroup samples into one overall sample.

FIGURE 5.4

The Population of a Major City Shown as Different Layers, or Strata, Defined by Annual Income

Families with Incomes
Above $250,000

Families with Incomes
Above $100,000 but Below $250,000

Families with Incomes
Above $40,000 but Below $100,000

Families with Incomes
Below $40,000

For example, suppose that we plan to select 50 individuals from a large introductory psychology class and want to ensure that psychology majors and nonmajors are equally represented. First, we select a random sample of 25 students from the psychology majors in the class and then a random sample of 25 students from those who are not psychology majors. Combining these two subgroup samples produces the desired stratified random sample.

Stratified random sampling is particularly useful when a researcher wants to describe each individual segment of the population or wants to compare segments. To do this, each subgroup in the sample must contain enough individuals to adequately represent its segment of the population. Consider the following example.

A sociologist conducts an opinion survey in a major city. Part of the research plan calls for describing and comparing the opinions of adults from three different age groups: Millennial, Gen-X, and Baby Boomer. If the researcher uses simple random sampling to select 150 individuals, the sample might contain only a few individuals from one (or more) of these groups. With only a handful of representatives of a particular group, the researcher could not make any definite statements about that group's opinion, and could not make any meaningful comparisons with other groups. A stratified random sample avoids this problem by ensuring that each subgroup contains a predetermined number of individuals (set by the researcher). For a total sample of 150, the researcher selects 50 representatives of each of the three age groups.

The main advantage of a stratified random sample is that it guarantees that each of the different subgroups will be well represented with a relatively large group of individuals in the sample. Thus, this type of sampling is appropriate when the purpose of a research study is to examine specific subgroups and make comparisons between them. However, stratified random sampling also has some negative consequences. First, stratified random sampling tends to produce a distorted picture of the overall population. Suppose, for example, that we are taking a stratified random sample of 50 children from an elementary school with a total population consisting of 50 students who are an only child and 250 who have siblings. When using stratified sampling the two subgroups would be represented equally in the sample (with 25 children from each group) but the subgroups are not equally represented in the population. Only children, for example, represent less than 17% of the population but make up 50% of the sample. Also, you should notice that stratified random sampling is not equivalent to simple random sampling. Specifically, every individual in the population does not have an equal chance of being selected for the sample. In our example, 25 of the 50 only-child students are selected so the probability of selecting an only child is 25/50 or ½. By comparison, 25 of the 250 children with siblings are selected so their probability is 25/250 or 1 out of 10. Thus, stratified random sampling does not produce a true random sample because all individuals in the population are not equally likely to be selected. The next sampling method does produce a true random sample by using a different definition of a *representative* sample.

Proportionate Stratified Random Sampling

Occasionally, researchers try to improve the correspondence between a sample and a population by deliberately ensuring that the composition of the sample matches the composition of the population. As with a stratified sample, we begin by identifying a set of subgroups or segments in the population. Next, we determine what proportion of the population corresponds to each subgroup. Finally, a sample is obtained such that the proportions in the sample exactly match the proportions in the overall population. This kind of sampling is called **proportionate stratified random sampling** or simply **proportionate random sampling**.

For example, suppose that the college administration wants a sample of students that accurately represent the distribution of freshmen, sophomores, juniors, and seniors in the college population. If the overall population contains 30% freshmen, 26% sophomores, 25% juniors, and 19% seniors, then the sample is selected so that it has exactly the same percentages for the four groups. First, determine the desired size of the sample, then randomly select from the freshmen in the population until you have a number corresponding to 30% of the sample size. Next, select sophomores until you have a number equal to 26% of the sample size. Continue this process with the juniors and seniors to obtain the full sample. Proportionate random sampling is used commonly for political polls and other major public opinion surveys in which researchers want to ensure that a relatively small sample provides an accurate, representative cross-section of a large and diverse population. The sample can be constructed so that several variables such as age, economic status, and political affiliation are represented in the sample in the same proportions in which they exist in the population.

Depending on how precisely we want sample proportions to match population proportions, the proportionate stratified sample can create a lot of extra work. Obviously, we must first determine the existing population proportions, which may require a trip to the library or another research center, and then we must find individuals who match the categories we have identified. One strategy is to obtain a very large sample (much bigger than ultimately needed), measure all of the different variables for each individual, and then randomly select those who fit the criteria (or randomly weed out the extras who do not fit). This process requires a lot of preliminary measurement before the study actually begins, and it discards many of the sampled individuals. In addition, a proportionate stratified sample can make it impossible for a researcher to describe or compare some subgroups or strata that exist within the population. For example, if a specific subgroup makes up only 1% of the population, they also make up only 1% of the sample. In a sample of 100 individuals, this means that there is only one person from the subgroup. It should be clear that you cannot rely on one person to adequately represent the entire subgroup.

Cluster Sampling

All of the sampling techniques we have considered so far are based on selecting individual participants, one at a time, from the population. Occasionally, however, the individuals in the population are already clustered in preexisting groups, and a researcher can randomly select groups instead of selecting individuals. For example, a researcher may want to obtain a large sample of third-grade students from the city school system. Instead of selecting 300 students one at a time, the researcher can randomly select 10 classrooms (each with about 30 students) and still end up with 300 individuals in the sample. This procedure is called **cluster sampling** and can be used whenever well-defined clusters exist within the population of interest. This sampling technique has two clear advantages. First, it is a relatively quick and easy way to obtain a large sample. Second, the measurement of individuals can often be done in groups, which can greatly facilitate the entire research project. Instead of selecting an individual and measuring a single score, the researcher can often test and measure the entire cluster at one time and walk away with 30 scores from a single experimental session.

The disadvantage of cluster sampling is that it can raise concerns about the independence of the individual scores. A sample of 300 individuals is assumed to contain 300 separate, individual, and independent measurements. However, the individuals within a cluster often have common characteristics or share common experiences that might influence the variables being measured. In this case, a researcher must question whether the individual measurements from the cluster actually represent separate and independent individuals.

Combined-Strategy Sampling

Occasionally, researchers combine two or more sampling strategies to select participants. For example, a superintendent of schools may first divide the district into regions (e.g., north, south, east, and west), which involves stratified sampling. From the different regions, the superintendent may then select two third-grade classrooms, which involves cluster sampling. Selection strategies are commonly combined to optimize the chances that a sample is representative of a widely dispersed or broad-based population such as in a wide market survey or a political poll.

A Summary of Probability Sampling Methods

Probability sampling techniques have a very good chance of producing a representative sample because they tend to rely on a random selection process. However, as we noted earlier, simple random sampling by itself does not guarantee a high degree of representativeness. To correct this problem, researchers often impose restrictions on the random process. Specifically, stratified random sampling can be used to guarantee that different subgroups are equally represented in the sample, and proportionate stratified sampling can be used to guarantee that the overall composition of the sample matches the composition of the population. However, probability sampling techniques can be extremely time consuming and tedious (i.e., obtaining a list of all the members of a population and developing a random, unbiased selection process). These techniques also require that researchers "know" the whole population and have access to it. For these reasons, probability sampling techniques are rarely used except in research involving small, contained populations (e.g., students at a school or prisoners at one correctional facility) or large-scale surveys.

LEARNING CHECK   1.   If each person in a large group has an equal chance of being included in an experiment, then what kind of sampling is being used?
   a. Systematic sampling
   b. Random sampling
   c. Convenience sampling
   d. Cluster sampling

2. A teacher obtains a sample of children from a fifth-grade classroom by randomly selecting the third, fifth, and eighth rows and taking all the students in those rows. What kind of sampling is being used?
    a. Simple random sampling
    b. Systematic sampling
    c. Cluster sampling
    d. Stratified sampling

3. A researcher would like to describe and compare the attitudes of four different ethnic groups of students at a local state college. What kind of sampling would be best to obtain participants for the study?
    a. Simple random sampling
    b. Stratified random sampling
    c. Proportionate stratified random sampling
    d. Systematic sampling

Answers appear at the end of the chapter.

5.3   Nonprobability Sampling Methods

LEARNING OBJECTIVES

LO5   Describe the process of convenience sampling, recognize examples of this technique in research reports, and explain why it is used and how researchers using this method can limit the risk of a biased sample.

LO6   Describe quota sampling, recognize examples of this technique in research reports, and explain why it is used.

Convenience Sampling

Convenience sampling is also known as accidental sampling or haphazard sampling.

The most commonly used sampling method in behavioral science research is probably **convenience sampling**. In convenience sampling, researchers simply use as participants those individuals who are easy to get. People are selected on the basis of their availability and willingness to respond. Examples are conducting research with students from an Introductory Psychology class or studying the children in a local daycare center. A researcher who teaches at the College at Brockport, State University of New York, and uses college students as participants is likely to use students enrolled at that college. A researcher at the University of California, Berkeley, is likely to use students enrolled there.

Convenience sampling is considered a weak form of sampling because it does not require knowledge of the population and does not use a random process for selection. The researcher exercises very little control over the representativeness of the sample and, therefore, there is a strong possibility that the obtained sample is biased. This is especially problematic when individuals actively come forward to participate as with phone-in radio surveys or mail-in magazine surveys. In these cases, the sample is biased because it contains only those individuals who listen to that station or read that magazine and feel strongly about the issue being investigated. These individuals are probably not representative of the general population.

Despite this major drawback, convenience sampling is probably used more often than any other kind of sampling. It is an easier, less expensive, more timely technique than the probability sampling techniques, which involve identifying every individual in the population and using a laborious random process to select participants.

Finally, although convenience sampling offers no guarantees of a representative and unbiased sample, you should not automatically conclude that this type of sampling is hopelessly flawed. Most researchers use two strategies to help correct most of the serious problems associated with convenience sampling. First, researchers try to ensure that their samples are reasonably representative and not strongly biased. For example, a researcher may select a sample that consists entirely of students from an Introductory Psychology class at a small college in Atlanta. However, if the researcher is careful to select a broad cross-section of students (different ages, different genders, different levels of academic performance, and so on), it is sensible to expect this sample to be reasonably similar to any other sample of college students that might be obtained from other academic departments or other colleges around the country. Unless the research study involves some special skill such as surfing or winter driving, it usually is reasonable to assume that a sample from one location is just as representative as a sample from any other location. The students in a state college in Florida are probably quite similar to the students in a state college in Idaho, and the children in a Seattle childcare center are probably similar to the children in a St. Louis childcare center. The exception to this simple concept occurs whenever a convenience sample is obtained from a location with unusual or unique characteristics, such as a music school for extremely talented students or a private childcare center for gifted children.

The second strategy that helps minimize potential problems with convenience sampling is simply to provide a clear description of how the sample was obtained and who the participants are. For example, a researcher might report that a sample of 20 children aged 3–5 was obtained from a childcare center in downtown Houston. Or a research report may state that a sample of 100 students, 67 females and 33 males, all between the ages of 18 and 22, was obtained from the Introductory Psychology class at a large Midwestern state university. Although these samples may not be perfectly representative of the larger population and each may have some biases, at least everyone knows what the sample looks like and can make their own judgments about representativeness.

Quota Sampling

One method for controlling the composition of a convenience sample is to use some of the same techniques that are used for probability sampling. In the same way that we used stratified sampling to ensure that different subgroups are represented equally, **quota sampling** can ensure that subgroups are equally represented in a convenience sample. For example, a researcher can guarantee equal groups of boys and girls in a sample of 30 preschool children by establishing quotas for the number of individuals to be selected from each subgroup. Rather than simply taking the first 30 children who agree to participate, you impose a quota of 15 girls and 15 boys. After the quota of 15 boys is met, no other boys have a chance to participate in the study. In this example, quota sampling ensures that specific subgroups are adequately represented in the sample.

A variation of quota sampling mimics proportionate stratified sampling. Specifically, a researcher can adjust the quotas to ensure that the sample proportions match a predetermined set of population proportions. For example, a researcher could ensure that 30% of the sample consists of participants under the age of 25 and 70% who are 25 or older so the sample has the same proportions that exist in a specific population. We should note that quota sampling is not the same as stratified and proportionate stratified sampling because it does not randomly select individuals from the population. Instead, individuals are selected on the basis of convenience within the boundaries set by the quotas.

It also is possible for a convenience sample to use techniques borrowed from systematic sampling or cluster sampling. For example, a researcher who is sampling shoppers at a local mall could systematically select every fifth person who passes by. This technique can help ensure that the researcher gets a broadly representative sample and does not focus on one particular subgroup of people who appear to be more approachable. Also, a researcher who is selecting children from the local school (because it is convenient) could still select classroom clusters rather than individual students.

Finally, there is not unanimous agreement about the terminology used to designate the different types of samples. For example, the procedure we call *quota sampling* has also been described as *convenience stratified sampling*. In general, you should rely on the description of the sampling technique rather than the name applied to it.

Different sampling techniques, including probability and nonprobability sampling, are summarized in Table 5.1.

TABLE 5.1

Summary of Sampling Methods

Type of Sampling	Description	Strengths and Weaknesses
Probability Sampling		
Simple random	A sample is obtained using a random process to select participants from a list containing the total population. The random process ensures that each individual has an equal and independent chance of selection.	The selection process is fair and unbiased, but there is no guarantee that the sample is representative.
Systematic	A sample is obtained by selecting every nth participant from a list containing the total population after a random start.	An easy method for obtaining an essentially random sample, but the selections are not really random or independent.
Stratified random	A sample is obtained by dividing the population into subgroups (strata) and then randomly selecting equal numbers from each of the subgroups.	Guarantees that each subgroup will have adequate representation, but the overall sample is usually not representative of the population
Proportionate stratified	A sample is obtained by subdividing the population into strata and then randomly selecting from each stratum a number of participants so that the proportions in the sample correspond to the proportions in the population.	Guarantees that the composition of the sample (in terms of the identified strata) will be perfectly representative of the composition of the population, but some strata may have limited representation in the sample.
Cluster	Instead of selecting individuals, a sample is obtained by randomly selecting clusters (preexisting groups) from a list of all the clusters that exist within the population.	An easy method for obtaining a large, relatively random sample, but the selections are not really random or independent.
Nonprobability Sampling		
Convenience	A sample is obtained by selecting individual participants who are easy to get.	An easy method for obtaining a sample, but the sample is probably biased.
Quota	A sample is obtained by identifying subgroups to be included, then establishing quotas for individuals to be selected through convenience from each subgroup.	Allows a researcher to control the composition of a convenience sample, but the sample probably is biased.

LEARNING CHECK

1. A researcher recruits a sample of 25 preschool children for a research study by posting an announcement in a local daycare center describing the study and offering a $10 payment for participation. What kind of sampling is the researcher using?
    a. Cluster sampling
    b. Quota sampling
    c. Simple random sampling
    d. Convenience sampling

2. Which of the following sampling techniques is most likely to result in a biased sample?
    a. Simple random sampling
    b. Convenience sampling
    c. Proportionate stratified random sampling
    d. Systematic sampling

3. A researcher would like to select a sample of 50 people so that five different age groups are equally represented in the sample. Assuming that the researcher does not know the entire list of people in the population, which sampling technique should be used?
    a. Quota sampling
    b. Stratified random sampling
    c. Proportionate stratified random sampling
    d. Cluster sampling

Answers appear at the end of the chapter.

CHAPTER SUMMARY

At this point you should review the learning objectives presented at the beginning of each section and be sure that you have mastered each objective.

The goal of the research study is to measure a sample and then generalize the results to the population. Therefore, the researcher should be careful to select a sample that is representative of the population. This chapter examines some of the common strategies for obtaining samples.

The two basic categories of sampling techniques are probability and nonprobability sampling. In probability sampling, the odds of selecting a particular individual are known and can be calculated. Types of probability sampling are simple random sampling, systematic sampling, stratified sampling, proportionate stratified sampling, and cluster sampling. In nonprobability sampling, the probability of selecting a particular individual is not known because the researcher does not know the population size or the members of the population. Types of nonprobability sampling are convenience and quota sampling. Each sampling method has advantages and limitations and differs in terms of the representativeness of the sample obtained.

KEY WORDS

population

sample

representativeness

representative sample

biased sample

selection bias, or sampling bias

sampling

probability sampling

random process

nonprobability sampling

EXERCISES

The exercises are identified with specific learning objectives and are intended to assess your mastery of the objectives. You should be aware that exam items are also generated to assess learning objectives.

1. In addition to the key words, you should also be able to define each of the following terms:

   target population
   accessible population
   law of large numbers
   sampling methods, or sampling techniques, or sampling procedures
   simple random sampling
   systematic sampling
   stratified random sampling
   proportionate random sampling
   proportionate stratified random sampling
   cluster sampling
   convenience sampling
   quota sampling

2. **(LO1)** A researcher conducting a political poll for a statewide election would like to know the attitudes of college students concerning the candidates. A sample of 200 upperclassmen from the state university is selected to participate in the survey. For this study:
   a. What is the target population?
   b. What is the accessible population?
   c. What is the sample?

3. **(LO1)** A researcher studying cyberbullying among middle-school students interviews a group of students from a local middle school about their cyberbullying experiences. For this study, identify the target population, the accessible population, and the sample.

4. **(LO2)** If a researcher selects a sample from each of the following populations, then which is likely to be a probability sample and which is likely to be a nonprobability sample?
   a. The population consists of the children enrolled in a prekindergarten program in a local school district.
   b. The population consists of adolescents from single-parent families.

5. **(LO3)** Explain how a researcher using simple random sampling can still obtain a biased sample.

6. **(LO4)** Under what circumstances is a stratified random sample preferred to a simple random sample?

7. **(LO4)** Under what circumstances is a proportionate stratified random sample preferred to a simple random sample?

8. **(LO4)** Explain the advantages and disadvantages of a stratified random sample compared with a proportionate stratified random sample.

9. **(LO5)** Describe the advantages and disadvantages of convenience sampling.

10. **(LO4** and **5)** For each of the following scenarios, identify which sampling method is used:
    a. The State College is conducting a survey of student attitudes and opinions. The plan is to use the list of all registered students and then select every 10th name on the list to make up the sample.
    b. The city population consists of four major ethnic groups. A researcher studying resident attitudes concerning a proposed city park surveys a large number of city residents and then selects the first 30 responders from each ethnic group to make up the sample.
    c. A second option for the survey in Part b is based on the observation that the four ethnic groups are not represented equally in the population. To ensure that the sample reflects these differences, the researcher first determines the number of residents in each ethnic group and then selects a sample so that the number for each group in the sample is in direct relation to the number in each group for the entire city population.
    d. The County Democratic Committee would like to determine which issues are most important to registered Democrats in the county. Starting with a list of registered Democrats, the committee uses a random process to select a sample of 30 names for telephone interviews.
    e. A medical research laboratory places ads in the local newspaper to recruit people with chronic migraine headaches to participate in clinical trials evaluating a new medication. Qualified individuals are asked to phone the lab for a screening appointment.

11. **(LO6)** Explain how the nonprobability technique of quota sampling can be used to mimic the probability technique of stratified random sampling.

LEARNING CHECK ANSWERS

Section 5.1
1. a, 2. a, 3. d

Section 5.2
1. b, 2. c, 3. b

Section 5.3
1. d, 2. b, 3. a

Research Strategies and Validity

© Nathan Jasowiak / Shutterstock

CHAPTER LEARNING OBJECTIVES

LO1 Describe, compare, and contrast the five research strategies (descriptive, correlational, experimental, quasi-experimental, and nonexperimental); the kinds of questions they address and the data structures they produce; and recognize examples of each.

LO2 Define *research strategy*, *research design*, and *research procedures*, and describe the choices and decisions involved during these three stages in the development of a research study.

LO3 Define the concept of external validity and a threat to external validity.

LO4 Define the concept of internal validity and a threat to internal validity.

LO5 Identify and explain the common threats to external validity and identify threats when they appear in a research report.

LO6 Describe how extraneous variables can become confounding variables and threaten the internal validity of a research study; identify threats when they appear in a research report.

LO7   Describe how environmental variables can be threats to internal validity for all studies, how some variables can threaten studies that compare different groups, and how other variables can threaten studies that compare scores for one group over time.

LO8   Define *experimenter bias*, *demand characteristics*, and *reactivity*, and explain how these artifacts can threaten both internal and external validity.

CHAPTER OVERVIEW

As a student, you probably have spent many hours of your life preparing for exams. Have you ever wondered how your study habits compare with those of other students? Is the time that you spend studying more or less than average? Should you be studying during the day or late at night? Are there any special study hints that might improve the effectiveness of your studying? Many of these same questions have interested researchers over the years and have produced several published research reports. For example, Babcock and Marks (2010) were interested in the average number of hours spent studying by full-time students at 4-year colleges in the United States. Reviewing survey data from 2003 to 2005, they obtained an average of 14 hours per week. By comparison, similar data from 1961 yielded an average of about 24 hours. Notice, that these researchers are asking a question about a single variable (student study time) and their results provide a description of that variable in the college student population.

Other researchers are interested in relationships between studying and other variables. Trockel, Barnes, and Egget (2000), for example, found a consistent relationship between student wake-up time and academic performance. Specifically, academic performance decreased as wake-up time moved later into the day. Notice, however, that these researchers are simply looking at two variables and observing the relationship between them. They are not attempting to explain the relationship or make any claim that sleeping later causes lower grades. For example, setting your alarm earlier in the morning probably will not improve your grade point average (GPA).

Some researchers, on the other hand, are interested in determining what factors are responsible for *causing* higher or lower grades. Muller and Oppenheimer (2014), for example, looked at academic performance for students taking notes on a laptop compared with those who used paper and pen. Students in one condition were given laptops and those in the other condition were given pen and paper. Each student viewed a 15-minute lecture and was asked to take notes just as you would in class. After a short break, the students were asked questions about the content of the lecture. The results showed that test performance was significantly worse for the students using laptops. Because the researcher carefully controlled other variables, they can conclude confidently that the method used for note taking causes a difference in learning performance.

Notice that the three studies that we have discussed are all in the topic area of student studying; however, each begins with a very different research question and has a very different goal. The first study simply wanted a number to describe the amount of time students spend studying. The second study was interested in two variables and the relationship between them. Although they could conclude that a relationship exists between wake-up time and academic performance, their study did not allow a conclusion that wake-up time causes a difference in grades. The final study, on the other hand, demonstrated a relationship between the method used for note taking and learning performance, and showed that the method you use for note taking can cause higher or lower grades.

Because these three studies begin with different questions, they also use very different approaches for answering the question. These different approaches are known as research strategies. Specifically, the first study is an example of descriptive research, the second is classified as correlational research, and the third is an experimental study. In this chapter, we introduce research strategies, identify the kinds of questions that each is designed to answer, and discuss the strengths and limitations of the answers they produce.

6.1   Research Strategies

LEARNING OBJECTIVES

LO1   Describe, compare, and contrast the five research strategies (descriptive, correlational, experimental, quasi-experimental, and nonexperimental); the kinds of questions they address and the data structures they produce; and recognize examples of each.

LO2   Define *research strategy*, *research design*, and *research procedures*, and describe the choices and decisions involved during these three stages in the development of a research study.

After you have identified a new idea for research, formed a hypothesis, decided how to define and measure your variables, and determined which individuals should participate in the study and how to treat them ethically, the next step is to select a research strategy (Step 5 in the research process; see more detail later in this section, pp. 135–136). The term *research strategy* refers to the general approach and goals of a research study. The selection of a research strategy is usually determined by the kind of question you plan to address and the kind of answer you hope to obtain—in general terms, what you hope to accomplish. For example, consider the following three research questions.

1. What is the average amount of daily time spent on social media sites by adolescents?
2. Is there a relationship between social media "lurking" and adults' satisfaction with life?
3. Do changes in social media use cause changes in depressive symptoms in young adults?

Notice that the first question, like the first question in the chapter overview about number of hours studied, is asking about a single variable (amount of time spend on social media sites). The second question, like the question in overview about the relationship between wake-up time and academic performance, is asking about a relationship between two variables (social media "lurking" and satisfaction with life). Specifically, this question is asking whether a relationship exists. The third question, like the question in the overview about the effects of method used for note taking on learning, is also asking whether a relationship exists; however, this question asks for an *explanation* for the relationship. In this form, the question is asking whether differences in social media use help explain why young adults experience different levels of depressive symptoms. These three different questions would require different research strategies. In this chapter, we introduce five research strategies that are intended to answer different types of research questions.

DEFINITION   A **research strategy** is a general approach to research determined by the kind of question that the research study hopes to answer.

As noted in Chapter 1 (p. 18), this book focuses on quantitative research, which involves measuring variables to obtain scores. The five strategies we introduce in this chapter are all intended to examine measurements of variables and relationships between variables and are presented as they apply to quantitative research. Nonetheless, some components of quantitative and qualitative research overlap and some of the methods and strategies we discuss can be used with either type of research. For example, observational research is discussed in Chapter 13 as it is used in quantitative research. However, this same procedure also forms the foundation for many qualitative research studies.

The Descriptive Research Strategy: Examining Individual Variables

Out of the five research strategies we discuss, the descriptive research strategy is the only one that focuses on individual variables. Specifically, this strategy is intended to answer questions about the current state of individual variables for a specific group of individuals. For example, for the students at a specific college, what is the typical number of text messages received each day? What is the average number of hours of sleep each day? What percentage voted in the latest presidential election? To answer these questions, a researcher could measure text messages, sleep time, and voting history for each student, and then calculate an average or percentage for each variable. Note that the **descriptive research strategy** is not concerned with relationships between variables but rather with the description of individual variables. The goal of the descriptive strategy is to obtain a snapshot (a description) of specific characteristics of a specific group of individuals. In Chapter 13, we discuss the details of the descriptive research strategy. In Chapter 15 Section 4, we identify the statistics used with the data from descriptive research studies.

Strategies That Examine Relationships between Variables

Relationships between Variables

Descriptive research studies are conducted simply to describe individual variables as they exist naturally. Most research, however, is intended to examine the relationships between variables. For example, is there a relationship between the quality of breakfast and academic performance for elementary-school children? Is there a relationship between the number of hours of sleep and GPA for college students? There are many different techniques for examining relationships and the four remaining research strategies presented in this chapter are intended to identify and describe relationships between variables.

Figure 6.1(a) shows the general relationship between wake-up time and academic performance for college students; when wake-up time changes from early to late, academic performance also changes from relatively high to relatively low (Trockel, Barnes, & Egget, 2000). In this example, both of the variables were initially measured with numerical scores and then converted to ordinal categories (early/late and high/low). In other situations, when both variables are measured using numbers or ranks, a variety of terms can be used to classify the relationships. For example, Figures 6.1(b) and 6.1(c) show **linear relationships** because the data points produced by the changing values of the two variables tend to form a straight-line pattern. Figure 6.1(d) shows an example of a **curvilinear relationship**. Again, there is a consistent, predictable relationship between the two variables, but now the pattern is a curved line. As we noted in Chapter 3 (p. 57), Figures 6.1(b) and 6.1(d) are examples of **positive relationships** because increases in one variable tend to be accompanied by increases in the other. Conversely, Figure 6.1(c) shows an example of a **negative relationship**, in which increases in one variable are accompanied by decreases in the other. Finally, recall that the terms describing relationships only apply when both variables consist of numbers or ranks. For example, Figure 6.1(a) shows a consistent and predictable relationship between wake-up time and academic performance; however, the relationship cannot be classified as linear, curvilinear, positive, or negative.

FIGURE 6.1

Examples of Different Types of Relationships between Variables

(a) A general relationship, (b) positive linear, (c) negative linear, (d) positive curvilinear. For graphs (b), (c), and (d), values for variable X increase from left to right, and values for variable Y increase from bottom to top.

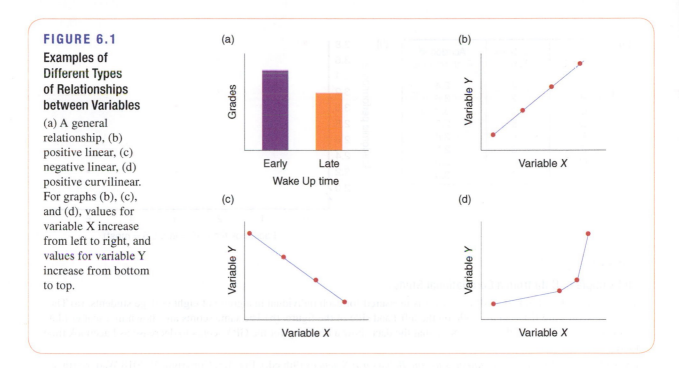

The Correlational Research Strategy: Measuring Two Variables for Each Individual

To establish the existence of a relationship, researchers must make observations—that is, measurements of the two variables. Depending on how the measurements are used, two distinct data structures can be produced. The two data structures also help to classify the different research strategies.

One technique for examining the relationship between variables is to observe the two variables as they exist naturally for a set of individuals. That is, simply measure the two variables for each individual. For example, researchers have found a relationship between GPA and time spent on Facebook, especially for college freshmen (Junco, 2015). Figure 6.2 shows an example of the kind of data found in the study.

Consistent patterns in the data are often easier to see if the scores are presented in a graph. The right-hand side of Figure 6.2 shows the Facebook time and GPA scores in a graph called a *scatter plot*. In the scatter plot, each individual is represented by a point so that the horizontal position corresponds to the Facebook time and the vertical position corresponds to the student's GPA. The scatter plot shows a clear relationship: As Facebook time increases, GPA tends to decrease.

A research study that simply measures two variables for each individual and produces the kind of data shown in Figure 6.2, in which each variable is measured with numerical scores, is an example of the **correlational research strategy**. Note that the correlational strategy only attempts to describe the relationship (if one exists); it is not trying to explain the relationship. For example, although there may be a relationship between Facebook time and GPA, this does not mean that limiting students' time on Facebook would cause them to get better grades. The details of the correlational research strategy are discussed in Chapter 12. In Chapter 15 Section 4, we identify the statistics used with the data from correlational research studies.

FIGURE 6.2

An Example of Data from a Correlational Study

Time spent on Facebook and GPA scores was measured for each individual in a group of eight college students. (a) The resulting scores are listed in the table on the left-hand side of the figure. (b) The same scores are shown in a scatter plot on the right-hand side of the figure. Note that the data show a tendency for the GPA scores to decrease as Facebook time increases.

From Gravetter, *Essentials of Statistics for the Behavioral Sciences* (9th ed.), Fig. 1.5. Copyright © 2018 Wadsworth, a part of Cengage Learning. Reproduced with permission.

Comparing Two or More Sets of Scores: The Experimental, Quasi-Experimental, and Nonexperimental Research Strategies

The second technique for examining the relationship between two variables involves comparing two or more groups of scores. In this situation, one of the variables is used to differentiate the groups. For example, one group of students is selected from high-income families and a second group is selected from low-income families. The second variable, each student's grade average, is then measured to obtain a score for each individual. An example of the resulting data is shown in Table 6.1. Note that the researcher compares the scores for the high-income group with the scores for the low-income group. A systematic difference between the two groups of scores provides evidence of a relationship between family income and academic performance.

There are three different research strategies that examine relationships between variables using the kind of data shown in Table 6.1. The differences among the three strategies are based on the questions that they address and their ability to produce unambiguous answers.

The Experimental Research Strategy

The **experimental research strategy** is intended to answer cause-and-effect questions about the relationship between two variables. For example, are increases in exercise responsible for causing decreases in cholesterol level? To answer this question, a researcher could create two treatment conditions by changing the amount of exercise from low in one condition to high in the other. Then, one group of individuals is assigned to the low-exercise condition, and a similar group is assigned to the high-exercise condition. Cholesterol is measured for each group, and the scores in the low-exercise condition are

TABLE 6.1

High School Grades for Students from High- and Low-Income Families

High Income	Low Income
72	83
86	89
81	94
78	90
85	97
80	89
91	95
Mean = 81.9 Compare the two groups	Mean = 91.0

compared with the scores in the high-exercise condition to determine whether changes in the level of exercise cause changes in cholesterol (Table 6.2a). Note that the purpose of the experimental research strategy is to explain the relationship by determining the underlying cause. An experimental study is conducted with rigorous control to help ensure an unambiguous demonstration of a cause-and-effect relationship. In Chapter 7, we discuss the details of the experimental research strategy. In Chapter 15 Section 4, we identify the statistics used with the data from experimental research studies.

The Quasi-Experimental Research Strategy

Although this strategy usually attempts to answer cause-and-effect questions about the relationship between two variables, it can never produce an unambiguous explanation. For example, a researcher would like to determine whether a specific treatment causes a reduction in cigarette smoking. Attempting to answer this question, a researcher identifies a large company with several offices across the country. Two of the offices are selected to participate in the study, and a group of people who smoke is identified in each office. The researcher then begins the smoking cessation treatment for one of the two groups. After two months, the smoking behavior for the individuals in both groups is recorded again, and the scores for the individuals in the smoking cessation treatment are compared with those obtained for the individuals who did not receive the treatment (see Table 6.2b). The **quasi-experimental research strategy** uses some of the rigor and control that exist in experiments; however, quasi-experimental studies always contain a flaw that prevents the research from obtaining an absolute cause-and-effect answer. For this example, the researcher used preexisting groups and did not control the assignment of individuals to groups. Therefore, there is no way to know whether the people in the treatment program are similar to those in the no-treatment program. The two groups could be very different in terms of age, income, motivation, or a variety of other variables. Although people who received the treatment may be more successful at quitting, you cannot conclude that the treatment *caused* greater success. It may be that the treatment has no effect and the smokers in the treatment condition were simply more motivated. As the name implies, quasi-experimental studies are almost, but not quite, experiments. In Chapter 10, we discuss the details of the quasi-experimental research strategy. In Chapter 15 Section 4, we identify the statistics used with the data from quasi-experimental research studies.

TABLE 6.2

Examples of Data for Experimental, Quasi-Experimental, and Nonexperimental Research Studies

a. Experimental		b. Quasi-Experimental		c. Nonexperimental	
Low Exercise	High Exercise	Without Treatment	With Treatment	Girls	Boys
168	122	still smoking	Quit	27	14
196	210	still smoking	Still smoking	30	16
175	130	Quit	Quit	19	18
210	124	still smoking	Quit	27	15
226	146	still smoking	Quit	24	21
183	133	still smoking	Quit	23	23
142	158	Quit	Still smoking	18	18
198	122	Quit	Quit	15	14
207	140	still smoking	Still smoking	29	21
195	135	still smoking	Quit	28	20
Compare cholesterol scores		Compare smoking behaviors		Compare verbal scores	

The Nonexperimental Research Strategy

The **nonexperimental research strategy** is intended to demonstrate a relationship between variables, but it does not attempt to explain the relationship. In particular, this strategy does not try to produce cause-and-effect explanations. For example, a researcher would like to determine whether the verbal skills for 6-year-old girls are different from those for 6-year-old boys. (Is there a relationship between verbal skills and gender?) To answer this question, a researcher could measure verbal skills for each individual in a group of boys and in a group of girls, then compare the two sets of scores (see Table 6.2c). Nonexperimental studies do not use the rigor and control that exist in experiments and in quasi-experimental studies and do not produce cause-and-effect explanations. For example, a study may demonstrate that girls have higher verbal skills than boys, but it does not explain *why* the girls' scores are higher. In Chapter 10, we discuss the details of the nonexperimental research strategy. In Chapter 15 Section 4, we identify the statistics used with the data from nonexperimental research studies.

Nonexperimental and Correlational Research

You may have noticed that nonexperimental and correlational research have exactly the same goal. Specifically, both are designed to demonstrate that a relationship exists between two variables but do not try to explain the relationship. The difference between the two research strategies is the kind of data used to accomplish this goal. The correlational strategy uses one group of participants and measures two variables for each individual, producing data structured like the scores shown in Figure 6.2. The nonexperimental strategy compares two or more groups of scores, measuring only one variable for each individual and produces data like the scores in Table 6.2c. Although these two research strategies take different approaches for collecting data, they reach the same conclusions and have exactly the same limitations.

Research Strategy Summary

The five research strategies are summarized in Table 6.3. For organizational purposes, we group the five research strategies into three broad categories based on the question being addressed and data structure:

1. Strategies that examine individual variables instead of relationships between variables.
2. Strategies that examine relationships between variables by measuring two (or more) variables for each participant.
3. Strategies that examine relationships between variables by comparing two (or more) groups of scores.

Note that the three research strategies in Category 3 (as seen in Table 6.3) form a hierarchy in terms of explaining relationships between variables. Experiments are designed

TABLE 6.3

Five Research Strategies Organized by the Data Structures They Use

Category 1: Strategies that examine individual variables.

Descriptive

Purpose: Produce a description of individual variables as they exist within a specific group.

Data: A list of scores obtained by measuring each individual in the group being studied.

Example: On average, students at the local college spend 12.5 hours studying outside of class each week and get 7.2 hours of sleep each night.

Category 2: Strategies that examine relationships between variables by measuring two (or more) variables for each participant.

Correlational

Purpose: Produce a description of the relationship between two variables but do not attempt to explain the relationship.

Data: Measure two variables (two scores) for each individual in the group being studied (see Figure 6.2).

Example: There is a relationship between Facebook time and GPA for college students, but we don't know why.

Category 3: Strategies that examine relationships between variables by comparing two (or more) groups of scores.

Experimental

Purpose: Produce a cause-and-effect explanation for the relationship between two variables.

Data: Create two treatment conditions by changing the level of one variable. Then measure a second variable for the participants in each condition (see Table 6.2a).

Example: Increasing the amount of exercise causes a decrease in cholesterol levels.

Quasi-Experimental

Purpose: Attempt to produce a cause-and-effect explanation but fall short.

Data: Measure before/after scores for one group that receives a treatment and for a different group that does not receive the treatment (see Table 6.2b).

Example: The treatment may cause a reduction in smoking behavior, but the reduced smoking may be caused by something else.

Nonexperimental

Purpose: Produce a description of the relationship between two variables but do not attempt to explain the relationship.

Data: Measure scores for two different groups of participants or for one group at two different times (see Table 6.2c).

Example: There is a relationship between gender and verbal ability. Girls tend to have higher verbal skills than boys, but we don't know why.

to demonstrate cause-and-effect relationships. That is, experimental studies produce unambiguous explanations by demonstrating that changes in one variable are responsible for causing changes to occur in a second variable. Quasi-experimental studies aim to demonstrate cause-and-effect relationships but fall short of achieving this goal. Finally, nonexperimental research simply attempts to demonstrate that a relationship exists and makes no attempt to explain why the two variables are related. Also notice that although the correlational and nonexperimental strategies use different data, they have the same purpose and produce the same kind of conclusion.

Research Strategies, Research Designs, and Research Procedures

We introduced the term *research strategy* to refer to the general approach to a research study that is intended to address a specific question. We should note, however, that the terms *research design* and *research procedures* are often used to refer to the same concept. We prefer that these three terms be defined individually to refer to three distinct stages of research development and the choices and decisions that comprise each stage. The following paragraphs discuss and define the three terms as they will be used throughout this book.

Research Strategies

The term *research strategy* refers to the general approach and goals of a research study (see p. 129). Research strategy is usually determined by the kind of question you plan to address and the kind of answer you hope to obtain. In general terms, a research strategy is concerned with what you hope to accomplish in a research study. Chapters 7, 10, 12, and 13 provide more details about these different approaches.

Research Designs

The next stage of research development, the research design, addresses how to implement the strategy. Determining a **research design** requires decisions about three basic aspects of the research study:

1. *Group versus individual.* Will the study examine a group of individuals, producing an overall description for the entire group, or should the study focus on a single individual? Although results from a large group can be generalized more confidently than results from a single individual, the careful examination of a single individual often can provide detail that is lost in averaging a large group.
2. *Same individuals versus different individuals.* Some research examines changes within the same group of individuals as they move from one treatment to the next. Other research uses a different group of individuals for each separate treatment and then examines differences between groups. Each design has advantages and disadvantages that must be weighed in the planning phase.
3. *The number of variables to be included.* The simplest study involves examining the relationship between two variables. However, some research involves three or more variables. For example, a researcher may be interested in multiple relationships, or a study may focus on two variables but ask how their relationship is affected by other variables. Thus, one factor in determining a research design is deciding how many variables will be observed, manipulated, or regulated.

A research design is a general framework for conducting a study. We discuss different designs and their individual strengths and weaknesses in Chapters 8, 9, 10, 11, 13, and 14.

DEFINITION

A **research design** is a general plan for implementing a research strategy. A research design specifies whether the study will involve groups or individual participants, will make comparisons within a group or between groups, and how many variables will be included in the study.

Research Procedures

The next stage in developing a research study involves filling in the details that precisely define how the study is to be done. This final, detailed stage is called the **research procedure**. It includes a precise determination of:

- exactly how the variables will be manipulated, regulated, and measured.
- exactly how many individuals will be involved.
- exactly how the individual participants or subjects will proceed through the course of the study.

The procedure contains the final decisions about all choices still open after the general design is determined and each study typically has its own unique procedures. The task of defining and measuring variables is discussed in Chapter 3; different ways of selecting individuals to participate in a study are discussed in Chapter 5. For each completed study, a description of the research procedure is typically presented in the method section of the research report, which is discussed briefly in Table 2.2 (p. 43) and in Chapter 16.

DEFINITION

A **research procedure** is an exact, step-by-step description of a specific research study.

Data Structures and Statistical Analysis

Experimental, quasi-experimental, and nonexperimental studies all involve comparing groups of scores (see Table 6.2). Usually, the comparison involves looking for mean differences or differences in proportions. For example:

- The average cholesterol score is 142 for people in the high-exercise group compared to an average of 190 for people in the low-exercise group.
- Of the individuals who were in the treatment program, 70% quit smoking compared with only 30% of those who did not receive the treatment.
- The average verbal score for the girls is 24, compared with an average score of 18 for the boys.

Because these three strategies produce similar data, they also tend to use similar statistical techniques. For example, *t*-tests and analysis of variance are used to evaluate mean differences, and chi-square tests are used to compare proportions.

Correlational studies do not involve comparing different groups of scores. Instead, a correlational study measures two different variables (two different scores) for each individual in a single group and then looks for patterns within the set of scores (see Figure 6.2). If a correlational study produces numerical scores, the data are usually evaluated by computing a correlation (such as the Pearson correlation). If the data consist of nonnumerical classifications, the statistical evaluation is usually a chi-square test.

Descriptive studies are intended to summarize single variables for a specific group of individuals. For numerical data, the statistical summary usually consists of a mean, or

Statistical techniques are discussed in Chapter 15.

average, score. If the data are nonnumerical classifications, the summary is typically a report of the proportion (or percentage) associated with each category. For example, the average student sleeps 7 hours a day and eats two pizzas a week. Or, 58% of the students report having failed at least one course.

Summary

Different research strategies are available to address the variety of questions with which research can begin. Each strategy is directed toward different types of questions, and each strategy has its own strengths and limitations. Although we have identified five research strategies, another common method differentiates only two: experimental research and nonexperimental, or nonmanipulative, research. The rationale for this two-way classification is that only the experimental strategy can establish the existence of cause-and-effect relationships; other strategies cannot.

LEARNING CHECK

1. Which of the following questions can be addressed with the descriptive strategy?
   a. What is the average number of text messages that a typical adolescent sends in a month?
   b. Is there a relationship between the number of text messages that adolescents send each month and the number of pages of leisure reading done by adolescents?
   c. Does decreasing the number of text messages sent by adolescents cause an increase in number of pages read for leisure?
   d. None of these questions can be addressed with this strategy

2. A research study attempts to describe the relationship between self-esteem and birth order position by measuring self-esteem for each individual in a group of first-born boys, and then comparing the results with self-esteem scores for a group of later-born boys. Which research strategy is being used?
   a. Nonexperimental
   b. Correlational
   c. Experimental
   d. Quasi-experimental

3. Which of the following is a general plan for implementing a research strategy?
   a. A research procedure
   b. A research design
   c. A research study
   d. A research protocol

Answers appear at the end of the chapter.

6.2   External and Internal Validity

LEARNING OBJECTIVES

LO3   Define the concept of external validity and a threat to external validity.

LO4   Define the concept of internal validity and a threat to internal validity.

In later chapters, we examine each of the research strategies in detail. For now, however, we focus on a more fundamental issue: How well does the research study actually answer the question it was intended to answer? This is a question concerning the *validity* of the research study. The dictionary defines *validity* as "the quality or state of being true." In the context of a research study, validity is concerned with the truth of the research or the accuracy of the conclusions.

In general, validity is the standard criterion by which researchers judge the quality of research. You probably have heard people talk about research studies that are "flawed," studies that are "poorly designed," or studies that produce "limited or non-applicable results." These are examples of research studies that lack validity. In this chapter, we examine how scientists define *validity* and how the concept of validity applies to different kinds of research. The goal for you is to learn how to design a valid research study, that is, a "good" study, and how to recognize validity (or the lack of it) in other people's research.

There is some potential for confusion about the use of the word *validity*. In Chapter 3, we introduced the concept of validity *as it applies to measurement*; the validity of a measurement procedure refers to whether the procedure actually measures the variable that it claims to measure. Here, however, we introduce the concept of validity *as it applies to an entire research study*. Specifically, we examine the quality of the research process and the accuracy of the results. The same word, *validity*, applies to both contexts. Therefore, we are careful to distinguish between the validity of a research study and the validity of measurement, and you should be careful to separate the two concepts in your own mind.

Any researcher's goal is to be able to summarize a research study by stating, "This is what happened, and this is what it means." Any factor that raises doubts about the limits of research results or about the interpretation of the results is a threat to the validity of the study. The *validity of a research study* is usually defined in terms of external validity and internal validity.

External Validity

Every research study is a unique event, conducted at a specific time and place with specific participants, instructions, measurement techniques, and procedures. Despite the unique nature of the study itself, researchers usually assume that the obtained results are not unique but can be generalized beyond that study. **External validity** concerns the extent to which the results obtained in a research study hold true outside that specific study. Can the results of the study be generalized to other populations, other settings, or other measurements? For example, Strack, Martin, and Stepper (1988) conducted a study showing that people rate cartoons as funnier when holding a pen in their teeth (which forced them to smile) than when holding a pen in their lips (which forced them to frown). Although this study was done in 1988 using undergraduate students from the University of Illinois, it seems reasonable to assume that the results are still valid today. That is, if the same study were conducted with today's undergraduate students from a different university, it would be reasonable to expect essentially the same results.

External validity focuses on any unique characteristics of the study that may raise questions about whether the same results would be obtained under different conditions. Any factor that limits the ability to generalize the results from a research study is a **threat to external validity**. For example, the results obtained from a group of 50-year-old males do not necessarily generalize to other genders or to other age groups. In this case, the limited range of participant characteristics is a threat to the external validity of the study.

DEFINITIONS

External validity refers to the extent to which we can generalize the results of a research study to people, settings, times, measures, and characteristics other than those used in that study.

A **threat to external validity** is any characteristic of a study that limits the ability to generalize the results from a research study.

There are at least three different kinds of generalization, and each can involve threats to external validity.

1. *Generalization from a sample to the general population.* Most research questions concern a large group of individuals known as a population. For example, a researcher may be interested in middle school children or adult caregivers for family members diagnosed with Alzheimer's disease. In each case, the population contains a very, very large number of individuals. However, the actual research study is conducted with a relatively small group of individuals known as a sample. For example, a researcher may select a sample of 50 middle school children to participate in a study. One concern for external validity is that the sample is representative of the population so that the results obtained for the sample can be generalized to the entire population. If, for example, a researcher finds that video game violence influences the behavior of middle school children in a sample, the researcher would like to conclude that video game violence affects the behavior of middle school children in general.

2. *Generalization from one research study to another.* As we noted earlier, each research study is a unique event, conducted at a specific time and place using specific procedures with a specific group of individuals. One concern for external validity is that the results obtained in one specific study will also be obtained in another similar study. For example, if I conduct a study with a specific group of 25 college students, will I obtain the same (or similar) results if I repeat the study 2 years later with a different group of students? If I do my study in New York, will another researcher using the same procedures obtain the same results in Kansas? If I measure IQ scores with the Stanford Binet Intelligence Scales, will another researcher get the same results measuring IQ with the Wechsler Adult Intelligence Scale–IV (WAIS–IV)?

3. *Generalization from a research study to a real-world situation.* Most research is conducted under relatively controlled conditions with individuals who know that they are participating in a research study. One concern for external validity is whether the results obtained in a relatively sterile research environment will also be obtained out in the real world. For example, a researcher may find that a new computer program is very effective for teaching mathematics to third-grade children. However, will the results obtained in the laboratory study also be found in a real third-grade classroom?

Internal Validity

For research studies using the experimental strategy, the goal is to obtain a cause-and-effect explanation for the relationship between two variables, and many other research studies hope to produce some support for a cause-and-effect explanation. For example, consider the following research questions:

- Does increased exercise cause a decrease in anxiety symptoms?
- Does a particular cognitive-behavioral therapy cause a reduction in depressive symptoms?
- Does a particular teaching technique cause an improvement in students' grades?

In each case, a valid research study would have to demonstrate that changes in one variable (e.g., the amount of exercise) are followed by changes in the other variable (anxiety symptoms), and that no other variable provides an alternative explanation for the results. This kind of validity is called **internal validity**. Internal validity is concerned with factors in the research study that raise doubts or questions about the interpretation of the results. A research study is said to have internal validity if it allows one and only one explanation of the results. Any factor that allows an alternative explanation for the results is a **threat to internal validity**.

For example, suppose a clinician obtains a group of clients diagnosed with depression and measures the level of depression for each individual. The clinician then begins therapy with the clients and measures depression again after 3 weeks. If there is a substantial decline in depression, the therapist would like to conclude that the therapy caused a reduction in depression. However, suppose that the weather was cold and miserable when the study began and changed to bright and sunny when the study ended 3 weeks later. In this case, the weather provides an alternative explanation for the results. Specifically, it is possible that the improved weather caused the reduction in depression. In this example, the weather is a threat to the internal validity of the research study.

DEFINITIONS

> A research study has **internal validity** if it produces a single, unambiguous explanation for the relationship between two variables.
>
> A **threat to internal validity** is any factor that allows for an alternative explanation.

Validity and the Quality of a Research Study

The value or quality of any research study is determined by the extent to which the study satisfies the criteria of external and internal validity. The general purpose of a research study is to answer a specific research question. A well-designed study produces results that accurately represent the variables being examined and justify a conclusion that accurately answers the original question. Any factor that generates doubts about the accuracy of the results or raises questions about the interpretation of the results is a threat to validity.

A good researcher is aware of these threats while planning a research study. Anticipating threats to validity allows a researcher to incorporate elements into a research design that eliminate or minimize threats to validity before the research is actually conducted. In this section, we identify and briefly describe some general threats to external and internal validity. In later chapters, we present a variety of different research designs and consider the specific threats to validity associated with each design. In addition, we identify methods of modifying or expanding each design to limit specific threats to validity.

One final caution: It is essentially impossible for a single research study to eliminate all threats to validity. Each researcher must decide which threats are most important for the specific study and then address those threats. Less-important threats can be ignored or treated casually. In fact, design changes that eliminate one threat may actually increase the potential for another threat; thus, each research study represents a set of decisions and compromises about validity. Although researchers typically try to make the best decisions and produce the best possible studies, most still contain some flaws. This basic "fact of life" has two implications:

1. Research studies vary in terms of validity. Some studies have both strong external and internal validity and their results and conclusions are highly respected. Some studies are strong in only one type of validity but not both. Other studies have only moderate validity, and some have little or no validity. Never accept a research result or conclusion as true simply because it is said to have been "scientifically demonstrated."

2. Being aware of threats to validity can help you critically evaluate a research study. As you read research reports, mentally scan the list of threats and ask yourself whether each one applies. A major learning objective of this book is to make you an informed consumer of research, capable of making your own decisions about its validity and quality.

LEARNING CHECK

1. Results from a research study suggest that a stop-smoking program is very successful. However, the participants who volunteered for the study were all highly motivated to quit smoking and the researcher is concerned that the same results may not be obtained for smokers who are not as motivated. What kind of validity is being questioned?
   a. Internal validity
   b. External validity ⓑ
   c. Experimental validity
   d. Validity of measurement

2. The degree to which your research results generalize beyond the specific characteristics of your study refers to
   a. internal validity.
   b. external validity. ⓑ
   c. general validity.
   d. reliability.

3. A researcher measures mood for a group of participants who have listened to happy music for 20 minutes and for a second group who have listened to sad music for 20 minutes. If different mood scores are obtained for the two groups, the researcher would like to conclude that music influences mood. However, the happy music group was tested in a room painted yellow and the sad music group was in a room painted dark brown and the researcher is concerned that the room color and not the music may influence mood scores. What kind of validity is being questioned?
   a. Internal validity ⓐ
   b. External validity
   c. Experimental validity
   d. Validity of measurement

Answers appear at the end of the chapter.

6.3   Threats to External Validity

LEARNING OBJECTIVE

LO5   Identify and explain the common threats to external validity and identify threats when they appear in a research report.

As discussed previously, external validity refers to the extent to which the results of the study can be generalized. That is, will the same (or similar) results be obtained with other populations, conditions, experimenters, other measurements, and so forth? When research findings can be generalized outside the confines of the specific study, the research is said to have external validity. Any characteristic of the study that limits the generality of the results is a threat to external validity. Some of the more common threats to external validity follow, grouped into three major categories.

Category 1: Generalizing across Participants or Subjects

The results of a study are demonstrated with a particular group of individuals. One question of external validity is, "To what extent can research results be generalized to individuals who differ from those who actually participated in the study?"

1. *Selection bias:* In Chapter 5 we defined a *biased sample* as one that has characteristics that are noticeably different from those of the population. A biased sample is usually the result of **selection bias**, which means that the sampling procedure favors the selection of some individuals over others. It should be obvious that selection bias is a threat to external validity. Specifically, if a sample does not accurately represent the population, then there are serious concerns that the results obtained from the sample will not generalize to the population. The question of external validity is always raised when a researcher selects participants based on convenience rather than using an unbiased selection process.

2. *College students:* The undergraduate shares with the laboratory rat the status of the most easily available and, therefore, most favored participant in behavioral research. However, evidence is accumulating to suggest that many of the characteristics of college students limit the ability to generalize the results to other adults. For example, Sears (1986) demonstrated that college students are likely to have a less formulated sense of self, a stronger tendency to comply with authority, less stable peer relationships, and higher intelligence than non-college-educated adults. We need to be cautious about generalizing research results obtained with this highly select group to the general adult population.

3. *Volunteer bias:* In most cases, someone who participates in research has volunteered for it. As noted in Chapter 4, the American Psychological Association (APA) guidelines for human research require (in most cases) that research participants be volunteers. This creates a basic problem for researchers known as **volunteer bias** because volunteers are not perfectly representative of the general population. The question of external validity is, "To what extent can we generalize results obtained with volunteers to individuals who may not volunteer to participate in studies?"

    In an extensive study of volunteer participants, Rosenthal and Rosnow (1975) identified a number of characteristics that tend to differentiate individuals who volunteer from those who do not. Table 6.4 presents a list of some of the characteristics they examined. Note that none of the individual characteristics is a perfectly reliable predictor of volunteerism, and some are better predictors than others. After an extensive review of previous research, Rosenthal and Rosnow grouped the items into categories based on the amount of evidence supporting the notion that these characteristics are, in fact, associated with volunteering.

    Remember, the items in Table 6.4 are general characteristics of volunteers; they are not intended to apply to each individual or to every situation. Nonetheless, the data clearly indicate that, on the average, volunteers are different from non-volunteers, which raises questions about the external validity of research conducted with volunteer participants.

4. *Participant characteristics:* Another threat to external validity occurs whenever a study uses participants who share similar characteristics. Demographic characteristics such as gender, age, race, ethnic identity, and socioeconomic status can limit the ability to generalize the results. For example, a study done in a Republican, suburban community with preschoolers may not generalize to other populations. You certainly would not expect to generalize the results to urban, Democratic young adults. It is always possible that the results of a study may be specific to participants with a certain set of characteristics and may not extend to participants with different characteristics.

5. *Cross-species generalizations:* External validity is also in question when research is conducted with nonhumans and presumed to be readily applicable to humans. Before we can consider whether the results obtained with one species can be generalized to another species, we must note the parallels and differences between the two species

TABLE 6.4

Participant Characteristics Associated with Volunteering

The characteristics are grouped according to the degree of confidence that the items are indeed related to volunteerism.

Maximum Confidence

Volunteers are more educated.

Volunteers are from a higher social class.

Volunteers are more intelligent.

Volunteers are more approval motivated.

Volunteers are more sociable.

Considerable Confidence

Volunteers are more arousal seeking.

Volunteers are more conventional.

Volunteers are more likely to be female than male.

Volunteers are more nonauthoritarian.

Volunteers are more likely to be Jewish than Protestant and more likely Protestant than Catholic.

Volunteers are more nonconforming.

Some Confidence

Volunteers are from smaller towns.

Volunteers are more interested in religion.

Volunteers are more altruistic.

Volunteers are more self-disclosing.

Volunteers are more maladjusted.

Volunteers are more likely to be young than old.

From Rosenthal and Rosnow (1975).

on the mechanism or process of interest. For example, rats are an excellent species to use for research on eating. Rats' eating behavior is similar to humans' eating behavior both physically and behaviorally (rats and humans have similar digestive systems, eating patterns, and food preferences). As a result, researchers can confidently generalize the results of research with rats to humans. In contrast, the blowfly is not a good species to use to generalize results to humans' eating because, unlike that of humans, the blowfly's eating behavior is purely reflexive and not learned (Logue, 1991). All of this is not to imply that nonhuman research is worthless and not applicable to humans; many major scientific advances in understanding humans have been made from research conducted with nonhumans. We must be careful not to presume, however, that all nonhuman research is directly applicable to humans.

Category 2: Generalizing across Features of a Study

In addition to the fact that each research study is conducted with a specific group of individuals, the results of a study are demonstrated with a specific set of procedures. Another question of external validity is, "To what extent can the results of the study be generalized to other procedures for conducting the study?"

1. *Novelty effect:* Participating in a research study is a novel, often exciting or anxiety-provoking experience for most individuals. In this novel situation, individuals may perceive and respond differently than they would in the normal, real world. This is called the **novelty effect**. In addition, the treatment(s) administered are typically clearly defined and unusually salient to the participants. Thus, the behavior (scores) of individuals participating in a research study may be quite different from behavior (scores) they would produce in other, more routine, situations in everyday life.

2. *Multiple treatment interference:* When individuals are tested in a series of treatment conditions, participation in one condition may have an effect on the participants that carries over into the next treatment and influences their performance or behavior. Common examples are **fatigue** and **practice**, which can occur in one treatment and then affect performance in the following treatment. In either case, participation in a previous treatment can be a threat to external validity. Specifically, the results obtained from individuals who have participated in previous conditions may not generalize to individuals who do not have the same previous experience. Again, any factor that limits the ability to generalize results is a threat to external validity. In this case, the potential influence of experience in earlier treatments is called **multiple treatment interference**.

3. *Experimenter characteristics:* As we have noted, each research study is conducted with a specific group of participants and a particular set of procedures. In addition, the results of a study are demonstrated with a specific experimenter conducting the study. The question of external validity is, "To what extent can the results of the study be generalized to other experimenters?"

   Experimenter characteristics can be a threat to external validity. The results of a study can be specific to an experimenter with a certain set of characteristics. Both demographic and personality characteristics of the experimenter can limit the generality of the results. Demographic characteristics can include gender, age, race, and ethnic identity; personality characteristics can include degree of friendliness, prestige, anxiety, and hostility. For example, a study conducted by a hostile experimenter is likely to produce different results from a study conducted by a kind experimenter.

Category 3: Generalizing across Features of the Measures

As we have noted, each research study is conducted with a specific group of participants, a particular set of procedures, and a specific experimenter. In addition, the results of a study are demonstrated with a specific set of measurements. Another question of external validity is, "To what extent can the results of the study be generalized to other ways of measuring in the study?"

1. *Sensitization:* Occasionally, the process of measurement, often called the assessment procedure, can alter participants so that they react differently to treatment. This phenomenon is called **sensitization** or **assessment sensitization**. Sensitization is a threat to external validity because it raises the question of whether the results obtained in a research study using assessment are different from results in the real world, where the treatment is used without assessment. For example, a self-esteem program for school children might be tested in a study in which self-esteem is actually measured, but then the program is applied throughout the school district without any measurement. Assessment sensitization commonly occurs in studies in which participants' behavior is measured before they are given a treatment, and they are measured again after treatment. The concern with regard to external validity is that the pretest (the before-treatment measurement) may in some way sensitize the participants so that

they become more aware of their own attitudes or behaviors. The increased awareness may cause the participants to be affected differently by the treatment. This threat to external validity is also known as **pretest sensitization**.

Assessment sensitization also commonly occurs in studies that use self-monitoring as a means of measuring scores. Harmon, Nelson, and Hayes (1980) demonstrated that the process of self-monitoring significantly reduced depression. That is, depressed patients who simply observed and recorded their own behavior showed significant improvement without any clinical treatment or therapy. Again, this is an example of a measurement procedure (not a treatment) affecting scores. You may recognize the self-monitoring effect as a common component of diet plans and smoking cessation programs, in which simply observing habits sensitizes people to their behavior and thereby changes it.

2. *Generality across response measures:* Many variables can be defined and measured in different ways. The variable fear, for example, can be defined in terms of physiological measures (e.g., heart rate), self-report measures, or behavior. In a research study, a researcher typically selects one definition and one measurement procedure. In this case, the results of the study may be limited to that specific measurement and may not generalize to other definitions or other measures. For example, a study may find that a particular therapy is effective in treating phobias when fear is defined and measured by heart rate. In actual practice, however, the therapy may not have any effect on the behavior of clients diagnosed with phobias.

3. *Time of measurement:* In a research study, the scores for individuals are measured at a specific time after (or during) the treatment. However, the actual effect of the treatment may decrease or increase with time. For example, a stop-smoking program may appear to be very successful if the participants are measured immediately after the program, but may have a much lower rate of success if participants are measured 6 months later. Thus, the results obtained in a research study in which responses are measured at a specific time may differ from the results obtained when measured at a different time.

Table 6.5 provides a summary of the three major categories of threats to the external validity of research results.

TABLE 6.5

General Threats to the External Validity of a Research Study

Source of the Threat	Description of the Threat
Participants	Characteristics that are unique to the specific group of participants in a study may limit ability to generalize the results of the study to individuals with different characteristics. For example, results obtained from college students may not generalize to noncollege adults.
Features of the study	Characteristics that are unique to the specific procedures used in a study may limit ability to generalize the results to situations in which other procedures are used. For example, the results obtained from participants who are aware that they are being observed and measured may not generalize to situations in which the participants are not aware that measurement is occurring. Also, results obtained with one experimenter might not generalize to a different experimenter.
Measurements	Characteristics that are unique to the specific measurement procedure may limit ability to generalize the results to situations in which a different measurement procedure is used. For example, the results obtained from measurements taken immediately after treatment may not generalize to a situation in which measurements are taken 3 months after treatment.

LEARNING CHECK

1. A journal article reports that a new teaching strategy is very effective for first-grade students. A teacher wonders if the same strategy would be effective for a class of third-grade students. What is the teacher questioning?
   a. The external validity of the report
   b. The internal validity of the report
   c. The reliability of the report
   d. The accuracy of the report

2. How can sensitization threaten external validity of a study?
   a. The results may be limited to the novel situation of the research study.
   b. The results may be limited to individuals who have experienced a pretest.
   c. The results may be limited to individuals who have experienced a series of different treatment conditions.
   d. The results may be limited to participants taking on different subject roles.

Answers appear at the end of the chapter.

6.4 Threats to Internal Validity

LEARNING OBJECTIVES

LO6 Describe how extraneous variables can become confounding variables and threaten the internal validity of a research study; identify threats when they appear in a research report.

LO7 Describe how environmental variables can be threats to internal validity for all studies, how some variables can threaten studies that compare different groups, and how other variables can threaten studies that compare scores for one group over time.

Extraneous Variables

A typical research study concentrates on two variables and attempts to demonstrate a relationship between them. For example, Hallam, Price, and Katsarou (2002) conducted a research study examining the effects of background music (variable #1) on task performance (variable #2) for primary school students. The results showed that calming and relaxing music led to better performance on an arithmetic task when compared to a no-music condition. Although the study focuses on two variables, there are countless other elements that vary within the study; that is, there are many additional variables (beyond the two being studied) that are part of every research study. Some of these extra variables are related to the individuals participating. For example, different students enter the study with different personalities, different IQs, different genders, different skills and abilities, and so on. Other variables involve the study's environment—for example, some participants may be tested in the morning and others in the afternoon; or part of the study may be conducted on a dark and dreary Monday and another part on a sunny Friday. The researcher is not interested in differences in IQ or weather, but these factors are still variables in the study. Additional variables that exist in a research study but are not directly investigated are called **extraneous variables**, and every research study has thousands of them.

DEFINITION   An **extraneous variable** is any variable in a research study other than the specific variables being studied.

Confounding Variables

Occasionally, an extraneous variable is accidentally allowed to creep into a study in a way that can influence or distort the results. When this happens, there is a risk that the observed relationship between two variables has been artificially produced by the extraneous variable. Consider the following scenario in which the researcher is attempting to demonstrate a relationship between background music and student performance.

> Suppose the research study starts with a group of students in a room with calm and relaxing background music for one treatment condition; later, the music is turned off to create a second treatment condition. In each condition, the students are given arithmetic problems to solve and their performance is measured. The results show that performance declines after the music is turned off. Although it is possible that the music is influencing performance, it also is possible that the participants are just getting tired. They do well on the first set of problems (with music) but are wearing down by the time they get to the second set (with no music). In this scenario, the observed decline in performance may be explained by fatigue. We now have an alternative explanation for the observed result: The decline in problem-solving performance may be explained by the removal of the music, or it may be explained by fatigue. Although the results of the study are clear, the interpretation of the results is questionable.

Recall that any factor allowing an alternative explanation for the results is a threat to internal validity. In this example, a third variable—fatigue—might explain the observed relation between background music and problem-solving performance. A third variable of this sort is called a confounding variable.

DEFINITION

> A **confounding variable** is an extraneous variable (usually unmonitored) that changes systematically along with the two variables being studied. A confounding variable provides an alternative explanation for the observed relationship between the two variables and, therefore, is a threat to internal validity.

Extraneous Variables, Confounding Variables, and Internal Validity

For a research study to have internal validity, there must be one, and only one, explanation for the research results. If a study includes a confounding variable, then there is an alternative explanation and the internal validity is threatened. Therefore, the key to achieve internal validity is to ensure that no extraneous variable is allowed to become a confounding variable. Because every research study involves thousands of extraneous variables, avoiding a confounding variable can be quite a task. Fortunately, however, confounding variables can be classified in a few general categories that make it somewhat easier to monitor them and keep them out of a research study. Before we examine the different categories of confounding variables, we look more closely at the general structure of a research study for which internal validity is a concern.

When the goal of a research study is to explain the relationship between two variables, it is common practice to use one of the variables to create different *treatment conditions* and then measure the second variable to obtain a set of *scores* within each condition. For example, Hallam, Price, and Katsarou (2002) conducted a second study in which they created three background conditions by playing pleasant, calming music in one room; unpleasant, aggressive music in one room; and no music in one room. The researchers then measured problem-solving performance (variable 2) for a group of students in each of the three rooms. Because they found differences in the problem-solving scores from one room to another, the researchers successfully demonstrated that problem solving depends on background music; that is, there is a relationship between the two variables. The general structure of this study is shown in Figure 6.3.

To ensure the internal validity of the study, it is essential that the only difference between the treatment conditions is the single variable that was used to define the conditions. In Figure 6.3, for example, the only difference between the three rooms is the background music. If there is any other factor that differentiates the treatment conditions, then the study has a confounding variable and the internal validity is threatened. For example, if the pleasant and calming music room is painted green, the no-music room yellow, and the unpleasant and aggressive music room red, then the color of the room is a confounding variable and therefore confounds the study. Specifically, any differences in performance from one room to another may be explained by the music but they also may be explained by room color. Similarly, if the three music conditions are administered at different times of day (morning, noon, and afternoon), then the time of day is a confounding variable.

In the following sections, we identify three different ways that internal validity can be threatened. That is, we examine three different categories of confounding variables: environmental variables, individual differences, and time-related variables.

Environmental Variables: General Threats to Internal Validity for All Studies

It is possible that variables in the general environment of the study—such as size of room, time of day, or gender of the experimenter—can become threats to internal validity. If one treatment is administered in a large, cheerful room and another treatment is administered in a small, dreary room, it is possible that the type of room (and not the treatment) is responsible for any differences between the scores in the two treatment conditions. Another example of this type of problem is a taste-test study that compared consumer preference for Coca-Cola versus Pepsi-Cola. In this study, individuals were asked to taste the colas in two different glasses and identify the one they preferred. The participants were not told which cola was in each glass but the glasses were marked with a Q and an M so

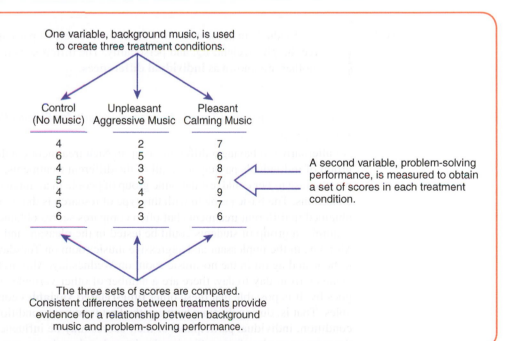

FIGURE 6.3

The Structure of a Research Study Designed to Explain the Relationship between Variables

In this example, the goal of the study is to demonstrate that changes in the background music produce changes in problem-solving performance.

One variable, background music, is used to create three treatment conditions.

Control (No Music)	Unpleasant Aggressive Music	Pleasant Calming Music
4	2	7
6	5	6
4	3	8
5	3	7
4	4	9
5	2	7
6	3	6

A second variable, problem-solving performance, is measured to obtain a set of scores in each treatment condition.

The three sets of scores are compared. Consistent differences between treatments provide evidence for a relationship between background music and problem-solving performance.

that the researcher could record the responses. However, the glass containing Coca-Cola was always marked with the letter Q, and the Pepsi-Cola glass was always marked with the letter M. Although the results indicated that people prefer Pepsi, an alternative explanation is that people prefer the glass labeled with the letter M (Huck & Sandler, 1979). In this study, the identifying letter was allowed to vary systematically with the brand of cola, so the letters M and Q became a confounding variable. To avoid confounding variables and ensure the internal validity of a research study, it is necessary that there are no systematic differences in the general environment from one treatment condition to another. Whenever a difference exists, there is an alternative explanation for the results and the internal validity of the study is threatened.

Participant Variables: Threats to Internal Validity for Studies Comparing Different Groups

Personal characteristics that can differ from one individual to another are known as **participant variables**. Examples are height, weight, gender, age, IQ, and personality. Because no two people (or animals) are identical, the individuals who participate in research studies will be different on a wide variety of participant variables. These differences, known as **individual differences**, are a part of every research study. For research studies that use a different group of individuals for each of the treatment conditions, the concern is that there may be consistent differences between groups for one or more participant variables. For example, the individuals in one treatment condition may be consistently smarter (or older, or faster) than the individuals in another treatment condition. In this situation, the participant variable becomes a confounding variable and is a threat to the internal validity of the study. Specifically, there are now two alternative explanations for any differences observed between treatments:

1. It is possible that the scores in one treatment are higher than the scores in another treatment because there are real differences between the treatments.
2. It is possible that the scores are different because the individuals in one treatment are smarter (or older, or faster) than those in the other treatment.

DEFINITION

> The individuals in a research study differ on a variety of participant variables such as age, height, weight, IQ, and personality. The differences from one participant to another are known as **individual differences**.

Time-Related Variables: Threats to Internal Validity for Studies Comparing One Group over Time

An alternative to having a different group in each treatment condition is to have the same group of individuals participate in all of the different treatments. In Figure 6.3, for example, the researcher could test the same group of people in all three of the background-music conditions. The basic problem with this type of research is that it not only compares scores obtained in different treatments but often compares scores obtained at different times. For example, a group of students could be tested in the pleasant and calming music room on Monday, in the unpleasant and aggressive music room on Tuesday, and then brought back to be tested again in the no-music room on Wednesday. Although the background music changes from day to day, there are a number of other variables that also change as time goes by. It is possible that these other **time-related variables** could be confounding variables. That is, during the time between the first treatment condition and the final treatment condition, individual participants or their scores may be influenced by factors other than the treatments. Any factor affecting the data other than the treatment is a threat to the internal validity of the study. Note that time-related variables can be participant variables, such

TABLE 6.6
General Threats to the Internal Validity of a Research Study

Source of the Threat	Description of the Threat
Environmental variables	General threats for all designs: If two treatments are administered in noticeably different environments, then the internal validity of the study is threatened. For example, if one treatment is administered in the morning and another at night, then any difference obtained may be explained by the time of day instead of treatment.
Participant variables: individual differences	Participant-related threats for designs that compare different groups: If the participants in one treatment condition have personal characteristics that are noticeably different from the participants in another treatment, then the internal validity of the study is threatened. For example, if the participants in one treatment are consistently older than the participants in another treatment, then any difference between the treatments may be explained by age instead of the treatment.
Time-related variables	Threats for designs that compare one group over time: Any variable that changes over time and influences the participants differently in one treatment than in another is a threat to the internal validity of the study. Possibilities are outside events or factors such as practice or fatigue. Any differences between treatments could be explained by the time-related variable.

as mood or physical state, outside events such as the weather, or factors like practice and fatigue that accumulate over time.

Table 6.6 provides a summary of the general threats to the internal validity of a research study.

LEARNING CHECK

1. Which of the following describes a variable that exists in a study but is not being directly examined?
   a. Independent
   b. Dependent
   c. Extraneous
   d. External

2. A study examining the relationship between humor and memory compares memory performance scores for one group presented with humorous sentences and a second group presented with nonhumorous sentences. The participants in one group are primarily 8-year-old students and those in the second group are primarily 10-year-old students. In this study, age is potentially a(n) _____ variable.
   a. independent
   b. dependent
   c. extraneous
   d. confounding

3. What aspect of a study is threatened if the participants are tested in one treatment condition at one time and then tested in a second treatment condition at a different time?
   a. Internal validity
   b. External validity
   c. Reliability
   d. Accuracy

Answers appear at the end of the chapter.

6.5   More about Internal and External Validity

LEARNING OBJECTIVE

LO8   Define *experimenter bias*, *demand characteristics*, and *reactivity*, and explain how these artifacts can threaten both internal and external validity.

The obvious goal of any research study is to maximize internal and external validity; that is, every researcher would like to be confident that the results of a study are true, and that the truth of the results extends beyond the particular individuals, conditions, and procedures used in the study. However, it is almost impossible to design and conduct a perfect research study. In fact, the steps taken to reduce or eliminate one threat to validity often increase others. As a result, designing and conducting research is usually a balancing act filled with choices and compromises that attempt to maximize validity and provide the best possible answer to the original research question. As we introduce specific research designs in later chapters, we discuss in more detail the choices and consequences involved in developing a research study. In particular, we consider the specific threats to internal and external validity associated with specific designs. For now, we outline some of the general constraints on validity to consider when planning or reading research, and discuss some of the necessary trade-offs between internal and external validity.

Balancing Internal and External Validity

To gain a high level of internal validity, a researcher must eliminate or minimize confounding variables. To accomplish this, a study must be tightly controlled so that no extraneous variables can influence the results. However, controlling a study may create a research environment that is so artificial and unnatural that results obtained within the study may not occur in the outside world. Thus, attempts to increase internal validity can reduce external validity. In general, the results from a tightly controlled research study should be interpreted as demonstrating what can happen but not necessarily what will happen in an outside environment where other variables are free to operate.

On the other hand, research that attempts to gain a high level of external validity often creates a research environment that closely resembles the outside world. The risk in this type of research comes from the fact that the real world is often a chaotic jumble of uncontrolled variables, especially in comparison with the highly regulated environment of a controlled study. Thus, striving for increased external validity can allow extraneous and potentially confounding variables into a study and thereby threaten internal validity.

In very general terms, there tends to be a trade-off between internal and external validity. Research that is very strong with respect to one kind of validity often tends to be relatively weak with respect to the second type. This basic relationship must be considered in planning a research study or evaluating someone else's work. Usually the purpose or goals of a study help you decide which type of validity is more important and which threats must be addressed.

Artifacts: Threats to Both Internal and External Validity

In Chapter 3 (pp. 73–76) we described an **artifact** as an external factor that may influence or distort measurements. Because an artifact can threaten the validity and reliability of measurements, it also can threaten both the internal and external validity of the research study. Experimenter bias and participant reactivity are just two of the many potential artifacts.

Experimenter Bias

Experimenter bias occurs when the experimenter's expectations or personal beliefs regarding the outcome of the study influence the findings of a study. Experimenter bias threatens external validity because the results obtained in a study may be specific to the experimenter who has the expectations. The results may not be the same with an experimenter who did not have such a bias. Experimenter bias also threatens internal validity because the data may show a pattern that appears to be a real treatment effect but was actually caused by the experimenter's influence. As discussed in Chapter 3 (p. 74), **single-blind** and **double-blind** studies minimize the potential for experimenter bias.

Demand Characteristics and Participant Reactivity

Also discussed in Chapter 3 (pp. 75–76), the combination of **demand characteristics** and participant **reactivity** can change a participant's normal behavior and thereby influence the outcome of the study. Recall that demand characteristics refer to any of the potential cues or features of a study that (1) suggest to the participants what the purpose and hypothesis is and (2) influence the participants to respond or behave in a certain way. Also recall that reactivity occurs when participants modify their natural behavior in response to the fact that they are participating in a research study or the knowledge that they are being measured. Some participants may assume *subject roles* becoming overly cooperative or uncooperative, and some may become defensive. Additional discussion of the subject roles adopted by research participants is presented in Chapter 3 (p. 76). If the participants are not acting normally, the internal validity of the study is threatened because the obtained results can be explained by participant reactivity instead of the different treatment conditions. Also, demand characteristics and reactivity can threaten the external validity of the study because the results obtained under the influence of demand characteristics may not generalize to a new situation where the environmental demands are different. Recall also from Chapter 3 that reactivity is particularly a problem in studies conducted in a **laboratory** setting, where participants are fully aware that they are participating in a study. In contrast, in a **field** study individuals are observed in their natural environment and are much less likely to know that they are being investigated. Laboratories and field studies are discussed in more detail in Chapter 7 (pp. 180–181). Steps to help reduce the effects of reactivity are discussed in Chapter 3 (p. 76).

Exaggerated Variables

Most research is undertaken in the hope of demonstrating a relationship between variables. To accomplish this goal, a research study often maximizes the differences for one of the variables to increase the likelihood of revealing a relationship with a second variable. In particular, researchers often exaggerate the differences between treatment conditions to increase the chance that the scores obtained in one treatment are noticeably different from the scores obtained in another treatment. To evaluate the effects of temperature on learning, for example, a researcher probably would not compare a 70-degree room and a 72-degree room. The study has a greater chance of success if it involves comparison of 70 degrees and 90 degrees. Although the larger temperature difference is likely to reveal a relationship between temperature and learning, the researcher should be cautious about generalizing the result to a normal classroom situation in which 20-degree temperature changes are unlikely.

Validity and Individual Research Strategies

Because different research strategies have different goals, they tend to have different levels of internal validity and external validity. For example, descriptive, correlational, and nonexperimental studies tend to examine variables in their natural, real-world settings and, therefore, tend to have relatively good external validity. On the other hand, experimental research tends to be rigorously controlled and monitored and, therefore, has high internal validity. Quasi-experimental studies tend to fall somewhere in between; they attempt to mimic the control of true experiments, which helps internal validity, and they tend to take place in applied, real-world situations, which helps external validity.

LEARNING CHECK

1. Cues given to participants about how they are expected to behave define which of the following terms?
   a. Reactivity
   b. Demand characteristics
   c. Experimenter bias
   d. Volunteer bias

2. Experimental research studies tend to have very _____ internal validity but often have relatively _____ external validity.
   a. high; low
   b. low; high
   c. high; high
   d. low; low

Answers appear at the end of the chapter.

CHAPTER SUMMARY

At this point, you should review the learning objectives presented at the beginning of each section and be sure that you have mastered each objective.

There are five general categories of research strategies: experimental, quasi-experimental, nonexperimental, correlational, and descriptive. The experimental strategy assesses whether there is a causal relationship between two variables. The quasi-experimental strategy attempts to obtain evidence for a causal relationship between two variables, but this strategy cannot unambiguously demonstrate cause and effect. The nonexperimental strategy examines relationships between variables by demonstrating differences between groups or treatment conditions. The correlational strategy determines whether there is a relationship or association between two variables by measuring both variables for each individual. The descriptive strategy assesses the variables being examined as they exist naturally.

Central to selecting a research strategy and design is validity, which is concerned with the truth of the research or the accuracy of the results. Any factor that raises doubts about the research results or the interpretation of the results is a threat to validity. Questions about the validity of research are traditionally grouped into two general categories: external validity and internal validity. A study has external validity if the results of the study can be generalized to people, settings, times, measures, and characteristics other than those in the study. The generality of a study's findings may be a function of virtually any characteristic of the study, including the participants or subjects, the features of the study, and the features of the measures. A research study has internal validity if it produces a single, unambiguous explanation for the relationship between variables. Any factor that allows for an alternative explanation of the relationship is a threat to the internal validity of the research. Confounding variables are the most common threats to internal validity. Artifacts threaten both internal and external validity.

There tends to be a trade-off between internal and external validity. Research that is very strong with respect to one kind of validity is often relatively weak with respect to the second type. This basic relationship must be considered in planning a research study or evaluating someone else's work. Research strategies also vary in terms of validity. Descriptive, correlational, and nonexperimental studies tend to have high external validity and relatively low internal validity; experimental studies tend to have high internal validity and relatively low external validity. Quasi-experimental studies tend to fall in between these extremes.

KEY WORDS

research strategy	external validity	threat to internal validity	individual differences
research design	threat to external validity	extraneous variable	
research procedure	internal validity	confounding variable	

EXERCISES

The exercises are identified with specific learning objectives and are intended to assess your mastery of the objectives. You should be aware that exam items are also generated to assess learning objectives.

1. In addition to the key words, you should also be able to define each of the following terms:
   descriptive research strategy
   linear relationship
   curvilinear relationship
   positive relationship
   negative relationship
   correlational research strategy
   experimental research strategy
   quasi-experimental research strategy
   nonexperimental research strategy
   selection bias
   volunteer bias
   novelty effect
   multiple treatment interference
   sensitization, or assessment sensitization, or pretest sensitization
   participant variables
   time-related variables
   fatigue
   practice
   artifact
   experimenter bias
   single-blind
   double-blind
   demand characteristics
   reactivity
   laboratory
   field

2. (**LO1**) For each of the following scenarios, identify which research strategy is used: descriptive, correlational, experimental, or nonexperimental. (Note: For now, do not differentiate between nonexperimental and quasi-experimental studies. The distinction between them is discussed in Chapter 10.)

   a. Dr. Jones conducts a study examining the relationship between sugar consumption and activity level for 5-year-old children. Sugar consumption scores are obtained by interviewing each child's parents and activity level is measured by observing the children during an outdoor play period.

   b. Dr. Jones conducts a study examining the relationship between sugar consumption and activity level for 5-year-old children. Sugar consumption scores are obtained by interviewing each child's parents. Based on the interview results, the children are divided into two groups: those who consume large amounts of sugar and those who eat relatively small amounts. Then activity level is measured by observing the children during an outdoor play period to determine if there is any difference between the two groups.

   c. Dr. Jones conducts a study examining the relationship between sugar consumption and activity level for 5-year-old children. A group of children is randomly separated into two groups. One group is given a sugary cereal for breakfast and the other is given oatmeal. Activity level is then measured by observing the children during an outdoor play period to determine if there is any difference between the two groups.

   d. Dr. Jones conducts a study examining activity level for 5-year-old children. Each afternoon for 1 week, a group of children in a childcare center is observed during a 30-minute period while they play outdoors. Activity level for each child is recorded during the 30-minute period.

3. (**LO1**) How is the descriptive strategy different from the other four research strategies?

4. (**LO2**) Explain the difference among the terms *research strategy*, *research design*, and *research procedure*.

5. (**LO3**) A researcher conducts a study with 6-year-old children at a summer computer camp for gifted

children. However, the researcher suspects that different results would be obtained if the study were conducted with regular 6-year-old children. Does this study have a problem with internal validity or external validity?

6. (**LO4**) A researcher finds that college students are more anxious near final exams in December than at the beginning of the semester in September. However, it is not clear whether the anxiety is caused by exams or by the change in season. Does this study have a problem with internal validity or external validity?

7. (**LO5**) Explain how using college students as participants in a study may limit the external validity of a study's research findings.

8. (**LO5**) What is the novelty effect, and how does it affect a study's external validity?

9. (**LO6**) Suppose that you wake up in the morning with all the symptoms of a head cold. You take a cold pill and eat a big bowl of your mother's chicken soup. By midday your cold symptoms are gone, and you are feeling much better. Can you conclude that the chicken soup cured your cold? Explain why or why not.

10. (**LO7**) What is the primary threat to internal validity for a study that compares different groups of participants?

11. (**LO8**) Describe how experimenter bias can be a threat to internal validity; that is, how can experimenter bias provide an explanation for the scores in one condition being higher than the scores in a second condition?

12. (**LO8**) Describe how participant reactivity can be a threat to external validity; that is, how can participant reactivity limit the ability to generalize research results?

13. (**LO5** and **7**) Selection bias and individual differences are both potential problems dealing with the participants in a study.
    a. Identify which of these is a threat to internal validity and which is a threat to external validity, and describe how each one is a threat.
    b. Suppose that you were planning a research study in which the individuals who participate will be put into separate groups and each group will participate in one of the treatment conditions that are being compared. Explain how you could minimize the risk of selection bias and how you could minimize the risk that individual differences become a confounding variable.

LEARNING CHECK ANSWERS

Section 6.1	Section 6.2	Section 6.3	Section 6.4	Section 6.5
1. a, 2. a, 3. b	1. b, 2. b, 3. a	1. a, 2. b	1. c, 2. d, 3. a	1. b, 2. a

The Experimental Research Strategy

© Nathan Jasowiak / Shutterstock

CHAPTER LEARNING OBJECTIVES

LO1 Describe the general purpose of an experimental research study, differentiate experiments from other types of research, and identify examples of experiments.

LO2 Define *independent, dependent,* and *extraneous variables* and identify examples of each in an experiment.

LO3 Describe the third-variable problem and the directionality problem, identify these problems when they appear in a research study, and explain why they must be eliminated before an experiment can demonstrate a cause-and-effect relationship.

LO4 Explain why manipulation of an independent variable is a critical component of an experiment.

LO5 Explain why control of extraneous variables is a critical component of an experiment.

LO6 Explain how an extraneous variable can become a confounding variable and identify confounding variables when they appear in a research study.

LO7 Describe the three primary techniques for controlling extraneous variables (holding constant, matching, and randomization), explain how each one works, and identify these techniques when they appear in a research report.

LO8 Describe the purpose for control conditions in experimental research, define the two basic types of control conditions (*no-treatment* and *placebo*), and identify control conditions when they appear in research reports.

LO9 Explain when a manipulation check is needed, describe what it is intended to accomplish, and identify a manipulation check when one appears in a research report.

LO10 Define *field studies* and *simulation*, explain why they are used as alternatives to laboratory experiments, and identify these techniques when they appear in a research report.

CHAPTER OVERVIEW

In this chapter, we discuss details of the experimental research strategy. The goal of experimental research is to establish and demonstrate a cause-and-effect relationship between two variables. To accomplish this goal, an experiment must manipulate one of the two variables and isolate the two variables being examined from the influence of other variables. Consider the following example.

In recent years, a number of research studies have examined the relationship between violent video games and aggressive behavior. For example, Gentile, Lynch, Linder, and Walsh (2004) surveyed over 600 eighth- and ninth-grade students asking about their gaming habits and other behaviors. Their results clearly showed that the adolescents who were exposed to more video game violence were more hostile, had more frequent arguments with teachers, more physical fights, and poorer performance in school than their peers who had less exposure to video game violence. Although this study established a strong relationship between violent video games and negative behaviors, the authors could not conclude that the games were responsible for *causing* the behaviors. It is possible, for example, that students who were already more aggressive and disruptive choose to play games with more violence and their more passive peers prefer less violence in their video games. In other words, it is possible that the violent games are not causing students to become aggressive; instead, it is the preexisting level of aggressiveness that is causing students to play certain games.

Other researchers took a different approach to examining the relationship between video game violence and aggressive behavior. For example, Polman, de Castro, and van Aken (2008) randomly divided a sample of 19 boys, all around 10 years old, between two treatment conditions: playing a violent video game or playing a nonviolent game. After the game-playing session, the children went to a free-play period and were monitored for aggressive behaviors, which were defined as hitting, kicking, pushing, frightening, name calling, fighting, quarreling, or teasing another child. The results clearly showed that the boys in the violent game condition displayed significantly more aggression than did the boys in the nonviolent game condition. Based on this result, the authors confidently concluded that the violence in the video games was responsible for causing the increase in aggressive behavior.

Notice that the Polman et al. study makes a cause-and-effect conclusion but the Gentile et al. study does not. How is this possible? The answer is in the details of the two studies. Specifically, the Polman et al. study used the experimental research strategy and the Gentile study did not. In this chapter, we discuss experimental research, and identify the characteristics that define true experiments and differentiate these studies from other kinds of research.

7.1 Cause-and-Effect Relationships

LEARNING OBJECTIVES

LO1 Describe the general purpose of an experimental research study, differentiate experiments from other types of research, and identify examples of experiments.

LO2 Define *independent*, *dependent*, and *extraneous variables* and identify examples of each in an experiment.

LO3 Describe the third-variable problem and the directionality problem, identify these problems when they appear in a research study, and explain why they must be eliminated before an experiment can demonstrate a cause-and-effect relationship.

In Chapter 6, we identified five basic strategies for investigating variables and their relationships: descriptive, correlational, experimental, quasi-experimental, and nonexperimental. In this chapter, we discuss details of the experimental research strategy. (The nonexperimental and quasi-experimental strategies are discussed in Chapter 10, the correlational strategy in Chapter 12, and the descriptive strategy in Chapter 13.)

> More complex experiments may involve several variables. In its simplest form, however, an experiment focuses on only one variable that may cause changes in one other variable.

The goal of the **experimental research strategy** is to establish the existence of a cause-and-effect relationship between two variables. To rule out the possibility of a coincidental relationship, an **experiment**, often called a **true experiment**, must demonstrate that changes in one variable are directly responsible for causing changes in the second variable. To accomplish this goal, an experimental study contains the following four basic elements, which are also shown in Figure 7.1:

1. *Manipulation.* The researcher manipulates one variable by changing its value to create a set of two or more treatment conditions.
2. *Measurement.* A second variable is measured for a group of participants to obtain a set of scores in each treatment condition.
3. *Comparison.* The scores in one treatment condition are compared with the scores in another treatment condition. Consistent differences between treatments provide evidence that the manipulation has caused changes in the scores (see Box 7.1).
4. *Control.* All other variables are controlled to be sure that they do not influence the two variables being examined.

Although the term *experiment* is often used casually to describe any scientific research study, only those studies satisfying these four requirements are actually real experiments.

> Caution! Not all research studies are experiments.

Earlier in the chapter, for example, we described a study by Polman et al. (2008) examining the relationship between video game violence and aggressive behavior. In the study, one group of boys was given a violent video game and another group received a nonviolent game. Notice that the researchers are *manipulating* the violence of the game by changing from violent to nonviolent. They then *measured* the behavior of the boys during a free-play period after the video games. Aggressive behavior for boys with the violent game was then *compared* with behavior for boys with the nonviolent game. During the study, the researchers *controlled* other variables by ensuring that both groups consisted of 10-year-old boys (same age and same gender) and randomly assigning participant to the different games to ensure that other variables were balanced across the two conditions. The results showed more aggressive behavior after playing a violent game than after playing a nonviolent game.

FIGURE 7.1

The Basic Components of an Experimental Research Study

An experiment involves manipulating one variable, measuring a second variable, comparing the scores between treatments, and controlling all other variables.

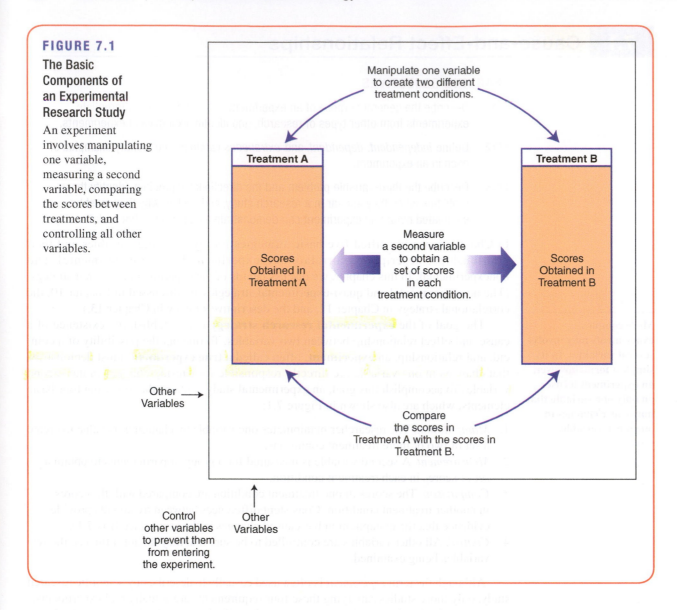

Manipulate one variable to create two different treatment conditions.

Treatment A

Scores Obtained in Treatment A

Measure a second variable to obtain a set of scores in each treatment condition.

Treatment B

Scores Obtained in Treatment B

Other Variables

Compare the scores in Treatment A with the scores in Treatment B.

Control other variables to prevent them from entering the experiment.

Other Variables

Terminology for the Experimental Research Strategy

In an experiment, the variable that is manipulated by the researcher is called the **independent variable**. Typically, the independent variable is manipulated by creating a set of **treatment conditions**. The specific conditions that are used in the experiment are called the **levels** of the independent variable. The variable that is measured in each of the treatment conditions is called the **dependent variable**. All other variables in the study are **extraneous variables**. For the Polman et al. (2008) video violence example, the independent variable is the level of violence in the video game, and there are two levels: violent and nonviolent. The dependent variable is the aggressive behavior observed after each of the two games. Other variables, such as the participants' personality, height, and weight, as well as environmental variables, such as the season and the weather conditions, are extraneous variables.

BOX 7.1 Statistical Significance

Whenever you compare two sets of scores that were obtained at different times or came from different people, the two sets will never be *exactly* the same. Small differences from one person to another (or from one time to another) always produce small differences between the two sets of scores. As long as the differences are small and random (one set does not have consistently larger scores than the other), they probably are meaningless and can be attributed to chance. For example, if you drew a line through the center of your classroom and computed the average age for students on the right side and for students on the left side, the two averages would be different. However, the age difference is simply the result of chance and should not be interpreted as evidence for some mysterious force that causes older students to gravitate toward one side of the room.

In an experiment, the scores in one treatment condition are compared with the scores in another condition. If there is a difference between the scores, however, you cannot automatically conclude that the treatments have *caused* a difference. As we noted earlier, the difference may simply be the result of chance. Before you can interpret the difference as a cause-and-effect relationship, you must conduct a hypothesis test and demonstrate that the difference is statistically significant. A significant result means that the difference is large enough and consistent enough for a hypothesis test to rule out chance as a plausible explanation, and thereby conclude that the difference must have been caused by the treatments. Chapter 15 presents a detailed presentation of hypothesis testing and statistical significance. For now, you should realize that any difference between treatment conditions must be evaluated statistically before you can conclude that the difference was caused by the treatments.

DEFINITIONS

The **experimental research strategy** establishes the existence of a cause-and-effect relationship between two variables. To accomplish this goal, an experiment manipulates one variable while a second variable is measured and other variables are controlled.

An **experiment** or a **true experiment** attempts to show that changes in one variable are directly responsible for changes in a second variable.

In an experiment, the **independent variable** is the variable manipulated by the researcher. In behavioral research, the independent variable usually consists of two or more treatment conditions to which participants are exposed.

In an experiment, a **treatment condition** is a situation or environment characterized by one specific value of the manipulated variable. An experiment contains two or more treatment conditions that differ according to the values of the manipulated variable.

Levels are the different values of the independent variable selected to create and define the treatment conditions.

The **dependent variable** is the variable that is observed for changes to assess the effects of manipulating the independent variable. The dependent variable is typically a behavior or a response measured in each treatment condition.

Extraneous variables are all variables in the study other than the independent and dependent variables.

Finally, you should note that in this book, we use the terms *experiment* and *true experiment* in a well-defined technical sense. Specifically, a research study is called an experiment only if it satisfies the specific set of requirements that are detailed in this chapter. Thus, some research studies qualify as true experiments whereas other studies, such as correlational studies, do not. In casual conversation, people tend to refer to any kind of research study as an experiment. ("Scientists" do "experiments" in the "laboratory.") Although this casual description of research activity is acceptable in some contexts, we are careful to distinguish between experiments and other research studies. Therefore, whenever the word experiment is used in this text, it is in this more precise, technical sense. This chapter introduces the characteristics that differentiate a true experiment from other kinds of research studies.

Causation and the Third-Variable Problem

One problem for experimental research is that variables rarely exist in isolation. In natural circumstances, changes in one variable are typically accompanied by changes in many other related variables. For example, in the video game violence experiment (p. 158), the researchers manipulated the level of violence in the game. Under normal circumstances, however, the violence level of the game depends on the set of games that the child owns, and which game is selected on a specific day and time. As a result, in natural circumstances researchers are often confronted with a tangled network of interrelated variables. Although it is relatively easy to demonstrate that one variable is related to another, it is much more difficult to establish the underlying cause of the relationship. To determine the nature of the relationships among variables, particularly to establish the causal influence of one event on another, it is essential that an experiment separate and isolate the specific variables being studied. The task of teasing apart and separating a set of naturally interconnected variables is the heart of the experimental strategy.

Earlier we noted that a relationship between two variables can be simply coincidental and not causal. For example, if a researcher measures weight and mathematical ability for a group of children who are 6–12 years old, there will be a strong relationship between the two variables: as weight increases from child to child, mathematical ability also tends to increase. However, this does not mean that an increase in weight causes an increase in mathematics ability. Instead, it is the age of the children that is responsible for the observed relationship: As age increases from 6 to 12, the children tend to weigh more and as age increases from 6 to 12, children tend to have more mathematics education. This is an example of the **third-variable problem**. Although a study may establish that two variables are related, it does not necessarily mean that there is a direct (causal) relationship between the two variables. It is always possible that a third (unidentified) variable is controlling the two variables and is responsible for producing the observed relation. For example, although there is a relationship between weight and mathematical ability for children, common sense suggests that this is not a causal relationship. A more reasonable interpretation is that another variable, such as age, is responsible for the systematic differences in both weight and mathematical ability.

Causation and the Directionality Problem

A second problem for researchers attempting to demonstrate cause-and-effect relationships is demonstrated in the Gentile et al. (2004) video gaming example described at the beginning of this chapter. In this study the researchers simply asked the students about their video game habits and other behaviors. Although the study found higher aggressive behavior for students who reported using more violent games, the results do not support a conclusion that an increase in video game violence causes an increase in aggressive behavior. Instead, it could be that aggressive behavior causes an increase in video game violence. As noted earlier, it is possible that students who are naturally more aggressive prefer to play games that are more violent.

This example is a demonstration of the **directionality problem**. Although a research study may establish a relationship between two variables, the existence of a relationship does not always explain the direction of the relationship. The remaining problem is to determine which variable is the cause and which is the effect.

Controlling Nature

The preceding examples demonstrated that we cannot establish a cause-and-effect relationship by simply observing two variables. In particular, the researcher must actively unravel the tangle of relationships that exists naturally. To establish a cause-and-effect relationship, an experiment must control nature, essentially creating an unnatural situation wherein the two variables being examined are isolated from the influence of other variables and wherein the exact character of a relationship can be seen clearly.

We acknowledge that it is somewhat paradoxical that experiments must interfere with natural phenomena to gain a better understanding of nature. How can observations made in an artificial, carefully controlled experiment reveal any truth about nature? One simple answer is that the contrived character of experiments is a necessity: To see beneath the surface, it is necessary to dig. A more complete answer, however, is that there is a difference between the conditions in which an experiment is conducted and the results of the experiment. Just because an experiment takes place in an unnatural environment does not necessarily imply that the results are unnatural.

For example, you are probably familiar with the law of gravity, which states that all objects fall at the same rate independent of mass. You are, no doubt, equally familiar with the "natural" fact that if you drop a brick and a feather from the roof of a building, they will not fall at the same rate. Other factors in the natural world, such as air resistance, conceal the true effects of gravity. To demonstrate the law of gravity, we must create an artificial, controlled environment (specifically, a vacuum) wherein forces such as air resistance have been eliminated. This fact does not invalidate the law of gravity; the law accurately describes the underlying force of gravity and explains the behavior of falling objects, even though natural conditions may conceal the basic principle. In the same way, the goal of any experiment is to reveal the natural underlying mechanisms and relationships that may be otherwise obscured. Nonetheless, there is always a risk that the conditions of an experiment are so unnatural that the results are questionable. To use the terminology presented in Chapter 6, an experimenter can be so intent on ensuring internal validity that external validity is compromised. Researchers are aware of this problem and have developed techniques to increase the external validity (natural character) of experiments. We discuss some of these techniques in Section 7.5.

LEARNING CHECK   1.   How do studies using the experimental research strategy differ from other types of research?
  (a) Only experiments can demonstrate a cause-and-effect relationship between variables.
  b. Only experiments involve comparing two or more groups of scores.
  c. Only experiments can demonstrate that relationships exist between variables and provide a description of the relationship.
  d. Only experiments can demonstrate a bidirectional relationship between variables.

2. Dr. Jones is interested in studying how indoor lighting can influence people's moods during the winter. A sample of 100 households is selected. Fifty of the homes are randomly assigned to the bright-light condition where Dr. Jones replaces all the lights with 100-watt bulbs. In the other 50 houses, all the lights are changed to 60-watt bulbs. After two months, Dr. Jones measures the level of depression for the people living in the houses. In this example, how many dependent variables are there?
    a. 100
    b. 50
    c. 2
    d. 1

3. Research indicates the people who suffer from depression also tend to experience insomnia. However, it is unclear whether the depression causes insomnia or the lack of sleep causes depression. What problem is demonstrated by this example?
    a. the directionality problem
    b. the third-variable problem
    c. the extraneous variable problem
    d. the manipulation-check problem

Answers appear at the end of the chapter.

7.2   Distinguishing Elements of an Experiment

LEARNING OBJECTIVES

LO4   Explain why manipulation of an independent variable is a critical component of an experiment.

LO5   Explain why control of extraneous variables is a critical component of an experiment.

LO6   Explain how an extraneous variable can become a confounding variable and identify confounding variables when they appear in a research study.

The general purpose of the experimental research strategy is to demonstrate the existence of a cause-and-effect relationship between two variables. That is, an experiment attempts to demonstrate that changing one variable (the independent variable) causes changes in a second variable (the dependent variable). This general purpose can be broken down into two specific goals.

1. The first step in demonstrating a cause-and-effect relationship is to demonstrate that the "cause" happens before the "effect" occurs. In the context of an experiment, this means that you must show that a change in the value of the independent variable is followed by a change in the dependent variable. To accomplish this, a researcher first manipulates the independent variable and then observes the dependent variable to see if it also changes.
2. To establish that one specific variable is responsible for changes in another variable, an experiment must rule out the possibility that the changes are caused by an extraneous variable.

Earlier, we described the experimental research strategy as consisting of four basic elements: manipulation, measurement, comparison, and control. Two of these elements, measurement and comparison, are also components in a number of other research strategies. However, the two elements that are unique to experiments and distinguish experimental research from other strategies are manipulation of one variable and control of extraneous variables. These two unique elements of experimental research are discussed in the following sections.

Manipulation

A distinguishing characteristic of the experimental strategy is that the researcher manipulates one of the variables under study. **Manipulation** is accomplished by first deciding which specific values of the independent variable you would like to examine. Then you create a series of treatment conditions corresponding to those specific values. As a result, the independent variable changes from one treatment condition to another. For example, if you wanted to investigate the effect of temperature (independent variable) on appetite (dependent variable), you would first determine which levels of temperature you wanted to study. Assuming that 70 degrees Fahrenheit is a "normal" temperature, you might want to compare 60 degrees, 70 degrees, and 80 degrees to see how warmer- or colder-than-normal temperatures affect appetite. You would then set the room temperature to 60 degrees for one treatment condition, change it to 70 degrees for another condition, and change it again to 80 degrees for the third condition. A group of participants or subjects is then observed in each treatment condition to obtain measurements of appetite.

DEFINITION

> In an experiment, **manipulation** consists of identifying the specific values of the independent variable to be examined and then creating a set of treatment conditions corresponding to the set of identified values.

Manipulation and the Directionality Problem

The primary purpose of manipulation is to allow researchers to determine the direction of a relationship. Suppose, for example, there is a systematic relationship between temperature and ice-cream sales at major-league baseball stadiums, so that temperature and ice-cream sales rise and fall together. This relationship is shown in Figure 7.2. As we have noted, however, simply observing that a relationship exists does not explain the relationship and certainly does not identify the direction of the relationship. One technique for determining the direction of a relationship is to manipulate one of the variables (cause it to increase and decrease) and watch the second variable to determine whether it is affected by the manipulation. We could, for example, select enclosed baseball stadiums and use the heating/cooling system to manipulate the temperature while monitoring ice-cream consumption. In this situation, it is reasonable to expect that increasing the temperature would produce an increase in ice-cream consumption. On the other hand, we could manipulate ice-cream consumption (hand out free ice cream) and monitor temperature. In this case, it is unlikely that more ice-cream consumption would result in higher temperatures. Note that manipulation of the individual variables allows us to demonstrate the direction of the relationship: Changes in temperature are responsible for causing changes in ice-cream consumption, not the other way around. In general, whenever there is a relationship between two variables, a researcher can use manipulation to determine which variable is the cause and which is the effect.

For an example more closely related to psychology, consider the relationship between depression and insomnia. It has been observed repeatedly that people suffering from depression also tend to have problems sleeping. However, the observed relationship does not answer the causal question, "Does depression cause sleep problems, or does the lack of sleep cause depression?" Although it may be difficult to manipulate depression

FIGURE 7.2

Using Manipulation to Determine the Direction of a Cause-and-Effect Relationship

Ice-cream consumption and temperature rise and fall together. Manipulating temperature (increasing or decreasing) causes a corresponding change in ice-cream consumption. However, increasing ice-cream consumption by handing out free ice cream has no influence on temperature.

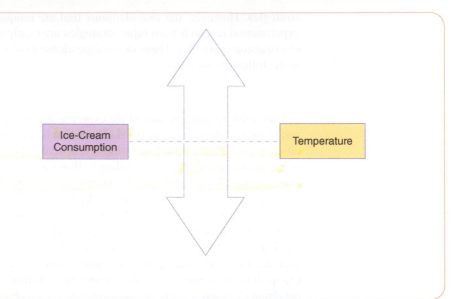

directly, it certainly is possible to manipulate the amount of sleep. One group of individuals, for example, could be allowed only 4 hours of sleep each night and a comparison group allowed 8 hours. After a week, depression scores could be obtained and compared for the two groups. If the 4-hour group is more depressed, this is evidence that a lack of sleep causes depression. Notice that the researcher is not directly manipulating depression. Instead, the researcher hopes and expects that manipulating the amount of sleep will produce a change in depression.

Manipulation and the Third-Variable Problem

A second purpose for manipulation is to help researchers control the influence of outside variables. In an experiment, researchers must actively manipulate the independent variable rather than simply waiting for the variable to change by itself. If you let variables change on their own, it is always possible that other variables are also changing, and these other variables may be responsible for the relationship you are observing. Earlier, we speculated about a relationship between ice-cream consumption and temperature: Increasing temperature is related to increased ice-cream consumption. Similarly, there is a relationship between temperature and crime (Cohn & Rotton, 2000). These two relationships are shown together in Figure 7.3. Notice that increasing temperature is related to both an increase in ice-cream consumption and an increase in crime. If a researcher simply observed ice-cream consumption and crime rates, the results would indicate a strong relationship: Increases in ice-cream consumption are accompanied by increases in crime. However, the existence of a relationship does not necessarily mean that there is a direct connection between the two variables. As in Figure 7.3, it is possible that a third, outside variable is responsible for the apparent relationship. The lack of any direct connection between variables can be demonstrated using manipulation. In this example, we could manipulate ice-cream consumption (hand out free ice cream) and monitor crime rates. Presumably, increasing ice-cream consumption would have no influence on crime rates. Similarly, we could manipulate crime rates (start a massive police initiative) and monitor ice-cream consumption. Again, it is unlikely that changing the crime rate would have any effect on ice-cream consumption. Notice that we are using manipulation to show that there is not a direct cause-and-effect relationship between crime and ice-cream consumption.

FIGURE 7.3

Manipulation and the Third-Variable Problem

Ice-cream consumption and crime rate rise and fall together as temperature increases and decreases. However, there is no direct connection between ice-cream consumption and crime rate. Manipulating either of the two variables will have no influence on the other.

Specifically, you can manipulate either crime rate or ice-cream consumption and it will have no effect on the other variable.

In an experiment, the researcher is responsible for causing the independent variable to change by direct manipulation. In this way, the researcher can be confident that changes in the independent variable are not being caused by some outside variable (a third variable) that could influence the outcome of the study. Thus, the act of manipulation helps eliminate one aspect of the third-variable problem in an experiment.

Control

The second distinguishing characteristic of an experiment is control of other variables; specifically, variables other than the independent and dependent variables. To accurately evaluate the relationship between two specific variables, a researcher must ensure that the observed relationship is not contaminated by the influence of other variables.

Control and the Third-Variable Problem

In general, the purpose of an experiment is to show that the manipulated variable is responsible for causing the changes observed in the dependent variable. To accomplish this, an experiment must rule out any other possible explanation for the observed changes; that is, eliminate all **confounding variables**. In Chapter 6 (p. 148) we defined a *confounding variable* as a third variable that is allowed to change systematically along with the two variables being studied. In the context of an experiment, the particular concern is to identify and control any third variable that changes systematically along with the independent variable and has the potential to influence the dependent variable.

A confounding variable and the need for control are illustrated in the following example. A researcher designs a study to determine whether preschool children prefer sweetened or unsweetened cereal. For one group, the researcher uses a box of colorful sweetened cereal and for the other group, a box of tan-colored unsweetened cereal. The results showed that the preschoolers ate more of the sweetened colorful cereal and therefore prefer the sweetened cereal.

However, you should realize that this study contains a potentially confounding variable. Specifically, the color of the cereal varies systematically with the sweetness of the cereal. In this experiment, it is impossible to tell whether the preference for the colorful sweetened cereal is caused by the color or the sweetness. The structure of this study, including the confounding variable, is shown in Figure 7.4.

To establish an unambiguous causal relationship between sweetness and preference, it is necessary to eliminate the possible influence of the confounding variable. For this study, one solution is to eliminate the color variable. For example, one group is given colorful sweetened cereal and the second group gets colorful unsweetened cereal. The structure of the controlled experiment is shown in Figure 7.5. In the controlled experiment, the confounding variable has been eliminated, and the true relation between sweetness and cereal preference can be observed.

The cereal example provides an opportunity to make another important point. Specifically, the independent variable in an experiment is determined by the hypothesis. Because the original study intended to examine the effect of sweetness on cereal preference, the independent variable was the sweetness of the cereal. If we wanted to examine the effect of color on cereal preference, then the independent variable would have been the color of the cereal. In a study in which color was the independent variable, the sweetness of the cereal would be a confounding variable. Thus, the classification as an independent variable or a confounding variable depends on the hypothesis.

Extraneous Variables and Confounding Variables

Although the focus in an experiment is on two specific variables, the independent and the dependent variables, there are thousands of other variables that exist within any experiment. Different individuals enter the experiment with different backgrounds, ages, genders, heights, weights, IQs, personalities, and the like. As time passes, room temperature

---

FIGURE 7.4

Confounding Variables

Because the sweetness of the cereal and the color of the cereal vary together systematically, they are confounded, and it is impossible to determine which variable is responsible for the differences in preferences.

Is the difference in preference caused by the change from sweetened to unsweetened, or by the change from colorful to tan colored?

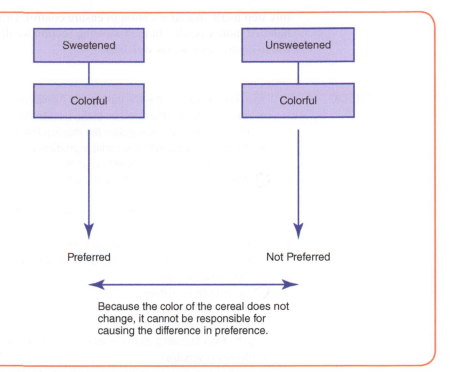

FIGURE 7.5

Eliminating a Confounding Variable

Because the level of sweetness of the cereal does not change systematically with the color of the cereal, the two variables are not confounded. In this study, you can be confident that the level of sweetness (not color) is responsible for the differences in preference.

and lighting fluctuate, weather changes, people get tired or bored or excited or happy, they forget things or remember things, and develop itches or aches and pains that distract them from the task at hand. Any of these extraneous variables have the potential to become a confounding variable.

With thousands of potentially confounding variables, however, the problem of controlling (or even monitoring) every extraneous variable appears insurmountable. Close inspection of the definition of a confounding variable (see Chapter 6, p. 148), however, reveals some hints. Note that a confounding variable has two important characteristics:

1. First, an extraneous variable becomes a confounding variable only if it influences the dependent variable. Something totally unrelated to the dependent variable is not a threat. In most experiments, for example, the participants are wearing different types of shoes (sneakers, flats, heels, loafers, or sandals); however, it is unlikely that the type of shoe has any influence on the dependent variable. Thus, it is not necessary to take any steps to control the shoe variable.

2. Second, a confounding variable must vary systematically with the independent variable. A variable that changes randomly, with no relation to the independent variable, is not a threat. The concept of random versus systematic change is an important part of control.

The first step in controlling extraneous variables is to identify those variables most likely to influence the dependent variable. This identification process is based primarily on common sense, simple logical reasoning, and past experience in controlling extraneous variables. For example, if you are measuring memory performance, IQ is a reasonable choice as a potentially confounding variable. If very young and/or very old participants are used, then age is also a variable that could reasonably affect memory performance. If memory performance is being measured in different settings or at different times, these variables also could influence performance. (A loud, busy room can create distractions that lower performance, as opposed to a quiet, empty room.) The variables you identify at this step merit special attention to ensure control. Other variables are not ignored but are handled more casually. In the following section we discuss the techniques that researcher use to control extraneous variables.

1. In an experiment, what is the purpose for manipulating the independent variable?
   a. It helps establish the direction of the relationship by showing that the dependent variable changes when you manipulate the independent variable.
   b. It helps eliminate the third-variable problem because you decide when to manipulate rather than waiting for the variable to change.
   c. It helps establish the direction of the relationship and it helps eliminate the third-variable problem.
   d. Manipulation does not establish the direction of the relationship or eliminate the third-variable problem.

2. In order to establish an unambiguous relationship between two variables, it is necessary to eliminate the possible influence of which of the following variables?
   a. Extraneous variables
   b. Confounding variables
   c. Independent variables
   d. Dependent variables

3. Which of the following characteristics are necessary for an extraneous variable to become a confounding variable?
   a. It must change systematically from one participant to the next.
   b. It must change systematically when the independent variable is changed.
   c. It must have no systematic relationship with the dependent variable.
   d. It must have no systematic relationship to either the independent or the dependent variables.

Answers appear at the end of the chapter.

7.3 Controlling Extraneous Variables

LEARNING OBJECTIVE

LO7   Describe the three primary techniques for controlling extraneous variables (holding constant, matching, and randomization), explain how each one works, and identify these techniques when they appear in a research report.

Once a limited set of specific extraneous variables with real potential as confounding variables is identified, it is possible to exercise some control over them. There are three standard methods for controlling extraneous variables. Two methods involve actively intervening to control variables by holding the variable constant or by matching values across the treatment conditions. The third method is randomization.

Control by Holding Constant or Matching

For now, we focus attention on the two active methods for controlling extraneous variables.

Holding a Variable Constant

An extraneous variable can be eliminated completely by holding it constant. For example, all individuals in the experiment could be observed in the same room, at the same time of day, by the same researcher. Because these factors are the same for every observation, they do not vary and, therefore, cannot be confounding variables. By standardizing the environment and procedures, most environmental variables can be held constant. This technique can also be used with participant variables. For example, by selecting only 6-year-old children to participate in an experiment, age is held constant.

Often, it is unreasonable to hold a variable completely constant. For example, it would not be practical to hold IQ constant by requiring all participants to have IQs of exactly 109. Similarly, it would be a bit overzealous to hold age constant by requiring all participants to have been born on June 13, 1999. Instead, researchers often choose to restrict a variable to a limited range instead of holding it absolutely constant. For example, a researcher may require participants to be between 18 and 21 years of age and to have IQ scores between 100 and 110. Although age and IQ are not perfectly constant here, the restricted range should ensure that the participants in one treatment are not noticeably older or smarter than the participants in another treatment.

Holding a variable constant eliminates its potential to become a confounding variable. However, this method also may have negative consequences because it can limit the external validity of an experiment. For example, if an experiment is conducted exclusively with participants from one ethnic group, the results may not generalize to another ethnic group. Recall from Chapter 6 that any factor limiting the generalization of research results is a threat to external validity.

Matching Values across Treatment Conditions

Control over an extraneous variable can also be exercised by matching the levels of the variable across treatment conditions. For example, a researcher using two samples of college students could assign 20 younger students (under age 25) and 10 older students (25 or older) to each separate treatment condition. Age still varies within treatment conditions, but it is now balanced and does not vary across treatments. Another common form of matching is to ensure that the average value is the same (or nearly the same) for all treatments. For example, participants could be assigned so that the average age is the same for all of the different treatment conditions. In this case, age is balanced across treatments and, therefore, cannot be a confounding variable. Matching can also be used to control environmental variables. For example, a study using two different rooms could match the rooms across treatment conditions by measuring half of the participants in one room and the other half in the other room for every treatment condition. Finally, matching can be used to control time-related factors. By varying the order of two treatments, I and II, some participants experience treatment I early in the series, and others experience the same treatment later. In the same way, some participants experience treatment II early and others later. In this way, the treatment conditions are matched with respect to time. The process of matching treatment conditions over time is called *counterbalancing* and is discussed in detail in Chapter 9.

Typically, controlling a variable by matching or holding constant requires some time and effort from the researcher and can intrude on the experimental participants. Matching individuals for IQ, for example, requires the researcher to obtain an IQ score for each participant before the experiment can begin. Although it is possible to control a few variables by matching or holding constant, the demands of these control techniques make them impractical or impossible to use to control all extraneous variables. Therefore, active control by matching or holding constant is recommended for a limited set of specific variables identified as potentially serious threats to an experiment.

Control by Randomization

Because it is essentially impossible to actively control the thousands of extraneous variables that can intrude on an experiment, researchers usually rely on a simpler, more passive control technique known as **randomization**. The goal of randomization is to disrupt any systematic relation between extraneous variables and the independent variable, thereby preventing the extraneous variables from becoming confounding variables.

Randomization involves using an unpredictable and unbiased procedure (such as a coin toss) to distribute different values of each extraneous variable across the treatment conditions. The procedure that is used must be a **random process**, which simply means that all the different possible outcomes are equally likely. For example, when we toss a coin, the two possible outcomes—heads and tails—are equally likely (see Chapter 5, p. 115).

One common use of randomization is **random assignment**, in which a random process such as a coin toss or a random number table (see Appendix A) is used to assign participants to treatment conditions. For an experiment comparing two treatment conditions, a researcher could use a coin toss to assign participants to treatment conditions. Because the assignment of participants to treatments is based on a random process, it is reasonable to assume that individual participant variables (such as age, gender, height, IQ, and the like) are also distributed randomly across treatment conditions. Specifically, the use of random assignment should ensure that the participant variables do not change systematically from one treatment to another and, therefore, cannot be confounding variables.

DEFINITIONS

> **Randomization** is the use of a random process to help avoid a systematic relationship between two variables.
>
> **Random assignment** is the use of a random process to assign participants to treatment conditions.

Randomization can also be used to control environmental variables. If the research schedule requires some observations in the morning hours and some in the afternoon, a random process can be used to assign treatment conditions to the different times. For example, a coin is tossed each day to determine whether treatment I or treatment II is to be administered in the morning. In this way, a morning hour is equally likely to be assigned to treatment condition I or treatment condition II. Thus, time of day is randomly distributed across treatments and does not have a systematic effect on the outcome.

Randomization is a powerful tool for controlling extraneous variables. Its primary advantage is that it offers a method for controlling a multitude of variables simultaneously and does not require specific attention to each extraneous variable. However, randomization does not guarantee that extraneous variables are really controlled; rather, it uses chance to control variables. If you toss a coin 10 times, for example, you expect to obtain a random mixture of heads and tails. This random mixture is the essence of randomization. However, it is possible to toss a coin 10 times and obtain heads every time; chance can produce a biased (or systematic) outcome. If you are using a random process (such as a coin toss) to assign people to treatment conditions, it is still possible for all the high-IQ individuals to be assigned to the same condition. In the long run, with large numbers (i.e., a large sample), a random process guarantees a balanced result. In the short run, however, especially with small numbers (i.e., a small sample), there is a chance that randomization will not work. Because randomization cannot be relied on to control extraneous variables, specific variables that have been identified as having high potential for influencing results should receive special attention and be controlled by matching or holding constant. Then, other variables can be randomized with the understanding that they probably will be controlled by chance, but with the risk that randomization may not succeed in providing adequate control.

Comparing Methods of Control

The goal of an experiment is to show that the scores obtained in one treatment condition are consistently different from the scores in another treatment and that the differences are caused by the treatments. In the terminology of the experimental design, the goal is to show that differences in the dependent variable are caused by the independent variable. In this context, the purpose of control is to ensure that no variable, other than the independent variable, could be responsible for causing the scores to differ.

We have examined three different methods for controlling extraneous variables, and an example of each is shown in Table 7.1. The table shows how participant IQ can be a confounding variable and how the three methods are used to prevent confounding.

a. Column A shows two treatment conditions with 10 participants in each treatment. In this column, IQ (high and low) is confounded with the treatments; 80% of the participants in treatment I are low IQ but in treatment II, only 20% are low IQ. If this study found differences between the scores in treatment I and treatment II, the differences in scores could have been caused by the differences in IQ.

b. In column B, IQ is held constant. All the participants in treatment I are low IQ, and all the participants in treatment II are low IQ. In this case, there is absolutely no IQ difference between the two treatments, so IQ cannot be responsible for causing differences in the scores.

c. In column C, IQ is matched across the treatments. In treatment I, 40% are classified as high IQ, and in treatment II, 40% are high IQ. Again, the two groups are balanced with respect to IQ, so any differences in scores for the two treatments cannot be caused by IQ.

d. Finally, in column D, IQ is randomized across treatments. By using a random process to assign high and low IQ participants to the treatment conditions, it is reasonable to expect that IQ will be balanced across treatments. If there are no substantial IQ differences between treatments, then IQ cannot cause the scores in one treatment to be different from the scores in the other treatment.

TABLE 7.1

A Confounding Variable and Three Methods to Prevent Confounding

(A) IQ Confounded		(B) IQ Held Constant		(C) IQ Matched		(D) IQ Randomized	
Treatment		Treatment		Treatment		Treatment	
I	II	I	II	I	II	I	II
High	High	Low	Low	High	High	High	Low
High	High	Low	Low	High	High	Low	High
Low	High	Low	Low	High	High	Low	Low
Low	High	Low	Low	High	High	High	Low
Low	High	Low	Low	Low	Low	Low	High
Low	High	Low	Low	Low	Low	High	High
Low	High	Low	Low	Low	Low	High	Low
Low	High	Low	Low	Low	Low	Low	Low
Low	Low	Low	Low	Low	Low	High	High
Low	Low	Low	Low	Low	Low	Low	High

Advantages and Disadvantages of Control Methods

The two active methods of control (holding constant and matching) require some extra effort or extra measurement and, therefore, are typically used with only one or two specific variables identified as real threats for confounding. In addition, holding a variable constant has the disadvantage of limiting generalization (external validity). On the other hand, randomization has the advantage of controlling a wide variety of variables simultaneously. However, randomization is not guaranteed to be successful; chance is trusted to balance the variables across the different treatments. Nonetheless, randomization is the primary technique for controlling the huge number of extraneous variables that exist within any experiment.

LEARNING CHECK

1. In an experiment comparing two treatments, the researcher assigns participants to treatment conditions so that each condition has fifteen 7-year-old children and ten 8-year-old children. For this study, what method is being used to control participant age?
   a. Randomization
   (b) Matching
   c. Holding constant
   d. Limiting the range
2. Holding a variable constant is a technique for removing one threat to _____, but it can limit the _____ of an experiment.
   (a) internal validity, external validity
   b. external validity, internal validity
   c. internal validity, reliability
   d. external validity, reliability
3. Which of the following is the primary goal for randomly assigning participants to treatment conditions in an experiment?
   a. Increase the ability to generalize the results
   b. Avoid selection bias
   c. Ensure that the individuals in the sample are representative of the individuals in the population
   (d) Minimize the likelihood that a participant variable (such as age or gender) becomes a confounding variable

Answers appear at the end of the chapter.

7.4 | Control Conditions and Manipulation Checks

LEARNING OBJECTIVES

LO8 Describe the purpose for control conditions in experimental research, define the two basic types of control conditions (*no-treatment* and *placebo*), and identify control conditions when they appear in research reports.

LO9 Explain when a manipulation check is needed, describe what it is intended to accomplish, and identify a manipulation check when one appears in a research report.

Control Conditions

The experimental condition is often called the *experimental group* and the control condition is called the *control group*.

An experiment always involves comparison. The experimental strategy requires comparing observations of the dependent variable across different levels of the independent variable. In general terms, an experiment compares observations across different treatment conditions. However, sometimes a researcher wishes to evaluate only one treatment rather than compare a set of different treatments. In this case, it is still possible to conduct an experiment. The solution is to compare the treatment condition with a baseline "no-treatment" condition. In experimental terminology, the treatment condition is called the *experimental condition*, and the no-treatment condition is called the *control condition*.

DEFINITIONS

In an experiment, the **experimental condition** is the condition in which the treatment is administered and the **control condition** is the condition in which the treatment is not administered.

The variety of different ways to construct a control **condition** for an experiment can be classified into two general categories: no-treatment control **conditions** and placebo control **conditions**.

No-Treatment Control Conditions

As the name implies, a **no-treatment control condition** simply means that the participants do not receive the treatment being evaluated. The purpose of the no-treatment control is to provide a standard of normal behavior, or baseline, against which the treatment condition can be compared. To evaluate the effects of a drug, for example, an experiment could include one condition in which the drug is administered and a control condition in which there is no drug. To evaluate the effectiveness of a training procedure, the experimental group receives the training and the control group does not.

DEFINITION

In an experiment, a **no-treatment control condition** is a condition in which the participants do not receive the treatment being evaluated.

At first glance, it may appear that a treatment versus no-treatment experiment eliminates the independent variable. However, the researcher still creates treatment conditions by manipulating different values of the treatment variable; the no-treatment condition is simply a zero value of the independent variable. Thus, the experiment compares one condition having a "full amount" of the treatment with a second condition having a "zero amount" of the treatment. The independent variable still exists, and its two levels now consist of treatment and no-treatment control.

Placebo Control Conditions

The opposite of a placebo is a nocebo, which is an inert substance that produces a negative or harmful effect (a "nocebo effect") simply because an individual expects or believes it will happen.

A **placebo** is an inert or innocuous medication, a fake medical treatment such as a sugar pill or a water injection that, by itself, has absolutely no medicinal effect, but produces a positive or helpful effect simply because an individual expects or believes it will happen. Although there is no biological or pharmacological reason for a placebo to be effective, a placebo can have a dramatic effect on health and behavior (Long, Uematsu, & Kouba, 1989). The **placebo effect** is believed to be psychosomatic: The mind (psyche), rather than the placebo itself, has an effect on the body (somatic). The fact that an individual thinks or believes a medication is effective can be sufficient to cause a response to the medication.

> The **placebo effect** refers to a positive response by a participant to an inert medication that has no real effect on the body. The placebo effect occurs simply because the individual thinks the medication is effective.

In psychotherapy, the term nonspecific is often used in place of placebo to refer to the elements of therapy that are not specifically therapeutic.

Although the concept of the placebo effect originated in medical research, it has been generalized to other situations in which a supposedly ineffective treatment produces an effect. Common examples in behavioral research are the use of inactive drugs (especially when participants believe they are receiving psychotropic drugs), nonalcoholic beverages (when participants are expecting alcohol), and nonspecific psychotherapy (therapy with the therapeutic components removed).

In the context of experimental research, the placebo effect can generate serious questions about the interpretation of results. When a researcher observes a significant difference between a treatment condition and a no-treatment control condition, can the researcher be sure that the observed effect is really caused by the treatment, or is part (or all) of the effect simply a placebo effect? The importance of this question depends on the purpose of the experimental research. Investigators often differentiate between outcome research and process research.

1. *Outcome research* simply investigates the effectiveness of a treatment. The goal is to determine whether a treatment produces a substantial or clinically significant effect. It is concerned with the general outcome of the treatment rather than identifying the specific components that cause the treatment to be effective.
2. *Process research,* on the other hand, attempts to identify the active components of the treatment. In process research, it is essential that the placebo effect be separated from other, active components of the treatment.

To separate placebo effects from "real" treatment effects, researchers include one or more **placebo control conditions** in an experiment. The placebo control is simply a treatment condition in which participants receive a placebo instead of the actual treatment. Comparison of the placebo control condition with the treatment condition reveals how much treatment effect exists beyond the placebo effect. It is also common to include a third, no-treatment control condition. Comparison of the placebo control with the no-treatment condition reveals the magnitude of the placebo effect. In situations in which it is possible to identify several different elements of a treatment, researchers may conduct a component analysis, or dismantling of the treatment, using multiple control conditions in which selected elements (or combinations of elements) are included or excluded in each condition.

> A **placebo control condition** is a condition in which participants receive a placebo instead of the actual treatment.

As a final word of caution, you should recognize that using a control condition and the control of extraneous variables are two completely different aspects of an experiment. Control of extraneous variables is an essential component of all experiments and is required to prevent extraneous variables from becoming confounding variables and threatening the internal validity of the study. However, a control condition is an optional component that is used in some experiments but certainly not all. In particular, a research study does not need a control condition to qualify as a true experiment.

Manipulation Checks

In an experiment, a researcher always manipulates the independent variable. Although this manipulation and its results are obvious to the researcher, occasionally, there is a question about how the manipulation is perceived by the participants. Specifically, are the participants even aware of the manipulation and, if so, how do they interpret it? When these questions are important to the results or interpretation of an experiment, researchers often include a ==manipulation check== as part of the study. A manipulation check directly measures whether the independent variable had the intended effect on the participant.

DEFINITION

> A **manipulation check** is an additional measure to assess how the participants perceived and interpreted the manipulation and/or to assess the direct effect of the manipulation.

There are two ways to check the manipulation. First, a manipulation check may be an explicit measure of the independent variable. Suppose, for example, a researcher wants to examine the effects of mood on performance. The study involves manipulating people's moods (i.e., mood is the independent variable). The researcher may include a mood measure to make sure that the desired moods were actually induced.

A second way to check the manipulation is to embed specific questions about the manipulation in a questionnaire that participants complete after their participation in the experiment. For example, participants may be given an exit questionnaire that asks for their responses to the experiment:

Did you enjoy participating?

How long did the experiment seem to take?

Were you bored?

What do you think was the purpose of the experiment?

Did you suspect that you were being deceived?

Embedded in the questionnaire are specific questions that address the manipulation. Participants can be asked directly whether they noticed a manipulation. For example, if the room lighting was adjusted during the experimental session, you could simply ask, "Did you notice that the lights were dimmed after the first 15 minutes?" Or, "Did you notice any change in the lights during the experiment?" In an experiment in which the researcher manipulates "praise" versus "criticism" by making verbal comments to the participants, the researcher might ask, "How did the researcher respond when you failed to complete the first task?" Notice that the intent of the manipulation-check questions is to determine whether the participants perceived the manipulation and/or how they interpreted the manipulation.

Although a manipulation check can be used with any study, it is particularly important in four situations.

1. *Participant Manipulations.* Although researchers can be confident of the success of environmental manipulations (such as changing the lighting), there often is good reason to question the success of manipulations that are intended to affect participants. For example, a researcher who wanted to examine the effects of frustration on task performance might try to induce a feeling of frustration by giving one group of participants a series of impossible tasks to perform. To determine whether the participants actually are frustrated, the researcher might include a measure of frustration as a manipulation check.

2. *Subtle Manipulations.* In some situations, the variable being manipulated is not particularly salient and may not be noticed by the participants. For example, a researcher might make minor changes in the wording of instructions or in his or her apparent mood (smiling versus not smiling). Small changes from one treatment condition to another might be overlooked completely, especially when participants are not explicitly told that changes are being made.

3. *Placebo Controls.* As with a simulation, the effectiveness of a placebo depends on its credibility. It is essential that participants believe that the placebo is real; they must have no suspicion that they are being deceived. A manipulation check can be used to assess the realism of the placebo.

4. *Simulations.* In simulation research, the researcher attempts to create a real-world environment by manipulating elements within the experimental situation. The effectiveness of the simulation, however, depends on the participants' perception and acceptance. A manipulation check can be used to assess how participants perceive and respond to an attempted simulation. (Simulation is discussed in the following section.)

LEARNING CHECK

1. What is the purpose for using a control condition in an experiment?
    a. It provides a baseline that can be used to evaluate the size of the treatment effect.
    b. It minimizes the threat of a confounding variable.
    c. It is necessary to ensure the internal validity of the study.
    d. It is necessary to ensure the external validity of the study.

2. An experiment includes a treatment condition, a no-treatment control, and a placebo control. Which two conditions should be compared to determine the size of the effect that is actually caused by the treatment?
    a. Placebo versus treatment
    b. Placebo versus no treatment
    c. Treatment versus no treatment
    d. You only need to look at the scores in the placebo control condition

3. A researcher exposes people to a stressful situation (such as public speaking) to examine the effect of stress on depressed mood. Why would the researcher also include a measure of stress?
    a. It is a measure of the dependent variable.
    b. It is a measure of extraneous variables.
    c. It is a control for confounding variables.
    d. It is a manipulation check.

Answers appear at the end of the chapter.

7.5 Increasing External Validity: Simulation and Field Studies

LEARNING OBJECTIVE

LO10 Define *field studies* and *simulation*, explain why they are used as alternatives to laboratory experiments, and identify these techniques when they appear in a research report.

Once again, the goal of the experimental strategy is to establish a cause-and-effect relationship between two variables. To do this, an experiment creates an artificial, controlled environment in which the two variables being studied are isolated from outside influences.

As a result, experiments are commonly conducted in a laboratory setting. A controlled environment increases the internal validity of the research (see Chapter 6). However, by creating an artificial environment, experimenters risk obtaining results that do not accurately reflect events and relations that occur in a more natural, real-world environment. As we discussed in Chapter 6, in research terminology, this risk is a threat to external validity. One example of this problem occurs when demand characteristics are present. Recall that demand characteristics are cues given to the participant that may influence the participant to behave in a certain way. Demand characteristics, as well as reactivity, are much more likely to be problems in experiments conducted in a laboratory setting. For some research questions, a threat to external validity can be extremely serious. In particular, when research seeks cause-and-effect explanations for behavior in real-world situations, it is essential that the experimental results generalize outside the confines of the experiment. In these situations, researchers often attempt to maximize the realism of the experimental environment to increase the external validity of the results. Two standard techniques are used to accomplish this: simulation and field studies.

Simulation

Simulation is the creation of conditions within an experiment that simulate or closely duplicate the natural environment being examined. The term *natural environment* is used in a very broad sense to mean the physical characteristics of the environment, and more important, its atmosphere or mood. Most people are familiar with flight simulators that duplicate the cockpit of an airplane and allow pilots to train and be tested in a safe, controlled environment. In the same way that a flight simulator duplicates the natural environment of an airplane, researchers often use simulation so they can control the "natural environment" and observe how people behave in real-world situations.

DEFINITION

> A **simulation** is the creation of conditions within an experiment that simulate or closely duplicate the natural environment in which the behaviors being examined would normally occur.

Researchers often differentiate between mundane realism and experimental realism in the context of simulation (Aronson & Carlsmith, 1968). **Mundane realism** refers to the superficial, usually physical, characteristics of the simulation, which probably have little positive effect on external validity. For example, converting a research laboratory into a mock singles bar probably would not do much to promote "natural" behavior of participants. In fact, most participants would probably view the situation as phony and respond with artificial behaviors. **Experimental realism,** on the other hand, concerns the psychological aspects of the simulation; that is, the extent to which the participants become immersed in the simulation and behave normally, unmindful of the fact that they are involved in an experiment. Obviously, a successful simulation is far more dependent on experimental realism than on mundane realism, and often the more mundane aspects of a simulation can be minimized or eliminated.

One of the most famous and most detailed simulation experiments was conducted in 1973 by researchers at Stanford University (Haney, Banks, & Zimbardo, 1973). The intent of the research was to study the development of interpersonal dynamics and relationships between guards and inmates in a prison. An actual prison, consisting of three barred cells, a solitary confinement facility, guards' quarters, and an interview room, was built in the basement of the psychology building. A sample of 24 normal, mature, emotionally stable male college students was obtained. On a random basis, half were assigned the role of "guard" and half were assigned the role of "prisoner." The guards were issued khaki uniforms, nightsticks, and sunglasses. The prisoners' uniforms were loose smocks with ID numbers on the front and back. The prisoners were publicly arrested, charged, searched, handcuffed, and led off to jail where they were fingerprinted, photographed, stripped, sprayed with a delousing preparation, and finally given uniforms and locked up. Except for an explicit prohibition against physical punishment or aggression, little specific instruction was given to the guards or the prisoners. Almost immediately, the prisoners and guards became immersed in their roles. The interactions became negative, hostile, dehumanizing, and impersonal. Five prisoners had to be released because they developed extreme depression, crying, rage, and anxiety. When the experiment was stopped prematurely after only 6 days, the remaining prisoners were relieved, but the guards were distressed at the idea of giving up the control and power that had been part of their roles. Clearly the simulation was successful; perhaps too much so.

The Stanford prison study is an extreme example of a simulation experiment involving role-playing and a detailed simulated environment. However, this degree of detail is not always necessary for a successful simulation. For example, multiple studies have examined the process by which jurors reach their verdicts by using simulations that do not attempt to duplicate a real courtroom situation but simply provide information about the case (Bornstein et al, 2016). These studies place the emphasis was on experimental realism rather than mundane realism.

Field Studies

A simulation experiment can be viewed as an effort to bring the real world into the laboratory to increase the external validity of experimental results. An alternative procedure that seeks the same goal is to take the laboratory into the real world. Research studies conducted in a real-world environment are called **field studies**, and researchers often speak of "going into the field" as a euphemism for taking research outside the laboratory. Field settings were discussed briefly in Chapters 3 and 6 and are detailed here.

DEFINITION

> **Field study** is research conducted in a place that the participant or subject perceives as a natural environment.

Not all studies conducted in the field are experiments. For example, observational research is often conducted in a field setting.

Although it can be difficult to maintain the necessary control of a true experiment in a field study, it is possible to conduct field study experiments. Many of the more famous field study experiments involve the investigation of helping behavior or "bystander apathy" in emergency situations. In these studies, the researchers create an emergency situation, then manipulate variables within the emergency and observe bystander responses (Hornstein, Fisch, & Holmes, 1968; Piliavin & Piliavin, 1972; Piliavin, Rodin, & Piliavin, 1969).

Brown, Flint, and Fuqua (2014) conducted a field study examining how nutrition information affected vending machine purchases on a university campus. They identified five high-use machines and recorded purchases before the study began. Then, they placed colored stickers by each selection with red indicating less-healthy items, yellow for moderately healthy, and green for more-healthy items. Purchases after the stickers were added showed a significant increase for green sticker items and a decrease for red and yellow sticker items. Apparently, nutrition matters, at least for university students.

Advantages and Disadvantages of Simulation and Field Studies

Although simulation and field studies can be used to increase the realism of experiments, there are risks as well as advantages to these techniques. The obvious advantage of both procedures is that they allow researchers to investigate behavior in more lifelike situations and, therefore, should increase the chances that the experimental results accurately reflect natural events. The disadvantage of both procedures is that allowing nature to intrude on an experiment means that the researcher often loses some control over the situation and risks compromising the internal validity of the experiment. This problem is particularly important for field experiments for which researchers have no control over the "participants" who show up. Simulation experiments, on the other hand, do provide researchers with the opportunity to control the assignment of participants to treatment conditions. However, simulation experiments are totally dependent on the participants' willingness to accept the simulation. No matter how realistic the simulation, participants still know that it is only an experiment and they know that their behaviors are being observed. This knowledge could influence behavior and compromise the experimental results.

LEARNING CHECK

1. A researcher moves an experiment out of the laboratory and into the real world. This type of research is called
   a. a simulation study.
   b. a field study.
   c. a transported study.
   d. a quasi-experimental study.

2. Researchers often use simulation experiments in an attempt to obtain the _____ of an experiment and still keep much of the _____ of research conducted in the real world.
   a. external validity, internal validity
   b. internal validity, external validity
   c. experimental realism, mundane realism
   d. mundane realism, experimental realism

3. Although field studies tend to have higher external validity than traditional laboratory studies, what risk do they tend to have?
   a. Lower internal validity
   b. Lower reliability
   c. An increased risk of confounding from history effects
   d. An increased risk that the manipulation of the independent variable will not be effective.

Answers appear at the end of the chapter.

CHAPTER SUMMARY

At this point you should review the learning objectives presented at the beginning of each section and be sure that you have mastered each objective.

In general, an experiment attempts to demonstrate that changes in one variable are directly responsible for changes in a second variable. The two basic characteristics that distinguish the experimental research strategy from other research strategies are (1) manipulation of one variable while measuring a second variable and (2) control of extraneous variables. In an experiment, the independent variable is manipulated by the researcher, the dependent variable is measured for changes, and all other variables are controlled to prevent them from influencing the results.

To establish an unambiguous causal relationship between the independent and dependent variables, it is necessary to eliminate the possible influence of a confounding variable. Extraneous variables become confounds when they change systematically along with the independent variable. After identifying a short list of extraneous variables that have the potential to become confounding variables, it is possible to actively or passively control these variables. The two standard methods of active control are (1) holding a variable constant and (2) matching values across the treatment conditions. The method for passive control is to randomize variables across the treatment conditions.

An experiment always involves comparison of measures of the dependent variable across different levels of the independent variable. To accomplish this, a treatment condition (an experimental condition) and a no-treatment condition (a control condition) often are created. The no-treatment condition serves as a baseline for evaluating the effect of the treatment. There are two general categories of control conditions: (1) the no-treatment control condition, a condition that involves no treatment whatsoever (participants receive a zero level of the independent variable); and (2) the placebo control condition, a condition that involves the appearance of a treatment but from which the active, effective elements have been removed.

In an experiment, a researcher always manipulates the independent variable. Occasionally, a researcher may include a manipulation check to assess whether the participants are aware of the manipulation. A manipulation check is an additional measure to assess whether the manipulation was successful. It is particularly useful to use a manipulation check when participant manipulations, subtle manipulations, simulations, or placebo control conditions are used.

To establish a cause-and-effect relationship between two variables, an experiment necessarily creates an artificial, controlled environment in which the two variables being studied are isolated from outside influences. This high level of control required by an experiment can be a threat to external validity. To gain higher external validity, a researcher may use a simulation or a field study. A simulation involves creating a real-world atmosphere in a laboratory to duplicate a natural environment or situation; a field study involves moving an experiment from the laboratory into the real-world environment.

KEY WORDS

experimental research strategy	levels	random assignment	placebo effect
experiment, or true experiment	dependent variable	experimental condition	placebo control condition
	extraneous variables	control condition	manipulation check
independent variable	manipulation	no-treatment control condition	simulation
treatment condition	randomization		field study

EXERCISES

The exercises are identified with specific learning objectives and are intended to assess your mastery of the objectives. You should be aware that exam items are also generated to assess learning objectives.

1. In addition to the key words, you should also be able to define the following terms:

    third-variable problem   placebo
    directionality problem   mundane realism
    confounding variable   experimental realism
    random process

2. (**LO1**) Dr. Jones conducted a study examining the relationship between the amount of sugar in a child's diet and the activity level of the child. A sample of thirty 4-year-old children from a local preschool was used in the study. Sugar consumption was measured by interviewing the parents about each child's diet. Based on the result of the interview, each child was then placed into one of two groups: high sugar consumption and low sugar consumption. Activity level was measured by observing the children during a regular preschool afternoon. Finally, Dr. Jones compared the activity level for the high-sugar group with the activity level for the low-sugar group. Explain why Dr. Jones's study is not an example of the experimental research strategy.

3. (**LO2**) In an experiment examining human memory, two groups of participants are used. One group is allowed 5 minutes to study a list of 40 words and the second group is given 10 minutes of study time for the same list of words. Then, both groups are given a memory test, and the researcher records the number of words correctly recalled by each participant. For this experiment, identify the independent variable and the dependent variable.

4. (**LO3**) It has been demonstrated that students with high self-esteem tend to have higher grades than students with low self-esteem. Does this relationship mean that higher self-esteem causes better academic performance? Does it mean that better academic performance causes higher self-esteem? Explain your answer, and identify the general problem that can preclude a cause-and-effect explanation.

5. (**LO3**) A researcher would like to compare two methods for teaching math to third-grade students. Two third-grade classes are obtained for the study. Mr. Jones teaches one class using method A, and Mrs. Smith teaches the other class using method B. At the end of the year, the students from the method-B class have significantly higher scores on a mathematics achievement test. Does this result indicate that method B causes higher scores than method A? Explain your answer, and identify the general problem that precludes a cause-and-effect explanation.

6. (**LO2** and **6**) Define *extraneous variable* and explain how extraneous variables can become confounding variables.

7. (**LO4** and **5**) Identify the two characteristics needed for a research study to qualify as an experiment.

8. (**LO7**) Identify the two active methods of preventing extraneous variables from becoming confounding variables.

9. (**LO7**) Explain how the process of randomly assigning participants to treatment conditions should prevent a participant variable such as age or gender from becoming a confounding variable.

10. (**LO8**) Can a research study be an experiment without a control group? Can a study be an experiment without controlling extraneous variables?

11. (**LO9**) What is the general purpose of a manipulation check?

12. (**LO10**) What is the general purpose for using a simulation or a field study for experimental research?

LEARNING CHECK ANSWERS

Section 7.1	Section 7.2	Section 7.3	Section 7.4	Section 7.5
1. a, 2. d, 3. a	1. c, 2. b, 3. b	1. b, 2. a, 3. d	1. a, 2. a, 3. d	1. b, 2. b, 3. a

Experimental Designs: Between-Subjects Design

© Nathan Jasowiak / Shutterstock

CHAPTER LEARNING OBJECTIVES

LO1 Describe, compare, and contrast the defining characteristics of a between-subjects design and a within-subjects design, and recognize examples of each.

LO2 Explain the general advantages and disadvantages of between-subjects design compared to within-subjects design.

LO3 Define *individual differences* and explain how individual differences between groups and confounding from environmental variables can threaten the internal validity of a between-subjects design.

LO4 Identify the three primary techniques for limiting confounding by individual differences in between-subjects experiments (random assignment, matched assignment, and holding variables constant) and explain how each one works.

LO5 Describe how individual differences influence variability within-treatments and explain how variance within treatments can influence the interpretation of research results.

LO6 Identify the options for reducing or controlling the variance within treatment condition and explain how each option works.

LO7 Describe how differential attrition and communication between participants can threaten the internal validity of between-subjects designs and identify these problems when they appear in a research study.

LO8 Describe how between-subjects designs are used to compare means and proportions for two or more groups, identify the statistical techniques that are appropriate for each application, and explain each design's strengths and weaknesses.

CHAPTER OVERVIEW

Research suggests that it is more effective for students to study text on printed hardcopy than to study text displayed on a computer screen (Ackerman & Goldsmith, 2011). In the study, college students were randomly assigned to one of the two media conditions to study text of 1,000–1,200 words and then were given a multiple-choice test on the material. When the students controlled their own amount of study time, test performance was significantly worse for students who studied on a computer screen. Because the researcher carefully controlled other variables, they can conclude confidently that the type of media causes a difference in learning performance.

You should recognize this study as an example of an experiment. The researchers manipulated the type of media to create two treatment conditions and randomly assigned students to conditions to control extraneous variables. They recorded scores on the multiple-choice test and then compared the two sets of scores. Another characteristic of this study is that the two groups of scores are obtained from two separate groups of participants.

An experiment always involves the comparison of different groups of scores. However, each group of scores can be obtained from a separate group of participants (as in this experiment), or they can be obtained from the same group of participants. You may recall, for example, in Section 1.2 we discussed an experiment showing that people are able to tolerate more pain when they are shouting swear words than when they shout neutral words (Stephens, Atkins, & Kingston, 2009). In that experiment, each participant was measured in both the swearing and the neutral word condition so that the two groups of scores came from the same group of participants.

The choice between one group and multiple groups of participants is one of the characteristics that differentiate one type of experiment from another, and hence determines for a particular research strategy, the selection of a research design (see Step 6 of the research process). In this chapter, we discuss in detail one type of experimental research design: the between-subjects design. The between-subjects design uses a separate group of individuals for each of the different treatment conditions. We consider the advantages, disadvantages, and different versions of between-subjects designs.

8.1   Introduction to Between-Subjects Experiments

LEARNING OBJECTIVES

LO1 Describe, compare, and contrast the defining characteristics of a between-subjects design and a within-subjects design, and recognize examples of each.

LO2 Explain the general advantages and disadvantages of between-subjects design compared to within-subjects design.

Review of the Experimental Research Strategy

In Chapter 7, we introduced the experimental research strategy, as well as its major goal, which is to demonstrate a cause-and-effect relationship between two variables. To accomplish this goal, the experimental strategy requires several basic characteristics: (1) manipulation of one variable to create a set of two or more treatment conditions; (2) measurement of a second variable to obtain a set of scores within each treatment condition; (3) comparison of the scores between treatments; and (4) control of all other variables to prevent them from becoming confounding variables.

At the end of the study, the researcher compares the scores from each treatment with the scores from every other treatment. If consistent differences exist between treatments, the researcher can conclude that the differences have been *caused* by the treatment conditions. For example, a researcher may compare memory scores for a list of one-syllable words with scores for a list of two-syllable words. By showing that there are consistent differences between the two groups of scores, the researcher can demonstrate that memory is related to the number of syllables in the words (i.e., the number of syllables causes differences in memory).

Two basic research designs are used to obtain the groups of scores that are compared in an experiment:

1. The different groups of scores all can be obtained from the same group of participants. For example, one group of individuals is given a memory test using a list of one-syllable words, and the same set of individuals is also tested using a list of two-syllable words. Thus, the researcher gets two sets of scores, both obtained from the same sample. This strategy is called a **within-subjects design** and is discussed in Chapter 9.
2. An alternative strategy is to obtain each group of scores from a different group of participants. For example, one group of individuals is given a list of one-syllable words to memorize and a separate group receives a list of two-syllable words. This type of design, comparing scores from separate groups, is called a **between-subjects design**. We examine the characteristics of a between-subjects research design in this chapter.

Characteristics of Between-Subjects Designs

The defining characteristic of a between-subjects design is that it compares different groups of individuals. In the context of an experiment, a researcher manipulates the independent variable to create different treatment conditions, and a separate group of participants is assigned to each of the different conditions. The dependent variable is then measured for each individual, and the researcher examines the data, looking for differences between the groups (Figure 8.1).

This chapter focuses on the **between-subjects experimental design**, that is, the between-subjects design as it is used in *experimental* research, wherein a researcher manipulates an independent variable. The general goal of a between-subjects experiment is to determine whether differences exist between two or more treatment conditions. For example, a researcher may want to compare two teaching methods (two treatments) to determine whether one is more effective than the other. In this case, two separate groups of individuals would be used, one for each of the two teaching methods. We should note that between-subjects designs are also commonly used for other research strategies, such as nonexperimental and quasi-experimental designs. However, nonexperimental and quasi-experimental between-subjects designs do not contain a manipulated variable. Nonexperimental and quasi-experimental strategies are examined in Chapter 10.

Independent Scores

One additional characteristic of the between-subjects design deserves special mention. A between-subjects design allows only one score for each participant. Every individual score represents a separate, unique participant. If a between-subjects experiment produces 30 scores in treatment A and 30 scores in treatment B, then the experiment must have employed a group of 30 individuals in treatment A and a separate group of 30 individuals in treatment B, for a total of 60 participants. In the terminology of experimental research, a between-subjects experimental design uses a different group of participants for each level of the independent variable, and each participant is exposed to only one level of the independent variable.

Occasionally, a researcher may combine several measurements for each individual into a single score. In particular, when the variable being measured is not particularly stable (e.g., reaction time), a researcher may choose to measure the variable several times and then average the measurements to produce a single, more reliable score. However, the net result is always one score per individual participant.

FIGURE 8.1

The Structure of a Between-Subjects Experiment

The key element is that separate groups of participants are used for the different treatment conditions.

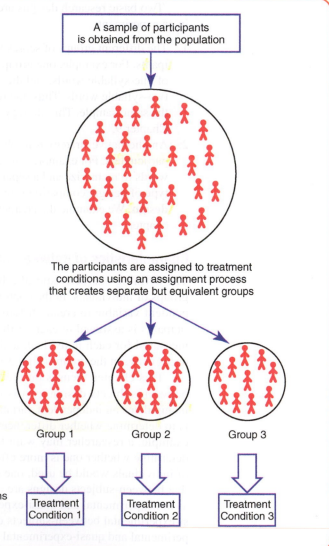

A sample of participants is obtained from the population

The participants are assigned to treatment conditions using an assignment process that creates separate but equivalent groups

Group 1   Group 2   Group 3

Separate treatment conditions created by the researcher (the independent variable)

| Treatment Condition 1 | Treatment Condition 2 | Treatment Condition 3 |

DEFINITION

A **between-subjects experimental design** requires a separate, independent group of individuals for each treatment condition. As a result, the data for a between-subjects design contain only one score for each participant. To qualify as an experiment, the design must satisfy all other requirements of the experimental research strategy, such as manipulation of an independent variable and control of extraneous variables.

Advantages and Disadvantages of Between-Subjects Designs

A main advantage of a between-subjects design is that each individual score is independent from the other scores. Because each participant is measured only once, the researcher can be reasonably confident that the resulting measurement is relatively clean and uncontaminated by other treatment factors. For this reason, a between-subjects experimental design is often called an **independent-measures experimental design**. In an experiment comparing performance under different temperature conditions, for example, each participant is exposed to only one treatment condition. Thus, the participant's score is not influenced by such factors as:

- practice or experience gained in other treatments;
- fatigue or boredom from participating in a series of different treatments; and
- contrast effects that result from comparing one treatment to another (a 60-degree room might feel cold after a 70-degree room, but the same 60-degree room might feel warm after a 50-degree room).

In addition, between-subjects designs can be used for a wide variety of research questions. For any experiment comparing two (or more) treatment conditions, it is always possible to assign different groups to the different treatments; thus, a between-subjects design is always an option. It may not always be the best choice, but it is always available.

One disadvantage of between-subjects designs is that they require a relatively large number of participants. Remember, each participant contributes only one score to the final data. To compare three different treatment conditions with 30 scores in each treatment, the between-subjects design requires 90 participants. This can be a problem for research involving special populations in which the number of potential participants is relatively small. For example, a researcher studying preschool children with a specific learning disability might have trouble finding a large number of individuals to participate.

Individual Differences

The primary disadvantage of a between-subjects design stems from the fact that each score is obtained from a unique individual who has personal characteristics that are different from all of the other participants. Consider the following descriptions of two individuals participating in the same research study.

John	Mary
John is a 21-year-old white male. He is 5'10" tall; weighs 180 pounds; and has blue eyes, blond hair, and an IQ of 110. He comes from a middle-class family with one older sister. John is a chemistry major and was awake until 2:00 a.m. this morning after celebrating his success on a chemistry exam. He comes to the experiment with only 4 hours of sleep, suffering from a mild hangover.	Mary is a 20-year-old black female. She is 5'3" tall, has brown eyes, black hair, and an IQ of 142. Her mother and father are both doctors, and she is an only child. Mary is a history major with a minor in psychology. She had a head cold yesterday and went to bed at 8:00 p.m. She arrived at the experiment well-rested and feeling much b[...] However, she skipped breakfast and is hu[...]

Clearly, these two individuals differ on a variety of dimensions. It should also be clear that we have identified only a few of the countless variables that differentiate the two people. Differences between participants on variables such as gender, age, personality, and family background that exist at the beginning of an experiment are called **individual differences**. The concern with individual differences is that they can cause two different individuals to produce two different scores when a dependent variable is measured in a research study.

DEFINITION

> **Individual differences** are personal characteristics that differ from one participant to another.

Occasionally, research is designed with the intention of examining a specific individual difference; for example, a study may be designed to compare behavior or attitudes for people in different age groups (this type of research is discussed in Chapter 10). Most of the time, however, individual differences are simply extraneous variables that are not directly addressed in the research design. For a between-subjects experimental design, individual differences are a particular concern and can create serious problems. The two major concerns are:

1. Individual differences can become confounding variables. Suppose that a researcher finds that participants in treatment A have higher scores than participants in treatment B. The researcher would like to conclude that the higher scores were caused by the treatment; however, individual differences may also provide an explanation for the difference in the scores. If the individuals in one treatment are generally older (or smarter, or stronger) than the individuals in another treatment, then the individual differences between groups may explain why one group has higher scores.
2. Individual differences can produce high variability in the scores, making it difficult to determine whether the treatment has any effect. The unpredictable variability caused by individual differences can obscure patterns in the data and cloud a study's results.

One more look at our two hypothetical participants, John and Mary, illustrates the problems that individual differences can cause.

1. Suppose John is assigned to treatment A, where he produces a score of 45, and Mary is assigned to treatment B and has a score of 51. The researcher has found a 6-point difference between the two scores. The researcher must determine what caused the difference. Notice that the difference in scores could be caused by the different treatment conditions. However, the difference could also be explained by the obvious fact that John and Mary are different people with different characteristics. Thus, the 6-point difference in scores could be caused by individual differences.
2. If John and Mary are both assigned to the same treatment condition, then you still expect them to have different scores. In this case, the difference between their scores increases the variance within the treatment, which reduces the likelihood of finding a significant difference between treatments.

The problems of confounding variables and high variability are discussed in detail in the following sections.

LEARNING CHECK

1. Which statement best characterizes a between-subjects experimental design?
   a. Participants are randomly selected from two different populations.
   b. Each participant is assigned to one condition of the experiment.
   c. Each participant is assigned to every condition of the experiment.
   d. Participants with the same characteristics are assigned to the different conditions of the experiment.

2. Which of the following accurately describes the scores in a between-subjects experiment?
   a. Only one score is obtained for each participant.
   b. At least two scores are obtained for each participant.
   c. One score is obtained for each treatment condition for each participant.
   d. Each score represents multiple participants.

3. If a between-subjects experiment produces 50 scores in treatment 1 and 50 scores in treatment 2, then how many participants were in the entire experiment?
   a. 50 participants
   b. 100 participants
   c. 25 participants
   d. 200 participants

Answers appear at the end of the chapter.

8.2   Individual Differences as Confounding Variables

LEARNING OBJECTIVE

LO3 Define *individual differences* and explain how individual differences between groups and confounding from environmental variables can threaten the internal validity of a between-subjects design.

In a between-subjects design, each level of the independent variable (each treatment condition) is represented by a separate group of participants. In this situation, a primary concern is to ensure that the different groups are as similar as possible except for the independent variable used to differentiate the groups. Any extraneous variable that systematically differentiates the groups is a confounding variable. For example, in a between-subjects experiment comparing two treatments (I and II), one group of participants is assigned to treatment I and a separate group to treatment II. If the participants in one group are generally older (or smarter, or taller, or faster, etc.) than the participants in the other group, then the experiment is confounded by individual differences.

Figure 8.2 shows an example of an experiment in which the participant's age is a confounding variable. In the figure, the two groups of participants are differentiated by treatment (I vs. II) and age (one group is older than the other). If the results from this example showed that the scores in one group were consistently higher than scores in the other group, it would be impossible to determine whether treatment or age is responsible for causing the difference between groups. Because the experiment is confounded, it is impossible to draw any clear conclusions. Note that this problem applies exclusively to research designs comparing different groups; that is, between-subjects designs. Whenever the individuals in one group have characteristics that are different from those in another group, the internal validity of the study is threatened.

Other Confounding Variables

In addition to the threat of individual differences between groups, a between-subjects design must also be concerned with threats to internal validity from environmental variables that can change systematically from one treatment to another (Chapter 6, p. 149). Thus, there are two major sources of confounding that exist in a between-subjects design.

FIGURE 8.2

An Experiment in Which Individual Difference (Participant Age) Is a Confounding Variable

1. *Confounding from individual differences.* Individual differences are any participant characteristics that can differ from one participant to another. If these characteristics are different from one group to another, then the experiment is confounded. For example, the participants in one group may be older, smarter, taller, or have higher socioeconomic status than the participants in another group. One group may have a higher proportion of males or a higher proportion of divorced individuals than another group. Any of these variables may produce differences between groups that can compromise the research results.
2. *Confounding from environmental variables.* Environmental variables are any characteristics of the environment that may differ. If these variables are different between groups, then the experiment is confounded by environmental variables. For example, one group may be tested in a large room and another group in a smaller room. Or one group may be measured primarily during the morning and another group during the afternoon. Any such variable may cause differences between groups that cannot be attributed to the independent variable.

Equivalent Groups

In Chapter 7, we identified three general techniques for controlling confounding variables: randomization, matching, and holding constant. These techniques can be used to protect a study from confounding environmental variables. With a between-subjects design, however, a researcher must also protect the study from individual differences between groups. Fortunately, with a between-subjects experimental design, the researcher has control over the assignment of individuals to groups. Thus, the researcher has both the opportunity and the responsibility to create groups that are equivalent. Specifically, the separate groups must be:

1. *Created equally.* The process used to obtain participants should be as similar as possible for all of the groups.
2. *Treated equally.* Except for the treatment conditions that are deliberately varied between groups, the groups of participants should receive exactly the same experiences.
3. *Composed of equivalent individuals.* The characteristics of the participants in any one group should be as similar as possible to the characteristics of the participants in every other group.

The techniques available for establishing equivalent groups of participants are discussed in the following section.

LEARNING CHECK

1. In a between-subjects experiment, if the participants in one group have characteristics that are different from the participants in another group, then which of the following is threatened?
   a. Internal validity
   b. External validity
   c. Reliability
   d. Accuracy

2. For a between-subjects experiment, which of the following is a possible threat to internal validity?
   a. Individual differences that exist within treatments
   b. Individual differences that exist between treatments
   c. The risk that one treatment condition may influence scores in another treatment
   d. All of the above are threats.

Answers appear at the end of the chapter.

8.3 | Limiting Confounding by Individual Differences

LEARNING OBJECTIVE

LO4 Identify the three primary techniques for limiting confounding by individual differences in between-subjects experiments (random assignment, matched assignment, and holding variables constant) and explain how each one works.

The first step in conducting a between-subjects experiment is to assign participants to different groups corresponding to the treatment conditions. If the assignment process produces groups of participants with different characteristics, then the study is confounded from individual differences. Specifically, any difference in the scores from one group to another may be caused by individual differences between groups instead of the treatments. Therefore, the initial groups must be as similar as possible. To accomplish this, researchers typically use one of the following three procedures to set up groups for a between-subjects experimental study. The three procedures are the same methods that were identified for controlling potentially confounding variables in an experiment (Chapter 7).

Random Assignment (Randomization)

Probably the most common method of establishing groups of participants is random assignment. Recall from Chapter 7 that **random assignment** simply means that a random process (such as a coin toss) is used to assign participants to groups. The goal is to ensure that all individuals have the same chance of being assigned to a group. Because group assignment is based on a random process, it is reasonable to expect that characteristics such as age, IQ, and gender are also distributed randomly across groups. Thus, we minimize the potential for confounding from individual differences because it is unlikely that any group is systematically older, or smarter, or more feminine than another.

It should be obvious that assigning participants with a simple random process such as a coin toss or drawing numbers out of a hat is likely to create groups of different sizes. If it is desirable to have all groups the same size (equal *n*s), which is typically the case, then the process can be modified to guarantee equal-size groups. To divide 90 participants into three equal groups, for example, the researcher could start with 90 slips of paper, 30 with #1, 30 with #2, and 30 with #3, and then draw one slip for each individual to determine the group assignment. In this case, the process is a **restricted random assignment**; the restriction is that the groups must be equal in size.

In **restricted random assignment**, the group assignment process is limited to ensure predetermined characteristics (such as equal size) for the separate groups.

The advantage of using a random process to establish groups is that it is fair and unbiased. Just as football teams use a coin toss to determine who receives the opening kickoff, random assignment eliminates prejudice from the decision process. However, a random process does not guarantee a perfectly balanced outcome. When tossing a coin, for example, we can expect an equal 50–50 distribution of heads and tails in the long run (with a large sample). However, in the short run (with a small sample), there are no guarantees. A sample of only 10 coin tosses, for example, can easily contain eight or nine heads and only one or two tails. With any random process, we trust chance to create a balanced outcome. In the long run, chance proves to be fair, but in the short run, anything can happen by chance. Specifically, there is always a possibility that random assignment will produce groups that have different characteristics and thus confound the experiment. Because pure chance is not a dependable process for obtaining balanced and equivalent groups, researchers often modify random processes by placing some limitations on or exerting some control over the outcomes. One such modification, restriction of equal group sizes, has been discussed; two additional techniques follow.

Matching Groups (Matched Assignment)

In many situations, a researcher can identify a few specific variables that are likely to influence the participants' scores. In a learning experiment, for example, it is reasonable to expect that intelligence is a variable that can influence learning performance. In this case, it is important that the researcher not allow intelligence to become a confounding variable by permitting one group of participants to be noticeably more intelligent than another group. Instead of hoping that random assignment produces equivalent groups, a researcher can use **matching** to guarantee that the different groups of participants are equivalent (or nearly equivalent) with respect to intelligence.

For example, a researcher comparing two different methods for teaching fifth-grade math wants to be sure that the two groups of participants are roughly equivalent in terms of IQ. School records are used to determine the IQs of the participants, and each student is classified as high IQ, medium IQ, or low IQ. The high-IQ participants are distributed equally between the two groups; half is assigned to one group and the other half is assigned to the second group using restricted random assignment. The medium-IQ participants and the low-IQ participants are evenly distributed between the two groups in the same way. The result is two separate groups of participants with roughly the same level of intelligence on average.

A similar matching process can be used to equate groups in terms of proportions. If a sample consists of 60% older adults (age 40 or more) and 40% younger adults (age less than 40), restricted random assignment could be used to distribute the older adults equally among the different groups. The same process is then used to distribute the younger adults equally among the groups. The result is that the groups are matched in terms of age, with each group containing exactly 60% older and 40% younger participants. Notice that the matching process requires three steps.

1. Identification of the variable (or variables) to be matched across groups
2. Measurement of the matching variable for each participant

This section discusses methods of creating matched groups. An alternative process is one in which each participant in one group is matched one-to-one with an "equivalent" participant in another group. The process is called matching subjects (as opposed to matching groups). Technically, a matched-subjects design is not classified as a between-subjects design and is discussed separately in Chapter 9.

3. Assignment of participants to groups by means of a restricted random assignment that ensures a balance between groups

DEFINITION

> **Matching** involves assigning individuals to groups so that a specific participant variable is balanced, or matched, across the groups. The intent is to create groups that are equivalent (or nearly equivalent) with respect to the variable matched.

Matching groups of participants provides researchers with a relatively easy way to ensure that specific participant variables do not become confounding variables. However, there is a price to pay for matching, and there are limitations that restrict the usefulness of this process. To match groups with respect to a specific participant variable, the researcher first must measure the variable. The measurement procedure can be tedious or costly and always adds another level of work to the study. In addition, it can be difficult or impossible to match groups on several different variables simultaneously. To match groups in terms of intelligence, age, and gender could require some fairly sophisticated juggling to achieve the desired balance of all three variables. Finally, groups cannot be matched on every single variable that might differentiate participants. Therefore, researchers typically use matching only for variables that are judged to have strong potential to be confounding. In a learning experiment, for example, intelligence is a variable that is likely to affect learning performance, but eye color is a variable that probably has little to do with learning. In this case, it would make sense to match groups for intelligence but not for eye color.

Holding Variables Constant or Restricting Range of Variability

Another method of preventing individual differences from becoming confounding variables is simply to hold the variable constant. For example, if a researcher suspects that gender differences between groups might confound a research study, one solution is to eliminate gender as a variable. By using only female participants, a researcher can guarantee that all of the groups in a study are equivalent with respect to gender; all groups are all female.

An alternative to holding a variable completely constant is to restrict its range of values. For example, a researcher concerned about potential IQ differences between groups could restrict participants to those with IQs between 100 and 110. Because all groups have the same narrow range of IQs, it is reasonable to expect that all groups would be roughly equivalent in terms of IQ.

Although holding a variable constant (or restricting its range) can be an effective way to prevent the variable from confounding a research study, this method has a serious drawback. Whenever a variable is prevented from reaching its natural range of variation, the external validity of the research is limited. A research study that uses only young adults, for example, cannot be generalized to the entire population of all adults. Similarly, results obtained for participants within a narrow range of IQs cannot be generalized to the whole population. As we noted in Chapter 6, attempting to improve internal validity by exercising control within a research study can threaten external validity or the ability to generalize the results.

Summary and Recommendations

Individual differences between groups are always a potential confounding variable in a between-subjects design. Therefore, it is important for researchers to create groups of participants that are as equivalent as possible at the beginning of a research study. Most of the time, researchers attempt to create equivalent groups by using random assignment because it is relatively easy and does not require any measurement or direct control of extraneous variables. The number of participant variables that could produce differences between groups is essentially infinite, and random assignment provides a simple method of balancing them across groups without addressing each individual variable. However, random assignment is not perfect and cannot guarantee equivalent groups, especially when a small sample is used. Pure chance is not a dependable process for obtaining balanced equivalent groups.

When one or two specific variables can be identified as likely to influence the dependent variable, these variables can be controlled either by matching groups or by holding the variable constant. However, matching requires pretesting to measure the variable(s) being controlled, and it can become difficult to match several variables simultaneously. Holding a variable constant guarantees that the variable cannot confound the research, but this process limits the external validity of the research results.

LEARNING CHECK

1. Which of the following does not guarantee that a specific participant variable will not become a confounding variable?
   a. Matching the variable across treatments
   b. Randomizing the variable across treatment
   c. Holding the variable constant
   d. All of the other options guarantee that the variable does not become a confounding variable
2. Which of the following is a limitation of using matching rather than random assignment to form groups in a between-subjects experiment?
   a. Matching requires another measurement procedure.
   b. Matching reduces error due to participant differences.
   c. Matching is easier than randomization.
   d. Matching eliminates any systematic relationship between participant characteristics and the treatment conditions.
3. How does holding a variable constant prevent the variable from becoming a confound?
   a. It eliminates the possibility that the variable will be substantially different from one group to another.
   b. It reduces error.
   c. It ensures a nonbiased sample.
   d. It increases the differences between the groups.

Answers appear at the end of the chapter.

8.4 Individual Differences and Variability

LEARNING OBJECTIVES

LO5   Describe how individual differences influence variability within-treatments and explain how variance within treatments can influence the interpretation of research results.

LO6   Identify the options for reducing or controlling the variance within treatment condition and explain how each option works.

In addition to becoming confounding variables, individual differences have the potential to produce high variability in the scores within a research study. As we noted earlier, high variability can obscure any treatment effects that may exist and therefore can undermine the likelihood of a successful study. In general, the goal of most research studies is to demonstrate a difference between two or more treatment conditions. For example, a study may be designed to show that one therapy technique is more effective than another. To accomplish this goal, it is essential that the scores obtained in one condition are noticeably different (higher or lower) than the scores in a second condition. Usually, the difference between treatments is described by computing the average score for each treatment, then comparing the two averages. However, simply comparing two averages is not enough to demonstrate a noticeable difference. The problem comes from the fact that in some situations, a 10-point difference is large, but in other circumstances, a 10-point difference is small. The absolute size of the difference must be evaluated in relation to the *variance* of the scores. **Variance** is a statistical value that measures the size of the differences from one score to another (see Chapter 15, p. 381). If the scores all have similar values, then the variance is small; if there are big differences from one score to the next, then variance is large. The following example demonstrates how individual differences influence variance and how variance can influence the interpretation of research results.

We begin with two distinct populations, one in which the individual differences are relatively small, and one in which the individual differences are large. The two populations are shown in Table 8.1. In the table, each number represents the score for a single individual. Notice that in population A, the scores are all very similar, indicating that the individual differences (the differences from one person to another) are relatively small and the variance is small. In population B, the differences between scores are large, indicating large individual differences and large variance. We then conduct the following hypothetical research study, first with population A and then with population B.

1. We select a random sample of 20 scores from the population and randomly divide the sample into two groups with 10 in each group.
2. One group is then assigned to a control condition that has no effect whatsoever on the participants' scores. The second group is assigned to a treatment that increases each participant's score by 10 points. To simulate this treatment effect, we simply add 10 points to the original score for each individual.

TABLE 8.1

Two Simulated Populations

In population A, the individual differences are relatively small. In population B, the individual differences are relatively large.

Population A						Population B			
42	39	41	39	39	32	48	28	24	20
41	40	41	41	40	24	32	56	60	44
40	38	38	40	40	44	20	40	52	40
42	39	40	41	40	44	36	36	48	60
40	42	40	38	39	36	56	56	52	28
38	41	40	39	38	56	32	60	24	28
38	42	41	42	39	36	52	48	40	20
41	38	42	39	40	48	28	20	60	40
40	39	41	40	40	40	44	32	24	48
41	40	40	42	39	40	32	36	44	52

For population A, the results of this hypothetical research study are shown as a table and as a graph in Figure 8.3. From either the numbers in the table or the piles of scores in the graph, it is easy to see the 10-point difference between the two conditions. Remember, in population A, the individual differences are small, which means that the variance of the scores is small. With small variance, the 10-point difference between treatments shows up clearly.

Next, we repeat the study using scores selected from population B. The results of this simulation are shown in Figure 8.4. This time, it is very difficult to see any difference between the two conditions. With the large individual differences in population B, the variance is large and the 10-point treatment effect is completely obscured. Although Figures 8.3 and 8.4 illustrate the effects of increasing (or decreasing) variance, you should realize that variance also has a dramatic influence on the statistical interpretation of the results. Specifically, the difference between treatments in Figure 8.3 is statistically significant but the difference in Figure 8.4 is not significant.

It may be helpful to think of the variance within each group as similar to interference to a cell phone or radio signal. When there is a lot of interference, it is difficult to get a clear signal. Similarly, when a research study has a lot of variance, it is difficult to see a real treatment effect. In between-subjects research, much of the variance is caused by individual differences. Remember, each individual score represents a different individual. Whenever there are large differences between individuals, there is large variance.

The term significant means that it is very unlikely that the difference would occur if there was not a consistent difference between the treatment conditions (see Box 7.1, p. 161).

Differences between Treatments and Variance within Treatments

In general, the goal of a between-subjects research study is to establish the existence of a treatment effect by demonstrating that the scores obtained in one treatment condition are significantly different (higher or lower) than the scores in another treatment condition. For example, if we can demonstrate that people in a bright yellow room are consistently happier and have more positive moods than people in a dark brown room, then we have reason to conclude that room color (the treatment) has an effect on mood. Thus, big differences *between* treatments are good because they provide evidence of differential

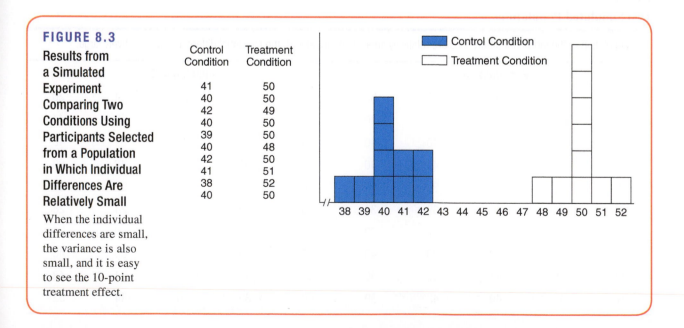

FIGURE 8.3
Results from a Simulated Experiment Comparing Two Conditions Using Participants Selected from a Population in Which Individual Differences Are Relatively Small

When the individual differences are small, the variance is also small, and it is easy to see the 10-point treatment effect.

Control Condition	Treatment Condition
41	50
40	50
42	49
40	50
39	50
40	48
42	50
41	51
38	52
40	50

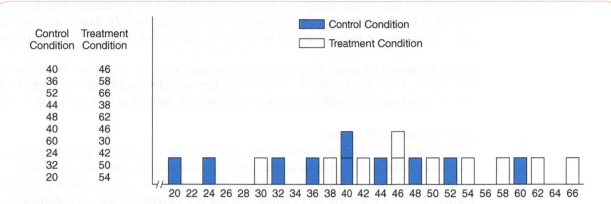

Control Condition	Treatment Condition
40	46
36	58
52	66
44	38
48	62
40	46
60	30
24	42
32	50
20	54

FIGURE 8.4

Results from a Simulated Experiment Comparing Two Conditions Using Participants Selected from a Population in Which Individual Differences Are Relatively Large

When the individual differences are large, the variance is also large, and it is not at all easy to see the 10-point treatment effect.

treatment effects. On the other hand, big differences *within* treatments are bad because the differences that exist inside the treatment conditions determine the variance of the scores, and, as we demonstrated in Figure 8.4, large variance can obscure patterns in the data.

Notice that we are distinguishing differences *between treatments* and variance (differences) *within treatments*. Researchers typically try to increase the differences between treatments and to decrease the variance within treatments. For example, if we were examining the effects of room color on mood, it would not be wise to compare two rooms that were slightly different shades of green. With only a subtle difference between the two colors, we would be unlikely to find a noticeable difference in mood. Instead, the best strategy would be to maximize the difference between room colors to increase our chances of finding a large difference in mood between treatments. Again, the goal is to increase the difference between treatments. At the same time, however, we would like to decrease the **variance within treatments**. Because a between-subjects design has a separate group of participants for each treatment condition, the variance within treatments is also the **variance within groups**. In the following section, we examine some of the methods that can be used to reduce or minimize the variance within treatments. In addition, we consider some of the design decisions that a researcher must make when developing a between-subjects research study and look at how those decisions affect variance within treatments.

Minimizing Variance within Treatments

As we have noted, large individual differences can lead to large variance within treatments, which can undermine the potential success of a between-subjects research study. Therefore, researchers are well-advised to take whatever steps are possible to reduce the variance inside each of the treatment conditions. The following options provide some ways to accomplish this.

Standardize Procedures and Treatment Setting

In a between-subjects design, each group of participants represents a single treatment condition. One obvious way to help minimize the variability within each group is to be sure that all participants within a group are treated exactly the same. Although existing individual differences are not reduced, at least care is taken not to increase them. Thus, researchers should avoid making any changes in the treatment setting or the procedures used from one individual to another. Whenever two individuals are treated differently, there is a chance that differences between their scores will be increased, thus increasing the variance within the group. In general, if two participants are in the same group (the same treatment condition), a researcher should not do anything that might cause their scores to be different. Standardizing procedures also makes it easier for other researchers to understand exactly how your study was done and makes it possible for them to replicate your study in their own research facility.

Limit Individual Differences

In Section 8.3, we suggested that holding a participant variable constant or restricting its range could be effective techniques used for limiting confounding from individual differences (see p. 195). This technique also reduces the variance within a group of participants. If it is known, for example, that age is a variable related to the participants' scores (e.g., older adults tend to have higher scores than younger adults), then a mixed group of older and younger adults will have higher variance than a group consisting of only younger adults. In the mixed group, the age differences (older vs. younger) will contribute to the variance within the group. By holding age constant (older only), age differences are eliminated and the variance within the group is reduced.

In the same way, restricting a participant variable to a narrow range of values creates a more homogeneous group and, therefore, can reduce the variability in the scores. For example, if the participants within a group are limited to those between the ages of 18 and 20, then age differences between participants make a very small contribution to the variance of scores within the group. In general, any attempt to minimize the differences between participants within a group tends to reduce the variance within the group.

Random Assignment and Matching

In Section 8.3, we also suggested that random assignment or matching groups could be used to help limit confounding from individual differences. However, these techniques have no effect on the variance within groups. If we randomly assign older and younger adults to each group, for example, then we can expect relatively little age difference between groups, but we still have a mixture of older and younger adults (age differences) within groups. In the same way, matching groups so that each group has exactly 50% older adults does not eliminate or reduce the age differences within each group.

Sample Size

Although sample size does not affect individual differences or variance directly, using a large sample can help minimize the problems associated with high variance. Sample size exerts its influence in the statistical analyses such that some of the negative effects of high variance can be statistically overcome by use of a very large sample. However, this technique has limitations because the influence of sample size occurs in relation to the *square root* of the sample size. The square-root relationship means that it takes a dramatic increase in sample size to have a real effect. To reduce the effects of high variance by a factor of 4, for example, the sample size must be increased by a factor of 16; a sample of 20 would need to be increased to a sample of 320. Usually, it is much more efficient to control variance by either standardizing procedures or directly limiting individual differences.

Summary and Recommendations

The best techniques for minimizing the negative consequences of high variance are to standardize treatments and to minimize individual differences between the participants in the study. Both of these techniques help eliminate factors that can cause differences between scores and therefore can reduce the variance within treatments. The technique of minimizing individual differences by holding a variable constant or restricting its range has two advantages:

1. It helps create equivalent groups, which reduces the threat of confounding variables.
2. It helps reduce the variance within groups, which makes treatment effects easier to see.

As we noted earlier, however, limiting individual differences has the serious disadvantage of limiting external validity. If participation in a study is limited to females between the ages of 18 and 20, for example, then the results cannot be generalized to other ages or to other genders. (An alternative method for reducing individual differences without threatening external validity is presented in Chapter 11, wherein we introduce factorial research designs.)

LEARNING CHECK

1. Which of the following maximizes the likelihood of a successful research result?
    a. Increase the differences between treatments and decrease the variance within treatments
    b. Decrease the differences between treatments and increase the variance within treatments
    c. Increase the differences between treatments and increase the variance within treatments
    d. Decrease the differences between treatments and decrease the variance within treatments
2. Which of the following is an option for limiting the variance within treatment conditions?
    a. Hold a participant variable constant
    b. Randomize participant variables across treatments
    c. Match participant variables across treatments
    d. All of the above are options for limiting variance within treatments
3. Which of the following is a potential problem with holding a participant variable constant?
    a. It threatens the internal validity of the study.
    b. It threatens the external validity of the study.
    c. It lowers the likelihood of obtaining a significant difference between treatments.
    d. None of the above is a potential problem.

Answers appear at the end of the chapter.

8.5 Other Threats to Internal Validity of Between-Subjects Experimental Designs

LEARNING OBJECTIVE

LO7 Describe how differential attrition and communication between participants can threaten the internal validity of between-subjects designs and identify these problems when they appear in a research study.

Remember that the goal of the between-subjects experimental design is to look for differences between groups for the dependent variable and to demonstrate that the observed differences are caused by the different treatments (i.e., by the manipulation of the independent variable). If the differences between the groups can be explained by any factor other than the treatments, the research is confounded and the results cannot be interpreted without some ambiguity. Also recall from Chapter 6 that any factor that allows for an alternative explanation for the research results is a threat to internal validity. Earlier in this chapter, we discussed the two major threats that can undermine the internal validity of a between-subjects study: confounding due to individual differences between groups and confounding from environmental variables. Now, we consider additional potential confounds that are specifically related to between-subjects designs.

Differential Attrition

The term *attrition* refers to participant withdrawal from a research study before it is completed. As long as the rate of attrition is fairly consistent from one group to another, it usually is not a threat to internal validity. However, big differences in attrition rates between groups can create problems. The different groups are initially created to be as similar as possible; if large numbers of individuals leave one group, the group may no longer be similar to the others. Again, whenever the groups of participants are noticeably different, the research is confounded. **Differential attrition** refers to differences in attrition rates from one group to another and can threaten the internal validity of a between-subjects experiment.

For example, a researcher may want to test the effectiveness of a dieting program. Using a between-subjects design, the researcher forms two groups of participants with approximately equal characteristics (weight, gender, dieting history). Next, one group of participants begins the 10-week dieting program, and the other group receives no treatment (this group, recall from Chapter 7, is the no-treatment control group). At the end of 10 weeks, the weights of the two groups are compared. During the course of 10 weeks, however, it is likely that some participants will drop out of the study. If more participants drop out of one group than the other, there is a risk that the two groups will no longer be similar. For example, some of the individuals in the dieting program may decide that it is too demanding and withdraw from the study. As a result, only the most motivated participants stay in the diet program. Although the study started with two equivalent groups, the individuals who are left in the program at the end have a higher level of motivation than those in the control group. In this case, the difference in dropout rate between the groups could account for the obtained differences in mean weight. Differential attrition is a threat to internal validity because we do not know whether the obtained differences between treatment conditions are caused by the treatments or by differential attrition. Whenever participants drop out of a study, a researcher must be concerned about differential attrition as an alternative explanation for treatment effects.

Communication between Groups

Whenever the participants in one treatment condition are allowed to talk with the participants in another condition, there is the potential for a variety of problems to develop. For example, a researcher may want to test the effectiveness of a new treatment for depression. Using a between-subjects design, the researcher randomly assigns half the clients of an inpatient facility to receive the new treatment and half to receive the standard treatment for depression. If the participants talk to each other, however, then those individuals receiving the old treatment may learn about the new treatment and may begin to use some elements from the new treatment. **Diffusion** refers to the spread of the treatment from the experimental group to the control group, which tends to reduce the difference between the two conditions. This is a threat to the internal validity of a between-subjects design because the true effects of the treatment can be masked by the shared information (i.e., it appears that there is no difference between the groups because both groups are actually getting much of the same treatment).

Another risk is that an untreated group learns about the treatment being received by the other group and demands the same or equal treatment. This is referred to as **compensatory equalization**. For example, in a study examining the effects of violent television viewing on boys in a residential facility, one team of researchers faced this problem. The boys in the nonviolent television group learned that those in the violent television group were allowed to watch the television series *Batman* and demanded the right to watch it too (Feshbach & Singer, 1971). This threat commonly occurs in medical and clinical studies when one group receives a treatment drug and another does not. A similar problem arises when researchers try to assess the effectiveness of large-scale educational enrichment programs (involving such improvements as computers in the classrooms). Parents and teachers of the classes or schools that do not receive the enrichment (the control group) hear about the special program other classes or schools (the experimental group) receive and demand that their children receive the same program or something equal in value. If the demand is met, the research study no longer has a no-treatment condition for comparison. Again, this is a threat to the internal validity of a between-subjects design because it can wipe out the true effects of the treatment (i.e., make it look as if there are no differences between the groups on the dependent variable).

Finally, problems can occur when participants in an untreated group change their normal behavior when they learn about a special treatment that is given to another group. One possibility is that the untreated group works extra hard to show that they can perform just as well as the individuals receiving the special treatment. This is referred to as **compensatory rivalry**. In this case, the performance observed by the researcher is much higher than would normally occur. It is also possible that the participants in an untreated group simply give up when they learn that another group is receiving special treatment. This is referred to as **resentful demoralization**. In this case, the untreated group becomes less productive and less motivated because they resent the expected superiority of the treated group. As a result, the effect of the treatment appears to be much greater than it really is.

In each case, internal validity is threatened because the observed difference between groups can be explained by factors other than the effects of the treatment. The best way to minimize each of these threats to internal validity resulting from communication between the groups is to separate the groups of participants as much as possible and keep them from being aware of one another. Notice that these problems are exclusive to between-subjects experimental designs in which different groups of participants are used to compare different treatment conditions.

LEARNING CHECK

1. Which of the following accurately defines compensatory equalization?
   a. One group demands the same benefits received by another group.
   b. One group works extra hard to make up for not receiving the benefits received by another group.
   c. One group stops trying because it is not receiving the benefits received by another group.
   d. Elements of the treatment in one group have spread to another group.

2. Which of the following accurately defines compensatory rivalry?
   a. One group demands the same benefits received by another group.
   b. One group works extra hard to make up for not receiving the benefits received by another group.
   c. One group stops trying because it is not receiving the benefits received by another group.
   d. Elements of the treatment in one group have spread to another group.

3. Which of the following accurately defines diffusion?
   a. One group demands the same benefits received by another group.
   b. One group works extra hard to make up for not receiving the benefits received by another group.
   c. One group stops trying because it is not receiving the benefits received by another group.
   d. Elements of the treatment in one group have spread to another group.

Answers appear at the end of the chapter.

8.6   Applications and Statistical Analyses of Between-Subjects Designs

LEARNING OBJECTIVE

LO8   Describe how between-subjects designs are used to compare means and proportions for two or more groups, identify the statistical techniques that are appropriate for each application, and explain each design's strengths and weaknesses.

Two-Group Mean Difference

The simplest version of a between-subjects experimental design involves comparing only two groups of participants: The researcher manipulates one independent variable with only two levels. This design is often referred to as the **single-factor two-group design** or simply the **two-group design**. This type of design can be used to compare treatments or to evaluate the effect of one treatment by comparing a treatment group and a control group. When the measurements consist of numerical scores, typically, a mean is computed for each group of participants, and then an independent-measures *t*-test is used to determine whether there is a significant difference between the means (see Chapter 15).

The primary advantage of a two-group design is its simplicity. It is easy to set up a two-group study, and there is no subtlety or complexity when interpreting the results; either the two groups are different or they are not. In addition, a two-group design provides the best opportunity to maximize the difference between the two treatment conditions; that is, you may select opposite extreme values for the independent variable. For example, in a study comparing two types of therapy, the two therapies can be structured to maximize or even exaggerate the differences between them. Or, in a research study comparing a treatment and a no-treatment control, the treatment group can be given the full-strength version of the treatment. This technique increases the likelihood of obtaining noticeably different scores from the two groups, thereby demonstrating a significant mean difference.

The primary disadvantage of a two-group design is that it provides relatively little information. With only two groups, a researcher obtains only two real data points for comparison. Although two data points are sufficient to establish a difference, they often are not sufficient to provide a complete or detailed picture of the full relationship between an independent and a dependent variable. Figure 8.5 shows a hypothetical relationship between dosage levels for a drug (independent variable) and activity (dependent variable). Notice that the complete set of five data points, representing five different drug doses, gives a good picture of how drug dosage affects behavior. Now, consider the limited data that would be available if the researcher had used only two different drug doses. If, for example, the researcher had used only a zero-dose and a one-dose group (points A and B in the figure), the data would seem to indicate that increasing the drug dose produces an increase in activity. However, a researcher comparing a two-dose versus a four-dose group (points C and E) would reach exactly the opposite conclusion. Although both of the two-group studies are accurate, neither provides a complete picture. In general, several groups (more than two) are necessary to obtain a good indication of the functional relationship between an independent and a dependent variable.

A two-group study also limits the options when a researcher wishes to compare a treatment group and a control group. Often, it is necessary to use several control groups to obtain a complete picture of a treatment's effectiveness. As we noted in Chapter 7, two common controls that often are used together are a no-treatment control and a placebo control. With these two control groups, researchers can separate the real treatment effects

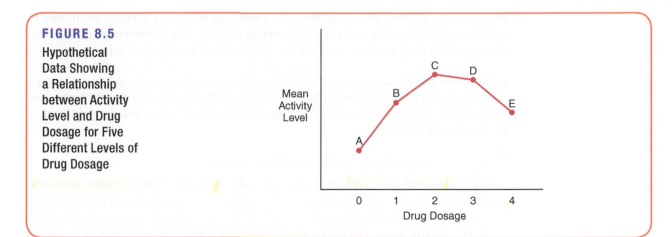

FIGURE 8.5

Hypothetical Data Showing a Relationship between Activity Level and Drug Dosage for Five Different Levels of Drug Dosage

from the placebo effects that occur simply because participants think that they are receiving treatment. However, as we noted in Chapter 4 (p. 109), there is some ethical concern regarding the use of no-treatment or placebo groups in clinical research. Rather than denying treatment to some participants, it is suggested that an established, standard therapy be used for the control comparison (LaVaque & Rossiter, 2001).

Comparing Means for More Than Two Groups

As noted in the previous section, research questions often require more than two groups to evaluate the functional relation between an independent and a dependent variable or to include several different control groups in a single study. In these cases, a **single-factor multiple-group design** may be used. For example, a researcher may want to compare driving performance under three telephone conditions: while talking on a cell phone, while texting on a cell phone, and without using a phone. Another researcher may want to examine five different dosages of a drug to evaluate the relation between dosage and activity level for laboratory rats. In the first example, the independent variable is the telephone condition with three levels compared. In the second example, the researcher compares five levels of drug dosage. For either study, the mean is computed for each group of participants, and a single-factor analysis of variance (ANOVA) (independent measures) is used to determine whether there are any significant differences among the means (see Chapter 15). When the ANOVA concludes that significant differences exist, some form of post hoc test or posttest is used to determine exactly which groups are significantly different from each other.

In addition to revealing the full functional relationship between variables, a multiple-group design also provides stronger evidence for a real cause-and-effect relationship than can be obtained from a two-group design. With a multiple-group design, the researcher changes the treatment conditions (independent variable) several times across several groups, demonstrating differences in performance for each different treatment condition. By contrast, a two-group design changes the treatment condition only once and observes only one difference in performance.

A Word of Caution about Multiple-Group Designs

Although a research study with more than two groups can give a clear and convincing picture of the relationship between an independent and a dependent variable, it is possible to have too many groups in a research design. One advantage of a simple, two-group design is that it allows the researcher to maximize the difference between treatments by selecting opposite extremes for the independent variable. The mirror image of this argument is that a design with more than two groups tends to reduce or minimize the difference between treatments. At the extreme, there is a risk of reducing the differences between treatments so much that the differences are no longer significant. Therefore, when designing a single-factor multiple-group research study, be sure that the levels used for the independent variable are sufficiently different to allow for substantial differences for the dependent variable.

Comparing Proportions for Two or More Groups

Often, the dependent variable in a research study is measured on a nominal or ordinal scale. In this case, the researcher does not have a numerical score for each participant and cannot calculate and compare averages for the different groups. Instead, each individual is simply classified into a category, and the data consist of a simple frequency count of the participants in each category on the scale of measurement. Examples of nominal scale measurements are:

- academic major for college students
- occupation

Examples of ordinal scale measurements are:

- college class (freshman, sophomore, etc.)
- birth order (first born, second born)
- high, medium, or low performance on a task

Because you cannot compute means for these variables, you cannot use an independent-measures *t*-test or an ANOVA (*F*-test) to compare means between groups. However, it is possible to compare proportions between groups using a chi-square test for independence (see Chapter 15, p. 406). As with other between-subjects experiments, the different groups of participants represent different treatment conditions (manipulated by the researcher). For example, Loftus and Palmer (1974) conducted a classic experiment demonstrating how language can influence eyewitness memory. A sample of 150 students watched a film of an automobile accident, and participants were then questioned about what they saw. One group was asked, "About how fast were the cars going when they smashed into each other?" Another group received the same question except that the verb was changed to "hit" instead of "smashed into." A third group served as a control and was not asked any question about the speed of the two cars. A week later, the participants returned and were asked additional questions about the accident, including whether they remembered seeing any broken glass in the accident. (There was no broken glass in the film.) Notice that the researchers are manipulating the form of the initial question and then measuring a yes/no response to a follow-up question 1 week later. Figure 8.6 shows the structure of this design represented by a matrix with the independent variable (different groups) determining the rows of the matrix and the two categories for the dependent variable (yes/no) determining the columns. The number in each cell of the matrix is the frequency count showing how many participants are classified in that category. For example, of the 50 students who heard the word *smashed,* there were 16 (32%) who claimed to remember seeing broken glass even though there was none in the film. By comparison, only 7 out of 50 (14%) of the students who heard the word *hit* claimed to have seen broken glass. The chi-square test compares the proportions across one row of the matrix (one group of participants) with the proportions across other rows. A significant outcome

	Response to the Question Did You See Any Broken Glass?	
	Yes	No
Smashed into	16	34
Hit	7	43
Control (Not Asked)	6	44

Verb Used to Ask About the Speed of the Cars

FIGURE 8.6

Results from an Experiment Comparing Three Different Questions Asked of Witnesses about the Speed of Cars They Observed in a Collision (Loftus & Palmer, 1974)

The dependent variable is the participants' response to a question about whether they recall seeing any broken glass. Note that the dependent variable is not a numerical score, so you cannot compute a mean score for each treatment condition.

means that the proportions in one row are different from the proportions in another row, and the difference is more than would be expected if there was not a systematic treatment effect. Loftus and Palmer found that participants who had been asked a leading question about the cars smashing into each other were significantly more likely to recall broken glass than participants who were not asked a leading question.

LEARNING CHECK

1. Which of the following is the primary limitation of a two-group design?
   a. It is simple to interpret.
   b. It increases the chances of demonstrating a significant mean difference.
   c. It tends to reduce the differences between the groups.
   d. It may not provide a complete picture of the relationship between the variables.

2. When comparing means in a two-group design, which statistical analysis is most appropriate?
   a. Independent-measures *t*-test
   b. Repeated-measures *t*-test
   c. Single-factor ANOVA
   d. Chi-square test for independence

3. When comparing means in a single-factor multiple group design, which statistical analysis is most appropriate?
   a. Independent-measures *t*-test
   b. Repeated-measures *t*-test
   c. Single-factor ANOVA
   d. Chi-square test for independence

Answers appear at the end of the chapter.

CHAPTER SUMMARY

At this point, you should review the learning objectives presented at the beginning of each section and be sure that you have mastered each objective.

In this chapter, we examined the characteristics of the between-subjects experimental research design. The general goal of a between-subjects experiment is to determine whether differences exist between two or more treatment conditions. The defining characteristic of a between-subjects design is that different but equivalent groups of individuals are compared.

The primary advantage of a between-subjects design is the fact that each individual score is independent of the other scores because each participant is measured only once. The primary disadvantage of a between-subjects design is individual differences. In between-subjects designs, individual differences can become confounding variables and produce high variance.

The potential confounding influence of individual differences is a particular problem for between-subjects designs. Because a between-subjects design compares different groups of individuals, there is always the possibility that the characteristics of one group can be substantially different from the characteristics of another group. Techniques for establishing equivalent groups of participants include random assignment, matched assignment, and holding variables constant. Individual differences also have the potential to produce high variance in the scores within each group or treatment condition. High variance within groups can obscure any treatment effects that may exist. Several methods that can be used to minimize the variance (differences) within treatments are discussed.

In addition to individual differences, there are other threats to the internal validity of between-subjects designs. Each of these potential confounds is also discussed in this chapter. Finally, different applications of the between-subjects design are considered along with the appropriate statistical analysis.

KEY WORDS

between-subjects experimental design, or	independent-measures experimental design	individual differences	restricted random assignment
			matching

EXERCISES

The exercises are identified with specific learning objectives and are intended to assess your mastery of the objectives. You should be aware that exam items are also generated to assess learning objectives.

1. In addition to the key words, you should also be able to define the following terms:
   within-subjects design
   between-subjects design
   independent-measures design
   random assignment
   variance within treatments, or variance within groups
   differential attrition
   diffusion
   compensatory equalization
   compensatory rivalry
   resentful demoralization
   single-factor two-group design, or two-group design

   single-factor multiple-group design

2. (**LO1**) At the beginning of this chapter (p. 186) we described a study comparing the effectiveness of studying material printed on paper to studying material displayed on a computer screen (Ackerman & Goldsmith, 2011). Explain why this study is an example of a between-subjects design and describe how the same question could be addressed with a within-subjects design.

3. (**LO2**) In a between-subjects design, each individual score is obtained from a separate participant. Briefly explain why this is an advantage. Briefly explain why this is a disadvantage.

4. (**LO2**) A researcher has a sample of 30 rats that are all cloned from the same source. The 30 rats are genetically identical and have been raised in exactly the

same environment since birth. The researcher conducts an experiment, randomly assigning 10 of the clones to treatment A, 10 to treatment B, and the other 10 to treatment C. Explain why the clone experiment is better than a between-subjects study using 30 regular rats that are randomly assigned to the three treatments. In other words, explain how the clone experiment eliminates the basic problems with a between-subjects study.

5. (**LO3**) Briefly explain how a participant characteristic, such as personality, could be a confounding variable in a between-subjects experiment.

6. (**LO4**) Explain the advantages and disadvantages of using random assignment as a method to prevent individual differences from becoming confounding variables.

7. (**LO3** and **4**) A recent survey at a major corporation found that employees who regularly participated in the company fitness program tended to have fewer sick days than employees who did not participate. However, because the study was not a true experiment, you cannot conclude that regular exercise causes employees to have fewer sick days.
   a. Identify another factor (a confounding variable) that might explain why some employees participated in the fitness program, and why those same employees have fewer sick days.

   b. Describe the design for a between-subjects experiment that would determine whether participation in the exercise program *caused* fewer sick days.
   c. Describe how the factor you identified in Part A is controlled in your experiment.

8. (**LO5**) Describe how individual differences can produce large variance within treatments and explain why this is a problem in a between-subjects experiment.

9. (**LO4** and **6**) Explain how holding a participant variable such as gender constant prevents the variable from becoming a confounding variable and can help reduce the variance within treatments. Identify the problem with using this method.

10. (**LO7**) Describe some of the problems that can arise when the participants in one treatment condition of a between-subjects experiment are allowed to communicate with participants in a different condition.

11. (**LO8**) Describe the advantages of a two-group design compared to an experiment with more than two groups.

12. (**LO8**) Identify the advantages of a multiple-group design compared to an experiment with only two groups.

LEARNING CHECK ANSWERS

Section 8.1	Section 8.2	Section 8.3	Section 8.4	Section 8.5	Section 8.6
1. b, 2. a, 3. b	1. a, 2. b	1. b, 2. a, 3. a	1. a, 2. a, 3. b	1. a, 2. b, 3. d	1. d, 2. a, 3. c

Experimental Designs: Within-Subjects Design

© Nathan Jasowiak / Shutterstock

CHAPTER LEARNING OBJECTIVES

LO1 Describe the general characteristics of a within-subjects experimental design and identify these designs when they appear in a research report.

LO2 Describe how time-related factors such as history, maturation, instrumentation, statistical regression, and order effects can threaten the internal validity of some within-subjects experiments.

LO3 For a within-subjects experiment, explain how the time delay between treatments can influence time-related threats to internal validity and why it may be better to switch to a between-subjects design.

LO4 Define counterbalancing and explain how it is used to minimize or eliminate threats to internal validity from time-related factors.

LO5 Describe the limitations of counterbalancing and explain why partial counterbalancing is sometimes used.

LO6 Explain the general advantages and disadvantages of within-subjects designs compared to between-subjects designs and be able to decide which design would be better under specific circumstances.

LO7 Define a matched-subject design and explain how it attempts to achieve the advantages of both

within- and between-subjects designs without their disadvantages.

LO8 Describe the different ways that within-subjects designs are used to compare two or more treatment conditions, identify the statistical techniques that are appropriate for each application, and explain the strengths and weaknesses of each application.

CHAPTER OVERVIEW

Step 6 of the research process involves selecting a research design. In this chapter, we discuss in detail another type of experimental research design: the within-subjects design. We also consider the threats to internal validity for this design and discuss the relative advantages and disadvantages of within-subjects experiments compared to the between-subjects experiments that were presented in Chapter 8.

9.1   Within-Subjects Experiments and Internal Validity

LEARNING OBJECTIVES

LO1 Describe the general characteristics of a within-subjects experimental design and identify these designs when they appear in a research report.

LO2 Describe how time-related factors such as history, maturation, instrumentation, statistical regression, and order effects can threaten the internal validity of some within-subjects experiments.

Characteristics of Within-Subjects Designs

In Chapter 8, we described the basic elements of the between-subjects experimental research design. Recall that the defining characteristic of a between-subjects experiment is that it requires separate but equivalent groups of participants for the different treatment conditions compared. In this chapter, we introduce an alternative research procedure: the **within-subjects design.** The defining characteristic of a within-subjects design is that it uses a single group of participants and tests or observes each individual in all of the different treatments being compared. The different treatments can be administered sequentially, with participants receiving one treatment condition followed, at a later time, by the next treatment (Figure 9.1a). In Chapter 1, for example, we described an experiment by Stephens, Atkins, and Kingston (2009) examining the effect of swearing on the experience of pain (pp. 10–14). In the study, participants were asked to place one hand in icy cold water for as long as they could bear the pain. In one condition, the participants were told to repeat their favorite swear word over and over for as long as their hands were in the water. In the second condition, the participants repeated a neutral word. Each participant started in one condition and, after a brief rest, repeated the ice water plunge switching words to the other condition. Thus, all the participants experienced both conditions with a brief rest period in between. The results clearly showed that swearing significantly increased pain tolerance and decreased the perceived level of pain. It also is possible that the different treatment conditions are administered all together in one experimental session (Figure 9.1b). For example, Schmidt

FIGURE 9.1

Two Possible Structures for a Within-Subjects Design

The same group of individuals participates in all of the treatment conditions. Because each participant is measured in each treatment, this design is sometimes called a repeated-measures design. The different treatments can be administered sequentially, with participants receiving one treatment condition followed, at a later time, by the next treatment (a). It also is possible that the different treatment conditions are administered all together in one experimental session (b). Note: All participants go through the entire series of treatments but not necessarily in the same order.

(1994) presented participants with a list containing a mix of humorous and nonhumorous sentences, and then asked them to recall as many as possible. The results showed that significantly more humorous sentences were recalled, indicating the humor plays an important role in human memory. In this case, the researcher switched back and forth between the two treatment conditions (humorous and nonhumorous) with only a few seconds between one treatment and the next. Whether the treatment conditions are administered in a sequence over time or are presented all together, the key element of a within-subjects design is that all the individuals in one sample participate in all of the treatment conditions.

In one sense, a within-subjects study is the ultimate in equivalent groups because the group in one treatment condition is absolutely identical to the group in every other condition. In the context of statistical analysis, a within-subjects design is often called a **repeated-measures design** because the research study repeats measurements of the same individuals under different conditions.

In this chapter, we examine the **within-subjects experimental design** or **repeated-measures experimental design;** that is, the within-subjects design as it is used in *experimental* research comparing different treatment conditions. Using the terminology of experimental research, in a within-subjects experimental design the same group of individuals participates in every level of the independent variable so that each participant experiences all of the different levels of the independent variable. We should note, however, that the within-subjects design is also well suited to other, nonexperimental types of research that investigate changes occurring over time. For example, studies in human development often observe a single group of individuals at different ages to monitor development over time. Examples of nonexperimental within-subjects designs are examined in Chapter 10.

DEFINITION

A **within-subjects experimental design,** or **repeated-measures experimental design,** compares two or more different treatment conditions (or compares a treatment and a control) by observing or measuring the same group of individuals in all of the treatment conditions being compared. Thus, a within-subjects design looks for differences between treatment conditions within the same group of participants. To qualify as an experiment, the design must satisfy all other requirements of the experimental research strategy, such as manipulation of an independent variable and control of extraneous variables.

Threats to Internal Validity of Within-Subjects Experiments

When a within-subjects experimental study compares different treatments that are administered at different times, it must be concerned with threats to internal validity from environmental variables and time-related factors that may change systematically from one treatment to another and may influence the participants' scores (Chapter 6, pp. 149–151). Thus, there are two major sources of potential confounding for a within-subjects design.

1. *Confounding from environmental variables.* Environmental variables are characteristics of the environment that may change from one treatment condition to another. For example, one treatment may be evaluated during the morning and another treatment during the afternoon. Any such variable may cause differences in scores from one treatment to another and, therefore, provides an alternative explanation for the differences between treatments.

2. *Confounding from time-related variables.* A serious concern of within-subjects designs comes from the fact that the design often requires a series of measurements made over time. During the time between the first measurement and the final measurement, the participants may be influenced by a variety of factors other than the treatments being investigated, and these other factors may affect the participants' scores. If this occurs, then the internal validity of the study is threatened because a change in a participant's score from one treatment to the next could be caused by an outside factor instead of the different treatments. In this section, we identify five time-related threats to internal validity.

   a. *History:* The term **history** refers to environmental events other than the treatment that change over time and may affect the scores in one treatment differently than in another treatment. Events that occur in participants' lives at home, in school, or at work may affect their performance or behavior in different sections of the research study. For example, a research study that extends over several days with a different treatment condition each day can be influenced by an outside event that is likely to affect some of the participants on one particular day, but not on another day, then the event may provide an explanation for unusual performance on that particular day. For example, a long power outage on campus could cause anxiety and confusion that affects the participants' performance on one specific day. Notice that a history effect becomes a confounding variable only if it influences at least one treatment condition differently and influences enough of the participants to have an effect on the overall group performance.

DEFINITION   When a group of individuals is being tested in a series of treatment conditions, any outside event(s) that influences the participants' scores in one treatment differently than in another treatment is called a history effect. **History** is a threat to internal validity because any differences that are observed between treatment conditions may be caused by history instead of the treatments.

b. *Maturation:* Any systematic changes in participants' physiology or psychology that occur during a research study and affect the participants' scores are referred to as **maturation.** Maturation effects are of particular concern when the research participants are young children or elderly adults. Young children, for example, can gather new knowledge and skills or simply grow bigger and stronger in a relatively short time. As a result, their performance at the end of a series of treatment conditions may be very different from their performance at the beginning, and the change in performance may not have been caused by the treatments but by maturation. In general, maturation threatens the internal validity of a research study conducted over time because it weakens our confidence that the different treatment conditions are responsible for observed changes in the participants' scores. Maturation is of particular concern in research situations in which the series of treatments extends over a relatively long time.

DEFINITION   **Maturation** is when a group of individuals is being tested in a series of treatment conditions, any physiological or psychological change that occurs in participants during the study and influences the participants' scores. Maturation is a threat to internal validity because observed differences between treatment conditions may be caused by maturation instead of the treatments.

c. *Instrumentation:* The term **instrumentation** (sometimes called **instrumental bias** or **instrumental decay**) refers to changes in a measuring instrument that occur over time. Instrumentation is much more likely to occur with behavioral observation measures (discussed in Chapters 3 and 13) than with other types of measures. Consider, for example, a researcher observing a group of children and recording occurrences of aggressive behavior. In this situation, part of the measurement depends on the subjective interpretation of the observer, whose criteria may change from one time to another. As a result, the same behavior may be judged differently at different times. Notice that the changes in the participants' scores are not caused by the treatment but by a change in the measurement instrument (the researcher). Like history and maturation, instrumentation is of particular concern in research situations in which the series of treatments extends over a relatively long time.

DEFINITION   **Instrumentation** refers to changes in the measuring instrument that occur during a research study in which participants are measured in a series of treatment conditions. Instrumentation is a threat to internal validity because any observed differences between treatment conditions may be caused by changes in the measuring instrument instead of the treatments.

d. *Regression toward the mean:* **Statistical regression,** or **regression toward the mean,** refers to the tendency for extreme scores on any measurement to move toward the mean (regress) when the measurement procedure is repeated. Individuals who score extremely high on a measure during the first testing are likely to score lower on the second testing, and, conversely, individuals who score extremely low on a measure during the first testing are likely to score higher on the second testing.

Statistical regression occurs because an individual's score is a function both of stable factors such as skill and of unstable factors such as chance. Although the stable factors remain constant from one measurement to another, the unstable factors can change substantially. Your grade on an exam, for example, is based on a combination of knowledge and luck. Some of the answers you really know; others you guess. The student who gets the highest score on the first exam probably combines knowledge and good luck. On the second exam, this student's knowledge is still there, but luck is likely to change; thus, the student will probably score lower on the second exam. This is regression toward the mean.

In research, regression is a concern whenever participants are selected for their exceptionally high (or low) scores in the first treatment condition. When the same participants are tested a second time, their scores are likely to be lower (or higher) based on regression. Notice that the change in scores is not caused by a new treatment but rather by the statistical phenomenon of regression. In general, statistical regression threatens the internal validity of a research study because it creates the possibility that the observed changes in the participants' scores are caused by regression instead of by the treatments.

DEFINITION

> **Statistical regression,** or **regression toward the mean,** is a mathematical phenomenon in which extreme scores (high or low) on one measurement tend to be less extreme on a second measurement. Regression is a threat to internal validity because changes that occur in participants' scores from one treatment to the next can be caused by regression instead of the treatments.

e. *Order effects (practice, fatigue, and carry-over effects):* Whenever individuals are tested in a series of treatment conditions, participation in one treatment may have an influence on the participants' scores in the following treatments. For example, becoming fatigued in one treatment may lead to poorer performance in the next treatment. You should recognize this problem as a threat to internal validity. Specifically, the experience of being tested in one treatment may explain why the participants' scores are different in the following treatment. Remember, an alternative explanation for an observed difference is a threat to internal validity. In this case, the researcher does not know whether the observed change in performance is caused by the different treatments or by fatigue. Any possible change in performance caused by participation in a previous treatment is called an **order effect** and is a threat to internal validity because it provides an alternative explanation for the results. Common examples of order effects include **fatigue** effects (progressive decline in performance as a participant works through a series of treatment conditions) and **practice** effects (progressive improvement in performance as a participant gains experience through the series of treatment condition).

It also is possible that a specific treatment causes changes in the participants so that the lingering aftereffects of the treatment carry over to the next treatment (or treatments) and alter the participants' scores. For example, participants in a memory study may learn a new rehearsal strategy in one treatment condition, and continue to use the strategy to help improve their memory scores when participating in later treatment conditions. Appropriately, these effects are called **carry-over effects.** Another common example of carryover is a **contrast effect** in which the subjective perception of a treatment condition is influenced by its contrast with the previous treatment. For example, participants entering a room with moderate lighting for their second treatment may perceive it as dark if they are coming from a brightly lit room for their first treatment. However, the same moderately lit room may be perceived as bright if participants are coming from a dimly lit room. Notice that carry-over effects are caused by experiencing a specific treatment. Other order effects, such as practice effects and fatigue, come from the general experience of being in the study. Occasionally, these other order effects are called **progressive error** to differentiate them from carry-over effects.

DEFINITIONS

> **Order effects** occur when the experience of being tested in one treatment condition (participating and being measured) has an influence on the participants' scores in a later treatment condition(s). Order effects threaten internal validity because any observed differences between treatment conditions may be caused by order effects rather than the treatments.
>
> **Carry-over effects** occur when one treatment condition produces a change in the participants that affects their scores in subsequent treatment conditions.
>
> **Progressive error** refers to changes in a participant's behavior or performance that are related to general experience in a research study but not related to a specific treatment or treatments. Common examples of progressive error are practice effects and fatigue.

Separating Time-Related Factors and Order Effects

Although the time-related threats to internal validity are commonly grouped together in one category, researchers occasionally distinguish between those that are related exclusively to time and those that are related to previous experience within the research study. Specifically, threats from history, maturation, instrumentation, and regression are related exclusively to time and are not directly connected to experience in a previous treatment. On the other hand, order effects are directly related to experience obtained by participating in previous treatment conditions. For example, participants may learn new skills in one treatment that can influence future behavior, or become fatigued from participation in one treatment, which then affects their scores in later treatments. Based on this distinction, researchers often separate order effects from the other time-related threats to internal validity. Throughout the remainder of this chapter, we will use both terms, order effects and time-related threats, to refer to the general set of time-related factors that can threaten the internal validity of a within-subjects experiment. Finally, you should realize that time-related effects and order effects are only threats for within-subjects experiments that compare different treatments at different times. In studies that administer the different treatments all together, there is no opportunity for these threats to exist (see Figure 9.1).

Order Effects as a Confounding Variable

Order effects can produce changes in the scores from one treatment condition to another that are not caused by the treatments and can confound the results of a research study. To demonstrate this confounding effect, we examine a hypothetical experiment in which a researcher uses a within-subjects design to compare two treatment conditions with a sample of eight participants. We also assume that there is no difference between the two treatments; on average, the scores in treatment I are the same as in treatment II. Results for this hypothetical study are shown in Table 9.1a. Notice that some individual participants show a small increase or decrease between treatment conditions, representing error that can occur in any measurement process (see the discussion of reliability in Chapter 3). However, on average, there is no difference between the treatment conditions; both produce an average score of 20.

Now, consider the data shown in Table 9.1b. For these data, we assume that each participant started the experiment in treatment I and then was moved to treatment II. In addition, we assume that participation in treatment I produces an order effect (e.g., a practice effect) that causes the subsequent measurements to be 5 points higher than they would be normally. Thus, we have added a 5-point order effect to each participant's score in treatment II. Notice that the 5-point increase is not caused by the second treatment but is rather an order effect resulting from earlier participation in treatment I. The resulting data in Table 9.1b illustrate two important points:

1. The order effect varies systematically with the treatments; that is, it always contributes to the second treatment but never to the first. Whenever something changes systematically with the independent variable, it is a confounding variable. Thus, the results of this study are confounded by the order effects.
2. In this example, the confounding from the order effects makes the data look like there is a 5-point difference between the treatments. With the help of order effects, the individual participants and the group mean show consistently higher scores in the second treatment. These data could lead the researcher to conclude that there is a significant difference between the treatments when, in fact, no such difference exists (remember, we constructed the original data so there is no difference between treatments). Thus, order effects, like any confounding variable, can distort the results of a research study. In this example, the order effect creates what looks like a treatment effect but actually is just an order effect. In other situations, order effects can diminish or exaggerate a real effect, thereby posing a real threat to the internal validity of the research.

TABLE 9.1

Hypothetical Data Showing How Order Effects Can Distort the Results of a Research Study

(a) Original Scores with No Order Effect		(b) Modified Scores with a 5-Point Order Effect	
Treatment I	Treatment II	Treatment I	Treatment II
20	21	20	26 (21 + 5)
23	23	23	28 (23 + 5)
25	23	25	28 (23 + 5)
19	20	19	25 (20 + 5)
26	25	26	30 (25 + 5)
17	16	17	21 (16 + 5)
14	14	14	19 (14 + 5)
16	18	16	23 (18 + 5)
Mean = 20	Mean = 20	Mean = 20	Mean = 25

LEARNING CHECK

1. How many participants would be needed for a within-subjects experiment comparing four different treatment conditions with a total of 20 scores in each treatment?
   - **a** 20
   - **b.** 40
   - ⊗ 80
   - **d.** Cannot answer without more information

2. In a within-subjects research study comparing different treatment conditions at different times, what kind of validity is threatened by factors that change over time, such as history and maturation?
   - **a** Internal validity
   - **b.** External validity
   - **c.** Both internal and external validity
   - **d.** Neither internal nor external validity

3. In a within-subjects study that extends over a relatively long time, it is possible that there will be systematic changes in the participants' skills or knowledge during the time of the study. If these changes influence the participants' scores, causing scores at the end of the study to be different from scores at the beginning, then what is the effect is called?
   - **a.** History
   - **b.** Instrumentation
   - **c** Maturation
   - **d.** Regression toward the mean

Answers appear at the end of the chapter.

9.2

Dealing with Time-Related Threats and Order Effects

LEARNING OBJECTIVES

LO3   For a within-subjects experiment, explain how the time delay between treatments can influence time-related threats to internal validity and why it may be better to switch to a between-subjects design.

LO4   Define counterbalancing and explain how it is used to minimize or eliminate threats to internal validity from time-related factors.

LO5   Describe the limitations of counterbalancing and explain why partial counterbalancing is sometimes used.

Within-subjects designs can control environmental threats to internal validity using the same techniques that are used in between-subjects designs. Specifically, environmental factors such as the room, the experimenter, or the time of day, can be controlled by (1) randomization, (2) holding them constant, or (3) matching across treatment conditions. Time-related factors and order effects, on the other hand, require special attention and new strategies for control.

Because order effects and time-related threats to internal validity can be serious problems whenever a within-subjects design is selected, researchers have developed a variety of ways to control these potential threats. In this section, we examine some of the methods for dealing with order effects and time-related threats to gain the full benefit of within-subjects designs.

Controlling Time

The possibility that a research study will be affected by a time-related threat such as history or maturation is directly related to the length of time required to complete the study. For example, if participants go through a series of two or three treatment conditions in a single 45-minute laboratory session, it is very unlikely that time-related threats will have any influence on the results. On the other hand, if the different treatment conditions are scheduled over a period of weeks, the chances greatly increase that an outside event (history), maturation, or change in the measurement instrument will have an influence on the results. By controlling the time from one treatment condition to the next, a researcher has some control over time-related threats to internal validity.

Although shortening the time between treatments can reduce the risk of time-related threats, this technique can often increase the likelihood that order effects will influence the results. For example, in situations in which order effects are expected to be temporary, one strategy is to increase the time between treatment conditions so the order effects can dissipate. Fatigue, for example, is less likely to be a problem if participants are allowed ample opportunity to rest and recover between treatments. As we have noted, however, increasing the time between treatments increases the risk of time-related threats to internal validity.

Switch to a Between-Subjects Design

Often, researchers begin a research study with some knowledge or expectation of the existence and magnitude of order effects. For example, if the study involves measuring skill or performance over a series of treatment conditions, it is reasonable to assume that practice gained in the early treatments is likely to affect performance in later treatments. If the study involves a tedious or boring task repeated under different conditions, the researcher can expect fatigue or boredom to develop during the course of the study. In some situations, order effects are so strong and so obvious that a researcher probably would not even consider using a within-subjects design. For example, a within-subjects design is a poor choice for a study comparing two methods of teaching reading to first-grade children. After the children have been taught with method I, they are permanently changed. You cannot erase what they have learned and try to teach them again with method II. In this extreme case, the obvious strategy for avoiding order effects is to use a between-subjects design with a separate group for each of the two teaching methods. Usually, a between-subjects design (with a separate group for each treatment) is available as an alternative and completely eliminates any threat of confounding from order effects. Although the potential for order effects is not always as severe as with learning to read, a between-subjects design is often the best strategy whenever a researcher has reason to expect substantial order effects.

Counterbalancing: Matching Treatments with Respect to Time

In Chapter 7 (p. 171), we discussed the technique of matching variables across treatments to prevent the variables from becoming threats to internal validity. At that time, we also mentioned that a similar process could be used to help control time-related threats. The process of matching treatments with respect to time is called **counterbalancing.** In counterbalancing, different participants undergo the treatment conditions in different orders so that every treatment has some participants who experience the treatment first, some for whom it is second, some third, and so on. As a result, the treatments are matched, or balanced, with respect to time. With two treatments, for example, half of the participants begin in treatment I, and then move to treatment II. The other half begin in treatment II, then receive treatment I. As a result, the two treatments are matched; for both treatments, 50% of the participants experience the treatment first and 50% experience the treatment second. This procedure disrupts any systematic relationship between time and the order of treatment conditions, and thereby eliminates potential confounding from time-related threats or order effects.

In the previous section, for example, we described an experiment by Stephens, Atkins, and Kingston (2009) examining the effect of swearing in response to pain (p. 212). In one condition, the participants were told to shout their favorite swear words while experiencing a painful stimulus (ice water) and in the second condition they shouted a neutral word. Half of the participants started with the swearing condition and half started with the neutral word condition. After a brief rest, the two groups switched words. Thus, the two conditions (curse and neutral) were counterbalanced, with half of the participants swearing first and half swearing second.

DEFINITION

> For a within-subjects design, **counterbalancing** is defined as changing the order in which treatment conditions are administered from one participant to another so that the treatment conditions are matched with respect to time. The goal is to use every possible order of treatments with an equal number of individuals participating in each sequence. The purpose of counterbalancing is to eliminate the potential for confounding by disrupting any systematic relationship between the order of treatments and time-related factors.

You may have noticed that counterbalancing requires separate groups of participants, with each group going through the series of treatments in a different order. The existence of separate groups may appear to contradict the basic definition of a within-subjects design. The solution to this apparent contradiction is based on the observation that although the groups go through the treatments in different orders, they all receive the full set of treatments. Thus, we still have a within-subjects design, with one combined group of individuals participating in all of the different treatment conditions. In Chapter 11 (p. 287), we return to this issue when we re-examine a counterbalanced study as a combination of a within-subjects design (with one group in all the treatments) and a between-subjects design (with different groups receiving the treatments in different orders).

Counterbalancing and Order Effects

Although counterbalancing has exactly the same effect on time-related threats and order effects, the process of counterbalancing is usually discussed in terms of order effects. Therefore, throughout the rest of this section, we focus on counterbalancing and order effects. Keep in mind, however, that counterbalancing is just as effective for controlling factors such as history and maturation as for controlling order effects.

The hypothetical data in Table 9.2 provide a numerical demonstration of counterbalancing, and how it controls threats to validity. The table shows the results from an experiment in which a researcher uses a within-subjects design to compare two treatments. The design is counterbalanced with four of the eight participants starting in treatment I and ending with treatment II, and the other four participants receiving the treatments in the reverse order. Table 9.2a shows scores as they would appear if there were no order effects.

The data have been constructed to produce a 6-point difference between the two treatment conditions (mean I = 20 vs. mean II = 26). The modified scores in Table 9.2b show how order effects influence the data. For this example, we assume that experience in one treatment condition produces an order effect that causes a 5-point increase in scores for the next treatment.

TABLE 9.2

Hypothetical Data Showing How Counterbalancing Distributes Order Effects Evenly between the Treatment Conditions

(a) Original Scores with No Order Effect		(b) Modified Scores with a 5-Point Order Effect		
Treatment I	**Treatment II**	**Treatment I**		**Treatment II**
20	27	20	— order →	32 (27 + 5)
23	29	23	→	34 (29 + 5)
25	29	25	→	34 (29 + 5)
19	26	19	→	31 (26 + 5)
26	31	(26 + 5) 31	← order —	31
17	22	(17 + 5) 22	←	22
14	20	(14 + 5) 19	←	20
16	24	(16 + 5) 21	←	24
Mean = 20	Mean = 26	Mean = 22.5		Mean = 28.5

Because the design is counterbalanced, the first four participants begin the experiment in treatment I, and the 5-point order effect adds to their scores in treatment II. The remaining four participants receive the treatments in the opposite order, so the order effect adds to their scores in treatment I. Notice that the result of the counterbalancing is to distribute the order effects evenly between the two treatments; that is, the order effects are balanced across the treatment conditions. Although the treatment means are affected by the order effects, they are affected equally. As a result, there is still a 6-point difference between the two treatment means, exactly as it was without any order effects. The point of this demonstration is to show that order effects can change individual scores and can change means, but when a design is counterbalanced, the changes do not influence the mean differences between treatments. Because the treatment differences are not affected, the order effects do not threaten the internal validity of the study.

The value of counterbalancing a within-subjects design is that it prevents any order effects from accumulating in one particular treatment condition. Instead, the order effects are spread evenly across all the different conditions so that it is possible to make fair, unbiased comparisons between treatments (no single treatment has any special advantage or disadvantage). On the other hand, counterbalancing does not eliminate the order effects; they are still embedded in the data. Furthermore, the order effects are hidden in the data so that a researcher cannot see whether they exist or how large they are. In Table 9.2, we identify and expose hypothetical order effects to demonstrate how they influence a counterbalanced design. In real life, however, all you see are the final scores, which may or may not include order effects.

Limitations of Counterbalancing

As demonstrated in Table 9.2, counterbalancing can be used to prevent order effects (or other time-related effects) from confounding the results of a within-subjects research study. In the same way that random assignment is a routine technique for maintaining validity in between-subjects research, counterbalancing is a routine technique used in within-subjects research. However, this apparently simple and effective technique has some limitations.

Counterbalancing and Variance

The purpose of counterbalancing is to distribute order effects evenly across the different treatment conditions. However, this process does not eliminate the order effects. In particular, the order effects are still part of the data, and they can still create problems. One is that they can distort the treatment means. In Table 9.2, the order effects are present in both treatments and inflate both of the treatment means. Usually, this kind of distortion is not important because researchers typically are interested in the amount of difference between treatments rather than the absolute magnitude of any specific mean. When counterbalancing works as intended, the differences between means are not changed. However, in situations in which the absolute level of performance (the true mean) is important, the process of counterbalancing can disguise the true value of a treatment mean.

A more serious problem is that counterbalancing adds the order effects to some of the individuals within each treatment but not to all of the individuals. In the example shown in Table 9.2, some of the individuals in treatment I receive an extra 5 points and some do not. As a result, the differences between scores are increased within each treatment, which adds to the variance within treatments. Recall from Chapter 8 (p. 196) that large variance within treatments can obscure treatment effects. In statistical terms, high variance within treatments decreases the likelihood that a research study will obtain significant differences between treatments. Thus, in situations in which order effects are relatively large, the process of counterbalancing can undermine the potential for a successful experiment.

Asymmetrical Order Effects

In Chapter 11 (p. 287), we present a method that allows researchers to measure and evaluate order effects.

In Table 9.2, we use exactly the same 5-point order effect whether participants started in treatment I or in treatment II. That is, we assume that the order effects are symmetrical. This assumption of symmetry is not always justified. It is definitely possible that one treatment might produce more of an order effect than another treatment. For example, one treatment condition might provide more opportunity for practice than the other conditions. Or one treatment might be more demanding and create more fatigue than the other treatment conditions. In such situations, the order effects are not symmetrical, and counterbalancing the order of treatments does not balance the order effects.

Counterbalancing and the Number of Treatments

To completely counterbalance a series of treatments, it is necessary to present the treatments in every possible sequence. The idea behind **complete counterbalancing** is that a particular series of treatment conditions may create its own unique order effect. For example, treatments II and III, in sequence, may produce a unique effect that carries over into the next treatment. Treatments I and III, in sequence, may produce a different order effect. To completely balance these combined effects, the research design should use every possible ordering of treatment conditions.

With only two treatment conditions, complete counterbalancing is easy: There are only two possible sequences. However, as the number of treatments increases, complete counterbalancing becomes more complex. If the number of different treatment conditions is identified as n, then the number of different sequences is $n!$ (n factorial).

$$n! = n(n-1)(n-2)(n-3)\ldots(1)$$

For example, with four treatment conditions, there are $4! = 4 \times 3 \times 2 \times 1 = 24$ different sequences. If the four treatments are identified as A, B, C, and D, the 24 sequences can be listed as follows:

ABCD	BACD	CABD	DABC	Note that the sequence ABCD indicates
ABDC	BADC	CADB	DACB	that treatment A is first, B is second, C is
ACBD	BCAD	CBAD	DBAC	third, and D is fourth.
ACDB	BCDA	CBDA	DBCA	
ADBC	BDAC	CDAB	DCAB	
ADCB	BDCA	CDBA	DCBA	

To completely counterbalance a within-subjects experiment with four treatment conditions, the researcher must divide the participants into 24 equal-sized groups and assign one group to each of the 24 different sequences. Obviously, this study would require at least 24 participants (one per group), which may be more than the researcher needs or wants. With even more treatments, the demands of complete counterbalancing can become outrageous. With $n = 6$ treatments, for example, there are $6! = 720$ different treatment sequences, which means that the study would require a minimum of 720 participants.

One solution to this problem is to use what is known as **partial counterbalancing**. Instead of every possible sequence, partial counterbalancing simply uses enough different orderings to ensure that each treatment condition occurs first in the sequence for one group of participants, occurs second for another group, third for another group, and so on. With four treatments, for example, this requires only four different sequences, such as: ABCD, CADB, BDAC, DCBA. To conduct a partially counterbalanced study with four treatments, a researcher needs to divide the participants into four equal sized groups and assign one group to each of the four sequences. One group of participants receives treatment A first, one group has A second, one has A third, and one has A fourth. Similarly, each of the other treatments appears once in each ordinal position.

Because partial counterbalancing does not use every possible sequence of treatment conditions, one problem is to decide exactly which sequences to select. A simple and unbiased procedure for selecting sequences is to construct a Latin square. To create a **Latin square** for four treatment conditions, start with a 4×4 matrix and fill it in with the letters A, B, C, and D, as follows:

List the letters ABCD in order in the top row of the matrix. To create the next row, simply move the last letter in line to the beginning. This creates DABC for the second row. Continue moving the last letter to the beginning of the line to create each new row. The result is the following Latin square:

A B C D   By definition, a Latin square is a matrix of n elements (letters)
D A B C   where each element appears exactly once in each column
C D A B   and in each row.
B C D A

Each row in the square provides a sequence of treatment conditions for one group of participants. For this example, the first group receives the four treatments in the order ABCD. A second group receives the order DABC, and so on.

The Latin square in the preceding paragraph is not a particularly good example of partial counterbalancing because it does not balance every possible sequence of treatment conditions. For example, the first three groups all receive treatment A followed immediately by treatment B. On the other hand, no one receives treatment B followed by treatment A. Whenever possible, a Latin square should ensure that every possible sequence of treatments is represented. One method for improving the square is to use a random process to rearrange the columns (e.g., a coin toss to decide whether or not each column is moved), then use a random process to rearrange the rows. The resulting rows in the square should provide a better set of sequences for a partially counterbalanced research study.

LEARNING CHECK

1. What is the effect of increasing the time between treatment conditions in a within-subjects experiment?
   a. It decreases the threat of time-related history effect.
   b. It decreases the threat of the order effect fatigue.
   c. It decreases the threat of a time-related maturation effect.
   d. None of the other options is an effect of increasing time between treatments.

2. For a within-subjects study comparing two treatments, A and B, a researcher expects that practice in the first treatment will improve the participants' scores in the second treatment. If the order of treatments is counterbalanced, then what scores will be influenced by the practice?
   a. Scores in treatment A but not in treatment B.
   b. Scores in treatment B but not in treatment A.
   c. Scores in treatment A for half the participants and scores in treatment B for half the participants.
   d. Practice will not influence the scores because the treatments are counterbalanced.

3. Which of the following describes a completely counterbalanced within-subjects experiment?
   a. Each group receives a different treatment.
   b. Each participant receives each treatment in the same order.
   c. A series of treatments is presented in every possible sequence.
   d. Participants receive a random order of treatment conditions.

Answers appear at the end of the chapter.

9.3 Comparing Within-Subjects and Between-Subjects Designs

LEARNING OBJECTIVES

LO6 Explain the general advantages and disadvantages of within-subjects designs compared to between-subjects designs and be able to decide which design would be better under specific circumstances.

LO7 Define a matched-subject design and explain how it attempts to achieve the advantages of both within- and between-subjects designs without their disadvantages.

Often a research question can be addressed with either a between-subjects or a within-subjects experiment. The between-subjects design would use a different group of participants for each of the treatment conditions and the within-subjects design would use the same individuals in all of the treatments. The decision about which design to use is often based on the relative advantages and disadvantages of the two designs.

Advantages of Within-Subjects Designs

One advantage of a within-subjects design is that it requires relatively few participants in comparison to between-subjects designs. For example, to compare three different treatment conditions with 30 participants in each treatment, a between-subjects design requires a total of 90 participants (three separate groups with 30 participants in each). A within-subjects design, however, requires only 30 participants (the same group of 30 participants is used in all three conditions). Because a within-subjects study requires only one group, it is particularly useful in situations in which participants are difficult to find. For example, it might be difficult to recruit a large sample of people for a study examining twins who are at least 80 years old.

The primary advantage of a within-subjects design, however, is that it essentially eliminates all of the problems based on individual differences that are the primary concern of a between-subjects design. Recall from Chapter 8 that in a between-subjects design, individual differences can create two major problems for research:

1. Individual differences between groups can become a confounding variable. If the individuals in one treatment condition are noticeably different from the individuals in another treatment (e.g., smarter, faster, bigger, or older), then the individual differences, rather than the treatments, may explain any observed differences.

2. The individual differences within each treatment condition can create high variance, which can obscure any differences between treatments.

These problems are reduced or eliminated in a within-subjects design. First, obviously, a within-subjects design has no individual differences between groups because there is only one group of participants. The group in one treatment is exactly the same as the group in every other treatment, which means that there are no individual differences between groups to confound the study. Second, because each participant appears in every treatment condition, each individual serves as his own control or baseline. This makes it possible to measure and remove the variance caused by individual differences. The following example demonstrates how the problems associated with individual differences are reduced in a within-subjects design.

Table 9.3 shows two sets of hypothetical data. The first set is from a typical between-subjects experiment and the second set represents a within-subjects experiment. Each score is labeled with the participant's name so that we can examine the effects of individual differences. For the between-subjects data, every score represents a different person. For the within-subjects data, on the other hand, the same people are measured in all three treatment conditions. The difference between the two designs has some important consequences:

1. Both research studies have exactly the same scores, and both show the same differences between treatments. In each case, the researcher would like to conclude that the differences between treatments were caused by the treatments. However, with the between-subjects design (see Table 9.3a), the participants in treatment I may have characteristics that make them different from the participants in treatment II. For example, the four individuals in treatment II may be more intelligent than the participants in treatment I, and their higher intelligence may have caused their higher scores. This problem disappears in the within-subjects design (see Table 9.3b); the participants in one treatment cannot differ from the participants in another treatment because the same individuals are used in all the treatments.

2. Although the two sets of data contain exactly the same scores, they differ greatly in the way that the individual differences contribute to the variance. For the between-subjects experiment, the individual differences and the treatment effects are tied together and cannot be separated. To measure the difference between treatments, we must also measure the differences between individuals. For example, John scored 5 points lower than Sue, but it is impossible to determine whether this 5-point difference is caused by the treatments or is simply a matter of individual differences (John is different from Sue).

TABLE 9.3

Hypothetical Data Showing the Results from a Between-Subjects Experiment and a Within-Subjects Experiment

The two sets of data use exactly the same numerical scores.

(a) Between-Subjects Experiment—Three Separate Groups

Treatment I		Treatment II		Treatment III	
(John)	20	(Sue)	25	(Beth)	30
(Mary)	31	(Tom)	36	(Bob)	38
(Bill)	51	(Dave)	55	(Don)	59
(Kate)	62	(Ann)	64	(Zoe)	69
Mean =	41	Mean =	45	Mean =	49

(b) Within-Subjects Experiment—One Group in All Three Treatments

Treatment I		Treatment II		Treatment III	
(John)	20	(John)	25	(John)	30
(Mary)	31	(Mary)	36	(Mary)	38
(Bill)	51	(Bill)	55	(Bill)	59
(Kate)	62	(Kate)	64	(Kate)	69
Mean =	41	Mean =	45	Mean =	49

Individual differences are an integral part of a between-subjects design, and they are automatically a part of the variance in the scores. For the within-subjects data, however, the treatment effects are not connected to the individual differences. To evaluate the difference between treatments I and II, for example, we never compare John to Mary. Instead we compare John (in treatment I) to John (in treatment II), and we compare Mary (in treatment I) to Mary (in treatment II). Because the treatment effects and individual differences are not connected, we can separate the individual differences from the rest of the variance in a within-subjects design.

Once again, consider the within-subjects experiment (see Table 9.3b). Although individual differences are part of the variance in the data (e.g., John's scores are different from Mary's scores), we can determine how much of the variance is caused by the individual differences. For these data, for example, there is a consistent difference of about 10 points between John and Mary in each of the three treatments. Similarly, there is a 30-point difference between John and Bill and a 40-point difference between John and Kate. Whenever the individual differences are reasonably consistent across treatment conditions, they can be measured and separated from the rest of the variance. Thus, in a within-subjects design, the following measurements are possible:

- It is possible to measure the differences between treatments without involving any individual differences. Because the same participants are in every treatment condition, the treatment effects and the individual differences are not linked.
- It is possible to measure the differences between individuals. When the individual differences are consistent across treatments, they can be measured and removed from the rest of the variance in the data. This can greatly reduce the negative effects of large variance.

To demonstrate the actual process of separating the individual differences from the rest of the variance, consider once again the within-subjects data in Table 9.3b. For these data, Kate consistently has the highest score in each treatment. Specifically, the average score for the four participants across all three treatments is 45; however, the average score for Kate is 65. This is an example of an individual difference; clearly, Kate is different from the other participants. However, we can eliminate this difference by simply subtracting 20 points from each of Kate's scores. As a result, Kate becomes a more "normal" participant.

Similarly, John's average score is 20 points lower than the group average, so we can make John "normal" by adding 20 points to each of his scores. Finally, we subtract 10 points from each of Bill's scores and then add 10 points to each of Mary's scores. The resulting data are shown in Table 9.4. Notice that we have removed the individual differences by making the four individuals equal (all four participants now have an average score of 45) but we have not changed any of the treatment effects. For example, John's score still increases by 5 points as he goes from treatment I to treatment II, and increases another 5 points as he goes from treatment II to treatment III. Also, all of the treatment means are exactly the same as they were before we started adding and subtracting. Thus, the newly created scores preserve all of the important characteristics of the original scores. That is, the changes (treatment effects) that occur for the participants, individually and collectively, are the same as in the original data. However the big differences from one participant to another in Table 9.3b are now gone, and the resulting scores show only a 1- or 2-point difference between individuals. Removing the individual differences drastically reduces the variance of the scores and makes the 4-point mean differences from treatment to treatment much easier to see.

The differences between treatments for the data in Table 9.4 are even more obvious when the scores are presented in a graph. Figure 9.2 shows the original within-subjects data from Table 9.3b and the adjusted data from Table 9.4. When the individual differences are removed, the treatment effects are much easier to see.

By measuring and removing individual differences, the within-subjects design reduces variance and reveals treatment effects that might not be apparent in a between-subjects design. In statistical terms, a within-subjects design is generally more powerful than a between-subjects design; that is, a within-subjects design is more likely to detect a treatment effect than a between-subjects design.

TABLE 9.4

Removing Individual Differences from Within-Subjects Data

This table shows the same data from Table 9.3b, except that we have eliminated the individual differences from the data. For example, we subtracted 20 points from each of Kate's scores to make her more "average," and we added 20 points to each of John's scores to make him more "average." This process of eliminating individual differences makes the treatment effects much easier to see.

Treatment I		Treatment II		Treatment III	
(John)	40	(John)	45	(John)	50
(Mary)	41	(Mary)	46	(Mary)	48
(Bill)	41	(Bill)	45	(Bill)	49
(Kate)	42	(Kate)	44	(Kate)	49
Mean =	41	Mean =	45	Mean =	49

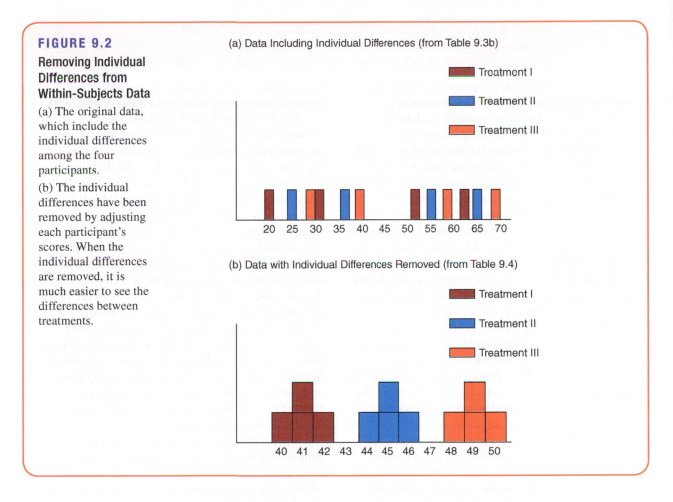

FIGURE 9.2

Removing Individual Differences from Within-Subjects Data

(a) The original data, which include the individual differences among the four participants.

(b) The individual differences have been removed by adjusting each participant's scores. When the individual differences are removed, it is much easier to see the differences between treatments.

(a) Data Including Individual Differences (from Table 9.3b)

Treatment I
Treatment II
Treatment III

20 25 30 35 40 45 50 55 60 65 70

(b) Data with Individual Differences Removed (from Table 9.4)

Treatment I
Treatment II
Treatment III

40 41 42 43 44 45 46 47 48 49 50

In the preceding example, we removed the individual differences by equalizing all the participants. In a normal research situation, this equalizing process is accomplished by statistical analysis (instead of manipulation of the data). However, the result is the same: The variance caused by individual differences is removed. The statistical removal of individual differences is demonstrated in Box 9.1. Finally, we should note that you cannot use this equalizing process to remove the individual differences from the data in a between-subjects design. In between-subjects data, every score is from a separate individual and an attempt to equalize the participants as in Table 9.4 would simply change *all* the scores to the same value, which would also eliminate the treatment effects.

Disadvantages of Within-Subjects Designs

Although a within-subjects design has some definite advantages relative to a between-subjects design, it also has some disadvantages. The primary disadvantage comes from the fact that each participant often goes through a series of treatment conditions, with each treatment administered at a different time. Whenever the treatments occur at different times, there is an opportunity for time-related factors, such as fatigue or the weather, to influence the participants' scores. For example, if a participant's performance steadily declines over a series of treatment conditions, you cannot determine whether the decline is being caused by the different treatments or is simply an indication that the participant is getting tired. You should recognize this problem as an example of a confounding variable that threatens

BOX 9.1 Statistical Consequences of Removing Individual Differences in a Within-Subjects Design

As we noted in the text, the process of removing individual differences from the variance in a within-subjects design is accomplished during the statistical analysis. To demonstrate this phenomenon, we consider the statistical evaluation for the two sets of data shown in Table 9.3. Both sets of data contain exactly the same scores and produce exactly the same means: the mean for treatment I is 41, for treatment II the mean is 45, and for treatment III the mean is 49. The purpose of the statistical analysis is to determine whether these mean differences are statistically significant; that is, are the differences large enough to conclude that they are very unlikely to have occurred by chance alone, and probably represent real differences between the treatments (see Box 7.1, p. 161)?

With three treatment conditions, the appropriate statistical procedure is an analysis of variance (ANOVA). The analysis first computes a variance that measures the size of the actual mean differences; the bigger the differences, the bigger the variance. The analysis then computes a second variance, called the error variance, which estimates the size of the mean differences that would be expected if there were no treatment effects. This second variance, the error variance, is the one that is influenced by individual differences. Finally, the analysis compares the two variances to determine whether the actual mean differences (variance 1) are significantly

bigger than the mean differences that would be expected without any treatment effects (variance 2).

For the data in Table 9.3, both designs, between-subjects and within-subjects, have exactly the same mean differences and produce exactly the same value for variance 1, $V_1 = 64$. For the between-subjects design, the error variance includes individual differences, and the data in Table 9.3 produce a value of $V_2 = 334$. In this case, the actual mean differences ($V_1 = 64$) are definitely not bigger than would be expected if there were no treatment effects ($V_2 = 334$), and we conclude that there are no significant differences. For the within-subjects design, however, the individual differences are eliminated from the error variance. As a result, the size of the error variance (V_2) is substantially reduced. For the data in Table 9.3, the error variance is $V_2 = 1$. For the within-subjects design, the actual mean differences ($V_1 = 64$) are substantially bigger than would be expected without any treatment effects ($V_2 = 1$), and we conclude that there are significant mean differences.

Once more, the general point from this demonstration is that a within-subjects design removes the individual differences from the data, which reduces the variance and can greatly increase the likelihood of detecting significant differences between treatment conditions.

---

the internal validity of the experiment. Specifically, whenever there is an alternative explanation for the results, the experiment is confounded. In Chapter 6 (p. 150), we noted that time-related factors can threaten the internal validity of a within-subjects experiment. These time-related factors, which are discussed in Section 9.1, are the major disadvantages of a within-subjects experimental design.

Caution: In Chapter 8, we discussed differential attrition as a threat to internal validity for between-subjects experiments. The attrition discussed here simply means the loss of participants from a research study.

Another potential problem for a within-subjects design with different treatments administered at different times is **participant attrition.** In simple terms, some of the individuals who start the research study may be gone before the study is completed. Because a within-subjects design often requires repeated measurements under different conditions for each individual, some participants may be lost between the first measurement and the final measurement. This problem is especially serious when the study extends over a period of time and participants must be called back for additional observation. Participants may forget appointments, lose interest, quit, move away, or even die. In addition to shrinking the sample size, the attrition problem may exaggerate volunteer bias if only the most dedicated volunteers continue from start to finish. As noted in Chapter 6, volunteer bias can threaten the external validity of a research study.

In situations in which participant attrition is anticipated, it is advisable to begin the research study with more individuals than are actually needed. In this way, the chances are increased of having a reasonable number of participants left when the study ends.

Choosing Within- or Between-Subjects Design

By now, it should be clear that a within-subjects design has some distinct advantages and some unique disadvantages compared to a between-subjects design. It should also be clear that the advantages of one design are essentially the same as the disadvantages of the other. Three factors that differentiate the designs are:

1. *Individual differences*. The prospect that individual differences may become confounding variables or increase variance is a major disadvantage of between-subjects designs. However, these problems are eliminated in a within-subjects design. Because the within-subjects design reduces variance, it is generally more likely to detect a treatment effect (if one exists) than is a between-subjects design. If you anticipate large individual differences, it is usually better to use a within-subjects design.

2. *Time-related factors and order effects*. There is often the potential for factors that change over time to distort the results of within-subjects designs. However, this problem is eliminated in a between-subjects design, in which each individual participates in only one treatment and is measured only once. Thus, whenever you expect one (or more) of the treatment conditions to have a large and long-lasting effect that may influence the participants in future conditions, it is better to use a between-subjects design.

3. *Fewer participants*. Although it is a relatively minor advantage, we should note once again that a within-subjects design typically requires fewer participants. Because a within-subjects design obtains multiple scores for each individual, it can generate a lot of data from a relatively small set of participants. A between-subjects design, on the other hand, produces only one score for each participant and requires a lot of participants to generate a lot of data. Whenever it is difficult to find or recruit participants, a within-subjects design is a better choice.

Matched-Subjects Designs

In Chapter 8 (p. 194), we discussed matching groups as a technique for ensuring that the different groups in a between-subjects design all have essentially the same characteristics. Now, we are matching subjects, one-to-one, as an attempt to simulate a within-subjects design.

Occasionally, researchers attempt to approximate the advantages of within- and between-subjects designs by using a technique known as a **matched-subjects design**. A matched-subjects design uses a separate group for each treatment condition, but each individual in one group is matched one-to-one with an individual in every other group. The matching is based on a variable considered to be particularly relevant to the specific study. Suppose, for example, that a researcher wants to com____ ____ferent methods for teaching mathematics in the third grade. For this study, the re____ ____math-ematics achievement test to a large sample of students, then ____ their test scores. Thus, if Tom and Bill have identical math ____ students can be treated as a matched pair with Tom assigne____ Bill assigned to the other. If the study compares three treatm____ to find triplets of matched individuals. Although a matche____ exactly the same individuals in each treatment condition (____ does have equivalent (matched) individuals in each treatr____

DEFINITION

> In a **matched-subjects design,** each individual in one group is matched with a participant in each of the other groups. The matching is done so that the matched individuals are equivalent with respect to a variable that the researcher considers to be relevant to the study.

The goal of a matched-subjects design is to duplicate all the advantages of within- and between-subjects designs without the disadvantages of either one. For example, a matched-subjects design attempts to mimic a within-subjects design by having "equivalent" participants in all of the treatment conditions. In a within-subjects design, the equivalent participants are literally the same people, and in a matched-subjects design, the equivalent participants are matched sets of people. Thus, a researcher does not need to worry that the participants in one treatment are noticeably different from the participants in another treatment. In addition, the statistics used to evaluate a matched-subjects design are the same as those used for within-subjects designs. In both designs, the variance caused by individual differences is measured and removed. The matched-subjects design also mimics a between-subjects design by using a separate group for each treatment condition with each individual measured only once. Thus, there is no chance for the scores to be influenced by time-related factors or order effects.

It is possible to match participants on more than one variable. For example, a researcher could match participants on the basis of age, gender, race, and IQ. In this case, for example, a 22-year-old white female with an IQ of 118 who was in one group would be matched with another 22-year-old white female with an IQ of 118 in another group. Note, however, that matching can become extremely difficult as the number of matched variables increases and the number of different groups increases.

In general, a matched-subjects design attempts to eliminate the problems associated with between-subjects experiments (individual differences) and the problems associated with within-subjects experiments (order effects). However, a matched-subjects design is only a crude approximation to a repeated-measures design. The matched pairs of participants in a matched-subjects design are not really the same people. Instead, they are merely "similar" individuals with the degree of similarity limited to the variable(s) that are used for the matching process. Simply because two individuals have the same IQ is no guarantee that they are also the same or even similar on other variables. Thus, matched-subjects designs are not nearly as effective at removing individual differences as are within-subjects designs.

LEARNING CHECK

1. What is measured and removed to reduce the variance in within-subjects design compared to a between-subjects design.
    (a) The individual differences
    b. The carry over effects
    c. The progressive error effects
    d. The instrumentation effects

2. Which of the following is an advantage of the between-subjects design versus the within-subjects design?
    a. It generally requires fewer participants.
    b. It usually is a more sensitive test (more likely to detect a treatment effect).
    (c) It eliminates the risk of order effects.
    d. It eliminates potential problems that may be caused by individual differences.

3. For an experiment that compares two treatment conditions with ten scores in each treatment, which design would require fewer subjects?
    a. Between-subjects design
    b. Within-subjects design
    c. Matched-subjects design
    d. All would require the same number of subjects.

Answers appear at the end of the chapter.

9.4 | Applications and Statistical Analysis of Within-Subjects Designs

LEARNING OBJECTIVE

LO8 Describe the different ways that within-subjects designs are used to compare two or more treatment conditions, identify the statistical techniques that are appropriate for each application, and explain the strengths and weaknesses of each application.

Commonly, a within-subjects design is preferred to a between-subjects design to take advantage of one or more of the special characteristics of this type of research. For example:

1. Because the within-subjects design requires only one group, it often is used when obtaining a large group of research participants is difficult or impossible. If a researcher studies a population with a rare characteristic (Olympic athletes, people with multiple-personality disorder, or women taller than 7 feet), then a within-subjects design is more efficient because it requires fewer participants.
2. We have noted repeatedly that one big advantage of a within-subjects design is that it reduces or eliminates variability caused by individual differences. Whenever a researcher anticipates that the data will show large variability caused by differences between participants, a within-subjects design is the preferred choice.

Two-Treatment Designs

The simplest application of a within-subjects design is to evaluate the difference between two treatment conditions. The two-treatment within-subjects design has many of the same advantages and disadvantages as the two-group between-subjects design discussed in Chapter 8 (see pp. 204–205). On the positive side, the design is easy to conduct and the results are easy to understand. With only two treatment conditions, a researcher can easily maximize the difference between treatments by selecting two treatment conditions that are clearly different. This usually increases the likelihood of obtaining a significant difference. In addition, with only two treatment conditions, it is very easy to counterbalance the design to minimize the threat of confounding from time-related factors or order effects. On the negative side, a study with only two treatments provides only two data points. In this situation, it is possible to demonstrate a difference between conditions, but the data do not provide any indication of the functional relationship between the independent and dependent variables. That is, we cannot determine how the dependent variable would respond to small, gradual changes of the independent variable.

With data measured on an interval or ratio scale, the most common strategy for data analysis is to compute a mean score for each treatment condition. The means are used to describe (summarize) the individual treatments, and the difference between means is used to describe the differential effects of the treatments. With two treatment conditions, a repeated-measures t or a single-factor ANOVA (repeated measures) can be used to evaluate the statistical significance of the mean difference, that is, to determine whether the obtained mean difference is greater than what would be reasonably expected from sampling error (see Chapter 15). If the data do not permit the calculation of treatment means, there are alternative methods for statistically evaluating the difference between treatments. If the data are measured on an ordinal scale (or can be rank ordered), a Wilcoxon Signed-Ranks test can be used to evaluate significant differences. Occasionally, a within-subjects study comparing two treatments produces data that show only the direction of difference between the two treatments. For example, a therapist may be able to classify individual clients as showing improvement or showing decline after treatment. In this situation, the data can be statistically evaluated using a sign test to determine whether the changes are consistently in one direction (enough to satisfy statistical significance).

Multiple-Treatment Designs

As we discussed in Chapter 8, the primary advantage of using more than two treatment conditions is that the data are more likely to reveal the functional relationship between the two variables being studied (see Figure 8.5, p. 205). A researcher can create a series of conditions (independent variable), and then observe how the participants' behavior (dependent variable) changes as they move through the series of treatments. A multiple-treatment design also produces a more convincing demonstration of a cause-and-effect relationship than is provided by a two-treatment design. Demonstrating repeatedly that a dependent variable responds each time an independent variable is changed produces compelling evidence that the independent variable is responsible for causing changes in the dependent variable.

The disadvantages of using multiple treatments in a within-subjects design include the same basic problem introduced in Chapter 8 (see p. 205). If a researcher creates too many treatment conditions, the distinction between treatments may become too small to generate significant differences in behavior. In addition, multiple treatments for a within-subjects design typically increase the amount of time required for each participant to complete the full series of treatments. This can increase the likelihood of participant attrition. Finally, the ability to completely counterbalance a design becomes more difficult as the number of treatment conditions increases.

With data measured on an interval or ratio scale, the typical statistical analysis consists of computing a mean for each treatment condition, then using a repeated-measures ANOVA to test for any significant differences among the treatment means (see Chapter 15). For more complex within-subjects designs, consult an advanced statistics text to verify that an appropriate analysis technique exists before beginning the research study.

LEARNING CHECK

1. What is the appropriate hypothesis test for a within-subjects design comparing mean differences for three treatment conditions?
   a. An independent-measures t test
   b. A repeated-measures t test
   c. A repeated-measures analysis of variance.
   d. A chi-square test for independence

2. Which of the following is an advantage of a two-treatment within-subjects design compared to a multiple-treatment design?
   a. There is a reduced risk of participant attrition.
   b. There is a reduced risk that time-related factors influence the data.
   c. It is easier to counterbalance a design with only two treatments.
   d. All of the above are advantages of a two-treatment design.

Answers appear at the end of the chapter.

CHAPTER SUMMARY

At this point, you should review the learning objectives presented at the beginning of each section and be sure that you have mastered each objective.

This chapter examined the characteristics of the within-subjects experimental design. The general goal of a within-subjects experiment is to determine whether differences exist between two or more treatment conditions. The defining characteristic of a within-subjects design is that it uses a single group of individuals, and tests or observes each individual in all of the different treatments being compared.

The primary advantage of a within-subjects design is that it essentially eliminates all the problems based on individual differences that are the primary concern of a between-subjects design. First, a within-subjects design has no individual differences between groups. There is only one group of participants, so the group of individuals in treatment I is exactly the same as the group of individuals in treatment II; hence, there are no individual differences between groups to confound the study. Second, because each participant appears in every treatment condition, each individual serves as his own control or baseline. This makes it possible to measure and remove the variance caused by individual differences.

The primary disadvantage of a within-subjects design is that the scores obtained in one treatment condition are directly related to scores in every other condition. The relationship between scores across treatments creates the potential for the scores in one treatment to be influenced by previous treatments, previous measurements, or previous experience.

This general problem is called an order effect because the current scores may have been affected by events that occurred earlier in the order of treatments. Order effects can be a confounding variable in a within-subjects design. In addition to order effects, other threats to the internal validity of within-subjects designs are discussed. A technique for dealing with such problems is to counterbalance the conditions.

Finally, different applications of the within-subjects design are considered along with the appropriate statistical analysis.

KEY WORDS

within-subjects experimental design or repeated-measures experimental design

history

maturation

instrumentation or instrumental bias or instrumental decay

statistical regression, or regression toward the mean

order effects

carry-over effects

progressive error

counterbalancing

matched-subjects design

EXERCISES

The exercises are identified with specific learning objectives and are intended to assess your mastery of the objectives. You should be aware that exam items are also generated to assess learning objectives.

1. In addition to the key words, you should also be able to define the following terms:

   within-subjects design
   repeated-measures design
   practice
   fatigue
   contrast effect
   complete counterbalancing
   partial counterbalancing
   Latin square
   participant attrition

2. (**LO1**) Describe the characteristics of a within-subjects experimental research design.

3. (**LO2**) Time-related factors and order effects can threaten internal validity for some within-subjects experiments. Describe the kind of study for which these factors can be a problem and explain how they can be a confounding variable in some within-subjects designs.

4. (**LO3**) For a within-subjects experiment that includes a time delay between treatment conditions, explain the possible advantages and the disadvantages of increasing the time delay between one treatment and the next.

5. (**LO3**) Under what circumstances is it advisable to switch to a between-subjects design instead of using a within-subjects design?

6. (**LO4**) Describe the circumstances in which counterbalancing is used and explain what it is trying to accomplish.

7. (**LO5**) Explain why partial counterbalancing is sometimes necessary.

8. (**LO6**) Describe the problems that can be caused by individual differences in a between-subjects experiment and explain how these problems are eliminated or reduced in a within-subjects experiment.

9. (**LO6**) A researcher has a sample of 30 rats that are all cloned from the same source. The 30 rats are genetically identical and have been raised in exactly the same environment since birth. The researcher conducts an experiment, randomly assigning 10 of the clones to treatment A, 10 to treatment B, and the other 10 to treatment C. Explain why the clone experiment is better than a within-subjects study using 10 regular rats that are tested in each of the three treatments. In other words, explain how the clone experiment eliminates the basic problems with a within-subjects study.

10. (**LO7**) Explain how a matched-subjects design attempts to avoid the major problem with between-subjects experiments (individual differences) and the major problem with within-subjects experiments (time-related factors).

11. (**LO8**) Describe the disadvantages of a multiple-treatment design, compared to a two-treatment design, for a within-subjects experiment.

12. (**LO8**) At the beginning of this chapter, we described a study in which participants shouted either a swear word or a neutral word over and over while holding one hand in a bowl of ice water. The study obtained two scores for each participant: how long the pain could be tolerated while swearing and how long while shouting a neutral word. Which statistical procedure should be used to evaluate the significance of the mean difference between the two groups of rating scores?

LEARNING CHECK ANSWERS

Section 9.1
1. a, 2. a, 3. c

Section 9.2
1. b, 2. c, 3. c

Section 9.3
1. a, 2. c, 3. b

Section 9.4
1. c, 2. d

The Nonexperimental and Quasi-Experimental Strategies: Nonequivalent Group, Pre–Post, and Developmental Designs

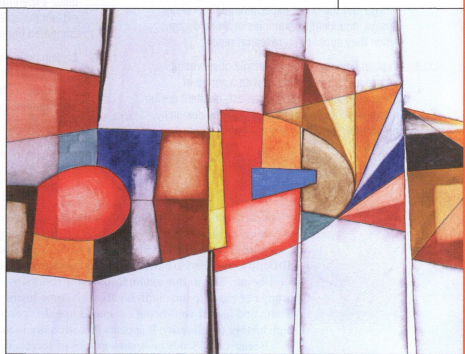

© Nathan Jasowiak / Shutterstock

CHAPTER LEARNING OBJECTIVES

LO1 Define, compare, and contrast the experimental, nonexperimental, and quasi-experimental research strategies, and identify these strategies when they appear in a research report.

LO2 Define a nonequivalent group design and identify examples of this research design when it appears in a research report.

LO3 Explain how individual differences threaten the internal validity of a nonequivalent group design.

LO4 Describe the two nonexperimental nonequivalent group designs (differential research and the posttest-only nonequivalent control group design) and the quasi-experimental nonequivalent group design (pretest–posttest nonequivalent control group design), and identify examples of these designs when they appear in a research report.

LO5 Explain how a simple modification of the posttest-only nonequivalent control group design increases internal validity and produces a quasi-experimental design.

LO6   Define a pre–post design and identify examples of this research design when it appears in a research report.

LO7   Identify the threats to internal validity for pre–post designs.

LO8   Describe the nonexperimental pretest–posttest design and the quasi-experimental time-series design, and identify examples of these designs when they appear in a research report.

LO9   Explain how replacing the single observation before and after treatment with a series of observations converts the pretest–posttest design into a quasi-experimental time-series design by minimizing threats to internal validity.

LO10   Define cross-sectional and longitudinal designs, identify these designs when they appear in a research report, and describe the strengths and weaknesses of each design.

LO11   Identify the statistical techniques that are appropriate for each nonexperimental, quasi-experimental, and developmental design and explain the strengths and weaknesses of two-group compared to multiple-group designs.

LO12   Explain how the terms quasi-independent variable and dependent variable are used in nonexperimental, quasi-experimental, and developmental research.

CHAPTER OVERVIEW

It appears that there is some truth to the old adage that whatever does not kill us makes us stronger. Seery, Holman, and Silver (2010) asked participants to report their lifetime exposure to a list of negative events such as illness, injury, assault, abuse, financial difficulty, and bereavement, and they obtained a variety of measurements of mental well-being. The authors summarize their results by comparing the outcomes for three groups of participants: individuals with some history of adversity report better mental health and higher well-being compared to either people with no history or people with a high history of adversity. It appears that adversity in moderation does make us stronger.

Because this study compares groups of scores, it may appear to be another example of the experimental strategy covered in Chapters 7–9. Specifically, it strongly resembles the between-subjects experiments presented in Chapter 8. However, you should also realize that the Seeley et al. study is missing one or two of the characteristics that are essential for a true experiment. Specifically, there is no manipulated independent variable. Instead, the three groups of participants are defined by the levels of adversity that they have experienced, which is not controlled or manipulated by the researchers. Also, the researchers have no control over the assignment of individuals to groups; a person who enters the study with a high level of adversity is automatically put into the high adversity group. Without manipulation and control, the study is definitely not an experiment. In fact, this kind of research is known as nonexperimental.

In Chapter 6, we noted that both the nonexperimental and quasi-experimental research strategies compare groups of scores, like true experiments, but do not manipulate an independent variable to create the groups. As a result, these two strategies do not have the internal validity of true experiments and cannot establish unambiguous cause-and-effect relationships. The distinction between the two strategies is that quasi-experimental studies make some attempt to minimize threats to internal validity, whereas nonexperimental studies typically do not. In this chapter, we discuss details of these two strategies, as well as different types of nonexperimental and quasi-experimental designs. Developmental designs, which are closely related to nonexperimental designs, are also presented.

10.1 Nonexperimental and Quasi-Experimental Research Strategies

LEARNING OBJECTIVE

LO1 Define, compare, and contrast the experimental, nonexperimental, and quasi-experimental research strategies, and identify these strategies when they appear in a research report.

In Chapter 6, we identified five basic research strategies: experimental, nonexperimental, quasi-experimental, correlational, and descriptive. In this chapter, we discuss the details of the nonexperimental and quasi-experimental strategies. (The experimental strategy is discussed in Chapter 7, the correlational strategy is discussed in Chapter 12, and the descriptive strategy is discussed in detail in Chapter 13.) The experimental research strategy was introduced in Chapter 7 as a means for establishing a cause-and-effect relationship between variables. Recall that the experimental strategy is distinguished from other research strategies by two basic requirements: manipulation of one variable and control of other, extraneous variables.

In many research situations, however, it is difficult or impossible for a researcher to satisfy completely the rigorous requirements of an experiment. This is particularly true for applied research in natural settings such as educational research in the classroom and clinical research with real clients. In these situations, a researcher can often devise a research strategy (a method of collecting data) that involves comparing groups of scores, like an experiment, but fails to satisfy at least one of the requirements of a true experiment. Although these studies resemble experiments, they always contain a confounding variable or other threat to internal validity that is an integral part of the design and simply cannot be removed. The existence of a confounding variable means that these studies cannot establish unambiguous cause-and-effect relationships and, therefore, are not true experiments. Such studies are generally called nonexperimental research studies.

Occasionally, a nonexperimental study is modified in an attempt to minimize the threats to internal validity. The resulting designs are called quasi-experimental studies. The distinction between the **nonexperimental research strategy** and the **quasi-experimental research strategy** is the degree to which the research strategy limits confounding and controls threats to internal validity. If a research design makes little or no attempt to minimize threats, it is classified as nonexperimental. A quasi-experimental design, on the other hand, makes some attempt to minimize threats to internal validity and approaches the rigor of a true experiment. As the name implies, a quasi-experimental study is almost, but not quite, a true experiment. In this chapter, we focus on nonexperimental designs and introduce some of the modifications that produce some closely related quasi-experimental designs. In each case, we discuss the aspect of the design that prevents it from being a true experiment.

DEFINITION

> Like true experiments, the **nonexperimental research strategy** and the **quasi-experimental research strategy** typically involve comparison of scores from different groups or different conditions. However, these two strategies use a nonmanipulated variable to define the groups or conditions being compared. The nonmanipulated variable is usually a participant variable (such as college graduate vs. no college) or a time variable (such as before vs. after treatment). The distinction between the two strategies is that nonexperimental designs make little or no attempt to control threats to internal validity, whereas quasi-experimental designs actively attempt to limit threats to internal validity.

At the end of this chapter, we examine developmental research, which includes research designs intended to investigate how age is related to other variables. Because age is a variable that cannot be manipulated, developmental designs are not true experiments and can be included in other categories of nonexperimental research. However, developmental designs are generally presented as a separate group of research designs with their own terminology. As we introduce the basic developmental research designs, we discuss how they are related to other types of nonexperimental research.

The term *significant* means that it is very unlikely that the difference between the groups of scores would occur if there were no corresponding difference in the population (see Box 7.1, p. 161).

The Structure of Nonexperimental and Quasi-Experimental Designs

Nonexperimental and quasi-experimental studies often look like experiments in terms of the general structure of the research study. In an experiment, for example, a researcher typically creates treatment conditions by manipulating an independent variable, and then measures participants to obtain a set of scores within each condition. If the scores in one condition are significantly different from the scores in another condition, the researcher can conclude that the two treatment conditions have different effects (Figure 10.1).

Similarly, a nonexperimental or quasi-experimental study also produces groups of scores to be compared for significant differences. One variable is used to create the groups or conditions, and then a second variable is measured to obtain a set of scores within each condition. In nonexperimental and quasi-experimental studies, however, the different groups or treatment conditions are not created by manipulating an independent variable. Instead, the groups are usually defined in terms of a specific participant variable (e.g., college graduate/no college) or in terms of time (e.g., before and after treatment). These two methods of defining groups produce two general categories of nonexperimental and quasi-experimental designs:

1. Between-subjects designs, also known as nonequivalent group designs
2. Within-subjects designs, also known as pre–post designs

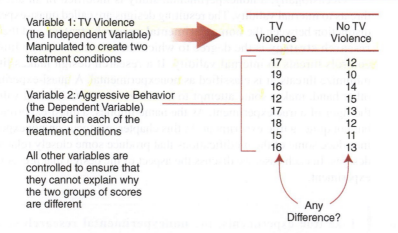

FIGURE 10.1

The Structure of an Experiment

An independent variable (in this case, violence on TV) is manipulated to create treatment conditions. Participants are then measured to obtain scores within each condition. Here, participants are observed during a free period at school and the score for each participant is a measure of aggressive behaviors. If there is a consistent difference between the scores in one condition and the scores in another condition, the difference is attributed to the treatment. In this case, a consistent difference would indicate that TV violence has an effect on aggressive behavior.

Examples of the two general types of nonexperimental and quasi-experimental research are shown in Figure 10.2, and Table 10.1 presents an overview of the nonexperimental and quasi-experimental research designs that are discussed in the following sections.

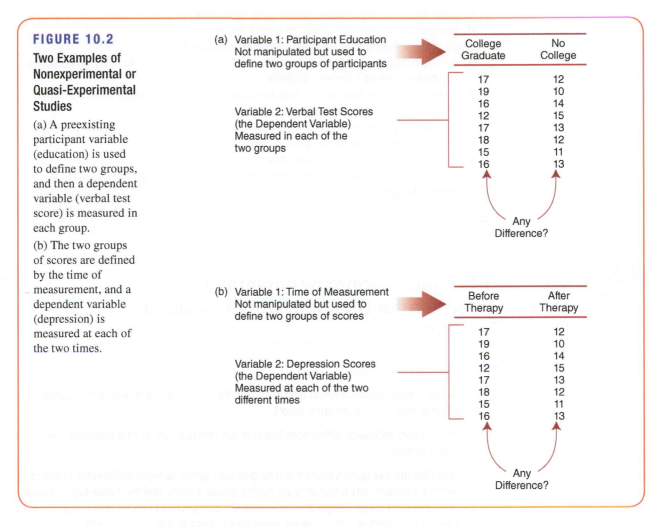

FIGURE 10.2

Two Examples of Nonexperimental or Quasi-Experimental Studies

(a) A preexisting participant variable (education) is used to define two groups, and then a dependent variable (verbal test score) is measured in each group.

(b) The two groups of scores are defined by the time of measurement, and a dependent variable (depression) is measured at each of the two times.

(a) Variable 1: Participant Education
Not manipulated but used to define two groups of participants

Variable 2: Verbal Test Scores (the Dependent Variable) Measured in each of the two groups

College Graduate	No College
17	12
19	10
16	14
12	15
17	13
18	12
15	11
16	13

Any Difference?

(b) Variable 1: Time of Measurement
Not manipulated but used to define two groups of scores

Variable 2: Depression Scores (the Dependent Variable) Measured at each of the two different times

Before Therapy	After Therapy
17	12
19	10
16	14
12	15
17	13
18	12
15	11
16	13

Any Difference?

TABLE 10.1

An Overview of Research Designs for the Nonexperimental and Quasi-Experimental Research Strategies

	Between-Subjects Designs	Within-Subjects Designs
Type	**Nonequivalent Group Designs**	**Pre–Post Designs**
Purpose	Compares preexisting groups of individuals (i.e., groups that are not randomly assigned)	Compares two or more scores for one group of participants
Examples of designs	• Differential research • Posttest-only nonequivalent control group design • Pretest–posttest nonequivalent control group design • Cross-sectional developmental design	• Pretest–posttest design • Time-series design • Longitudinal developmental design

LEARNING CHECK

1. A nonexperimental design
   ⓐ makes no attempt to minimize threats to validity.
   b. makes some attempts to minimize threats to validity.
   c. controls extraneous variables, similar to an experiment.
   d. manipulates one variable, similar to an experiment.
2. Which of the following is an example of a nonexperimental study?
   ⓐ A study comparing self-esteem scores for children with a learning disability versus scores for children without a learning disability
   b. A study comparing depression scores for one group that is assigned to receive a therapy versus another group that is assigned not to receive a therapy
   c. A study comparing performance in a room where the walls have been painted yellow versus performance in a room painted blue
   d. A study comparing cognitive functioning scores for one group of Alzheimer's patients who are assigned to receive memory therapy versus another group that is assigned not to receive therapy

Answers appear at the end of the chapter.

10.2 Between-Subjects Nonexperimental and Quasi-Experimental Designs: Nonequivalent Group Designs

LEARNING OBJECTIVES

LO2 Define a nonequivalent group design and identify examples of this research design when it appears in a research report.

LO3 Explain how individual differences threaten the internal validity of a nonequivalent group design.

LO4 Describe the two nonexperimental nonequivalent group designs (differential research and the posttest-only nonequivalent control group design) and the quasi-experimental nonequivalent group design (pretest–posttest nonequivalent control group design), and identify examples of these designs when they appear in a research report.

LO5 Explain how a simple modification of the posttest-only nonequivalent control group design increases internal validity and produces a quasi-experimental design.

In Chapter 8, we introduced the between-subjects experimental design as a method of comparing two or more treatment conditions using a different group of participants in each condition. A common element of between-subjects experiments is the control of individual differences by assigning participants to specific treatment conditions. The goal is to balance or equalize the groups by using a random assignment process or by deliberately matching participants across treatment conditions. Note that the researcher attempts to create equivalent groups of participants by actively controlling which individuals go into which groups. There are occasions, however, when a researcher must examine preexisting groups. For example, a researcher may want to compare student performance for a high school that encourages students to use their phones and tablets during class with student performance in a high school that bans the use of electronic devices. In this study, the researcher does not have control over which individuals are assigned to which group; the two groups of participants already exist. Because the researcher cannot use random assignment or matching to minimize the individual differences between groups, there is no assurance that the two groups are equivalent. In this situation, the research study is called a **nonequivalent group design**.

DEFINITION

> A **nonequivalent group design** is a research study in which the different groups of participants are formed under circumstances that do not permit the researcher to control the assignment of individuals to groups, and the groups of participants are, therefore, considered nonequivalent. Specifically, the researcher cannot use random assignment to create groups of participants.

Threats to Internal Validity for Nonequivalent Group Designs

A general example of a nonequivalent group design is shown in Figure 10.3. Notice that the groups are differentiated by one specific factor that identifies the groups. In the example evaluating in-class electronic devices, the differentiating factor was the school policy: one high school encouraged use and one banned use. Typically, the purpose of the study is to show that the factor that differentiates the groups is responsible for causing the participants' scores to differ from one group to the other. For this example, the goal is to show that the school policy concerning electronic devices is responsible for the different levels of student performance in the two schools.

However, a nonequivalent group design has a built-in threat to internal validity that precludes an unambiguous cause-and-effect explanation. That threat was introduced in Chapter 6 as **individual differences** between groups. Recall that individual differences create a confound whenever the assignment procedure produces groups that have different participant characteristics. For example, the two high schools in the electronic device

FIGURE 10.3

The General Structure of a Nonequivalent Group Study

Nonequivalent groups (usually preexisting). The researcher has no control over the assignment of individuals to groups. The groups may experience different conditions or treatments.

Group 1 (Condition 1)	Group 2 (Condition 2)
23	14
21	19
28	13
25	20
18	19
22	19
26	13

Scores obtained for the individuals in each group

Any Difference?

study may differ in terms of student IQs, socioeconomic background, racial mixture, student motivation, and so on. These variables are all potentially confounding variables because any one of them could explain the differences between the two groups. Because the assignment of participants is not controlled in a study using nonequivalent groups, this type of research always is threatened by individual differences. You may recognize that a nonequivalent groups study is similar to the between-subjects experimental design presented in Chapter 8. However, the experimental design always uses some form of random assignment or matching to ensure equivalent groups. In a nonequivalent groups design, there is no random assignment and there is no assurance of equivalent groups.

In this section, we consider three common examples of nonequivalent group designs: (1) the differential research design, (2) the posttest-only nonequivalent control group design, and (3) the pretest–posttest nonequivalent control group design. The first two designs make no attempt to control or minimize individual differences as a confound and are nonexperimental designs. The third design is a modification of the posttest-only design and is classified as quasi-experimental because it does attempt to minimize the threat of individual differences as a confound.

Nonexperimental Designs with Nonequivalent Groups

The Differential Research Design

In most between-subjects research, individual differences are considered to be a problem that must be controlled by random assignment, matching groups, or some other process. However, there are research studies for which individual differences are the primary interest. For example, researchers are often interested in how behavior is influenced by gender differences, or how performance is influenced by age differences. In these situations, researchers deliberately create separate groups of participants based on a specific individual difference such as gender or age. Note that these studies involve no manipulation but simply attempt to compare preexisting groups that are defined by a particular participant characteristic. For example, a researcher may want to compare self-esteem scores for children from two-parent households with children from single-parent households. Note that the researcher does not control the assignment of participants to groups; instead, the participants are automatically assigned to groups based on a preexisting characteristic. For this example, the children are assigned to groups based on the number of parents in the household. Although this type of study compares groups of participants (like a between-subjects experiment), the researcher does not manipulate the treatment conditions and does not have control over the assignment of participants to groups. Again, this is not a true experiment.

A research study that simply compares preexisting groups is called a **differential research design** because its goal is to establish differences between the preexisting groups. This type of study often is called ex post facto research because it looks at differences "after the fact," that is, at differences that already exist between groups. Because the differential research design makes no attempt to control the threat of individual differences between groups, it is classified as a nonexperimental research design. For example, a study by InsuranceHotline.com (Romanov, 2006) found significant differences in the number of car accidents and tickets for people with different astrological signs. Libras and Aquarians were the worst offenders, while Leos and Geminis had the best overall records. Clearly, people who have different astrological signs form preexisting groups that were not manipulated or created by the researchers. In another somewhat bizarre study, DeGoede, Ashton-Miller, Liao, and Alexander (2001) swung a pendulum at their participants and measured how quickly the participants moved their hands to intercept the approaching object. This study examined gender differences and age differences, once again comparing scores for preexisting groups.

Many research questions in social psychology and personality theory are focused on differences between groups or categories of people. Personality theorists, for example, often classify people according to attachment style, and then examine differences between individuals with different styles. Many research studies have demonstrated that the style of mother/child attachment formed in infancy persists as an individual develops and is related to adult intimacy and romantic relationships (Brennan & Morris, 1997; Feeney, 2004). Differential research and correlational research, which also examines relationships between variables, are compared in Box 10.1.

DEFINITION

> A **differential research design** is a research study that simply compares preexisting groups. A differential study uses a participant characteristic such as gender, race, or personality to automatically assign participants to groups. The researcher does not randomly assign individuals to groups. A dependent variable is then measured for each participant to obtain a set of scores within each group. The goal of the study is to determine whether the scores for one group are consistently different from the scores of another group. Differential research is classified as a nonexperimental research design.

BOX 10.1 Differential Research and Correlational Research

Many researchers place differential research in the same category as correlational research. In many ways, differential research is similar to the correlational research strategy (introduced in Chapter 6 and discussed in Chapter 12). In differential and correlational studies, a researcher simply observes two naturally occurring variables without any interference or manipulation. The subtle distinction between differential research and correlational research is whether one of the variables is used to establish separate groups to be compared. In differential research, participant differences in one variable are used to create separate groups, and measurements of the second variable are made within each group. The researcher then compares the measurements for one group with the measurements for another group, typically looking at mean differences between groups (Figure 10.4a). A correlational study, on the other hand, treats all the participants as a single group and simply measures the two variables for each individual (Figure 10.4b). Although differential research and correlational research produce different kinds of data and involve different statistical analyses, their results should receive the same interpretation. Both designs allow researchers to establish the existence of relationships and to describe relationships between variables, but neither design permits a cause-and-effect explanation of the relationship.

The Posttest-Only Nonequivalent Control Group Design

Nonequivalent groups are commonly used in applied research situations in which the goal is to evaluate the effectiveness of a treatment administered to a preexisting group of participants. A second group of similar but nonequivalent participants is used for the control condition. Note that the researcher uses preexisting groups and does not control the assignment of participants to groups. In particular, the researcher does not randomly assign individuals to groups.

For example, Skjoeveland (2001) used a nonequivalent group study to examine the effects of street parks on social interactions among neighbors. Parks were constructed in one area, and the people living in that neighborhood were compared with two control groups that did not get new parks. Similarly, Goldie, Schwartz, McConnachie, and

FIGURE 10.4

Comparison of Differential Research and Correlational Research

(a) The structure of a differential study examining the relationship between self-esteem and academic performance. Note that one of the two variables (self-esteem) is used to create groups, and the other variable (academic performance) is measured to obtain scores within each group.

(b) The structure of a correlational study examining the relationship between self-esteem and academic performance. Note that there is only one group of participants with two scores (self-esteem and academic performance) measured for each individual.

(a) A differential study examining the relationship between self-esteem and academic performance.

Variable 1: Self-Esteem
Not manipulated but used to define two groups of participants

Variable 2: Academic Performance (the Dependent Variable)
Measured in each of the two groups

High Self-Esteem Group	Low Self-Esteem Group
17	12
19	10
16	14
12	15
17	13
18	12
15	11
16	13

Any Difference?

(b) A correlational study examining the relationship between self-esteem and academic performance.

Participant	Variable 1 Self-Esteem	Variable 2 Academic Performance
A	84	16
B	72	10
C	90	19
D	68	13
E	77	16
F	81	12
G	85	17
H	76	13

Morrison (2001) evaluated a new ethics course for medical students by comparing the group of students who took the new course with a nonequivalent group who did not take the course. This type of research is called a **nonequivalent control group design**.

DEFINITION

A **nonequivalent control group design** uses preexisting groups, one of which serves in the treatment condition and the other in the control condition. The researcher does not randomly assign individuals to the groups.

A **posttest-only nonequivalent control group design** is one common example of a nonequivalent control group design. This type of study is occasionally called a *static group comparison*. In this design, one group of participants is given a treatment and then is measured after the treatment (this is the posttest). The scores for the treated group are then compared with the scores from a nonequivalent group that has not received the treatment (i.e., the control group). This design can be represented schematically using a series of Xs and Os to represent the series of events experienced by each group. In this notation system, developed by Campbell and Stanley (1963), the letter X corresponds to the treatment, and the letter *O* corresponds to the observation or measurement. Thus, the treatment group experiences the treatment first (X) followed by observation or measurement (O). The control group does not receive any treatment but is simply observed (O). The two groups are represented as follows:

> X   O   (treatment group)
>   O   (nonequivalent control group)

If a design includes random assignment of participants to groups in the study, an R is placed as the first symbol in each line of notation. The absence of an R in this schematic reflects the use of preexisting groups, as in a nonequivalent control group design.

DEFINITION

A **posttest-only nonequivalent control group design** compares two nonequivalent groups of participants. One group is observed (measured) after receiving a treatment, and the other group is measured at the same time but receives no treatment. This is an example of a nonexperimental research design.

The posttest-only nonequivalent control group design is commonly used when a treatment is given to a well-defined, isolated cluster of individuals, such as the students in a classroom or the patients in a clinic. In these situations, a separate cluster (e.g., another classroom or another clinic) is often selected as the nonequivalent control group. The neighborhood parks program discussed earlier is a good example of this type of study. The program is administered in one neighborhood, and other neighborhoods that do not receive the parks serve as a nonequivalent control group. Note that the purpose of the study is to show that the parks have an effect by demonstrating a difference in social interactions for the two groups.

Although this kind of research design appears to ask a cause-and-effect question (Do the parks cause a difference?), the research design does not protect against individual differences as a confound. As we noted earlier, the people in the two neighborhoods could differ on a variety of variables (in addition to the parks), and any of these other variables could be responsible for the difference in social interactions. Because the posttest-only nonequivalent control group design does not address the threat of individual differences as a confound, it is considered a nonexperimental design.

A Quasi-Experimental Design with Nonequivalent Groups

The Pretest–Posttest Nonequivalent Control Group Design

A much stronger design can be created with a small modification of the posttest-only nonequivalent control group design. The modification involves adding a pretest that obtains measurements of both groups before the treatment is administered. The resulting design is called a **pretest–posttest nonequivalent control group design** and can be represented as follows:

> O   X   O   (treatment group)
> O   O   (nonequivalent control group)

In this design, the first step is to observe (measure) both groups. The treatment is then administered to one group, and, following the treatment, both groups are observed again.

The addition of the pretest measurement allows researchers to address the problem of individual differences as a confound that exists with all nonequivalent group research. Specifically, the researcher can now compare the observations before treatment to establish whether the two groups really are similar. If the groups are found to be similar before treatment, the researcher has evidence that the participants in one group are not substantially different from the participants in another group, and the threat of individual differences is reduced. Note, however, that the pretest scores simply allow the researcher to ensure that the two groups are similar with respect to one specific variable. Other potentially important variables are not measured or controlled. Thus, the threat of individual differences is reduced, but it is certainly not eliminated.

This type of design also allows a researcher to compare the pretest scores and posttest scores for both groups to help determine whether the treatment or some other, time-related factor is responsible for changes. In Chapter 9, we introduced a set of time-related factors such as history and maturation that can threaten internal validity. In the pretest–posttest nonequivalent groups design, however, these time-related threats are minimized because both groups are observed over the same time period and, therefore, should experience the same time-related factors. If the participants are similar before treatment but different after treatment, the researcher can be more confident that the treatment has an effect. On the other hand, if both groups show the same degree of change from the pretest to the posttest, the researcher must conclude that some factor other than the treatment is responsible for the change. Thus, the pretest–posttest nonequivalent control group design reduces the threat of individual differences, limits threats from time-related factors, and can provide some evidence to support a cause-and-effect relationship. As a result, this type of research is considered quasi-experimental.

DEFINITION

> A **pretest–posttest nonequivalent control group design** compares two non-equivalent groups. One group is measured twice, once before a treatment is administered and once after. The other group is measured at the same two times but does not receive any treatment. Because this design attempts to limit threats to internal validity, it is classified as quasi-experimental.

Although the addition of a pretest to the nonequivalent control group design reduces some threats to internal validity, it does not eliminate them completely. In addition, the fact that the groups are nonequivalent and often are in separate locations creates the potential for other threats. Specifically, it is possible for a time-related threat to affect the groups differently. For example, one group may be influenced by outside events that are not experienced by the other group. The students in one high school may be enjoying a winning football season, whereas students in another school may be depressed because their team is losing every game. In Chapter 9, we identified the influence of outside events as history effects. When history effects differ from one group to another, they are called differential history effects. The **differential effects** can be a confounding variable because any differences observed between the two groups may be explained by their different histories. In a similar way, other time-related influences such as maturation, instrumentation, testing effects, and regression may be different from one group to another, and these differential effects can threaten the internal validity of a nonequivalent group study.

LEARNING CHECK

1. For which of the following studies does the researcher not control which individuals are assigned to which group?
   a. Between-subjects experiment
   b. Within-subjects experiment
   c. Nonequivalent group design
   d. Pre–post design

2. Which of the following is the primary threat to internal validity for nonequivalent group designs?
   a. History effects
   b. Instrumentation effects
   c. Regression toward the mean
   d. Individual differences between treatment groups

3. Which research design is used by a researcher comparing self-esteem scores for children from divorced families versus scores for children from families with no divorce?
   a. Differential research design
   b. Pretest-only nonequivalent control group design
   c. Pretest–posttest nonequivalent control group design
   d. Time-series design

4. Which of the following is the primary advantage of a pretest-posttest nonequivalent control group design, in comparison to other nonequivalent group designs?
   a. The posttest scores can help reduce threats from history effects.
   b. The posttest scores can eliminate threats from history effects.
   c. The pretest scores can help reduce the threat of individual differences between groups.
   d. The pretest scores can eliminate the threat of individual differences between groups.

Answers appear at the end of the chapter.

10.3   Within-Subjects Nonexperimental and Quasi-Experimental Designs: Pre–Post Designs

LEARNING OBJECTIVES

LO6   Define a pre–post design and identify examples of this research design when it appears in a research report.

LO7   Identify the threats to internal validity for pre–post designs.

LO8   Describe the nonexperimental pretest–posttest design and the quasi-experimental time-series design, and identify examples of these designs when they appear in a research report.

LO9   Explain how replacing the single observation before and after treatment with a series of observations converts the pretest–posttest design into a quasi-experimental time-series design by minimizing threats to internal validity.

The second general category of nonexperimental and quasi-experimental designs consists of studies in which a series of observations is made over time. Collectively, such studies are known as **pre–post design**s. In a typical pre–post study, one group of participants is observed (measured) before and after a treatment or event. The goal of the pre–post design is to evaluate the influence of the intervening treatment or event by comparing the observations made before treatment with the observations made after treatment.

You may have noticed that a pre–post design is similar to the pretest–posttest nonequivalent control group design discussed earlier. However, a pre–post design has no control group. In addition, the primary focus of a pretest–posttest nonequivalent control group design is to compare the treatment group and the control group, not to compare the pretest scores with the posttest scores. As a result, the pretest–posttest nonequivalent control group design is primarily a nonequivalent group design, and we have classified it in that category.

DEFINITION

> A **pre–post design** is a research study in which a series of observations is made over time for one group of participants.

Threats to Internal Validity for Pre–Post Designs

Whenever the same group of individuals is observed repeatedly over time, time-related factors can threaten internal validity. As we noted in Chapter 9, the five categories of time-related threats are **history**, **instrumentation**, **order effects**, **maturation**, and **statistical regression**. Clearly, pre–post studies are vulnerable to these threats; any differences found between the pretreatment observations and the posttreatment observations could be explained by history, instrumentation, order effects, maturation, or regression (see Chapter 9, pp. 214–217). You may recognize that a pre–post design is similar to the within-subjects experimental design presented in Chapter 9. However, the experimental design uses counterbalancing to control order effects and other time-related threats to internal validity. In a pre–post design, it is impossible to counterbalance the order of treatments. Specifically, the before-treatment observations (pretest) must always precede the after-treatment observations (posttest).

In general, the internal validity of a pre–post study is threatened by a variety of factors related to the passage of time. During the time between the first observation and the last observation, any one of these factors could influence the participants and cause a change in their scores. Unless these factors are controlled or minimized by the structure of the research design, a pre–post study cannot approach the internal validity of a true experiment. In this section, we introduce two examples of pre–post studies: the one-group pretest–posttest design and the time-series design. The first of these designs makes no attempt to control the threats to internal validity and, therefore, is classified as nonexperimental. The second design manages to minimize most threats to internal validity and is classified as quasi-experimental.

A Nonexperimental Pre–Post Design

The Pretest–Posttest Design

The simplest version of the pre–post design consists of one observation for each participant made before the treatment or event, and one observation made after it. Schematically, this simple form can be represented as follows:

$$O \quad X \quad O$$

This type of study is called a **pretest–posttest design**. For example, a political consultant could evaluate the effectiveness of a new political television commercial by assessing voters' attitudes toward a candidate before and after they view the commercial. The results from this study may demonstrate a change in attitude. However, because this design makes no attempt to control the many threats to internal validity, the study cannot conclude that the change was caused by the intervening commercial. Because the pretest–posttest study precludes a cause-and-effect conclusion, this type of research is classified as nonexperimental.

DEFINITION

> In the nonexperimental **pretest–posttest design**, each individual in a single group of participants is measured once before treatment and once after treatment.

A Quasi-Experimental Pre–Post Design

The Time-Series Design

A simple modification of the pretest–posttest design minimizes the threats to internal validity and produces a much stronger research design. The modification consists of using a series of observations, in place of the single observation, before and after the treatment or event. The result is called a **time-series design** and can be represented as follows:

$$O \quad O \quad O \quad X \quad O \quad O \quad O$$

DEFINITION

> A **time-series design** has a series of observations for each participant before a treatment or event and a series of observations after the treatment or event. A treatment is a manipulation administered by the researcher, and an event is an outside occurrence that is not controlled or manipulated by the researcher.

The intervening treatment or event (X) may or may not be manipulated by the researcher. For example, a doctor may record blood pressure for a group of executives before and after they complete relaxation training. Or a researcher may evaluate the effect of a natural disaster such as earthquake or flood on the well-being of a group of students by recording visits to the school nurse for the months before and after the disaster. In one case, the researcher is manipulating a treatment (the relaxation training) and in the other case, the researcher is studying a nonmanipulated event (an earthquake). A study in which the intervening event is not manipulated by the researcher is sometimes called an **interrupted time-series design**.

Occasionally, a time-series study is used to investigate the effect of a predictable event such as a legal change in the drinking age or speed limit. In this case, researchers can begin collecting data before the event actually occurs. However, it often is impossible to predict the occurrence of an event such as an earthquake, so it is impossible for researchers to start collecting data just before one arrives. In this situation, researchers often rely on archival data, such as police records or hospital records, to provide the observations for the time-series study.

In a time-series design, the pretest and posttest series of observations serve several valuable purposes. First, the pretest observations allow a researcher to see any trends that may already exist in the data before the treatment is even introduced. Trends in the data are an indication that the scores are influenced by some factor unrelated to the treatment. For example, practice or fatigue may cause the scores to increase or decrease over time before a treatment is introduced. Similarly, instrumentation effects, maturation effects, or regression should produce noticeable changes in the observations before treatment. On the other hand, if the data show no trends or major fluctuations before the treatment, the researcher can be reasonably sure that these potential threats to internal validity are not influencing the participants. Thus, the series of observations allows a researcher to minimize most threats to internal validity. As a result, the time-series design is classified as quasi-experimental.

It is possible for an external event (history) to be a threat to internal validity in time-series designs, but only if the event occurs simultaneously with the treatment. If the outside event occurs at any time other than the introduction of the treatment, it should be easy to separate the history effects from the treatment effects. For example, if the participants are affected by an outside event that occurs before the treatment, the effect should be apparent in the observations that occur before the treatment. Figure 10.5 shows three possible outcomes in which the treatment has no effect but instead the participants are

FIGURE 10.5

How Data in a Time-Series Study Might Be Affected by an Outside Event

(a) The event occurs and influences scores before the treatment is introduced.

(b) The event occurs and influences scores after the treatment.

(c) The event and the treatment occur simultaneously, and it is impossible to determine which is influencing the scores.

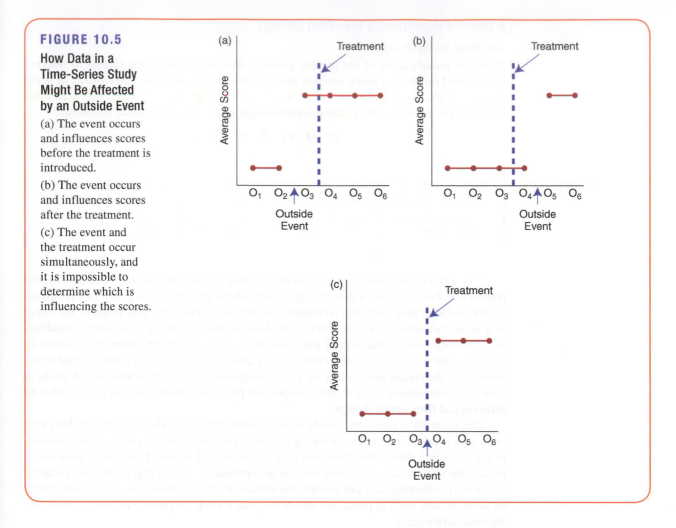

influenced by an outside event. Notice that a problem occurs only when the treatment and the outside event coincide perfectly. In this case, it is impossible to determine whether the change in behavior was caused by the treatment or by the outside event. Thus, history effects (outside events) are a threat to validity only when there is a perfect correspondence between the occurrence of the event and the introduction of the treatment. Suppose, for example, that a clinical researcher uses a time-series design to evaluate a treatment for depression. Observations are made for a group of depressed clients for a week before therapy begins, and a second series of observations is made for a week after therapy. The observations indicate significant improvement after therapy. However, suppose that, by coincidence, there is an abrupt change in the weather on the same day that therapy starts; after weeks of cold, dark, rainy days, it suddenly becomes bright, sunny, and unseasonably warm. Because the weather changed at the same time as the treatment, it is impossible to determine what caused the clients' improvement. Was the change caused by the treatment or by the weather?

The series of observations after the treatment or event also allows a researcher to observe any posttreatment trends. For example, it is possible that the treatment has only a temporary effect that quickly fades. Such a trend would be seen in the series of posttreatment observations. Figure 10.6 demonstrates how a series of observations can be more informative than single observations made before and after treatment. The figure shows a

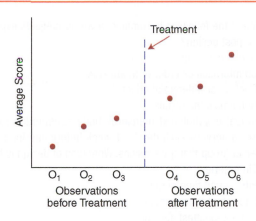

FIGURE 10.6

A Time Series Study with Multiple Observations before and after Treatment

The series of observations makes it possible to see the trend in the data that existed before the treatment was administered and that continues after the treatment.

series of scores that are consistently increasing before treatment and continue to increase in an uninterrupted pattern after treatment. In this case, it does not appear that the treatment has any effect on the scores. However, if the study included only one observation before treatment and only one observation after treatment (O_3 and O_4), the results would indicate a substantial increase in scores following the treatment, suggesting that the treatment did have an effect.

Single-Case Applications of Time-Series Designs

The time-series design was introduced as a research study that involves observing a group of participants at several different times. However, this design is often applied to single individuals or single organizations. For example, a high school could evaluate the effects of an anger-management program by monitoring the number of fights at the school for 3 months before the program is enacted and for 3 months afterward. This is an example of a time-series design, but it involves measurements for one high school, not for individual participants. Similarly, a therapist could monitor instances of compulsive behavior in one client for 3 weeks before therapy and for 3 weeks after. This is an example of a time-series design applied to a single individual. Research designs that focus on a single case, rather than a group of participants, are occasionally called single-case time-series designs but are more often classified as **single-case** or **single-subject designs**. Single-case designs are discussed in Chapter 14.

LEARNING CHECK

1. What design is being used by a researcher comparing depression scores before and after treatment in one group of clients?
   a. Pretest–posttest nonequivalent control group design
   b. Differential research design
   c. Pre–post design
   d. Posttest-only nonequivalent control group design

2. Which of the following is common in within-subjects experimental designs but is impossible in a pre–post design?
   a. Randomly assign participants
   b. Counterbalance order of treatments
   c. Control for differential effects
   d. Generalize the results

3. A clinical psychologist measures body satisfaction for a group of clients diagnosed with anorexia nervosa each day for 1 week before and for 1 week after the psychologist begins a series of group therapy sessions. What kind of design is being used?
   a. Time-series
   b. Interrupted time-series
   c. Equivalent time-samples
   d. Pretest–posttest design

4. What can a researcher determine by using a series of observations before treatment?
   a. If the treatment has a temporary effect.
   b. If the treatment has a permanent effect.
   c. If scores are influenced by individual differences between groups.
   d. If scores are influenced by some factor unrelated to the treatment.

Answers appear at the end of the chapter.

10.4 Developmental Research Designs

LEARNING OBJECTIVE

LO10 Define cross-sectional and longitudinal designs, identify these designs when they appear in a research report, and describe the strengths and weaknesses of each design.

Developmental research designs are another type of nonexperimental research that can be used to study changes in behavior that relate to age. The purpose of developmental research designs is to describe the relationship between age and other variables. For example, if a researcher is interested in how language ability changes with age, a developmental research design would be appropriate.

DEFINITION

> **Developmental research designs** are used to examine changes in behavior related to age.

Two basic types of developmental research designs are the cross-sectional design and the longitudinal design. Each has its strengths and weaknesses.

The Cross-Sectional Developmental Research Design

The **cross-sectional developmental research design** is a between-subjects design that uses a separate group of participants for each of the ages being compared. A dependent variable is measured for the individuals in each group, and the groups are compared to determine whether there are age differences. For example, a researcher who wants to examine the relationship between IQ and aging could select three different groups of people—40-year-olds, 60-year-olds, and 80-year-olds—and could then measure IQ for each group (see Figure 10.7).

DEFINITION

> The **cross-sectional developmental research design** uses different groups of individuals, each group representing a different age. The different groups are measured at one point in time and then compared.

The term *cross-sectional* is also used to describe surveys that classify people into different categories or subgroups. Here we are discussing cross-sectional developmental designs.

For example, Oppenheimer (2006) used a cross-sectional study to examine changes in people's belief in a just and orderly world as they mature from 12 to 22 years of age. Comparing results from six age groups of students from secondary school through college, the study found that belief in a just world declined as the students aged.

A cross-sectional design is an example of a between-subjects nonexperimental design, specifically, a nonequivalent group design. The different groups of participants are not created by manipulating an independent variable; instead, the groups are defined by a preexisting participant variable (age). Also, the researcher does not randomly assign participants to groups; instead, group assignment is predetermined by each participant's age. Earlier in this chapter, we defined this kind of study as differential research. However, when a study evaluates differences related to age, the design is typically called a cross-sectional study.

Strengths and Weaknesses of the Cross-Sectional Developmental Design
One obvious advantage of the cross-sectional design is that a researcher can observe how behavior changes as people age without waiting for a group of participants to grow older. The example in Figure 10.7 shows that we do not need to follow a group of people over the next 40 years to observe the differences that occur during 40 years of aging. With the cross-sectional design, data can be collected in a short period of time. In addition, cross-sectional research does not require long-term cooperation between the researcher

FIGURE 10.7

The Structure of a Cross-Sectional Developmental Research Design

Three separate groups of participants are selected to represent three different ages.

Three separate groups of participants selected from the population

A group of 40-year-old participants measured today

A group of 60-year-old participants measured today

A group of 80-year-old participants measured today

and the participant; that is, the researcher does not have to incur the time and expense of tracking people down for 40 years and encouraging them to continue in the research.

The cross-sectional research design is not without its weaknesses. One weakness is that a researcher cannot say anything about how a particular individual develops over time because individuals are not followed over years. A more serious problem is that factors other than age may differentiate the groups. For example, 40-year-old women not only are younger than 80-year-old women but also grew up in very different environments. Opportunities for education, employment, and social expectations were very different for these two groups of women. In general, individuals who are the same age and have lived in similar environments are called **cohorts**. For example, today's preschool children, today's adolescents, and today's college students would be three sets of cohorts. In addition to being different ages, these three groups have also experienced different social and cultural environments. The environmental factors that differentiate one age group from another are called **cohort effects**, or **generation effects**, and they may be responsible for differences observed between the groups instead of age. As a result, generation effects are a threat to internal validity for a cross-sectional design. Specifically, in a cross-sectional study, the generation of the participants changes from one group to another so that the apparent relationship between age and other variables may actually be caused by generation differences. For example, suppose that you compared computer literacy for three groups: one with 40-year-olds, one with 60-year-olds, and one with 80-year-olds. Almost certainly, the data would show a decline in literacy as the participants grow older. However, you should not assume that this difference should be attributed to age. Specifically, you should not conclude that losing computer literacy is a consequence of aging. The 80-year-old participants did not lose computer literacy as they aged; instead, they spent most of their lives in an environment without computers and never had computer literacy to start with.

DEFINITIONS

> **Cohorts** are individuals who were born at roughly the same time and grew up under similar circumstances.
>
> The terms **cohort effects** and **generation effects** refer to differences between age groups (or cohorts) caused by unique characteristics or experiences other than age.

A great example of how cohort effects can influence the results of research comes from studies on the relationship between IQ and age (Baltes & Schaie, 1974). Many research studies show that IQ declines between the ages of 20 and 50. On the other hand, a separate group of studies shows little or no decline in IQ between the ages of 20 and 50. How can these two sets of data be so completely different? One answer lies in the designs of the studies. The data that show IQ declining with age are generally obtained with cross-sectional studies. The problem with cross-sectional designs is that the results may be influenced by cohort effects because the groups being compared are not only different in age but also lived in different decades. The fact that the groups grew up and lived in different environments could affect their IQ scores and be the source of the IQ differences between the groups. Cohort effects are more likely when there are large age differences between groups. The second set of studies, showing stable IQ, monitored the same set of people over a long period of time. This type of research design is called the longitudinal research design and is discussed next. Incidentally, other researchers have raised serious questions about this interpretation of the aging and IQ relationship (Horn & Donaldson, 1976).

The Longitudinal Developmental Research Design

The **longitudinal developmental research design** involves measuring a variable in the same group of individuals over a period of time (typically every few months or every few years). The individuals are usually cohorts, roughly the same age, who have grown up in similar circumstances. Several measurements of a particular variable are made in the same individuals at two or more times in their lives to investigate the relationship between age and that variable. For example, to examine IQ and age using the longitudinal approach, a researcher might measure IQ in a group of 40-year-olds and then measure the same individuals again at ages 60 and 80 (Figure 10.8).

DEFINITION

> The **longitudinal developmental research design** examines development by observing or measuring a group of cohorts over time.

A longitudinal study is an example of a within-subjects nonexperimental design, specifically, a one-group pretest–posttest design. In a longitudinal design, however, no treatment is administered; instead, the "treatment" is age. That is, a longitudinal study can be described as a set of observations followed by a period of development or aging, then another set of observations. The differences between the initial observations and the final observations define the effects of development. Thus, longitudinal studies can be viewed as a kind of pretest–posttest study. However, when this type of research is used to evaluate development or the effects of age, the design is typically called a longitudinal study.

The distinction between a longitudinal design and a time-series design is not always clear. For example, Sun (2001) examined the well-being of a group of adolescents for an extended period before and after their parents' divorces. This can be viewed as a longitudinal study because it examined the changes that occur over time for a group of participants. However, it also can be viewed as a pre–post time-series study that compared a series of observations made before an event (the divorce) with a series of observations made after the event.

FIGURE 10.8

The Structure of a Longitudinal Developmental Research Design

One group of participants is measured at different times as the participants age.

Strengths and Weaknesses of the Longitudinal Developmental Design

A major strength of the longitudinal research design is the absence of cohort effects because the researcher examines one group of people over time rather than comparing groups that represent different ages and come from different generations. Second, with longitudinal research, a researcher can discuss how a single individual's behavior changes with age. However, longitudinal research is extremely time-consuming, both for the participants (it requires a big commitment to continue in the study) and the researcher (the researcher must stay interested in the research and wait for years to see the final results). In addition, these designs are very expensive to conduct because researchers need to track people down and persuade them, when necessary, to come back to participate in the study. If the study spans many years, there is the additional expense of training new experimenters to take over the study. Furthermore, these designs are subject to high dropout rates of participants. People lose interest in the study, move away, or die. When participants drop out of a study, it is known as **participant attrition** (or **participant mortality**), and it may weaken the internal validity of the research. Specifically, if the participants who drop out are systematically different from those who stay, the group at the end of the study may have different characteristics from the group at the beginning. For example, if the less-motivated individuals drop out, then the group at the end is more motivated than the group at the beginning. The higher level of motivation (rather than age) may explain any changes that are observed over time. (The issue of participant attrition is discussed in more detail in Chapter 9.) A final weakness of the longitudinal research design is that the same individuals are measured repeatedly. It is possible that the scores obtained late in the study are partially affected by previous experience with the test or measurement procedure. (In Chapter 9, we discussed order effects as a threat to internal validity.)

Table 10.2 summarizes the strengths and weaknesses of cross-sectional and longitudinal developmental research designs.

Cross-Sectional Longitudinal Designs

Although the term cross-sectional longitudinal design may appear to be internally contradictory, there are research studies for which this label is appropriate. Specifically, many research studies compare the results obtained from separate samples (like a cross-sectional design) that were obtained at different times (like a longitudinal design). Typically, this type of research is examining the development of phenomena other than individual aging. For example, Pope, Ionescu-Pioggia, and Pope (2001) examined how drug use and lifestyle have changed over the past 30 years by returning to the same college every 10 years to measure freshman attitudes and behaviors. Because Pope and his colleagues measured different individuals every 10 years, this research combines elements of cross-sectional

TABLE 10.2

Strengths and Weaknesses of Cross-Sectional and Longitudinal Developmental Research Designs

	Longitudinal Research	Cross-Sectional Research
Strengths	No cohort or generation effects Assesses individual behavior changes	Time-efficient No long-term cooperation required
Weaknesses	Time-consuming Participant dropout may create bias Potential for practice effects	Individual changes not assessed Cohort or generation effects

TABLE 10.3

A Summary of Nonexperimental and Quasi-Experimental Research Designs

(Note that each quasi-experimental design is created by modifying a nonexperimental design.)

	Between-Subjects Designs (Nonequivalent Group Designs)	**Within-Subjects Designs (Pre–Post Designs)**
Nonexperimental	**Differential research**	**Pretest–posttest design**
	Compares preexisting groups (i.e., college grad/no college)	Compares pretreatment and posttreatment scores for one group of participants
	Posttest-only nonequivalent control group design	**Longitudinal developmental design**
	Compares preexisting groups after one group receives a treatment	Observes one group of individuals at different points in time
	Cross-sectional developmental design	
	Compares preexisting groups differing in age	
Quasi-experimental	**Pretest–posttest nonequivalent control group design**	**Time-series design**
	Adds a pretest to the posttest-only design	Replaces the single pre and post scores in a pretest–posttest design with a series of measurements

and longitudinal designs. In a similar study, Mitchell, Wolak, and Finkelhor (2007) examined trends in youth reports of unwanted exposure to pornography on the Internet. This study compared results from a survey of 10- to 17-year-old Internet users in the year 2000 with an equivalent survey of a different sample in the year 2005. Although both of these studies are examining development (or social evolution) over time, neither is a purely longitudinal or a purely cross-sectional design. Nonetheless, you are likely to find this type of research is occasionally described as longitudinal or cross-sectional. Because the design is not clearly one or the other, we hedge a little and classify this research *cross-sectional longitudinal.*

The complete set of quasi-experimental and nonexperimental research designs, including developmental designs, is summarized in Table 10.3.

LEARNING CHECK

1. A research study evaluates changes in behavior related to age by examining different groups of individuals with each group representing a different age. What is the name for this research design?
   a. A time-series design
   b. An interrupted time-series design
   c. A cross-sectional developmental design
   d. A longitudinal developmental design

2. A research study evaluates changes in behavior related to age by examining one group of participants who are all roughly the same age, at different times. What is the name for this research design?
   a. A time-series design
   b. An interrupted time-series design
   c. A cross-sectional developmental design
   d. A longitudinal developmental design

3. A cross-sectional developmental design is an example of which general category of research designs?
   (a.) Nonequivalent group designs
   b. Pretest–posttest designs
   c. Time-series designs
   d. Interrupted time-series designs

Answers appear at the end of the chapter.

10.5 Applications, Statistical Analysis, and Terminology for Nonexperimental, Quasi-Experimental, and Developmental Designs

LEARNING OBJECTIVES

LO11 Identify the statistical techniques that are appropriate for each nonexperimental, quasi-experimental, and developmental design and explain the strengths and weaknesses of two-group compared to multiple-group designs.

LO12 Explain how the terms quasi-independent variable and dependent variable are used in nonexperimental, quasi-experimental, and developmental research.

Application and Analysis

The application and analysis of the between-subjects designs presented in this chapter (nonequivalent group designs, including cross-sectional designs) follows exactly the same pattern as the application and analysis of between-subjects experiments presented in Chapter 8 (pp. 204–207). Similarly, the application and analysis of within-subjects designs (pre–post and longitudinal) is the same as that presented for within-subjects experiments in Chapter 9 (pp. 233–234). The only exception to this rule is the quasi-experimental pretest–posttest nonequivalent control group design, which includes within-subjects and between-subjects components and is discussed at the end of this section.

Two group designs have the advantage of simplicity; they are easy to set up and the results are easy to understand. However, a two-group does not provide the full functional relationship between variables that is available in a multigroup design. When the data consist of numerical scores, then the statistical analysis consists of comparing means with either a *t* test (independent- or repeated-measures) for two means or a single-factor analysis of variance (independent- or repeated-measures) for multiple means. For non-numerical data, the appropriate statistical analysis for a between-subjects design is a chi-square test for independence. These statistical tests are presented in Chapter 15.

The Pretest–Posttest Nonequivalent Control Group Design

If the data consist of numerical scores, then the appropriate statistical analysis is a two-factor, mixed design analysis of variance (the pre–post factor is within-subjects and the group factor is between-subjects). This analysis is not covered in this book but is available on most statistical software programs such as SPSS. If you are comparing the pre–post means for one of the groups, then a repeated-measures *t* test can be used. Also, if you are comparing the two group means for either the pretest or the posttest scores, then an independent-measures *t* test is appropriate.

Terminology in Nonexperimental, Quasi-Experimental, and Developmental Designs

In a true experiment, the researcher manipulates an independent variable to create treatment conditions and then measures a dependent variable (scores) in each condition; scores in one condition are compared with the scores obtained in another condition. In nonexperimental and quasi-experimental research, no independent variable is manipulated. Nonetheless, nonexperimental studies do involve comparing groups of scores. In nonequivalent group studies, for example, the scores from one group of participants are compared with the scores from a different group. In pre–post studies, the scores obtained before the treatment are compared with the scores obtained after the treatment. In general, the variable that differentiates the groups (or sets of scores) is similar to the independent variable in an experiment and is often called an independent variable. However, this variable is more accurately referred to as a **quasi-independent variable**. As in an experiment, the score obtained for each participant is called the **dependent variable**.

DEFINITIONS

> Within the context of nonexperimental and quasi-experimental research, the variable that is used to differentiate the groups of participants or the groups of scores being compared is called the **quasi-independent variable**, and the variable that is measured to obtain the scores within each group is called the **dependent variable**.

In nonequivalent control group studies, for example, one group receives the treatment and one does not. The group difference, treatment versus nontreatment, determines the quasi-independent variable. In time-series studies, the researcher compares one set of observations (scores) before treatment with a second set of observations after treatment. For these studies, the quasi-independent variable is defined as "before versus after treatment."

Note that the same terminology is used for nonexperimental research as well as quasi-experimental studies. In differential research, for example, the participant variable used to differentiate the groups is called the quasi-independent variable. In a differential study comparing self-esteem scores for children from two-parent and single-parent homes, the number of parents is the quasi-independent variable, and self-esteem is the dependent variable. In a developmental study (either longitudinal or cross-sectional) examining changes in memory that occur with aging, the different ages are the quasi-independent variable and the memory scores are the dependent variable.

LEARNING CHECK

1. What is the appropriate statistical analysis for comparing non-numerical data for a differential design comparing samples representing two populations?
    a. Independent-measures *t* test
    b. Repeated-measures *t* test
    c. Independent-measures analysis of variance
    d. Chi-square test for independence

2. What is the appropriate statistical analysis for evaluating the after treatment mean difference for a posttest-only nonequivalent control group design?
    a. Independent-measures t test
    b. Repeated-measures t test
    c. Repeated-measures analysis of variance
    d. Chi-square test for independence
3. In a differential research design, what term is used identify the participant variable that is used to define the groups?
    a. Independent
    b. Dependent
    c. Quasi-independent
    d. Quasi-dependent

Answers appear at the end of the chapter.

CHAPTER SUMMARY

At this point, you should review the learning objectives presented at the beginning of each section and be sure that you have mastered each objective.

In many research situations, it is difficult or impossible for a researcher to satisfy completely the rigorous requirements of an experiment, particularly when doing applied research in natural settings. In these situations, a researcher may use the nonexperimental or the quasi-experimental research strategy. Nonexperimental and quasi-experimental studies always contain a threat to internal validity that is integral to the design and cannot be removed. As a result, these two research strategies cannot establish unambiguous cause-and-effect explanations. Quasi-experimental studies make some attempt to control threats to internal validity but nonexperimental studies typically do not.

Nonexperimental and quasi-experimental studies often look like experiments because they involve comparing groups of scores. Unlike experiments, however, the different groups are not created by manipulating an independent variable; instead, the groups are defined in terms of a preexisting participant characteristic (e.g., college graduate/no college) or defined in terms of time (e.g., before and after treatment). These two methods for defining groups produce two general categories of nonexperimental and quasi-experimental designs: nonequivalent group designs and pre–post designs.

In nonequivalent group designs, the researcher does not control the assignment of individuals to groups because the two groups already exist. Therefore, there is no assurance that the two groups are equivalent in terms of extraneous variables and internal validity is threatened by individual differences between groups. Three types of nonequivalent group designs are discussed: (1) the differential research design, (2) the posttest-only nonequivalent control group design, and (3) the pretest–posttest nonequivalent control group design. The first two designs make no attempt to limit the threat of individual differences between groups and are classified as nonexperimental. The pretest–posttest nonequivalent control group design does reduce the threat of individual differences and is classified as quasi-experimental.

The second general category is the pre–post design. The goal of a pre–post design is to evaluate the influence of the intervening treatment or event by comparing the observations before treatment with the observations made after treatment. Two examples of pre–post designs are considered: (1) the pretest–posttest design and (2) the time-series design. The first design makes no attempt to control time-related threats and is classified as nonexperimental. The second is quasi-experimental.

Developmental research designs are another type of nonexperimental research. The purpose of developmental designs is to describe the relationship between age and other variables. There are two types of developmental research designs. The cross-sectional research design compares separate groups of individuals with each group representing a different age. The obvious advantage of this design is that the researcher need not wait for participants to age to examine the relationship between a variable and age. However, the cohort or generation effect is a major weakness. In the longitudinal research design, the same group of individuals is followed and measured at different points in time; hence, cohort effects are not a problem. However, longitudinal research is extremely time-consuming for participants and researchers, and participant dropout can create a biased sample.

KEY WORDS

nonexperimental research strategy

quasi-experimental research strategy

nonequivalent group design

differential research design

nonequivalent control group design

posttest-only nonequivalent control group design

pretest–posttest nonequivalent control group design

pre–post design

pretest–posttest design

time-series design

developmental research designs

cross-sectional developmental research design

cohorts

cohort effects, or generation effects

longitudinal developmental research design

quasi-independent variable

dependent variable

EXERCISES

The exercises are identified with specific learning objectives and are intended to assess your mastery of the objectives. You should be aware that exam items are also generated to assess learning objectives.

1. In addition to the key words, you should also be able to define the following terms:

   individual differences
   differential effects
   history
   instrumentation
   order effects
   maturation
   statistical regression
   interrupted time-series designs
   single-case, or single-subject designs
   participant attrition, or participant mortality

2. (**LO1**) Explain the distinction between experimental and nonexperimental research strategies.

3. (**LO1**) Why are studies that examine the effects of aging not considered true experiments?

4. (**LO1**) Explain why we can be more confident about causal relationships between variables when a quasi-experimental design is used instead of a nonexperimental design.

5. (**LO2**) Give an example of a situation (aside from gender) in which a researcher must examine preexisting groups.

6. (**LO3**) Mueller and Oppenheimer (2014) conducted a series of studies comparing the effectiveness of taking classroom notes on laptops versus writing longhand. In one study, students were instructed to use their normal classroom note taking strategy using either a notebook or a laptop while they watched a brief lecture. A short time later, the students were given a quiz on the lecture material. Although the quiz results showed no difference between the two strategies for factual questions, the students using longhand had significantly higher scores for conceptual questions. Explain why the researchers cannot conclude that taking longhand notes causes better conceptual learning that taking notes on a laptop.

7. (**LO4**) A researcher measures personality characteristics for a group of participants who successfully lost weight in a diet program, and compared their scores with a second group consisting of individuals who failed to lose weight in the program. Is this study a differential design? Explain your answer.

8. (**LO4 & 8**) A researcher wants to describe the effectiveness of a new program (compared to the old program) for teaching reading to elementary school children. Describe how this study could be done as a posttest-only nonequivalent control group design. Next, describe how this study could be done as a nonexperimental pretest-posttest design.

9. (**LO5**) Explain how the pretest helps minimize the threat to internal validity from individual differences in a pretest–posttest nonequivalent control group design.

10. (**LO6**) Describe the basic characteristics of a pre–post design and explain why these designs are not true experiments.

11. (**LO7**) To evaluate the effectiveness of a new television commercial, a researcher measures attitudes toward the advertised product for a group of consumers before and after they view the commercial. Identify one factor that threatens the internal validity of this study.

12. (**LO8**) What characteristic differentiates a pretest–posttest design from a time-series design?

13. (**LO9**) Explain how a time-series design minimizes most threats to internal validity from time-related variables.

14. (**LO10**) A researcher wants to describe how fine motor skills change as a group of infants age from 18 to 24 months. Describe how this study could be done as a cross sectional design. Next, describe how this study could be done as longitudinal design.

15. (**LO10**) Although the cohort effect can be a serious problem for cross-sectional research, it is not a problem for longitudinal designs. Explain why not.

16. (**LO11**) Identify the appropriate statistical test for each of the following nonexperimental and quasi-experimental designs.
    a. A differential design
    b. A cross-sectional design comparing children at ages 10, 14, and 18

17. (**LO12**) The college offers all students an optional seminar on note taking and study skills. Suppose that a researcher compares personality scores for students who elected to take the seminar with the scores for students who did not. Identify the quasi-independent variable and the dependent variable for this study.

LEARNING CHECK ANSWERS

Section 10.1	Section 10.2	Section 10.3	Section 10.4	Section 10.5
1. a, 2. a	1. c, 2. d, 3. a, 4. c	1. c, 2. b, 3. a, 4. d	1. c, 2. d, 3. a	1. d, 2. a, 3. c

Factorial Designs

© Nathan Jasowiak / Shutterstock

CHAPTER LEARNING OBJECTIVES

LO1 Define a factorial research design, including the terms factor and level, and identify and describe factorial designs when they appear in a research report.

LO2 Define a main effect for one factor and an interaction between factors, and be able to identify main effects and interactions in the results from a two-factor design.

LO3 Explain how the existence of an interaction can influence the interpretation of main effects.

LO4 Describe and explain the independent relationship between main effects and interactions.

LO5 Explain how a factorial study can combine different research designs (between and within subjects) and different research strategies (experimental and nonexperimental) and identify these features when they appear in a research report.

LO6 Identify the statistical analyses that are appropriate to evaluate the mean differences for two-factor designs, and explain the strengths and weaknesses of using two levels versus multiple levels for each factor.

LO7 Describe three specific applications of the factorial design: (1) adding a factor to an existing study;

(2) using a participant variable as a second factor to control the variance in a between-subjects design; and (3) using the order of treatments as a second factor to evaluate the order effects in a within-subjects design; explain the advantage of using a factorial design in these situations.

CHAPTER OVERVIEW

Often, a research question requires a design that is more complex than the relatively simple experimental, nonexperimental, and quasi-experimental designs presented in Chapters 8–10. For example, Bartholow and Anderson (2002) designed a study to determine whether experiencing violence in video games has an effect on the players' behavior. Their results suggest that the answer is yes and no. In the study, male and female undergraduate students were randomly assigned to play either a violent video game or a nonviolent game. After the game, each participant was asked to take part in a competitive reaction time game with another student who was actually part of the research team (a confederate). After each trial, the winner was allowed to punish the loser with a blast of white noise delivered through headphones and the participants were allowed to set the intensity of the punishment noise. The researchers used the intensity level for the punishment noise as a measure of aggressive behavior. The results of the study are shown in Table 11.1.

Notice the level of violence in the video game had essentially no effect on the behavior of the female participants, but the males who played a violent game were significantly more aggressive than the males who played the nonviolent game.

From a research methods perspective, this study is interesting because it uses two variables (game violence and gender) to create four groups of participants and allows the researchers to examine how aggressive behavior is influenced by the two variables acting together. This study is an example of what is called a factorial design, specifically a two-factor design. If the study had used only females, the data would suggest that game violence has little or no effect on aggressive behavior. If only males were used, the conclusion would be that experiencing violence in video games increases aggressive behavior. Neither of these conclusions is completely correct. The real answer is: "It depends."

In this chapter, we introduce factorial designs, examine their components, and discuss different types and applications of factorial designs.

TABLE 11.1

Aggressiveness, as Measured by the Mean Intensity of Punishment (Noise Level) Administered to an Opponent in a Reaction Time Competition, after Playing either a Nonviolent or a Violent Video Game (Bartholow & Anderson, 2002)

	Nonviolent Game	Violent Game
Females	$M = 4.61$	$M = 5.05$
Males	$M = 4.60$	$M = 7.01$

11.1 Introduction to Factorial Designs

LEARNING OBJECTIVE

LO1 Define a factorial research design, including the terms *factor* and *level*, and identify and describe factorial designs when they appear in a research report.

In most research situations, the goal is to examine the relationship between two variables by isolating those variables within the research study. The idea is to eliminate or reduce the influence of any outside variables that may disguise or distort the specific relationship under investigation. For example, experimental research (discussed in Chapters 7–9) typically focuses on one independent variable (which is expected to influence behavior) and one dependent variable (which is a measure of the behavior). Similarly, the nonexperimental and quasi-experimental designs described in Chapter 10 usually investigate the relationship between one quasi-independent variable and one dependent variable. For example, developmental studies typically examine how a behavior (dependent variable) is related to age (quasi-independent). In real life, however, variables rarely exist in isolation. That is, behavior usually is influenced by a variety of different variables acting and interacting simultaneously. For example, weight loss may be related to diet, exercise, health, and a variety of other variables. To examine these more complex, real-life situations, researchers often design research studies that include more than one independent variable (or quasi-independent variable). These studies are called factorial designs.

> Recall from Chapter 10 (p. 261) that in nonexperimental and quasi-experimental research, the variable that differentiates the groups of participants or the groups of scores is called the quasi-independent variable.

To simplify our discussion of factorial designs, we begin by looking exclusively at experimental studies; that is, studies that involve the manipulation of two or more independent variables. However, it is also possible for factorial designs to involve variables such as age or gender that are not manipulated and, therefore, are quasi-independent variables. At the beginning of this chapter, for example, we discussed a study examining how video game violence and gender are related to aggressive behavior. In this case, gender is a quasi-independent variable because it is not manipulated. Factorial studies involving quasi-independent variables are discussed on page 279. The following example introduces experimental factorial designs.

Ackerman and Goldsmith (2011) conducted two experimental studies comparing the effectiveness of studying text printed on paper compared to text presented on a computer screen. In both studies, one group of participants studied from paper and the second from a screen and both groups were given a multiple-choice test on the material they had studied. In the first experiment, study time was fixed by the researchers and test performance was the same for the two groups. In the second study, however, study time was self-regulated and test performance was significantly worse for the students studying on-screen text. It appears that students who are studying on-screen material are unable to judge how well they have mastered the material and show more erratic study-time regulation.

Although the paper/on-screen study was actually done as two separate experiments, we are combining the two experiments into a single study to help introduce a new kind of experimental design. Figure 11.1 shows the general structure of this experiment. Notice that the study involves two independent variables. The mode of presentation is manipulated by having the participants read either from paper or a screen. The amount of control of study time is manipulated by fixing the time for some participants and letting the other group of participants self-regulate their study time. The two independent variables create a matrix with the different values of presentation defining the columns and the different levels of time control defining the rows. The resulting 2×2 matrix shows four different combinations of the variables, producing four treatment conditions to be examined. The

	On Paper	On Screen
Fixed Time	Exam scores for a group of participants who studied text presented on paper for a fixed time.	Exam scores for a group of participants who studied text presented on screen for a fixed time.
Self-Regulated Time	Exam scores for a group of participants who studied text presented on paper for a self-regulated time.	Exam scores for a group of participants who studied text presented on screen for a self-regulated time.

FIGURE 11.1

The Structure of a Two-Factor Experiment in Which Mode of Presentation (Factor A) and Control of Study Time (Factor B) Are Manipulated in the Same Study

The purpose of the experiment is to examine how different combinations of presentation mode and time control affect performance on a multiple-choice exam.

dependent variable for each of the four conditions is each student's score on the multiple-choice test.

To simplify further discussion of this kind of research study, some basic terminology and definitions are in order. When two or more independent variables are combined in a single study, the independent variables are commonly called **factors**. For the study in our example, the two factors are mode of presentation and control of time. A research study involving two or more factors is called a **factorial design**. This kind of design is often described by the number of its factors, such as a two-factor design or a three-factor design. Our example is a **two-factor design**. A research study with only one independent variable is often called a **single-factor design**.

Nonexperimental studies using quasi-independent variables as factors are discussed in Section 11.3.

DEFINITIONS

> A **factor** is an independent variable in an experiment, especially those that include two or more independent variables.
> A **factorial design** is a research design that includes two or more factors.

Generically, each factor is denoted by a letter (A, B, C, and so on). In addition, factorial designs use a notation system that identifies both the number of factors and the number of values or **levels** that exist for each factor (see Chapter 7, p. 261). The previous example has two levels for the mode-of-presentation factor (factor A) and two levels for the time-control factor (factor B), and can be described as a 2 × 2 (read as "two by two") factorial design. The total number of treatment conditions can be determined by multiplying the levels for each factor. For example, a 2 × 3 factorial design would represent a two-factor design with two levels of the first factor and three levels of the second, with a total of six treatment conditions; and a 2 × 3 × 2 design would represent a **three-factor design** with two, three, and two levels of each of the factors, respectively, for a total of 12 conditions. Factorial designs including more than two independent variables are discussed in Section 11.3.

As we have noted, one advantage of a factorial design is that it creates a more realistic situation than that which can be obtained by examining a single factor in isolation.

Because behavior is influenced by a variety of factors usually acting together, it is sensible to examine two or more factors simultaneously in a single study. At first glance, it may appear that this kind of research is unnecessarily complicated. Why not do two separate, simple studies looking at each factor by itself? The answer to this question is that combining two (or more) factors within one study provides researchers with an opportunity to see how each individual factor influences behavior and how the group of factors, acting together, can influence behavior. Returning to the presentation-mode and time-control example, a researcher who compared paper versus on-screen studying for a controlled-time condition only would conclude that the mode of presentation makes no difference. In the same way, a researcher who compared the two presentation modes only for self-regulated time would conclude that paper presentation is significantly better. Notice that neither answer is completely correct. However, combining the two variables permits researchers to see how changing the way that time is controlled can influence the effects of the presentation mode. The idea that two factors can act together, creating unique conditions that are different from either factor acting alone, underlies the value of a factorial design.

LEARNING CHECK

1. How many independent variables are there in a $2 \times 2 \times 2$ factorial design?
   a. 2
   b. 3
   c. 4
   d. 8

2. How many separate groups of participants would be needed for a between-subjects, two-factor study with three levels of factor A and four levels of factor B?
   a. 3
   b. 4
   c. 7
   d. 12

3. A researcher who is examining the effects of temperature and humidity on the eating behavior of rats uses a factorial experiment comparing three different temperatures (70°, 80°, and 90°) and two humidity conditions (low and high). How many factors are in the experiment?
   a. 1
   b. 2
   c. 3
   d. 6

Answers appear at the end of the chapter.

11.2 Main Effects and Interactions

LEARNING OBJECTIVES

LO2 Define a main effect for one factor and an interaction between factors, and be able to identify main effects and interactions in the results from a two-factor design.

LO3 Explain how the existence of an interaction can influence the interpretation of main effects.

LO4 Describe and explain the independent relationship between main effects and interactions.

The primary advantage of a factorial design is that it allows researchers to examine how unique combinations of factors acting together influence behavior. To explore this feature in more detail, we focus on designs involving only two factors, that is, the simplest possible factorial design. In Section 11.3, we look briefly at more complex situations involving three or more factors.

The structure of a two-factor design can be represented by a matrix in which the levels of one factor determine the columns and the levels of the second factor determine the rows (see Figure 11.1). Each cell in the matrix corresponds to a specific combination of the factors, that is, a separate treatment condition. The research study would involve observing and measuring a group of individuals under the conditions described by each cell.

The data from a two-factor study provide three separate and distinct sets of information describing how the two factors independently and jointly affect behavior. To demonstrate the three kinds of information, the general structure of the presentation-mode and time-control study is repeated in Table 11.2, with hypothetical data added showing the mean test score for participants in each of the cells. (Note that the data in this table do not correspond to the actual results of the study.) The data provide information about the effect of each factor separately and how they interact together.

Main Effects

Each column of the matrix corresponds to a specific mode of presentation. For example, all of the participants tested in the first column (both sets of scores) read the text on paper. By computing the mean score for each column, we obtain an overall mean for each of the presentation-mode conditions. Comparison of the two column means provides an indication of how the mode of presentation affects test performance. The difference between the two column means is called the **main effect** for mode of presentation. In more general terms, the mean differences among the columns determine the main effect for one factor. Notice that each column includes both levels of time control (half the scores were obtained with a fixed time and half were obtained with self-regulated time). Thus, time control is balanced or matched across both presentation modes, which means that any differences obtained between the columns cannot be explained by differences in how time was controlled.

For the data in Table 11.2, the participants in the paper condition have an average test score of 20. This column mean was obtained by averaging the two groups in the paper column (mean = 22 and mean = 18). In a similar way, the participants who read from a screen have an average score of 16. These two means show a general tendency for higher test scores with paper presentation than for on-screen presentation. This relationship between presentation mode and test scores is the main effect for the mode of presentation.

TABLE 11.2

Hypothetical Data Showing the Treatment Means for a Two-Factor Study Examining How Different Modes of Presentation and Methods of Controlling Study Time Affect Performance on a Multiple-Choice Test

The data are structured to create main effects for both factors but no interaction.

	On Paper	On Screen	
Fixed time	$M = 22$	$M = 18$	Overall $M = 20$
Self-regulated time	$M = 18$	$M = 14$	Overall $M = 16$
	Overall $M = 20$	Overall $M = 16$	

Finally, note that the mean difference between the columns simply describes the main effect for presentation mode. A statistical test is necessary to determine whether the mean difference is significant.

Just as we determine the overall main effect for mode of presentation by calculating the column means for the data in Table 11.2, we can determine the overall effect of time control by examining the rows of the data matrix. For example, all of the participants in the top row were tested with a fixed study time. The mean score for these participants (both sets of scores) provides a measure of test performance when study time is fixed. Similarly, the overall mean for the bottom row describes test scores when study time is self-regulated. The difference between these two means is called the main effect for time control. As before, notice that the process of obtaining the row means involves averaging both levels of presentation mode. Thus, each row mean includes exactly the same presentation-mode conditions. As a result, presentation mode is matched across rows and cannot explain the mean differences between rows. In general terms, the differences between the column means define the main effect for one factor, and the differences between the row means define the main effect for the second factor.

For the data shown in Table 11.2, the overall mean for the first row (fixed time) is 20. This mean is obtained by averaging the two treatment means in the top row (22 and 18). Similarly, the overall mean for participants in the self-regulated condition is 16. The 4-point difference between the two row means (20 and 16) describes the main effect for time control. In this study, fixing the study time increases test scores by an average of 4 points.

The Interaction between Factors

A factorial design allows researchers to examine how combinations of factors working together affect behavior. In some situations, the effects of one factor are completely independent of the levels of the second factor. In this case, neither factor has a direct influence on the other. For the paper/on-screen study, independent factors means that the difference between paper versus on-screen presentation does not depend on how study time is controlled. In this case, the main effect for presentation mode (the 4-point difference in test scores) applies equally to both time-control conditions. This is exactly what exists for the data in Table 11.2. There is a 4-point difference between paper and on-screen in the top row (fixed time) and in the bottom row (self-regulated time).

In other situations, however, one factor does have a direct influence on the effect of a second factor, producing an **interaction between factors**, or **interaction**. To demonstrate an interaction, we have created a new set of data, shown in Table 11.3. (Note that the data in this table reflect the pattern of results that was obtained in the original study.) These data have exactly the same main effects that existed in Table 11.2. Specifically, students studying text on paper have test scores that average 4 points higher than the scores for students studying on a screen, and students with a fixed study time score 4 points higher than students whose study time is self-regulated. For these data however, we have modified the cell means to create an interaction between factors. Now, the main effects for the two factors do not explain the mean differences within the matrix. For example, the 4-point main effect for paper versus on-screen does not explain either of the two time-control conditions. In the top row, for example, there is no difference between paper and on-screen but there is an 8-point difference in the bottom row (self-regulated time).

Probably the most familiar example of an interaction between factors is a drug interaction, in which one drug modifies the effects of a second drug. In some cases, one drug can exaggerate the effects of another, and, in other cases, one drug may minimize or completely block the effectiveness of another. In either case, the effect of one drug is being modified by a second drug, and there is an interaction.

TABLE 11.3

Hypothetical Data Showing the Treatment Means for a Two-Factor Study Examining How Different Modes of Presentation and Methods of Controlling Study Time Affect Performance on a Multiple-Choice Test

The data are structured to create the same main effects as in Table 11.2, but the cell means have been adjusted to produce an interaction.

	On Paper	**On Screen**	
Fixed time	$M = 20$	$M = 20$	Overall $M = 20$
Self-regulated time	$M = 20$	$M = 12$	Overall $M = 16$
	Overall $M = 20$	Overall $M = 16$	

DEFINITIONS

The mean differences among the levels of one factor are called the **main effect** of that factor. When the research study is represented as a matrix with one factor defining the rows and the second factor defining the columns, then the mean differences among the rows define the main effect for one factor, and the mean differences among the columns define the main effect for the second factor. Note that a two-factor study has two main effects; one for each of the two factors.

An **interaction between factors** (or simply an **interaction**) occurs whenever two factors, acting together, produce mean differences that are not explained by the main effects of the two factors. On the other hand, if the main effect for either factor applies equally across all levels of the second factor, then the two factors are independent and there is no interaction.

Alternative Views of the Interaction between Factors

The concept of an interaction has been defined as unique mean differences that are not explained by the main effects of the two factors. Now we look at interactions in more detail and consider two alternative points of view. For simplicity, we continue to examine two-factor designs and postpone discussion of more complex designs (and more complex interactions).

A slightly different perspective on the concept of an interaction focuses on the notion of independence, as opposed to dependence, between the factors. More specifically, if the two factors are independent so that the effect of one is not influenced by the other, then there is no interaction. On the other hand, if the effect of one factor depends on the influence of the other factor, then there is an **interaction**. The notion of interdependence is consistent with our earlier discussion of interactions; if the effect of one factor depends on the other, then unique combinations of the factors produce unique effects. This new perspective leads to an alternative definition of the interaction between factors.

DEFINITION

An **interaction** exists between the factors when the effects of one factor depend on the different levels of a second factor.

This alternative definition uses different terminology but is equivalent to the first definition. When the effects of one factor vary depending on the levels of a second factor, the two factors are combining to produce unique effects. For the data in Table 11.3, the difference between paper and on-screen depends on how study time is controlled. In the fixed-time condition, there is no difference between the two modes of presentation; both groups have a mean test score of 20. However, in the self-regulated condition, the paper group scores an average of 8 points higher on the test. Again, the effect of one factor (mode of presentation) depends on the levels of the second factor (time control), which indicates an interaction. By contrast, the original data in Table 11.2 show that the effect of presentation mode does not depend on time control. For these data, the students studying from paper score 4 points higher than students studying on screen for both time-control conditions. Thus, the effect of switching from paper to on-screen does not depend on the method of time control and there is no interaction.

A second view of an interaction focuses on the pattern that is produced when the means from a two-factor study are presented in a graph. Figure 11.2 shows the original data from Table 11.2, for which there is no interaction. To construct this figure, one of the factors was selected as the independent variable to appear on the horizontal axis; in this case, the two different modes of presentation are displayed. The dependent variable—test score—is shown on the vertical axis. Notice that the figure actually contains two separate graphs; the top line shows the relationship between mode of presentation and test scores when study time is fixed, and the bottom line shows the relationship when study time is self-regulated. In general, the graph matches the structure of the data matrix; the columns of the matrix appear as values along the *X*-axis, and each row of the matrix appears as a separate line in the graph.

For this particular set of data (see Figure 11.2), notice that the lines in the graph are parallel. As you move from left to right, the distance between the lines is constant. For these data, the distance between the lines corresponds to the time-control effect, that is, the mean difference in test scores with fixed time and with self-regulated time. That this difference is constant indicates that the time-control effect does not depend on the mode of presentation and there is no interaction between factors.

Now consider data for which there is an interaction between factors. Figure 11.3 shows the data from Table 11.3. In this case, the two lines are not parallel. The distance between the lines changes as you move from left to right, indicating that the effect of controlling time is different for on-paper presentation than for on-screen presentation. For these data, the time-control effect does depend on the mode of presentation and there is

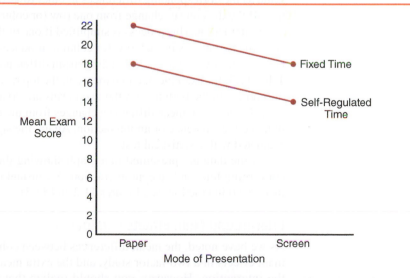

FIGURE 11.2

A Line Graph of the Data from Table 11.2

The hypothetical data are structured to show main effects for both factors but no interaction.

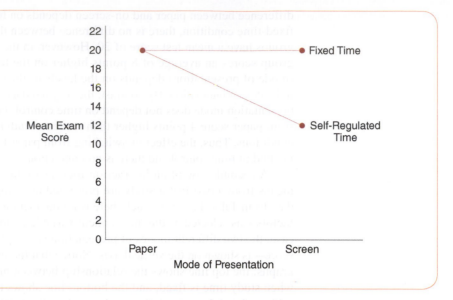

FIGURE 11.3

A Line Graph of the Data from Table 11.3

The hypothetical data are structured to show main effects for both factors and an interaction.

an **interaction** between factors. Viewing the graph produced by the means in a two-factor study leads to another alternative definition of an interaction.

DEFINITION

> When the results of a two-factor study are graphed, the existence of nonparallel lines (lines that cross or converge) is an indication of an **interaction** between the two factors. (Note that a statistical test is needed to determine whether the interaction is significant.)

Identifying Interactions

To identify an interaction in a data matrix such as Table 11.3, you must compare the mean differences in any individual row (or column) with the mean differences in other rows or columns. If the size and the direction of the differences in one row (or column) are the same as the corresponding differences in other rows (or columns), then there is no interaction. If the differences change from one row (or column) to another, then there is evidence of an interaction. This process is simplified if one of the factors has only two levels. In this case, the two means in each row (or column) produce one mean difference, which can then be compared with the corresponding mean difference in the other rows (or columns). In Table 11.3, for example, the two means in the top row are 20 and 20 and produce a 0-point difference. In the bottom row, the two means are 20 and 12 and produce an 8-point difference. Because the mean difference changes from the top row to the bottom row, these data indicate the existence of an interaction. Again, the significance of the interaction must be evaluated with a statistical test.

If the data are presented in a graph showing the treatment means, then crossing or converging lines indicate an interaction. A constant distance between lines indicates that there is no interaction (see Figures 11.2 and 11.3).

Interpreting Main Effects and Interactions

As we have noted, the mean differences between columns and between rows describe the main effects in a two-factor study, and the extra mean differences between cells describe the interaction. However, you should realize that these mean differences are simply descriptive and must be evaluated by a statistical hypothesis test before they can be considered significant. That is, the obtained mean differences may not represent a real treatment effect but rather may be caused by chance or error. Until the data are evaluated by a hypothesis test, be cautious about interpreting any results from a two-factor study (see Box 7.1, p. 161).

When a statistical analysis does indicate significant effects, you must still be careful about interpreting the outcome. In particular, if the analysis results in a significant interaction, then the main effects, whether significant or not, may present a distorted view of the actual outcome. Remember, the main effect for one factor is obtained by averaging all the different levels of the second factor. Because each main effect is an average, it may not accurately represent any of the individual effects that were used to compute the average. To illustrate this point, Figure 11.4 presents the general results from research examining the relationship between the TV viewing habits of 5-year-old children and their future performance in high school.

In general, research results indicate that 5-year-old children who watched a lot of educational programming such as *Sesame Street* and *Mister Rogers' Neighborhood* had higher high-school grades than their peers (Anderson, Huston, Wright, & Collins, 1998). The same study reported that 5-year-old children who watched a lot of noneducational TV programs had relatively low high-school grades compared to their peers. Figure 11.4 shows a data matrix and a graph presenting this combination of results. Notice that the data show no main effect for the factor representing the amount of time that the children watched TV. Overall, the grades for students who watched a lot of TV as children are the same as the grades for students who watched a small or moderate amount of TV. However, the lines in the graph show an interaction, suggesting that the effect of watching a lot of TV depends on the type of programs the children are watching. Educational programs are related to an increase in grades and noneducational programs are related to a decrease. Averaging these two results produces the zero value for the main effect. However, the main effect does not accurately

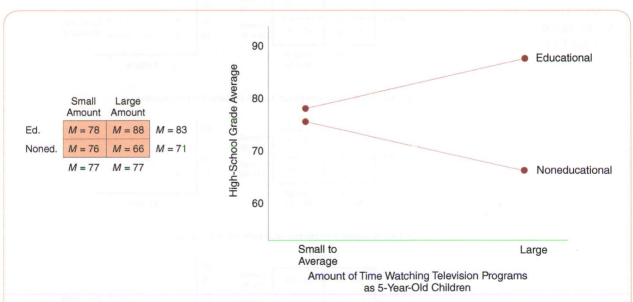

FIGURE 11.4

The Relationship between the TV Viewing Habits of 5-Year-Old Children and Their Future High-School Grades
Based on results from Anderson, Huston, Wright, and Collins (1998).

describe the results. In particular, it would be incorrect to conclude that there is no relationship between the amount of time spent watching TV as a child and future high-school grades.

In general, the presence of an interaction can obscure or distort the main effects of either factor. Whenever a statistical analysis produces a significant interaction, you should take a close look at the data before giving any credibility to the main effects.

Independence of Main Effects and Interactions

The two-factor study allows researchers to evaluate three separate sets of mean differences: (1) the mean differences from the main effect of factor A, (2) the mean differences from the main effect of factor B, and (3) the mean differences from the interaction between factors. The three sets of mean differences are separate and completely independent. Thus, it is possible for the results from a two-factor study to show any possible combination of main effects and interaction.

The data sets in Figure 11.5 show several possibilities. To simplify discussion, the two factors are labeled A and B. The two levels of factor A (A1 and A2) define the rows of the data matrix, and the two levels of factor B (B1 and B2) define the columns.

Figure 11.5a shows data with a mean difference between levels of factor A, but no mean difference for factor B and no interaction. To identify the main effect for factor A, notice that the overall mean for the top row is 10 points higher than the overall mean for the bottom row. This 10-point difference is the main effect for factor A, or, simply, the A effect. To evaluate the main effect for factor B, notice that both columns have exactly the same overall mean, indicating no difference between levels of factor B; hence, no B effect.

FIGURE 11.5

Three Possible Combinations of Main Effects and Interactions in a Two-Factor Experiment

(a) Data showing a main effect for factor A but no main effect for factor B and no interaction

(b) Data showing main effects for both factor A and factor B but no interaction

(c) Data showing no main effect for either factor, but an interaction

Finally, the absence of an interaction is indicated by the fact that the overall A effect (the 10-point difference) is constant within each column; that is, the A effect does not depend on the levels of factor B. (Alternatively, the data indicate that the overall B effect is constant within each row.)

Figure 11.5b shows data with an A effect and a B effect, but no interaction. For these data, the A effect is indicated by the 10-point mean difference between rows, and the B effect is indicated by the 20-point mean difference between columns. The fact that the 10-point A effect is constant within each column indicates no interaction.

Finally, Figure 11.5c shows data that display an interaction but no main effect for factor A or for factor B. For these data, there is no mean difference between rows (no A effect) and no mean difference between columns (no B effect). However, within each row (or within each column) there are mean differences. The "extra" mean differences within the rows and columns cannot be explained by the overall main effects and, therefore, indicate an interaction.

LEARNING CHECK

1. The following data represent the means for each treatment condition in a two-factor experiment. What pattern of results is shown in the data?

	A1	A2
B1	$M = 30$	$M = 20$
B2	$M = 40$	$M = 10$

   a. Main effects for both factors and an interaction
   b. Main effects for both factors and no interaction
   c. A main effect for factor A, no main effect for factor B, and no interaction
   d. A main effect for factor A and an interaction but no main effect for factor B

2. The results from a two-factor ANOVA show no main effect for factor A but a significant interaction. What can you conclude based on this pattern of results?
   a. Factor A has no effect on the participants' scores.
   b. Factor A may have an effect but, if so, it depends on the levels of factor B.
   c. Because the interaction is significant, factor A must also have an effect.
   d. The effect of factor A is constant across all levels of factor B.

3. Which of the following is not a possible outcome from a 2×2 factorial design?
   a. Two main effects and an interaction
   b. Two main effects and no interaction
   c. No main effect for either factor but an interaction
   d. All of the above are all possible outcomes

Answers appear at the end of the chapter.

11.3 Types of Factorial Designs and Analysis

LEARNING OBJECTIVES

LO5 Explain how a factorial study can combine different research designs (between and within subjects) and different research strategies (experimental and nonexperimental) and identify these features when they appear in a research report.

LO6 Identify the statistical analyses that are appropriate to evaluate the mean differences for two-factor designs, and explain the strengths and weaknesses of using two levels versus multiple levels for each factor.

Thus far, we have examined only one version of all of the many different types of factorial designs. In particular:

- All of the designs that we have considered use a separate group of participants for each of the individual treatment combinations or cells. In research terminology, we have looked exclusively at between-subjects designs.
- All of the previous examples use factors that are true independent variables. That is, the factors are manipulated by the researcher so that the research study is an example of the experimental strategy.

Although it is possible to have a separate group for each of the individual cells (a between-subjects design), it is also possible to have the same group of individuals participate in all of the different cells (a within-subjects design). In addition, it is possible to construct a factorial design in which the factors are not manipulated but rather are quasi-independent variables (see Chapter 10, p. 261). Finally, a factorial design can use any combination of factors. As a result, a factorial study can combine elements of experimental and nonexperimental research strategies, and it can combine elements of between-subjects and within-subjects designs within a single research study. A two-factor design, for example, may include one between-subjects factor (with a separate group for each level of the factor) and one within-subjects factor (with each group measured in all the different treatment conditions). The same study could also include one experimental factor (with a manipulated independent variable) and one nonexperimental factor (with a preexisting, nonmanipulated variable). The ability to mix designs within a single research study provides researchers with the potential to blend several different research strategies within one study. This potential allows researchers to develop studies that address scientific questions that could not be answered by any single strategy. In the following sections, we examine some of the possibilities for factorial designs.

Between-Subjects and Within-Subjects Designs

It is possible to construct a factorial study that is purely a between-subjects design; that is, a study in which there is a separate group of participants for each of the treatment conditions. As we noted in Chapter 8, this type of design has some definite advantages as well as some disadvantages. A particular disadvantage for a factorial study is that a between-subjects design can require a large number of participants. For example, a 2×4 factorial design has eight different treatment conditions. A separate group of 30 participants in each condition requires a total of 240 (8×30) participants. As noted in Chapter 8, another disadvantage of between-subject designs is that individual differences (characteristics that differ from one participant to another) can become confounding variables and increase the variance of the scores. On the positive side, a between-subjects design completely avoids any problem from order effects because each score is completely independent of every other score. In general, between-subjects designs are best suited to situations in which a lot of participants are available, individual differences are relatively small, and order effects are likely.

At the other extreme, it is possible to construct a factorial study that is purely a within-subjects design. In this case, a single group of individuals participates in all of the separate treatment conditions. As we noted in Chapter 9, this type of design has some definite advantages and disadvantages. A particular disadvantage for a factorial study is the number of different treatment conditions that each participant must undergo. In a 2×4 design, for example, each participant must be measured in eight different treatment conditions. The large number of different treatments can be very time-consuming, which increases the chances that participants will quit and walk away before the study is ended (participant attrition). In addition, having each participant undergo a long series of treatment conditions can increase the potential for testing effects (such as fatigue or practice effects) and make it more difficult to counterbalance the design to control for order effects. Two advantages of within-subjects designs are that they require only one group of participants and eliminate or greatly reduce the problems associated with individual differences. In general, within-subjects designs are best suited for situations in which individual differences are relatively large, and there is little reason to expect order effects to be large and disruptive.

Mixed Designs: Within-Subjects and Between-Subjects

Often, a researcher encounters a situation in which the advantages or convenience of a between-subjects design apply to one factor but a within-subjects design is preferable for a second factor. For example, a researcher may prefer to use a within-subjects design to take maximum advantage of a small group of participants. However, if one factor is expected to produce large order effects, then a between-subjects design should be used for that factor. In this situation, it is possible to construct a **mixed design**, with one between-subjects factor and one within-subjects factor. If the design is pictured as a matrix with one factor defining the rows and the second factor defining the columns, then the mixed design has a separate group for each row with each group participating in all of the different columns.

DEFINITION

> A **mixed design** is a factorial study that combines two different research designs. A common example of a mixed design is a factorial study with one between-subjects factor and one within-subjects factor.

Figure 11.6 shows a mixed factorial design in a study examining the effect of acetaminophen (the active ingredient in Tylenol) on the experience of pain and pleasure (Durso, Luttrell, & Way, 2015). Half of the participants were given a 1,000 milligram dose of acetaminophen and half were given a placebo. The participants were then shown a series of 40 photographs with some showing highly positive images such as children with kittens and some showing highly negative images such as starving children, and they rated the pleasantness/unpleasantness of each photograph. The results showed that the participants who took acetaminophen rated both types of picture less extremely than the participants with the placebo; that is, the pleasant photographs were rated less positively and the unpleasant photographs were rated less negatively. Apparently acetaminophen reduces the experience of both pain and pleasure.

Because each participant saw and rated all the photographs, the type of photograph (pleasant vs. unpleasant) is a within-subjects factor corresponding to the two columns in Figure 11.6. The researchers also created a between-subjects factor consisting of an acetaminophen group and a placebo group. In Figure 11.6, the two groups correspond to the two rows in the matrix.

Experimental and Nonexperimental or Quasi-Experimental Research Strategies

As we demonstrated earlier in this chapter (p. 267) with an example that compared studying text presented on paper versus text presented on screen, it is possible to construct a factorial study that is a purely experimental research design. In this case, both factors are true independent variables that are manipulated by the researcher. It also is possible to construct a factorial study for which all the factors are nonmanipulated, quasi-independent

FIGURE 11.6

Results from a Mixed Two-Factor Study That Combines One Between-Subjects Factor and One Within-Subjects Factor

The graph shows the pattern of results obtained by Durso, Luttrell, and Way (2015). The researchers showed participants a series of photographs of positive and negative images to create a within-subjects factor (positive/negative). The researchers manipulated acetaminophen by dividing the participants into two groups and having one group given 1,000 milligram dose and the other group given a placebo, creating a between-subjects factor (acetaminophen/placebo). The participants in both groups rated the pleasantness/unpleasantness of each photograph.

variables. For example, several studies have reported a negative relationship between the amount of time spent on Facebook and academic performance. Other researchers, however, have suggested that the observed relationship may be caused by the fact that many students try to multitask by combining Facebook and studying. To look into this issue, Junco (2015) examined the time that students spent on Facebook by itself and the time they spent multitasking with Facebook for different class ranks. Notice that one factor for this study consists of four different college classes (Freshmen, Sophomores, Juniors, Seniors), which are preexisting groups. The second factor, which also is not manipulated, simply compares two ways of using Facebook (by itself or multitasking). Because both factors are nonmanipulated quasi-independent variables, the study is a purely nonexperimental design. Incidentally, the results showed that seniors spent significantly less time using Facebook, either alone or multitasking, than students in the other classes.

Combined Strategies: Experimental and Quasi-Experimental or Nonexperimental

In the behavioral sciences, it is common for a factorial design to use an experimental strategy for one factor and a quasi-experimental or nonexperimental strategy for another factor. This type of study is an example of a **combined strategy**. This kind of study involves one factor that is a true independent variable consisting of a set of manipulated treatment conditions, and a second factor that is a quasi-independent variable that typically falls into one of the following categories.

1. The second factor is a preexisting participant characteristic such as age or gender. For example, a researcher may want to determine whether the set of treatment conditions has the same effect on males as on females, or the question is whether the treatment effects change as a function of age. Note that preexisting participant characteristics create nonequivalent groups; thus, this factor is a quasi-independent variable. Occasionally, designs that add a participant characteristic as a second factor are called *person-by-environment* (P × E) designs or *person-by-situation* designs.

2. The second factor is time. In this case, the concern of the research question is how the different treatment effects persist over time. For example, two different therapy techniques may be equally effective immediately after the therapy is concluded, but

one may continue to have an effect over time, whereas the other loses effectiveness as time passes. Note that time is not controlled or manipulated by the researcher, so this factor is a quasi-independent variable.

DEFINITION

A **combined strategy** study uses two different research strategies in the same factorial design. One factor is a true independent variable (experimental strategy) and one factor is a quasi-independent variable (nonexperimental or quasi-experimental strategy).

At the beginning of the chapter, for example, we discussed a two-factor study examining the relationship between video game violence and aggressive behavior (Bartholow & Anderson, 2002). The results showed that experiencing video game violence increased aggression for males but had little or no effect on females (Figure 11.7). In the study, the researchers manipulated the level of violence in the video game, so this factor is a true independent variable. The second factor in the study is gender, which is a preexisting participant variable and, therefore, a quasi-independent variable.

Notice that Figure 11.7 uses a bar graph to show the results. This kind of graph is often considered more appropriate than the typical line graph when the two factors are non-numerical measurements from nominal or ordinal scales. You should note, however, that the graph clearly shows an interaction between the two factors. Specifically, the level of game violence had a large effect on male participants, but had essentially no effect on the females.

Pretest–Posttest Control Group Designs

In Chapter 10, we introduced a quasi-experimental design known as the pretest–posttest nonequivalent control group design (p. 247). This design involves two separate groups of participants. One group—the treatment group—is measured before and after receiving

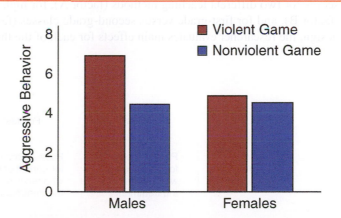

FIGURE 11.7

Results from a Two-Factor Study That Combines One Experimental Factor and One Nonexperimental Factor

The researchers manipulated whether the participants played a violent or a nonviolent videogame. This is an independent variable (violent vs. nonviolent). Within each experimental condition, the participants were divided into two groups (male vs. female). The gender of the participants is a nonmanipulated, quasi-independent variable. The dependent variable is the intensity level for the punishment noise as a measure of aggressive behavior.

a treatment. A second group—the control group—also is measured twice (pretest and posttest) but does not receive any treatment between the two measurements. Using the notation introduced in Chapter 10, this design can be represented as follows:

O X O   (treatment group)

O   O   (nonequivalent control group)

Each O represents an observation or measurement, and the X indicates a treatment. Each row corresponds to the series of events for one group.

You should recognize this design as an example of a two-factor mixed design. One factor—treatment/control—is a between-subjects factor. The other factor—pretest–posttest—is a within-subjects factor. Figure 11.8 shows the design using the matrix notation customary for factorial designs.

Finally, the design introduced in Chapter 10 was classified as quasi-experimental because it used nonequivalent groups (e.g., students from two different high schools or clients from two different clinics). On the other hand, if a researcher has one sample of participants and can randomly assign them to the two groups, then the design is classified as a combined strategy with one experimental factor (treatment/control) and one nonexperimental factor (pre–post). This version of the pretest–posttest control group design can be represented as follows:

R O X O   (treatment group)

R O   O   (control group)

The letter R symbolizes random assignment, which means that the researcher has control over assignment of participants to groups and, therefore, can create equivalent groups.

Higher-Order Factorial Designs

The basic concepts of a two-factor research design can be extended to more complex designs involving three or more factors; such designs are referred to as **higher-order factorial designs**. A three-factor design, for example, might look at academic performance scores for two different teaching methods (factor A), for high IQ versus low IQ students (factor B), and for first-grade versus second-grade classes (factor C). In the three-factor design, the researcher evaluates main effects for each of the three factors, as well as a set

FIGURE 11.8

The Structure of a Pretest–Posttest Control Group Study Organized as a Two-Factor Research Design

Notice that the treatment/control factor is a between-subjects factor and the pre–post factor is a within-subjects factor.

of two-way interactions: A × B, B × C, and A × C. In addition, the extra factor introduces the potential for a three-way interaction: A × B × C.

The logic for defining and interpreting higher-order interactions follows the pattern set by two-way interactions. For example, a two-way interaction such as A × B indicates that the effect of factor A depends on the levels of factor B. Extending this definition, a three-way interaction such as A × B × C indicates that the two-way interaction between A and B depends on the levels of factor C. For example, two teaching methods might be equally effective for high- and low- IQ students in the first grade (no two-way interaction between method and IQ), but in the second grade, one of the methods works better for high IQ students and the other method works better for low IQ students (an interaction between method and IQ). Because the method-by-IQ pattern of results is different for the first graders and the second graders, there is a three-way interaction. Although the general idea of a three-way interaction is easily grasped, most people have great difficulty comprehending or interpreting a four-way (or higher) interaction. Although it is possible to add factors to a research study without limit, studies that involve more than three factors can produce complex results that are difficult to understand and, therefore, often have limited practical value.

Statistical Analysis of Factorial Designs

The statistical evaluation of the results from a factorial study depends in part on whether the factors are between-subjects, within-subjects, or some mixture of between-subjects and within-subjects. The standard practice is to compute the mean for each treatment condition (cell) and use an analysis of variance (ANOVA) to evaluate the statistical significance of the mean differences. However, the specific version of the analysis depends on the between-subjects and within-subjects factors. In this section, we will focus on two-factor designs, but the same principles generalize to higher-order factorial designs.

The two-factor ANOVA (see Chapter 15) conducts three separate hypothesis tests: one each to evaluate the two main effects and one to evaluate the interaction. In each case, the test uses an *F*-ratio to determine whether the actual mean differences in the data are significantly larger than reasonably would be expected by chance. The existence of a significant interaction suggests that you should be cautious about interpreting the interaction. Remember: an interaction means that the effect of one factor is not necessarily consistent but instead depends on the levels of the other factor.

A two-factor ANOVA is usually conducted using a statistical computer program such as SPSS. For two between-subjects factors, the correct choice is an independent-measures two-factor ANOVA (see p. 490). If only one of the two factors is between-subjects, then you must specify which it is and use a mixed-design two-factor ANOVA (see p. 492). For two within-subjects factors, you use a repeated-measures two-factor ANOVA.

As with other tests evaluating mean differences, the simplest design compares only two groups for each factor. The results from a 2 × 2 design are much easier to describe and to understand than results from a larger design. However, a 2 × 2 design provides only two data points for each factor and may not produce an accurate picture of the full relationship between the dependent and the independent variables. On the other hand, a 4 × 8 design can result in a complex interaction and can require a large number of participants if one or both of the factors is between-subjects. Also, a large number of treatment conditions within one study tends to reduce the size of the mean differences from one treatment to another and can produce results that are not statistically significant.

1. A factorial study measures allergy symptoms before and after taking medication for a group taking the real medication and a control group taking a placebo. What kind of design is being used?
   a. Between-subjects design
   b. Within-subjects design
   c. Repeated measures design
   (d.) Mixed design

2. The students in one gym class receive a self-esteem program as part of their sports training. To evaluate the program, a researcher measures self-esteem for the students before and after the program and compares their scores with those from another class that did not receive the program but was measured at the same two times. What kind of design is being used?
   a. Between-subjects design
   b. Within-subjects design
   c. Repeated measures design
   (d.) Mixed design

3. Which of the following accurately describes a two-factor analysis of variance?
   a. It conducts one hypothesis test and produces one F-ratio.
   b. It conducts two separate hypothesis tests and produces two F-ratios.
   (c.) It conducts three separate hypothesis tests and produces three F-ratios.
   d. None of the other options is an accurate description.

Answers appear at the end of the chapter.

11.4   Applications of Factorial Designs

LEARNING OBJECTIVE

LO7   Describe three specific applications of the factorial design: (1) adding a factor to an existing study; (2) using a participant variable as a second factor to control the variance in a between-subjects design; and (3) using the order of treatments as a second factor to evaluate the order effects in a within-subjects design; explain the advantage of using a factorial design in these situations.

Factorial designs provide researchers with a tremendous degree of flexibility and freedom for constructing research studies. As noted earlier, the primary advantage of factorial studies is that they allow researchers to observe the influence of two (or more) variables acting and interacting simultaneously. Thus, factorial designs have an almost unlimited range of potential applications. In this section, however, we focus on three specific situations in which adding a second factor to an existing study answers a specific research question or solves a specific research problem.

Expanding and Replicating a Previous Study

Often, factorial designs are developed when researchers plan studies that are intended to build on previous research results. For example, a published report may compare a set of treatment conditions or demonstrate the effectiveness of a particular treatment by comparing the treatment condition with a control condition. The critical reader asks questions such as:

> Would the same treatment effects be obtained if the treatments were administered under different conditions?

> Would the treatment outcomes be changed if individuals with different characteristics had participated?

Developing a research study to answer these questions would involve a factorial design. Answering the first question, for example, requires administering the treatments (one factor) under a variety of different conditions (a second factor). The primary prediction for this research is to obtain an interaction between factors; that is, the researcher predicts that the effect of the treatments depends on the conditions under which they are administered. Similarly, the second question calls for a factorial design involving the treatments (factor one) and different types of participants (factor two). Again, the primary prediction is for an interaction.

Because current research tends to build on past research, factorial designs are fairly common and very useful. In a single study, a researcher can replicate and expand previous research. The replication involves repeating the previous study by using the same factor or independent variable exactly as it was used in the earlier study. The expansion involves adding a second factor in the form of new conditions or new participant characteristics to determine whether the previously reported effects can be generalized to new situations or new populations.

One example of adding a new factor to an existing study comes from the video game violence experiment discussed at the beginning of this chapter (Bartholow & Anderson, 2002). Years of previous research had established a link between media violence, primarily on television, and aggressive behavior in children and adults (Andison, 1977; Bushman & Huesmann, 2001). Some studies had found that participants who played violent video games in the lab displayed more aggressive behaviors that those who played a nonviolent game (Anderson & Dill, 2000). Notice that these are single-factor studies examining only the effect of media violence. Although it was clear that there was a relationship between video game violence and aggressive behavior, there was still some question as to whether the effects of media violence were the same for males and females. To address this issue, the researchers decided to create a two-factor study with video violence as one factor and adding gender (male/female) as a second factor (Figure 11.9).

Reducing Variance in Between-Subjects Designs

In Chapter 8, we noted that individual differences such as age or IQ can create serious problems for between-subjects research designs. One such problem is the simple fact that differences between participants can result in large variance for the scores within a treatment condition. Recall that large variance can make it difficult to establish any significant differences between treatment conditions (see p. 198). Often a researcher has reason to suspect that a specific participant characteristic such as age or IQ is a major factor contributing to the variance of the scores. In this situation, it often is tempting to eliminate or reduce the influence of the specific characteristic by holding it constant or by restricting its range. For example, suppose that a researcher compares two treatment conditions using a separate group of children for each condition. Within each group, the children range in age from 6 to 14 years of age. The study is shown in Figure 11.10a.

However, the researcher is concerned that the older children may have higher scores than the younger children simply because they are more mature. If the scores really are related to age, then there will be big individual differences and high variance within each

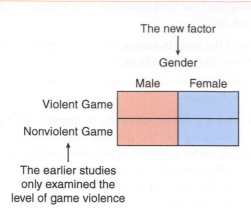

FIGURE 11.9

Creating a New Research Study by Adding a Second Factor to an Existing Study

Bartholow and Anderson (2002) repeated previous research studies examining the effect of media violence on aggressive behavior and then extended the study by adding gender as a second factor. The results showed that the effect of videogame violence (first factor) depends on the gender of the participants (second factor), resulting in an interaction.

group. In this situation, the researcher may be tempted to restrict the study by holding age constant (e.g., using only 10-year-old participants). This will produce more homogeneous groups with less variance, but it will also limit the researcher's ability to generalize the results. Recall that limiting generalization reduces the external validity of the study. Fortunately, there is a relatively simple solution to this dilemma that allows the researcher to reduce variance within groups without sacrificing external validity. The solution involves using the specific variable as a second factor, thereby creating a two-factor study. For this example, the researcher could use age as a second factor to divide the participants into three groups within each treatment: a younger age group (6–8 years), a middle age group (9–11 years), and an older group (12–14 years). The result is the two-factor experiment shown in Figure 11.10b, with one factor consisting of the two treatments (I and II) and the second factor consisting of the three age groups (younger, middle, and older).

By creating six groups of participants instead of only two, the researcher has greatly reduced the individual differences (age differences) within each group, while still keeping the full range of ages from the original study. In the new two-factor design, age differences still exist, but now they are differences between groups rather than variance within groups. The variance has been reduced without sacrificing external validity. Furthermore, the researcher has gained all of the other advantages that go with a two-factor design. In addition to examining how the different treatment conditions affect memory, the researcher can now examine how age (the new factor) is related to memory and can determine whether there is any interaction between age and the treatment conditions.

Evaluating Order Effects in Within-Subjects Designs

In Chapter 9, we noted that order effects can be a serious problem for within-subjects research studies. Specifically, in a within-subjects design, each participant goes through a series of treatment conditions in a particular order. In this situation, it is possible that treatments that occur early in the order may influence a participant's scores for treatments

FIGURE 11.10

A Participant Characteristic (Age) Used as a Second Factor to Reduce the Variability of Scores in a Research Study

(a) Each treatment condition contains a wide range of ages, which probably produces large variability among the scores. (b) The participants have been separated into more homogeneous age groups, which should reduce the variability within each group.

(a) A study comparing two treatments with large age differences among the participants in each group

	Treatment I	Treatment II
	A group of 12 participants ranging in age from 6 to 14 years old	A group of 12 participants ranging in age from 6 to 14 years old

(b) Using participant age as a second factor, the participants have been separated into smaller, more homogeneous groups. The smaller age differences within each group should reduce the variability of the scores.

	Treatment I	Treatment II
Younger (Six to Eight Years Old)	A group of four participants ranging in age from 6 to 8 years old	A group of four participants ranging in age from 6 to 8 years old
Middle (Nine to 11 Years Old)	A group of four participants ranging in age from 9 to 11 years old	A group of four participants ranging in age from 9 to 11 years old
Older (12 to 14 Years Old)	A group of four participants ranging in age from 12 to 14 years old	A group of four participants ranging in age from 12 to 14 years old

that occur later in the order. Because order effects can alter and distort the true effects of a treatment condition, they are generally considered a confounding variable that should be eliminated from the study. In some circumstances, however, a researcher may want to investigate the order effects (where and how big they are). For example, a researcher may be specifically interested in how the order of treatments influences the effectiveness of treatments (is treatment I more effective if it comes before treatment II or after it?). Or a researcher simply may want to remove the order effects to obtain a clearer view of the data. In any of these situations, it is possible to create a research design that actually measures the order effects and separates them from the rest of the data.

Using Order of Treatments as a Second Factor

To measure and evaluate order effects, it is necessary to use counterbalancing (as discussed in Chapter 9). Remember that counterbalancing requires separate groups of participants with each group going through the set of treatments in a different order. The simplest example of this procedure is a within-subjects design comparing two treatments: I and II. The design is counterbalanced so that half of the participants begin with treatment I and then move to treatment II. The other half of the participants start with treatment II and then receive treatment I. The structure of this counterbalanced design can be presented as a

FIGURE 11.11

Order of Treatments Added as a Second Factor to a Within-Subjects Study

The original study uses a counterbalanced design to compare two treatment conditions. Thus, half of the participants have treatment I first, and half have treatment II first. Similarly, half of the participants have treatment I second, and half have treatment II second.

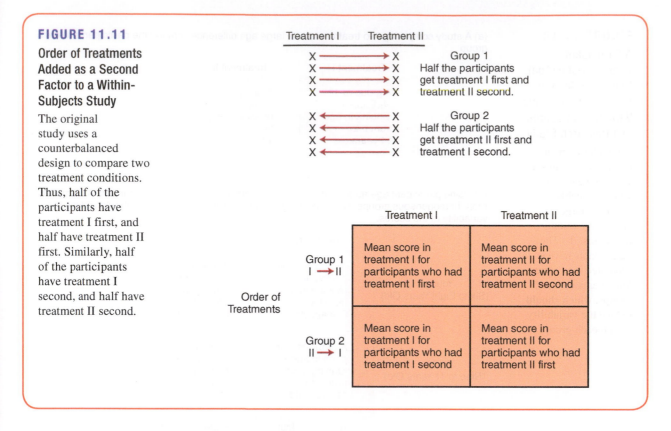

matrix with the two treatment conditions defining the columns and the order of treatments defining the rows (Figure 11.11).

You should recognize the matrix structure in Figure 11.11 as a two-factor research design and an example of a mixed design. In particular, the two treatments form a within-subjects factor, and the two orders form a between-subjects factor. By using the order of treatments as a second factor, it is possible to evaluate any order effects that exist in the data. There are three possible outcomes that can occur, and each produces its own pattern of results.

1. *No order effects.* When there are no order effects, it does not matter if a treatment is presented first or second. An example of this type of result is shown in Figure 11.12. For these data, when treatment I is presented first (group 1), the mean is 20, and when treatment I is presented second (group 2), the mean is still 20. Similarly, the order of presentation has no effect on the mean for treatment II. As a result, the difference between treatments is 10 points for both groups of participants. Thus, the treatment effect (factor 1) does not depend on the order of treatments (factor 2). You should recognize this pattern as an example of data with no interaction. When there are no order effects, the data show a pattern with no interaction. It makes no difference whether a treatment is presented first or second; the mean is the same in either case.

2. *Symmetrical order effects.* When order effects exist, the scores in the second treatment are influenced by participation in the first treatment. For example, participation in one treatment may produce practice effects, which lead to improved performance in the second treatment. An example of this situation is shown in Figure 11.13. Notice that the data now include a 5-point order effect. For both groups of participants, the mean score is raised by 5 points for the treatment that occurs second. For group 1, the order

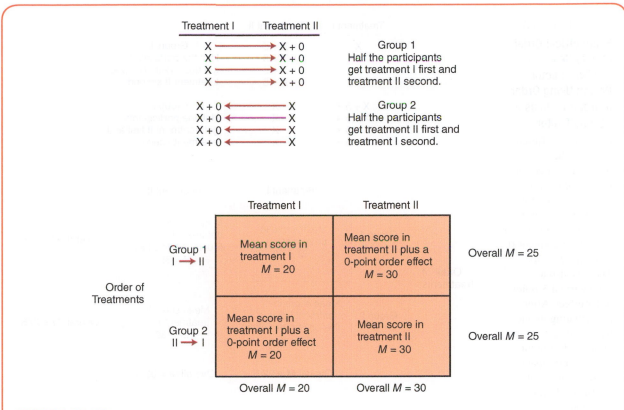

FIGURE 11.12

Treatment Effects and Order Effects Revealed in a Two-Factor Design Using Order of Treatment as a Second Factor

A 10-point difference between the two treatment conditions is assumed, with the mean score for treatment I equal to $M = 20$ and the mean score for treatment II equal to $M = 30$. It is also assumed that there are no order effects. Thus, participating in one treatment has no effect (0 points) on an individual's score in the following treatment. In the two-factor analysis, the treatment effect shows up as a 10-point main effect for the treatment factor, and the absence of any order effects is indicated by the absence of an interaction between treatments and order of treatments.

effect influences the scores in treatment II, and for group 2, the order effect influences scores in treatment I. Also notice that the order effect is symmetrical; that is, the second treatment always gets an extra 5 points, whether it is treatment I or treatment II.

In this situation, the size of the treatment effect (I vs. II) depends on the order of treatments. Thus, the effect of one factor depends on the other factor. You should recognize this as an example of interaction. When order effects exist, they show up in the two-factor analysis as an interaction between treatments and the order of treatments.

For these data, the order effect is symmetrical and the symmetry of the order effect appears in the data as a symmetrical interaction. In the graph of the data, for example, the two lines cross exactly at the center. Also, the 5-point difference between the two groups in treatment I (left-hand side of the graph) is exactly equal to the 5-point difference between the groups in treatment II (right-hand side of the graph). This symmetry only exists in situations in which the order effects are symmetrical.

FIGURE 11.13

Symmetrical Order Effects Revealed in a Two-Factor Design Using Order of Treatments as a Second Factor

A 10-point difference between the two treatment conditions is assumed, with the mean score for treatment I equal to $M = 20$ and the mean score for treatment II equal to $M = 30$. There is also a symmetrical 5-point order effect. After participating in one treatment, the order effect adds 5 points to each participant's score in the second treatment. In this situation, the order effect appears as an interaction between treatments and the order of treatments.

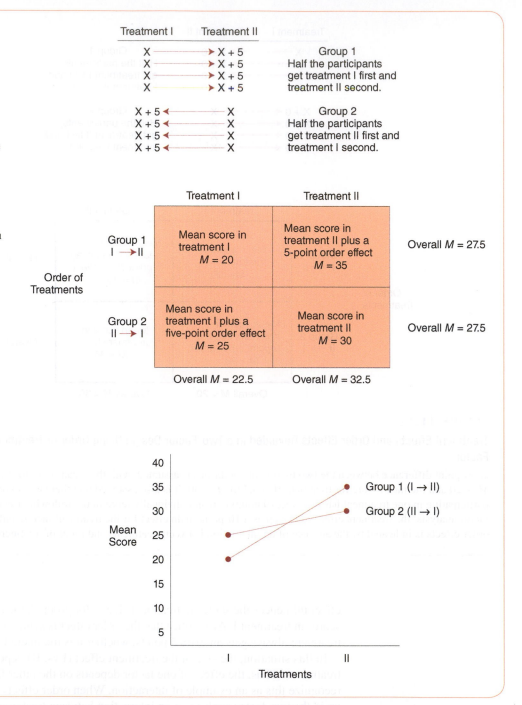

3. *Nonsymmetrical order effects.* Often, order effects are not symmetrical. For example, participation in different treatment conditions may produce different levels of fatigue or practice. This situation is shown in Figure 11.14. Notice the following characteristics for the data in the figure:

   a. The participants in group 1 received treatment I first. This treatment produces a relatively large, 10-point order effect. For these participants, the 10-point order effect increases the mean for treatment II by 10 points.

b. The participants in group 2 receive treatment II first. This treatment produces a relatively small, 5-point order effect that increases the mean for treatment I by 5 points.

Notice that the graph in Figure 11.14 shows an interaction, just as with symmetrical order effects. Again, the existence of an interaction in this analysis is an indication that order effects exist. For these data, however, the interaction is not symmetrical; in the graph, the two lines do not intersect at their midpoints. Also, the difference between groups in treatment I is much smaller than the difference in treatment II. In general, nonsymmetrical order effects produce a lopsided, or nonsymmetrical, interaction between treatments and orders as seen in Figure 11.14.

FIGURE 11.14

Nonsymmetrical Order Effects Revealed in a Two-Factor Design Using Order of Treatments as a Second Factor

A 10-point difference between the two treatment conditions is assumed, with the mean score for treatment I equal to $M = 20$ and the mean score for treatment II equal to $M = 30$. An asymmetrical order effect is added. After participating in treatment I, the order effect adds 10 points to each participant's score, and after participating in treatment II, the order effect adds 5 points to each participant's score. In this situation, the order effects appear as an interaction between treatments and order of treatments. Because the order effects are not symmetrical, the structure of the interaction is also not symmetrical.

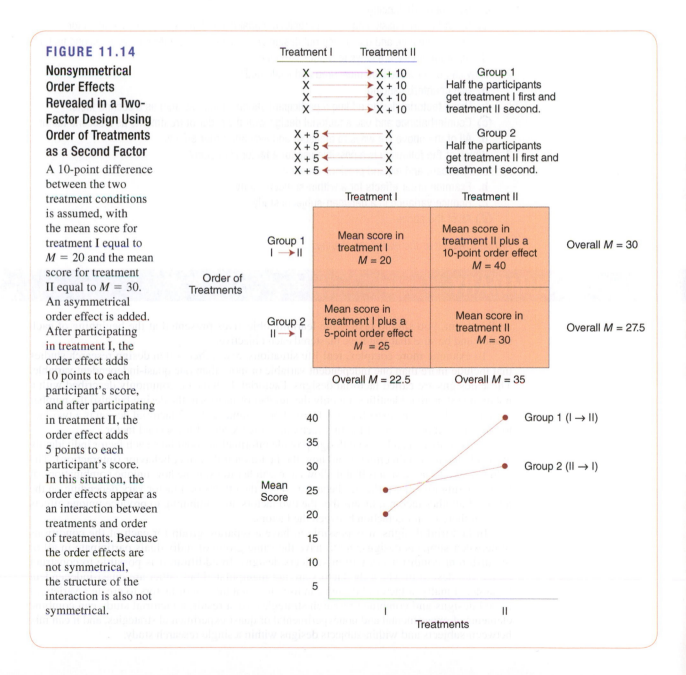

In the preceding examples, the order effects were clearly displayed in the data. In this artificial situation, we knew that order effects existed and how big they were. In an actual experiment, however, a researcher cannot see the order effects. However, as we have demonstrated in the three examples, using order of treatments as a second factor makes it possible to examine any order effects that exist in a set of data; their magnitude and nature are revealed in the interaction. Thus, researchers can observe the order effects in their data and separate them from the effects of the different treatments.

LEARNING CHECK

1. How can variance be reduced in a between-subjects design?
   a. Use counterbalancing
   b. Use a factorial design adding a participant variable (such as age) as a second factor
   c. Counterbalance and use a factorial design with the order of treatments as a second factor
   d. All of the above are ways to reduce variance

2. How can order effects be measured and evaluated?
   a. Use counterbalancing
   b. Use a factorial design adding a participant variable (such as age) as a second factor
   c. Counterbalance and use a factorial design with the order of treatments as a second factor
   d. All of the above are ways to measure and evaluate order effects

3. Which of the following is a possible use for a factorial design?
   a. Replicate and expand previous research
   b. Examine order effects for a within-subjects study
   c. Reduce variance in a between-subjects study
   d. All of the above

Answers appear at the end of the chapter.

CHAPTER SUMMARY

At this point, you should review the learning objectives presented at the beginning of each section and be sure that you have mastered each objective.

To examine more complex, real-life situations, researchers often design research studies that include more than one independent variable or more than one quasi-independent variable. These designs are called factorial designs. Factorial designs are commonly described with a notation system that identifies not only the number of factors in the design but also the number of values or levels that exist for each factor. For example, a 2×3 factorial design is a two-factor design with two levels of the first factor and three levels of the second factor.

The results from a factorial design provide information about how each factor individually affects behavior (main effects) and how the factors jointly affect behavior (interaction). The value of a factorial design is that it allows a researcher to examine how unique combinations of factors acting together influence behavior. When the effects of a factor vary depending on the levels of another factor, it means that the two factors are combining to produce unique effects and that there is an interaction between the factors.

In factorial designs, it is possible to have a separate group for each of the conditions (a between-subjects design) and to have the same group of individuals participate in all of the different conditions (a within-subjects design). In addition, it is possible to construct a factorial design in which the factors are not manipulated but rather are quasi-independent variables. Finally, a factorial design can use any combination of factors to create a variety of mixed designs and combined research strategies. As a result, a factorial study can combine elements of experimental and nonexperimental or quasi-experimental strategies, and it can mix between-subjects and within-subjects designs within a single research study.

Although factorial designs can be used in a variety of situations, three specific applications were discussed: (1) Often, a new study builds on existing research by adding another factor to an earlier research study; (2) using a participant variable such as age or gender as a second factor can separate participants into more homogeneous groups and thereby reduce variance in a between-subjects design; and (3) when the order of treatments is used as a second factor in a counterbalanced within-subjects design, it is possible to measure and evaluate the order effects.

KEY WORDS

factor

factorial design

main effect

interaction between factors, or interaction

mixed design

combined strategy

EXERCISES

The exercises are identified with specific learning objectives and are intended to assess your mastery of the objectives. You should be aware that exam items are also generated to assess learning objectives.

1. In addition to the key words, you should also be able to define the following terms:

   two-factor design
   single-factor design
   levels
   three-factor design
   higher-order factorial design

2. (**LO1**) In a classic study, Shrauger (1972) examined the effect of an audience on performance for two groups of participants: high self-esteem and low self-esteem individuals. The participants in the study were given a problem-solving task with half of the individuals in each group working alone and the other half working with an audience. Performance on the problem-solving task was measured for each individual. The results showed that the presence of an audience had little effect on high self-esteem participants but significantly lowered performance for the low self-esteem participants.
   a. How many factors does this study have? What are they?
   b. Describe this study using the notation system that indicates factors and numbers of levels of each factor.
   c. Use a matrix to diagram the structure of the study.

3. (**LO2**) Suppose a researcher conducts a two-factor study comparing two treatments (I and II) for college graduates versus adults with no college experience. The structure of the study is shown in the following matrix.

   Treatment

   I   II

   College graduate

   No college

   a. If the results show that college graduates have higher scores than the no-college adults in treatment I and equivalent scores in treatment II, is it likely that there will be a main effect for the education factor? Is it likely that there will be an interaction?
   b. If the results show that college graduates have higher scores than the no-college adults in treatment I and lower scores than the no-college adults in treatment II, is it likely that there will be a main effect for the education factor? Is it likely that there will be an interaction?

3. (**LO2**) The following matrix represents the results (the means) from a 2 × 2 factorial study. One mean is not given.

	A1	A2
B1	10	20
B2	20	

   a. What value for the missing mean would result in no main effect for factor A?
   b. What value for the missing mean would result in no main effect for factor B?
   c. What value for the missing mean would result in no interaction?

4. (**LO2**) The following data show the pattern of results that was obtained in a study by Liguori and Robinson (2001) examining how different levels of alcohol and caffeine consumption influenced response time in a simulated driving test. The means show the average response time in milliseconds for different combinations of alcohol and caffeine. For these data:
   a. Is there a main effect for alcohol?
   b. Is there an interaction?
   c. Does caffeine improve response time (produce faster times) for people who have consumed alcohol?
   d. Does caffeine eliminate the effect of alcohol on response time?

	No Caffeine	200 mg Caffeine	400 mg Caffeine	Overall
No alcohol	$M = 620$	$M = 600$	$M = 590$	$M = 603$
Alcohol	$M = 720$	$M = 700$	$M = 690$	$M = 703$
Overall	$M = 670$	$M = 650$	$M = 640$	

5. (**LO3**) Explain why the main effects in a factorial study may not provide an accurate description of the results?

6. (**LO4**) Explain what is meant by the concept that main effects and interactions are independent.

7. (**LO2, 4**) In Figure 11.5, we show three combinations of main effects and interactions for a 2×2 factorial design. Using the same 2×2 structure, with factor A defining the rows and factor B defining the columns, create a set of means that produce each of the following patterns:
   a. A main effect for factors A and B, but no interaction.
   b. A main effect for factor A and an interaction, but no main effect for factor B.
   c. A main effect for both factors and an interaction.

8. (**LO5**) For a two-factor research study with two levels for factor A and four levels for factor B, how many participants are needed to obtain five scores in each treatment condition for each of the following situations?
   a. Both factors are between-subjects.
   b. Both factors are within-subjects.
   c. Factor A is a between-subjects factor and factor B is a within-subjects factor.

9. (**LO5**) A researcher would like to use a factorial study to compare two programs designed to help people stop smoking. The smoking behavior of each participant will be measured at the beginning of the program, at the end of the program, and again 4 months after the program has ended. Thus, the two treatment programs make up one factor, the three measurement times make up the second factor. For this study, which factor(s) should be between-subjects and which should be within-subjects? Explain your answer.

10. (**LO6**) A two-factor analysis of variance is used to evaluate the significance of the mean differences for the two-factor research study shown in the following table. The study is evaluating the effects of sugary versus nonsugary snacks on the activity level of preschool children. Identify the three F-ratios and, using the following data from a 2×2 design, identify the means (or mean differences) that are compared by each F-ratio.

	Before Snack	After Snack	
Sugary snack	$M = 20$	$M = 24$	$M = 22$
Nonsugary Snack	$M = 22$	$M = 26$	$M = 24$
Overall	$M = 21$	$M = 25$	

11. (**LO7**) A researcher has demonstrated that a new non-competitive physical education program significantly improves self-esteem for children in a kindergarten program.
   a. What additional information can be obtained by introducing participant motor skill ability (high and low) as a second factor to the original research study?
   b. What additional information can be obtained by adding participant age (third grade, fifth grade, etc.) to the original study?

LEARNING CHECK ANSWERS

Section 11.1
1. b, 2. d, 3. b

Section 11.2
1. d, 2. b, 3. d

Section 11.3
1. d, 2. d, 3. c

Section 11.4
1. b, 2. c, 3. d

The Correlational Research Strategy

© Nathan Jasowiak / Shutterstock

CHAPTER LEARNING OBJECTIVES

LO1 Define the goal or purpose of the correlational research strategy and distinguish between a correlational study and experimental and differential research.

LO2 Explain how a correlation describes the direction, form, and strength of a relationship and identify these characteristics for a set of data, especially data presented in a scatter plot.

LO3 Identify the statistical procedure used to determine a correlation for different types of data and explain what each correlation measures.

LO4 Describe how correlations are used for prediction, measuring reliability and validity of measurement, and evaluating theories.

LO5 Describe the strengths and weaknesses of the correlational research strategy including the third-variable problem and the directionality problem, and identify these problems when they appear in a research study.

CHAPTER OVERVIEW

As part of a large study concerning the health and well-being of undergraduate students, Lederer, Autr, Day, and Oswalt (2015) examined how work hours are related to sleep and feelings of being overwhelmed. The students reported the number of hours spent at work each week as well as the number of days they had enough sleep to feel rested and how often they felt overwhelmed. Not surprisingly, the results showed that increased hours at work was related to a decreased amount of sleep but that increased hours of work was related to an increased likelihood of feeling overwhelmed. For each relationship, notice that the data consist of two scores for each individual in a single group of participants; for example, a work score and a sleep score for each person are used to determine the relationship between work and sleep. This kind of study is an example of the correlational research strategy. In this chapter, we discuss the details of the correlational research strategy, discuss its strengths and weaknesses, and describe several specific applications.

12.1 | An Introduction to Correlational Research

LEARNING OBJECTIVE

LO1   Define the goal or purpose of the correlational research strategy and distinguish between a correlational study and experimental and differential research.

In Chapter 6, we identified five basic research strategies for investigating variables and their relationships: experimental, nonexperimental, quasi-experimental, correlational, and descriptive. In this chapter, we deal with the details of the **correlational research strategy.** (The experimental strategy is discussed in Chapter 7, the nonexperimental and quasi-experimental strategies are discussed in Chapter 10, and details of the descriptive strategy are discussed in Chapter 13.)

A correlational study can involve measuring more than two variables but usually involves relationships between two variables at a time.

The goal of the correlational research strategy is to examine and describe the associations and relationships between variables. More specifically, the purpose of a correlational study is to establish that a relationship exists between variables and to describe the nature of the relationship. Notice that the correlational strategy does not attempt to explain the relationship and makes no attempt to manipulate, control, or interfere with the variables.

The data for a correlational study consist of two or more measurements, one for each of the variables being examined. Usually, the scores are obtained from the same individual. For example, a researcher might record on-task behavior and grades for each child in a classroom of elementary school students. Or a researcher could record food consumption and activity level for each animal in a colony of laboratory rats. Measurements can be made in natural surroundings or the individuals can be measured in a laboratory setting. The important factor is that the researcher simply measures the variables being studied. The measurements are then examined to determine whether they show any consistent pattern of relationship.

DEFINITIONS

In the **correlational research strategy,** two or more variables are measured to obtain a set of scores (usually two scores) for each individual. The measurements are then examined to identify any patterns of relationship that exist between the variables and to measure the strength of the relationship.

For example, in Chapter 6, we described a correlational study by Junco (2015) examining the relationship between GPA and time spent on Facebook for college students (p. 131 and Figure 6.2). The researchers measured the grade point average and Facebook time for each individual in a group of college students and found that larger amounts of time spent on Facebook were consistently related to lower grade point averages. Although the study demonstrated a relationship between the two variables, it does not explain why the relationship exists. Specifically, the results do not justify a conclusion that time spent on Facebook causes lower grades (or that lower grades cause students to spend more time on Facebook).

In the definition of correlational research, we state that a correlational study usually obtains two or more scores for each individual. Usually, the word *individual* refers to a single person. However, the individual is intended to be a single source, not necessarily a single person. For example, several studies have demonstrated a relationship between family income and children's academic performance (for example, Elstad & Bakken, 2015). In general, higher family income is associated with higher grades. Note that the researchers have two scores for each child, however, one score comes from the parents and one from the child. In this case, each *individual* is a family rather than a single person.

Comparing Correlational, Experimental, and Differential Research

In Chapter 7 (p. 159), we noted that the goal of an experimental study is to demonstrate a cause-and-effect relationship between two variables. To accomplish this goal, an experiment requires the manipulation of one variable to create treatment conditions and the measurement of the second variable to obtain a set of scores within each condition. All other variables are controlled. The researcher then compares the scores from each treatment with the scores from other treatments. If there are differences between treatments, the researcher has evidence of a causal relationship between variables. Specifically, the researcher can conclude that manipulating one variable causes changes in the second variable. Note that an experimental study involves measuring only one variable and looking for differences between two or more groups of scores.

A correlational study, on the other hand, is intended to demonstrate the existence of a relationship between two variables. Note that a correlational study is not trying to explain the relationship. To accomplish its goal, a correlational study does not involve manipulating, controlling, or interfering with variables. Instead, the researcher simply measures two different variables for each individual. The researcher then looks for a relationship within the set of scores.

In Chapter 10 (p. 245), we noted that differential research, an example of a nonexperimental design, is very similar to correlational research. The difference between these two research strategies is that a correlational study views the data as two scores, *X* and *Y*, for each individual, and looks for patterns within the pairs of scores to determine whether there is a relationship. A differential design, on the other hand, establishes the existence of a relationship by demonstrating a difference between groups. Specifically, a differential design uses one of the two variables to define groups of participants and then measures the second variable to obtain scores within each group. For example, a researcher could divide a sample of students into two groups corresponding to high and low self-esteem, and then measure academic performance scores in each group. If there is a consistent difference between groups, the researcher has evidence for a relationship between self-esteem and academic performance. A correlational study examining the same relationship would first measure a self-esteem score and an academic performance score for each student, and then look for a pattern within the set of scores. Note that the correlational study involves one group of participants with two scores for each individual. The primary focus of the correlational study is on the relationship between the two variables. The differential study involves two groups of scores and focuses on the difference between groups. However, both designs are asking the same basic question: "Is there a relationship between self-esteem and academic performance?"

LEARNING CHECK

1. Which of the following is a defining characteristic of the correlational research strategy?
   a. The research is conducted in field settings rather than in a laboratory.
   b. The intent is simply to describe behaviors.
   c. The intent is to demonstrate the relationship between variables.
   d. The other three options are all defining characteristics of the correlational study

2. Which of the following commonly occurs in a correlational study?
   a. One variable is measured.
   b. Two variables are measured.
   c. One individual is described in great detail.
   d. One individual is treated.

3. A researcher would like to examine the relationship between self-esteem and academic performance for high school students. Instead of a correlational study, what other kind of study could the researcher use?
   a. A differential study comparing academic performance scores for a group of high self-esteem students and a group of low self-esteem students
   b. An experimental study comparing academic performance scores for a group of high self-esteem students and a group of low self-esteem students
   c. A descriptive study examining self-esteem for a group of students who are in the top 25% of their high school class
   d. None of the other options could be used to examine the relationship

Answers appear at the end of the chapter.

12.2 The Data and Statistical Analysis for Correlational Studies

LEARNING OBJECTIVES

LO2 Explain how a correlation describes the direction, form, and strength of a relationship and identify these characteristics for a set of data, especially data presented in a scatter plot.

LO3 Identify the statistical procedure used to determine a correlation for different types of data and explain what each correlation measures.

A correlational research study produces two or more scores for each individual. However, researchers are usually interested in the relationship between two variables at a time. Therefore, multiple scores are typically grouped into pairs for evaluation. In this section, we focus on relationships between pairs of scores. Relationships among multiple variables are discussed in Section 12.4.

Evaluating Relationships for Numerical Scores (Interval or Ratio Scales) and Ranks (Ordinal Scale)

When the data consist of numerical values, the scores in each pair are traditionally identified as X and Y. The data can be presented in a list showing the two scores for each individual or the scores can be shown in a graph known as a **scatter plot.** In the scatter plot, each individual is represented by a single point with a horizontal coordinate determined by the individual's X score and the vertical coordinate corresponding to the Y value. Figure 12.1 shows hypothetical data from a correlational study presented as a list of scores and as a scatter plot. The benefit of a scatter plot is that it allows you to see the characteristics of the relationship between the two variables.

Researchers typically calculate a numerical value known as a **correlation**, or **correlation coefficient**, to measure and describe the relationship between two variables. A correlation describes three characteristics of a relationship.

1. *The direction of the relationship.* In Figure 12.1, there is a clear tendency for individuals with larger X values to also have larger Y values. Equivalently, as the X values get smaller, the associated Y values also tend to get smaller. A relationship of this type is called a **positive relationship**. For example, there is a positive relationship between height and weight for college students; taller students also tend to weigh more. Positive relationships are indicated by positive values (greater than zero) for the correlation. In a scatter plot, a positive relationship is indicated by data points that cluster around a line that slopes up to the right. On the other hand, a relationship in which X and Y tend to change in opposite directions (as X increases, Y decreases) is called a **negative relationship**. On most performance tasks, for example, there is a negative relationship between speed and accuracy; going faster tends to result in lower accuracy. Negative relationships are indicated by negative values (less than zero) for the correlation. In a scatter plot, a negative relationship is indicated by data points that cluster around a line that slopes down to the right.

DEFINITIONS

> In a **positive relationship,** there is a tendency for two variables to change in the same direction; as one variable increases, the other also tends to increase.
>
> In a **negative relationship,** there is a tendency for two variables to change in opposite directions; increases in one variable tend to be accompanied by decreases in the other.

FIGURE 12.1

Data from a Correlational Study

Two scores, X and Y, for each of five people are shown in a table and in a scatter plot.

Person	X	Y
A	1	3
B	6	8
C	4	4
D	7	12
E	9	10

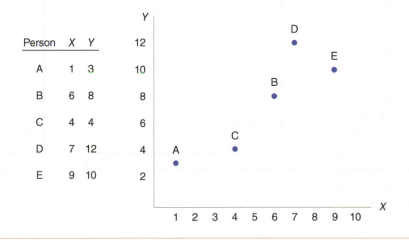

2. *The form of the relationship.* Typically, researchers are looking for a pattern in the data that suggests a consistent and predictable relationship between the two variables. In most situations, researchers look for a **linear relationship,** in which the data points in the scatter plot tend to cluster around a straight line. In a positive linear relationship, for example, each time the *X* variable increases by 1 point, the *Y* variable also increases, and the size of the increase is a consistently predictable amount. Figure 12.2a shows an example of a positive linear relationship. A **Pearson correlation** is used to describe and measure linear relationships when both variables are numerical scores from interval or ratio scales (see Chapter 15, pp. 384–387).

    It is possible for a relationship to be consistent and predictable, but not linear. For example, there tends to be a consistent relationship between practice and performance; for most skills, increased practice leads to improved performance. However, the amount of improvement is not constant from one week to another, so the relationship is not linear. During the first few weeks of practice, the increases in performance are large. However, after years of practice, one more week produces a hardly noticeable change in performance. A relationship that is consistently one-directional, either consistently positive or consistently negative, is called a **monotonic relationship**. In a positive monotonic relationship, for example, increases in one variable tend to be accompanied by increases in the other variable. However, the amount of increase need not be constantly the same size. Figure 12.2b shows an example of a positive monotonic relationship similar to the practice and performance example. A **Spearman correlation** is used to measure and describe monotonic relationships when both variables are ranks from an ordinal score or have been transformed to ranks (see Chapter 15, pp. 384–387).

3. *The consistency or strength of the relationship.* You may have noticed that the data points presented in Figure 12.2 do not form perfectly linear or perfectly monotonic relationships. In Figure 12.2a, the points are not perfectly on a straight line and in Figure 12.2b, the relationship is not perfectly one directional (there are reversals in the positive trend). In fact, perfectly consistent relationships are essentially never found in real behavioral sciences data. Instead, real data show a degree of consistency. In correlational studies, the consistency of a relationship is typically measured and

FIGURE 12.2

Linear and Monotonic Relationships

(a) An example of a linear relationship. The data points cluster around a straight line.

(b) An example of a monotonic relationship. The data points show a one-directional trend; as the *X* values increase from left to right, the *Y* values also tend to increase from bottom to top.

(a)

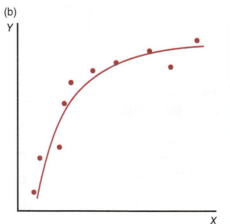

(b)

described by the numerical value obtained for a correlation coefficient. A correlation of +1.00 (or –1.00) indicates a perfectly consistent relationship, and a value of zero indicates no consistency whatsoever. Intermediate values indicate different degrees of consistency. For example, a Pearson correlation coefficient of 0.8 (or –0.8) indicates a nearly perfect linear relationship in which the data points cluster closely around a straight line. Each time the value of X changes, the value of Y also changes by a reasonably predictable amount. By contrast, a correlation of 0.2 (or –0.2) describes a relationship in which there is only a weak tendency for the value of Y to change in a predictable manner when the value of X changes. In this case, the data points are widely scattered around a straight line. Note that the sign of the correlation (+/–) and the numerical value are independent. A correlation of +0.8 has the same degree of consistency as a correlation of –0.8, and both correlations indicate that the data points cluster closely around a straight line; the lines simply tilt in different directions. Figure 12.3 shows a series of scatter plots demonstrating different degrees of linear relationship and the corresponding correlation values. As a final point, we should note once again that a correlation coefficient simply *describes* the consistency or strength of a relationship between variables. Even the strongest correlation of 1.00 (or –1.00) does not imply that there is a cause-and-effect relationship between the two variables.

DEFINITION

> A **correlation**, or **correlation coefficient**, is a numerical value that measures and describes the relationship between two variables. The sign of the correlation (+/–) indicates the direction of the relationship. The numerical value of the correlation (0.0 to 1.0) indicates the strength or consistency of the relationship. The type of correlation (Pearson or Spearman) indicates the form of the relationship.

Evaluating Relationships for Non-Numerical Scores from Nominal Scales

Occasionally, a correlational research study produces two or more scores for each individual with at least one score that does not consist of numerical values. For example, a researcher may be interested in the relationship between college (college graduate/no

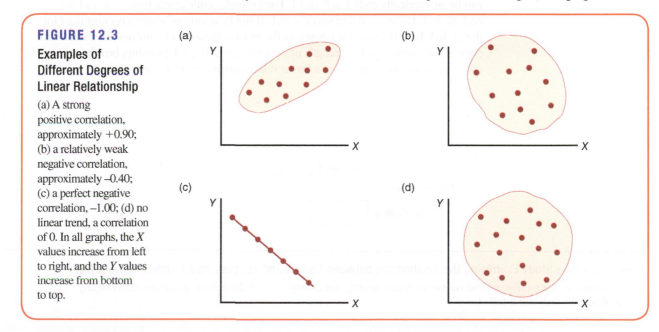

FIGURE 12.3

Examples of Different Degrees of Linear Relationship

(a) A strong positive correlation, approximately +0.90; (b) a relatively weak negative correlation, approximately –0.40; (c) a perfect negative correlation, –1.00; (d) no linear trend, a correlation of 0. In all graphs, the X values increase from left to right, and the Y values increase from bottom to top.

college) and success on a problem-solving task (succeed/fail). In this case, there are two measurements for each individual, but neither is a numerical score suitable for computing a correlation. In this situation, there are several alternatives for evaluating the relationship.

1. If one of the scores is numerical, like IQ, and the other is non-numerical, like college, the most common strategy is to use the non-numerical variable to organize the scores into separate groups. For this example, the data would consist of a group of IQ scores for the college graduates and a group of scores for people without college. The two groups are then compared using an independent-measures t test (for two groups) or an analysis of variance (for more than two groups). These hypothesis tests are discussed in Chapter 15 (see pp. 409–410). Note that when the data are organized into groups of scores, the research strategy is generally considered to be nonexperimental rather than correlational (see p. 297).

    If the non-numerical variable consists of exactly two categories, it is also possible to calculate a special correlation. First, the two categories are numerically coded as 0 and 1. For example college graduate = 0 and no college = 1. The data then consist of two scores per person, an IQ score and a coded score for college, and the Pearson correlation can be computed for the coded data. The resulting correlation is called a *point-biserial* correlation. The numerical value of the correlation is a measure of the strength or consistency of the relationship; however, the sign of the correlation is meaningless (because 0 and 1 are assigned arbitrarily), and the concept of a linear relationship is not meaningful (because the scores are simply separated into two groups).

2. If both variables are non-numerical, the relationship is typically evaluated by organizing the data in a matrix, with the categories of one variable forming the rows and the categories of the second variable forming the columns. Each cell of the matrix shows the frequency or number of individuals in that cell and the data are evaluated using a chi-square hypothesis test (see Chapter 15, p. 406). Figure 12.4 shows an example of data from a study examining the relationship between college experience and success on a problem-solving task.

    If the two non-numerical variables both consist of exactly two categories, each can be numerically coded as 0 and 1. For example, college graduate = 0 and no college = 1; failure = 0 and success = 1. If the Pearson correlation is computed for the coded data, the result is known as the *phi-coefficient*. The numerical value of the correlation measures the strength or consistency of the relationship, but the sign of the correlation and the concept of a linear relationship are not meaningful.

	Succeed	Fail
College Graduate	17	3
No College	12	8

FIGURE 12.4

Results from a Study Examining the Relationship between College and Success on a Problem-Solving Task

The values are the number of individuals in each category; for example, 12 of the college graduates successfully completed the task and 8 failed.

Interpreting and Statistically Evaluating a Correlation

For both numerical and non-numerical data, the value of a correlation, which ranges from 0.00 to 1.00, describes the consistency of the relationship with 1.00 (or −1.00) indicating a perfectly consistent relationship and 0.00 indicating a complete lack of consistency. However, there are two additional factors that must be considered when interpreting the strength of a relationship. One is the coefficient of determination, which is obtained by squaring the correlation, and the other is the significance of the correlation. Each of these factors is discussed in the following sections.

The Strength of a Relationship

The most common technique for measuring the strength of the relationship between two variables is to compute the **coefficient of determination**, which is obtained by squaring the numerical value of the correlation. Because a correlation is typically identified by the letter r, the coefficient of determination is r^2. This coefficient measures how much of the variability in one variable is predictable from its relationship with the other variable. For example, if two college students are randomly selected, they will almost certainly have different grade point averages. Although there are many explanations for different grades, one possibility is that the two students have different IQs. In general, there is a tendency for higher IQs to correlate with higher grades. If the correlation between IQ and grade point average is calculated and then squared, the result provides a measure of how much of the differences in grade point averages can be predicted by IQ scores. A correlation of $r = 0.80$ would mean that $r^2 = 0.64$ (or 64%) of the differences in grade point average can be predicted by difference in IQ. A correlation of $r = 0.30$ would mean that only 0.09 (9%) of the differences are predictable.

DEFINITION

> The **coefficient of determination** is the squared value of a correlation and measures the percentage of variability in one variable that is determined, or predicted, by its relationship with the other variable.

In the behavioral sciences, the differences that exist from one individual to another tend to be large and are usually difficult to predict or explain. As a result, the ability to predict only a small portion of the differences in behavior is typically considered a major accomplishment. With this in mind, the guidelines in Table 12.1 are commonly used to interpret the strength of the relationship between two variables (Cohen, 1988).

We should note that the values in Table 12.1 are a general guide for interpreting the correlations obtained in most behavioral science research. There are some situations, however, in which a correlation of 0.50 would not be considered to be large. For example, when using correlations to measure the reliability of measurement, researchers usually

TABLE 12.1

Guidelines for Interpreting the Strength of a Correlation

Degree of Relationship	Value of the Correlation Coefficient, or Coefficient of Determination
Small	$r = 0.10$ or $r^2 = 0.01$ (1%)
Medium	$r = 0.30$ or $r^2 = 0.09$ (9%)
Large	$r = 0.50$ or $r^2 = 0.25$ (25%)

look for large values, typically much greater than $r = 0.50$. Similarly, a research study that finds a theoretically important relationship between two variables might view a "small" correlation of $r = 0.10$ as a substantial relationship.

The Significance of a Relationship

The **statistical significance of a correlation** is the second important factor for interpreting the strength of a correlation. In the context of a correlation, the term *significant* means that a correlation found in the sample data is very unlikely to have been produced by random variation. Instead, whenever a sample correlation is found to be significant, you can reasonably conclude that it represents a real relationship that exists in the population.

With a small sample, it is possible to obtain what appears to be a very strong correlation when, in fact, there is absolutely no relationship between the two variables being examined. For example, with a sample of only two individuals, there are only two data points, and they are guaranteed to fit perfectly on a straight line. Thus, with a sample of two individuals, you will always obtain a perfect correlation of 1.00 (or −1.00) no matter what variables you are measuring. As the sample size increases, it becomes increasingly more likely that the sample correlation accurately represents the real relationship that exists in the population. A correlation found in a relatively large sample is usually an indication of a real, meaningful relationship and is likely to be significant. You should be warned, however, that a statistically significant correlation does not necessarily mean that the correlation is large or strong. With a very large sample, for example, it is possible for a correlation of $r = 0.10$ or smaller to be statistically significant. Clearly, this is not a strong correlation. (See Appendix B, p. 470 for additional information concerning the significance of a correlation.)

LEARNING CHECK

1. A college professor reports that students who finish exams early tend to get better grades than students who hold on to exams until the last possible moment. The correlation between exam score and amount of time spent on the exam is an example of
   a. a positive correlation.
   b. a negative correlation.
   c. a correlation near zero.
   d. a correlation near one.

2. A researcher reports that there is no consistent relationship between grade point average and the number of hours spent studying for college students. Which of the following is the best description for the correlation between grade point average and the number of hours studying?
   a. A positive correlation
   b. A negative correlation
   c. A correlation near zero
   d. A correlation near one

3. What is measured by the Pearson correlation?
   a. The degree of relationship without regard to the form of the relationship
   b. The degree to which the relationship is consistently one directional
   c. The degree of linear relationship
   d. The degree of curvilinear relationship

Answers appear at the end of the chapter.

12.3   Applications of the Correlational Strategy

LEARNING OBJECTIVE

LO4   Describe how correlations are used for prediction, measuring reliability and validity of measurement, and evaluating theories.

As noted earlier, the correlational design is used to identify and describe relationships between variables. Following are three examples of how correlational designs can be used to address research questions.

Prediction

One important use of correlational research is to establish a relationship between variables that can be used for purposes of prediction. For example, research shows a good positive relationship between SAT scores and future grade point average in college (Camera & Echternacht, 2000; Geiseer & Studley, 2002). College administrators can use this relationship to help predict which applicants are most likely to be successful students. High school students who do well on the SAT are likely to do well in college, and those who have trouble with the SAT are likely to have difficulty in college classes.

The use of correlational results to make predictions is not limited to predictions about future behavior. Whenever two variables are consistently related, it is possible to use knowledge of either variable to help make predictions about the other. For example, because there is a consistent, positive relationship between parents' IQs and their children's IQs, we can use either score to predict the other. Specifically, parents with above-average IQs are likely to have children with above-average IQs. Often, one of the two variables is simply easier to measure or more readily available than the other. In these situations, it is possible to use the available knowledge of one variable to predict the value of the unavailable variable. By establishing and describing the existence of a relationship, correlational studies provide the basic information needed to make predictions.

Within a correlational study, the two variables being examined are essentially equivalent. Nonetheless, correlational studies often identify one variable as the **predictor variable** and the second variable as the **criterion variable**. In a correlational study used for prediction, the designation of the two variables is usually quite clear. University admissions offices occasionally use the graduate record exam (GRE) scores to predict graduate school success. In this situation, the GRE scores are the predictor variable, and graduate performance is the criterion variable. Clearly, one variable (the predictor) is used to predict the other (the criterion).

The statistical process for using one variable to predict another is called **regression.** Typically, the goal is to find the equation that produces the most accurate predictions of Y (the criterion variable) for each value of X (the predictor variable). In a recent study, for example, regression was used to demonstrate that higher positive affect (low depression score) predicts better problem-solving ability for older adults (Paterson, Yeung, & Thornton, 2016).

In situations in which a correlational study is not used for prediction, researchers still tend to refer to a predictor and a criterion variable. In these situations, the labels are usually determined by the purpose of the study. Typically, a correlational study begins with one of the two variables relatively simple and well defined, and the second variable is relatively complex or unknown. Thus, the purpose of the study is to gain a better understanding of the complex variable by demonstrating that it is related to an established, known variable. In this situation, the known variable is designated as the predictor and the unknown variable as the criterion. For example, researchers are constantly looking for environmental and genetic factors that are related to the risk of Alzheimer's disease to gain a better understanding of this complex disorder.

DEFINITIONS

When a correlational study demonstrates a relationship between two variables, it allows researchers to use knowledge about one variable to help predict or explain the second variable. In this situation, the first variable is called the **predictor variable** and the second variable (being explained or predicted) is called the **criterion variable**.

Reliability and Validity

In Chapter 3 (p. 56), the concepts of reliability and validity were introduced as the two basic criteria for evaluating a measurement procedure. In general terms, reliability evaluates the consistency or stability of the measurements, and validity evaluates the extent to which the measurement procedure actually measures what it claims to be measuring. Both reliability and validity are commonly defined by relationships that are established using the correlational research design. For example, test–retest reliability is defined by the relationship between an original set of measurements and a follow-up set of measurements. If the same individuals are measured twice under the same conditions, and there is a consistent relationship between the two measurements, then the measurement procedure is said to be reliable.

The concurrent validity of a measurement procedure can also be defined in terms of a relationship (see Chapter 3, p. 59). If a new test is developed to detect early-stage Alzheimer's disease, for example, the validity of the test can be established by demonstrating that the scores from the test are strongly related to scores from established tests. This is exactly what was done by Ijuin et al. (2008) to validate a relatively new 7-minute test that was developed as an alternative to other commonly used screening tests for Alzheimer's. Correlations were computed to measure the relationship between the scores from the 7-Minute Screen and the scores from each of the three established cognitive tests for Alzheimer's. The researchers obtained a correlation of around 0.70 for each test, indicating a strong positive relationship and high concurrent validity between the 7-Minute Screen and established screening tests.

Evaluating Theories

Many theories generate research questions about the relationships between variables that can be addressed by the correlational research design. A good example comes from the age-old nature/nurture question as it applies to intelligence: "Is intelligence primarily an inherited characteristic, or is it primarily determined by environment?" A partial answer to this question comes from correlational studies examining the IQs of identical twins separated at birth and placed in different environments. Because these twins have identical heredity and different environments, they provide researchers with an opportunity to separate the two factors. The original work in this area, conducted by British psychologist Cyril Burt, showed a strong relationship between the twins' IQs, suggesting that hereditary factors overwhelmed environment (Burt, 1972). However, later evidence showed that Burt probably falsified much of his data (Kamin, 1974). Nonetheless, correlational results suggest a strong relationship between twins' IQs. Note that the correlational research design is being used to address a theoretical issue.

LEARNING CHECK

1. Dr. Jones hopes to demonstrate that children who eat a more nutritious breakfast tend to have more academic success than their peers. If this result is obtained, then _____ would be the predictor variable and _____ would be the criterion variable for the study.
   a. the nutrition in the breakfast; the level of success
   b. the level of success; the nutrition in the breakfast
   c. those who eat a high nutrition breakfast; those who eat a low nutrition breakfast
   d. the children; the level of success

2. Which research design is commonly used to help establish the reliability or validity of a measurement procedure?
   a. The observational research design
   b. The survey research design
   c. The case study design
   d. The correlational design

3. A researcher uses a correlation to demonstrate that a new 5-minute test for intelligence produces scores that are strongly related to the scores from traditional IQ tests. What is the researcher attempting to demonstrate about the new 5-minute test?
   a. Reliability
   b. Validity
   c. A cause-and-effect relationship
   d. None of the above

Answers appear at the end of the chapter.

12.4 | Strengths and Weaknesses of the Correlational Research Strategy

LEARNING OBJECTIVE

LO5 Describe the strengths and weaknesses of the correlational research strategy including the third-variable problem and the directionality problem and identify these problems when they appear in a research study.

The correlational research strategy is often used for the preliminary work in an area that has not received a lot of research attention. The correlational design can identify variables and describe relationships between variables that might suggest further investigation using the experimental strategy to determine cause-and-effect relationships. In addition, the correlational research design allows researchers an opportunity to investigate variables that would be impossible or unethical to manipulate. For example, a correlational study could investigate how specific behaviors or skills are related to diet deficiencies or exposure to pollution. Although it is possible and ethical to record diet deficiencies and environmental pollution as they exist naturally, it would not be ethical to create these conditions in the laboratory. Countless other variables such as family size, personality, alcohol consumption, level of education, income, and color preferences can be interesting topics for behavioral research but cannot be manipulated and controlled in an experimental research study. However, these variables can be easily measured and described in correlational research.

One of the primary advantages of a correlational study is that the researcher simply records what exists naturally. Because the researcher does not manipulate, control, or otherwise interfere with the variables being examined or with the surrounding environment, there is good reason to expect that the measurements and the relationships accurately reflect the natural events being examined. In research terminology, correlational studies tend to have high external validity. In general, a correlational study can establish that a relationship exists, and it can provide a good description of the relationship. However, a correlational study usually does not produce a clear and unambiguous explanation for the relationship. In research terminology, correlational studies tend to have low internal validity. In particular, two limitations arise in explanations of results from a correlational study.

The third-variable and directionality problems are discussed in more detail in Chapter 7, pp. 162–163.

1. *The third-variable problem*. Although a correlational study may establish that two variables are related, it does not mean that there must be a direct relationship between the two variables. It is always possible that a third (unidentified) variable is controlling the two variables and is responsible for producing the observed relation. As noted in Chapter 7 (p. 162), this is known as the **third-variable problem**. For example, sales figures show a positive relationship between temperature and ice cream consumption; as temperature increases, ice cream consumption also increases. Other research shows a positive relationship between temperature and crime rate (Cohn & Rotton, 2000). When the temperature increases, both ice cream consumption and crime rates tend to increase. As a result, there is a positive correlation between ice cream consumption and crime rate. However, no one would suggest that there is a direct relationship between ice cream sales and crime. Instead, a third variable—temperature—is responsible for the observed correlation (Figure 12.5).

2. *The directionality problem*. A correlational study can establish that two variables are related; that is, changes in one variable tend to be accompanied by changes in the other variable. However, a correlational study does not determine which variable is the cause and which is the effect. As noted in Chapter 7 (p. 163), this is known as the **directionality problem**. For example, Collins et al. (2004) found a relationship between exposure to sexual content on television and sexual behavior among adolescents. Given this relationship, it is tempting to conclude that watching sex on television causes adolescents to engage in sexual behavior. However, it is possible that the true causal relationship is in the opposite direction. Adolescents who tend to be

FIGURE 12.5

The Third-Variable Problem

Although ice cream sales (variable *A*) and crime rate (variable *B*) appear to vary together, there is no direct connection between these two variables. Instead, both are influenced by a third variable. In this example, the temperature (variable *X*) influences ice cream sales. In addition, temperature influences the crime rate.

sexually active could simply choose to watch television programs that are consistent with their own behaviors. In this case, sexual behavior causes the teenager to prefer television programs with sexual content (Figure 12.6).

The study linking sexual content on television and sexual behavior provides one more opportunity to discuss the fact that the correlational research strategy does not establish the existence of cause-and-effect relationships. The study consisted of a survey of 1,792 adolescents, 12–17 years of age, who reported their television viewing habits and their sexual behaviors. Notice that this is a correlational study; specifically, there is no manipulated variable. The title of the research report correctly states that watching sex on television *predicts* adolescent sexual behavior. However, when the study was presented in newspaper articles, it often was interpreted as a demonstration that sex on television *causes* adolescent sexual behavior. It was even suggested that reducing the sexual content of television shows could substantially reduce adolescent sexual behavior. As an analogy, consider the fact that the beginning of football season *predicts* the onset of fall and winter. However, no reasonable person would suggest that we could substantially postpone the change of seasons by simply delaying the opening day of football.

Table 12.2 summarizes the strengths and weaknesses of the correlational research design.

Relationships with More than Two Variables

Thus far, we only have considered correlational research in which the investigators are examining relationships between two variables. In most situations, however, an individual variable, especially a behavior, is related to a multitude of other variables. For example,

FIGURE 12.6

The Directionality Problem

Although a correlational study can demonstrate a relationship between the sexual content of television programs that adolescents watch and their sexual behaviors, the study cannot determine if the television content is influencing behavior or whether the behavior is influencing the choice of television programs.

TABLE 12.2

A Summary of the Strengths and Weaknesses of the Correlational Research Design

Strengths	Weaknesses
Describes relationships between variables	Cannot assess causality
Nonintrusive—natural behaviors	Third-variable problem
High external validity	Directionality problem
	Low internal validity

academic performance is probably related to IQ as well as to a number of other cognitive variables such as motivation, self-esteem, social competence, and a variety of other personal characteristics. One commonly used technique for studying multivariate relationships is a statistical procedure known as **multiple regression**. The underlying concept is that one criterion variable such as academic performance can be explained or predicted from a set of predictor variables such as IQ and motivation. IQ predicts part of academic performance, but you can get a better prediction if you use IQ and motivation together. For example, Collins and Ellickson (2004) evaluated the ability of four psychological theories to predict smoking behavior for adolescents in 10th grade. Although all four theories were good independent predictors, an integrated model using multiple regression to combine predictors from all four theories was more accurate than any of the individual models.

One interesting use of multiple regression is to examine the relationship between two specific variables while controlling the influence of other, potentially confounding variables. By adding predictor variables one at a time into the regression analysis, it is possible to see how each new variable adds to the prediction after the influence of the earlier predictors has already been considered. Earlier, we discussed a correlational study examining the relationship between adolescents' sexual behavior and the sexual content of the television programs they watch (Collins et al., 2004). Because the age of the participants ranged from 12 to 17 years, the researchers were aware that participant age could create a third-variable problem. Specifically, the older the participants are, the more likely it is that they watch television programs with sexual content and that they engage in sexual behaviors. Thus, the participants' age can create an artificial relationship between sexual content and sexual behavior; individuals who watch less sexual content tend to engage in less sexual behavior (the younger participants), and individuals who watch more sexual content tend to engage in more sexual behavior (the older participants). However, the researchers were able to use multiple regression to eliminate this problem. Sexual content of the television programs was entered into the regression equation after the effects of age (and other variables) had been removed. The results indicated that sexual content still was a significant predictor of adolescent sexual behavior.

As a final note, we should warn you that the language used to discuss and report the results from a multiple regression can be misleading. For example, you will occasionally see reports that the predictor variables *explained* the observed differences in the criterion variable. For example, a report might say that regression has demonstrated that variables such as intelligence, personality, and work drive *explain* differences in student grades. The truth is that the predictor variables only *predict* student grades; they do not really explain them. To get a cause-and-effect explanation, you must use the experimental research strategy. Unless a research study is using the experimental strategy (including manipulation and control), the best you can do is to describe relationships, not explain them.

LEARNING CHECK

1. The results from a correlational study show a positive relationship between aggressive behavior for 6-year-old children and the amount of violence they watch on television. Based on this relationship, which of the following conclusions is justified?
   a. Decreasing the amount of violence that the children see on TV will reduce their aggressive behavior
   b. Increasing the amount of violence that the children see on TV will increase their aggressive behavior
   c. Children who watch more TV violence exhibit more aggressive behavior
   d. All of the other options are justified conclusions

2. A researcher reports a positive relationship between sugar consumption and activity level for a group of 8-year-old children. However, the researcher cannot be sure whether the extra sugar is causing the children to be more active or whether the extra activity is causing the children to eat more sugar. Which of the following is demonstrated by this example?
    a. The third-variable problem
    b. The directionality problem
    c. The reversal problem
    d. The criterion problem

Answers appear at the end of the chapter.

CHAPTER SUMMARY

At this point, you should review the learning objectives presented at the beginning of each section and be sure that you have mastered each objective.

The goal of the correlational research strategy is to examine the relationship between variables and to measure the strength of the relationship. The data typically consist of measurements of two different variables for each individual. A graph of the data provides an opportunity to see the characteristics of the relationship (if one exists). Typically, researchers examine three characteristics of a relationship: the direction, the form, and the degree of consistency.

Correlational research can be used for prediction, to establish validity and reliability, and to evaluate theories. However, because of the third-variable and directionality problems, correlational research cannot be used to determine the causes of behavior.

The correlational research strategy is extremely useful as preliminary research and valuable in its own right as a source of basic knowledge. However, this strategy simply describes relationships between variables, and does not explain the relationships or determine their underlying causes.

KEY WORDS

correlational research strategy	negative relationship	coefficient of determination	criterion variable
positive relationship	correlation, or correlation coefficient	predictor variable	

EXERCISES

The exercises are identified with specific learning objectives and are intended to assess your mastery of the objectives. You should be aware that exam items are also generated to assess learning objectives.

1. In addition to the key words, you should also be able to define each of the following terms:
    scatter plot
    linear relationship
    Pearson correlation
    monotonic relationship
    Spearman correlation
    statistical significance of a correlation
    regression

third-variable problem
directionality problem
multiple regression

2. (**LO1**) Explain how the purpose of a correlational study differs from the purpose of an experimental study.

3. (**LO1**) Each of the following studies examines the relationship between sugar consumption and activity level for preschool children. Identify which is correlational, which is experimental, and which is nonexperimental.

    Study 1: A researcher obtains a sample of 100 preschool children. Each child's parents are interviewed to determine the child's typical diet, and the child is assigned a score describing the amount of sugar consumed daily. Also, the child's activity level is obtained from direct observation on the playground. The results show that higher sugar consumption tends to be associated with a higher level of activity.

Study 2: A researcher obtains a sample of 100 preschool children. The children are randomly assigned to two groups. On arriving at school each morning, one group is given a high-sugar breakfast, and the other group is given a breakfast relatively low in sugar. After 1 week, each child's activity level is measured by direct observation on the playground. On average, the children in the high-sugar breakfast group had a higher level of activity than the children in the low-sugar group.

Study 3: A researcher obtains a sample of 100 preschool children. Based on interviews with the parents, the children are divided into two groups corresponding to high-sugar and low-sugar diets. The children are then observed on the playground to obtain an activity-level score for each child. On average, the children in the high-sugar group had higher activity scores than the children in the low-sugar group.

4. (**LO2**) Describe the pattern that would appear in a scatter plot showing the data points for each of the following correlations: $r = -0.9$ and $r = +0.3$.

5. (**LO2**) Suppose that there is a negative relationship between grade point average and the number of hours spent playing video games for high school boys. What

grades would you predict for boys who spend more than the average amount of time playing video games?

6. (**LO1** and **2**) The following list contains several variables that differentiate college students.
   a. Select two variables from the list that should have a consistent relationship (either positive or negative). Briefly describe how you would do a correlational study to evaluate the relationship.
   b. Describe how you would do a nonexperimental, differential research study to evaluate the same relationship (see Box 10.1, p. 245).

physical attractiveness
intelligence
alcohol consumption
shyness
exam anxiety
hours of sleep per night
hours of television per week

7. (**LO3**) Explain the difference between a linear relationship and a monotonic relationship, and identify which correlation is used to measure each.

8. (**LO4**) Describe how the reliability of a personality test could be established using the results from a correlational study.

9. (**LO5**) Describe how the third-variable problem and the directionality problem limit the interpretation of results from correlational research designs.

LEARNING CHECK ANSWERS

Section 12.1
1. c, 2. b, 3. a

Section 12.2
1. b, 2. c, 3. c

Section 12.3
1. a, 2. d, 3. b

Section 12.4
1. c, 2. b

The Descriptive Research Strategy

© Nathan Jasowiak / Shutterstock

CHAPTER LEARNING OBJECTIVES

LO1 Describe the purpose of the descriptive research strategy, explain how it differs from the purpose of other research strategies, and identify this strategy when it is used in a research study.

LO2 Describe the two general problems (observer influence and subjectivity) that can exist with behavioral observation and explain how researchers attempt to minimize them.

LO3 Describe the three techniques used to quantify behavioral observations and the three techniques used for sampling observations.

LO4 Define content analysis and archival research.

LO5 Describe the general characteristics of the observational research design; explain its strengths and weaknesses; and differentiate between natural observation, participant observation, and contrived observation.

LO6 Describe the general characteristics of the survey research design.

LO7 Define open-ended, restricted, and rating-scale questions; identify examples of these three types of questions; and describe the strengths and weaknesses of each.

LO8 Describe the four methods for administering a survey (mail, phone, Internet, and in person) and

explain the strengths and weaknesses of each, including the problems of nonresponse bias and interviewer bias.

LO9 Describe the general characteristics of the case study design, identify the different situations for which this type of research is well suited, and explain its strengths and weaknesses.

CHAPTER OVERVIEW

The following items appeared in our local newspaper or on the Internet in the early spring of 2017:

- One third of Americans get less than 6 hours of sleep each night.
- According to the CDC, the prevalence of obesity was 36.5% among adults during 2011–2014.
- The average class of 2016 graduate has $37,172 in student loan debt (U.S. Student Loan Department Statistics, 2017).
- Over 40% of Americans say that they eat breakfast for dinner two or three times a month.
- A survey of over 2,000 adults found that 63% of Americans would have trouble meeting basic needs if they lost income for 3 months.
- Tooth Fairy payments hit an all time high, averaging $4.66 in 2016.
- The average American spends more than 7 hours each day looking at a screen.
- More than 119,000 people are on the national transplant waiting list.
- A survey of corporate professionals found that 85% would rather be CEO of the company than be the President of the United States.

These reports are examples of descriptive research studies. In each case, the intent of the study is simply to describe a phenomenon. In essence, a descriptive research study takes a snapshot showing the current status of a specific variable or a behavior. Much of what we know about human and nonhuman behavior is based on descriptions of variables.

In Chapter 6, we identified five basic research strategies for investigating variables and their relationships: experimental, nonexperimental, quasi-experimental, correlational, and descriptive. In this chapter, we discuss the details of the descriptive research strategy. Unlike the other four strategies, descriptive research is not concerned with trying to explain relationships, determine why specific behaviors occur, or identify underlying causes for behaviors. Instead, the goal of descriptive research is simply to describe individual variables as they exist naturally.

13.1 An Introduction to Descriptive Research

LEARNING OBJECTIVE

LO1 Describe the purpose of the descriptive research strategy, explain how it differs from the purpose of other research strategies, and identify this strategy when it is used in a research study.

Descriptive research typically involves measuring a variable or set of variables as they exist naturally. Unlike the other research strategies, the **descriptive research strategy** is not concerned with relationships between variables but rather with the description of individual variables. The goal is to describe a single variable or to obtain separate descriptions for each variable when several are involved. This strategy is extremely useful as preliminary research (i.e., in the early stages of research) and in its own right. The first step in understanding a new phenomenon is to gain some idea of the variable of interest as it naturally exists. In addition, the results from descriptive research can help us capture interesting, naturally occurring behavior.

In the following sections, three descriptive research designs are considered: observational research, survey research, and case study research. In the observational research design, we describe observations of behaviors as they occur in natural settings. In survey research design, we describe people's responses to questions about behavior and attitudes. In case studies, we describe a single individual in great detail.

LEARNING CHECK

1. A researcher conducts a survey to determine the average number of text messages that college students send or receive during a typical 1-hour class. Which research strategy is being used?
   a. The descriptive research strategy
   b. The correlational research strategy
   c. The experimental research strategy
   d. The nonexperimental research strategy

2. How does the descriptive research strategy differ from the experimental or nonexperimental research strategies?
   a. It involves comparing groups of scores.
   b. It does not concern relationships between variables.
   c. It attempts to describe and explain relationships between variables.
   d. It does not involve the measurement of variables.

Answers appear at the end of the chapter.

13.2 The Observational Research Design

Caution! Many students assume all research studies that use behavioral observation are observational research designs. However, observation is used in a variety of different designs. The defining element of an observational research design is that the results are used simply to describe the variable being studied.

LEARNING OBJECTIVES

LO2 Describe the two general problems (observer influence and subjectivity) that can exist with behavioral observation, and explain how researchers attempt to minimize them.

LO3 Describe the three techniques used to quantify behavioral observations and the three techniques used for sampling observations.

LO4 Define content analysis and archival research.

LO5 Describe the general characteristics of the observational research design; explain its strengths and weaknesses; and differentiate between natural observation, participant observation, and contrived observation.

In the observational research design, the researcher observes and systematically records the behavior of individuals for the purpose of describing behavior, for example, the mating behavior of birds, parent–child interactions on a playground, or the shopping behavior of adolescents in a mall. In Chapter 3, we discussed behavioral observation (i.e., the observation and recording of behavior) as a technique for measuring variables. As a measurement technique, behavioral observation can be used in a variety of research strategies including experimental and correlational designs. In this chapter, we focus on the **observational research design**, which involves studies using behavioral observation simply for descriptive purposes. However, you should keep in mind that the techniques of behavioral observation are valuable for other research strategies. Following are details of the process of behavioral observation.

DEFINITION

> In the **observational research design**, the researcher observes and systematically records the behavior of individuals to describe the behavior.

Behavioral Observation

The process of **behavioral observation** simply involves the direct observation and systematic recording of behaviors, usually as the behaviors occur in a natural situation. For example, a researcher may observe children on a playground or tropical birds in a rain forest. This measurement technique, however, introduces two special measurement problems.

1. Because the goal is to observe natural behavior, it is essential that the behaviors are not disrupted or influenced by the presence of an observer. This raises the question of demand characteristics and reactivity (see Chapter 3, pp. 75–76).
2. Observation and measurement require at least some degree of subjective interpretation by the observer. If we observe two preschool children bumping into each other, we must decide whether the contact was accidental or deliberate, and if it was deliberate, which child initiated the contact and whether it was aggression or simply play. The fact that the measurements are based, in part, on a subjective judgment raises the question of reliability (see Chapter 3, pp. 61–64); that is, would two different occurrences of the same behavior be judged in the same way?

The first problem can be addressed by concealing the observer so that the individuals do not know that their behaviors are being observed and recorded. As long as we observe public behaviors in public places, there is no ethical problem with this technique. An alternative procedure is to habituate the participants to the observer's presence. **Habituation** requires repeated exposure until the observer's presence is no longer a novel stimulus. For example, an observer might sit in a classroom for an hour every day for a week before the actual observation begins. On the first day or two, the observer is a novel event, and the children modify their behaviors. After a few days, however, the children become accustomed to the observer's presence (like a piece of furniture) and return to their normal behaviors.

To address the second problem, subjectivity, researchers typically employ three interrelated devices to help ensure the objectivity of their behavioral observations. First, they develop a list of well-defined categories of behavior; next, they use well-trained observers; and finally, they use multiple observers to assess inter-rater reliability. As noted, the first step in the process is to prepare a list of behaviors called **behavior categories**. Developing a set of behavior categories means that before observation begins, we identify the categories of behavior we want to observe (such as group play, play alone, aggression, or social interaction) and then construct a list of specific behaviors that are examples for each category. A preexisting list enables observers to know exactly what to look for and how to categorize each behavior. For example, observers do not have to make a subjective decision about whether an observed behavior is aggressive; they simply need to decide whether the observed behavior is on the preexisting list of aggressive behaviors. In addition, a set of pre-established behavior categories provides a clear operational definition of each construct being examined. In a study examining the effects of playing violent video games on children's aggressive behavior, for example, Polman, de Castro, and van Aken (2008) defined aggression using the following list of behaviors: hit, kick, or push someone; fight with someone; name calling or have a quarrel; tease someone; frighten someone to get what he or she wanted; and gossip.

During the observation period, normally only one individual observes and records behaviors using the set of behavioral categories as a guide. To establish reliability, however, it is required that two or more individuals observe and record simultaneously during some of the observation periods (see Chapter 3, pp. 63–64). The degree of agreement between the two observers is then computed, either by computing a correlation between the scores for the two observers (Chapter 3 and Figure 3.1) or by computing a proportion of agreement (see Chapter 15, pp. 414–417), ranging from 1.00, perfect agreement, to 0, no agreement, as a measure of **inter-rater reliability**.

Quantifying Observations

Behavioral observation also involves converting the observations into numerical scores that can be used to describe individuals and groups. The creation of numerical values is usually accomplished by one of three techniques:

1. The **frequency method** involves counting the instances of each specific behavior that occur during a fixed-time observation period. For example, the child committed three aggressive acts during the 30-minute period.
2. The **duration method** involves recording how much time an individual spends engaged in a specific behavior during a fixed-time observation period. For example, the child spent 18 minutes playing alone during the 30-minute period.
3. The **interval method** involves dividing the observation period into a series of intervals and then recording whether a specific behavior occurs during each interval. For example, the 30-minute observation period is divided into thirty 1-minute intervals. The child was observed in group play during 12 of the intervals.

The first two techniques are often well suited for specific behaviors but can lead to distorted measurements in some situations. For example, a bird that sings continuously for the entire 30-minute observation period would get a *frequency* score of only 1. Another bird that sings 25 times with each song lasting 2 seconds would get a *duration* score of only 50 seconds. In such situations, the *interval method* provides a way to balance frequency and duration to obtain a more representative measurement.

Sampling Observations

When an observer is confronted with a complex situation, it can be impossible to observe many different individuals and record many different behaviors simultaneously. One solution is to record the situation so the scene can be replayed repeatedly to gather observations. A second solution is to take a sample of the potential observations rather than attempt to watch and record everything. The first step in the process of sampling observations is to divide the observation period into a series of time intervals. The sampling process then consists of one of the following three procedures:

1. **Time sampling** involves observing for one interval, then pausing during the next interval to record all the observations. The sequence of observe–record–observe–record is continued through the series of intervals.
2. **Event sampling** involves identifying one specific event or behavior to be observed and recorded during the first interval, then shifting attention to a different event or behavior during the second interval, and so on, for the full series of intervals.
3. **Individual sampling** involves identifying one participant to be observed during the first interval, then shifting attention to a different individual for the second interval, and so on.

Content Analysis and Archival Research

The same techniques that are used in behavioral observation can be applied to other situations that do not involve the direct observation of ongoing behaviors. For example, it is possible to measure behaviors that unfold in movies or books, and it is possible to study documents recording behaviors that occurred long ago. Thus, researchers can measure and record incidences of violence in movies or television programs, and they can look into the past to see whether adults with personality disorders displayed any evidence of abnormal behavior as children. When researchers measure behaviors or events in books, movies, or other media, the measurement process is called **content analysis**. For example, Brooks, Bichard, and Craig (2016) used content analysis to examine the demographics of characters shown in Super Bowl commercials from 2010 to 2014. Their results showed that mature adults (aged 65 or more) were featured in over 30% of the commercials. Surprisingly, 30% is much greater than the actual proportion of mature adults in the general population. Recording behaviors from historical records is called **archival research**. For example, Jones, Pelham, Carvallo, and Mirenberg (2004) used a series of four archival studies to demonstrate that people tend to marry individuals whose first or last names resemble their own significantly more often than would be expected by randomly pairing names. The data for all four studies were obtained from Internet sites containing birth records (parents' names), marriage records, and joint telephone listings.

DEFINITIONS

> **Content analysis** involves using the techniques of behavioral observation to measure the occurrence of specific events in literature, movies, television programs, or similar media that present replicas of behaviors.
>
> **Archival research** involves looking at historical records (archives) to measure behaviors or events that occurred in the past.

To ensure that the measurements are objective and reliable, the processes of content analysis and archival research follow the same rules that are used for behavioral observation. Specifically, the measurement process involves the following:

1. Establishing behavioral categories and preparing a list of specific examples to define exactly which events are included in each category being measured; for example, a list of specific examples is prepared to define television violence.
2. Using the frequency method, the duration method, or the interval method to obtain a numerical score for each behavioral category; for example, an observer records how many examples of violence are seen in a 30-minute television program or how many disciplinary actions appear on an individual's school records.
3. Using multiple observers for at least part of the measurement process to obtain a measure of inter-rater reliability.

Types of Observation and Examples

Ethologists (researchers who study nonhumans in their natural environment) and researchers interested in human behavior commonly use the observational research design. There are three basic kinds of observation: naturalistic observation, participant observation, and contrived observation.

Naturalistic Observation

When a researcher observes and records behavior in a natural setting without intervening in any way, it is called **naturalistic observation**, or **nonparticipant observation**. A natural setting is one in which behavior ordinarily occurs and that has not been arranged in any way for the purpose of modifying behavior. In naturalistic observation, researchers try to be as inconspicuous and unobtrusive as possible, passively recording whatever occurs.

DEFINITION

> In **naturalistic observation**, or **nonparticipant observation**, a researcher observes behavior in a natural setting as unobtrusively as possible.

Naturalistic observation could be used to describe any behavior, for example, the behavior of children in a classroom, the behavior of protestors in a riot, or the behavior of patrons at a bar. A classic example of naturalistic observation used to describe non-human behavior is Jane Goodall's research (1971, 1986). Goodall lived with a colony of chimpanzees in Gombe, Tanzania, for a number of years during the 1960s and observed behaviors in chimps that had never before been recorded (e.g., tool use in nonhumans). She observed chimpanzees stripping leaves off twigs, inserting the twigs into a termite hill, then withdrawing the twigs and licking off the termites that clung to them. More recently, Wang and Repetti (2016) used video recordings of natural interactions between couples to examine supportive behaviors for husbands and wives.

Naturalistic observation is particularly useful in providing insight into real-world behavior. The results of studies using naturalistic observation also have high degrees of external validity because the behavior is examined in real-world settings as opposed to laboratories. Furthermore, naturalistic observation is useful for examining behaviors that, for practical or ethical reasons, cannot be manipulated by the researcher. For example, a researcher interested in investigating spanking behavior in parents obviously could not make parents spank their children for the purposes of scientific exploration. A researcher could, however, stroll through public places such as malls and watch parents disciplining their children.

One limitation of naturalistic observation is the time needed to conduct this type of research. To observe the mating behavior of a particular species of bird, for example, a researcher would need to wait until two opposite sex members of that species appeared. In addition, both birds would need to be sexually ready before a researcher could observe their courtship and mating behaviors. Similarly, using naturalistic observation of parent–child interactions on a playground means waiting for a parent with a child of the appropriate age and gender to arrive at the playground, then engage in the behavior the researcher wants to observe. A second problem with naturalistic observation is that the observer must take extra care not to disrupt or influence the behavior being observed because the goal is to observe natural behavior.

Participant Observation

In **participant observation**, a researcher does not observe from afar as in naturalistic observation. Instead, the researcher interacts with the participants and becomes one of them to observe and record behavior. This type of observation is needed in situations in which inconspicuous observation is not possible. For example, researchers certainly could not set up observation in the middle of a cult or gang meeting and expect that no one would notice them, that their presence would not alter behavior, or that the observed behaviors would be at all natural.

DEFINITION

> In **participant observation**, the researcher engages in the same activities as the people being observed in order to observe and record their behavior.

A great example of participant observation is Rosenhan's (1973) research investigating the experiences of mental patients and patient–staff interactions in psychiatric hospitals. In this research, Rosenhan had eight individuals misrepresent their names and occupations and claim they heard voices in order to be admitted to various mental hospitals. All eight individuals were admitted. The pseudo-patients observed hospital conditions, their own treatment, and the behaviors of staff and patients. The eight researchers were admitted to 12 different hospitals, and apparently, no hospital staff realized that they were not real patients. In a much less risky study, a researcher joined the members of an alternative-medicine group who used poetry and song writing as a medium of health care (Holmes, 2017). The participants experienced healing by using themes of mothering, loving and being loved, and dealing with grief in their original works and performances.

Participant observation allows researchers to observe behaviors that are often not open to scientific observation—for example, occult activities—and to get information that may not be accessible to outside observation. Additionally, by having the same experiences as the participants in the study, the observer gains a unique perspective, obtaining insight into behavior not obtainable by observing from afar. The results of participant-observation studies have high external validity because the behaviors are examined in real-world settings, not laboratories.

There are several limitations of this type of observation. It is extremely time-consuming; for example, the observers' stays in the mental hospitals in Rosenhan's study ranged from 7 to 52 days. In addition, participant observation is potentially dangerous for the observer. Furthermore, the observer may inadvertently alter participants' behavior by directly interacting with them; and, finally, by interacting with the participants and identifying closely with the individuals in the study, an observer may lose objectivity.

Contrived Observation

Another type of observation is **contrived observation**, or **structured observation**. In contrast to observing behavior in natural settings, the observer sets up a situation that is likely to produce the behaviors to be observed so that it is not necessary to wait for them to occur naturally. The purpose of contrived observation is to precipitate a behavior that occurs naturally but infrequently and to create a situation wherein a natural behavior will probably occur and be observed in a timelier fashion.

DEFINITION

> **Contrived observation**, or **structured observation**, is the observation of behavior in settings arranged specifically to facilitate the occurrence of specific behaviors.

Often, such studies are conducted in laboratory settings. For example, if a researcher wants to observe parent–child interactions, the parents and children could be brought into a laboratory and given a task to perform while being observed or videotaped. This process is much quicker than waiting for parents and children to show up at a playground and interact with one another, which is how natural observation would proceed. To observe the development of child conduct problems, for example, Fleming, McMahon, and King (2016) instructed pairs of parents and children to engage in parent-directed play analogs so they could observe the child's response to adult authority.

Developmental psychologists frequently use structured observation. The most notable example is Jean Piaget (1896–1980). In many of Piaget's studies, a child is given a problem to solve (e.g., which cylinder contains more water), and the researcher observes and records how the child solves the problem. These descriptions have provided a wealth of information regarding children's cognitive abilities and are the basis for Piaget's stage theory of cognitive development.

Contrived observation may also take place in a natural but "set up" arena: a field setting (which the participant perceives as a natural environment) arranged by the researcher for the purposes of observing and recording a behavior. For example, to observe the eating behaviors of birds, a researcher could set up a bird feeder. Structured observation is a compromise between the purely descriptive naturalistic observation discussed earlier and manipulative field experiments (discussed in Chapter 7). Ethologists frequently use contrived observation to study animals' responses. For example, Nobel Prize–winning ethologist Konrad Lorenz discovered the phenomenon of imprinting by observing the behavior of graylag goslings. Imprinting is the establishment of a strong, stable preference for or attachment to an object when that object is encountered during a sensitive period in an animal's life; normally, a gosling imprints on its parent immediately after hatching. Lorenz discovered imprinting by naturalistic observation when the goslings pursued him as if he were their parent! He and others then used contrived observation to see if the young goslings would imprint on other models as well. (Indeed they will; graylag goslings will imprint on almost any moving object in the environment.)

An advantage of contrived observation over both natural and participant observation is that researchers do not have to wait for behaviors to occur naturally. Instead, the environment is structured in such a way that the desired behaviors are more likely to occur. However, a disadvantage of contrived observation is that, because the environment is less natural, the behavior may be as well.

Strengths and Weaknesses of Observational Research Designs

The strengths and weaknesses of the three types of observation are summarized in Table 13.1. Here, we discuss some additional strengths and weaknesses of observational research designs in general. A major strength of observational research is that the researcher observes and records actual behavior; in contrast, survey research, for example, relies on the participants' *reports* of their behavior. Participants can distort or conceal the accuracy or truthfulness of their responses and thus not reflect their actual behavior. Observational research results often have high external validity as well. With the exception of contrived observation in a laboratory, most observational research is conducted in a field setting, and field research tends to have higher external validity. Another strength of observational research is its flexibility. A researcher can complete a comprehensive observation of antecedents, behaviors, and consequences of the behaviors, whereas other studies examine a single, discrete behavior.

TABLE 13.1

A Summary of the Strengths and Weaknesses of the Observational Research Design

Research Design	Strengths	Weaknesses
Naturalistic observation	Behavior observed in the real world Useful for nonmanipulated behaviors Actual behaviors observed and recorded	Time-consuming Potential for observer influence Potential for subjective interpretation
Participant observation	When natural observation is impossible Get information not accessible otherwise Participation gives unique perspective	Time-consuming Potential for loss of objectivity Increased chance for observer influence
Contrived observation	Do not have to wait for behaviors to occur	Less natural

A potential problem with observational research is the ethical concern about spying on people. If participants are not aware that their behavior is being observed, the researcher may be violating a person's privacy and right to choose to participate in the study. (In Chapter 4, we discussed when it is not necessary to obtain informed consent before individuals participate in a research study.) Finally, a general weakness of the descriptive research strategy and, therefore, of all observational research designs, is that they simply describe behavior and do not examine its causes.

LEARNING CHECK

1. During a study using the behavioral research strategy, it is common to have two observers record behavior simultaneously. What is the purpose for this procedure?
   - **a.** It is used to ensure the objectivity of the measurements.
   - **b.** It is used to convert observations into numerical scores.
   - **c.** It provides an operational definition for the variables being measured.
   - **d.** It helps ensure that the behaviors are not influenced by the presence of an observer.

2. In an observational study of children diagnosed with autism spectrum disorder, you record how much time each child spends playing alone during a 30-minute observation period. Which method of quantifying behavior is being used?
   - **a.** Frequency
   - **b.** Duration
   - **c.** Interval
   - **d.** Individual

3. When researchers use behavioral observation techniques to measure behaviors in movies, what is the measurement process called?
   - **a.** Behavioral observation
   - **b.** Event sampling
   - **c.** Content analysis
   - **d.** Archival research

4. Which technique would probably be used by a researcher who wanted to observe behaviors in a private social club?
   - **a.** Naturalistic observation
   - **b.** Participant observation
   - **c.** Contrived observation
   - **d.** Unstructured observation

Answers appear at the end of the chapter.

13.3 The Survey Research Design

LEARNING OBJECTIVES

LO6 Describe the general characteristics of the survey research design.

LO7 Define open-ended, restricted, and rating-scale questions; identify examples of these three types of questions; and describe the strengths and weaknesses of each.

LO8 Describe the four methods for administering a survey (mail, phone, Internet, and in person) and explain the strengths and weaknesses of each, including the problems of nonresponse bias and interviewer bias.

Caution! Simply because a study uses a survey does not mean that it is a survey research design. The defining element of the survey research design is that the results of the survey are used simply to describe the variables being studied.

Surveys and questionnaires are used extensively in the behavioral sciences as relatively efficient ways to gather large amounts of information. By presenting people with a few carefully constructed questions, it is possible to obtain self-reported answers about attitudes, opinions, personal characteristics, and behaviors. The simple notion behind a survey is that it is not necessary to observe directly where people shop or what foods they prefer, or how many hours they sleep each night; instead, we simply ask. With a survey, a researcher does not have to wait until a behavior or response occurs; for example, it is not necessary to wait until after an election to discover people's attitudes about candidates or issues; we can ask at any time. Although surveys can be used to obtain scores for a variety of different research designs, a survey often is conducted simply to obtain a description of a particular group of individuals. A study using the results from a survey simply for descriptive purposes is classified as a **survey research design**.

DEFINITION

A **survey research design** is a research study that uses a survey to obtain a description of a particular group of individuals.

As noted earlier, surveys are used to collect data for many different research designs including experimental, correlational, and nonexperimental studies. In this chapter, however, we focus on the survey research design, which involves studies using survey results exclusively for descriptive purposes. Nonetheless, you should keep in mind that the techniques of planning, constructing, and administering surveys are valuable for other research strategies.

The goal of the survey research design is to obtain an accurate picture of the individuals being studied. The survey provides a "snapshot" of the group at a particular time. Sometimes, survey research focuses on a specific characteristic such as eating behavior or political attitudes; other survey research may seek a more complex picture of a variety of behaviors and opinions. For example, a researcher could use a survey to investigate alcohol use at a local high school. Depending on the questions asked, the results could provide a description of how many students drink alcohol, how much they drink, and when and where. Other questions could yield a description of student attitudes toward alcohol use among their peers.

A common application of survey research is by companies to obtain more accurate descriptions of their customers. When you buy any electronic device, for example, a warranty registration card usually accompanies it. In addition to your name and address and the serial number of the product, other demographic questions are usually asked:

What is your age?

What is your occupation?

What is your income?

How did you hear about our product?

Clearly, the purpose of these questions is to obtain the demographic characteristics of customers; that is, to put together a description of the people who are likely to buy this product so that the company can do a better job of targeting its advertising.

Conducting survey research presents researchers with four issues that must be addressed for the results to be accurate and meaningful. First, survey questions must be developed. Second, the questions must be assembled and organized to produce a well-constructed survey. Third, a selection process must be developed to determine exactly who will participate in the survey and who will not; survey participants must be representative of the general group to be studied. Finally, researchers must determine how the survey will be administered. Will participants receive printed surveys through the mail; will the survey questions be read to people over the telephone; or will participants complete the questions online in an Internet survey, or in person? These four issues are discussed in the following sections.

Types of Questions

There are different ways to ask participants for self-report information. Sometimes, you may be satisfied with a simple yes or no answer (Have you ever…), but in other circumstances, you may want a quantitative answer (how much, how often). Different types of questions encourage different types of responses. Also, different types of questions permit different degrees of freedom in the participants' answers. For example, a question may severely restrict response options (Which of the following three flavors of ice cream do you prefer?), or a question may give each participant complete freedom in choosing a response (What is your favorite ice cream flavor?). The wording of a question also can introduce bias into participants' answers (Are you one of those bland, unimaginative people who prefer vanilla ice cream?). Finally, different types of questions permit different types of statistical analysis and interpretation. If answers are limited to non-numerical categories on a nominal scale, for example, you cannot compute a group average. In this section, we consider three general types of self-report questions. Each type has its own individual strengths and weaknesses and is designed to obtain specific information.

Open-Ended Questions

An open-ended question simply introduces a topic and allows participants to respond in their own words. For example:

1. What do you think about the current availability of food on this campus?
2. In your view, what are the most important factors in choosing a college or university?

The primary advantage of an open-ended question is that it allows an individual the greatest flexibility in choosing how to answer. An open-ended question imposes few restrictions on the participant and, therefore, is likely to reveal each individual's true thoughts or opinions. Although the question may lead the participant in a particular direction or suggest a specific point of view, individuals are free to express their own thoughts. However, this can also be a major disadvantage. For example, different participants may approach the question from entirely different perspectives, leaving you with answers that are impossible to compare or summarize. To the question about food on the college campus, for example, one individual may respond with a list of food suggestions, another may suggest new locations for selling food, and a third participant may state simply that the current situation is "okay." All three answers may be useful, but they are clearly not compatible with each other, and they may be very different from the issue you had in mind when the original question was written.

A second disadvantage of open-ended questions is that the answers are often difficult to summarize or analyze with conventional statistical methods. As with the food question, different participants may provide responses that are difficult to group together or to average in any meaningful way. Often, the researcher must impose some subjective interpretation on the answer, such as classifying a rambling response as generally positive or generally negative. Finally, the responses to open-ended questions may be limited by a participant's ability or willingness to express his or her thoughts. Inarticulate or tired people may give very brief answers that do not completely express the true breadth of their thinking.

Restricted Questions

A restricted question presents the participant with a limited number of response alternatives, thereby restricting the response possibilities. Like a multiple-choice question, a restricted question typically asks the participant to select the best or most appropriate answer in a series of choices. For example:

1. If the election were held today, which of the following candidates would receive your vote?
   a. Mr. Jones
   b. Ms. Smith
   c. Mr. Johnson

2. Which of the following alternatives is the best description of your current occupation?
   a. Blue collar
   b. White collar (sales/service)
   c. Professional
   d. Managerial
   e. Student
   f. Unemployed

Because these questions produce a limited and predetermined set of responses, they are easy to analyze and summarize. Typically, the data are tabulated and reported as percentages or proportions of participants selecting each alternative.

It also is possible to obtain quantitative information from restricted questions by using an ordered set of response alternatives. For example:

1. During a typical week, how often do you eat at a fast-food restaurant?
   a. Not at all
   b. Once
   c. Twice
   d. Three times
   e. Four times or more

With this type of question, it is often possible to compute some kind of average response for a group of participants.

Finally, an element of open-endedness can be allowed in a restricted question by including a blank category where participants are free to fill in their own responses. For example:

1. Which of the following is your favorite local grocery store?
   a. Wegmans
   b. Trader Joe's
   c. Whole Foods
   d. Publix
   e. Other (please specify) _____

Rating-Scale Questions

A rating-scale question requires a participant to respond by selecting a numerical value on a predetermined scale. Movie critics often use this type of scale to evaluate films with a number from 1 to 10. The numerical scale that accompanies each question typically presents a range of response alternatives from very positive to very negative. A common example uses a 5-point scale on which individuals rate their level of agreement or disagreement with a simple statement:

1. Strongly disagree
2. Disagree
3. Neither agree or disagree
4. Agree
5. Strongly agree

The rating scale is usually presented as a horizontal line divided into categories so that participants can simply circle a number or mark an X at the location corresponding to their response (Figure 13.1). This type of rating-scale question is often called a **Likert scale** (or a Likert-type scale) after Rensis Likert, who developed the 5-point response scale as part of a much more sophisticated scaling system (Likert, 1932). Notice that the scale is presented with equal spacing between the different response choices. The idea is to simulate an interval scale of measurement, and the responses from rating scales are usually treated as interval measurements. Thus, the distance between agree and strongly agree is treated as a 1-point distance that is equivalent to any other 1-point difference on the scale.

There is no absolute rule for determining the number of categories for a rating-scale question; however, researchers commonly use from 5 to 10 numerical values. The reasoning behind this range of values is based on two observations:

1. Participants tend to avoid the two extreme categories at the opposite ends of the scale, especially if they are identified with labels that indicate extreme attitudes or opinions. Thus, the actual scale is effectively reduced by two categories.
2. Participants have trouble discriminating among more than 9 or 10 different levels. If the scale offers more than 10 options, the participants usually blend categories and effectively create their own 10-point scale.

FIGURE 13.1

A Likert-Type Rating Scale and a Series of Questions Examining Elementary School Students' Attitudes about Mathematics

The participants' responses consist of numerical ratings for each of the five questions. The numbers can be added and averaged and are compatible with most standard statistical procedures.

Questionnaire

Use the following scale (numbers 1 through 5) to describe how you feel about each of the statements below. For each statement, circle the number that gives the best description of how you feel.

Strongly Disagree	Disagree	Undecided	Agree	Strongly Agree
1	2	3	4	5

1. I have a natural talent for mathematics. 1 2 3 4 5
2. I am a good math student. 1 2 3 4 5
3. I like mathematics. 1 2 3 4 5
4. Math is easier for me than it is for most students. 1 2 3 4 5
5. I probably will use mathematics in my future job. 1 2 3 4 5

There is also no absolute rule for labeling the categories. Typically, the opposite extremes are identified with verbal labels called **anchors** that establish the endpoints of the scale. In addition, the central category is often labeled, especially if it represents a neutral response. Beyond the endpoints and the middle, however, labeling categories is optional.

One criticism of rating-scale questions is that whenever questions in a series all have the same choices for responding, participants tend to use the same response to answer all (or most) of the questions. This tendency is called a **response set**. With a Likert-type scale, for example, some participants use the neutral (#3) answer for everything. One rationalization is that they do not feel strongly about any of the items, so they really are neutral. (A more likely explanation is that they simply want to finish quickly.) Another possibility is that a participant may use the agree category for all responses except to those few items where there is serious disagreement. To minimize this problem, it is recommended that the items include a mixture of positive and negative statements, including some alternate phrasing of the same item. For example, one item might be:

Today's teenagers are rude and disrespectful.

Later in the series, an alternate item might be:

Today's teenagers are polite and courteous.

The intent is to force respondents to move back and forth between opposite sides of the scale so that they cannot fall into a single response set for answering the questions.

The primary advantage of rating-scale questions is that they produce numerical values that can be treated as measurements from an interval scale. (Recall from Chapter 3 that an interval scale consists of a series of equal-sized categories, which makes it possible to measure distances on the scale.) Using the five items in Figure 13.1 as an example, each participant receives a total score obtained by adding the responses from the five items. A participant who answered 1 (strongly disagree) to all five items would have a total score of 5. Someone who answered 5 (strongly agree) to all five items would have a total score of 25. Thus, we can position each individual on a scale that represents attitudes toward mathematics. This way, we can compare different individuals and compute means to describe different groups of participants. In general, it is very easy to use standard statistical procedures to summarize and interpret the results from a rating-scale question.

A secondary advantage of rating-scale questions is that participants usually find them easy to understand and easy to answer. Because the scale permits different degrees of response, participants are not forced into an absolute yes or no, all-or-none choice. Instead, they can qualify their answers by indicating degrees of agreement or approval. It is also easy for participants to breeze through a long series of questions after the rating scale has been introduced at the beginning of the survey. Thus, it is possible to collect a lot of data on a variety of different topics in a single, relatively efficient survey.

Constructing a Survey

Once the survey questions are determined, the next step is to organize the questions into a coherent survey that participants can easily understand and complete. The details of constructing a survey are beyond the scope of this text, but there are a few general guidelines for creating a well-organized survey.

1. Demographic questions (such as age, gender, level of education) should be placed at the end of the survey. These items are considered boring, and you do not want participants to quit because they are bored by the first few questions. In addition, identifying age, race, or gender first may influence how the participant answers survey questions that relate to these variables.

2. Sensitive questions or items that may cause embarrassment or discomfort should be placed in the middle of the survey. By the time participants encounter these items, they are more likely to have warmed up to the topic and to have become committed to completing the survey.

3. Questions dealing with the same general topic should be grouped together. Also, questions in the same format should be grouped together; for example, all rating-scale questions should be grouped together. Grouping questions simplifies the survey so participants do not have to jump from one topic to another or switch from one type of question to another.

4. If participants are going to read the survey, the format for each page should be relatively simple and uncluttered. Questions that are crammed together and seem to fill every square inch of the page create an overwhelming appearance that can intimidate participants.

5. Finally, vocabulary and language style should be easy for participants to understand. A survey with language appropriate for college students probably would not be appropriate for elementary school students.

These guidelines address only a few of the considerations involved in designing a survey. If you plan to construct your own survey, you probably should seek more detailed guidance. Two excellent sources are Rea and Parker (2014) and Dillman, Smyth, and Christian (2014).

Selecting Relevant and Representative Individuals

Researchers typically want to generalize their results from the study's sample to the target population. (See Chapter 5 for information about selecting a sample.) In addition, the external validity of a research study is limited, in part, by the representativeness of the sample to the population (see Chapter 6). The survey research design introduces a few additional concerns regarding sample selection. First, many surveys address a specific issue that is relevant to only a small subset of the general population. For such a survey, care must be taken to select survey participants to whom the questions are relevant. For a survey about childcare issues, for example, participants should be parents with small children. A sensible strategy might be to hand out surveys to parents as they pick up their children at childcare centers around the city. Or you might obtain mailing lists or e-mail addresses from the different childcare centers. Similarly, participants for a shopping survey might be selected from the people in a shopping mall, and participants for an education survey could come from the parents of children in the local school district.

Second, although some surveys focus on a specific topic or group of people, some surveys seek to describe a broad cross-section of the general population. In this case, the sample of survey participants must not be too restricted. For example, administering surveys to the students in a psychology class would not result in an accurate description of the political attitudes of people in the community. A researcher should take some time to identify the group to be described, and then make an effort to select individuals who accurately represent the group. This often means that the individuals who participate in the survey are not necessarily the ones who are easiest or most convenient to obtain.

Occasionally, individual researchers seek professional help preparing surveys and identifying participants. In most major metropolitan areas, there are several research companies that design, administer, and analyze surveys. These companies usually have access to specialized mailing lists that can focus on a specific, well-defined population. Typically, a researcher supplies specific demographic characteristics, and the computer generates a list of individuals who meet the criteria, for example, single mothers between the ages of 20 and 29 who have an annual income greater than $35,000. Focusing a survey in this way can increase the chances of obtaining a reasonable number of useful responses.

Administering a Survey

Once you have developed the survey questions, constructed the survey, and identified the participants, the next step is to distribute the survey to the individuals you would like to investigate. There are a number of options for administering a survey, each of which has advantages and disadvantages. In this section, we examine some of the most common methods for administering surveys: on the Internet, by mail, by telephone, and in person.

Internet Surveys

In recent years, it has become increasingly common to administer surveys over the Internet. Occasionally, you will find links to surveys on existing websites or Facebook pages of businesses or organizations. Commonly, people are sent an e-mail or other invitation sending them a link or asking them to visit the survey website. Today, setting up a survey online is relatively easy and fast. There are a number of survey authoring software packages and online survey services available (Wright, 2005). SurveyMonkey and Qualtrics are examples of companies that, for a monthly fee, provide software to create and conduct a survey. The survey is housed on their server and they provide additional support as well. Google, through Google Forms, provides free software for online survey development as well.

Internet surveys provide an economical and efficient medium for reaching a large number of potential respondents. A related advantage of Internet surveys is that a researcher has greater access to participants with a particular characteristic (McKenna & Bargh 2000; Wright, 2005). It is easier to find people who share a specific interest, belief, or characteristic than asking many more people by mail or on the phone. Hence there is a saving of time, as well as the cost of printing surveys, postage, and phone bills.

Another advantage of an Internet survey is the flexibility in presenting questions and response alternatives. For example, if a survey question asks whether you have flown on a commercial airline during the past 7 months, it is possible to select the next question(s) based on an individual's response. For individuals who answer no, the survey can jump immediately to the next topic and skip all the other questions about airline travel. For individuals who answer yes, the survey can move to a series of questions concerning the travel experience. For example, the next question might be "On what airline did you travel?" accompanied by a drop box that presents 20 response choices. The ability to skip irrelevant questions or move to a set of related questions based on an individual's responses makes it possible to individualize a survey to obtain the maximum amount of information from each individual. In addition, the ability to control response alternatives with pop-ups and drop-down boxes increases the options for types of questions.

However, administering a survey on the Internet has numerous disadvantages related to issues of the sample. Because participants are often recruited from users of specific social media, the individuals in the sample may differ from Internet users in general and other people who are not on the Internet. Internet surveys, similarly to mail surveys, are subject to **nonresponse bias** (Wright, 2005), which means that the people who complete surveys are a self-selected sample that may not be representative of the population. Furthermore, it can be difficult to control the sample of respondents. For example, there is no simple system for organizing e-mail addresses. Many households have several computers with several different users, all of whom have different e-mail addresses. In addition, many people have more than one e-mail address. This makes it difficult to identify and select a sample of individuals or households who will be asked to participate in the survey.

Internet surveys are controlled best when they are administered to a closed group of e-mail users such as a university or other organization with a common address. For example, e-mails directing people to a survey website can be sent to all the students at a university by using the university list serve. If a link to a survey is simply posted on an existing website, you have no idea who might visit the site and decide to participate in the survey. Although people who visit a website are likely to be interested in the content, and therefore are a relevant sample, you have no ability to control or even determine the composition of the sample.

Mail Surveys

Another common method of administration is to mail the survey to a large sample of individuals. For individual participants, a mailed survey is very convenient and nonthreatening. Individuals can complete the survey at their own convenience, and can be relatively confident that responses are anonymous and confidential. On the other hand, the fact that the survey is anonymous means that a researcher can never be sure exactly who in the household completed and returned the survey.

Mailing surveys is usually a relatively simple and easy process, although printing a large number of surveys, addressing them, and paying postage can be expensive and time-consuming. The expense is compounded by the fact that response rates tend to be very low for mailed surveys. A response rate of 10%–20% is fairly typical. This means that you need to distribute at least five times the number of surveys you hope to have returned.

In addition to the costs of a low response rate, there may be a bias differentiating those who do and those who do not return surveys. One obvious possibility is that people who are most interested in the survey topic (those with the most intense feelings) are most likely to complete and return the survey. As we noted with Internet surveys, this trend creates nonresponse bias in the sample, which simply means that the individuals who return surveys are usually not representative of the entire group who receives them. Imagine, for example, a survey about blocking Internet sites on the computers at a public library. Although the surveys are mailed to all library patrons, they are most likely to be completed by people who are passionate about free speech and those who are paranoid about pornography. Neither group accurately represents the people who typically use the library. As a result, nonresponse bias can limit your ability to generalize survey results and poses a threat to the external validity of your study.

Although it is impossible to eliminate nonresponse bias completely, several actions can increase the overall response rate for a mail survey and thereby reduce the bias. First, response rates can be significantly improved if a good cover letter accompanies the survey. A cover letter should introduce the survey and ask for participation and should include the following elements:

1. An explanation of why the topic is important. For a survey on television program preferences, for example, you should point out the major role that television plays in the entertainment and education of most people.
2. An explanation of the usefulness of the results. Usually, the results of a survey are used in future planning or to help determine a future course of action. This should be explained in the cover letter so that participants know that the information they are providing may actually influence them in the future.
3. An emphasis on the importance of each individual response. The intent is to encourage all people to respond, whether or not they feel strongly about the issues in the survey. The cover letter should point out the importance of results that represent the entire population (not just a small group with special interests) and that it is, therefore, especially important that each person respond.
4. A contact person (name, address, and telephone number) whom participants can call or write to if they have any questions or comments. Participants rarely contact this person, but a real name and address help personalize the survey.
5. The signature of a person who is recognized and respected by individuals in the sample. People are more likely to respond if they are asked to by someone they know and like.

A second technique for improving response rates is to include a gift or token of appreciation with each survey (James & Bolstein, 1992). Common examples include a pen ("Please use this pen to fill out the survey, then keep the pen as our gift to you.") or money. Some surveys arrive with a dollar taped to the top and a note suggesting that the recipient use the money to buy a cup of coffee ("Sit back and enjoy your coffee while you complete the survey.").

Finally, it is possible to increase response rates by giving participants advance warning of the survey, then providing a follow-up reminder after the survey has been received (Dillman, Clark, & Sinclair, 1995). Typically, participants are notified about 1 week before the survey is mailed, that they have been selected to participate. The advance warning helps make the individuals feel special (they are a select group) and helps ensure that they will be watching for the survey in the mail. Approximately 1 week after the surveys have been received, a follow-up is sent to remind each person to complete and return the survey (if they have not done so already) and to thank each person for participating. Essentially, the advance notice and reminder provide a polite way to add an extra *please* and *thank-you* to the recruitment process and can significantly increase the response rate.

Telephone Surveys

Another method of administering a survey is to contact individuals by telephone. However, administering a survey by telephone can be incredibly time-consuming. The obvious problem with a telephone survey is that there is a direct, one-to-one relationship between the time spent by the researcher and the time spent by the participants; to complete 60 minutes of survey questions and responses, a researcher must spend 60 minutes on the telephone. Therefore, most telephone surveys are restricted to situations in which a large number of researchers or assistants can share the telephone assignments.

Administering a survey by telephone does have some advantages. First, the survey can be conducted from home or office. If several people place the calls and the survey is relatively brief, it is possible to contact a fairly large number of participants in only a few days. If you are considering a telephone survey, here are a few important notes for improving your chances for success.

1. Keep the questions short and use a small number of response alternatives. With a telephone survey, the participants do not have a written copy for reference, so you must depend on the listener's memory. If a participant gets confused or lost in the middle of a long, complicated question, you may not get a sensible response.
2. Practice reading the survey aloud. Listening to a question can be different from reading a question. On the telephone, participants cannot see the punctuation and other visual cues that help communicate the content of a written question. A good strategy is to pretest your survey questions by reading them to a set of friends. Be sure that your listeners understand the questions as you intended.
3. Beware of **interviewer bias**. Whenever a researcher has direct contact with participants, even over the telephone, there is a risk that the researcher will influence their natural responses. On the telephone, the primary problem is exerting influence by tone of voice or by rephrasing questions. The standard solutions are to practice reading the survey questions in a consistent, neutral tone, and never to alter a survey question. If a participant does not understand a question and asks for clarification, your only option is to reread the question. If you paraphrase a question or try to explain what it means, then you have changed the question and maybe even changed the participant's answer. Consider the following two versions of the same question. The first version uses neutral wording and focuses on the library hours. The second version is phrased in a leading way; that is, it appears to be an invitation for the participant to join a happy little group (especially if the question is read in a very friendly tone of voice).

Do you think there should be an increase in the hours that the library is open on weekends?

Don't you think we should increase the hours that the library is open on weekends?

4. Begin by identifying yourself and your survey. People are constantly bombarded by "junk" telephone calls and are inclined to hang up whenever a stranger calls. You can help avoid this problem if you immediately identify yourself and your topic, and make it clear that you are conducting a survey and not trying to sell anything. Your first few sentences on the telephone are similar to the cover letter for a mail survey and should contain the same elements (see p. 330).

In-Person Surveys and Interviews

Probably the most efficient method for administering a survey is to assemble a group of participants and have all of them complete the survey at the same time. You can ask people to sign up for predetermined meeting times, or simply ask for volunteers to gather at a specific time and place. Another possibility is to approach preexisting groups such as those in school classrooms or workplace lunchrooms. By having participants volunteer before the survey is presented, you guarantee a 100% response rate. The efficiency comes from the fact that you give instructions once to the entire group and then collect a whole set of completed surveys in the time it takes one participant to finish.

It also is possible to administer a survey in person to a single participant. In this case, the survey becomes a one-on-one interview. Although this appears to be a very inefficient method of collecting information, an interview can be quite valuable. Usually, interviews are reserved for a very small group of specially selected individuals, often called key informants. Typically, these are people who have unique perspectives on the issues or unique access to information (such as a college president, a chief of police, or a mayor). Interviews are also useful in situations in which you are willing to accept the limitations of a small group of participants in exchange for the in-depth information that can come from a detailed interview. An interview provides an opportunity for follow-up questions, and it is possible to explore complex issues more fully than could be done with a few isolated paper-and-pencil questions. Finally, interviews allow you to gather information from individuals who are unable to read and answer printed questions such as young children, people who cannot read, and people with low IQs.

A major concern with the interview is that interviewer bias can distort the results. For example, a participant may perceive a smile or nod from the researcher as a sign of approval or encouragement to continue on the current topic. Thus, the participant's response may be influenced by subtle actions on the part of the interviewer. Although it is impossible to completely eliminate this problem, it can be limited if the interviewer maintains a consistent attitude throughout the entire interview. A common strategy is to adopt a universal, mildly positive response to anything the participant says.

Strengths and Weaknesses of Survey Research

Table 13.2 summarizes the strengths and weaknesses of each method for administering a survey. In general, one of the real strengths of survey research is its flexibility. Surveys can be used to obtain information about a wide variety of different variables including attitudes, opinions, preferences, and behaviors. In fact, some of these variables are very difficult to describe in any other way. In addition, surveys typically provide a relatively easy and efficient means of gathering a large amount of information.

We have already noted some of the disadvantages of survey research, such as low response rates and nonresponse bias. Responses to survey questions can also be difficult to analyze or summarize. This problem is especially important with open-ended questions,

TABLE 13.2

A Summary of the Strengths and Weaknesses of the Survey Research Design

Survey Type	Strengths	Weaknesses
Internet surveys	Efficient to administer to a large number of participants Access to large number of individuals with common characteristics Survey can be individualized based on participant's responses	Initial expense for site Sample may not be representative Cannot control composition of the sample
Mail surveys	Convenient and anonymous Nonthreatening to participants Easy to administer	Can be expensive Low response rate and nonresponse bias Unsure exactly who completes the survey
Telephone surveys	Can be conducted from home or office Participants can stay at home or office	Time-consuming Potential for interviewer bias
In-person surveys	Efficient to administer with groups, 100% response rate, and flexible (groups or individual interviews)	Time-consuming, with individual interviews, and risk of interviewer bias

to which participants are allowed to respond in their own words. A final concern about survey research is that the information obtained is always a self-report. Ultimately, the quality of a survey study depends on the accuracy and truthfulness of the participants. It is certainly possible that at least some participants will distort or conceal information, or simply have no knowledge about the topic when they answer certain questions. Therefore, if your survey results show that 43% of the high school students use alcohol at least once a month, keep in mind that the results actually show that 43% of the students *report* using alcohol at least once a month.

LEARNING CHECK

1. Although surveys can be used with a variety of different research strategies, which of the following is the defining characteristic of the survey research design?
   a. The research is conducted in field settings rather than in a laboratory.
   b. The intent is simply to describe behaviors.
   c. The intent is to demonstrate a relationship between behavior and other variables.
   d. The intent is to explain the causes of the behaviors being surveyed.
2. The multiple-choice questions in an exam are examples of which type of survey question.
   a. Open-ended
   b. Restricted
   c. Rating-scale
   d. Physiological
3. What is an advantage to administering a survey over the Internet?
   a. 100% response rate
   b. Survey can be individualized based on responses
   c. Risk of interviewer bias
   d. None of the options are advantages

Answers appear at the end of the chapter.

13.4   The Case Study Design

LEARNING OBJECTIVE

LO9   Describe the general characteristics of the case study design, identify the different situations for which this type of research is well suited, and explain its strengths and weaknesses.

Research in the behavioral sciences tends to emphasize the study of groups rather than single individuals. By focusing on groups, researchers can observe the effects of a treatment across a variety of different personal characteristics and form a better basis for generalizing the results of the study. At the same time, however, some fields within the behavioral sciences are more concerned with individual behavior than with group averages. This is particularly true in the field of clinical psychology, in which clinicians concentrate on treatments and outcomes for individual clients. For clinicians, research results averaged over a large group of diverse individuals may not be as relevant as the specific result obtained for an individual client. In fact, it has been argued that intensive study of individuals (called the **idiographic approach**) is just as important as the study of groups (called the **nomothetic approach**) for clinical research (Allport, 1961).

> Caution! Other types of research also involve the detailed study of single individuals (see Chapter 14). The defining element of a case study design is that its goal is simply to obtain a description of the individual.

Although it is possible to conduct experimental research with individual participants (see Chapter 14), most individual-participant research studies can be classified as case studies. A **case study design** is a study of a single individual for the purpose of obtaining a description of the individual. The description is typically prepared as a report, usually containing a detailed description of observations and experiences during the diagnosis and treatment of a specific clinical client, including a detailed description of the unique characteristics and responses of the individual. If no treatment is administered to the individual being studied, the term **case history** often is used instead of case study. The information included in a case study can be obtained in a variety of ways, such as interviews with the client and/or close relatives, observation of the client, surveys, and archival data.

DEFINITION

> The **case study design** involves the in-depth study and detailed description of a single individual (or a very small group). A case study may involve an intervention or treatment administered by the researcher. When a case study does not include any treatment or intervention, it often is called a **case history**.

Applications of the Case Study Design

The case study design is most commonly used in clinical psychology. However, the case study has a long history of successful application throughout the behavioral sciences. Although group studies probably offer a more direct path to discovering general laws of behavior, it can also be argued that group studies are necessarily limited because they overlook the importance of the individual. By highlighting individual variables, case studies can offer valuable insights that complement and expand the general truths obtained from groups. In some instances, case studies can lead directly to general laws or theories. The developmental theories of Jean Piaget, for example, are largely based on detailed observations of his own children. The following sections identify specific applications of the case study design.

Rare Phenomena and Unusual Clinical Cases

The case study design is often used to provide researchers with information concerning rare or unusual phenomena such as multiple personality, a dissociative disorder in which two or more distinct personalities exist within the same individual. Although multiple personality is fairly common in television and popular fiction, it is actually an extremely rare condition. With a disorder this rare, it is essentially impossible to gather a group of individuals to participate in any kind of experimental investigation. As a result, most of what is known about multiple personality and its treatment comes from case studies. One of the most famous cases involved a relatively quiet and humble 25-year-old woman (Eve White) who also exhibited a more playful and mischievous personality (Eve Black), as well as a more mature and confident personality (Jane) (Thigpen & Cleckley, 1954, 1957). You may recognize this highly publicized case study by the title of the 1957 publication, *The Three Faces of Eve.*

Unique or unusual examples of individuals with brain injuries are often used to help identify the underlying neurological mechanisms for human memory and mental processing. A classic example is the case study of a patient identified as H. M. (Scoville & Milner, 1957). In an attempt to control severe epileptic seizures, H. M.'s hippocampus was surgically severed in both the left and right hemispheres of the brain. After surgery, H. M. had normal memory of events that occurred prior to surgery and his overall intelligence was unchanged. In addition, his immediate memory (short-term memory) also appeared to function normally. For example, he could repeat a string of digits, such as a telephone number. However, H. M. had lost the ability to permanently store any new information in memory. You could introduce yourself and talk briefly with H. M., then leave the room while he was occupied with some other task; when you returned to the room after only a few minutes, H. M. would have no memory of ever having met you and no memory of your conversation. In general, H. M. was unable to learn any new information presented to him after the surgery. This remarkable case study completely changed the way psychologists think about memory. Prior to the H. M. case, psychologists tended to view memory as a location in the brain. Now, memory is viewed as a process. H. M.'s injury did not destroy any specific memories; instead it seems to have disrupted a process. As a consequence of the study of H. M.'s case, evidence was provided that the hippocampus appears to play a crucial role in the process by which our current experiences are transformed into permanent memories. Finally, we should note that the initials H. M. were used in research reports to protect the identity of Henry Molaison, whose name was revealed when he died in December 2008 (Bhattacharjee, 2008). Over a period of more than 50 years, Mr. Molaison participated in hundreds of research studies examining human learning and memory.

New Therapy Methods or Applications

A case study can be a means of presenting the successful application of a new therapy technique or the application of an existing technique in a new area. In particular, it is not necessary to perform a long series of complicated clinical trials with hundreds of patients if you can provide one convincing, detailed example of a successful therapy procedure.

One example is a case study demonstrating a novel approach for treating the eating disorder anorexia nervosa (Glasofer, Albano, Simpson, & Steinglass, 2016). The researchers added exposure therapy to the regular treatment for one woman with anorexia nervosa. Exposure therapy is an established, effective treatment for anxiety disorders and involves exposing the patient to the feared object in a safe, controlled situation to help their anxiety. Although anxiety disorders and eating disorders are normally viewed as two distinct illnesses, the researchers noted that many people who had been successfully treated for anorexia nervosa still used various food rituals to help control their fears about food and how it could affect their weight. If food anxiety is commonly associated with anorexia, then adding an anxiety therapy to the standard anorexia therapy makes sense. The researchers used the case study to demonstrate that the combination therapy was effective.

Strengths and Weaknesses of the Case Study Design

One of the primary strengths of a case study is the intense detail that is typically included. A case study exposes a wide variety of different variables, events, and responses that would probably be overlooked or deliberately eliminated (controlled) in an experiment. Thus, a case study can identify or suggest new variables that might account for a particular outcome and can thereby generate hypotheses for future research.

Case studies provide researchers with a good opportunity to identify special situations or unique variables that can modify a general treatment effect. For example, a specific treatment may be especially effective (or ineffective) in specific situations or with specific individuals. There are very few absolute laws of behavior; most have exceptions, limitations, and qualifications, and often the qualifiers are discovered in case studies.

One final strength of the case study strategy is that case studies can be extremely powerful and convincing. The detailed description in a case study tends to make it more personal, more vivid, and more emotional than the "cold" facts and figures that result from a traditional laboratory study. These factors have all been demonstrated to have a strong, positive effect on memory (Tversky & Kahneman, 1973), suggesting that case studies may be more memorable and have a greater effect than experiments. As an analogy, consider your own response to witnessing an automobile accident versus reading an article on accident statistics. Witnessing one accident usually has more influence than reading a statistical summary of all the accidents across the state during the past year. In addition, case studies are typically descriptions of the everyday work of clinicians. This fact gives a case study a sense of realism that can be lacking in an "artificial" laboratory study. As a result, case studies often have an appearance of credibility and a degree of acceptance that far exceed a more objective evaluation of their true levels of internal and external validity.

Like all descriptive designs, the case study is necessarily limited because it simply describes and does not attempt to identify the underlying mechanisms that explain behavior. For example, a case study can provide a detailed description of the individual participant's characteristics (age, gender, family background, and the like), but it provides no means of determining how these variables influence the participant's response to treatment. A case study can tell how a specific individual with specific characteristics responded to a specific treatment, but it cannot explain why. Although a case study may offer an explanation for the observed results, alternative explanations are always possible. In research terminology, case studies lack internal validity.

In addition to lacking internal validity, case studies also tend to be weak in external validity. Because a case study reports results for a single individual in a specific situation, it is difficult to justify generalizing the results to other individuals in other situations. It is always possible that a case study concerns a unique event in the life of a unique person, and there is no reason to expect the same outcome outside the confines of the study. Again, this threat can be tempered by the extent and detail of description within the study. If the study describes a relatively typical client and a relatively straightforward treatment procedure, there is good reason to expect the results to generalize to a broader population. On the other hand, if the case includes odd or unusual circumstances, a strange historical background, bizarre behaviors, or a uniquely individualized treatment program, it is less likely that the results will generalize beyond the specific case being described.

Finally, case studies can suffer from bias that distorts or obscures the results and interpretations, and thus, threaten internal validity. First, there is always a degree of selective bias that determines which cases are reported and which are not. Obviously, a researcher is likely

TABLE 13.3

A Summary of the Strengths and Weaknesses of the Case Study Research Design

Strengths	Weaknesses
Not averaged over a diverse group	Limited generalization
Detailed description	Potential for selective bias
Vivid, powerful, convincing	Potential for subjective interpretation
Compatible with clinical work	
Can study rare and unusual events	
Can identify exceptions to the rule	

to report the most successful or dramatic case. It is unlikely that a researcher would write a detailed report (and that a journal would publish the report) of an elaborate new treatment that has absolutely no effect. More subtle biases can operate within a reported case study. Remember, a case study consists of observations made by the researcher. These observations are subject to interpretations, impressions, and inferences. In general, the reports of participants are filtered through the researcher who decides what is important and what is not. In addition, the client may provide a biased or falsified report. Clients may exaggerate, minimize, lie about, or simply imagine events that are reported to a clinician/researcher.

Although case studies are exposed to serious threats to both internal and external validity and are subject to bias, many of these problems are reduced by replication. A case study rarely exists by itself but rather is accompanied by several similar reports. Repeated examples of the same basic finding by different researchers with different clients clearly helps bolster the validity and the credibility of the results. Table 13.3 summarizes the strengths and weaknesses of the case study research design.

LEARNING CHECK

1. Which of the following accurately describes the idiographic approach to research?
   a. Direct observation of individuals without their knowledge
   b. Interviewing people in a small group setting
   © The intensive study of one individual
   d. The study of groups
2. Which of the following is typically examined in case study?
   a. A single disease or psychiatric disorder
   b. A single clinical treatment
   c. A single group such as a fraternity or an athletic team
   ⓓ A single individual
3. What kind of research was used to study the brain surgery patient H. M. who lost the ability to store new memories?
   a. Participant observation
   b. Naturalistic observation
   c. Correlational research
   ⓓ Case study research

Answers appear at the end of the chapter.

CHAPTER SUMMARY

At this point, you should review the learning objectives presented at the beginning of each section and be sure that you have mastered each objective.

The goal of the descriptive research strategy is to describe the variables being examined as they exist naturally. Three different types of descriptive research designs were discussed: observational research, survey research, and case study research.

In the observational research design, researchers observe behaviors for the purpose of describing behaviors. There are three kinds of observation. In naturalistic observation, a researcher tries as unobtrusively as possible to observe behavior in a natural setting. Although the results of naturalistic observation have high external validity, a major weakness is the time it takes to conduct such research. Participant observation is used in situations in which inconspicuous observation is not possible; instead, the researcher interacts with the participants to observe and record behaviors. Participant observation allows researchers to observe behaviors not usually open to scientific observation; however, it, too, is time-consuming. In contrived observation, the observer sets up a situation that is likely to produce the behaviors to be observed. A major strength of the observational research design is that the researcher observes and records actual behaviors.

In the survey research design, we describe people's responses to questions about behaviors and attitudes. The four most common methods for administering a survey are Internet surveys, mail surveys, telephone surveys, and in-person surveys and interviews; each has strengths and weaknesses. Surveys are relatively easy to administer and can be used to obtain information about a wide variety of different variables. However, major weaknesses of survey research include low response rates, nonresponse bias, and the self-report nature of the design.

In case study research, a single individual is described in great detail. Case studies can be used to provide information about rare and unusual behaviors, and to demonstrate new treatment methods or applications. Furthermore, case studies can suggest new variables that might account for a particular outcome and thereby generate hypotheses for future research. However, case studies tend to be weak in both internal and external validity.

Overall, the descriptive research strategy is extremely useful as preliminary research and is valuable in its own right as a source of basic knowledge. However, the strategy is simply intended to provide a description of behavior and does not examine causal factors.

KEY WORDS

observational research design

content analysis

archival research

naturalistic observation, or nonparticipant observation

participant observation

contrived observation, or structured observation

survey research design

case study design

case history

EXERCISES

The exercises are identified with specific learning objectives and are intended to assess your mastery of the objectives. You should be aware that exam items are also generated to assess learning objectives.

1. In addition to the key words, you should also be able to define each of the following terms:

   descriptive research strategy
   behavioral observation

   habituation
   behavior categories
   inter-rater reliability
   frequency method
   duration method
   interval method
   time sampling
   event sampling
   individual sampling

Likert scale
anchors
response set
nonresponse bias
interviewer bias
idiographic approach
nomothetic approach

2. (**LO1**) In this chapter, we introduced the observational research design, the survey research design, and the case study research design as examples of the descriptive research strategies. What differentiates these three designs from other research that uses behavioral observation, surveys, or case studies to obtain measurements?

3. (**LO2**) What is the purpose for determining a set of behavior categories and creating a list of specific behaviors to define each category before making behavioral observations.

4. (**LO3**) Describe how time, event, or individual sampling is done during behavioral observation, and explain why sampling may be necessary?

5. (**LO4**) Define content analysis, and explain how it is different from regular behavioral observational.

6. (**LO5**) Explain the distinction between naturalistic observation and participant observation, and describe the situations in which participant observation may be particularly useful.

7. (**LO5**) Explain the distinction between naturalistic observation and contrived observation, and describe the situations in which contrived observation may be particularly useful.

8. (**LO5** and **6**) What is the general advantage of using the survey research design instead of the observational design? In the same context, what is the disadvantage of survey research?

9. (**LO1** and **6**) Each of the following research studies uses a survey as a method for collecting data. However, not all of the studies are examples of the *survey research design.* Based on the information provided for each study, (a) indicate whether it is or is not an example of the survey research design and (b) briefly explain the reason for your answer.

a. Based on a survey of 12,344 U.S. college students and 6,729 Canadian college students, Kuo et al. (2002) report that alcohol use is more common among Canadian than U.S. students, but heavy drinking (five or more drinks in a row for males, four or more for females) is significantly higher among U.S. students than Canadian students.

b. To examine adolescent substance abuse, Li, Pentz, and Chou (2002) surveyed 1,807 middle school students from 57 schools. The results showed that a greater risk of adolescent substance abuse was associated with increasing numbers of parents and friends who were substance abusers. However, friends' use did not affect adolescent substance abuse when parents were nonusers.

c. Wolak, Mitchell, and Finkelhor (2002) used a survey of 1,501 adolescents to examine online relationships. The results showed that 14% reported close online friendships during the past year, 7% reported face-to-face meetings with online friends, and 2% reported romantic online relationships.

10. (**LO7**) Define the three types of survey questions (open-ended, restricted, and rating-scale) and identify the relative strengths and weaknesses of each.

11. (**LO8**) Outline the major advantages and disadvantages of administering a survey by mail.

12. (**LO9**) Most research in the behavioral sciences involves gathering information from a group of participants. However, the case study design focuses on a single individual. Under what circumstances is the case study approach preferred to a group design?

LEARNING CHECK ANSWERS

Section 13.1
1. a, 2. b

Section 13.2
1. a, 2. b, 3. c, 4. b

Section 13.3
1. b, 2. b, 3. b

Section 13.4
1. c, 2. d, 3. d

Single-Case Experimental Research Designs

© Nathan Jasowiak / Shutterstock

CHAPTER LEARNING OBJECTIVES

LO1 Describe the goal of single-case research and explain how single-case designs are related to other experimental designs, the descriptive case study, and the quasi-experimental time-series design.

LO2 Identify the basic elements of a single-case experimental research design that make it a true experiment: manipulation and control (including baseline observations, multiple and stable observations, and replication of treatment effects).

LO3 Describe the purpose of a phase in a single-case design and explain how patterns within a phase are defined, including the importance of stability of data.

LO4 Explain how researchers identify a "significant" difference between two phases in a single-case study.

LO5 Describe the structure of an ABAB reversal design and explain how the results from this design can demonstrate a cause-and-effect relationship.

LO6 Identify the strengths and weaknesses of an ABAB reversal design and describe the circumstances in which it should or should not be used.

LO7 Explain the circumstances in which an ABAB reversal design should be modified to create a more complex phase-change design and identify some options for the modification.

LO8 Describe the structure of a multiple-baseline design and explain how the results from this design can demonstrate a cause-and-effect relationship.

LO9 Identify and describe the component-analysis design and describe the circumstances in which it is used.

LO10 Identify the strengths and weaknesses of a multiple-baseline design and describe the circumstances in which it should or should not be used.

LO11 Identify the general advantages and disadvantages of single-case designs compared to traditional group designs.

CHAPTER OVERVIEW

Disruptive behavior is a common problem that interferes with education and learning, especially in elementary classrooms. However, a recently developed intervention, known as tootling, has proven to be effective in reducing disruptions and promoting academic engagement (McHugh, Tingstrom, Radley, Barry, & Walker, 2016). The opposite of tattling, tootling involves students reporting examples of positive behaviors by their classmates. The researchers identified a few individual target students who were regular disruptors. Disruptive behaviors were recorded for the target students for several days before the tootling intervention was started. The concept of tootling was explained to the class, and the students were given a target number of tootles to be reached each day. For several days following the intervention, the target students were monitored and disruptive behaviors were recorded. Next, the tootling program was withdrawn, the amount of tootling decreased, and the researchers recorded disruptive behaviors for several more days. Finally, the tootling program was restored, and disruptive behaviors were recorded again for the final stage of the study. Figure 14.1 shows the pattern of results for one of the targeted students. Clearly, disruptive behaviors were substantially reduced during the tootling periods as compared to the initial baseline period and the withdrawal portion of the

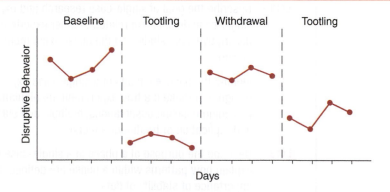

FIGURE 14.1

Simplified Data Showing the Pattern of Results Obtained by McHugh, Tingstrom, Radley, Barry, and Walker (2016)

The graphs show a noticeable decrease in disruptive behaviors when tootling periods as compared to the initial baseline period and the withdrawal portion of the study.

study. In this chapter, we discuss in detail this unique type of experimental research: the single-case design. We discuss the general characteristics of this design, as well as the evaluation of the data it produces. We consider different types of single-case designs, followed by the general strengths and weaknesses of this type of design.

14.1   Introduction

LEARNING OBJECTIVES

LO1   Describe the goal of single-case research and explain how single-case designs are related to other experimental designs, the descriptive case study, and the quasi-experimental time-series design.

LO2   Identify the basic elements of a single-case experimental research design that make it a true experiment: manipulation and control (including baseline observations, multiple and stable observations, and replication of treatment effects).

Single-case designs, or **single-subject designs**, are experimental research designs that can be used with only one participant (or subject) in the entire research study. We use the term *experimental* to describe these single-case designs because the designs presented in this chapter allow researchers to identify relatively unambiguous cause-and-effect relationships between variables. Although these designs can also be used with a small number of participants, their particular advantage is that they allow researchers to conduct experiments in situations where a single individual is available or is being treated, observed, and measured. This option is especially valuable when researchers want to obtain cause-and-effect answers in applied situations. For example, a clinician would like to demonstrate that a specific treatment actually causes a client to make changes in behavior, or a school psychologist would like to demonstrate that a counseling program really helps a student in academic difficulty.

DEFINITION

> **Single-case designs**, or **single-subject designs**, are experimental research designs that use the results from a single participant or subject to establish the existence of cause-and-effect relationships. To qualify as experiments, these designs must include manipulation of an independent variable and control of extraneous variables to prevent alternative explanations for the research results.

Historically, most single-case designs were developed by behaviorists examining operant conditioning. The behavior of a single subject (usually a laboratory rat) was observed, and changes in behavior were noted while the researcher manipulated the stimulus or reinforcement conditions. Although clinicians have adopted the designs, their application is still largely behavioral, especially in the field of applied behavior analysis (previously called behavior modification). Despite this strong association with behaviorism, however, single-case research is not tied directly to any single theoretical perspective and is available as a research tool for general application.

The goal of single-case research, as with other experimental designs, is to identify cause-and-effect relationships between variables. In common application, this means demonstrating that a treatment (variable 1) implemented or manipulated by the researcher causes a change in the participant's responses (variable 2). Although single-case studies are experimental, their general methodology incorporates elements of descriptive case studies and quasi-experimental time-series designs (see Chapters 13 and 10, respectively). Like a case study, single-case research focuses on a single individual and allows a detailed description of the observations and experiences related to that unique individual. Like time-series research, the single-case approach involves a series of observations made over time. Usually, a set of observations made before treatment is contrasted with a set of observations made during or after treatment. Although single-case designs are similar to descriptive case studies and quasi-experimental time-series studies, the designs discussed in this chapter are capable of demonstrating cause-and-effect relationships and, therefore, are true experimental designs.

Critical Elements of a Single-Case Experimental Design

As we noted in Chapter 7, the goal of any experimental research design is to demonstrate the existence of a cause-and-effect relationship between two variables. That is, an experiment must demonstrate that changes in one variable are directly responsible for causing changes in a second variable. To accomplish this goal, all experiments have two distinct basic elements:

1. Manipulation
2. Control

Single-case experimental studies always involve manipulation of one variable. Researchers determine exactly which treatment conditions will be compared and decide exactly when the treatment is changed from one condition to another. Control of other variables is achieved with a combination of three components in all single-case designs:

1. Baseline. There is a clear measure of baseline behavior prior to administering any treatment.
2. Repeated Observations: Multiple measures are obtained during baseline and each treatment condition to ensure that outside factors are not influencing behavior until the researcher intervenes and changes to the next treatment condition. The success of a single-case design requires that the series of observations/measurements during baseline and each treatment are stable. That is, there are no large fluctuations from one observation to the next that suggest the behavior is being influenced by some factor other than the treatment condition established by the researcher.
3. Replication. If the results show a clear change in behavior when the researcher changes the treatment condition, the same change must be demonstrated a second time before the researcher can conclude that the change in treatment is responsible for *causing* the change in behavior. Specifically, the study must rule out the possibility that some other, outside variable changed at the same time that the researcher changed the treatment condition, and it is the outside variable that actually caused behavior to change. A second demonstration of the treatment effect minimizes the likelihood of a coincidental outside influence: One coincidence is possible, but two would be very unlikely.

Evaluating the Results from a Single-Case Study

Unlike other experimental methods, the results of a single-case design do not provide researchers with a set of scores from a group of participants or subjects that can be used to conduct traditional statistical tests for significance. Instead, the presentation and interpretation of results from a single-case experiment are based on visual inspection of a simple graph of the data. Figure 14.2, for example, shows hypothetical results from a study examining the effects of a behavior intervention program designed to treat the classroom-disruption behavior of a single student. The student's behavior (number of disruptions)

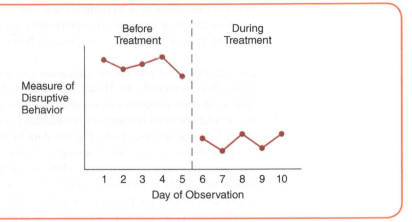

FIGURE 14.2

Data Obtained from a Single-Case Research Study

was observed and recorded for 5 days prior to implementing the treatment. In the graph, each day's observation is recorded as a single point, with the series of days presented on the horizontal axis and the magnitude of the behavior (number of disruptions) on the vertical axis. The intervention program was implemented on day 6, and the student's behavior was recorded for five additional days while the program was being administered (days 6–10 on the graph). The vertical line in the graph between days 5 and 6 indicates when the treatment was started; the five points to the left of the line are before treatment and the five points to the right are during treatment. Also notice that the individual data points are connected by straight lines to help emphasize the pattern of behavior before treatment and the change in the pattern that occurred with treatment.

The graph in Figure 14.2 appears to indicate that a substantial change in behavior occurred when the treatment program was started. However, the graph by itself is not a convincing demonstration that the treatment actually caused a change in behavior. In fact, there are two reasons for skepticism concerning the results.

1. The results as presented do not represent a true experiment because there is no control over extraneous variables. In particular, it is possible that factors other than the treatment are responsible for the apparent change in behavior. Variables outside the study such as the weather, changes in the student's family situation, or changes in the student's relationships with peers, may be responsible for causing the change in behavior. Because the study cannot measure or control all these potentially confounding variables, it is impossible to interpret the results as a clear, unambiguous demonstration of the treatment's effectiveness. To demonstrate a cause-and-effect relationship, single-case designs must demonstrate convincingly that it is the treatment, not coincidental extraneous variables, causing the changes in behavior.

2. The second problem with interpreting results such as those shown in Figure 14.2 is that the apparent difference between the before-treatment observations and the after-treatment observations may simply be the result of chance. Notice that there is variability in the day-to-day observations; this variability is a natural part of behavior and measurement. Although the results appear to suggest a pattern of higher scores before treatment and lower scores after treatment, the "pattern" may be nothing more than normal variability. You may recognize this problem as the traditional question of statistical significance.

In a traditional group design (e.g., a between-subjects or a within-subjects design), a researcher is able to obtain a precise measurement of how much difference is reasonable to expect by chance. A hypothesis test can then be used to determine whether the differences found in the data are significantly greater than the differences that are likely to occur by chance. In single-case research, however, there is no group of scores that allows a researcher to calculate the patterns that are reasonable to occur by chance alone. Instead, a researcher must rely on the appearance of the graph to convince others that the treatment effect is significant. Hence, it is essential that the obtained data be unquestionably clear so that an observer can see the treatment effect by inspecting a graph of the results. We should note that researchers occasionally do compute means to describe the treatment effect in a single-case study. For the data in Figure 14.2, for example, it is possible to compute the mean number of disruptive behaviors before treatment and compare it with the mean number after treatment. However, that mean difference only supplements what should be clearly evident from simply looking at the graph. Guidelines for inspection of single-case graphs are presented in Section 14.2.

To qualify as a true experiment, the graph must also provide convincing evidence that the treatment has *caused* a change in behavior. In Sections 14.3 and 14.4, we introduce single-case designs that produce graphs containing additional elements that clearly demonstrate cause-and-effect relationships.

14.2 | Phases and Phase Changes

LEARNING OBJECTIVES

LO3 Describe the purpose of a phase in a single-case design and explain how patterns within a phase are defined, including the importance of stability of data.

LO4 Explain how researchers identify a "significant" difference between two phases in a single-case study.

Before beginning discussion of specific single-case experimental designs, we introduce and define the general concept of a **phase**, which is the basic building block used to construct most single-case designs. A phase is a series of observations made under the same conditions. The results shown in Figure 14.2, for example, consist of two phases: the series of five observations before treatment constitutes one phase and the final five observations constitute a second phase (during treatment). In the terminology of single-case research, observations made in the absence of a treatment are called **baseline observations**, and a series of baseline observations is called a **baseline phase**. Similarly, observations made during treatment are called **treatment observations**, and a series of treatment observations is called a **treatment phase**. By convention, a baseline phase is identified by the letter *A*, and a treatment phase is usually identified by the letter *B*. Designating different phases by different letters allows researchers to describe the sequence of phases in a study by using a sequence of letters. For example, the study producing the results shown in Figure 14.2 would be described as an AB design; that is, the study consists of a baseline phase (A) followed by a treatment phase (B).

DEFINITIONS

A **phase** is a series of observations of the same individual under the same conditions.

Baseline observations are observations made when no treatment is being administered. A series of baseline observations is called a baseline phase and is identified by the letter A.

Treatment observations are observations made when a treatment is being administered. A series of treatment observations is called a **treatment phase** and is identified by the letter B.

Although the letter B usually identifies the treatment phase of a single-case study, there are situations in which other letters may be used. Specifically, when a study contains two or more distinct treatments, B identifies the first treatment condition, and C, D, and so on identify other treatments. Also, when a study contains modifications of a basic treatment, B identifies the basic treatment, and the different modifications are called B$_1$, B$_2$, and so on. Finally, when one phase involves administering two or more treatments simultaneously, the single phase can be identified by a pair of letters representing the two different treatments. Thus, a single-case research design might be described as an A-B-B$_1$-A-BC-C design. This letter sequence indicates that the researcher first made a series of baseline observations, and then implemented a treatment (B) while continuing to make observations. Next, the researcher tried a modification of the treatment (perhaps treatment B was not effective), followed by withdrawal of all treatment (back to baseline). Then, the original treatment (B) was administered in combination with a new treatment (C) and finally, treatment C was administered by itself.

Level, Trend, and Stability

The purpose of a phase within a single-case experiment is to establish a clear picture of the participant's behavior under the specific conditions that define the phase. That is, the series of observations that make up the phase should show a clear pattern that describes the behavior. Ultimately, the researcher changes phases by implementing or withdrawing a treatment, and the goal is to show that the pattern of behavior changes from one phase to the next. Before it is possible to demonstrate a change in patterns, however, it is essential that the pattern within a phase be clearly established.

One way to define a pattern within a phase is in terms of the **level** of behavior. The term *level* simply refers to the magnitude of the participant's responses. If all of the observations within a phase indicate approximately the same magnitude, or level, of behavior, then the data have demonstrated a consistent or stable level of behavior within the phase. Figure 14.3a shows data demonstrating a stable level of behavior. Although there are minor differences in magnitude from one observation to another, the data points generally line up at the same level of magnitude. Notice that the concept of a stable level simply means that the data points within a phase tend to form a horizontal line on the graph.

An alternative way to define a pattern within a phase is in terms of a **trend**. The term *trend* refers to a consistent increase (or a consistent decrease) in the magnitude of behavior across the series of observations that make up the phase. Figure 14.3b shows data demonstrating a consistent or stable trend in behavior. Again, notice that the data points tend to form a relatively straight line, but now the line slopes upward to the right, indicating a consistent increase in the magnitude of behavior over time.

Thus, the pattern within a phase can be described in terms of level or trend. In either case, however, the critical factor is the consistency of the pattern. Remember that single-case research does not use statistical analysis to summarize or interpret the results but depends on the visual appearance of the data in a graph. To establish that a treatment causes a change in behavior, for example, the graph must show a clear change in the pattern of behavior as the participant moves from a baseline phase to a treatment phase. Therefore, it is essential that the graph show a clear picture that establishes an unambiguous pattern (either a level or a trend) within each phase. In the terminology of single-case research, the critical factor is the **stability** of the data. When the data points form a straight line with only minor deviations, the data are said to be stable, and the pattern is easy to see. Note that the data points do not have to form a perfectly straight line to be considered stable; some variability is allowed, but it should be relatively small.

On the other hand, if there are large differences (high variability) from one observation to the next, so that no obvious pattern emerges, the data are said to be unstable. Figure 14.3c shows unstable data. Unstable data are disastrous to the goals of single-case research. When the data points vary wildly, it is impossible to define any pattern within a phase and, therefore, it is impossible to determine whether changing the phase (e.g., implementing a treatment) produces any change in the pattern.

FIGURE 14.3

Three Patterns of Results for the Data from One Phase in a Single-Case Research Study

(a) A stable level, (b) a stable trend, and (c) unstable data.

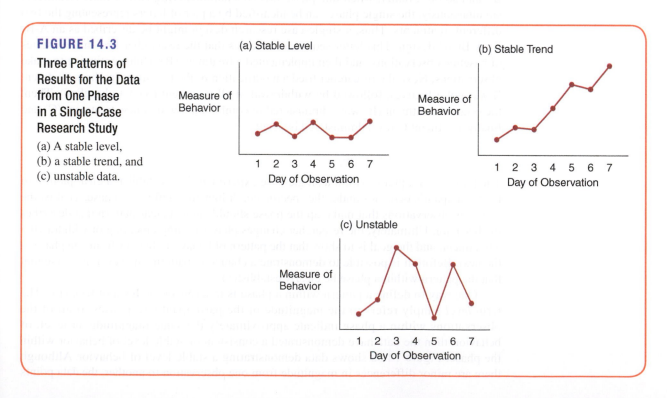

DEFINITIONS

A consistent **level** occurs when a series of measurements are all approximately the same magnitude. In a graph, the series of data points cluster around a horizontal line.

A consistent **trend** occurs when the differences from one measurement to the next are consistently in the same direction and are approximately of the same magnitude. In a graph the series of data points cluster around a sloping line.

The **stability** of a set of observations refers to the degree to which the observations show a pattern of consistent level or consistent trend. Stable data may show minor variations from a perfectly consistent pattern, but the variations should be relatively small and the linear pattern relatively clear.

Dealing with Unstable Data

Usually, behavior is fairly consistent over time, which means that a series of observations shows a consistent pattern (either a consistent level or consistent trend in behavior). Where data appear to be unstable, however, researchers can employ several techniques to help uncover a consistent pattern.

1. First, the researcher can simply wait; that is, keep making observations and hope that the data will stabilize and reveal a clear pattern. Occasionally, a participant reacts unpredictably to the novelty of being observed. When this happens, the first few days of observation are distorted by the participant's reactivity and may appear unstable. After several days, however, the novelty wears off, participants habituate to being observed, and they return to normal, consistent behavior.

2. A second method for stabilizing data is simply to average a set of two (or more) observations. Figure 14.4a shows a set of observations made over a 10-day period. Notice that the large, day-to-day differences produce a relatively unstable set of data. Figure 14.4b shows the same data after they have been smoothed by averaging over two-day periods. To create Figure 14.4b, the first two days' observations were averaged to produce a single data point. Similarly, days 3 and 4 were averaged and so on. Notice that the averaging process tends to reduce the variability of the data points and produces a more stable set of data making it easier to see the pattern of behavior.

3. A final strategy for dealing with unstable data is to look for patterns within the inconsistency. For example, a researcher examining disruptive classroom behavior

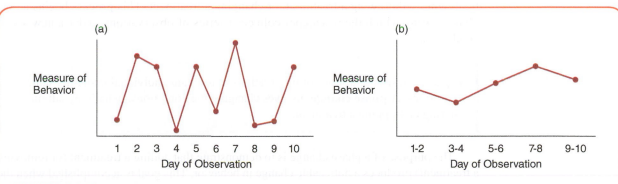

FIGURE 14.4

Stabilizing Data by Averaging over Successive Data Points

(a) The original unstable data. (b) The results of averaging over 2-day periods.

may find that a student exhibits very high levels of disruption on some days and very low levels on other days. Although the data appear to be very unstable, closer examination reveals that the high levels tend to occur on Mondays, Wednesdays, and Fridays, and the low levels are observed on Tuesdays and Thursdays. The obvious question is "Why are Tuesdays and Thursdays different?" Checking the class schedule reveals that the student is in gym class immediately prior to the Tuesday/Thursday observation periods. Perhaps the exercise in gym allows the student to burn off excess energy and results in more subdued behavior. The researcher could try changing the time of observation to early morning to eliminate the influence of the gym class. Or the researcher could simply limit the data to observation made on the nongym days. In general, unstable data may be caused by extraneous variables; it is often possible to stabilize the data by identifying and controlling them.

Length of a Phase

To establish a pattern (level or trend) within a phase and to determine the stability of the data within a phase, a phase must consist of a minimum of three observations. You may have noticed that the graphs in Figure 14.3 were constructed so that the first two data points are identical in all three graphs. In Figure 14.3a, the difference between the first two observations is simply minor variation that eventually becomes part of a consistent level. In Figure 14.3b, the difference signifies the beginning of a consistent trend, and in Figure 14.3c, the difference between the two points is part of an unstable set of data. Our point is that the first two observations, by themselves, do not provide enough information to determine a pattern. Additional observations beyond the first two are essential to establish level, trend, and stability. Although three data points are the absolute minimum for determining a phase, typically five or six observations are necessary to determine a clear pattern. However, when high variability exists in the data points, additional observations should be made. In general, there is no single number that defines the optimal length for a phase. Instead, the length of a phase is determined by the number of data points needed to establish a clear and stable pattern in the data.

Changing Phases

After a researcher has obtained the necessary data points to establish a clear and stable pattern within a phase, it is possible to initiate a **phase change**. A phase change is essentially a manipulation of the independent variable and is accomplished by implementing a treatment, withdrawing a treatment, or changing a treatment. This process begins a new phase, during which the researcher collects a series of observations under a new set of conditions.

DEFINITION

> A phase consists of a series of observations of the same individual under the same conditions. A **phase change** involves changing the conditions, usually by administering or stopping a treatment.

The purpose of a phase change is to demonstrate that adding a treatment (or removing a treatment) produces a noticeable change in behavior. This goal is accomplished when the data show a clear difference between the pattern that exists before the phase change and the pattern that exists after the phase change. For example, a dramatic drop in the level of behavior when the treatment is started (phase change) is evidence that the treatment has an effect on behavior.

Deciding When to Change Phases

As we have discussed, the primary factor determining when a new phase should be started is the emergence of a clear pattern within the preceding phase. However, there are several other factors that can influence the decision concerning when and if a phase change is appropriate.

The first consideration involves changing from a baseline phase to a treatment phase. When the data in a baseline phase show a trend indicating improvement in the client's behavior, a researcher should not intervene by introducing a treatment phase. There are two good reasons for this no-action strategy; one clinical and one experimental. From a clinical point of view, if the client is already showing improvement, the simplest and safest decision is to stand back and let the improvement run its course. The client's improvement indicates that there is no need for immediate intervention. From an experimental perspective, initiating a treatment when the participant is already showing a trend toward improvement can only result in ambiguous results. Specifically, if a treatment is started and the participant continues to improve, the researcher cannot determine whether the continued improvement is caused by the treatment or is simply the continuation of an established trend. Because the results cannot be interpreted as a clear demonstration of the treatment's effect, the experiment is compromised.

Another possibility is that the baseline data indicate a seriously high level of dangerous or threatening behavior. In this case, a researcher probably should not wait for the full set of five or six observations necessary to establish a clear pattern. Instead, the researcher/clinician has an ethical obligation to begin treatment immediately (after one or two observations). After the behavior is brought under control during a treatment phase, the researcher can consider resuming the experiment by changing back to a baseline (no-treatment) phase or by introducing a different treatment phase.

It is also possible that the data within a treatment phase can dictate a premature phase change. If, for example, a treatment appears to produce an immediate and severe deterioration in behavior, the researcher/clinician should stop, change, or modify the treatment immediately without waiting for a clear pattern to emerge.

In general, the decision to make a phase change is based on the participant's responses. If the responses establish a clear pattern, then a change is appropriate. If the responses indicate a serious problem, then a change is necessary. In either case, the step-by-step progress of the experiment is controlled by the participant and does not necessarily follow a predetermined plan developed by the researcher. This aspect of single-case research creates a very flexible and adaptive research strategy that is particularly well suited to clinical application. We return to this point later when the strengths and weaknesses of single-case designs are discussed in Section 14.6.

Visual Inspection Techniques

In very general terms, the goal of single-case research is to demonstrate that manipulation of one variable (the treatment) causes a change in a second variable (the participant's behavior). More specifically, the goal is to demonstrate that the pattern of behavior established in a baseline phase changes to a different pattern when the researcher switches to a treatment phase. Because the interpretation of the experimental results depends entirely on the visual appearance of a graph, it is important that the change in pattern from baseline to treatment be easy to see when the results are presented in a graph. The most convincing results occur when the change in pattern is immediate and large.

Unfortunately, there are no absolute, objective standards for determining how much of a change in pattern is sufficient to provide a convincing demonstration of a treatment effect. The visual inspection of single-case data is very much a subjective task, and different observers often interpret data in different ways, that is, there is often disagreement about particular data patterns (Normand & Bailey, 2006; Stewart, Carr, Brandt, & McHenry, 2007). Nonetheless, there are guidelines that focus attention on specific aspects of the data and help observers decide whether a phase change produced a real change in pattern. Kazdin (2016) has identified four specific characteristics of single-case data that help determine whether there is a meaningful change between phases.

1. *Change in average level.* Although statistical means and variances are typically not computed for single-case data, the average level of behavior during a phase provides a simple and understandable description of the behavior within the phase. Figure 14.5 shows hypothetical data from a single-case design for which the average level for each phase is indicated by a dashed line. Notice that the data show clear differences in the average level from one phase to another. In general, large differences in the average level are a good indication that there is a real difference between phases.

2. *Immediate change in level.* Another indicator of a difference between phases is the initial response of the participant to the change. This involves comparing the last data point in one phase with the first data point in the following phase. A large difference between these two points is a good indication that the participant showed an immediate response to the addition (or removal) of the treatment. In Figure 14.5, for example, the data show a large difference between the final score in the first baseline phase and the first score in the first treatment phase. Apparently, the participant showed an immediate reaction when the treatment was introduced.

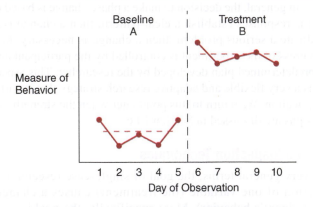

FIGURE 14.5

Data Showing a Change in Average Level from One Phase to the Next

The horizontal dashed lines in each phase correspond to the average level. A clear difference between averages is a good indication of a real difference between phases. Also note the large difference between the final point in the baseline phase and the first point in the treatment phase. This difference also indicates that the participant's behavior changed when the treatment was introduced.

FIGURE 14.6

Two Examples of a Clear Change in Trend from One Phase to the Next

(a) A clear change from no trend (consistent level) to an increasing trend.

(b) A reversal in trend from increasing to decreasing.

(a)

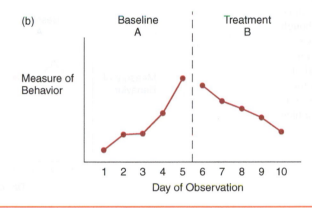

(b)

3. *Change in trend.* When the trend observed in one phase is noticeably different from the trend in the previous phase, it is a clear indication of a difference between phases. Figure 14.6 demonstrates changes in trend. Figure 14.6a shows a change from no trend (consistent level) to a clear, increasing trend. The data in Figure 14.6b are even more convincing. Here, the trends change direction from increasing to decreasing. Again, clear changes in trend are evidence of a real difference between phases.

4. *Latency of change.* The most convincing evidence for a difference between phases occurs when the data show a large, immediate change in pattern. A delay between the time the phase is changed and the time behavior begins to change undermines the credibility of a cause-and-effect explanation. Figure 14.7 shows two examples of a baseline-to-treatment phase change. In Figure 14.7a, the data show an immediate change in behavior when the treatment is introduced, providing clear evidence that the treatment is affecting behavior. In Figure 14.7b, however, there is no immediate change in behavior. Although there is an eventual change in behavior, it does not occur until several sessions after the treatment starts. In this case, the data do not provide unambiguous evidence that the treatment is causing the changes in behavior.

FIGURE 14.7

Latency of Change Affects Interpretation

(a) An immediate change in trend when treatment is introduced. This pattern provides good evidence that the treatment is influencing behavior.
(b) The behavior remains at the baseline level for several days after the treatment is introduced. Although the behavior does eventually show a decreasing trend, it is not clear that the decrease occurs as a result of the treatment.

(a)

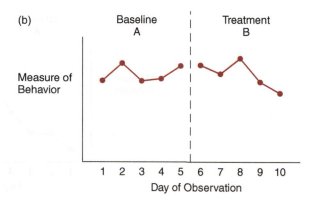

(b)

LEARNING CHECK

1. In a single-case design, what is the series of observations called when no treatment is being administered?
   a. No-treatment phase
   b. Baseline phase
   c. Treatment observations
   d. None of the above

2. Which of the following is the definition of a treatment phase?
   a. A series of observations made when a treatment is being administered
   b. The first observation made after a treatment is administered
   c. The amount of change between the final observation before treatment and the first observation after treatment
   d. The boundary between pretreatment and posttreatment observations

3. How are the results from a single-case study typically evaluated?
   a. Descriptive statistics such as the mean and standard deviation
   b. Inferential statistics such as a hypothesis test
   c. Visual inspection of a graph
   d. Consensus among at least three researchers

Answers appear at the end of the chapter.

Reversal Designs: ABAB and Variations

LEARNING OBJECTIVES

LO5 Describe the structure of an ABAB reversal design and explain how the results from this design can demonstrate a cause-and-effect relationship.

LO6 Identify the strengths and weaknesses of an ABAB reversal design and describe the circumstances in which it should or should not be used.

LO7 Explain the circumstances in which an ABAB reversal design should be modified to create a more complex phase-change design and identify some options for the modification.

We have introduced the concept of a phase as the basic building block of most single-case experiments. A specific research design, therefore, consists of a sequence of phases that can be represented by a sequence of letters (e.g., ABB_1AC). Because each unique sequence of letters represents a unique experimental design, the number of potential designs is essentially unlimited. We address the issue of complex designs later in this section. For now, we focus on one type of single-case experimental design, the **reversal design**. In a reversal design, phase changes alternate between baseline and treatment phases, and are done over time in a single individual. The most common form of the reversal design is the **ABAB design**.

As the letters indicate, the ABAB design consists of four phases: a baseline phase (A), followed by treatment (B), then a withdrawal of treatment which is a return (or reversal) to baseline (A), and finally a repetition of the treatment phase (B). The goal of the ABAB design is to demonstrate that the treatment causes a change in behavior by showing that:

- The pattern of behavior in each treatment phase is clearly different from the pattern in each baseline phase. This demonstration is necessary to establish a relationship between the treatment and the behavior.
- The changes in behavior from baseline to treatment and from treatment to baseline are the same for each of the phase-change points in the experiment. This demonstration is necessary to establish a causal relationship between treatment and behavior. That is, the results demonstrate that the researcher can cause the behavior to turn on and off simply by starting and stopping the treatment.

DEFINITIONS

A **reversal design** consists of a series of phases including a baseline phase followed by a treatment phase and at least one replication of a baseline followed by a treatment.

The **ABAB design** is the most commonly used reversal design and consists of four phases: a baseline phase, a treatment phase, a return-to-baseline phase, and a second treatment phase. The goal of the design is to demonstrate that the treatment causes changes in the participant's behavior.

The single-case ABAB design is used in the tootling example discussed at the beginning of the chapter. The pattern of results obtained in the study was shown in Figure 14.1 and is repeated here in Figure 14.8a. Close examination of the graph reveals the elements that make it possible to infer a causal relationship between the treatments and the changes in behavior.

1. The first phase change (baseline to treatment) shows a clear change in the pattern of behavior. This first change by itself simply demonstrates that a behavior change accompanies the treatment. At this point, we cannot conclude that the treatment has caused the change in behavior, because some extraneous variable that changed coincidentally with the treatment might be responsible for changing the behavior. It is possible, for example, that, on the same day when the treatment was first introduced, the participant woke up feeling much better after suffering with a cold for the previous week. If so, it could be that the change in behavior was caused by the change in health rather than the treatment.

2. The second phase change (treatment to baseline) shows the participant's behavior returning to the same level observed during the initial baseline phase. This component of the experiment is often called the *reversal*, or *return to baseline*. The reversal component is important because it begins to establish the causal relationship between the treatment and behavior. Although the participant's behavior may have been influenced by extraneous variables at the first phase change, it now appears more likely that the treatment (not extraneous variables) is responsible for the change. Behavior changed when the treatment was introduced, and behavior reverted back to baseline when the treatment was withdrawn. During the return-to-baseline phase, it is not essential that behavior return to exactly the same level observed during the initial baseline. However, there must be a clear and immediate change toward the pattern established in the initial baseline phase.

3. The final phase change (baseline back to treatment) shows the same treatment effect that was observed in the initial phase change. This component of the experiment, the

FIGURE 14.8

Two Examples of Optimal Results from an ABAB Reversal Design

(a) The data show a clear change in level when the treatment is introduced, a clear return to baseline when the treatment is withdrawn, and a clear replication of the treatment effect when the treatment is reintroduced. (b) A similar pattern, except that the treatment stops the baseline trend and restores behavior to a higher, more stable level.

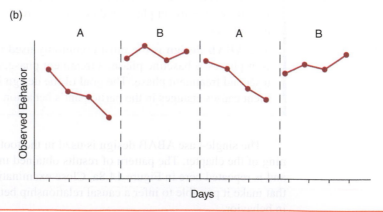

second AB in the sequence, provides a replication of the first AB. This replication clinches the argument for a causal interpretation of the results. By showing that behavior changes repeatedly when the treatment is implemented, the results minimize the likelihood that a coincidence (extraneous variables) is responsible for the changes in behavior. Although it is possible that coincidence is responsible for the first change in behavior, it is very unlikely that another coincidence occurred the second time the treatment was introduced. By using replication, the ABAB design maximizes the likelihood that the observed changes in behavior are caused by the treatment.

In Figure 14.8a, the data provide evidence for a cause-and-effect relationship by showing a change in level each time the treatment is introduced or withdrawn. It is also possible to demonstrate a cause-and-effect relationship by showing a change in trend. In Figure 14.8b, for example, the decreasing trend is stopped when the treatment is introduced. Behavior returns to the baseline trend when the treatment is withdrawn, and the stable level returns when the treatment is reintroduced.

Limitations of the ABAB Design

Like other experimental designs, the ABAB research design can establish, with good credibility, the existence of a cause-and-effect relationship between the manipulation of a treatment and corresponding changes in behavior. However, the credibility of this causal interpretation depends in large part on the reversal (return to baseline) that is a component of the design. Withdrawing treatment in the middle of the experiment can create some practical and ethical problems that can limit the application and success of this specific design.

The first issue related to the withdrawal of treatment focuses on the participant's response; withdrawing treatment may not result in a change in behavior. That is, although the researcher may return to baseline by removing the treatment, the participant's behavior may not return to baseline. From a purely clinical point of view, this phenomenon is not a problem; in fact, it is an excellent outcome. The clinician has implemented a treatment that has corrected a problem behavior, and when the treatment is removed, the correction continues. In simple terms, the client is cured. From an experimental perspective, however, the credibility of the treatment effect is seriously compromised if the participant's behavior does not respond to removal of the treatment. If a manipulation of the treatment fails to produce any response in the participant, the researcher is left with doubts about the treatment's effect. One obvious consequence of this problem is that an ABAB design is not appropriate for evaluating treatments that are expected to have a permanent or long-lasting effect.

Thus far, we have discussed the failure to return to baseline as an absolute, all-or-none phenomenon. Degrees of failure are also possible. That is, the participant may show some response to the withdrawal of treatment but not a complete or immediate return to the original baseline behavior. As long as there is some noticeable response when the treatment is removed, the experiment is not severely compromised. However, the degree of credibility generally depends on the degree of the response. Large responses that produce a pattern similar to the original baseline are more convincing than small responses. In addition, the final phase of the experiment (reintroducing the treatment) provides an opportunity to reestablish the credibility of the treatment effect. If the second application of the treatment produces another clear change in behavior, the problem of a less-than-perfect return to baseline becomes less critical.

A second problem with an ABAB design concerns the ethical question of withdrawing a successful treatment. The ABAB design asks a clinician to withdraw a treatment that has been shown to be effective. Furthermore, the treatment is withdrawn with the intention of having the client's behavior revert to its original problem condition. Although this reversal component is an integral part of the ABAB design, it appears to be contrary to good clinical practice. The ethical question is compounded by the practical problem of convincing the client, therapist, and family members to agree to stop treatment. Although this problem cannot be eliminated completely, two considerations help to minimize (or rationalize) its effect. First, everyone can be reassured that the withdrawal of treatment is a temporary event; the treatment will be returned. Second, the eventual withdrawal of treatment is often a practical necessity. Eventually, the client must be released to return to a normal life. In this sense, the return-to-baseline phase can be viewed as a trial period to assess the permanence or long-term effectiveness of the treatment.

Variations on the ABAB Design: Creating More Complex Phase-Change Designs

Although researchers often begin a research study intending to use an ABAB design, circumstances that develop during the study may require adding new treatments or modifying the sequence of baseline and treatment phases. As a result, the exact sequence of baseline and treatment phases evolves during the course of the study creating an essentially unlimited number of potential designs. For example, a researcher may plan for an ABAB design but switch to a new treatment (C) when the participant fails to respond to the first treatment phase, thus creating a more complex phase-change design.

Although the number of potential phase sequences is unlimited, not every sequence qualifies as an experimental design. Remember, a true experiment should produce a reasonably unambiguous cause-and-effect explanation for the relationship between treatment and behavior. In single-case research, the experiment must show a clear change in behavior when the treatment is introduced, and it must provide at least one replication of the change. These two criteria can produce some interesting consequences in a study with two or more different treatment phases. Consider the following example.

Suppose that a researcher begins with the traditional baseline phase, and then moves to a specific treatment (B). However, the participant's responses indicate that the treatment has little or no effect, so the researcher modifies the treatment, creating a new phase (B_1). Again, there is little or no response, so a completely different treatment (C) is started. Finally, the data show a clear change in pattern, indicating that treatment C may be effective. Thus far, the sequence of phases can be described as A-B-B_1-C, and the pattern of results we have described is presented as a graph in Figure 14.9a. Although the data seem to suggest that treatment C has produced a change in behavior, there are several alternative explanations for the observed data.

- It is possible that the change in behavior is simply a coincidence caused by some extraneous variable that coincided with the beginning of treatment C.
- The change in behavior may be a delayed effect from one of the previous treatments (B or B_1). That is, treatment B or B_1 really was effective, but the effect did not become visible until several days after the treatment was administered.
- It is possible that the observed change is not the result of treatment C by itself. Instead, treatment C may be effective only when B and/or B_1 precede it. That is, either treatment B or treatment B_1 is a necessary catalyst that made the participant more receptive to treatment C.

To qualify as an experiment, the study must consider these alternatives and eventually produce one unambiguous explanation for the results. The problem for the researcher is to

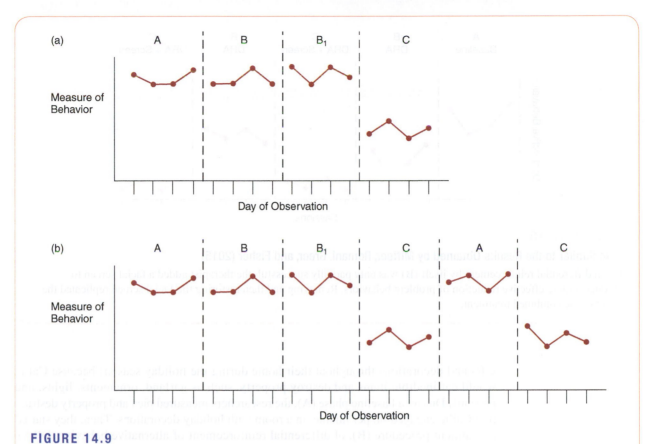

FIGURE 14.9

Hypothetical Data from a More Complex Phase-Change Design

(a) The first treatment B and its modification B$_1$ appear to have no effect; however, treatment C produces a change in level.

(b) An extension of the study by addition of a return-to-baseline phase and a replication of treatment C.

decide what to do next. One course of action is to begin a second baseline phase, hoping that the participant's behavior returns to baseline, then to try repeating treatment C. In symbols, the sequence of phases would become A-B-B$_1$-C-A-C. If the observed behavior replicates the patterns seen in the original A and C phases (see Figure 14.9b), you can be reasonably confident that treatment C is causing the changes. Notice that the confidence in a cause-and-effect interpretation comes from the replication of the treatment effect. In this example, treatment C was shown to be effective when it was first administered, and the demonstration of effectiveness was repeated in the final phase of the study. On the other hand, failure to replicate the original effects of treatment C would suggest that this treatment by itself is not the causal agent. In this case, the study would need to be extended to evaluate the potential of a delayed effect from one of the preceding treatments or the potential of a catalyst effect. For example, the researcher could attempt another return to baseline followed by a B$_1$-C sequence to determine whether the presence of treatment B$_1$ is a necessary prerequisite for the effectiveness of treatment C.

Mitteer, Romani, Greer, and Fisher (2015) used a complex phase change design to evaluate the treatment of pica and destruction of holiday decorations for a 6-year-old girl named Callie who was diagnosed with autism spectrum disorder. Callie's family had been unable to conduct their usual holiday celebrations for several years (e.g., have wrapped

Pica is the constant, compulsive eating of inappropriate, inedible items such as dirt or paint.

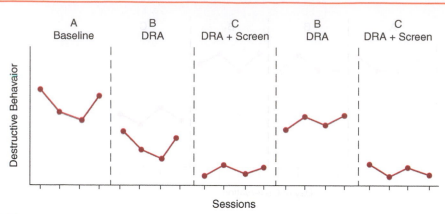

FIGURE 14.10

Data Similar to the Results Obtained by Mitteer, Romani, Greer, and Fisher (2015)

When differential reinforcement by itself (B) was only partially successful, the therapist added a facial screen to produce a more effective reduction of problem behaviors. Removing and then restoring the facial screen replicated the effect of the combined treatment.

gifts and decorations throughout their home during the holiday season) because Callie would eat inedible items and destroy property, such as garland, ornaments, lights, and presents. During a baseline phase (A), the researchers measured pica and property destruction Callie engaged in, per minute, in a room with holiday decorations. Then, they started a treatment procedure (B), of differential reinforcement of alternative behavior (DRA), which involved giving Callie an edible item each time she played with an appropriate toy. Although both problem behaviors decreased, they still persisted at unacceptable rates. At this point, the researchers added a facial screen (i.e., the therapist placed one hand over Callie's hands and one over her face, covering her eyes for 30 seconds) to the DRA treatment by creating a new phase identified as C (for the DRA treatment and the added facial screen). Adding the facial screen produced a dramatic decrease in problem behaviors. Following the C phase, the researchers removed the facial screen for several sessions (B) and then returned the facial screen to the DRA treatment (C). In symbols, this design can be described as ABCBC reversal design. Figure 14.10 shows a simplified version of the data obtained by Mitteer et al. (2015).

As you can see, a single-case design can easily grow into a complex sequence of phases before a clear cause-and-effect relationship emerges. At any time during the study, the researcher's decision concerning the next phase is determined by the pattern of responses observed during the preceding phases.

LEARNING CHECK

1. What name is given to a single-case design consisting of the following four phases in the order given: baseline, treatment, baseline, treatment?
   a. BABA design
   b. ABA design
   c. ABAB design
   d. Multiple-baseline design

2. Which of the following is an ethical concern for the ABAB design?
   a. Continuing to administer the treatment after it has already been shown to be effective
   b. Administering the treatment immediately after the initial baseline phase
   c. Removing the treatment after it has already been shown to be effective
   d. Reintroducing the treatment after it has already been shown to be effective
3. Which of the following would cause a researcher who planned to use an ABAB design to switch to a more complex phase-change design.
   a. The participant shows unstable behavior during the initial baseline.
   b. The participant shows no change in behavior when the treatment is introduced.
   c. The participant returns to baseline behavior when the treatment is removed.
   d. All of the above.

Answers appear at the end of the chapter.

14.4   Multiple-Baseline Designs

LEARNING OBJECTIVES

LO8   Describe the structure of a multiple-baseline design and explain how the results from this design can demonstrate a cause-and-effect relationship.

LO9   Identify and describe the component-analysis design and describe the circumstances in which it is used.

LO10   Identify the strengths and weaknesses of a multiple-baseline design and describe the circumstances in which it should or should not be used.

One basic problem with the single-case designs considered thus far is the reversal, or return-to-baseline, component that is essential to provide a replication of the initial treatment effect. Specifically, reversal designs require that the participant's behavior revert to baseline as soon as the treatment is removed. In addition to the ethical dilemma created by withdrawing treatment, these studies are also limited to evaluation of treatments with only a temporary effect. The **multiple-baseline design** provides an alternative technique that eliminates the need for a return to baseline and therefore is particularly well suited for evaluating treatments with long-lasting or permanent effects.

Characteristics of a Multiple-Baseline Design

A multiple-baseline design requires only one phase change—from baseline to treatment—and establishes the credibility of the treatment effect by replicating the phase change for a second participant or for a second behavior. The general plan for a multiple-baseline study is shown in Figure 14.11. The figure shows hypothetical results for a study involving two different participants, both of whom are exhibiting the same problem behavior; the top half of the figure presents data for one participant and the bottom half shows the data for the second participant. Notice that the study begins with a baseline phase with simultaneous observations, beginning at the same time, for both participants. After a baseline pattern is established for both participants, the treatment phase is initiated for one participant only. Meanwhile, the baseline phase is continued for the second participant. Finally, the treatment phase is initiated for the second participant, but at a different time from that at which treatment is begun for the first participant. Thus, this study consists of simultaneous

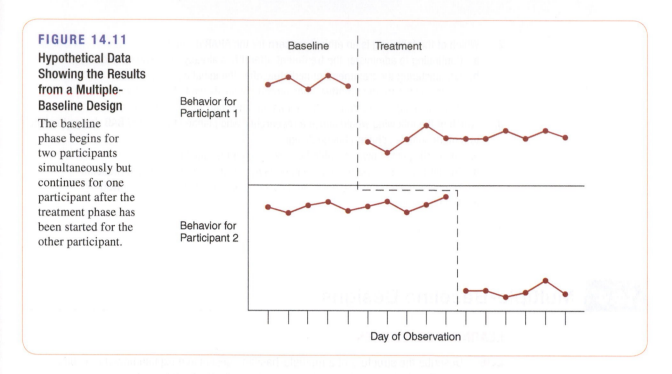

FIGURE 14.11

Hypothetical Data Showing the Results from a Multiple-Baseline Design

The baseline phase begins for two participants simultaneously but continues for one participant after the treatment phase has been started for the other participant.

observations of two participants who experience two different baseline periods before the treatment is administered. When a multiple-baseline design uses two separate participants, it is called a **multiple-baseline across subjects**.

An example of a multiple-baseline across subjects design involves relatively simple intervention intended to improve class attendance for college athletes (Bicard, Lott, Mills, Bicard, & Baylot-Casey, 2012). Part of the study involved two male athletes at an NCAA Division I university who were considered to be at high risk for academic failure and had a history of poor class attendance. For each student, the researchers monitored attendance for one class. At the beginning of the semester, the researcher recorded the time that each student arrived at the selected class. If the student was more than 30 minutes late, he was recorded as absent from class. A few weeks into the semester, each student met with an academic counselor and was asked to begin texting "in class" when he arrived at the classroom. The researchers continued to monitor arrival time to ensure that the participants were texting from the classroom. Figure 14.12 presents the pattern of results found in the study, showing the minutes late for class for each week of the semester for the two students. The vertical dashed line in the figure indicates when each student started texting his arrival in class.

Notice that both students show an abrupt change in behavior when they are required to text their arrival at class. Early in the semester, they are chronically late, but on-time attendance improves dramatically when they begin texting. Also notice that the researchers started the texting intervention at different times for the two students. This was done to help ensure that the change in behavior was caused by the texting and not by an outside influence such as a demand by the coach for better class attendance.

Unlike other single-case designs, we should note that the multiple-baseline designs across subjects require a minimum of two participants. However, we still examine the behavior of each individual, separately. Specifically, we do not consider the two participants to be a group and attempt to examine the average behavior for the group.

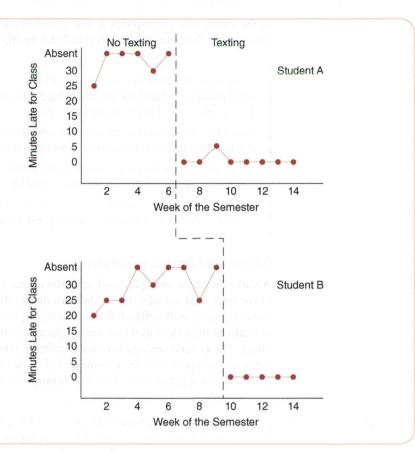

FIGURE 14.12

Simplified Data Showing the Pattern of Results Obtained by Bicard, Lott, Mills, Bicard, and Baylot-Casey (2012)

The graphs show a noticeable change in class attendance and punctuality when a school counselor asked two at-risk students to begin texting their arrival at class.

As we noted earlier, it is also possible to conduct a multiple-baseline study using two or more different behaviors for a single participant. The key to the single-case version of the design is that the different behaviors are independent (one does not influence another) and can be treated separately by focusing a treatment on one behavior at a time. For example, a student may show disruptive behavior (speaking out and interrupting) and aggressive behavior (picking on other students). Each of these problem behaviors can be treated using a behavior modification program directed specifically at the problem behavior. Or a clinical client may have several different phobias, each of which can be treated with a specific desensitization program. Note that the same treatment is used for each of the different behaviors. After clear baseline patterns are established for both behaviors, the treatment is started for one of the behaviors and baseline observations continue for the second behavior. After a short period, the treatment is started for the second behavior. The single-case design follows exactly the same pattern that was shown in Figure 14.12; however, the top half of the figure now corresponds to one behavior, and the bottom half represents the second behavior. This type of design, using two behaviors for a single participant, is called a **multiple-baseline across behaviors**.

Finally, the multiple-baseline design can be used to evaluate the treatment of one behavior that is exhibited in two different situations. For example, a child may exhibit disruptive behavior at school and at home. When it is possible to treat the two situations separately, we can begin baseline measurements for both situations simultaneously, and then administer treatment at two different times for the two different situations. As before, the design follows the same pattern that was shown in Figure 14.12; however, the top half of the figure now corresponds to one situation and the bottom half represents the second situation. In this case, the design is called a **multiple-baseline across situations**.

A **multiple-baseline design** begins with two simultaneous baseline phases. A treatment phase is initiated for one of the baselines while baseline observations continue for the other. At a later time, the treatment is initiated for the second baseline.

When the initial baseline phases correspond to the same behavior for two separate participants, the design is called a **multiple-baseline across subjects**.

When the initial baseline phases correspond to two separate behaviors for the same participant, the design is called a **multiple-baseline across behaviors**.

When the initial baseline phases correspond to the same behavior in two separate situations, the design is called a **multiple-baseline across situations**.

Component Analysis Designs

A variation of the multiple-baseline or the reversal design is used in situations where parts of the treatment are added or withdrawn during different phases. When a treatment consists of several well-defined, distinct elements, it is possible to use a phase-change design to evaluate the extent to which each separate element contributes to the overall treatment effect. The general strategy is to use a series of phases, in which each phase adds or eliminates one component of the treatment. This type of design, in which a treatment is broken down into its separate parts, is called a **component-analysis design**.

A **component-analysis design** consists of a series of phases in which each phase adds or subtracts one component of a complex treatment to determine how each component contributes to the overall treatment effectiveness.

There are two general strategies for conducting a component-analysis design. The first is to begin with a full-treatment phase (including all the different components), then remove or withdraw components one by one to see whether the effectiveness of the treatment is reduced. The second strategy is to begin with a baseline phase, then add components one by one to see how each individual component contributes to the effectiveness of the total treatment package. The process of adding or withdrawing components can be accomplished using either a reversal design or a multiple-baseline design.

Component Analysis with a Reversal Design   The key component of a reversal design is a return to baseline followed by a second demonstration of the treatment effect. The second demonstration provides a replication of the initial treatment effect and helps demonstrate that the treatment, and not some outside influence, is causing the changes in behavior. A typical study would consist of the following phases:

1. Baseline phase
2. A series of phases adding treatment components one by one
3. Return to a baseline phase
4. Repeat the series of phases adding treatment components.

It is also possible for a study to add one component, return to baseline, add a different component followed by another return to baseline. This procedure evaluates the effect of each component separately.

As noted in the earlier discussion of reversal designs, the limitation of this type of single-case research is that the treatment effect must be temporary. If a treatment or treatment component has a permanent effect on behavior, then the return to baseline will not be effective. If a permanent or long-lasting effect is expected, then a multiple-baseline design is preferred.

Component Analysis with a Multiple-Baseline Design   A multiple-baseline design replicates the demonstration of a treatment effect by repeating the effect for a different participant (or behavior or situation) at a different time. An example of this type of study evaluated the effectiveness of three commonly used components of toilet training for young children (Greer, Neidert, & Dozier, 2016). Because toilet training produces a permanent change in behavior, the researchers used a multiple-baseline across participants design to evaluate the following training components:

1. Cotton underwear instead of diapers or pull-ons.
2. A dense sit schedule, which required the child to sit on the toilet every 30 minutes. Each sit lasted 3 minutes or until success.
3. Differential reinforcement: Children were given preferred items if they were dry at underwear checks every 30 minutes or if they asked to use the potty.

Each child started with a baseline phase followed by the three components added sequentially in a different order for different children. The researchers recorded several variables including the number of appropriate eliminations (using the toilet) during each day in the early education classroom. Figure 14.13 presents simplified data showing the general pattern of results obtained in the study. Based on the results, the researchers concluded that wearing cotton underwear appeared to be the most effective component. Differential reinforcement also seemed to have an effect but only if it was used after the child started wearing underwear.

Rationale for the Multiple-Baseline Design

The goal of a multiple-baseline design is to show that the treatment causes a change in behavior. The data in Figure 14.11 provide an ideal example of how this goal is accomplished. Notice that the following criteria for a successful multiple-baseline experiment are essentially identical to the criteria described earlier to define the success of an ABAB design.

- There is a clear and immediate change in the pattern of behavior when the researcher switches from a baseline to a treatment phase. This demonstration is necessary to establish a relationship between the treatment and the behavior; that is, a change in behavior accompanies the manipulation of the treatment.
- The design includes at least two demonstrations that behavior changes when the treatment is introduced. This replication is necessary to establish a causal relationship between treatment and behavior. It might be argued that the change observed when the treatment is first administered is simply a coincidental effect caused by extraneous variables. However, the fact that the change is replicated when the treatment is administered again at a different time undermines the coincidence argument.

The study examining college athletes texting their arrival in class demonstrates this point (see Figure 14.12). Notice that there is an immediate and substantial chance in class attendance for both students when the treatment (texting) is initiated. Because the treatment and the accompanying change in behavior occur at different times for the two students, the authors can be confident that it is the texting intervention and not some outside factor that is responsible for the change.

FIGURE 14.13

Component Analysis with a Multiple-Baseline Design for Effectiveness of Three Components of Toilet Training for Young Children Showing Simplified Results Similar to Those Obtained by Greer, Neidert, and Dozier (2016)

After a baseline phase, the researchers sequentially added three components of toilet training in a different order for different children. The three components were (B) cotton underwear instead of diapers, (C) differential reinforcement, and (D) dense sitting. The data show the number of times each child used the toilet successfully each day.

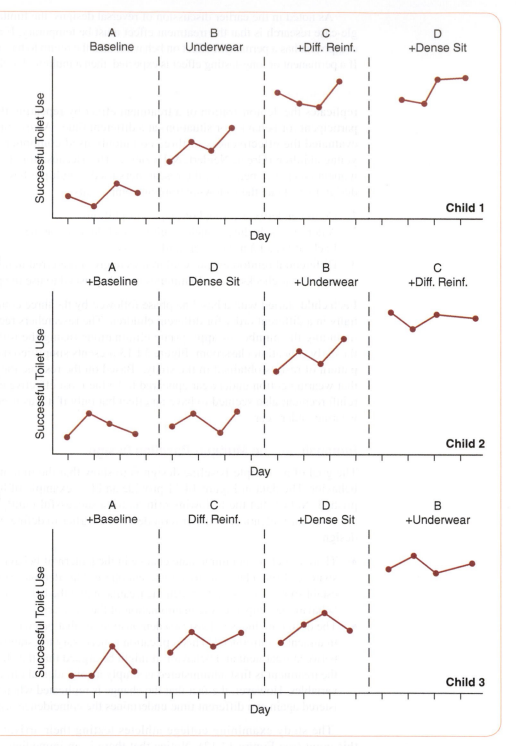

Strengths and Weaknesses of the Multiple-Baseline Design

The primary strength of the multiple-baseline design is that it eliminates the need for a reversal, or return-to-baseline, phase and, therefore, is well suited for evaluating treatment effects that are permanent or long-lasting. However, when this design is used with a single participant to examine two or more behaviors, it can be difficult to identify similar but independent behaviors. The risk is that a treatment applied to one behavior may generalize and produce changes in the second behavior. Once again, this problem illustrates a general conflict between clinical goals and experimental goals. From a clinical perspective, it is valuable for a single treatment to have a general effect, producing improvement in a variety of different problem behaviors. For the multiple-baseline experiment, however, it is essential that the treatment affect only the specific behavior to which it is applied. If both behaviors show a response to the initiation of treatment, the credibility of the treatment effect is undermined. That is, the observed changes may result from the treatment, or they may be caused by an outside variable that changes coincidentally with the treatment and affects both behaviors.

In addition, the clarity of the results can be compromised by individual differences between participants or between behaviors. In a multiple-baseline study across behaviors, for example, one behavior may show a large and immediate change, but the second behavior may show only a minor or gradual change when the treatment is introduced. When this happens, the pattern is different from one behavior to another and, therefore, creates doubts about the consistency of the treatment effect. The same problem can occur with research involving different participants with similar behavior problems. For example, Kercood and Grskovic (2009) examined the effects of color highlighting on mathematics performance for students with attention problems. The treatment consisted of giving the students colored highlighters to use while working on mathematics problems. The students were told that they could highlight important elements of each problem, color code problems according to the level of difficulty, or use the highlighters in any other way they wanted. For each of three student participants, the researchers recorded computational accuracy before and after the treatment. Somewhat simplified data similar to the research results are shown in Figure 14.14. Note that the first two participants show a clear increase in performance when they were given highlighters. For the third participant, however, there is so much variability in the pretreatment scores that it is difficult to see any change when the treatment is administered. Again, the lack of consistency across participants creates some doubt about the consistency of the treatment effect.

LEARNING CHECK

1. Which of the following accurately describes the two baseline phases in a multiple-baseline design?
   a. They are started simultaneously but ended at different times.
   b. They are started at different times but ended simultaneously.
   c. They are started at the same time and ended at the same time.
   d. They can be started and ended at completely different times.
2. Under what circumstances is a component-analysis design appropriate?
   a. When a treatment is expected to have a permanent or long-lasting effect.
   b. When a treatment is expected to have a temporary effect.
   c. When a treatment consists of several distinct elements.
   d. None of the above.
3. Which of the following is a strength of the multiple-baseline design?
   a. It can be used when a participant has more than one problem behavior.
   b. It can be used when a participant has a problem behavior that occurs in two different locations.
   c. It can be used when the treatment is expected to have a permanent or long-lasting effect.
   d. All of the above.

Answers appear at the end of the chapter.

FIGURE 14.14

Multiple-Baseline Data for Three Participants Showing Results Similar to Those Obtained by Kercood and Grskovic (2009)

For two of the three participants, there is a clear increase in mathematics performance when they are given highlighters. For participant 3, however, the large variability in the baseline data makes the results far less convincing.

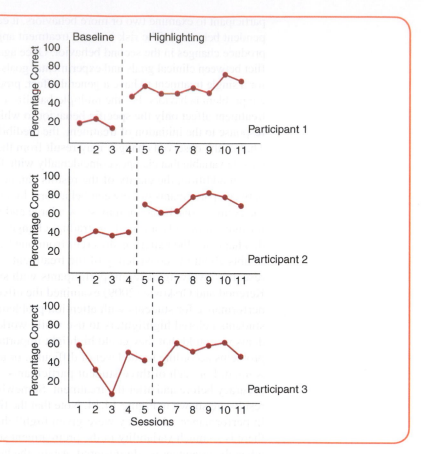

14.5 General Strengths and Weaknesses of Single-Case Designs

LEARNING OBJECTIVE

LO11 Identify the general advantages and disadvantages of single-case designs compared to traditional group designs.

There are three fundamental differences between single-case designs and traditional group designs.

1. The first and most obvious distinction is that single-case research is conducted with only one participant or occasionally a very small group.
2. Single-case research also tends to be much more flexible than a traditional group study. A single-case design can be modified or completely changed in the middle of a study without seriously affecting the integrity of the design, and there is no need to standardize treatment conditions across a large set of different participants.
3. Single-case designs require continuous assessment. In a traditional group design, an individual subject typically is observed and measured only once or twice. A single-case design, however, normally involves a series of 10–20 observations for each individual.

As a consequence of these differences, single-case designs have some advantages and some disadvantages in comparison with group designs. In this section, we identify and discuss the general strengths and weaknesses of single-case research, beginning with the strengths.

Advantages of Single-Case Designs

The primary strength of single-case designs is that they allow researchers to establish cause-and-effect relationships between treatments and behaviors using only a single participant. This simple fact makes it possible to integrate experimental research into applied clinical practice. As we noted in Chapters 7 and 10, the demands and restrictions of traditional group experiments are often at odds with conducting research in natural settings such as a clinic with real clients. As a result, clinicians tend to prefer alternative strategies such as case studies or quasi-experimental research. However, these alternative strategies do not permit clinicians to establish causal relations between the treatments they use and the resulting behaviors. As a result, clinical psychologists are often left in the unenviable position of using treatments that have not been scientifically demonstrated to be effective. Single-case designs provide a solution to this dilemma. By employing single-case designs, a clinician who typically works with individual clients or small groups can conduct experimental research and practice therapy simultaneously without seriously compromising either activity. By recording and graphing observations during the course of treatment, a clinician can demonstrate a cause-and-effect relationship between a treatment and a client's behavior. This scientific demonstration is an important part of establishing accountability in the field of clinical psychology. That is, clinicians should be able to demonstrate unambiguously that the treatments they use are effective.

A second major advantage of single-case designs comes from their flexibility. Although a researcher may begin a single-case experiment with a preconceived plan for the design, the ultimate development of the design depends on the participant's responses. If a participant fails to respond to treatment, for example, the researcher is free to modify the treatment or change to a new treatment without compromising the experiment. Once again, this characteristic of single-case research makes these designs extremely well suited to clinical research. In routine clinical practice, a therapist monitors a client's responses and makes clinical decisions based on those responses. This same flexibility is an integral part of most single-case research. That is, the clinical decision to begin a new treatment and the experimental decision to begin a new phase are both determined by observing the participant's response to the current treatment or current phase. In addition, single-case designs allow a clinician/researcher to individualize treatment to meet the needs of a specific client. Because these designs typically employ only one participant, there is no need to standardize a treatment across a group of individuals with different needs, different problems, and different responses.

In summary, the real strength of single-case designs is that they make experimental clinical research compatible with routine clinical practice. These designs combine the clinical advantages of case study research with the rigor of a true experiment. In particular, single-case research allows for the detailed description and individualized treatment of a single participant, and allows a clinician/researcher to establish the existence of a cause-and-effect relationship between the treatment and the participant's responses.

Disadvantages of Single-Case Designs

Earlier, we noted that one of the strengths of a single-case design is that it can establish the presence of a cause-and-effect relationship using only one participant. At the same time, however, a weakness of these designs is that the relationship is demonstrated only for one participant. This simple fact leaves researchers with some question as to whether the relationship can or should be generalized to other individuals. You should recognize this problem as the general concern of external validity. However, the problem of limited external validity is mitigated by the fact that single-case research seldom exists in isolation. Usually, the researcher or clinician has observed the treatment effect in multiple cases before one individual case is selected for the single-case research project. Also, the relationship between the treatment and outcome is commonly demonstrated in other nonexperimental research such as case studies or quasi-experimental studies. These other studies provide support for generalizing the treatment effect (external validity), and the single-case study demonstrates the causal nature of the effect (internal validity).

A second potential weakness of single-case designs comes from the requirement for multiple, continuous observations. If the observations can be made unobtrusively, without constantly interrupting or distracting the participant, there is little cause for concern. However, if the participant is aware that observations are continuously being made, this awareness may result in reactivity or sensitization that could affect the participant's responses (see Chapter 6). As a result, there is some risk that the participant's behavior may be affected not only by the treatment conditions but also by the assessment procedures. In experimental terminology, the continuous assessment can be a threat to internal validity.

Another concern for single-case designs is the absence of statistical controls. With traditional group designs, researchers can use standard inferential statistical techniques to quantify the likelihood that the results show a real treatment effect versus the likelihood that the results simply reflect chance behavior. Single-case designs, on the other hand, rely on the visual effect of a graph to convince others that the treatment effects are real. Problems can arise if there is any ambiguity at all in the graphed results. One observer, for example, may see clear indications of a treatment effect, whereas other observers may not. On the positive side, reliance on graphed results helps ensure that researchers report only results that are substantial; that is, the treatment effects must be sufficiently large that they are obvious to a casual observer when presented in a graph. Researchers often make a distinction between **statistical significance** and **practical significance**, or **clinical significance**. Practical significance means that the treatment effect is substantial and large enough to have practical application. A **statistically significant result**, on the other hand, simply means that the observed effect, whether large or small, is very unlikely to have occurred by chance. Using this terminology, the results from a single-case study tend to have practical significance, although they typically are not evaluated in terms of statistical significance.

The reliance on a graph to establish the significance of results places additional restrictions on the application of single-case designs. Specifically, the treatment effects must be large and immediate to produce a convincing graph. Treatments that produce small effects or effects that are slow to develop can generate ambiguous graphs and, therefore, are unlikely to appear in published reports. As a result, single-case research is likely to fail to detect such effects. From a research perspective, this tendency is unfortunate because many real treatments are overlooked. From a clinician's point of view, however, this aspect of single-case research simply means that marginally effective treatments are weeded out and only those treatments that are truly effective are reported.

LEARNING CHECK   1. Single-case research studies tend to have
      a. practical significance even though they do not have statistical significance.
      b. statistical significance even though they do not have practical significance.
      c. both practical and statistical significance.
      d. neither practical nor statistical significance.

2. Which of the following is an advantage of single-case designs compared to traditional group designs?
    a. They can be used with one participant.
    b. They are valuable in clinical settings.
    c. They allow for an experiment to be conducted on a single individual.
    d. The other three choices are all advantages of single-case designs.

Answers appear at the end of the chapter.

CHAPTER SUMMARY

At this point, you should review the learning objectives presented at the beginning of each section and be sure that you have mastered each objective.

In this chapter, we examined the characteristics of single-case designs. The general goal of single-case research, like other experimental designs, is to demonstrate the existence of a cause-and-effect relationship between variables. The defining characteristic of a single-case study is that it can be used with a single individual, by testing or observing the individual before and during or after the treatment is implemented by the researcher.

The basic building block of most single-case designs is the phase, a series of observations all made under the same conditions. Observations are made in a baseline phase (i.e., in the absence of a treatment) and in a treatment phase (i.e., during treatment). The series of observations that make up any phase should show a clear pattern that describes the behavior. The pattern within a phase can be described in terms of level or trend, but in either case, the critical factor is the consistency or stability of the pattern. Ultimately, the researcher changes phases by implementing or withdrawing a treatment. The purpose for a phase change is to demonstrate that adding or removing a treatment produces a noticeable change in the pattern of behavior from one phase to the next.

Unlike other experimental designs, the results of a single-case design are not evaluated with traditional tests for statistical significance. Instead, researchers must rely on graphs to convey the meaning of their results. The graph must show a clear change in behavior when the treatment is introduced. Also, the change in behavior must be replicated at least one more time to demonstrate that the first change was not a result of coincidence or chance.

Because the interpretation of the results depends entirely on the visual appearance of a graph, it is important that the change in pattern from baseline to treatment be easy to see when the results are presented in a graph. Visual inspection of single-case data is, unfortunately, a very subjective task. However, four specific characteristics help determine whether there is meaningful change between phases: (1) change in the average level of behavior, (2) immediate change in level of behavior, (3) change in trend of behavior, and (4) latency of change in behavior.

Different types of single-case designs were discussed, including the ABAB reversal design: more complex phase-change designs, variations of the multiple-baseline design, and component analysis designs. The primary advantage of single-case designs is that they allow cause-and-effect relationships to be established with a single participant. In addition, the flexibility of these designs makes them well suited for clinical and other applied research. The primary disadvantage of single-case research is that the results may be unique to the specific individual examined in the study.

KEY WORDS

single-case designs or
    single-subject design

phase

baseline observations

baseline phase

treatment observations

treatment phase

level

trend

stability

phase change

reversal design

ABAB design

multiple-baseline design

multiple-baseline across
    subjects

multiple-baseline across
    behaviors

multiple-baseline across
    situations

component-analysis design

EXERCISES

The exercises are identified with specific learning objectives and are intended to assess your mastery of the objectives. You should be aware that exam items are also generated to assess learning objectives.

1. In addition to the key words, you should also be able to define the following terms:

    statistical significance
    statistically significant result
    practical significance, or clinical significance

2. (**LO1**) What is the goal of a single-case experimental research design?

3. (**LO1**) Traditional statistics (means, variances, and hypothesis tests) are not used to evaluate the results from a single-case study. Explain how the results are evaluated.

4. (**LO2**) What elements are required for a single-case research study to qualify as an experiment?

5. (**LO3**) In a single-case research study consisting of a series of phases, how long should each phase be and what factor determines that it is time to change phases?

6. (**LO3**) Define the concept of "stability" within a phase, and explain why it is important.

7. (**LO4**) What pattern of results is needed to provide convincing evidence that behavior changed when the phase was changed?

8. (**LO5**) Identify the four phases that make up an ABAB (reversal) design, and describe how the participant's behavior is expected to change each time the phase is changed if the study is successful.

9. (**LO5**) In general, how does a phase-change design like the ABAB reversal design demonstrate that the treatment (rather than chance or coincidence) is responsible for causing changes in behavior?

10. (**LO6**) Explain why an ABAB reversal design is inappropriate for a treatment that has a permanent or long-lasting effect.

11. (**LO6** and **8**) Under what circumstances would you use a multiple-baseline design instead of an ABAB (reversal) design?

12. (**LO6**) Explain why a researcher might have some ethical reservations about beginning the second baseline phase in an ABAB single-case design.

13. (**LO7**) Although researchers typically begin a single-case reversal study with the intention of using an ABAB design, what outcome can cause the researcher to switch to a more complex phase-change design?

14. (**LO8**) How does a multiple-baseline design rule out chance or coincidence as the explanation for changes in behavior that occur when the treatment is started?

15. (**LO9**) Suppose that a complex therapy procedure contains one component that has absolutely no effect on behavior. Explain how a component design could be used to demonstrate that the component has no effect.

16. (**LO10**) Under what circumstances would it be difficult to interpret the results of a multiple-baseline design?

17. (**LO11**) Briefly explain why a clinical psychologist might prefer doing research with a single-case instead of traditional group design.

LEARNING CHECK ANSWERS

Section 14.1	Section 14.2	Section 14.3	Section 14.4	Section 14.5
1. b, 2. b	1. b, 2. a, 3. c	1. c, 2. c, 3. b	1. a, 2. c, 3. d	1. a, 2. d

Statistical Evaluation of Data

© Nathan Jasowiak / Shutterstock

CHAPTER LEARNING OBJECTIVES

LO1 Define the two general categories of statistics, descriptive and inferential, and explain the purpose for each.

LO2 Define a statistic and a parameter and explain the role that each plays in inferential statistics.

LO3 Construct a frequency distribution table or graph to organize and display an entire distribution of scores.

LO4 Define and compute the three measures of central tendency.

LO5 Explain how the mean and the standard deviation describe a distribution of scores.

LO6 Explain how the Pearson correlation describes the relationship between two variables and predicts the general appearance of the scatter plot for the data.

LO7 Identify the general purpose of a hypothesis test, and explain how the test accomplishes the researcher's goal.

LO8 Define a Type I and a Type II error, explain why they occur, and describe the consequences of each.

LO9 Explain how sample size and sample variance influence the outcome of a hypothesis test and why a measure of effect size is needed to supplement the test.

LO10 Identify the characteristics that differentiate different sets of data and identify the hypothesis test(s) appropriate for each data structure.

LO11 Describe the two basic concerns with the calculation of split-half reliability and explain how these concerns are addressed by the Spearman–Brown formula, the K-R-20, and Cronbach's alpha.

LO12 Describe the basic concern with measuring inter-rater reliability and explain how Cohen's kappa addresses this concern.

CHAPTER OVERVIEW

In this chapter, we consider Step 8 of the research process: evaluating the data. Both descriptive and inferential statistics are described in detail. In addition, special statistical analyses for research are considered.

Most of you were probably required to take a Statistics course as a prerequisite or a corequisite for the Research Methods course. Therefore, this chapter is intended to be a concise review of material that you have already studied. We focus on the conceptual side of statistics—what are they intended to do and how do they accomplish their goals—rather than the details of formulas and calculations. In addition, we present a roadmap to help direct you to the appropriate statistical procedures for your data. This chapter is supplemented by Appendix B, which presents examples demonstrating most of the statistical procedures mentioned in this chapter, and Appendix C, which presents step-by-step instructions for using the Statistical Package for the Social Sciences (SPSS) to perform most of the statistics that are needed for an introductory Research Methods course.

15.1 The Role of Statistics in the Research Process

LEARNING OBJECTIVES

LO1 Define the two general categories of statistics, descriptive and inferential, and explain the purpose for each.

LO2 Define a statistic and a parameter and explain the role that each plays in inferential statistics.

The exception is single-case research in which visual inspection is used in place of statistical techniques.

When the data collection phase of the research process is completed, a researcher typically is confronted with pages of data consisting of the scores, measurements, and observations recorded during the research study. The next step, Step 8 in the research process, is to use statistical methods to help make sense of the data. Statistical methods serve two principal purposes.

1. Statistics help organize and summarize the data so the researcher can see what happened in the study and communicate the results to others.
2. Statistics help the researcher answer the general questions that initiated the research by determining exactly what conclusions are justified based on the results.

These two general purposes correspond to the two general categories of statistical techniques: descriptive statistics and inferential statistics. **Descriptive statistics** are techniques that help describe a set of data. Examples of descriptive statistics include organizing a set of scores into a graph or a table and calculating a single value, such as the average score, that describes the entire set. The goal of descriptive statistics is to organize, summarize, and simplify data.

Inferential statistics, on the other hand, are methods that use the limited information from samples to answer general questions about populations. Recall from Chapter 5 that research questions concern a population, but research studies are conducted with relatively small samples. Although the sample is selected from the population and is intended to represent the population, there is no guarantee that a sample provides a perfectly accurate picture of the population. Thus, researchers must be cautious about assuming that the results obtained from a sample will generalize to the entire population. Inferential statistics help researchers determine when it is appropriate to generalize from a sample to a population.

DEFINITIONS

Descriptive statistics are methods that help researchers organize, summarize, and simplify the results obtained from research studies.

Inferential statistics are methods that use the results obtained from samples to help make generalizations about populations.

Planning Ahead

Although using statistics to evaluate research results appears as Step 8 in the research process, you should think about statistics long before you begin the research study. In particular, you should decide how you want to describe your results and exactly which descriptive statistics are needed. This task includes an evaluation of your planned measurement procedure to be sure that the scores you obtain are compatible with the statistics you plan to use. For example, if you intend to compute mean scores, you need to have numerical data. You also need to anticipate the inferential statistics you will use. This involves deciding exactly what kind of conclusion you would like to make and then ensuring that there is an appropriate inferential procedure to make your point.

In general, as soon as you begin to make decisions about how to define and measure the variables in your research study, you should also make decisions about the statistical analysis of your data. You should anticipate the appearance of your research data, plan the descriptive statistics that will allow you to present your data so that others can see and understand your results, and plan the inferential statistics that will allow you to interpret your results.

Statistics Terminology

Before we discuss descriptive and inferential statistical techniques, two additional terms should be introduced. The most commonly used descriptive technique is to compute one or two numerical values that summarize an entire set of data. When the set of data is a sample, the summary values are called **statistics**.

DEFINITION

A **statistic** is a summary value that describes a sample. A common example of a statistic is the average score for a sample.

Sample statistics serve a dual purpose.

1. They describe or summarize the entire set of scores in the sample. For example, the average IQ score for a sample of 100 people provides a summary description of the intelligence level of the entire sample.

2. They provide information about the corresponding summary values for the entire population. For example, the average reading score for a sample of 25 first-grade students provides information about the general reading level for the entire population of first graders.

Once again, summary values computed for a sample are called statistics. The corresponding summary values for a population are called **parameters**. For example, if a sample of 20 students is selected from a high school with a total population of 1,148 students, then the average age for the students in the sample would be a statistic and the average age for the entire population would be a parameter.

DEFINITION

> A **parameter** is a summary value that describes a population. A common example of a parameter is the average score for a population.

Each statistic (computed for a sample) has a corresponding parameter (for the entire population). As we show later in this chapter, most research questions concern population parameters and most research data consists of sample statistics. As a result the general purpose for inferential statistical techniques is to use sample statistics as the basis for drawing general conclusions about the corresponding population parameters.

LEARNING CHECK

1. Which general category of statistical methods is intended to answer questions about a population by using sample data?
   a. Parameters
   b. Statistics
   c. Descriptive statistics
   d. Inferential statistics

2. A researcher is interested in the sleeping habits of students at the local state college. The average number of hours spent sleeping each night for the entire set of students enrolled at the college is an example of a _____.
   a. statistic
   b. parameter
   c. sample
   d. population

3. A researcher uses an anonymous survey to investigate the study habits of American college students. Based on the set of 56 surveys that were completed and returned, the researcher finds that these students spend an average of 4.1 hours each week working on course material outside of class. For this study, the average of 4.1 hours is an example of a _____.
   a. parameter
   b. statistic
   c. population
   d. sample

Answers appear at the end of the chapter.

15.2 Descriptive Statistics

LEARNING OBJECTIVES

LO3 Construct a frequency distribution table or graph to organize and display an entire distribution of scores.

LO4 Define and compute the three measures of central tendency.

LO5 Explain how the mean and the standard deviation describe a distribution of scores.

LO6 Explain how the Pearson correlation describes the relationship between two variables and predicts the general appearance of the scatter plot for the data.

As noted earlier, the general goal of descriptive statistics is to organize or summarize a set of scores. Two general techniques are used to accomplish this goal.

1. Organize the entire set of scores into a table or a graph that allows researchers (and others) to see the whole set of scores.
2. Compute one or two summary values (such as the average) that describe the entire group.

Each of these techniques is discussed in the following sections.

Frequency Distributions

One method of simplifying and organizing a set of scores is to group them into an organized display that shows the entire set. The display is called a **frequency distribution** and consists of a tabulation of the number of individuals in each category on the scale of measurement. Thus, a frequency distribution displays two sets of information:

1. The set of categories that make up the scale of measurement.
2. The number of individuals with scores in each of the categories.

   Depending on the method used to display the scale of measurement and the frequencies, a frequency distribution can be a table or a graph. The advantage of a frequency distribution is that it allows a researcher to view the entire set of scores. The disadvantage is that constructing a frequency distribution without the aid of a computer can be somewhat tedious, especially with large sets of data.

Frequency Distribution Tables

A frequency distribution table consists of two columns of information. The first column presents the scale of measurement or simply lists the set of categories into which individuals have been assigned. The second column lists the frequency, or the number of individuals, located in each category. Table 15.1 is a frequency distribution table summarizing the scores from a 5-point quiz given to a class of $n = 15$ students. The first column lists the entire set of possible quiz scores (categories of measurement) in order from 5 to 0; it is headed X to indicate that these are the potential scores. The second column shows the frequency of occurrence for each score. In this example, one person had a perfect score of $X = 5$ on the quiz, three people had scores of $X = 4$, and so on.

Frequency Distribution Graphs

The same information that is presented in a frequency distribution table can be presented in a graph. The graph shows the scale of measurement (set of categories) along the horizontal axis and the frequencies on the vertical axis. Recall from Chapter 3 that there are

TABLE 15.1

A Frequency Distribution Table

The table shows the distribution of scores from a 5-point quiz.

X	F
5	1
4	3
3	4
2	3
1	2
0	2

FIGURE 15.1

Frequency Distribution Graphs

The same set of scores is shown in a histogram (a) and in a polygon (b).

four different scales of measurement: nominal, ordinal, interval, and ratio. When the measurement scale (scores) consists of numerical values (interval or ratio scale of measurement), there are two options for graphing the frequency distribution.

1. A **histogram** shows a bar above each score so that the height of the bar indicates the frequency of occurrence for that particular score. The bars for adjacent scores touch each other.
2. A **polygon** shows a point above each score so that the height of the point indicates the frequency. Straight lines connect the points, and additional straight lines are drawn down to the horizontal axis at each end to complete the figure.

Figure 15.1 shows a histogram and a polygon presenting the same data as Table 15.1. Figure 15.1a is a histogram with a bar above each category, and Figure 15.1b is an example of a polygon. Each of the graphs gives an organized picture of the entire set of scores, so you can tell at a glance where the scores are located on the scale of measurement.

When the categories on the scale of measurement are not numerical values (nominal or ordinal scales), the frequency distribution is presented as a **bar graph**. A bar graph is like a histogram except that a space is left between adjacent bars. Figure 15.2 is a bar graph that presents a frequency distribution of academic majors in an introductory college course. Notice that the height of each bar indicates the frequency associated with that particular category. In this example, the class contains 10 psychology majors, 6 biology majors, and so on.

Frequency distributions are generally considered to be preliminary methods of statistical analysis and are rarely shown in published research reports. Nonetheless, a frequency distribution graph is an excellent first step in examining a set of data. In addition, a

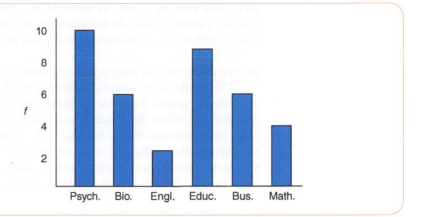

FIGURE 15.2

A Bar Graph Showing the Frequency Distribution of Academic Majors in an Introductory Psychology Class

Notice the space between adjacent bars.

frequency distribution graph is probably the single best method for thinking about a set of data. Whenever you encounter the concept of a sample or a set of scores, we suggest that you visualize the scores in a frequency distribution graph. The image of a frequency distribution graph gives you a concrete representation of all the individual scores as well as the appearance of the entire set of data.

Describing Interval and Ratio Data (Numerical Scores)

Although frequency distribution tables and graphs have the advantage of presenting a complete picture of a set of data, there are simpler methods for describing the scores in a sample. Perhaps the most commonly used descriptive statistic involves computing the average score for a set of data. In statistical terms, this process is called measuring **central tendency**. The purpose of measuring central tendency is to locate the center of the distribution of scores by finding a single score that represents the entire set. The goal is to find the average, or the most typical, score for the entire set.

> **DEFINITION**
>
> **Central tendency** is a statistical measure that identifies a single score that defines the center of a distribution. The goal of central tendency is to identify the value that is most typical or most representative of the entire group.

Researchers have developed three different measures of central tendency: the mean, the median, and the mode. When the scores consist of numerical values from an interval or ratio scale of measurement, the most commonly used measure is the mean. However, there are situations for which it is impossible to compute a mean or the mean does not produce a good representative value. In these situations, the median and mode provide alternative measures.

The Mean, Median, and Mode

The **mean** is computed by adding the scores and dividing the sum by the number of individuals. Conceptually, the mean is the amount each individual would receive if the total were divided equally. In research reports, the convention is to use the letter M to represent a sample mean.

The **median** is the score that divides a distribution in half, so that 50% of the individuals have scores that are less than or equal to the median. Usually, the median is used for data sets in which the mean does not provide a good representative value. In a distribution

In statistics textbooks, the symbol $\overline{X}$ (X-bar) is commonly used for a sample mean.

with a few extreme scores, for example, the extreme values can displace the mean so that it is not a central value. In this situation, the median often provides a better measure of central tendency. For example, demographic data such as family income or prices of new single-family homes often contain a few extreme values. In these situations, the median income or the median price is typically used to describe the average.

The **mode** is the score or category with the greatest frequency. In a frequency distribution graph, the mode identifies the location of the peak (highest point) in the distribution. When the scores consist of classifications that are not numerical values (e.g., measurements from a nominal scale of measurement), it is impossible to compute the mean or the median. In this case, the mode is the only available measure of central tendency. When the scores are numerical values, the mode is often reported along with the mean because it helps describe the shape of the distribution.

DEFINITIONS

The **mean** is a measure of central tendency obtained by adding the individual scores, then dividing the sum by the number of scores. The mean is the arithmetic average.

The **median** measures central tendency by identifying the score that divides the distribution in half. If the scores are listed in order, 50% of the individuals have scores at or below the median.

The **mode** measures central tendency by identifying the most frequently occurring score in the distribution.

Examples demonstrating calculation of the mean, the median, and the mode are presented in Appendix B, p. 453.

Standard Deviation and Variance

When the scores are numerical values, the mean is the most commonly used measure of central tendency, and the **standard deviation** is typically used to describe how the scores are scattered around the mean. Conceptually, the standard deviation describes the variability of the scores by measuring the average distance from the mean. When the scores are clustered close to the mean, the standard deviation is small; when the scores are scattered widely around the mean, the standard deviation is large. As a general rule, roughly 70% of the scores in a distribution are within a distance of one standard deviation of the mean, and roughly 95% of the scores are within two standard deviations.

Although the concept of the standard deviation is fairly straightforward, its actual calculation is somewhat more complicated. Instead of simply computing the average distance from the mean, the calculation of standard deviation begins by computing the average *squared* distance from the mean. This average squared value is called **variance**. Although variance is not an intuitively meaningful concept, it is an important statistical measure, especially in the context of inferential statistics. In summary, the calculation of variance and standard deviation can be viewed as a series of steps.

1. For each score, measure the distance away from the mean. This distance is often called a *deviation*. For example, if the mean is 80 and you have a score of 84, then the distance (or deviation) is 4 points.
2. Square each of the distances and compute the average of the squared distances. This is variance. (We should note that the average squared distance for a sample is computed by dividing the sum of the squared distances by $n - 1$, where n is the number of scores in the sample. The value of $n - 1$ is called **degrees of freedom**.)

3. Because the variance measures the average squared distance from the mean, simply take the square root to obtain the standard deviation. Thus, variance and standard deviation are directly related by a squaring or square root operation.

$$\text{Standard deviation} = \sqrt{\text{Variance}}$$

$$\text{Variance} = (\text{Standard deviation})^2$$

In statistics textbooks, the sample standard deviation is usually identified by the letter s, and the sample variance is s^2. In published reports, the sample standard deviation is identified as SD.

DEFINITIONS

> **Variance** measures the variability of the scores by computing the average squared distance from the mean. First, measure the distance from the mean for each score, then square the distances and find the sum of the squared distances. Next, for a sample, the average squared distance is computed by dividing the sum of the squared distances by $n - 1$.
>
> **Standard deviation** is the square root of the variance and provides a measure of variability by describing the average distance from the mean.

Sample Variance and Degrees of Freedom

Although sample variance is described as measuring the average squared distance from the mean, the actual calculations involve dividing the sum of the squared distances by $n - 1$ (instead of dividing by n). As we noted, the value of $n - 1$ is called degrees of freedom (df). Dividing by $n - 1$ is a necessary adjustment to ensure that the sample variance provides an accurate representation of its population variance. Without the adjustment, the sample variance tends to underestimate the actual variance in the population. With the adjustment, the sample variance—on average—gives an accurate and unbiased picture of the population variance.

It is not critical to understand the concept of degrees of freedom (df); however, this concept is encountered in nearly every situation in which statistics are computed or reported. In most cases, you should be able to find a relationship between the structure of the study and the value for degrees of freedom. For example, a research study with 20 participants has a sample variance with $df = 19$. Examples demonstrating the calculation of standard deviation and variance are presented in Appendix B, pp. 455–456.

Describing Non-Numerical Data from Nominal and Ordinal Scales of Measurement

Occasionally, the measurements or observations made by a researcher are not numerical values. Instead, a researcher may simply classify participants by placing them in separate nominal or ordinal categories. Examples of this kind of measurement include:

- Classification of people by level of education (college graduate or not).
- Classification of attitude (agree or disagree).
- Classification of self-esteem (high, medium, or low).

In each case, the data do not consist of numerical values: there are no numbers with which to compute a mean or a standard deviation. In this case, the researcher must find some other method of describing the data.

One of the simplest ways to describe nominal and ordinal data is to report the proportion or percentage in each category. These values can be used to describe a single sample or to compare separate samples. For example, a report might describe a sample of voters by stating that 43% prefer candidate Green, 28% prefer candidate Brown, and 29% are undecided. A research report might compare two groups by stating that 80% of the 6-year-old children were able to successfully complete the task, but only 34% of the 4-year-olds were successful.

In addition to percentages and proportions, you also can use the mode as a measure of central tendency for data from a nominal scale. Remember, the mode simply identifies the most commonly occurring category and, therefore, describes the most typical member of a sample. For example, if the modal response to a survey question is "no opinion," you can probably conclude that the people surveyed do not care much about the issue. However, the concept of *distance between scores* is meaningless with non-numerical values, and it is impossible to compute a meaningful measure of variability.

Using Graphs to Compare Groups of Scores

When a research study compares several different treatment conditions (or several different populations), it is common to use a graph to display the summary statistics for all the different groups being compared. The value of a graph is that it allows several different statistics to be displayed simultaneously so that an observer can easily see the differences (or similarities) between them. For example, it is possible to list the means from eight different treatment conditions, but it probably is easier to compare the eight means if they are all presented in a single picture.

The most common statistics to present in a graph are sample means, but it is possible to present sample medians or sample proportions. In each case, the graph is organized with the same basic structure.

1. The different groups or treatment conditions are listed on the horizontal axis. Usually, this involves the different levels of an independent variable or different values for a quasi-independent variable.
2. The values for the statistics are listed on the vertical axis. Usually, this involves values for the sample means that are being compared.

The graph can be constructed as either a **line graph** or a bar graph. Figure 15.3 shows each type of graph displaying the means from four different treatment conditions. To construct the line graph, we placed a point above each value on the horizontal axis (each treatment) so that the vertical position of the point corresponds to the mean for that treatment condition, and then connected the points by straight lines. The bar graph simply uses a bar above each of the treatment conditions so that the height of the bar corresponds to the mean for the treatment. By convention, line graphs are used when the values on the horizontal axis are measured on an interval or a ratio scale; bar graphs are used when the values are from a nominal or ordinal scale.

Similar graphs are used to display sample medians or sample proportions. Two examples are shown in Figure 15.4. The first graph shows the median incomes for three samples of 30-year-old men representing three different levels of education. The second graph shows the results from a study examining how preferences for wristwatch styles are related to age. Participants in three samples (representing three age groups) were asked whether they preferred a digital watch or a traditional analog watch. The graph shows the proportion preferring digital watches for each of the three samples.

Factorial research studies (Chapter 11) include two or more independent variables (or quasi-independent variables). For example, a researcher may want to examine the effects

FIGURE 15.3

Presenting Means and Mean Differences in a Graph

(a) A line graph and (b) a bar graph showing treatment means obtained from a research study.

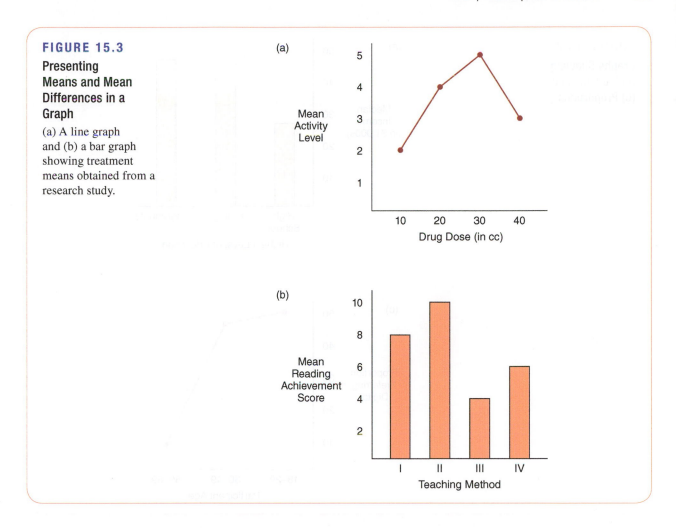

of heat and humidity on performance. For this study, both the temperature (variable 1) and the humidity (variable 2) would be manipulated, and performance would be evaluated under a variety of different temperature and humidity conditions. The structure of this type of experiment can be represented as a matrix, with one variable determining the rows and the second variable defining the columns. Each cell in the matrix corresponds to a specific combination of treatments. Figure 15.5 presents hypothetical data for the temperature and humidity experiment just described. The figure includes a matrix showing the mean level of performance for each treatment condition and demonstrates how the means would be displayed in a graph. As a general rule, graphs for two-factor studies are constructed by listing the values of one of the independent variables on the horizontal axis and listing the values for the dependent variable on the vertical axis. For this figure, we list temperature values on the horizontal axis and list values for the mean level of performance on the vertical axis. Then, a separate line is used to present the means for each level of the second independent variable. In this case, there is a separate line for each of the two levels of humidity. Notice that the top line presents the means in the top row of the data matrix and the bottom line shows the means from the bottom row. The result is a graph that displays all six means from the experiment, and allows comparison of means and mean differences.

FIGURE 15.4

Graphs Showing
(a) Medians and
(b) Proportions

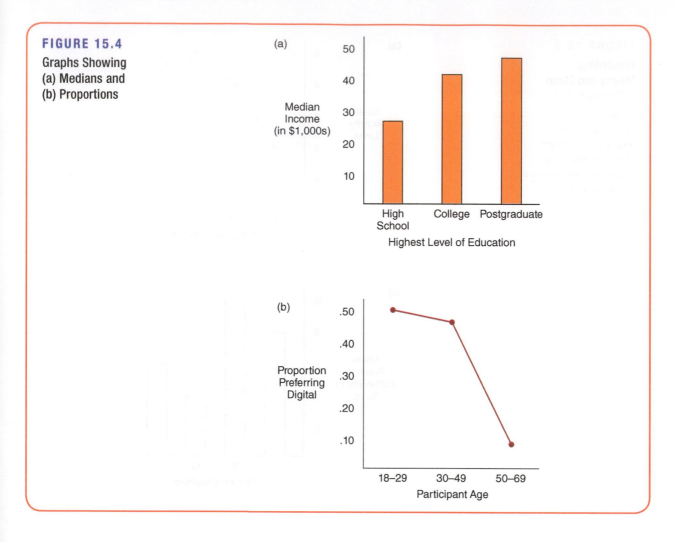

Correlations

Thus far, all of the statistics we have considered are intended to describe a group of scores and to permit a researcher to look for differences between groups. For example, a researcher interested in examining the relationship between self-esteem and task performance could conduct a differential study, selecting a sample of high self-esteem participants and a sample of low self-esteem participants (see Chapter 10, pp. 244–245). Each individual is given a task and performance is measured. An example of the data resulting from this type of study is shown in Table 15.2a. Notice that the researcher has two sets of scores. The mean would be computed for each set to describe the scores, and the difference between the two means would describe the relationship between self-esteem and performance.

An alternative research approach is to use a correlational design in which self-esteem and performance are measured for each participant (see Chapter 12). Instead of comparing two groups of scores, the researcher now has one group of participants with two scores for each individual. An example of the data that result from this type of study is shown in Table 15.2b. For this type of data, the researcher computes a **correlation** that measures and describes the relationship between the two variables. For this example, the correlation would measure and describe the relationship between self-esteem and performance.

FIGURE 15.5

A Matrix and a Graph Showing the Means from a Two-Factor Study

	Temperature (in °F)		
	70	80	90
Low Humidity	M = 30	M = 28	M = 24
High Humidity	M = 28	M = 20	M = 12

TABLE 15.2

Two Different Strategies for Evaluating the Relationship between Self-Esteem and Performance

One study (a) uses a nonexperimental strategy and evaluates the mean difference between two groups of participants. The other study (b) uses a correlational strategy, measuring two variables for each participant, and computing a correlation to evaluate the relationship between variables.

(a)

High Self-Esteem Group	Low Self-Esteem Group	
19	12	
23	14	
21	10	
24	17	←———————— Performance scores
17	13	
18	20	
20	13	
22	11	
M = 20.50	M = 13.75	

(b)

Participant	Self-Esteem Scores	Performance Scores	
A	62	13	
B	84	20	
C	89	22	
D	73	16	←———————— Two separate scores
E	66	11	for Each participant
F	75	18	
G	71	14	
H	80	21	

The data for a correlation always consist of two scores for each individual. By convention, the scores are identified as *X* and *Y* and can be presented in a table or in a graph called a **scatter plot**. Figure 15.6 shows a scatter plot for the self-esteem and performance data in Table 15.2b. In the scatter plot, each individual is represented by a point in the graph; the horizontal position of the point corresponds to the value of *X* (self-esteem) and the vertical position is the value of *Y* (performance). A scatter plot can be a great aid in helping you see the nature of a relationship between two variables.

A correlation measures and describes three aspects of the relationship between two variables:

1. The direction of the relationship is described by the sign of the correlation. A positive correlation indicates that *X* and *Y* tend to change in the same direction. For a negative correlation, *X* and *Y* change in opposite directions.
2. The form of the relationship is determined by the type of correlation. The **Pearson correlation**, usually identified by the letter *r* evaluates linear (straight line) relationships and is by far the most commonly used correlation. The Spearman correlation, identified by r_s, is simply the Pearson correlation applied to ordinal data (ranks). If the original scores are numerical values from an interval or ratio scale, it is possible to rank the scores and then compute a **Spearman correlation**. In this case, the Spearman correlation measures the degree to which the relationship is consistently one-directional, or monotonic.
3. The degree of consistency, or strength, of the relationship is described by the numerical value of the correlation. A correlation of 1.00 indicates a perfectly consistent relationship, and a correlation of 0.00 indicates no consistent relationship whatsoever. Different degrees of relationship were discussed in Chapter 12 (see Figure 12.3 on p. 301).

Finally, we should note that the sign of the correlation and the strength, or magnitude, of the correlation are independent. For example, correlations of *r* = +0.85 and *r* = −0.85

FIGURE 15.6

A Scatter Plot Showing the Data from Table 15.2b

The data show a strong, positive relationship between self-esteem and performance. The Pearson correlation is *r* = 0.933.

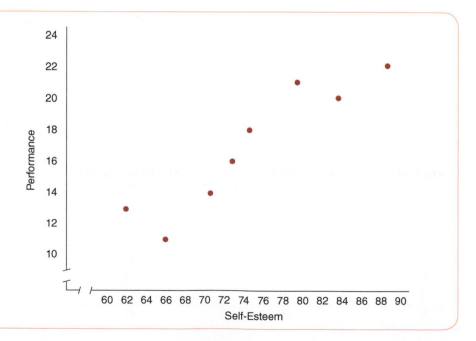

are equally strong, and Pearson correlations of $r = +1.00$ and $r = -1.00$ both indicate a perfect linear relationship.

DEFINITION

> A **correlation** is a statistical value that measures and describes the direction and degree of relationship between two variables.

Examples demonstrating the calculation of the Pearson and Spearman correlations are presented in Appendix B, 455–457.

Regression

The Pearson correlation describes the linear relationship between two variables. Whenever a linear relationship exists, it is possible to compute the equation for the straight line that provides the best fit for the data points. The process of finding the linear equation is called **regression**, and the resulting equation is called the **regression equation**.

All linear equations have the same general structure and can be expressed as

$$Y = bX + a$$

> The regression equation actually minimizes the total *squared* error between the actual Y values and the predicted Y values, and it is often called the least-squared error solution.

where b and a are fixed constants. The value of b is called the **slope constant** because it describes the slope of the line (how much Y changes when X is increased by 1 point). The value of a is called the **Y-intercept** because it is the point at which the line intersects the Y axis. The process of regression identifies the specific values for b and a that produce the most accurate predictions for Y. That is, regression identifies the specific equation that results in the smallest possible error between the predicted Y values on the line and the actual Y values in the data.

Figure 15.7 shows a scatter plot of X and Y values with a straight line drawn through the center of the data points. The straight line is valuable because it makes the relationship easier to see and it can be used for prediction. That is, for each value of X, the line provides a predicted value of Y that can be computed using the regression equation.

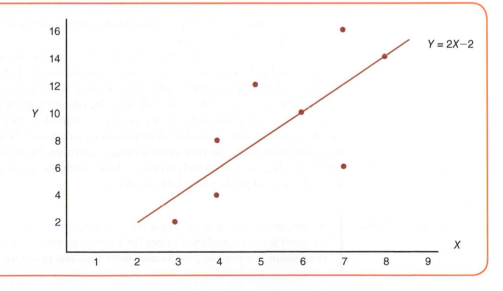

FIGURE 15.7

A Scatter Plot and Regression Line

For each value of X, it is possible to calculate a Y value on the line that serves as a predicted value of Y.

$Y = 2X - 2$

Often the regression equation is reported in standardized form, which means that the original X and Y scores were standardized, or transformed into z-scores, before the equation was computed. In standardized form, the equation for predicting Y values becomes

$$z_Y = \beta z_X$$

where z_Y and z_X are the standardized values (z-scores) for X and Y, and the Greek letter beta (β) is the standardized slope constant. For linear regression using one variable (X) to predict one variable (Y), the value of β is equal to the Pearson correlation between X and Y.

Unless there is a perfect linear relationship (a Pearson correlation of $+1.00$ or -1.00), there is some error between the predicted Y values and the actual Y values. The amount of error varies from point to point, but the average amount of error is directly related to the value of the Pearson correlation. For a correlation near 1.00 (plus or minus), the data points are clustered close to the line and the average error is small. For a correlation near zero, the data points are widely scattered around the line and the average error is large. The squared value of the correlation, r^2, describes the overall accuracy of the prediction. Specifically, r^2 equals the proportion of the Y-score variance that is predicted by the regression equation. An example demonstrating the calculation of the regression equation is presented in Appendix B, 471.

Multiple Regression

Often, researchers try to get more accurate predictions by using more than one predictor variable. For example, using a student's high school grades and SAT scores to predict college performance should result in more accurate predictions than those obtained from only one of the two predictors. The process of finding the most accurate prediction equations with multiple predictors is called **multiple regression**, and the resulting equation is called the **multiple-regression equation**.

When two variables, X_1 and X_2, are used to predict Y, the general form of the multiple-regression equation is

$$Y = b_1X_1 + b_2X_2 + a$$

Multiple regression determines the specific values of a, b_1, and b_2, which produce the most accurate predictions. In standardized form, the equation becomes

$$z_Y = \beta_1 z_{X1} + \beta_2 z_{X2}$$

where z_Y, z_{X1}, and z_{X2}, are the standardized values (z-scores) for Y, X_1, and X_2, and the β values are the slope constants.

Again, there usually is some error between the predicted Y values and the actual Y values in the data. In the same way that r^2 measures the proportion of variance that is predicted with one predictor variable, it is possible to compute a corresponding proportion for multiple regression. The symbol R^2 describes the proportion of the total variance of the Y scores that is accounted for by the regression equation. Occasionally, researchers use one predictor variable in the initial regression equation, and then add a second predictor to determine how much the prediction accuracy improves. In this situation, researchers often report a value for ΔR^2, which measures how much the value of R^2 changes (increases) when the second predictor variable is added.

DEFINITIONS

> **Regression** is the statistical process of finding the linear equation that produces the most accurate predicted values for Y using one predictor variable (X). **Multiple regression** is when the process uses more than one predictor variable.

LEARNING CHECK

1. The ages of the children in a summer camp range from 7 to 12 years old. A counselor constructs a frequency distribution graph showing the number of children for each of the six ages. What kind of graph would be appropriate for this distribution?
   a. Only a histogram
   b. Only a polygon
   c. Only a bar graph
   d. Either a histogram or a polygon

2. For scores measured on a nominal scale of measurement (e.g., job classification), which measure of central tendency is appropriate?
   a. Mean
   b. Median
   c. Mode
   d. Standard deviation

3. Which of the following is the definition of variance?
   a. The sum of the scores divided by the number of scores
   b. The average distance from the mean
   c. The square root of the average distance from the mean
   d. The average squared distance from the mean

4. What would the scatter plot show for data that produce a Pearson correlation of r = +.88?
   a. Points clustered close to a line that slopes up to the right
   b. Points clustered close to a line that slopes down to the right
   c. Points widely scattered around a line that slopes up to the right
   d. Points widely scattered around a line that slopes down to the right

Answers appear at the end of the chapter.

15.3 Inferential Statistics

LEARNING OBJECTIVES

LO7 Identify the general purpose of a hypothesis test and explain how the test accomplishes the researcher's goal.

LO8 Define a Type I and a Type II error, explain why they occur, and describe the consequences of each.

LO9 Explain how sample size and sample variance influence the outcome of a hypothesis test and why a measure of effect size is needed to supplement the test.

Although research questions typically concern an entire population, research studies typically involve a relatively small sample selected from the population (see Chapter 5, p. 111). For example, a researcher would like to know whether adolescents' social skills are influenced by their social experiences as infants. To answer this question, the researcher could select a sample of 25 adolescents, measure their social skills, and interview their parents to get a measure of their social experiences as infants. Notice that the researcher is relying on a specific group of 25 adolescents to provide an answer for a question about all adolescents. This creates a general problem for researchers. Does the sample accurately represent the population? If the researcher took a different sample, would different results be obtained? Addressing these questions is the purpose of inferential statistics.

The general goal of inferential statistics is to use the limited information from samples as the basis for reaching general conclusions about the populations from which the samples were obtained. Notice that this goal involves making a generalization or an inference from limited information (a sample) to a general conclusion (a population). The basic difficulty with this process is centered on the concept of **sampling error**. In simple terms, sampling error means that a sample does not provide a perfectly accurate picture of its population; that is, there is some discrepancy, or error, between the information available from a sample and the true situation that exists in the general population.

The concept of sampling error is illustrated in Figure 15.8. The figure shows a population of 1,000 college students and two samples, each with 5 students who were selected from the population. The figure also shows a set of parameters for the population and the corresponding statistics for the two samples. First, notice that none of the sample statistics are exactly equal to the population parameters. This is the fundamental idea behind sampling error; there is always some discrepancy between a sample statistic and the corresponding population parameter. Also note that the sample statistics differ from one sample to the other. This is another consequence of sampling error; each sample has its own individuals and its own scores, and each sample has its own statistics.

DEFINITION

Sampling error is the naturally occurring difference between a sample statistic and the corresponding population parameter.

FIGURE 15.8

A Demonstration of Sampling Error

Two samples are selected from the same population. Notice that the sample statistics are different from one sample to another, and all of the sample statistics are different from the corresponding population parameters.

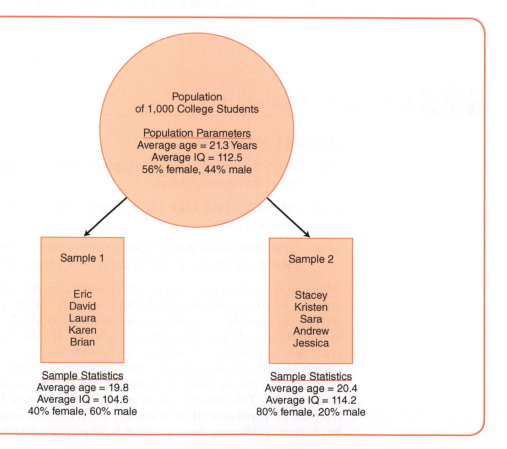

The fundamental problem for inferential statistics is to differentiate between research results that represent real patterns or relationships, and those that simply represent sampling error. Figure 15.9 shows a prototypical research situation. In this case, the research study is examining the relationship between violence on television and aggressive behavior for preschool children. Two groups of children (two samples) are selected from the population. One sample watches television programs containing violence for 30 minutes, and the other sample watches nonviolent programs for 30 minutes. Both groups are then observed during a play period, and the researcher records the amount of aggression displayed by each child. The researcher calculates a sample mean (a statistic) for each group and compares the two sample means. In Figure 15.9, there is a 4-point difference between the two sample means. The problem for the researcher is to decide whether the 4-point difference was caused by the treatments (the different television programs) or is just a case of sampling error (like the differences that are shown in Figure 15.8). That is, does the 4-point difference provide convincing evidence that viewing television violence has an effect on behavior, or is it simply a result of chance? The purpose of inferential statistics is to help researchers answer this question.

Hypothesis Tests

In Chapter 1, we presented an overview of the research process, and we have followed the research process step-by-step throughout this book. Recall that the second step in the research process was to use your research idea to form a specific, testable hypothesis, which is a tentative statement describing the relationship between variables. The following

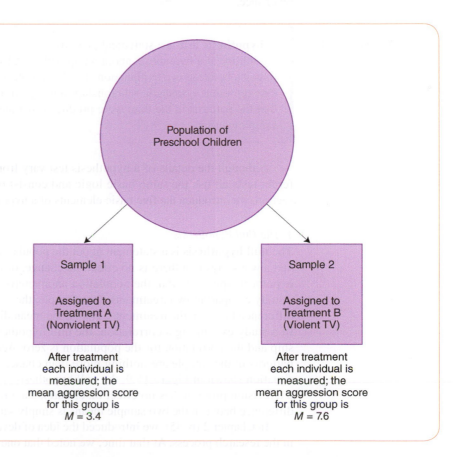

FIGURE 15.9

A Research Study Examining the Relationship between Television Violence and Aggressive Behavior for Preschool Children

Two groups of children (two samples) receive two different treatments and produce different means. The problem is to determine if the mean difference was caused by the treatments or is simply an example of sampling error (as in Figure 15.8).

Population of Preschool Children

Sample 1

Assigned to Treatment A (Nonviolent TV)

After treatment each individual is measured; the mean aggression score for this group is $M = 3.4$

Sample 2

Assigned to Treatment B (Violent TV)

After treatment each individual is measured; the mean aggression score for this group is $M = 7.6$

steps involved planning and conducting a research study to determine whether the hypothesis is correct. Now, the data have been collected, and it is time to use the data to test the credibility of the original hypothesis.

As we have noted, the original research question and the hypothesis concern the population. The research results, however, come from a sample. Thus, the task of evaluating a research hypothesis involves using the information from samples as the basis for making general conclusions about populations. This is the task of inferential statistics. One of the most commonly used inferential procedures is the **hypothesis test**. In very general terms, a hypothesis test is a systematic procedure that determines whether the sample data provide convincing evidence to support the original research hypothesis.

A hypothesis test can be viewed as a technique to help ensure the internal validity of a research study. Recall in Chapter 6 (p. 139) that internal validity is threatened whenever there is an alternative explanation for the results obtained in a research study. Because it is always possible that the results observed in a sample are simply random variation caused by sampling error, it is also always possible that pure chance (sampling error) is an alternative explanation. In Figure 15.9, for example, the 4-point difference between the two sample means could have been caused by the treatments, but it also could have been caused by chance.

The goal of a hypothesis test is to rule out chance as a plausible explanation for the results. The hypothesis test accomplishes this goal by first determining what kind of results can be reasonably expected from chance and what results are very unlikely to occur by chance. The test hopes to demonstrate that the actual results are very unlikely to occur by chance.

DEFINITION

> A **hypothesis test** is a statistical procedure that uses sample data to evaluate the credibility of a hypothesis about a population. A hypothesis test attempts to distinguish between two explanations for the sample data: (1) that the patterns in the data represent systematic relationships among variables in the population and (2) that the patterns in the data were produced by random variation from chance or sampling error.

Although the details of a hypothesis test vary from one situation to another, the different tests all use the same basic logic and consist of the same basic elements. In this section, we introduce the five basic elements of a hypothesis test.

1. The Null Hypothesis

The **null hypothesis** is a statement about the population, or populations, being examined, and always says that there is no effect, no change, or no relationship. In general, the null hypothesis specifies what the population parameter(s) should be if nothing happened. In a study comparing two treatments, for example, the null hypothesis states that there is no difference between the treatments; that is, the mean difference for the population is zero. In a study examining a correlation, the null hypothesis states that there is no relationship and the correlation for the population is zero. According to the null hypothesis, any patterns in the sample are nothing more than chance (sampling error). For the research situation shown in Figure 15.9, the null hypothesis states that the amount of violence in a television program has no effect on children's aggressive behavior and, therefore, any difference between the two sample means is simply sampling error.

In Chapter 2 (p. 45), we introduced the idea of developing a good hypothesis as Step 2 in the research process. At that time, we noted that one characteristic of a good hypothesis is that it must make a positive statement about the existence of a relationship or the existence of a treatment effect. The null hypothesis is exactly the opposite of the research hypothesis. The research hypothesis says that the treatment does have an effect, and the null hypothesis says that the treatment has no effect. The goal of the research study is to gather enough evidence to demonstrate convincingly that the treatment really does have an effect. The test determines whether the research study produces enough evidence to reject the null hypothesis and justify a conclusion that the treatment has an effect.

2. The Sample Statistic

The data from the research study are used to compute a sample statistic (or statistics) corresponding to the parameter (or parameters) specified in the null hypothesis. For example, if the null hypothesis states that there is no difference between two population means, the sample statistic would be the difference between two sample means. Or, if the null hypothesis states that the population correlation is zero, the sample statistic would be the sample correlation obtained in the research study.

3. The Standard Error

Earlier, we introduced the concept of sampling error as the natural difference between a sample statistic and the corresponding parameter. Figure 15.8, for example, shows several sample means (statistics) that are all different from the corresponding population means (parameters). Some samples are representative of the population and produce statistics that are very similar to the population parameters. It is also possible to obtain some extreme, unrepresentative samples whose statistics are very different from the population values. In most research situations, it is possible to calculate the average size of the sampling error, that is, the average difference between a statistic and a parameter. This average distance is called the **standard error**.

> **DEFINITION**
>
> **Standard error** is a measure of the average, or standard, distance between a sample statistic and the corresponding population parameter.

The advantage of computing the standard error is that it provides a measure of how much difference it is reasonable to expect between a statistic and a parameter. Notice that this distance is a measure of the natural discrepancy that occurs just by chance. Samples are intended to represent their populations but they are not expected to be perfect. Typically, there is some discrepancy between a sample statistic and the population parameter, and the standard error tells you how much discrepancy to expect.

4. The Test Statistic

A **test statistic** is a mathematical technique for comparing the sample statistic with the null hypothesis, using the standard error as a baseline. In many hypothesis tests, the test statistic is a ratio with the following structure:

$$\text{Test statistic} = \frac{\text{Sample statistic} - \text{Parameter from the null hypothesis}}{\text{Standard error}}$$

$$\text{Actual difference} = \frac{\text{Actual different between the data and the hypothesis}}{\text{Difference expected by chance}}$$

The null hypothesis states that the results of the research study represent nothing more than chance. If this is true, then the actual results (the numerator) and the chance results (the denominator) should be very similar, and the test statistic will have a value near 1.00. Thus, when the test statistic produces a value near 1.00, it is an indication that there is no treatment effect, no difference, or no relationship; that is, the results are consistent with the null hypothesis.

On the other hand, if there is a real treatment effect or a real relationship, the actual results should be noticeably bigger than those expected from chance. In this case, the test statistic should produce a value much larger than 1.00. Thus, a large value for a test statistic (much greater than 1.00) is an indication of a large discrepancy between the data and the hypothesis, and suggests that the null hypothesis should be rejected.

DEFINITION

> In the context of a hypothesis test, a **test statistic** is a summary value that measures the degree to which the sample data are in accordance with the null hypothesis. Typically, a large value for the test statistic indicates a large discrepancy between the sample statistic and the parameter specified by the null hypothesis, and leads to rejecting the null hypothesis.

5. The Alpha Level (Level of Significance)

The final element in a hypothesis test is the **alpha level**, or **level of significance**. The alpha level provides a criterion for interpreting the test statistic. As we noted earlier, a test statistic with a value greater than 1.00 usually indicates that the obtained result is greater than would be expected from chance. However, researchers typically demand research results that are not just greater than chance but *significantly* greater than chance. The alpha level provides a criterion for significance.

Remember, the goal of a hypothesis test is to rule out chance as a plausible explanation for the results. To achieve this, researchers determine which results are reasonable to expect just by chance (without any treatment effect), and which results are extremely unlikely to be obtained by chance alone. The alpha level is a probability value that defines what is *extremely unlikely*. By convention, alpha levels are very small probabilities, usually .05, .01, or .001. An alpha level of .01, for example, means that a sample result is considered to be extremely unlikely to occur by chance (without any treatment effect) if it has a probability that is less than .01. Such a sample results in rejection of the null hypothesis and the conclusion that a real treatment effect does exist.

With rare exceptions, a value of .05 is the largest acceptable alpha level.

DEFINITION

> The **alpha level**, or **level of significance**, for a hypothesis test is the maximum probability that the research result was obtained simply by chance. A hypothesis test with an alpha level of .01, for example, means that the test demands that there is less than a 1% (.01) probability that the results are caused only by chance.

The following scenario provides a concrete example for the concept of an alpha level and the role it plays in a hypothesis test.

Suppose that I get a brand new coin from the bank. The null hypothesis says that there is nothing wrong with the coin—it is perfectly balanced and should produce 50% heads if it is tossed repeatedly. I decide to test the hypothesis by counting the number of heads I obtain in a sample of 100 tosses, using an alpha level of .05.

According to the null hypothesis, I should get around 50 heads in a sample of 100 tosses. Remember, a sample is not expected to be perfect; there will be some sampling error, so I should not be surprised to obtain 47 heads or 52 heads in 100 tosses. However, it is very unlikely that I would obtain more than 60 heads. In fact, the probability of obtaining more than 60 heads in 100 tosses of a balanced coin is only 0.0228. Thus, any sample with more than 60 heads is very unlikely to occur if the null hypothesis is true (the probability is less than an alpha level of .05). Therefore, if I obtain a sample with more than 60 heads, my decision will be to reject the null hypothesis and conclude that the coin is not perfectly balanced.

Reporting Results from a Hypothesis Test

The goal of a hypothesis test is to establish that the results from a research study are very unlikely to have occurred by chance. "Very unlikely" is defined by the alpha level. When the result of a research study satisfies the criterion imposed by the alpha level, the result is said to be a **significant result**, or a **statistically significant result**. For example, when the difference between two sample means is so large that there is less than a 1% probability that the difference occurred by chance, it is said to be a significant difference at the .01 level of significance. Notice that a smaller level of significance means that you have more confidence in the result. A result that is significant at the .05 level means that there is a 5% risk that the result is just a result of chance. Significance at the .01 level, on the other hand, means that there is only a 1% probability that the result is caused by chance. If the research results do not satisfy the criterion established by the alpha level, the results are said to be not significant.

In the literature, significance levels are reported as p values. For example, a research paper may report a significant difference between two treatments with $p < .05$. The expression $p < .05$ simply means that the probability of the result being caused simply by chance is less than .05.

When statistics are done on a computer, the printouts usually report exact values for p. For example, a computer-based hypothesis test evaluating the mean difference between two treatments may report a significance level of $p = .028$. In this case, the computer has determined that there is a .028 probability that the mean difference could have occurred simply by chance or sampling error without any treatment effect. Based on this outcome and using an alpha level of .05, the researcher would:

• Reject the null hypothesis. In other words, the researcher rejects chance as a plausible explanation for the research results.
• Report a significant result with $p < .05$ or $p = .028$. In the past, research reports identified the probability of chance in relation to standard alpha levels. In this example, the exact probability of $p = .028$ is less than the standard alpha level of .05, so the researcher would report $p < .05$, indicating that it is very unlikely (probability less than .05) that the results can be explained by chance. More recent studies report the exact level of probability, in this case, $p = .028$. However, if the computer reported a value of $p = .067$, the researcher would have to conclude that the result is not statistically significant. Because the actual probability is larger than the standard value of .05, the researcher would accept chance as a plausible explanation for the research results, and report the result as not significant with $p > .05$.

DEFINITION

A **significant result**, or a **statistically significant result**, means that it is extremely unlikely that the research result was obtained simply by chance. A significant result is always accompanied by an alpha level that defines the maximum probability that the result is caused only by chance.

Errors in Hypothesis Testing

Because a hypothesis test is an inferential process (using limited information to reach a general conclusion), there is always a possibility that the process will lead to an error. Specifically, a sample always provides limited and incomplete information about its population. In addition, some samples are not good representatives of the population and can provide misleading information. If a researcher is misled by the results from the sample, it is likely that the researcher will reach an incorrect conclusion. Two kinds of errors can be made in hypothesis testing.

Type I Errors

One possibility for error occurs when the sample data appear to show a significant effect but, in fact, there is no effect in the population. By chance, the researcher has selected an unusual or extreme sample. Because the sample appears to show that the treatment has an effect, the researcher incorrectly concludes that there is a significant effect. This kind of mistake is called a **Type I error**.

Note that the consequence of a Type I error is a false report. This is a serious mistake. Fortunately, the likelihood of a Type I error is very small, and the exact probability of this kind of mistake is known to everyone who sees the research report. Recall that a significant result means that the result is very unlikely to have occurred by chance. It does not mean that it is impossible for the result to have occurred by chance. In particular, a significant result is always accompanied by an alpha level or an exact p value (e.g., $p < .01$ or $p = .006$). By reporting the p value, researchers are acknowledging the possibility that their result could be caused by chance. In other words, the alpha level or the p value identifies the probability of a Type I error.

Type II Errors

The second possibility for error occurs when the sample data do not show a significant effect when, in fact, there is a real effect in the population. This often occurs when an effect is very small and does not produce sample data that are sufficiently extreme to reject the null hypothesis. In this case, the researcher concludes that there is no significant effect when a real effect actually exists. This is a **Type II error**.

The consequence of a Type II error is that a researcher fails to detect a real effect. Whenever research results do not show a significant effect, the researcher may choose to abandon the research project under the assumption that either there is no effect or the effect is too small to be of any consequence. On the other hand, the researcher may be convinced that an effect really exists but failed to show up in the current study. In this case, the researcher may choose to repeat the study, often using a larger sample, a stronger version of the treatment, or some other refinement that might increase the likelihood of obtaining a significant result.

DEFINITIONS

> A **Type I error** occurs when a researcher finds evidence for a significant result when, in fact, there is no effect (no relationship) in the population. The error occurs because the researcher has, by chance, selected an extreme sample that appears to show the existence of an effect when there is none.
>
> A **Type II error** occurs when sample data do not show evidence of a significant effect when, in fact, a real effect does exist in the population. This often occurs when the effect is so small that it does not show up in the sample.

Although Type I and Type II errors are mistakes, they are not foolish or careless mistakes in the sense that the researcher is overlooking something that should be perfectly obvious. In fact, these errors are the direct result of a careful evaluation of the research results. The problem is that the results are misleading. For example, in the general population there is no difference in average IQ between males and females. However, it is possible for a researcher to select a random sample of 25 females who have exceptionally high (or low) IQ scores. Note that the researcher is not deliberately seeking exceptional people and is not using a biased selection process. Instead, the exceptional women are selected purely by chance. As a result, the researcher finds that the women in the study have significantly higher IQs than the men. This result appears to provide clear evidence that the average IQ is not the same for men and women. Based on this result, the researcher is likely to conclude that a real difference exists and, thereby, make a Type I error.

Factors That Influence the Outcome of a Hypothesis Test

There are several factors that help determine whether a hypothesis test will successfully reject the null hypothesis and conclude that there is a significant effect. When the test involves numerical scores that have been used to compute means or correlations, there are two factors that are particularly important:

1. The number of scores in the sample
2. The variability of the scores, typically described by the sample variance

The Number of Scores in the Sample

The key question for a hypothesis test is whether the sample data provide convincing evidence for a real mean difference between treatments or a real correlation between two variables. In general, results obtained from large samples are simply more convincing than results from small samples. For example, suppose a research study finds a 2-point mean difference between treatments using a sample of $n = 4$ participants in each treatment. Because there are only four people in each group, the sample means are considered to be relatively unstable. One new person in each group could change the means enough to erase the 2-point difference. Thus, the 2-point difference obtained for samples of $n = 4$ is not likely to be significant. On the other hand, suppose the study finds the same 2-point difference using samples of $n = 100$ participants. Now the sample means are quite stable; adding a few new people will not noticeably affect the means. As a result, the 2-point difference is viewed as solid evidence of a real difference between treatments and is likely to be statistically significant. In general, a mean difference or a correlation found with a large sample is more likely to be significant than the same result found with a small sample. The optimal sample size depends on a variety of factors including the expected size of the treatment effect and the size of the variance. However, increasing sample size always increases the chances for detecting a treatment effect if one exists. (Also see the discussion of sample size on pp. 113–115.)

The Size of the Variance

In simple terms, small variance means that the scores are clustered together with all of the individual scores close to each other and close to the mean. In this situation, any individual score that is selected is likely to be representative of the entire group. On the other hand, large variance means that the scores are widely scattered with relatively large distances between individual scores and the overall mean. When variance is large, it is easy to select an individual or a group of individuals whose scores are extreme and not representative. As a result, sample statistics are generally viewed as unreliable and unstable if the variance is high. With high variance, for example, adding one or two new people to a sample can drastically change the value of the mean. Remember, a few extreme scores can distort the mean (see p. 380) and extreme scores are common when the variance is high. In general, a sample mean difference or a correlation found with high variance is less convincing and less likely to be significant than the same result found with low variance.

The idea that large variance can obscure any meaningful patterns was first introduced in Chapter 8 (pp. 196–198) in the context of individual differences. Figure 15.10 reproduces Figures 8.3 and 8.4, which show the results from two research studies. Both studies use two samples to compare two treatment conditions and both studies find a mean difference between treatments of approximately 10 points. In Figure 15.10a, both samples have small variance and the 10-point mean difference between treatments is easy to see. In Figure 15.10b, however, the sample variances are increased and the same 10-point difference is no longer visible.

The effect of large variance that is shown visually in Figure 15.10 is supported by the two hypothesis tests. The appropriate test for comparing two means from two separate samples is the independent-measures t-test. For the data in Figure 15.10a (small variance), the test shows a statistically significant difference between the two sample means. In this case, it is very unlikely ($p < .001$) that the mean difference is caused by chance. For the data in Figure 15.10b (large variance), however, the test shows no significant mean difference. With the larger variance, there is a reasonable probability ($p = .084$) that the mean difference is simply the result of chance.

When the variance is small, the 10-point treatment effect is easy to see and is statistically significant (Figure 15.10a). However, the same 10-point treatment effect is obscured and is

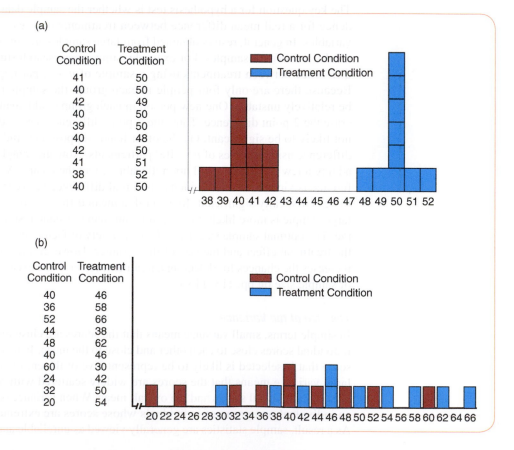

FIGURE 15.10

The Results from Two Research Studies Demonstrating the Role of Variance

(a) When the variance is small, the data show a clear mean difference between the two treatments.
(b) With large variance, the mean difference between treatments is obscured.

(a)

Control Condition	Treatment Condition
41	50
40	50
42	49
40	50
39	50
40	48
42	50
41	51
38	52
40	50

(b)

Control Condition	Treatment Condition
40	46
36	58
52	66
44	38
48	62
40	46
60	30
24	42
32	50
20	54

not significant when the variance is large (Figure 15.10b). Once again, the general point is that large variance reduces the likelihood of obtaining a statistically significant result.

Supplementing Hypothesis Tests with Measures of Effect Size

In the preceding section we noted that the outcome of a hypothesis test depends in part on the size of the sample. Specifically, increasing the sample size increases the likelihood of obtaining a significant result. As a result, a very small treatment effect can be statistically significant if the sample is large enough. Because a *significant* effect does not necessarily mean a *large* effect, many scientists have criticized hypothesis tests for providing inadequate or incomplete analyses of research results (Hunter, 1997; Killeen, 2005; Loftus, 1996). As a result, it is strongly recommended that researchers include an independent measure of **effect size** whenever they report a statistically significant effect (see the guidelines presented by Wilkinson & Task Force on Statistical Inference, 1999). The purpose for measuring and reporting effect size is to provide information about the absolute size of the treatment effect that is not influenced by outside factors such as sample size. Statisticians have developed several different methods for computing a standardized measure of effect size. We consider two examples that are representative of the most commonly used techniques for measuring and reporting effect size.

Measuring Effect Size with Cohen's d

Cohen (1961) recommended that the size of the mean difference between two treatments be standardized by measuring the mean difference in terms of the standard deviation. The resulting measure of effect size is defined as **Cohen's *d*** and is computed as

$$d = \frac{\text{Sample mean difference}}{\text{Sample standard deviation}}$$

For example, a value of $d = 2.00$ indicates that the mean difference is twice as big as the standard deviation. On the other hand, a value of $d = 0.5$ indicates that the mean difference is only half as large as the standard deviation. The concept of measuring effect size with Cohen's *d* is easier to understand if you visualize two frequency distributions corresponding to the scores from two different treatment conditions. In this context, Cohen's *d* corresponds to the amount of separation between the two distributions. For example, Figure 15.11a shows a situation in which Cohen's *d* is equal to 0.50. The distribution on the left corresponds to scores from treatment 1. Notice that we have marked the location of the mean and indicated the size of the standard deviation for this distribution. The distribution on the right corresponds to scores from treatment 2. The two distributions are drawn so that the distance between means is equal to exactly half of the standard deviation; that is, Cohen's $d = 0.50$. For comparison, Figure 15.11b shows a situation for which Cohen's $d = 2.00$; that is, the two means are separated by two full standard deviations. Cohen (1988) also provided objective criteria for evaluating the size of an effect. These criteria are presented in Table 15.3. Finally, we should note that Cohen's *d* is used primarily to evaluate effect size in research situations comparing two treatment means. Examples demonstrating the calculation of Cohen's *d* are presented in Appendix B, pp. 459–460.

Measuring Effect Size as a Percentage of Variance (r^2 and η^2)

When there is a consistent relationship between two variables, it is possible to predict whether a participant's score on one variable will be relatively high or relatively low if you know the participant's score on the second variable. For example, there is a consistent positive correlation between a child's IQ and the IQ of the child's mother. If you know that

FIGURE 15.11

Measuring Effect Size with Cohen's *d*

Cohen's *d* measures the mean difference between two distributions in terms of the standard deviation. (a) The two distributions are separated by half of a standard deviation, $d = 0.50$. (b) The two distributions are separated by two standard deviations, $d = 2.00$.

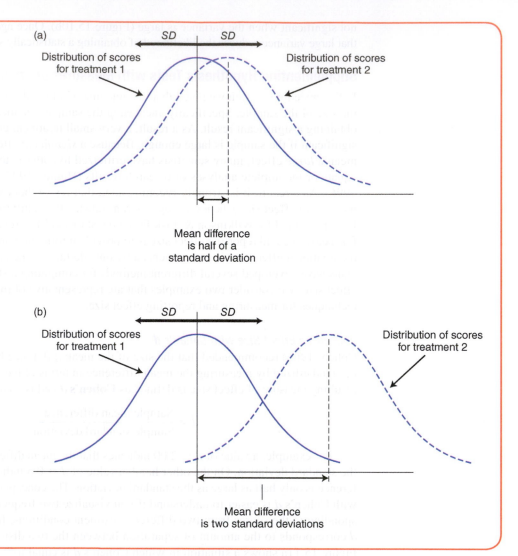

(a)

Distribution of scores for treatment 1

SD   SD

Distribution of scores for treatment 2

Mean difference is half of a standard deviation

(b)

SD   SD

Distribution of scores for treatment 1

Distribution of scores for treatment 2

Mean difference is two standard deviations

TABLE 15.3

Criteria for Evaluating Effect Size Using Cohen's *d*

Magnitude of *d*	Evaluation of Effect Size
$d = 0.2$	Small effect (mean difference around 0.2 standard deviation)
$d = 0.5$	Medium effect (mean difference around 0.5 standard deviation)
$d = 0.8$	Large effect (mean difference around 0.8 standard deviation)

the mother has a relatively high IQ, you can predict that the child also has a relatively high IQ. In the same way, if there is a consistent difference between two treatment conditions, it is possible to predict whether a participant's score will be relatively high or relatively low if you know which treatment the participant receives. For example, suppose one group of participants receives an effective cholesterol-lowering medication and a second group receives an ineffective placebo. In this case, we can predict that people who receive the drug will have lower cholesterol levels than people who do not receive the drug.

The ability to predict differences forms the basis of another method of measuring effect size by computing the **percentage of variance accounted for**. This calculation involves measuring the percentage of variance for one variable that can be predicted by knowing a second variable. For example, the participants in the cholesterol study all have different cholesterol levels. In statistical terms, their scores are variable. However, some of this variability can be predicted by knowing the treatment condition for each participant; individuals in the drug condition score lower than individuals in the no-drug condition. By measuring exactly how much of the variability is predictable, we can obtain a measure of how big the effect actually is. When the percentage of variance is measured for t-tests (comparing two sample means) or for correlations, it is typically called r^2. When the percentage is measured for analysis of variance, or ANOVA (comparing multiple sample means), it is usually called η^2 (the Greek letter eta squared). For a t-test evaluating the difference between two sample means, the value of r^2 can be obtained directly from the t statistic and its degrees of freedom (df) by the following formula:

$$r^2 = \frac{t^2}{t^2 + df}$$

Examples demonstrating the calculation of r^2 and η^2 are presented in Appendix B, pp. 459, 465, and 469. Criteria for evaluating the size of a treatment effect using r^2 or η^2 are presented in Table 15.4 (Cohen, 1988). Effect size is most commonly measured with r^2 in research situations that compare two treatment means or for research evaluating relationships, such as a correlational study. Effect size is measured with η^2 for research studies that compare more than two treatment means.

Confidence Intervals

An alternative technique for measuring or describing the size of a treatment effect or the strength of a relationship is to compute a confidence interval. The concept of a confidence interval is based on the observation that sample statistics tend to provide reasonably accurate estimates of the corresponding population parameters. For example, if a sample is selected from a population, you do not expect the sample mean to be exactly equal to the population mean, but the sample mean should give a good indication of the actual value for the population mean. Thus, a sample mean of $M = 85$ suggests that the population mean is probably around 85. Similarly, a sample correlation of $r = 0.64$ indicates that the population correlation is probably around 0.64.

The fact that sample statistics tend to be close to their population parameters means that we can use the sample values as estimators of the corresponding population values.

TABLE 15.4

Criteria for Evaluating Effect Size Using r^2 or η^2 (Percentage of Variance Accounted for)

Magnitude of r^2 or η^2	Evaluation of Effect Size
r^2 or $\eta^2 = 0.01$	Small effect (around 1%)
r^2 or $\eta^2 = 0.09$	Medium effect (around 9%)
r^2 or $\eta^2 = 0.25$	Large effect (around 25% or more)

A **confidence interval** involves estimating that an unknown population parameter is located within an interval, or range of values, around a known sample statistic. If a sample is selected from an unknown population and the sample mean is found to be $M = 60$, then we can estimate that the population mean is around 60. For example, the actual population mean is likely to be within 5 points of $M = 60$, that is, within an interval from 55 to 65. It is even more likely that the population mean is within 10 points of $M = 60$, somewhere in an interval from 50 to 70. Notice that the likelihood of the estimate being correct depends on the width of the interval. If the sample has a mean of $M = 60$, it is almost guaranteed that the population mean has a value between 30 and 90 ($M = 60 \pm 30$ points).

DEFINITION

> A **confidence interval** is a technique for estimating the magnitude of an unknown population value, such as a mean difference or a correlation. The logic behind a confidence interval is that a sample statistic should provide a reasonably accurate estimate of the corresponding population parameter. Therefore, the value of the parameter should be located in an interval, or a range of values, centered around the sample statistic.

Researchers construct confidence intervals by creating a range of values on each side of a known sample statistic. The wider the range of values, the more confidence the researchers have that the interval actually contains the unknown population value. Notice that there is a trade-off between the precision of the estimate and the confidence in the estimate. A very narrow interval provides a precise estimate but gives very little confidence. A wider interval gives more confidence but is less precise.

The width of a confidence interval is determined by two factors: the standard error for the sample statistic and the level of confidence desired by the researcher. Recall that the standard error provides a measure of the average or standard distance between a sample statistic and the corresponding population parameter (p. 393). A small standard error means that all the possible sample statistics are within a small distance of the population parameter. As a result, the unknown population parameter is likely to be contained in a relatively narrow interval around the sample statistic. A large standard error, on the other hand, tends to produce a relatively wide interval. The second factor, level of confidence, is also directly related to the width of the confidence interval, so that increasing confidence produces an increase in interval width.

Confidence intervals provide a good indication of how large a treatment effect actually is. For a study comparing two treatment conditions, for example, the difference between the two sample means provides an estimate of the difference between the two population means. If there is a 4-point difference between sample means, then the actual difference between the two treatments should be around 4 points. A confidence interval would produce a precise range of values and a specific level of confidence for estimating the true mean difference.

Finally, we should note that confidence intervals, like hypothesis tests, are influenced by the size of the sample(s). In general, larger samples lead to smaller standard errors, which increase the likelihood of finding a significant result and decrease the width of confidence intervals. Because confidence intervals are influenced by sample size they do not provide an unqualified measure of absolute effect size and are not an adequate substitute for Cohen's d or r^2.

LEARNING CHECK

1. When a sample is selected from a population, the sample mean is essentially guaranteed to be different from the population mean. What is the name for the naturally occurring difference between a sample statistic and the corresponding population parameter?
   a. Type I error
   b. Type II error
   c. Sampling error
   d. Inferential error

2. A researcher reports a significant correlation using an alpha level of .01. Which of the following is an accurate conclusion from this result?
   a. The probability that the researcher is making a Type I error is $p > .01$
   b. The probability that the researcher is making a Type I error is $p < .01$
   c. The probability that the researcher is making a Type II error is $p > .01$
   d. The probability that the researcher is making a Type II error is $p < .01$

3. What is measured by values such as Cohen's d or r^2 (the percentage of variance accounted for)?
   a. The validity of a hypothesis test
   b. The risk of committing a type I error
   c. The size of a treatment effect or the strength of a correlation
   d. The level of significance

Answers appear at the end of the chapter.

15.4   Finding the Right Statistics for Your Data

LEARNING OBJECTIVE

LO10 Identify the characteristics that differentiate different sets of data and identify the hypothesis test(s) appropriate for each data structure.

Three Data Structures

As we noted in Chapter 6, the five basic research strategies produce three distinct data structures, and each data structure determines the specific statistical techniques that are used to describe and evaluate the data. The three data structures and the corresponding research strategies are as follows:

1. One group of participants with one variable measured for each participant. These data are produced by studies using the descriptive research strategy (Chapter 13).
2. One group of participants with two (or more) variables measured for each participant. These data are produced by the correlational research strategy (Chapter 12).
3. Two or more groups of scores with each score a measurement of the same variable. These data are produced by the experimental, the nonexperimental, and the quasi-experimental research strategies (Chapters 7–11).

In this section, we present examples of each structure. Once you match your data to one of the examples, you can use the corresponding flowchart to determine the statistical procedures that apply to that example.

Scales of Measurement

Before we begin discussion of the three categories of data, there is one other factor that differentiates data within each category and helps to determine exactly which statistics are appropriate. In Chapter 3, we introduced four scales of measurement and noted that different measurement scales allow different kinds of mathematical manipulation, which result in different statistics. For most statistical applications, however, ratio and interval scales are equivalent so we group them together for the following review.

Ratio scales and **interval scales** produce numerical scores that are compatible with the full range of mathematical manipulation. Examples include measurements of height in inches, weight in pounds, the number of errors on a task, and IQ scores.

Ordinal scales consist of ranks or ordered categories. Examples include classifying cups of coffee as small, medium, and large or ranking job applicants as first, second, and third.

Nominal scales consist of named categories. Examples include eye color, academic major, or occupation.

Within each category of data, we present examples representing these three measurement scales and identify the statistics that apply to each.

Category 1: A Single Group of Participants with One Score per Participant

This type of data typically is produced by studies using the descriptive research strategy (Chapter 13). These studies are conducted simply to describe individual variables as they exist naturally. For example, a recent news report stated that half of American teenagers, ages 12–17, send 50 or more text messages a day. To get this number, the researchers had to measure the number of text messages for each individual in a large sample of teenagers. The resulting data consist of one score per participant for a single group.

It is also possible that the data are a portion of the results from a larger study examining several variables. For example a college administrator may conduct a survey to obtain information describing the eating, sleeping, and study habits of the college's students. Although several variables are being measured, the intent is to look at them one at a time. For example, the administrator will look at the number of hours each week that each student spends studying. These data consist of one score for each individual in a single group. The administrator will then shift attention to the number of hours per day that each student spends sleeping. Again, the data consist of one score for each person in a single group. The identifying feature for this type of research (and this type of data) is that there is no attempt to examine relationships between different variables. Instead, the goal is to describe individual variables, one at a time.

Table 15.5 presents three examples of data in this category. Note that the three data sets differ in terms of the scale of measurement used to obtain the scores. The first set (a) shows numerical scores measured on an interval or ratio scale. The second set (b) consists of ordinal, or rank-ordered, categories, and the third set (c) shows nominal measurements.

Statistics for Data in Category 1

Because the data in this category are usually intended to describe individual variables, the most commonly used statistical procedures are descriptive statistics that are used to summarize and describe the group of scores. In some limited situations, however, there is a logical basis for a null hypothesis and the data can be used for a hypothesis test. For example, if the scores are from a measurement scale with a well-defined neutral point, then a hypothesis test can be used to determine whether the scores are significantly different from neutral. On a 7-point rating scale, for example, a score of $X = 4$ is often identified as neutral. The null hypothesis would state that the population mean is equal to 4. For

TABLE 15.5

Three Examples of Data with One Score per Participant for One Group of Participants

(a) Number of Text Messages Sent in Past 24 Hours	(b) Rank in Class for High School Graduation	(c) Got a Flu Shot Last Season
X	X	X
6	23rd	No
13	18th	No
28	5th	Yes
11	38th	No
9	17th	Yes
31	42nd	No
18	32nd	No

measurements using non-numerical categories, it may be reasonable to hypothesize that the categories occur equally often (equal proportions) in the population and the hypothesis test would determine whether the sample proportions are significantly different.

The flowchart in Figure 15.12 identifies the appropriate statistical procedures for data in category 1, and the descriptive statistics are all demonstrated in Appendix B.

Category 2: A Single Group of Participants with Two Variables Measured for Each Participant

These data are typically produced by the correlational research strategy (Chapter 12). Research studies using this strategy are intended to examine relationships between variables. Note that different variables are being measured, so each participant has two or more scores, each representing a different variable. Typically, there is no attempt to manipulate or control the variables; they are simply observed and recorded as they exist naturally.

Although several variables may be measured, researchers usually select pairs of variables to evaluate specific relationships. Therefore, we present examples showing pairs of variables and focus on statistics that evaluate relationships between two variables. Table 15.6 presents four examples of data in this category. Once again, the four data sets differ in terms of the scales of measurement that are used. The first set of data (a) shows numerical scores for each set of measurements. For the second set (b), we have ranked the scores from the first set and show the resulting ranks. The third data set (c) shows numerical scores for one variable and nominal scores for the second variable. In the fourth set (d), both scores are measured on a nominal scale of measurement.

Statistics for Data in Category 2

The goal of the statistical analysis for data in this category is to describe and evaluate the relationships between variables, typically focusing on two variables at a time. With only two variables, the most commonly used statistics are correlations and regression. Correlations serve as their own descriptive statistics, identifying the direction and the strength of the relationship. Regression describes the relationship determining the equation for the straight line that is the best fit for the data points. The equation (or the line) provides a simplified description of the data.

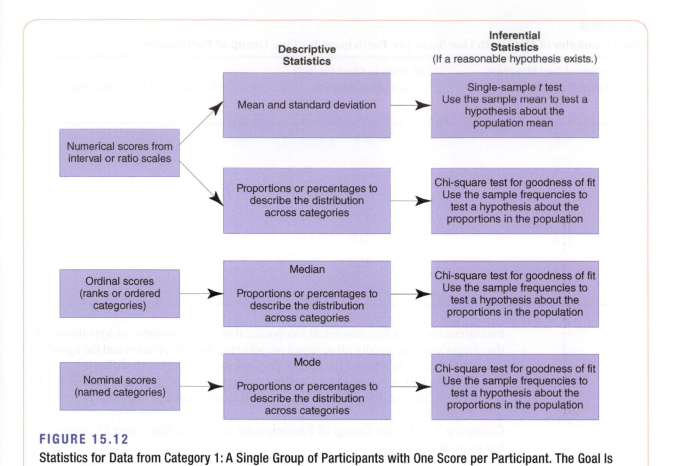

FIGURE 15.12

Statistics for Data from Category 1: A Single Group of Participants with One Score per Participant. The Goal Is Usually to Describe the Variable as It Exists Naturally.

For either correlations or regression, the null hypothesis states that there is no relationship between the two variables in the population. The hypothesis test determines whether the sample provides sufficient evidence to reject the null hypothesis and conclude that there is a significant relationship.

The **chi-square test for independence** provides an alternative to correlations for evaluating the relationship between two variables. For the chi-square test, each of the two variables can be measured on any scale, provided that the number of categories is reasonably small. For numerical scores covering a wide range of value, the scores can be grouped into a smaller number of ordinal intervals. For example, IQ scores ranging from 93 to 137 could be grouped into three categories described as high, medium, and low IQ.

For the chi-square test, the two variables are used to create a matrix showing the frequency distribution for the data. The categories of one variable define the rows of the matrix and the categories of the second variable define the columns. Each cell of the matrix contains the frequency or number of individuals whose scores correspond to the row and column of the cell. For example, the politics and academic major scores in Table 15.6d could be reorganized in a matrix as follows:

	Arts	Humanities	Sciences	Professions
Conservative				
Liberal				

TABLE 15.6

Examples of Data with Two Scores for Each Participant for One Group of Participants

(a) SAT Score (X) and College Freshman GPA (Y)		(b) Ranks for the Scores in Set (a)	
X	Y	X	Y
620	3.90	7	8
540	3.12	3	2
590	3.45	6	5
480	2.75	1	1
510	3.20	2	3
660	3.85	8	7
570	3.50	5	6
560	3.24	4	4

(c) Age (X) and Wrist Watch Preference (Y)		(d) Politics (X) and Academic Major (Y)	
X	Y	X	Y
27	Digital	Liberal	Sciences
43	Analog	Liberal	Humanities
19	Digital	Conservative	Arts
34	Digital	Liberal	Professions
37	Digital	Conservative	Professions
49	Analogue	Conservative	Humanities
22	Digital	Conservative	Arts
65	Analogue	Liberal	Sciences
46	Digital	Conservative	Humanities

The value in each cell is the number of students with the politics and major identified by the cell's row and column. The matrix provides a description of the data. The null hypothesis for the chi-square test would state that there is no relationship between politics and academic major in the population. The hypothesis test would determine whether the sample data are sufficient to reject the null hypothesis.

The flowchart in Figure 15.13 identifies the appropriate statistical procedures for different types of data in category 2 and most of the statistics are demonstrated in Appendix B.

Category 3: Two or More Groups of Scores with Each Score a Measurement of The Same Variable

A second method for examining relationships between variables is to use the categories of one variable to define different groups and then measure a second variable to obtain a set of scores within each group. The first variable, defining the groups, usually falls into one of the following general categories:

a. Participant Characteristic: for example occupation or age

b. Time: for example, before versus after treatment

c. Treatment Conditions: for example, with caffeine versus without caffeine

If the scores in one group are consistently different from the scores in another group, then the data indicate a relationship between variables. For example, if the performance scores for a group of doctors are consistently higher than the scores for a group of dentists, then there is a relationship between performance and occupation.

Another factor that differentiates data sets in this category is the distinction between within-subjects and between-subjects designs. Between-subjects designs include experimental studies (Chapter 8) and nonequivalent-group designs (Chapter 10). Within-subjects design include experimental designs (Chapter 9) and the pre–post designs (Chapter 10). You should recall that a *between-subjects design,* also known as an *independent-measures design,* requires a separate group of participants for each group of scores. For example, a study comparing scores for liberals with scores for conservatives would require two groups of participants. On the other hand, a *within-subjects design*, also known as

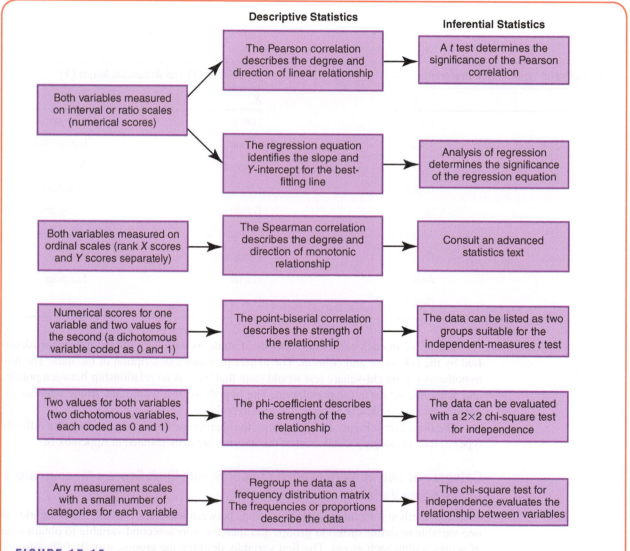

FIGURE 15.13

Statistics for Data from Category 2: One Group of Participants with Two Variables Measured for Each Participant. The Goal Is to Describe and Evaluate the Relationship between Variables.

a *repeated-measures design*, obtains several groups of scores from the same group of participants. A common example of a within-subjects design is the nonexperimental pre–post study in which one group of individuals is measured before a treatment and then measured again after the treatment.

Examples of data sets in this category are presented in Table 15.7. The table includes a sampling of between-subjects and within-subjects designs as well as examples representing several different scales of measurement.

Statistics for Data in Category 3

Data in this category includes single-factor and two-factor designs. In a single-factor study, the values of one variable are used to define different groups and a second variable (the dependent variable) is measured to obtain a set of scores in each group. For a two-factor design, two variables are used to construct a matrix with the values of one variable defining the rows and the values of the second variable defining the columns. A third variable

TABLE 15.7

Examples of Data Comparing Two or More Groups of Scores with All Scores Measuring the Same Variable

(a) Quiz Scores for Students Taking Notes Longhand or on a Laptop		(b) Performance Scores before and after 24 Hours of Sleep Deprivation		
Laptop	**Longhand**	**Participant**	**Before**	**After**
5	7	A	9	7
4	5	B	7	6
4	4	C	7	5
3	5	D	8	8
4	6	E	5	4
3	4	F	9	8
4	5	G	8	5

(c) Success or Failure on a Task for Participants Working Alone or in a Group		(d) Amount of Time Spent on Snapchat (small, medium, large) for Students from Each High School Class			
Alone	**Group**	**Freshman**	**Sophomore**	**Junior**	**Senior**
Fail	Succeed	Med	Small	Med	Large
Succeed	Succeed	Small	Large	Large	Med
Succeed	Succeed	Small	Med	Large	Med
Succeed	Succeed	Med	Med	Large	Large
Fail	Fail	Small	Med	Med	Large
Fail	Succeed	Large	Large	Med	Large
Succeed	Succeed	Med	Large	Small	Med
Fail	Succeed	Small	Med	Large	Large

(the dependent variable) is measured to obtain a set of scores in each cell of the matrix. To simplify discussion, we focus on single-factor designs now and address two-factor designs separately at the end of this section.

The goal for a single-factor research design is to demonstrate a relationship between the two variables by showing consistent differences between groups. When the scores in each group are numerical values, the standard procedure is to compute the mean and the standard deviation as descriptive statistics to summarize and describe each group.

If the scores are measurements on a nominal or ordinal scale and the scale consists of a relatively small number of categories, then the data can be displayed as a frequency-distribution matrix with the groups defining the rows and the categories defining the columns. The number in each cell is the frequency, or number of individuals in the group, identified by the cell's row, with scores corresponding to the cell's column. For example, the data in Table 15.7c show success or failure on a task for participants who are working alone or working in a group. These data could be regrouped as follows:

	Success	Failure
Work Alone		
Work in a Group		

Ordinal data are treated in exactly the same way. For example, a researcher could group high school students by class (freshman, sophomore, junior, senior) and measure the amount of time each student spends on Snapchat by classifying students into three ordinal categories (small, medium, large). An example of the resulting data is shown in Table 15.7d. However, the same data could be regrouped into a frequency-distribution matrix as follows:

	Amount of Time Spent on Snapchat		
	Small	Medium	Large
Freshman			
Sophomore			
Junior			
Senior			

These data are usually described by the distribution of individuals across categories. For example, the scores in one group may be clustered in one category or set of categories and the scores in another group may be clustered in different categories.

Hypothesis tests are used to determine whether there are significant differences between groups. For numerical scores, a **single-factor analysis of variance (ANOVA)** or **one-way ANOVA** and *t*-tests (independent- or repeated-measures) are used to evaluate the statistical significance of the mean differences between the groups of scores. For data from nominal or ordinal scales, the scores are regrouped into a frequency distribution matrix, and chi-square test for independence is used to evaluate the differences between groups.

Two-Factor Designs with Scores from Interval or Ratio Scales

Research designs with two independent (or quasi-independent) variables are known as two-factor designs (Chapter 11). These designs can be presented as a matrix with the levels of one factor defining the rows and the levels of the second factor defining the columns. A third variable (the dependent variable) is measured to obtain a group of scores in each cell of the matrix.

When the scores in each group are numerical values, the standard procedure is to compute the mean and the standard deviation as descriptive statistics to summarize and describe each group.

A **two-factor ANOVA**, or a **two-way ANOVA**, is used to evaluate the significance of the mean differences between cells. The ANOVA separates the mean differences into three categories and conducts three separate hypothesis tests:

1. The main effect for factor *A* evaluates the overall mean differences for the first factor, that is, the mean differences between rows in the data matrix.
2. The main effect for factor *B* evaluates the overall mean differences for the second factor, that is, the mean differences between columns in the data matrix.
3. The interaction between factors evaluates the mean differences between cells that are not accounted for by the main effects.

The flowchart in Figure 15.14 identifies the appropriate statistical procedures for different types of data in category 3. Most of the statistics are demonstrated in Appendix B.

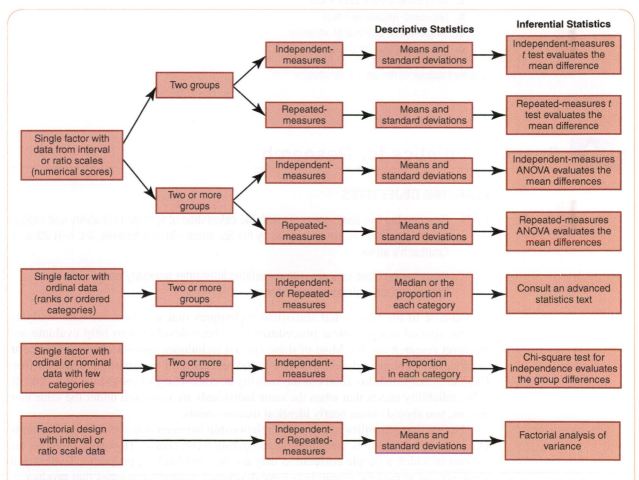

FIGURE 15.14

Statistics for Data from Category 3: Two or More Groups of Scores with One Score per Participant. The Goal Is to Evaluate Differences between Groups of Scores.

1. One category of data is obtained by measuring one variable for each individual in a single group of participants. What kind of statistics are most commonly used for data in this category?
   a. Descriptive statistics
   b. *t*-Tests or analysis of variance
   c. Correlations or chi-square tests
   d. Analysis of variance or chi-square tests

2. One category of data is obtained by measuring two different variables for each individual in a single group of participants. What kind of statistics are most commonly used for data in this category?
   a. Descriptive statistics
   b. *t*-Tests or analysis of variance
   c. Correlations or chi-square tests
   d. Analysis of variance or chi-square tests

3. For a between-subjects study evaluating the mean differences among three treatment conditions, which of the following is the appropriate hypothesis test?
   a. Independent-measures *t*-test
   b. Repeated-measures *t*-test
   c. Single-factor analysis of variance
   d. Chi-square test for independence

Answers appear at the end of the chapter.

15.5 | Special Statistics for Research

LEARNING OBJECTIVES

LO11 Describe the two basic concerns with the calculation of split-half reliability and explain how these concerns are addressed by the Spearman–Brown formula, the K–R 20, and Cronbach's alpha.

LO12 Describe the basic concern with measuring inter-rater reliability and explain how Cohen's kappa addresses this concern.

In addition to the traditional statistical techniques that are used for data analysis, several special mathematical procedures have been developed to help evaluate and interpret research results. Most of these special techniques address questions concerning measurement procedures, specifically the reliability of measurements. Recall from Chapter 3 that reliability refers to the stability or consistency of measurements. Specifically, reliability means that when the same individuals are measured under the same conditions, you should obtain nearly identical measurements.

Notice that reliability refers to the relationship between two sets of measurements. Often, the relationship is measured by computing a correlation. However, there are situations in which a simple correlation may not be completely appropriate. To deal with these special situations, researchers have developed several techniques that produce an adjustment to the correlation or an alternative measure of relationship. In this section, we examine four statistical techniques for adjusting or correcting measures of reliability: the Spearman–Brown formula, the Kuder–Richardson formula 20, Cronbach's coefficient alpha, and Cohen's kappa.

The Spearman–Brown Formula

When a single variable is measured with a test that consists of multiple items, it is common to evaluate the internal consistency of the test by computing a measure of **split-half reliability**. The concept behind split-half reliability is that all the different items on the test are measuring the same variable and, therefore, the measurement obtained from each individual item should be related to every other item. As a result, if you split the test items in half and compute a score for each half, then the score obtained from one half of the test should be related to the score obtained from the other half. A correlation can be used to measure the degree of relationship between the two scores. The value of the correlation defines the split-half reliability of the test.

Although computing a correlation appears to be a straightforward method for measuring the relationship between two halves of a test, this technique has a problem. In particular, the two split-half scores obtained for each participant are based on only half of the test items. In general, the score obtained from half of a test is less reliable than the score obtained from the full test. (With a smaller number of items, there is a greater chance for error or chance to distort the participant's score.) Therefore, a measure of split-half reliability (based on half the test) tends to underestimate the true reliability of the full test. A number of procedures have been developed to correct this problem, but the most commonly used technique is the **Spearman–Brown formula.** The formula adjusts the simple correlation between halves as follows:

$$\text{Spearman-Brown } R = \frac{2r}{1+r}$$

For a test consisting of 20 items, for example, each participant receives two scores with each score based on 10 items. If the split-half correlation between the two scores were $r = 0.80$, then the corrected correlation from the Spearman–Brown formula would be

$$R = \frac{2(0.80)}{1+0.80} = \frac{1.60}{1.80} = 0.89$$

Notice that the effect of the correction is to increase the size of the correlation to produce a better estimate of the true reliability for the full set of test items.

The Kuder–Richardson Formula 20

A second problem with split-half reliability is that here are many different ways to split a test in half. For a 20-item test, for example, you could compute one score for the first 10 items and a second score for the last 10 items. Alternatively, you could compute one score for the odd-numbered items and a second score for the even-numbered items. Depending on how the test is split, you are likely to obtain different measures of reliability. To deal with this problem, Kuder and Richardson (1937) developed a formula that estimates the average of all the possible split-half correlations that can be obtained from all of the possible ways to split a test in half. The formula is the 20th and best one they tried and is, therefore, called the **Kuder–Richardson formula 20** (often shortened to **K–R 20**).

The K–R 20 is limited to tests in which each item has only two possible answers such as true/false, agree/disagree, or yes/no, and the two responses are assigned numerical values of 0 and 1. Each participant's score is the total, added over all the items. The Kuder-Richardson measure of reliability is obtained by

$$\text{K-R } 20 = \left(\frac{n}{n-1}\right)\left(\frac{SD^2 - \Sigma\, pq}{SD^2}\right)$$

The elements in the formula are defined as follows:

The letter n represents the number of items on the test.

SD is the standard deviation for the set of test scores.

For each item, p is the proportion of the participants whose response is coded 0 and q is the proportion of the participants whose response is coded 1 (note that $p + q = 1$ for each item).

Σpq is the sum of the p times q products for all items.

Again, the K–R 20 is intended to measure the average correlation from every possible way to split a test in half. Like a correlation, the formula produces values ranging from 0 to 1.00, with higher values indicating a higher degree of internal consistency or reliability.

Cronbach's Alpha

One limitation of the K–R 20 is that it can only be used for tests in which each item has only two response alternatives. Cronbach (1951) developed a modification of the K–R 20 that can be used when test items have more than two alternatives, such as a Likert scale that has five response choices (see p. 326). **Cronbach's alpha** has a structure similar to the K–R 20 and is computed as follows:

$$\text{Cronbach's alpha} = \left(\frac{n}{n-1}\right)\left(\frac{SD^2 - \Sigma\text{variance}}{SD^2}\right)$$

The elements in Cronbach's formula are identical to the elements in the K-R 20 except for Σvariance. To compute this new term, first calculate the variance of the scores for each item separately. With 20 participants, for example, you would compute the variance for the 20 scores obtained for item 1, and the variance for the 20 scores on item 2, and so on. Then add the variances across all the test items to obtain the value for Σvariance.

Like the K–R 20, Cronbach's alpha is intended to measure split-half reliability by estimating the average correlation that would be obtained by considering every possible way to split the test in half. Also like the K–R 20, Cronbach's alpha produces values between 0 and 1.00, with a higher value indicating a higher degree of internal consistency or reliability.

Cohen's Kappa

When measurements are obtained by behavioral observation, it is customary to evaluate the measurement procedure by determining inter-rater reliability (see p. 63). Inter-rater reliability is the degree of agreement between two observers who have independently observed and recorded behaviors at the same time. The simplest technique for determining inter-rater reliability is to compute the percentage of agreement as follows:

$$\text{Percent agreement} = \frac{\text{Number of observation in agreement}}{\text{Total number of observations}} \times 100$$

For example, if two observers agree on 46 out of 50 observations, their percent agreement is $(46/50)100 = 92\%$.

The problem with a simple measure of percent agreement is that the value obtained can be inflated by chance. That is, the two observers may record the same observation simply by chance. As an extreme example, consider two individuals who are each tossing a coin. For each toss, they record whether the two coins agree. Note that in a series of coin tosses, they will observe several agreements, but the agreements are just chance.

Cohen's kappa is a measure of agreement that attempts to correct for chance (Cohen, 1961). Cohen's kappa is computed as follows:

$$\text{Cohen's kappa} = \frac{PA - PC}{1 - PC}$$

The elements in the formula are defined as follows: PA is the observed percent agreement and PC is the percent agreement expected from chance.

We use the data in Table 15.8 to demonstrate the calculation of Cohen's kappa. The data show the recorded observations of two observers watching a child over 25 observation periods. For every observation period, each observer records yes or no, indicating whether an example of aggressive behavior was observed. The number of agreements is obtained by counting the number of periods in which both observers record the same observation. For the data in Table 15.8, there are 21 agreements out of the 25 observation periods. Thus, the percent agreement is

$$PA = \frac{21}{25} = 84\%$$

To determine the percentage agreement expected from chance (PC), we must call on a basic law of probability. The law states:

> Given two separate events, A and B, with the probability of A equal to p and the probability of B equal to q, then the probability of A and B occurring together is equal to the product of p and q.

For example, if two coins are tossed simultaneously, the probability of each one coming up heads is 0.50 ($p = q = 0.50$). According to the rule, the probability that both coins will come up heads is $p \times q = (0.50)(0.50) = 0.25$.

Applying the probability rule to the data in Table 15.8, we can calculate the probability that both observers will say *yes* just by chance and the probability that both will say *no* just by chance. For the data in the table, the probability that observer 1 says *yes* is 20 out of 25, which equals 0.80. The probability that observer 2 says *yes* is 18 out of 25, or 0.72. According to the probability rule, the probability that both will say *yes* just by chance is:

Probability that both say *yes* $= (0.80)(0.72) = 0.576$ or 57.6%.

Similarly, the probability that both will say *no* just by chance is:

Probability that both say *no* $= (0.20)(0.28) = 0.056$ or 5.6%.

Combining these two values, we obtain an overall probability that the two observers will agree by chance:

$$PC = 57.6\% + 5.6\% = 63.2\%$$

TABLE 15.8

Data That Can Be Used to Evaluate Inter-Rater Reliability Using Either the Percentage of Agreement or Cohen's Kappa

Two observers record behavior for the same individual over 25 observation periods and record whether they observe aggressive behavior during each period.

Observation Period	Observer 1	Observer 2	Agreement
1	Yes	Yes	Agree
2	Yes	Yes	Agree
3	No	Yes	Disagree
4	No	No	Agree
5	Yes	Yes	Agree
6	Yes	Yes	Agree
7	Yes	Yes	Agree
8	Yes	Yes	Agree
9	Yes	Yes	Agree
10	No	No	Agree
11	No	No	Agree
12	No	No	Agree
13	Yes	No	Disagree
14	Yes	Yes	Agree
15	Yes	Yes	Agree
16	Yes	Yes	Agree
17	Yes	Yes	Agree
18	Yes	No	Disagree
19	Yes	Yes	Agree
20	Yes	Yes	Agree
21	Yes	Yes	Agree
22	Yes	No	Disagree
23	Yes	Yes	Agree
24	Yes	Yes	Agree
25	Yes	Yes	Agree

The value for Cohen's kappa can now be computed as follows:

$$\text{Kappa} = \frac{PA-PC}{1-PC} = \frac{84\%-63.2\%}{1-63.2\%} = \frac{20.8\%}{36.8\%} = 56.5\%$$

Because there is a large probability that the two observers will agree by chance, correcting for chance dramatically reduces the true percentage of agreement from 84% without correction to 56.5% with Cohen's correction.

LEARNING CHECK

1. Because measures of split-half reliability are based on only half the items in the test, they tend to be inaccurate estimates of the true reliability of the whole test. Which of the following is an attempt to correct this problem?
   a. Spearman–Brown formula
   b. Kuder–Richardson formula 20
   c. Cronbach's alpha
   d. All of the above

2. Of the following research statistics, which one is not designed to correct problems with the calculation of split-half reliability?
   a. Cohen's kappa
   b. Cronbach's alpha
   c. Kuder–Richardson formula 20
   d. Spearman–Brown formula

3. What problem is Cohen's Kappa intended to correct?
   a. Split-half reliability tends to underestimate the true reliability of the full test.
   b. Split-half reliability tends to overestimate the true reliability of the full test.
   c. The simple percentage of agreement tends to overestimate the true level of agreement between two observers.
   d. The simple percentage of agreement tends to underestimate the true level of agreement between two observers.

Answers appear at the end of the chapter.

CHAPTER SUMMARY

At this point, you should review the learning objectives presented at the beginning of each section and be sure that you have mastered each objective.

This chapter examined the statistical techniques that researchers use to help describe and interpret the results from research studies. Statistical methods are classified into two broad categories: descriptive statistics, which are used to organize and summarize research results, and inferential statistics, which help researchers generalize the results from a sample to a population.

Descriptive statistical methods include constructing frequency distribution tables or graphs that provide an organized view of an entire set of scores. Commonly, a distribution of numerical scores is summarized by computing measures of central tendency and variability. The mean is the most commonly used measure of central tendency, but the median and the mode are available for situations in which the mean does not provide a good representative value. Variability is commonly described by the standard deviation, which is a measure of the average distance from the mean. Variance measures the average squared distance from the mean. The relationship between two variables can be measured and described by a correlation. The Pearson correlation measures the direction and degree of linear relationship for numerical scores, and the Spearman correlation measures the direction and degree of relationship for ordinal data (ranks). If numerical scores are converted to ranks, the Spearman correlation measures the degree to which the relationship is consistently one directional.

In behavioral science research, the most commonly used inferential statistical method is the hypothesis test. A hypothesis test begins with a null hypothesis, which states that there is no treatment effect or no relationship between variables for the population. According to the null hypothesis, any treatment effect or relationship that appears to exist in the sample data is really just chance or sampling error. The purpose of the hypothesis test is to rule out chance as a plausible explanation for the obtained results. A significant result is one that is very unlikely to have occurred by chance alone. The alpha level, or level of significance, defines the maximum probability that the results are caused by chance. Hypothesis tests evaluate the significance of mean differences, differences between proportions, and correlational relationships.

The five basic research strategies produce three distinct data structures, and each data structure determines the specific statistical techniques that are used to describe and evaluate the data. Once you match your data to one of the structures and you consider the scale of measurement of your data, you can use one of the corresponding flowcharts to determine the statistical procedures that apply to your data.

The final section of the chapter introduced special statistical procedures used to evaluate the reliability of measurements. Three techniques (the Spearman–Brown formula, the Kuder–Richardson formula 20, and Cronbach's alpha) are used to measure split-half reliability. All three techniques address the general problems resulting from the fact that split-half reliability is based on only half the test items. Cohen's kappa provides a measure of inter-rater reliability. Cohen's kappa is intended to correct for inter-rater agreements that are simply the result of chance.

KEY WORDS

descriptive statistics	median	multiple regression	significant result
inferential statistics	mode	sampling error	statistically significant result
statistics	variance	hypothesis test	
parameters	standard deviation	standard error	Type I error
central tendency	correlation	test statistic	Type II error
mean	regression	alpha level, or level of significance	confidence interval

EXERCISES

The exercises are identified with specific learning objectives and are intended to assess your mastery of the objectives. You should be aware that exam items are also generated to assess learning objectives.

1. In addition to the key words, you should also be able to define each of the following terms:

    frequency distribution

    histogram

    polygon

    bar graph

    degrees of freedom, *df*

    line graph

    scatter plot

    Pearson correlation

    Spearman correlation

regression equation

slope constant

Y-intercept

multiple-regression equation

null hypothesis

effect size

Cohen's *d*

percentage of variance accounted for (r^2 or η^2)

ratio scale

interval scale

ordinal scale

nominal scale

chi-square test for independence

independent-measures *t*-test

repeated-measures *t*-test

single-factor analysis of variance or one-way ANOVA

two-factor analysis of variance or two-way ANOVA

split-half reliability

Spearman–Brown formula

Kuder–Richardson formula 20, or K–R 20

Cronbach's alpha

Cohen's kappa

2. (**LO1**) Identify the basic goals for descriptive statistics and for inferential statistics.

3. (**LO2**) A researcher who is interested in examining the eating behavior of adolescents records the number of calories consumed each day by each individual in a sample of 25 adolescents and computes the average for the sample. For this study, what is the statistic and what is the parameter of interest?

4. (**LO3**) Construct a frequency distribution histogram or polygon for the set of scores presented in the following frequency distribution table:

X	F
8	2
7	4
6	7
5	6
4	3
3	1

5. (**LO4**) Under what circumstances are the median and the mode considered to be better than the mean for describing central tendency.

6. (**LO5**) Describe a distribution of scores that has a mean of $M = 30$ and a standard deviation of $SD = 6$. (Where are the scores centered? What range of values contains most of the scores?)

7. (**LO6**) Describe the appearance of a scatter plot showing the data from a set of scores that produce a Pearson correlation of $r = -0.76$.

8. (**LO7**) Describe the general concept of sampling error and explain why this concept creates a problem to be addressed by inferential statistics.

9. (**LO7**) Briefly explain what is meant when a researcher reports "a significant mean difference between two treatment conditions."

10. (**LO7**) A hypothesis test attempts to rule out chance, or sampling error, as a plausible explanation for the results from a research study. Explain how a hypothesis test accomplishes this goal.

11. (**LO8**) Describe the relationship between the alpha level and the likelihood of making a Type I error.

12. (**LO9**) Explain how increasing the size of the sample can influence the outcome of a hypothesis test.

13. (**LO10**) The purpose of an independent-measures *t*-test is to determine whether the mean difference obtained between two groups in a between-subjects study is greater than could reasonably be expected by chance. In other words, the test determines whether the data provide enough evidence to show that the mean difference was caused by something other than chance. Briefly describe the purpose of each of the following hypothesis tests:

   a. Single-factor ANOVA
   b. Test for the significance of a correlation
   c. Chi-square test for independence

14. (**LO10**) Identify the appropriate hypothesis test for each of the following research situations.

   a. A researcher conducts a between-subjects study to determine whether there is a significant difference in problem-solving ability between older adults who are generally happy and those who are generally unhappy.
   b. A researcher gives a questionnaire to a group of 30-year-old married adults, including questions to measure the stability of their own marriages and the stability of their parents' marriages. The researcher would like to know whether the two variables are related.
   c. A researcher obtains a sample of 100 college students between 18 and 21 years old and a similar sample of 100 young adults who have no college experience. The researcher would like to know if

there is a difference in the proportion of registered voters for the two groups.

15. (**LO11**) Describe the basic problem with a split-half correlation that the K–R 20 and Cronbach's alpha are designed to correct.

16. (**LO12**) Cohen's kappa was developed to deal with a particular problem with measuring inter-rater reliability. Identify the problem that the technique attempts to solve.

LEARNING CHECK ANSWERS

Section 15.1	Section 15.2	Section 15.3	Section 15.4	Section 15.5
1. d, 2. b, 3. b	1. d, 2. c, 3. d, 4. a	1. c, 2. b, 3. c	1. a, 2. c, 3. c	1. a, 2. a, 3. c

Writing an APA-Style Research Report

16.1 The Goal of a Research Report

16.2 General APA Guidelines for Writing Style and Format

16.3 The Elements of an APA-Style Research Report

16.4 Writing a Research Proposal

© Nathan Jasowiak / Shutterstock

CHAPTER LEARNING OBJECTIVES

LO1 Describe the basic elements of APA-style writing including the use of verb tense and guidelines for citations and apply these elements in your own writing when APA-style is required.

LO2 Identify and describe the content of each section of an APA-style research report.

LO3 Write a research report using APA style.

LO4 Explain the purpose of a research proposal and how it differs from a research report.

CHAPTER OVERVIEW

Simply writing about your past experiences can be an effective therapy for mental or emotional problems that are associated with the experiences. For example, writing about traumatic experiences has been shown to reduce symptoms of post-traumatic stress disorder that resulted from the trauma (Van Emmerik, Kamphuis, & Emmelkamp, 2008). Therapeutic writing has also been used to improve quality-of-life for early breast cancer survivors (Craft, Davis, & Paulson, 2013) and as an effective tool to help manage chronic pain (Furnes & Dysvik, 2012).

In this chapter, we discuss the process of writing about your research experience. More specifically, this chapter presents the details of writing a research report (Step 9 of the research process) using the style elements developed by the American Psychological Association (APA). As you will see, writing an APA-style research report is a very structured writing process that produces a report that is divided into well-defined sections, with each section presenting specific content. The process is intended to produce a clear and concise report describing why the research was done, how it was done, and the results it produced. The process may even have therapeutic elements that make you feel better.

16.1 | The Goal of a Research Report

Preparing a **research report** is Step 9 in the overall research process (see Chapter 1, p. 24). When the study is completed and the data are in and analyzed, it is time to share your work with others who are interested in the topic. Ideally, this means preparing a written report for future publication in a scientific journal. Perhaps your report will be presented as a poster or paper at a professional conference. Possibly, your report will be simply a classroom project to fulfill a course requirement. In any case, the research report fulfills one of the basic tenets of scientific investigation: science is public. Thus, your research is not finished until you have made it available to the rest of the scientific community.

The basic purpose of a good research report is to provide three kinds of information about the research study.

1. *What was done.* The report should describe in some detail the step-by-step process you followed to complete the research project.
2. *What was found.* The report should contain an objective description of the outcome. Typically, this involves the measurements that were taken, and the statistical summary and interpretation of those measurements.
3. *How your research study is related to other knowledge in the area.* As we noted in Chapter 2, a good research study does not stand alone, but rather grows out of an existing body of knowledge and adds to that body of knowledge. The research report should show the connections between the present study and past knowledge.

Although the prospect of writing an entire research report may appear overwhelming at first glance, several factors make this task more manageable. First, throughout the research process, you have read and consulted many journal articles, each of which can be viewed as a good model of how your report should look. Second, if you have kept notes or maintained a journal of your research, you have an excellent foundation for preparing a formal report. Simply noting what background literature you consulted, how you used each journal article, how you obtained a sample for your study, what was done to individuals in your study, what each subject or participant actually did, and so on, should give you a very complete outline for the written report. Finally, you should realize that a research report is a very structured document. It is subdivided into separate, well-defined segments, and each segment has a specified content. You simply need to describe your own study, piece by piece, in each segment.

Although several styles exist for the preparation of research reports in various disciplines, in the following sections of this chapter, we examine the formal style and structure that have become the generally accepted convention for writing research reports in the behavioral sciences. This style and structure have evolved over the years, and the current guidelines are presented in the ***Publication Manual of the American Psychological Association*** (6th edition, 2010; henceforth referred to as the *Publication Manual*). The writing style developed by the American Psychological Association (known commonly as APA style) is used by many publications throughout the behavioral sciences; however, it is not universal. If you are planning to submit a manuscript to a specific journal to be considered for publication, you should consult the journal's Instructions to Authors for specific information on style and submission requirements. Incidentally, you probably will find that writing a research report is very different from any other writing you have done.

We should also note that this chapter is only a brief summary of some of the more important aspects of APA format and style; for final answers, you should consult the *Publication Manual* itself. In addition, to assist you with learning APA format and style, APA has also published a workbook, *Mastering APA Style: Student's Workbook and Training Guide*, 6th edition and a pocket guide, *Concise Rules of APA Style*. Information can also be obtained at http://www.apastyle.org/

DEFINITION

A **research report** is a written description of a research study that includes a clear statement of the purpose of the research, a review of the relevant background literature that led to the research study, a description of the methods used to conduct the research, a summary of the research results, and a discussion and interpretation of the results.

16.2 General APA Guidelines for Writing Style and Format

LEARNING OBJECTIVE

LO1 Describe the basic elements of APA-style writing including the use of verb tense and guidelines for citations and apply these elements in your own writing when APA-style is required.

Appendix D contains an example of a complete research report manuscript. Portions of the manuscript appear as figures in this chapter.

Although your research report may eventually be published in a professionally formatted, two- or three-column journal, everyone must start with a typed or word-processed manuscript. The *Publication Manual* provides detailed information on the proper method of preparing a manuscript to be submitted for publication. The methods it presents are generally accepted and appropriate for most scientific writing. The goal of the *Publication Manual* is to establish a standardized style and format for scientific reports so that readers will know exactly where to find specific information within a report and will not be distracted by tangential topics or personalized writing styles.

Some Elements of Writing Style

A research report is not the same as creative writing. You are not trying to amuse, entertain, challenge, confuse, or surprise your reader. Instead, the goal is to provide a simple, straightforward description and explanation of your research study. The *Publication*

Manual contains hundreds of guidelines and suggestions to help create a clear and precise manuscript, and we do not attempt to repeat all of them here. Because we present only a selected portion of the general guidelines, you would be wise to consult the *Publication Manual* directly when you actually write a research report. In addition, you can access some of its information, along with helpful tutorials, at www.apastyle.org. In the meantime, this discussion of four general elements of style will help you get a good start.

Impersonal Style

A research report is different from other types of literature and should be written in an objective style. Your goal is to provide a clear and concise report of the research study and its results. Avoid distracting the reader with literary devices such as alliteration, rhyming, deliberate ambiguity, or abrupt changes in topic. You should avoid colloquial expressions such as "once in a blue moon" (in place of "rarely"), and jargon such as "left-winger" (in place of "politically liberal"). You may use personal pronouns to describe what you did as a researcher, "I instructed the participants," but keep in mind that you are writing a research report, not a personal journal.

Verb Tense

When describing or discussing past events that occurred at a specific time, use the past tense (e.g., "They demonstrated"). If the event did not occur at a specific time or is continuing into the present, use the present perfect tense ("Several studies have demonstrated"). This applies to the presentation of background material and previous research that is used to introduce your study and to the description of the methods used to conduct the study. When you present your results, always use the past tense ("the scores increased"). After you have described the study and presented the results, switch to the present tense to discuss the results and your conclusions ("the data suggest").

Reducing Biased Language

Scientific writing should be free of implied or irrelevant evaluation of groups. Therefore, when describing or discussing characteristics of participants, avoid implying bias against people on the basis of gender, sexual orientation, racial or ethnic group, disability, or age. The *Publication Manual* gives three guidelines for avoiding biased language. First, describe people with a level of specificity that is accurate. For example, when describing ethnic groups, instead of general terms such as Asian American or Hispanic American, use Korean American or Mexican American. Second, be sensitive to labels; call people what they prefer to be called. For example, "people diagnosed with schizophrenia" and "older adults" are currently preferred to "schizophrenics" and "the elderly." In addition, for example, Black and African American are preferred to the older terms Negro and Afro-American. And keep in mind that over time, preferences change. Third, acknowledge people's participation in your study. For example, instead of "the participants were run in the study," write "the students completed the survey," or "participants completed the study." The *Publication Manual* provides the details of these guidelines as well as further information about avoiding biased language.

Citations

Throughout your manuscript, you will cite the published research of other scientists. Other research results are cited as background for your hypothesis, to establish a basis for any claims or facts you assert, and to credit those who prepared the foundation for your own work. Recall from Section 4.4 that using someone else's ideas or words as your own is **plagiarism**, a serious breach of ethics. See Chapter 4 (pp. 104–106) for further discussion and examples of plagiarism. Whenever you assert a fact that may not be common knowledge or refer to a previous research finding, you must provide a **citation** that identifies your source. Citation of a source means that you read the cited work. The APA convention for a citation requires that you identify the author(s) and the year of publication. Although there are a variety of methods for accomplishing this goal, two formats are commonly used for citation:

1. State a fact or make a claim in the text; then cite your source in parentheses within the same sentence. In this case, the author(s) last name(s) and the date of publication appear outside the body of the sentence (i.e., contained within parentheses). For example:

    It has been demonstrated that immediate recall is extremely limited for 5-year-old children (Jones, 2017).
    Previous research has shown that response to an auditory stimulus is much faster than response to a visual stimulus (Smith & Jones, 2016).

2. You may want to use the source as the subject of your sentence. In this case, the author(s) last name(s) appear within the body of the sentence and only the year of publication is noted in parentheses. For example:

    In a related study, Jones (2017) found that…
    Smith and Jones (2016) found that…

    With multiple authors, note that an ampersand (the symbol "&") is used before the last author's name when you cite your source in parentheses. Also note that the word "and" is used before the last author's name when your source is the subject of your sentence. A few additional commonly used citation rules include the following:

1. When a publication has one or two authors, you cite all the author's last names and the date every time you refer to this item in your text.
2. When a publication has three to five authors, you cite all of the author's last names and the date the first time you refer to this item in your text. In subsequent citations, you only include the first author's last name followed by "et al." and the date. For example:

    First time cited in text:

    > It has been found that word recall decreases as a function of age (Jones, Smith, & Brown, 2014).

    Or

    > In a related study, Jones, Smith, and Brown (2014) found that…

    Subsequent times cited in text:

    > It has also been found that word recognition decreases as a function of age (Jones et al., 2014).

    Or

    > Jones et al. (2014) found that…

3. When a publication has six or more authors, you only include the first author's last name followed by "et al." and the date for the first and subsequent citations.
4. When you are citing more than one publication within the same parentheses, you list them in alphabetical order by the first authors' last names and separate the items with a semicolon. For example,

    > Several studies (Jones, Smith, & Brown, 2014; Smith & Jones, 2016) found that…

In any case, the citation should provide enough information for the reader to find the complete reference in your list of references at the end of the paper. Note that the APA convention for a citation requires that you identify only the last name(s) of the author(s) and the year of publication. Specifically, you do not include the authors' first names, the name of the institution where the research was done, the title of the article, the name of the journal, or the volume number and pages. In addition, APA conventions allow you to simplify subsequent citations if a particular publication has already been cited within the same paper. See Table 16.1 for a summary of the rules and some examples of citations.

It is also customary to distinguish between citations of empirical results and citations of theory or interpretation. To report an empirical result, for example, you could use:

Jones (2017) demonstrated…

To cite a theory or speculation, for example, you might use:

Jones (2017) argued…

DEFINITION

A **citation** identifies the author(s) and the year of publication of the source of a specific fact or idea mentioned in a research report. The citation provides enough information for a reader to locate the full reference in the list of references at the end of the report.

As a general rule, be conservative about the references you include in a research report, especially a report of an empirical study. References should all be directly relevant to the study that you are presenting. Your goal is to describe and explain your study, not to provide readers with a complete literature review that summarizes every publication that may be remotely related. Select only those references that are truly useful and contribute to your arguments.

As a general rule, it is better to paraphrase a point using your own words than to quote directly from another work. There are rare occasions when direct quotations can be useful, but they should be used only when it is necessary to preserve the whole essence of the original statements. Thus, quotations should be used sparingly. When directly quoting from another work, in addition to identifying the author(s) and year of publication, you must also provide a page number (or paragraph number in the case of online sources without page numbers). For short quotations, fewer than 40 words, the quotation is embedded in the text with quotation marks at both ends. For example,

Resenhoeft, Villa, and Wiseman (2008) report that participants judged a model without a visible tattoo as "more attractive, athletic, and intelligent than the same model shown with a tattoo" (p. 594).

TABLE 16.1

Examples of Original and Subsequent Citations

Number of Authors	First Time in Text	Subsequent Times in Text	First Time in Parentheses	Subsequent Times in Parentheses
1	Jones (2017)	Jones (2017)	(Jones, 2017)	(Jones, 2017)
2	Smith and Jones (2016)	Smith and Jones (2016)	(Smith & Jones, 2016)	(Smith & Jones, 2016)
3-5	Jones, Smith, and Brown (2014)	Jones et al. (2014)	(Jones, Smith, & Brown, 2014)	(Jones et al., 2014)
6 or more	Jones et al. (2015)	Jones et al. (2015)	(Jones et al., 2015)	(Jones et al., 2015)

Quotations of 40 or more words are presented as an indented block, separate from the other text, and without any quotation marks. For example,

> Fontes (2004) offers several recommendations to help protect the confidentiality and safety of individuals participating in studies investigating violence against women and girls, including the following:
>
>> Interviewers should be trained to terminate or change the subject of discussion if the interview is interrupted by anyone. Researchers can have a questionnaire on a less sensitive topic in women's health (e.g., menstruation or eating habits) to "switch to" if they are interrupted. Researchers should forewarn respondents that they will switch to this other topic if the interview is interrupted. (p. 155)

But remember that, whenever you paraphrase someone else's work or use direct quotations, you need to provide a citation to give them credit.

Guidelines for Typing or Word Processing

The general APA guidelines require that a manuscript be double-spaced (with the exception that tables and figures may be single-spaced) with at least a 1" margin on all sides (8½ × 11" page). In addition, the text should have a straight left-hand margin but an uneven or ragged right-hand margin without hyphenation, (breaking words at the ends of lines). Indent the first line of each paragraph, five to seven spaces; indentation should be consistent throughout the manuscript. For APA publications, the preferred typeface is 12-point Times New Roman. This uniform format serves several purposes. First, it ensures a lot of blank space on every page to allow editors, reviewers, or professors to make comments or corrections. In addition, uniform spacing makes it possible for editors to estimate the length of a printed article from the number of pages in a manuscript.

Manuscript Pages

In addition to the body of the manuscript (the basic text that describes the research study), a research report consists of several other parts that are necessary to form a complete manuscript. In Section 16.3, we discuss each of these parts in much more detail, but, for now, note that they are organized in the following order, with each part starting on its own separate page:

Title Page: Title, author's name and affiliation, and the author note. Page 1.

Abstract: A brief summary of the research report. Page 2.

Text: This is the body of the research report (containing four sections: introduction, method, results, and discussion) beginning on page 3.

References: Listed together, starting on a new page.

Tables: Each table starts on a new page.

Figures: Each figure starts on a new page and includes a caption on the same page.

Appendices (if any): Each appendix starts on a new page.

LEARNING CHECK

1. Which of the following is the proper way to cite a source in a research report, when the author's name appears as the subject of the sentence?
   a. Smith, 2015
   b. Sam Smith, 2015
   c. Smith (2015)
   d. Smith (in 2015)

2. Which of the following is the proper way to cite a source with two authors in a research report, when the authors' names are in parentheses, outside the body of the sentence?
   a. (Smith and Jones, 2015)
   b. (Smith & Jones, 2015)
   c. (Sam Smith and Bill Jones, 2015)
   d. (Sam Smith & Bill Jones, 2015)

3. The second time you cite a publication with four authors in your report, what should be included in the citation?
   a. All four authors' last names and the date
   b. The first author's last name followed by et al. and the date
   c. The first author's last name and the date
   d. The first two authors' last names and the date

Answers appear at the end of the chapter.

16.3 | The Elements of an APA-Style Research Report

The APA-style webpage has information about how to format your paper so that the words "Running head" appear only on the first page. See www.apastyle.org/learn/faqs/running-head.aspx. The following procedure also works on most computers. To set up the running head, in Microsoft Word, click Insert on the toolbar and select Header. On the Header toolbar, click Blank. The popup box contains a checkbox for "different first page." Check that box to have the words *Running head:* followed by the abbreviated title, all in capital letters, appear in the header on the title page, and only the abbreviated title, all in capital letters (without the words *Running head)* appear in the header on all subsequent pages of the manuscript.

LEARNING OBJECTIVES

LO2 Identify and describe the content of each section of an APA-style research report.

LO3 Write a research report using APA style.

In the previous section, we identified the components of a complete manuscript. In this section, we look in more detail at the contents of each part, dividing the body of the manuscript into additional subsections that make up the majority of a research report.

Title Page

The **title page** is the first page of the manuscript and contains, in order from top to bottom of the page, the running head and page number (1), the title of the paper, the author names (byline) and affiliations, and author note.

Running Head and Page Number

The first line of the title page is the running head and the page number (1). The **running head** is a complete, but abbreviated, title that contains a maximum of 50 characters, including spaces and punctuation. On the title page, the running head begins at the left margin with the phrase, Running head: followed by the abbreviated title, all in capital letters. The page number appears at the right margin. An example of a running head and page number as they appear on a title page is shown in the top line in Figure 16.1 on page 430, which shows a complete title page.

The running head (without the phrase *Running head* typed out) and page number run consecutively on every page of the manuscript. An example of a running head and page number on all subsequent pages after the title page would appear as follows:

MAJOR DEPRESSIVE DISORDER TREATMENT AND RELAPSE   2

The pages are numbered consecutively, starting with the title page, so that the manuscript can be reassembled if the pages become mixed, and to allow editors and reviewers to refer to specific items by their page number. To have the running head and page number appear on each page of the manuscript, generate them using headers in a word-processing program. Do not manually type this information on each page. In a published article, the running head appears at the top of the pages to identify the article for the readers.

Title

The title, typed in upper and lower case letters, is positioned in the upper half of the page centered between the left and right margins. It is recommended that a title be no more than 12 words in length. The title should be a concise statement that describes your study as accurately and completely as possible. It should identify the main variables or theories, as well as the relationships being investigated. Keep in mind that the words used in the title are often the basis for indexing and referencing your paper. Also remember that the title gives the first impression of your paper and often determines whether an individual reads the rest of the article. (Recall that in Section 2.2, we discussed using the title of an article as a first basis for deciding whether or not to read the rest of the article.) Following are some general guidelines for writing a title:

1. Avoid unnecessary words. It is tempting to begin your title with "A Study of" or "The Relationship Between." However, these phrases usually do not add any useful information and can be deleted with no negative consequences.
2. If possible, the first word in the title should be of special relevance or importance to the content of the paper. If your main topic concerns gender stereotypes, try to begin your title with "Gender Stereotypes." Again, your title gives the first impression of the article and the first few words provide the first impression of the title.
3. Avoid cute or catchy titles. For example, newspaper headlines often use catchy phrases to attract the reader's attention. However, this type of title is usually not appropriate for a research study because it typically does not provide the reader with much information about the content of the article.

Author Name(s) (Byline) and Affiliation

Immediately following the title, centered on the next double-spaced lines, are the author's name(s), followed by the institution(s) where each researcher was when the research was conducted (without the words *by* or *from*). If there are multiple authors, the order of the names is usually significant; the first author listed is typically the individual who made the primary contribution to the research, and the remaining authors are listed in descending order of their contributions.

The **author note** is placed on the title page, several lines below the title, byline, and affiliation. The words Author Note are centered on one line with the paragraphs comprising the author note beginning on the next double-spaced line. Typically, the author note contains four paragraphs, each paragraph starting with an indent, that provide details about the authors, including:

- Departmental affiliation.
- Changes in affiliation (if any) since the time that the research was conducted.
- Acknowledgements of sources of financial support for the research (if any), and recognition of others who contributed or assisted with the study (if any). Disclosure of special circumstances (if any).
- Identification of a contact person if a reader wants further information.

You may have noticed that individual identification (such as your name) appears only on the title page. This allows editors to create a completely anonymous manuscript by simply removing the title page. The anonymous manuscript can then be forwarded to reviewers who will not be influenced by the author's reputation but can give an unbiased

Throughout this chapter, we use a series of figures to illustrate different parts of a manuscript. The figures present portions of an edited adaptation of a research manuscript prepared by undergraduate student Chad Mazzarella as part of a course requirement at The College at Brockport, State University of New York. A complete copy of the edited manuscript appears in Appendix D.

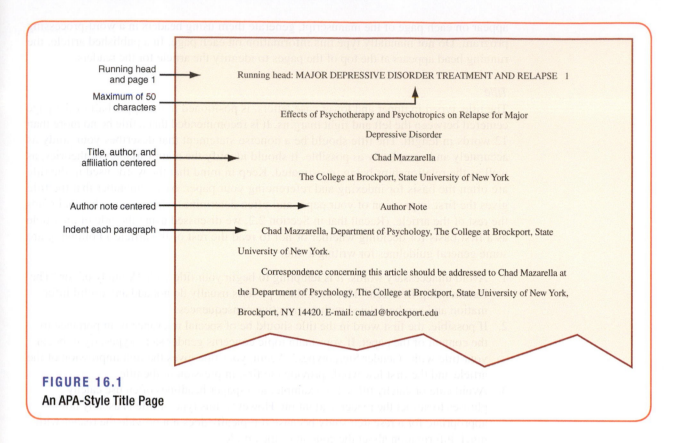

FIGURE 16.1

An APA-Style Title Page

review based solely on the quality of the research study. Many journals are now requesting that manuscripts be submitted electronically.

A title page from an APA-style manuscript, illustrating all of these elements, is shown in Figure 16.1. The complete manuscript is in Appendix D.

DEFINITIONS

The **title page** is the first page of a research report manuscript and contains the running head and page number (1), the title of the paper, the author names (byline) and affiliations, and the author note.

A **running head** is an abbreviated title for a research report containing a maximum of 50 characters and is printed on every page of the manuscript, flush left, on the same line as the page number, which is printed at the right margin. The running head appears at the top of the pages if the manuscript becomes a published article.

Abstract

The **abstract** is a concise summary of the paper that focuses on what was done and what was found. The abstract appears alone on page 2 of the manuscript. The word *Abstract* is centered at the top of page 2, and the one-paragraph summary starts on the next double-spaced line with no paragraph indentation. Although the abstract appears on page

2 of your manuscript, the abstract typically is written last, after the rest of the paper is done. It is considered as the most important section of a research report. With the possible exception of the title, the abstract is the section that most people read and use to decide whether to seek out and read the entire article. (In Section 2.2, we discussed using the abstract of an article as a second screening device, after the title, for deciding whether to read the rest of the article.)

For most journals, the word limit for an abstract ranges from 150 to 250 words. It should be a self-contained summary that does not add to or evaluate the body of the paper. The abstract of an empirical study should include the following elements, not necessarily in this order.

1. A one-sentence statement of the problem or research question
2. A brief description of the subjects or participants (identifying how many and any relevant characteristics)
3. A brief description of the research method and procedures
4. A report of the results
5. A statement about the conclusions or implications

The abstract of an APA-style manuscript is shown in Figure 16.2. The complete manuscript is in Appendix D.

DEFINITION

> The **abstract** is a brief summary of the research study totaling between 150 and 250 words. The abstract focuses on what was done and what was found in the study.

Introduction

The first major section of the body or text of a research report is the introduction. The **introduction** provides the background and orientation that introduces the reader to your research study. The introduction should identify the question or problem that your study addresses and explain why the problem is important, it should explain how you arrived at the question from the previous research in the area, it should identify the hypotheses and how they relate to the research design, and it should explain the implications of the study. A good introduction should address these issues in a few pages. The introduction begins on page 3 of your manuscript. It is identified by centering the title of the article (exactly as it appears on the title page) at the top of the page. The first paragraph of the introduction begins with a paragraph indentation on the next double-spaced line. An introduction typically consists of the following four parts, not necessarily in this order (the parts are not labeled).

1. Typically, this section begins with a general introduction to the topic of the paper. In a few paragraphs, describe the issue investigated and why this problem is important and deserves new research.
2. Next is a review of the relevant literature. You do not need to review and discuss everything that has been published in the area, only the articles that are directly relevant to your research question. Discuss only relevant sections of previous work. Identify and cite the important points along the way but do not provide detailed descriptions. The literature review should not be an article-by-article description of one study after another; instead, the articles should be presented in an integrated manner. Taken together, your literature review should provide a rationale for your study. Remember, you are taking your readers down a logical path that leads to your research question.

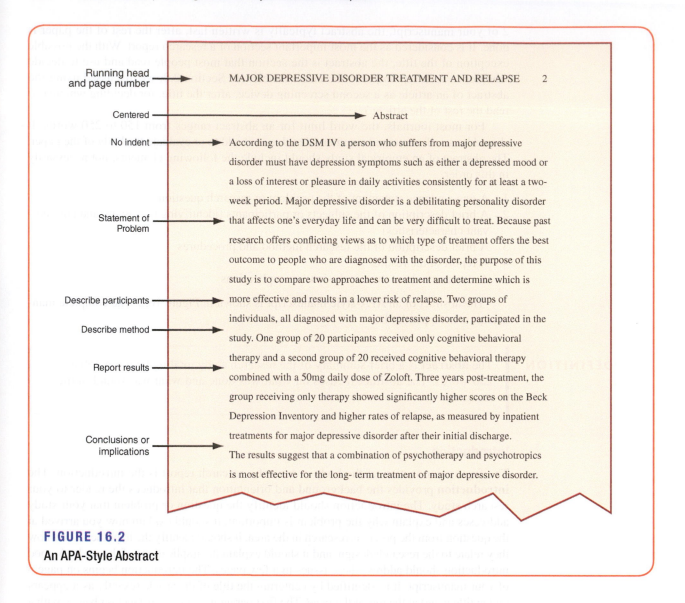

Running head and page number

MAJOR DEPRESSIVE DISORDER TREATMENT AND RELAPSE   2

Centered — Abstract

No indent — According to the DSM IV a person who suffers from major depressive disorder must have depression symptoms such as either a depressed mood or a loss of interest or pleasure in daily activities consistently for at least a two-week period. Major depressive disorder is a debilitating personality disorder that affects one's everyday life and can be very difficult to treat. Because past research offers conflicting views as to which type of treatment offers the best outcome to people who are diagnosed with the disorder, the purpose of this study is to compare two approaches to treatment and determine which is more effective and results in a lower risk of relapse. Two groups of individuals, all diagnosed with major depressive disorder, participated in the study. One group of 20 participants received only cognitive behavioral therapy and a second group of 20 received cognitive behavioral therapy combined with a 50mg daily dose of Zoloft. Three years post-treatment, the group receiving only therapy showed significantly higher scores on the Beck Depression Inventory and higher rates of relapse, as measured by inpatient treatments for major depressive disorder after their initial discharge. The results suggest that a combination of psychotherapy and psychotropics is most effective for the long- term treatment of major depressive disorder.

Statement of Problem

Describe participants

Describe method

Report results

Conclusions or implications

FIGURE 16.2

An APA-Style Abstract

3. Ultimately, the introduction reaches the specific problem, hypothesis, or question that the research study addresses. State the problem or purpose of your study, and clearly define the relevant variables. The review of the literature should lead directly to the purpose of or the rationale for your study.

4. Describe the research strategy that was used to evaluate your hypothesis or to obtain an answer to your research question. Briefly outline the methodology used for the study (the details of which are provided in the next section of the report, the method section). At this point, simply provide a snapshot of how the study was conducted so the reader is prepared for the upcoming details. Also, explain how the research strategy provides the information necessary to address your hypothesis or research question.

If the introduction is well written, your readers will finish the final paragraphs with a clear understanding of the problem you intend to address, the rationale that led to the problem, and a basic understanding of how you answered the problem. Figure 16.3 shows portions of the introduction of an APA-style manuscript. The complete introduction and the rest of the manuscript are in Appendix D.

Running head and page number → MAJOR DEPRESSIVE DISORDER TREATMENT AND RELAPSE   3

Center title → Effects of Psychotherapy and Psychotropics on Relapse for Major Depressive Disorder

General introduction → Major depressive disorder is a severe condition in which the person affected must meet at least 3 of the following 5 symptoms: low mood, loss of interest, guilt or worthlessness, impaired concentration of indecisiveness, and death wishes or suicidal thoughts, one of which is low mood or loss of interest (Zimmerman, Emmeret-Aronson, & Brown, 2011). Major depression is a chronic and ongoing condition that affects the individual for approximately 17 to 30 years and is a particularly disabling disorder which

Relevant literature → some form of psychotherapy or psychotherapy combined with psychotropic drugs (Kennard et al., 2008). The goal is for individuals diagnosed with major depressive disorder is to achieve remission with minimum relapse, and the question is which treatment will effectively allow this to be attained. Cuijpers, Andersson, Donker, and van Stratten (2011) concluded that psychotherapy is effective in the treatment of major depression and dysthymia but probably less than psychotropic drugs. This type of conclusion tends to make psychotherapy appear to be less effective. In contrast, some individuals diagnosed with major depressive disorder have been known to not respond to psychotropic medicine and according to Riedel et al. (2011) the longer the search for an effective antidepressant treatment is, the higher the risk for a chronic condition, the

Method → yet there is little evidence to show the relationship between the types of therapy and relapse rate. This is significant because major depressive disorder has such a large risk of relapse. We addressed this issue with a long-term study comparing individuals diagnosed with major depressive disorder who received only psychotherapy with patients who received both psychotherapy and psychotropic drugs three years after inpatient discharge.

Hypothesis → We hypothesized that patients receiving therapy with medication will have lower depression scores and a lower relapse rate than those who receive only therapy. This outcome would support and strengthen the results reported by Kennard et al. (2008).

FIGURE 16.3

Excerpts from an APA-Style Introduction

DEFINITION

The **introduction** is the first major section of text in a research report. The introduction presents a logical development of the research question, including a review of the relevant background literature, a statement of the research question or hypothesis, and a brief description of the methods used to answer the question or test the hypothesis.

Method

The second major section of the body or the text of a research report is the method section. The **method section** provides a relatively detailed description of exactly how the variables were defined and measured and how the research study was conducted. Other researchers should be able to read your method section and obtain enough information to determine whether your research strategy adequately addresses the question you hope to answer. It also allows other researchers to duplicate all of the essential elements of your research study. The method section immediately follows the introduction. Do not start a new page. Instead, after the last line of the introduction, on the next double-spaced line, type the word *Method*, centered and in boldface. Usually, a method section is divided into two subsections: Subjects or Participants and Procedure. Each subsection heading is presented at the left margin in boldface with uppercase and lowercase letters.

The first major subsection of the method section is either the **subjects subsection** (for nonhumans) or the **participants subsection** (for humans). This subsection describes the sample that participated in the study. For nonhumans, describe (1) the number of animals used in the study; (2) their genus, species, and strain; (3) the supplier; (4) how the animals were housed and handled; and (5) their specific characteristics, including sex, weight, and age. For humans, it is customary to report (1) the number of participants; (2) eligibility and exclusion criteria; (3) basic demographic characteristics of the group, including age, gender, and ethnicity; and (4) any other characteristics relevant to the study (e.g., IQ or psychopathology diagnosis).

The second major subsection of the method section is the procedure subsection. The **procedure subsection** provides a description of the step-by-step process used to complete the study. Include (1) a description of selection procedures, (2) the settings and locations in which data were collected, (3) any payments made to participants, (4) ethical standards met and safety-monitoring procedures, (5) any methods used to divide or assign participants into groups or conditions and how many individuals were in each condition, (6) a description of instructions given to participants, (7) the research design, (8) any experimental manipulation or intervention, and (9) any apparatus or materials that were used.

If portions of your study are complex or require detailed description, additional subsections can be added. One example is entitled either Apparatus or Materials. This subsection describes any apparatus (equipment) or materials (questionnaires and the like) used in the study. Occasionally, both subsections are included in a research report. In an **apparatus subsection**, common items such as chairs, tables, and stopwatches are mentioned without a lot of detail. The more specialized the equipment, the more detail is needed. For custom-made equipment, a figure or picture is required as well. For studies that use many questionnaires, a common additional subsection is a **materials subsection**. The materials subsection includes identification of the variables and how they were operationalized; that is, how they were defined and measured. Each questionnaire used in the study requires a description, a citation, and an explanation of its function in the study (what it was used to measure). Also include information on the instrument's psychometric properties (evidence of reliability and validity). For a new questionnaire that you developed for the purposes of your study, it is also necessary to provide a copy of the measure in an appendix.

The term *operationalized* is an example of jargon, meaning "operationally defined" (see p. 54).

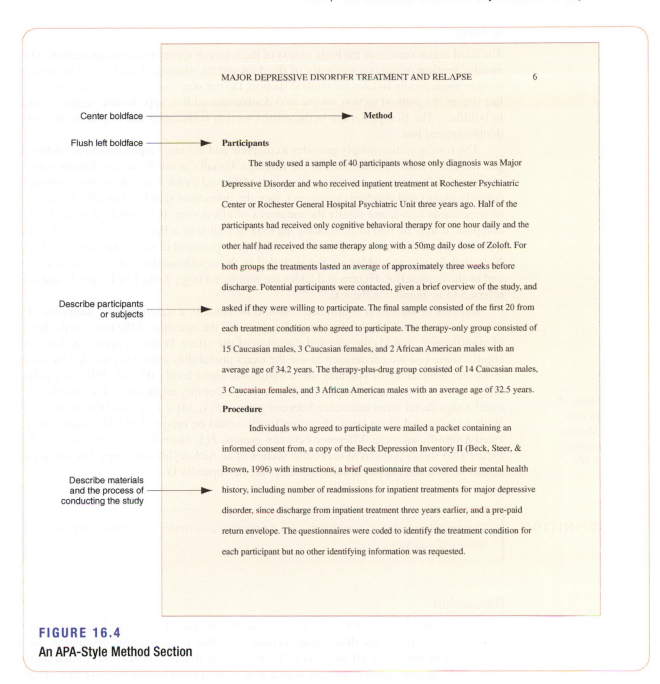

MAJOR DEPRESSIVE DISORDER TREATMENT AND RELAPSE   6

Center boldface →

Method

Flush left boldface →

Participants

    The study used a sample of 40 participants whose only diagnosis was Major Depressive Disorder and who received inpatient treatment at Rochester Psychiatric Center or Rochester General Hospital Psychiatric Unit three years ago. Half of the participants had received only cognitive behavioral therapy for one hour daily and the other half had received the same therapy along with a 50mg daily dose of Zoloft. For both groups the treatments lasted an average of approximately three weeks before discharge. Potential participants were contacted, given a brief overview of the study, and

Describe participants or subjects →

asked if they were willing to participate. The final sample consisted of the first 20 from each treatment condition who agreed to participate. The therapy-only group consisted of 15 Caucasian males, 3 Caucasian females, and 2 African American males with an average age of 34.2 years. The therapy-plus-drug group consisted of 14 Caucasian males, 3 Caucasian females, and 3 African American males with an average age of 32.5 years.

Procedure

    Individuals who agreed to participate were mailed a packet containing an informed consent from, a copy of the Beck Depression Inventory II (Beck, Steer, & Brown, 1996) with instructions, a brief questionnaire that covered their mental health

Describe materials and the process of conducting the study →

history, including number of readmissions for inpatient treatments for major depressive disorder, since discharge from inpatient treatment three years earlier, and a pre-paid return envelope. The questionnaires were coded to identify the treatment condition for each participant but no other identifying information was requested.

FIGURE 16.4

An APA-Style Method Section

Figure 16.4 shows portions of the method section of an APA-style manuscript. The complete method section and the rest of the manuscript are in Appendix D. Notice that the sample manuscript uses two subsections.

DEFINITION

The **method section** of a research report describes how the study was conducted, including information about the subjects or participants and the procedures used.

Results

The third major section of the body or text of the research report is the results section. The **results section** presents a summary of the data and the statistical analyses. The results section immediately follows the method section. Do not start a new page. Instead, after the last line of the method section, on the next double-spaced line, type Results, centered and in boldface. The first paragraph in the results section is indented and begins on the next double-spaced line.

The results section simply provides a complete and unbiased reporting of the findings, just the facts, with no discussion of the findings. Usually, a results section begins with a statement of the primary outcome of the study, followed by the basic descriptive statistics (usually means and standard deviations), then the inferential statistics (usually the results of hypothesis tests), and finally the measures of effect size. If the study was relatively complex, it may be best to summarize the data in a table or a figure. However, with only a few means and inferential tests, it is usually more practical to report the results as text. Note that figures and tables are not included in the results section but are placed at the end of the manuscript. Figures and tables are numbered (e.g., Table 1 or Figure 1) and are referred to by number in the text.

Reports of statistical significance should be made in a statement that identifies (1) the type of test used, (2) the degrees of freedom, (3) the outcome of the test, (4) the level of significance, and (5) the size and direction of the effect. When reporting the level of significance, you are encouraged to use the exact probability value (as provided by most computer programs), or you may use a traditional alpha level (.05, .01, .001) as a point of reference. For example, a report using an exact probability might state "The results indicated a significant mean difference between groups, $F(1, 36) = 4.37$, $p = .006$, $\eta^2 = 0.12$." With a traditional alpha level, the same result would be reported as "The results indicated a significant mean difference between groups, $F(1, 36) = 4.37$, $p < .01$, $\eta^2 = 0.12$." Figure 16.5 shows portions of the results section of an APA-style manuscript. The complete results section and the rest of the manuscript are in Appendix D.

> Statistical tests of significance and measures of effect size are discussed in Chapter 15.

DEFINITION

> The **results section** of a research report presents a summary of the data and the statistical analysis.

Discussion

The fourth and final major section of the body or text of a research report is the discussion section. In the **discussion section**, you offer interpretation, evaluation, and discussion of the implications of your findings. The discussion section immediately follows the results section. Do not start a new page. Instead, after the last line of the results, on the next double-spaced line, type word *Discussion*, centered and in boldface. The first paragraph of the discussion section is indented and begins on the next double-spaced line.

The discussion section should begin with a restatement of the hypothesis. (Recall that your hypothesis is first presented at the end of the introduction.) Next, briefly restate your major results, and indicate how they either support or fail to support your primary hypothesis. Note that the results are described in a sentence format without repeating all the numerical statistics that appear in the results section. Next, relate your results to the work of others, explaining how your outcome fits into the existing structure of knowledge of the

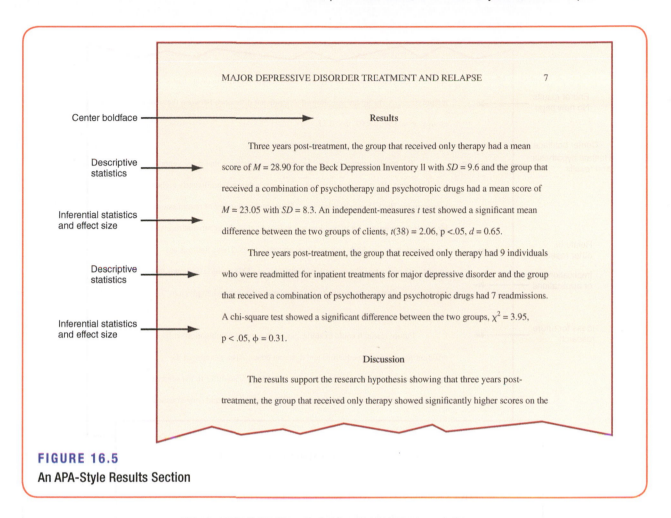

Center boldface

Descriptive statistics

Inferential statistics and effect size

Descriptive statistics

Inferential statistics and effect size

MAJOR DEPRESSIVE DISORDER TREATMENT AND RELAPSE   7

Results

Three years post-treatment, the group that received only therapy had a mean score of $M = 28.90$ for the Beck Depression Inventory ll with $SD = 9.6$ and the group that received a combination of psychotherapy and psychotropic drugs had a mean score of $M = 23.05$ with $SD = 8.3$. An independent-measures t test showed a significant mean difference between the two groups of clients, $t(38) = 2.06$, p $<.05$, $d = 0.65$.

Three years post-treatment, the group that received only therapy had 9 individuals who were readmitted for inpatient treatments for major depressive disorder and the group that received a combination of psychotherapy and psychotropic drugs had 7 readmissions. A chi-square test showed a significant difference between the two groups, $\chi^2 = 3.95$, p $< .05$, $\phi = 0.31$.

Discussion

The results support the research hypothesis showing that three years post-treatment, the group that received only therapy showed significantly higher scores on the

FIGURE 16.5

An APA-Style Results Section

area. It is also common to identify any limitations of the research, especially factors that affect the generalization of the results.

It can be helpful to think of the discussion section as a mirror image of the introduction. Remember, the introduction moved from general to specific, using items from the literature to focus on a specific hypothesis. Now, in the discussion section, you begin with a specific hypothesis (your outcome) and relate it back to the existing literature. Do not simply repeat statements from the introduction, but you may find it useful to mention some of the same references you used earlier to make new points relating your results to the other work.

In the last paragraphs of the discussion section, you may reach beyond the actual results and begin to consider their implications and/or applications. This corresponds to Step 10 in the research process, refining or reformulating a research idea (see Chapter 1, p. 25). Your results may support or challenge existing theories, suggest changes in practical and day-to-day interactions, or indicate new interpretations of previous research results. Any of these is an appropriate topic for a discussion section, and each can lead to new ideas for future research.

If your results support your original hypothesis, it is now possible to test the boundaries of your findings by extending the research to new environments or different populations. If the research results do not support your hypothesis, then more research is needed to find out why. It is common, at the end of the discussion section, to pose problems

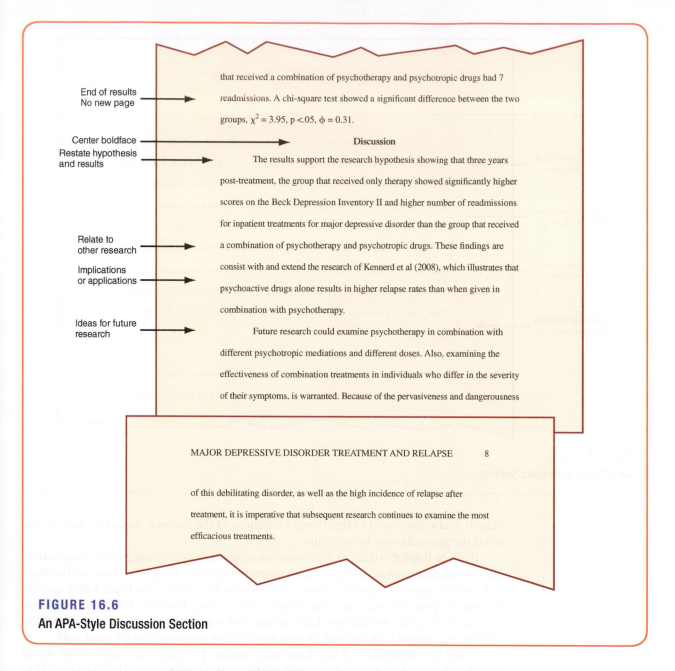

that received a combination of psychotherapy and psychotropic drugs had 7

**End of results
No new page**

readmissions. A chi-square test showed a significant difference between the two

groups, $\chi^2 = 3.95$, p <.05, $\phi = 0.31$.

Center boldface

Discussion

**Restate hypothesis
and results**

The results support the research hypothesis showing that three years

post-treatment, the group that received only therapy showed significantly higher

scores on the Beck Depression Inventory II and higher number of readmissions

for inpatient treatments for major depressive disorder than the group that received

**Relate to
other research**

a combination of psychotherapy and psychotropic drugs. These findings are

consist with and extend the research of Kennerd et al (2008), which illustrates that

**Implications
or applications**

psychoactive drugs alone results in higher relapse rates than when given in

combination with psychotherapy.

**Ideas for future
research**

Future research could examine psychotherapy in combination with

different psychotropic mediations and different doses. Also, examining the

effectiveness of combination treatments in individuals who differ in the severity

of their symptoms, is warranted. Because of the pervasiveness and dangerousness

MAJOR DEPRESSIVE DISORDER TREATMENT AND RELAPSE   8

of this debilitating disorder, as well as the high incidence of relapse after

treatment, it is imperative that subsequent research continues to examine the most

efficacious treatments.

FIGURE 16.6
An APA-Style Discussion Section

that remain unsolved as the result of the findings of the study. This never-ending process of asking questions, gathering evidence, and asking new questions is part of the general scientific method. The answer to a research question is always open to challenge. Figure 16.6 shows portions of the discussion section of an APA-style manuscript. The complete discussion section and the rest of the manuscript are in Appendix D.

DEFINITION   The **discussion section** of a research report restates the hypothesis; summarizes the results; and then presents a discussion of the interpretation, implications, and possible applications of the results.

References

Beginning on a new page, with the centered title, References, the **reference section** provides complete information about each item cited in the manuscript. Notice that there is a precise one-to-one relationship between the items listed in the references and the items cited in the paper. Each item cited must appear in the references, and each item in the references must have been cited in the body of the report. The references are listed alphabetically by the last name of the first author. One-author entries precede multiple-author entries beginning with the same first author. References with the same author, or authors in the same order, are listed chronologically from oldest to most recent publication date. Figure 16.7 shows the first page of the reference section of an APA-style manuscript. The complete reference section and the rest of the manuscript are in Appendix D.

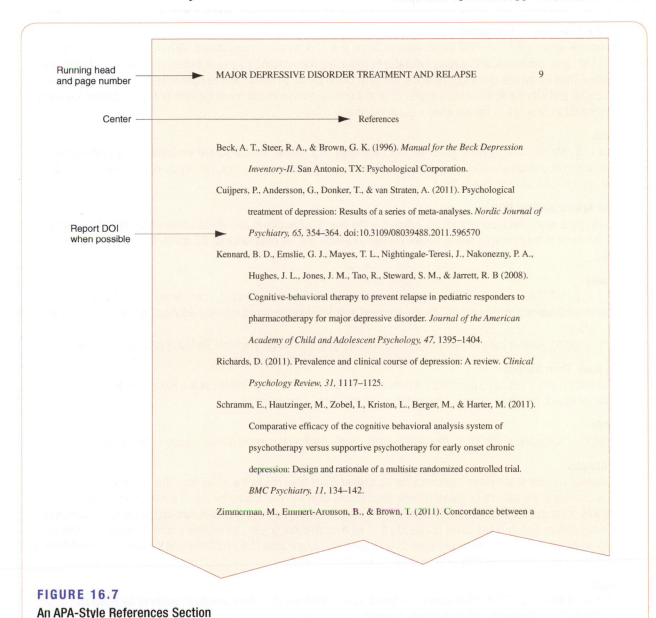

Running head and page number →

MAJOR DEPRESSIVE DISORDER TREATMENT AND RELAPSE   9

Center →

References

Beck, A. T., Steer, R. A., & Brown, G. K. (1996). *Manual for the Beck Depression Inventory-II*. San Antonio, TX: Psychological Corporation.

Cuijpers, P., Andersson, G., Donker, T., & van Straten, A. (2011). Psychological treatment of depression: Results of a series of meta-analyses. *Nordic Journal of Psychiatry, 65,* 354–364. doi:10.3109/08039488.2011.596570

Report DOI when possible →

Kennard, B. D., Emslie, G. J., Mayes, T. L., Nightingale-Teresi, J., Nakonezny, P. A., Hughes, J. L., Jones, J. M., Tao, R., Steward, S. M., & Jarrett, R. B (2008). Cognitive-behavioral therapy to prevent relapse in pediatric responders to pharmacotherapy for major depressive disorder. *Journal of the American Academy of Child and Adolescent Psychology, 47,* 1395–1404.

Richards, D. (2011). Prevalence and clinical course of depression: A review. *Clinical Psychology Review, 31,* 1117–1125.

Schramm, E., Hautzinger, M., Zobel, I., Kriston, L., Berger, M., & Harter, M. (2011). Comparative efficacy of the cognitive behavioral analysis system of psychotherapy versus supportive psychotherapy for early onset chronic depression: Design and rationale of a multisite randomized controlled trial. *BMC Psychiatry, 11,* 134–142.

Zimmerman, M., Emmert-Aronson, B., & Brown, T. (2011). Concordance between a

FIGURE 16.7

An APA-Style References Section

DEFINITION

> The **reference section** of a research report is a listing of complete references for all sources of information cited in the report, organized alphabetically by the last name of the first author.

Table 16.2 presents examples of proper formatting of the most commonly used types of references. Note that the *Publication Manual* provides formats for more than 100 types and variations of referenced works. As a general rule, direct readers as closely as possible

TABLE 16.2

Common Reference Formats and Examples

Journal Article with DOI Assigned

Begin with the author's last name and initials, followed by the year of publication in parentheses. With multiple authors, list each author's last name and initials, with authors separated by commas. An ampersand (&) is used instead of the word *and* before the final author. Then list the title of the journal article, the name of the journal (in italics), volume number (in italics), and the pages for the article. End with the digital object identifier (DOI) as a unique identifier of and link to the item. Note that no database name (e.g., PsycARTICLES) or URL is needed when a DOI is available.

Example

Forzano, L. B., Michels, J. L., Sorama, M., Etopio, A. L., & English, E. J. (2014). Self-control and impulsiveness in adult humans: Comparison of qualitatively different consumable reinforcers using a new methodology. *The Psychological Record, 64,* 719–730. doi:10.1007/s40732-014-0038-7

Journal Article without DOI

Begin with the author's last name and initials, followed by the year of publication in parentheses. Then list the title of the journal article, the name of the journal (in italics), volume number (in italics), and the page range for the article. If a URL is available, provide it.

Examples

Mazur, J. E. (2007). Choice in a successive-encounters procedure and hyperbolic decay of reinforcement. *Journal of the Experimental Analysis of Behavior, 88,* 73–86. Retrieved from http://seab.envmed.rochester.edu/jeab/ articles/2007/jeab-88-01-0073.pdf

Miller, R. J. (2007). Another slant on the oblique effect in drawings and paintings. *Empirical Studies of the Arts, 25,* 41–61.

Entire Book, Print Version

Begin with the author's last name and initials; if there are multiple authors, list them exactly as in a journal article. Follow with the book title (in italics), the city and state of the publisher, and the name of the publisher.

Example

Gravetter, F. J., & Forzano, L. B. (2019). *Research methods for the behavioral sciences* (6th ed.). Boston, MA: Cengage.

Book Chapter

This reference consists of two parts: a reference for the chapter and a reference for the edited book. The reference for the chapter or article consists of the author's (or authors') name listed exactly as in a journal article, the year of publication in parentheses, and the title of the chapter or article. The reference for the edited book begins with the word *In*, followed by the name (or names) of the editor (initials first, then last name) followed by (Ed.) for a single editor or (Eds.) for multiple editors. Then list the name of the book (in italics), the page numbers of the article or chapter, the city and state of the publisher, and the name of the publisher. If an electronic version of the book chapter is available, include the DOI or URL.

Example

McNall, L.A., & Nicklin, J. (2014). Work-family enrichment. In A. C. Michalos (Ed.), *Encyclopedia of quality of life research* (pp. 7215–7218). Dordrecht, the Netherlands: Springer.

to a persistent link for the source used. Many publishers now identify individual publications with a unique digital object identifier (DOI) that provides continuous access to the item. When a DOI is available, it is recommended that you include it for both print and electronic sources. DOIs are typically located at the top of the first page of a journal article or in the Detailed Record of PsycINFO. All DOIs begin with the number 10. If no DOI is available, provide the homepage URL of the journal or the book. In general, it is no longer necessary to include database information or retrieval dates unless the material may change over time.

Tables and Figures

The final sections of the manuscript contain any tables and figures used to illustrate points or present results. As a general rule, tables and figures supplement the text; they should not duplicate information that has already been presented in text form, and they should not be completely independent of the text. Instead, any table or figure should be mentioned in the text by number, and the text should point out some of the more important aspects of the figure or table.

Tables, formatted according to APA specifications, are each typed separately on a new page. The table number and title, respectively, are displayed at the top of the page, each at the left margin. The title or header for the table should describe what information is included in the table. The title is printed in italics. Three types of notes may appear below the table and are used to provide further explanation for elements of the table. *General notes* refer to the entire table and begin with *Note* (italic and followed by a period). *Specific notes* refer to items in the table that have been identified with superscript, lowercase letters (e.g., [a], [b]) and each note begins with the corresponding letter (superscript and lowercase). *Probability notes* identify the level of significance for statistics reported in the table that have been identified with one or more asterisks (e.g., $*p < .05$, $**p < .01$). Tables may be printed either single- or double-spaced to enhance readability.

The figures are included next, prepared according to APA specifications, each on a new page, as final artwork or photographs. A figure number and caption is placed directly below the figure. The caption is a concise explanation of the figure and serves as the figure title. The word *Figure* and the number appears at the left margin in italics. Only the "F" in *Figure* is capitalized, and the figure number is followed by a period. The figure caption immediately follows on the same line.

Appendix

An **appendix** may be included as a means of presenting detailed information that is useful but would interrupt the flow of text if it was presented in the body of the paper. Examples of items that might be presented in an appendix are a copy of a questionnaire, a computer program, a detailed description of an unusual or complex piece of equipment, and detailed instructions to participants. Appendices each start on a new page with the centered title, Appendix, and are identified by consecutive letters (A, B, C, etc.) if there is more than one (e.g., Appendix A).

Table 16.3 lists, in order, the parts of a complete research report. For each part, we have identified the APA formatting issues to be considered, in a checklist format.

Submitting a Manuscript for Publication

After you have prepared your research report, you are ready to submit the manuscript for publication in a scientific journal. Recall that communicating your research to the scientific community makes your finding public, which is necessary in the realm of science. The *Publication Manual* provides detailed information for preparation and submission of a manuscript for publication and you can access a checklist for manuscript submission in

TABLE 16.3
APA Format Checklist

Overall
- Double-spaced lines.
- 1" margins on all sides.
- Straight left-hand margin, with uneven, or ragged, right-hand margin, without hyphenation.
- Indent first line of each paragraph five to seven spaces.
- Typeface should be 12-point Times New Roman.
- Running head (positioned flush left) and page number (positioned flush right corner) on every page.

Title Page
- Running head and page number.
  - Top of title page.
  - Type the words Running head: (including the colon) flush left followed by the running head all in capitals.
  - Running head is a maximum of 50 characters including spaces and punctuation.
  - Across from the running head, on the same line, flush right, type the page number. For the title page, the page number is 1.
- A few lines down from running head, in the upper half of the page, centered, type the title.
  - The title is no more than 12 words in length.
  - Centered on the next available double-spaced lines, type author name(s) (byline) and affiliation(s).
- A few lines down, centered, type the words *Author Note*.
- On the following lines, type the author note consisting of two to four paragraphs (affiliation; changes of affiliation, if any; acknowledgments, if any; and person to contact), each paragraph starting with an indent.

Abstract
- Running head and page number.
  - Running head, flush left, in all capitals, appears in the header on its own (without the words Running head) for all remaining pages of the manuscript. Page 2 (flush right).
- Centered, type the word *Abstract.*
- On the next double-spaced line, begin typing the abstract.
- One paragraph, no indent.
- Between 150 and 250 words.

Introduction
- Begins on page 3.
- Centered, type the title of paper.
- Text begins on the next double-spaced line.

Method
- Begins immediately following the end of the introduction on the next available double-spaced line (do not begin a new page).
- Centered, boldfaced, type the word *Method.*
- Text begins on the next double-spaced line.
- Common subsection headings include: participants or subjects and procedure.
- Type subsection headings flush left in boldface with upper case and lowercase letters.

Results
- Begins immediately following the end of the method section on the next available double-spaced line (do not begin a new page).
- Centered, boldfaced, type the word *Results.*
- Text begins on the next double-spaced line.

Discussion
- Begins immediately following the end of the results section on the next available double-spaced line (do not begin a new page).
- Centered, boldfaced, type the word *Discussion*.
- Text begins on the next double-spaced line.

References
- Begins on a new page.
- Centered, type the word *References*.
- Entries begin on the next double-spaced line.
- Entries listed in alphabetical order by first author's last name.
- For multiple works by the same first author, list one-author entries first in chronological order (earliest first), followed by multiple-author entries, listed alphabetically by second author's last name.
- Entry formats (see Table 16.2).
- Hanging indents for each entry.

Tables
- Each begins on a new page.
- Top, flush left margin, type the word *Table* and the number. On the next available double-spaced line, type the table title (in italics). On the following lines, include the table in APA format.
- May be single- or double-spaced.

Figures
- Each on its own page.
- Identified with figure number (type the word *Figure* and the number in italics, followed by a period) and caption, directly below the figure.

Appendices
- Each begins on new page.
- Centered, type the word *Appendix*.
- Text begins on the next double-spaced line.
- Multiple appendices are identified by consecutive letters, A, B, C, and so on; for example, *Appendix A*.

section 8.03 of the *Publication Manual* or at www.apa.org/journals/authors/manuscript_ check .html. However, the following three steps will help you get a good start.

1. First, select a journal that is appropriate for the topic of your research report. Most journals focus on a few special topics. Consider the journals of the articles you cite in your research report. Then consult each journal's website, which describes what kinds of manuscripts are appropriate for that journal. In addition, there are a few journals that exclusively publish undergraduate research papers. *Psi Chi Journal of Undergraduate Research* and *Modern Psychological Studies* are such journals.
2. Consult the journal's Instructions to Authors for specific submission requirements. Instructions to Authors are typically found on the journal's website. Be sure to identify whether the manuscript is to be submitted electronically (and if so, in what format) or if a hard copy is to be mailed (and if so, be sure to include the number of additional photocopies required by the journal). Instructions for submitting manuscripts for all APA journals can be found at www.apa.org/pubs/authors/instructions.aspx
3. Attach a cover letter to the journal editor along with the manuscript. Detailed information concerning the contents of the cover letter can be founded in section 8.03 of the *Publication Manual*.

When a manuscript is received by a journal editor, the editor usually informs the author of its receipt and distributes copies of the manuscript to reviewers. The reviewers are selected on the basis of their expertise in the research area of your manuscript. Reviewers provide the editor with an evaluation of the manuscript, but, ultimately, the editor makes the decision to accept it, reject it, or request its revision. Note that most manuscripts are rejected for publication; only the best of the best get published.

Conference Presentations: Papers and Posters

Thus far our discussion has focused on preparing a written research report for future publication in a scientific journal. An alternative way to prepare a research report, and hence make your research available to the rest of the scientific community, is to present it as a paper or poster at a professional conference. Typically, this kind of research report consists of two phases: first, a written summary or abstract is submitted to the conference organizers for approval, and second, the actual oral presentation or poster is made.

Typically, a paper presentation at a conference is a 1-hour session during which several researchers each present their research in a related area. An oral presentation at a conference does not simply mean that you read aloud your written research report. Instead, you simplify your research to present orally to an audience, avoiding picky details. This typically includes preparing a PowerPoint presentation with slides that provide information on each of the elements of an APA-style research report, including: an introduction to your topic area; purpose or rationale for the study; and hypothesis, methodology, results, and conclusions. For an oral presentation, you are given a strict time limit (commonly between 10 and 20 minutes). You should practice your presentation, with your slides, until you are comfortable sticking to that time limit. You should also prepare a summary of your presentation and bring copies of this summary for distribution to those who are interested.

Typically, a poster session at a conference occurs in a large room filled with rows of bulletin boards, where individual researchers are given space to display their research for an hour or two. Researchers stand by their posters as attendees walk by to look and ask questions. Although poster presentations are very common at conferences, the *Publication Manual* provides no guidelines for their preparation. Therefore, there are big differences from one to another. When a poster is accepted for presentation, you receive some guidelines from the organization for preparation. In addition, Szuchman (2014) provides some helpful hints for preparing posters. All posters should be easy to read at a distance of approximately 3 feet. For example, text should be no smaller than 24 points, with headings and poster title being even larger, and in a font that is easy to read, such as Arial or Times New Roman. Your poster should be laid out in an organized, logical way, with as few words as possible, so that a reader can figure out the rationale of your study, based on a very brief introduction, the purpose or hypothesis of your study, the method, the results, and the conclusions, within 1–2 minutes. Use bulleted lists, tables, and graphs. Mounting each page of your poster on a colored board backing or sparingly using colored text for titles and headings is common, as is having professionally produced glossy vinyl posters that can simply be unrolled. For a poster, you are given a strict space limit (commonly 4 feet high by 6 feet wide). You should ensure that you keep your poster within the space limitation for the conference. You should also bring pushpins for mounting your poster, as well as copies of a summary of your poster for distribution to those who are interested.

1. If a research manuscript is printed in a journal, where does the running head appear?
   a. On every page of the manuscript and on every page of the journal article
   b. On every page of the manuscript and only on the first page of the journal article
   c. Only on the first page of the manuscript but on every page of the journal article
   d. Only on the first page of the manuscript and only on the first page of the journal article
2. What is typically described in the results section of an APA-style research report?
   a. The interpretation of the findings
   b. The results of descriptive and inferential statistics
   c. The implications of the findings
   d. The other three choices are all typically described in the results section
3. In APA style, where do page numbers appear?
   a. At the upper left hand corner of the page
   b. At the upper right hand corner of the page
   c. At the center bottom of the page
   d. At the lower right hand corner of the page

Answers appear at the end of the chapter.

16.4   Writing a Research Proposal

LEARNING OBJECTIVE

LO4   Explain the purpose of a research proposal and how it differs from a research report.

Although we have identified writing a research report as Step 9 in the research process, researchers often do some writing earlier. Before conducting a study, many researchers write a research proposal. A **research proposal** is basically a plan for a new study. As outlined in the research process (see Chapter 1), before data are collected, you must (1) find a research idea, (2) form a hypothesis, (3) define and choose your measures, (4) identify and select the individuals for your study and plan for their ethic treatment, (5) select a research strategy, and (6) select a research design and make a plan for analyzing and interpreting the data (discussed in Chapter 15). A research proposal is a written report that addresses these points.

Why Write a Research Proposal?

Research proposals are commonly used in the following situations.

- Researchers submit research proposals to government and local funding agencies to obtain financial support for their research.
- Researchers develop proposals for their own use to help develop and refine their thinking, and to remind themselves to attend to details they might otherwise overlook.
- Undergraduate honors thesis students and graduate students submit proposals to their thesis and dissertation committees for approval.
- Undergraduate students are asked to write research proposals for the purposes of research methods classes (even when they are not required to conduct the actual study).

In each case, the research proposal is evaluated, feedback is provided, and suggestions for modification are made. Like the research report, the basic purpose of a good research proposal is to provide three kinds of information about the research study.

1. *What will be done.* The proposal should describe in some detail the step-by-step process you will follow to complete the research project.
2. *What may be found.* The proposal should contain an objective description of the possible outcomes. Typically, this involves a description of the measurements that will be taken and the statistical methods that will be used to summarize and interpret those measurements.
3. *How your planned research study is related to other knowledge in the area.* The research proposal should show the connections between the planned study and past knowledge.

DEFINITION

> A **research proposal** is a written report presenting the plan and underlying rationale of a future research study. A proposal includes a review of the relevant background literature, an explanation of how the proposed study is related to other knowledge in the area, a description of how the planned research will be conducted, and a description of the possible results.

How to Write a Research Proposal

Writing a research proposal is very much like writing a research report. First, the general APA style guidelines discussed in Section 16.2 are identical, with the exception of verb tense. In a research proposal, always use the future tense when you describe your study. You will need to do this (1) at the end of the introduction when you introduce your study (e.g., "The purpose of this study will be"), (2) in the method section (e.g., "The participants will be" or "Participants will complete"), and (3) in the results/discussion (e.g., "It is expected that the scores will increase"). In a research proposal, unlike in a research report, the study has not been conducted yet and, therefore, it does not make sense to refer to it in the past tense.

Second, the content of each part of the manuscript body discussed in Section 16.3 is identical, with these exceptions.

1. An abstract is optional in a research proposal.
2. The literature review in the introduction is typically more extensive than the review in a research report.
3. The results and discussion sections are typically replaced either by a combined Results/Discussion section, or a section entitled Expected Results and Statistical Analysis or Data Analysis and Expected Results. Regardless of its heading, this final section of the body of the research proposal should describe (1) how the data will be collected and analyzed, (2) the expected or anticipated results, (3) other plausible outcomes, and (4) implications of the expected results.

LEARNING CHECK

1. Which of the following accurately describes a research proposal?
   a. They are written after the data for the study have been collected.
   b. They help researchers refine their thinking
   c. They do not include a review of previous research.
   d. They contain the same results section as a regular research report.
2. Which of the following is optional for a research proposal?
   a. An abstract
   b. An introduction
   c. A methods section
   d. A discussion

Answers appear at the end of the chapter.

16 | Writing An APA-Style Research Report

CHAPTER SUMMARY

At this point, you should review the learning objectives presented at the beginning of each section and be sure that you have mastered each objective.

Your research is not finished until you have made it available to the rest of the scientific community. Therefore, when the study is completed and the data are in and analyzed, it is time to prepare a research report (Step 9 in the overall research process). Briefly, a research report describes what was done, what was found, and how your research study is related to other knowledge in the area.

The current guidelines for the formal style and structure that are the convention for research reports in the behavioral sciences are presented in the *Publication Manual of the American Psychological Association* (6th edition, 2010). The *Publication Manual* provides detailed information on properly preparing a manuscript to be submitted for publication.

Although the *Publication Manual* contains hundreds of guidelines and suggestions for creating a clear, precisely written manuscript, four elements of writing style help you get a good start: using an impersonal writing style, past-tense verbs, unbiased language, and appropriate citations. We also describe elements of format, including general guidelines for word processing, and order of manuscript pages.

The contents of each part of a research report are described in detail. Submitting a manuscript for publication and writing a research proposal are briefly discussed as well.

KEY WORDS

research report	running head	method section	reference section
citation	abstract	results section	research proposal
title page	introduction	discussion section	

EXERCISES

The exercises are identified with specific learning objectives and are intended to assess your mastery of the objectives. You should be aware that exam items are also generated to assess learning objectives.

1. In addition to the key words, you should also be able to define each of the following terms:

   Publication Manual of the American Psychological Association
   plagiarism
   author note
   subjects subsection
   participants subsection
   procedure subsection
   apparatus subsection
   materials subsection
   appendix

2. **(LO1)** At the beginning of Chapter 2, we described a study by Jones, Jones, Thomas, and Piper (2003)

demonstrating that alcohol increases the perceived attractiveness of opposite-sex individuals. Write a sentence that presents this result as a statement of fact that cites this publication.

3. **(LO1)** Create an example of a citation for each of the following:

   a. A single author cited in parentheses
   b. Two or more authors cited as the subject of a sentence
   c. Seven authors cited in parentheses
   d. The second citation of a study with three authors as the subject of a sentence

4. **(LO2)** List the major sections of an APA-style report in order of appearance.

5. **(LO2)** What information should be included in the abstract of an APA-style research report?

6. **(LO2)** Describe the major elements of the introduction section for an APA-style empirical research report.

7. (**LO2**) For each of the following, identify the section of a research report that would probably contain the desired information:

How many individuals participated in the study, and what are their characteristics?

Why was the study done?

Did the study use any questionnaires or unusual measurement techniques?

Did the study produce a statistically significant result?

What are the implications of the results and how might they be applied?

8. (**LO4**) Identify the circumstances in which it is useful to write a research proposal before conducting the actual research study. In each case, explain why the proposal would be useful.

9. (**LO4**) Describe the similarities and differences between a research proposal and a research report.

LEARNING CHECK ANSWERS

Section 16.2
1. c, 2. b, 3. b

Section 16.3
1. a, 2. b, 3. b

Section 16.4
1. b, 2. a

Random Number Table and Instruction

In the text, we often discuss using a process such as a coin toss to randomly select participants from a population or to randomly assign participants to groups. Instead of tossing a coin, many researchers prefer to use a table of random numbers. A table of random numbers is simply a huge list of randomly generated digits (0–9) grouped into five-digit sequences and organized into rows and columns. A page of random numbers is shown in on p. 450 in Table A1 (RAND, 2001).

The process of using a table of random numbers is demonstrated in the following two examples.

Example A

For this example, we use the table of random numbers to randomly select a sample of 20 individuals from a population of 197 people. Each individual in the population is assigned a number from 1 to 197. The goal is to randomly pick a set of 20 numbers between 1 and 197 to identify the 20 individuals in the sample. To use the random number table, follow these steps.

1. Because you want to generate numbers from 001 to 197, limit the selections to three-digit numbers. However, each column consists of five-digit values; therefore, you need to decide how to identify three digits within each group. For example, you can use the first three digits, the middle three digits, the last three digits, or some other three-digit sequence.
2. Begin in a random spot; close your eyes and place your finger or a pen anywhere in the table. If your pen falls on one of the digits, you are ready to begin. Otherwise, try again.
3. The number on which your pen falls determines the first value. For example, if you have decided to use the final three digits in each sequence, and your pen lands on the 4 in the number 14225 in row 19, column 3, then the first number to consider is 225.
4. Numbers outside the range of the population are skipped. In our example, any value greater than 197 is outside the range. Therefore, 225 is not a usable number and is skipped.
5. The next number is determined by continuing down the column of numbers. In our example, 479, 940, and 157 are the next three numbers to consider. The first two are outside our range and are skipped. However, 157 is usable, and the participant numbered 157 is selected for the sample.
6. Continue down the column of numbers until you have selected the designated number of participants. If you are sampling without replacement, skip any number that has already been selected. When you cannot go any further down a column, go to the top of the next column.

Example B

For this example, we use the table of random numbers to assign participants to four different treatment conditions. Each treatment condition is assigned a number from 1 to 4, and the participants are organized sequentially (first, second, third, etc.). The goal is to

449

TABLE A1

A Page of Random Numbers

Row/Col	(1)	(2)	(3)	(4)	(5)	(6)	(7)	(8)	(9)	(10)
00000	10097	32533	76520	13586	34673	54876	80959	09117	39292	74945
00001	37542	04805	64894	74296	24805	24037	20636	10402	00822	91665
00002	08422	68953	19645	09303	23209	02560	15953	34764	35080	33606
00003	99019	02529	09376	70715	38311	31165	88676	74397	04436	27659
00004	12807	99970	80157	36147	64032	36653	98951	16877	12171	76833
00005	66065	74717	34072	76850	36697	36170	65813	39885	11199	29170
00006	31060	10805	45571	82406	35303	42614	86799	07439	23403	09732
00007	85269	77602	02051	65692	68665	74818	73053	85247	18623	88579
00008	63573	32135	05325	47048	90553	57548	28468	28709	83491	25624
00009	73796	45753	03529	64778	35808	34282	60935	20344	35273	88435
00010	98520	17767	14905	68607	22109	40558	60970	93433	50500	73998
00011	11805	05431	39808	27732	50725	68248	29405	24201	52775	67851
00012	83452	99634	06288	98083	13746	70078	18475	40610	68711	77817
00013	88685	40200	86507	58401	36766	67951	90364	76493	29609	11062
00014	99594	67348	87517	64969	91826	08928	93785	61368	23478	34113

randomly pick a number between 1 and 4 to determine the treatment condition for each of the participants. To use the random number table, follow these steps.

1. Because you want to generate numbers from 1 to 4, limit the selections to one-digit numbers. Decide how to identify one digit within each group of five digits. For example, you can use the first digit, the second digit, the third digit, and so on.

2. Begin in a random spot; close your eyes and place your finger or a pen anywhere in the table. If your pen falls on one of the digits, you are ready to begin. Otherwise, try again.

3. The number on which your pen falls determines the first value. For example, if you have decided to use the first digit in each sequence, and your pen lands on the number 14225 in row 19, column 3, then the first number to consider is 1.

4. Numbers outside the range are skipped. In our example, the range is values from 1 to 4. Therefore, the value 1 is a usable number. The first participant is assigned to treatment condition 1.

5. The next number to consider is determined by continuing down the column of numbers. In our example, numbers 6, 2, and 8 are the next three numbers to consider. The first and third numbers are outside our range and are skipped. However, 2 is a usable value, and the second participant is assigned to treatment condition 2.

6. Continue down the column of numbers until you have selected a treatment condition for each participant. When you cannot go any further down a column, go to the top of the next column.

A portion of a table of random numbers (from RAND Corporation, 2001) follows.

TABLE A1
A Page of Random Numbers—cont'd

Row/Col	(1)	(2)	(3)	(4)	(5)	(6)	(7)	(8)	(9)	(10)
00015	65481	17674	17468	50950	58047	76974	73039	57186	40218	16544
00016	80124	35635	17727	08015	45318	22374	21115	78253	14385	53763
00017	74350	99817	77402	77214	43236	00210	45421	64237	96286	02655
00018	69916	26803	66252	29148	36936	87203	76621	13990	94400	56418
00019	09893	20505	14225	68514	46427	56788	96297	78822	54382	14598
00020	91499	14523	68479	27686	46162	83554	94750	89923	37089	20048
00021	80336	94598	26940	36858	70297	34135	53140	33340	42050	82341
00022	44104	81949	85157	47954	32979	26575	57600	40881	22222	06413
00023	12550	73742	11100	02040	12860	74697	96644	89439	28707	25815
00024	63606	49329	16505	34484	40219	52563	43651	77082	07207	31790
00025	61196	90446	26457	47774	51924	33729	65394	59593	42582	60527
00026	15474	45266	95270	79953	59367	83848	82396	10118	33211	59466
00027	94557	28573	67897	54387	54622	44431	91190	42592	92927	45973
00028	42481	16213	97344	08721	16868	48767	03071	12059	25701	46670
00029	23523	78317	73208	89837	68935	91416	26252	29663	05522	82562
00030	04493	52494	75246	33824	45862	51025	61962	79335	65337	12472
00031	00549	97654	64051	88159	96119	63896	54692	82391	23287	29529
00032	35963	15307	26898	09354	38351	35462	77974	50024	90103	39333
00033	59808	08391	45427	26842	83609	49700	13021	24892	78565	20106
00034	46058	85236	01390	92286	77281	44077	93910	83647	70617	42941
00035	32179	00597	87379	25241	05567	07007	86743	17157	85394	11838
00036	69234	61406	20117	45204	15956	60000	18743	92423	97118	96338
00037	19565	41430	01758	75379	40419	21585	66674	36806	84962	85207
00038	45155	14938	19476	07246	43667	94543	59047	90033	20826	69541
00039	94864	31994	36168	10851	34888	81553	01540	35456	05014	51176
00040	98086	24826	45240	28404	44999	08896	39094	73407	35441	31880
00041	33185	16232	41941	50949	89435	48581	88695	41994	37548	73043
00042	80951	00406	96382	70774	20151	23387	25016	25298	94624	61171
00043	79752	49140	71961	28296	69861	02591	74852	20539	00387	59579
00044	18633	32537	98145	06571	31010	24674	05455	61427	77938	91936

Continued

TABLE A1

A Page of Random Numbers—cont'd

Row/Col	(1)	(2)	(3)	(4)	(5)	(6)	(7)	(8)	(9)	(10)
00045	74029	43902	77557	32270	97790	17119	52527	58021	80814	51748
00046	54178	45611	80993	37143	05335	12969	56127	19255	36040	90324
00047	11664	49883	52079	84827	59381	71539	09973	33440	88461	23356
00048	48324	77928	31249	64710	02295	36870	32307	57546	15020	09994
00049	69074	94138	87637	91976	35584	04401	10518	21616	01848	76938

RAND (2001). *A million random digits with 100,000 normal deviates.* Santa Monica, CA: RAND. Copyright RAND 2001 (RAND/MR-1418). (Originally published by The Free Press, Glencoe, IL, 1995.)

APPENDIX B

Statistics Demonstrations and Statistical Tables

Descriptive Statistics

The Mean

To compute the mean, you first find the sum of the scores (represented by ΣX) and then divide by the number of scores (represented by n).

    Scores: 4, 2, 1, 5, 2, 2, 3, 4, 3, 2, 3, 1

$$\Sigma X = 32 \text{ and } n = 12. \text{ The mean is } M = 32/12 = 2.67.$$

In a research report, this mean is reported as $M = 2.67$.
Instructions for computing the mean with SPSS are presented in Appendix C.

The Median

To compute the median, you first list the scores in order. With an odd number of scores, the median is the middle value. With an even number of scores, the median is the average of the middle two scores.

    Scores: 4, 2, 1, 5, 2, 2, 3, 4, 3, 2, 3, 1
    Listed in order: 1, 1, 2, 2, 2, 2, 3, 3, 3, 4, 4, 5
The middle two scores are 2 and 3. The median is 2.5.

The Mode

The mode is simply the most frequently occurring score.

Scores: 4, 2, 1, 5, 2, 2, 3, 4, 3, 2, 3, 1

There are more scores of $X = 2$ than any other value. The mode is 2.

Variance and *SS* (Sum of Squared Deviations)

Variance is the average squared distance from the mean and is usually identified with the symbol s^2. The calculation of variance involves two steps:

Step 1:

Compute the distance from the mean, or the deviation, for each score using the following equation:

$$\text{Deviation} = X - M$$

Note that each deviation will be a signed number with the sign indicating whether the score is above ($+$) or below ($-$) the mean. Also note that the sum of the deviations is always zero. Next, square each deviation and add the squared deviations. The result is called *SS*, or the sum of the squared deviations.

Score	Deviation from *M*	Squared Deviation	
5	1	1	For these scores:
6	2	4	$n = 5, \Sigma X = 20,$
1	−3	9	and $M = 20/5 = 4$.
5	1	1	
3	−1	1	$SS = 1 + 4 + 9 + 1 + 1 = 16$

Note: The value for *SS* can also be completed using a computational formula:

$$SS = \Sigma X^2 - \frac{(\Sigma X)^2}{n}$$

For these scores:

X	*X²*		
5	25	$\Sigma X = 20$	$SS = 96 - \dfrac{(20)^2}{5}$
6	36	$\Sigma X^2 = 96$	$= 96 - 80$
1	1		$= 16$
5	25		
3	9		
20	96		

Step 2:

Variance is obtained by dividing *SS* (the sum of standard deviations) by $n - 1$. Note that the value of $n - 1$ is also called degrees of freedom, or simply *df*.

For the scores we have been using,

$$\text{Variance} = s^2 = \frac{SS}{n - 1} = \frac{16}{4} = 4$$

Standard Deviation (*SD*)

Standard deviation is the square root of the variance and measures the standard distance from the mean.

In the demonstration of variance, we computed a variance of 4 for a set of $n = 5$ scores. For these scores, the standard deviation is

$$SD = \sqrt{4} = 2.$$

In a research report, this standard deviation is reported as $SD = 2$.

Instructions for computing the variance and the standard deviation with SPSS are presented in Appendix C.

Pearson Correlation and Regression

The Pearson correlation measures and describes the direction and degree of linear relationship between two variables. The data consist of two measurements (two different variables) for each individual in the sample. The process of regression determines the equation for the best fitting straight line for the X and Y data points. The following data will be used to demonstrate the calculation of the Pearson correlation and the regression equation. Note that the two variables are labeled X and Y, and that we have already computed the sum of squared deviations (*SS*) for the X values and for the Y values.

X	Y	
3	1	For the X scores, $M_X = 2$ and $SS = 10$
4	2	
0	5	For the Y scores, $M_Y = 4$ and $SS = 40$
2	3	
1	9	

In addition to the *SS* for the X scores and *SS* for the Y scores, the calculation of the Pearson correlation requires the sum or the products of the deviations, or *SP*. The value of *SP* can be computed directly by:

1. For each individual, find the distance from the mean for the X score and the distance from the mean for the Y score, including the sign $(+/-)$ for each distance.
2. Multiply the two distances to obtain the product for each individual.
3. Add the products.

This process is demonstrated as follows:

X	Y	Distance for X	Distance for Y	Products
3	1	1	−3	−3
4	2	2	−2	−4
0	5	−2	1	−2
2	3	0	−1	0
1	9	−1	5	−5
				−14 = SP

Note: The value for SP can also be found using a computational formula:

$$SP = \Sigma XY - \frac{(\Sigma X)(\Sigma Y)}{n}$$

For these data,

X	Y	XY
3	1	3
4	2	8
0	5	0
2	3	6
1	9	9
		$26 = \Sigma XY$

$$SP = 26 - \frac{(10)(20)}{5}$$
$$= 26 - 40$$
$$= -14$$

The Pearson correlation, identified by the letter r, can now be computed as follows:

$$r = \frac{SP}{\sqrt{(SS \text{ for } X)(SS \text{ for } Y)}}$$

For our data,

$$r = \frac{-14}{\sqrt{(10)(40)}} = \frac{-14}{\sqrt{400}} = -0.70$$

The regression equation has the general form of $Y = bX + a$, where

$$b = r\frac{s_Y}{s_X} \text{ or } b = \frac{SP}{SS_X} \text{ and } a = M_Y - bM_X$$

where r is the Pearson correlation, s_X is the standard deviation for the X scores, and s_Y is the standard deviation for the Y scores.

For these data, $b = \dfrac{-14}{10} = -1.4$ and $a = 4 - 1.4(2) = 1.2$

For these data the regression equation is $Y = -1.4X + 1.2$

Instructions for computing the Pearson correlation and the regression equation with SPSS are presented in Appendix C.

Spearman Correlation

The Spearman correlation measures and describes the degree of relationship between two variables that have been measured on an ordinal scale (ranks). This correlation also can be used to measure the degree of monotonic (one-directional) relationship between two variables measured on an interval or ratio scale (numerical scores) by first ranking the numerical values and then computing the Spearman correlation for the ranks. The Spearman correlation is computed by simply applying the Pearson correlation formula to ordinal data (ranks). The following data are used to demonstrate the calculation of the Spearman correlation. Notice that we begin with numerical scores from an interval or ratio scale.

The first step is to transform the numerical values into ranks. First, rank the X values: The smallest score gets a rank of 1, the next smallest gets a 2, and so on. Then rank the Y values.

	Original Scores			Ranks	
Person	X	Y	Person	X	Y
A	3	1	A	4	1
B	4	2	B	5	2
C	0	5	C	1	4
D	2	3	D	3	3
E	1	9	E	2	5

Then, use the Pearson correlation for the ranks.

For the X ranks, $\Sigma X = 15$, $M = 3$, and $SS = 10$

For the Y ranks, $\Sigma Y = 15$, $M = 3$, and $SS = 10$

Multiplying the X rank times the Y rank for each person produces 4, 10, 4, 9, and 10. These values add to $\Sigma XY = 37$, and the computational formula for SP produces

$$SP = \Sigma XY - \frac{(\Sigma X)(\Sigma Y)}{N} = 37 - \frac{(15)(15)}{5} = 37 - 45 = -8$$

Finally, the Spearman correlation, identified by the symbol r_s, is

$$r_S = \frac{SP}{\sqrt{(SS \text{ for } X)(SS \text{ for } Y)}} = \frac{-8}{\sqrt{(10)(10)}} = -0.80$$

The Spearman correlation can also be computed using a special formula that works only when the scores have already been converted to ranks. We introduce and demonstrate the special formula using the same ranked data that were used to demonstrate the Spearman correlation.

The special Spearman formula is

$$r_S = 1.00 - \frac{6\Sigma D^2}{n(n^2 - 1)}$$

where D is the difference between the X rank and the Y rank for each individual.

For these data, the ranks, the D values, and the D^2 values are as follows:

Person	X	Y	D	D²
A	4	1	3	9
B	5	2	3	9
C	1	4	3	9
D	3	3	0	0
E	2	5	3	9
				$36 = \Sigma D^2$

Using the special formula, we obtain:

$$r_S = 1.00 - \frac{6\Sigma D^2}{n(n^2 - 1)} = 1.00 - \frac{6(36)}{5(24)}$$

$$= 1.00 - 1.80$$

$$= -0.80$$

Note that this is exactly the same value we obtained for the Spearman correlation using the regular Pearson formula.

Inferential Statistics

Independent-Measures *t* Test

The independent-measures *t* test is a hypothesis test used to evaluate the mean difference between two separate groups. The test involves computing a *t* statistic (as is demonstrated) and then consulting a statistical table to determine whether the obtained value of *t* is large enough to indicate a significant mean difference. The following sample data are used to demonstrate the independent-measures *t* test. Note that each group is described by the number of scores (*n*), the mean (*M*), the sum of squared deviations (*SS*), and the degrees of freedom ($df = n - 1$):

Group 1	Group 2
$n_1 = 10$	$n_2 = 5$
$M_1 = 44$	$M_2 = 40$
$SS_1 = 280$	$SS_2 = 110$
$df_1 = 9$	$df_2 = 4$

The calculation of the *t* statistic involves three steps:

Step 1:

Pool the two sample variances.

$$\text{pooled variance} = s_p^2 = \frac{SS_1 + SS_2}{df_1 + df_2} = \frac{280 + 110}{9 + 4} = \frac{390}{13} = 30$$

The pooled variance can also be obtained using the *df* value and the variance (or squared standard deviation) for each of the two samples. The formula is as follows:

$$\text{pooled variance} = \frac{df_1(s_1^2) + df_2(s_2^2)}{df_1 + df_2}$$

This alternative formula is especially useful when you are dealing with summarized data, such as the printout from a computer program.

Step 2:

Compute the standard error (denominator of the *t* statistic).

$$\text{standard error} = \sqrt{\frac{s_p^2}{n_1} + \frac{s_p^2}{n_2}} = \sqrt{\frac{30}{10} + \frac{30}{5}} = \sqrt{3 + 6} = \sqrt{9} = 3$$

Step 3:

Compute the *t* statistic.

$$t = \frac{M_1 - M_2}{\text{Standard error}} = \frac{44 - 40}{3} = \frac{4}{3} = 1.33$$

You must consult a *t* distribution table to determine whether the obtained *t* statistic ($t = 1.33$) is large enough to indicate a significant difference. The *t* statistic has degrees of freedom equal to the sum of the *df* values for the two groups.

$$df \text{ for the } t \text{ statistic} = df_1 + df_2$$

For these data, $df = 9 + 4 = 13$. The *t* distribution table shows that a minimum value of $t = 2.160$ is needed for significance with an alpha level of .05. Our *t* value does not meet this criterion, so we must conclude that there is no significant difference between the two means.

Effect Size for the Independent-Measures t Test

It is customary to report a measure of effect size along with the results from a hypothesis test. For the independent-measures t test, effect size can be measured with Cohen's d or r^2. Cohen's d is a standardized measure of mean difference that is computed by:

$$d = \frac{\text{Mean difference}}{\text{Standard deviation}}$$

For the independent-measures t, the standard deviation is obtained by taking the square root of the pooled variance. Using the data from the previous demonstration:

$$d = \frac{M_1 - M_2}{\sqrt{s_p^2}} = \frac{44 - 40}{\sqrt{30}} = \frac{4}{5.48} = 0.73$$

The proportion of variance accounted for is represented by r^2 and is computed by:

$$r^2 = \frac{t^2}{t^2 + df}$$

For the data from the independent-measures t demonstration, we obtained $t = 1.33$ with $df = 13$. For these data:

$$r^2 = \frac{(1.33)^2}{(1.33)^2 + 13} = \frac{1.77}{14.77} = 0.12$$

In a research report, the results of this independent-measures t test (including df and the α level) and effect size are reported as $t(13) = 1.33$, $p > .05$, $d = 0.73$ (or $r^2 = 0.12$).

Instructions for performing an independent-measures t test with SPSS are presented in Appendix C.

Repeated-Measures t Test

The repeated-measures t test is a hypothesis test used to evaluate the mean difference between two sets of scores obtained from a single group of participants. The test involves computing a t statistic (as is demonstrated) and then consulting a statistical table to determine whether the obtained value of t is large enough to indicate a significant mean difference. The following sample data are used to demonstrate the repeated-measures t test. Notice that we have computed the difference between the first and second score for each participant by subtracting the first score from the second. Note that the signs ($+/-$) are important.

Participant	Score in Condition 1	Score in Condition 2	Difference
A	20	22	+2
B	24	23	−1
C	18	24	+6
D	21	24	+3
E	26	28	+2
F	19	25	+6

The calculation of the t statistic involves three steps.

Step 1:

Compute the mean and the variance for the set of difference scores. For these data, there are $n = 6$ difference scores with a mean of $M = 3.00$ and a variance of $s^2 = 7.2$.

Step 2:

Compute the standard error (denominator of the t statistic).

$$\text{standard error} = \sqrt{\frac{s^2}{n}} = \sqrt{\frac{7.2}{6}} = \sqrt{1.20} = 1.10$$

Step 3:

Compute the t statistic.

$$t = \frac{M}{\text{Standard error}} = \frac{3.00}{1.10} = 2.73$$

You must consult a t distribution table to determine whether the obtained t statistic ($t = 2.73$) is large enough to indicate a significant difference. The t statistic has degrees of freedom equal to $n - 1$.

For these data, $df = 5$. The t distribution table shows that a minimum value of $t = 2.571$ is needed for significance with an alpha level of .05. Our t value exceeds this criterion, so we conclude that there is a significant mean difference between the two treatment conditions.

Effect Size for the Repeated-Measures t Test

As with the independent-measures test, effect size can be measured with either Cohen's d or r^2. Cohen's d is a standardized measure of mean difference that is computed by:

$$d = \frac{\text{Mean difference}}{\text{Standard deviation}}$$

For the repeated-measures t, the standard deviation is simply the square root of the variance. Using the data from the previous demonstration:

$$d = \frac{M}{\sqrt{s^2}} = \frac{3}{\sqrt{7.2}} = \frac{3}{2.68} = 1.12$$

The proportion of variance accounted for is represented by r^2 and is computed by:

$$r^2 = \frac{t^2}{t^2 + df}$$

For the data from the repeated-measures t demonstration, we obtained $t = 2.73$ with $df = 5$. For these data:

$$r^2 = \frac{(2.73)^2}{(2.73)^2 + 5} = \frac{7.45}{12.45} = 0.60$$

In a research report the results of this repeated-measures t test (including df and the α level) and effect size are reported as $t(13) = 2.73$, $p < .05$, $d = 1.12$ (or $r^2 = 0.60$).

Instructions for performing a repeated-measures t test with SPSS are presented in Appendix C.

Single-Factor Analysis of Variance (Independent Measures)

The single-factor analysis of variance is a hypothesis test used to evaluate the mean differences among two or more separate groups when the groups are defined by separate values of the same variable or factor. The test involves computing an F-ratio (as is demonstrated) and then consulting a statistical table to determine whether the value obtained for the F-ratio is large enough to indicate significant mean differences. The following sample data are used to demonstrate the single-factor analysis of variance. Note that each group is described by the number of scores (n), the mean (M), the sum of squared deviations (SS), and the degrees of freedom ($df = n - 1$). Also note that we have computed ΣX and ΣX^2 for the entire set of $N = 15$ scores.

Treatment 1 Group 1	Treatment 2 Group 2	Treatment 3 Group 3	Totals
0	1	2	$N = 15$
2	5	5	
1	2	6	$\Sigma X = 60$
5	4	9	
2	8	8	$\Sigma X^2 = 354$
$n = 5$	$n = 5$	$n = 5$	
$M = 2$	$M = 4$	$M = 6$	
$SS = 14$	$SS = 30$	$SS = 30$	
$df = 4$	$df = 4$	$df = 4$	

The F-ratio for the analysis is a ratio of two variances:

$$F = \frac{\text{Variance between treatments}}{\text{Variance within treatments}}$$

where each variance is computed as

$$\text{Variance} = \frac{SS}{df}$$

The SS values and the df values for the two variances are obtained by an analysis process that first computes SS and df for the total set of scores, then separates the total into the two components: between treatments and within treatments. The analysis for SS and df can be pictured as follows:

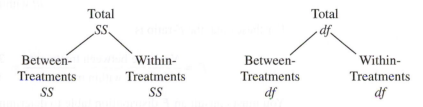

We demonstrate the analysis of variance in three steps: First, analyzing the SS values, then analyzing the df values, and finally using the SS and df values to compute the two variances and the F-ratio.

Step 1:

Analysis of the SS (sum of squared deviations).

Using the computational formula, SS for the total set of scores is

$$SS \text{ total} = \Sigma X^2 - \frac{(\Sigma X)^2}{n}$$

$$= 354 - \frac{(60)^2}{15}$$

$$= 354 - 240$$

$$= 114$$

The value for SS within treatments is obtained directly from the SS values that were computed inside each treatment.

$$SS \text{ within treatments} = \Sigma SS = 14 + 30 + 30 = 74$$

Finally, the value for SS between treatments is obtained by subtraction.

$$SS \text{ between treatments} = SS \text{ total} - SS \text{ within treatments}$$

$$= 114 - 74$$

$$= 40$$

Step 2:

Analysis of df (degrees of freedom).

Degrees of freedom for the total set of scores is simply:

$$df \text{ total} = N - 1 = 14$$

The value for df within treatments is obtained directly from the df values that were computed inside each treatment.

$$df \text{ within treatments} = \Sigma df = 4 + 4 + 4 = 12$$

Finally, the value for df between treatments is obtained by subtraction.

$$df \text{ between treatments} = df \text{ total} - df \text{ within treatments}$$

$$= 14 - 12$$

$$= 2$$

Step 3:

Compute the two variances and the F-ratio.

$$\text{Variance between treatments} = \frac{SS \text{ between}}{df \text{ between}} = \frac{40}{2} = 20$$

$$\text{Variance within treatments} = \frac{SS \text{ within}}{df \text{ within}} = \frac{74}{12} = 6.17$$

For these data, the F-ratio is

$$F = \frac{\text{Variance between treatments}}{\text{Variance within treatments}} = \frac{20.00}{6.17} = 3.24$$

You must consult an F distribution table to determine whether the obtained F-ratio, ($F = 3.24$), is large enough to indicate a significant difference. The F-ratio has two values for degrees of freedom, one for the variance in the numerator and one for the denominator. For our example, the F-ratio has $df = 2$ for the numerator and $df = 12$ for the denominator. Together, the F-ratio has $df = 2, 12$.

The F distribution table shows that a minimum value of $F = 3.88$ is needed for significance with an alpha level of .05. Our F-ratio does not meet this criterion, so we must conclude that the mean differences among the three groups are not significant.

Measuring Effect Size for the Single-Factor Independent-Measures ANOVA

For analysis of variance, it is customary to measure effect size with η^2 (the Greek letter *eta* squared), which measures the percentage of variance accounted for by the mean differences. For the independent-measures analysis we just completed, η^2 is computed as

$$\eta^2 = \frac{SS \text{ between treatments}}{SS \text{ total}} = \frac{40}{114} = 0.35$$

In a research report, the results from this single-factor, independent-measures ANOVA (including the df values and α level) and the measure of effect size are reported as $F(2, 12) = 3.24, p > .05, \eta^2 = 0.35$.

Instructions for performing this analysis using SPSS are presented in Appendix C.

Single-Factor Analysis of Variance (Repeated-Measures)

The repeated-measures analysis of variance serves exactly the same purpose as the independent-measures analysis in the previous demonstration. However, the repeated-measures analysis is used when the different sets of scores are all obtained from a single group of participants. To demonstrate the single-factor, repeated-measures analysis of variance, we use the same scores that were used for the independent-measures demonstration. Notice that the data are now presented as scores from one group of participants, with each individual measured three times. Also note that we have computed the mean score for each of the five participants.

Participant	Treatment 1	Treatment 2	Treatment 3	Participant Means	Total
A	0	1	2	$M = 1$	$N = 15$
B	2	5	5	$M = 4$	$\Sigma X = 60$
C	1	2	6	$M = 3$	$\Sigma X^2 = 354$
D	5	4	9	$M = 6$	
E	2	8	8	$M = 6$	
	$n = 5$	$n = 5$	$n = 5$		
	$M = 2$	$M = 4$	$M = 6$		
	$SS = 14$	$SS = 30$	$SS = 30$		
	$df = 4$	$df = 4$	$df = 4$		

Most of the repeated-measures analysis uses exactly the same computations that were used for the independent-measures analysis of variance. With repeated measures, however, we can use the participant means to measure the magnitude of the individual differences, and then subtract these differences from the denominator before computing a final F-ratio. Thus, the F-ratio for the repeated-measures analysis has the following structure:

$$F = \frac{\text{Variance between treatments}}{\text{Error variance (individual differences removed)}}$$

Each variance is computed as

$$\text{Variance} = \frac{SS}{df}$$

The *SS* values and the *df* values for the two variances are obtained by a two-stage analysis. The first stage is identical to the independent-measures analysis and can be pictured as follows:

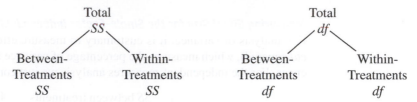

The second stage analyzes the within-treatment components by measuring and subtracting out the differences between subjects.

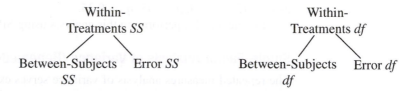

The first stage of this analysis is identical to the independent-measures analysis in the previous demonstration and produces exactly the same values.

SS total $= 114$ df total $= 14$
SS between treatments $= 40$ df between treatments $= 2$
SS within treatments $= 74$ df within treatments $= 12$

The second stage involves computing *SS* and *df* between subjects and then subtracting these values from the corresponding *SS* and *df* within treatments. The results provide the *SS* and *df* for the error variance in the denominator of the *F*-ratio.

Using the symbol *k* to represent the number of treatment conditions, the *SS* between subjects can be computed as follows:

$$SS \text{ between subjects} = k(SS \text{ for the participant means})$$

First, we compute *SS* for the set of means. The means and squared means are presented in the following table, and the computational formula is used to obtain *SS*.

X	X²		
1	1	$\Sigma X = 20$	$SS = 98 - \dfrac{(20)^2}{5}$
4	16		$= 98 - 80$
3	9	$\Sigma X^2 = 98$	$= 18$
6	36		
6	36		
20	98		

For these data we have $k = 3$ treatments, so:

$$SS \text{ between subjects} = 3(18) = 54$$

With a group of $n = 5$ participants:

$$df \text{ between subjects} = n - 1 = 4$$

Completing the second stage of the analysis, we obtain:

$$SS\ error = SS\ \text{within treatments} - SS\ \text{between subjects}$$
$$= 74 - 54$$
$$= 20$$

$$df\ error = df\ \text{within treatments} - df\ \text{between subjects}$$
$$= 12 - 4$$
$$= 8$$

Finally, the two variances and the F-ratio are

$$\text{Variance between treatments} = \frac{SS\ \text{between treatments}}{df\ \text{between treatments}} = \frac{40}{2} = 20$$

$$\text{Error variance} = \frac{SS\ error}{df\ error} = \frac{20}{8} = 2.50$$

For these data, the F-ratio is

$$F = \frac{\text{Variance between treatments}}{\text{Error variance}} = \frac{20.00}{2.50} = 8.00$$

You must consult an F distribution table to determine whether the obtained F-ratio ($F = 8.00$) is large enough to indicate a significant difference. The F-ratio has two values for degrees of freedom, one for the variance in the numerator and one for the denominator. For our example, the F-ratio has $df = 2$ for the numerator and $df = 8$ for the denominator. Together, the F-ratio has $df = 2, 8$.

The F distribution table shows that a minimum value of $F = 4.46$ is needed for significance with an alpha level of .05, and a minimum value of 8.65 is needed with an alpha level of .01. Our F-ratio ($F = 8.00$) is large enough to conclude that there are significant differences at the .05 level of significance.

Measuring Effect Size for the Single-Factor Repeated-Measures ANOVA

For a repeated-measures analysis of variance, it is customary to remove the variance accounted for by the individual differences before computing η^2, which measures the percentage of variance accounted for by the mean differences. For the repeated-measures analysis we just completed, η^2 is computed as

$$\eta^2 = \frac{SS\ \text{between treatments}}{SS\ \text{total} - SS\ \text{between subjects}} = \frac{40}{114 - 54} = \frac{40}{60} = 0.67$$

In a research report, the results from this single-factor, repeated-measures ANOVA (including the df values and α level), and the measure of effect size are reported as $F(2, 8) = 8.00$, $p < .05$, $\eta^2 = 0.67$.

Instructions for performing this analysis using SPSS are presented in Appendix C.

Two-Factor Analysis of Variance (Independent Measures)

The two-factor analysis of variance is a hypothesis test used to evaluate the mean differences in a research study with two factors. The different groups in the study can be represented as cells in a matrix, with the levels of one factor determining the rows and the levels of the second factor determining the columns. The test involves computing three separate F-ratios: one to evaluate the main effects of the first factor, one to evaluate the main effects of the second factor, and one to evaluate the interaction. The following sample data are used to demonstrate the two-factor analysis of variance. Note that each group is described by the number of scores (n), the mean (M), the sum of squared deviations (SS), and the degrees of freedom ($df = n - 1$). Also note that we have computed the overall mean for each row in the matrix (each level of factor A) and the overall mean for each column (each level of factor B). Finally, note that we have computed ΣX and ΣX^2 for the entire set of $N = 30$ scores.

Factor B

	B1	B2	B3	
A1	$n = 5$ $M = 10$ $SS = 400$ $df = 4$	$n = 5$ $M = 20$ $SS = 500$ $df = 4$	$n = 5$ $M = 30$ $SS = 400$ $df = 4$	$M = 20$
A2	$n = 5$ $M = 10$ $SS = 300$ $df = 4$	$n = 5$ $M = 10$ $SS = 300$ $df = 4$	$n = 5$ $M = 10$ $SS = 500$ $df = 4$	$M = 10$
	$M = 10$	$M = 15$	$M = 20$	

Factor A (label for rows A1, A2)

Overall
$N = 30$
$\Sigma X = 450$
$\Sigma X^2 = 10{,}900$

The two-factor analysis of variance can be viewed as a two-stage process. The first stage is identical to the single-factor analysis of variance with each cell of the matrix considered as a separate treatment condition. In this stage, we first compute SS and df for the total set of scores, then separate the total into the two components: between treatments and within treatments. This stage of the analysis for SS and df can be pictured as follows:

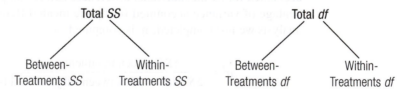

In the second stage of the analysis, the values for SS and df between treatments are further analyzed into the main effect for factor A, the main effect for factor B, and the interaction. This stage can be pictured as follows:

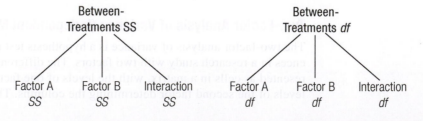

We demonstrate the two-factor analysis of variance in three steps: The first two steps correspond to the two stages of the analysis, and the third step will involve computing the variances and the F-ratios.

Step 1:

Analyze the total SS and df values into a between-treatments component and a within-treatments component.

SS total measures the SS for the entire set of $N = 30$ scores. Using the computational formula, SS for the total set of scores is

$$SS \text{ total} = \Sigma X^2 - \frac{(\Sigma X)^2}{n}$$

$$= 10{,}900 - \frac{(450)^2}{30}$$

$$= 10{,}900 - 6{,}750$$

$$= 4{,}150$$

The value for SS within treatments is obtained directly from the SS values that were computed inside each treatment (each cell of the matrix).

$$SS \text{ within treatments} = \Sigma SS = 400 + 500 + 400 + 300 + 300 + 500$$
$$= 2{,}400$$

Finally, the value for SS between treatments is obtained by subtraction.

$$SS \text{ between treatments} = SS \text{ total} - SS \text{ within treatments}$$
$$= 4{,}150 - 2{,}400$$
$$= 1{,}750$$

Degrees of freedom for the total set of scores is simply

$$df \text{ total} = N - 1 = 29$$

The value for df within treatments is obtained directly from the df values that were computed inside each treatment (each cell of the matrix).

$$df \text{ within treatments} = \Sigma df = 4 + 4 + 4 + 4 + 4 + 4 = 24$$

Finally, the value for df between treatments is obtained by subtraction.

$$df \text{ between treatments} = df \text{ total} - df \text{ within treatments}$$
$$= 29 - 24$$
$$= 5$$

Step 2:

Split the between-treatments SS and df values into three separate components that correspond to the main effect for factor A, the main effect for factor B, and the interaction.

The SS for factor A can be computed using the overall means for A1 and A2 (the means for the two rows). Each of these means was computed from a set of 15 scores (three groups, each with $n = 5$), so the SS for factor A can be computed as follows:

$$SS \text{ factor A} = 15(SS \text{ for the A1 and A2 means})$$

The first step is to compute SS for the set of means. The means and squared means are presented in the following table, and the computational formula is used to obtain SS.

X	X²
20	400
10	100
30	500

$\Sigma X = 30$

$\Sigma X^2 = 500$

$SS = 500 - \dfrac{(30)^2}{2}$

$= 500 - 450$

$= 50$

Multiplying by 15 gives us

$$SS \text{ factor A} = 15(50) = 750$$

The SS for factor B can be found using the means for B1, B2, and B3. Each of these means is based on 10 scores (2 groups, each with $n = 5$), so the SS for factor B can be computed as follows:

$$SS \text{ factor B} = 10(SS \text{ for the B1, B2, and B3 means})$$

The first step is to compute SS for the set of means. The means and squared means are presented in the following table and the computational formula is used to obtain SS.

X	X²
10	100
15	225
20	400
45	725

$\Sigma X = 45$

$\Sigma X^2 = 725$

$SS = 725 - \dfrac{(45)^2}{3}$

$= 725 - 675$

$= 50$

Multiplying by 10 gives us

$$SS \text{ factor B} = 10(50) = 500$$

Finally, we compute SS for the interaction by subtraction:

$$SS \text{ interaction} = SS \text{ between treatments} - SS \text{ factor A} - SS \text{ factor B}$$
$$= 1{,}750 - 750 - 500 = 500$$

There were only 2 means for factor A, so:

$$df \text{ factor A} = 2 - 1 = 1$$

There were 3 means for factor B, so:

$$df \text{ factor B} = 3 - 1 = 2$$

And df for the interaction is found by subtraction:

$$df \text{ interaction} = df \text{ between treatments} - df \text{ factor A} - df \text{ factor B}$$
$$= 5 - 1 - 2 = 2$$

Step 3:

Compute the variances and the F-ratios

$$\text{Variance for factor A} = \frac{SS \text{ for factor A}}{df \text{ for factor A}} = \frac{750}{1} = 750$$

$$\text{Variance for factor B} = \frac{SS \text{ for factor B}}{df \text{ for factor B}} = \frac{500}{2} = 250$$

$$\text{Variance for the interaction} = \frac{SS \text{ for the interaction}}{df \text{ for the interaction}} = \frac{500}{2} = 250$$

The variance within treatments will be the denominator for each F-ratio:

$$\text{Variance within treatments} = \frac{SS \text{ within treatments}}{df \text{ within treatments}} = \frac{2,400}{24} = 100$$

Finally, the three F-ratios are

$$F\text{-ratio for factor A} = \frac{\text{Variance for factor A}}{\text{Variance within treatments}} = \frac{750}{100} = 7.50$$

$$F\text{-ratio for factor B} = \frac{\text{Variance for factor B}}{\text{Variance within treatments}} = \frac{250}{100} = 2.50$$

$$F\text{-ratio for the interaction} = \frac{\text{Variance for the interaction}}{\text{Variance within treatments}} = \frac{250}{100} = 2.50$$

You must consult an F distribution table to determine whether the obtained F-ratios are large enough to indicate significant differences. Each F-ratio has two values for degrees of freedom: one for the variance in the numerator and one for the denominator. For our example, the F-ratio for factor A has $df = 1$ for the numerator and $df = 24$ for the denominator. With $df = 1, 24$, the F distribution table shows that a minimum value of $F = 4.26$ is needed for significance with an alpha level of .05, and a value of $F = 7.82$ for an alpha level of .01. Our F-ratio exceeds the .05 value (but not the .01 value), so we conclude that the mean difference between the two levels of factor A is significant at the .05 level of significance. That is, the main effect for factor A is significant.

The F-ratios for factor B and for the interaction both have $df = 2, 24$. For these degrees of freedom, the F distribution table shows that a minimum value of $F = 3.40$ is needed for significance with an alpha level of .05. Both of our F-ratios fail to meet this criterion, so we must conclude that there is no significant main effect for factor B and no significant interaction between factors.

Measures of Effect Size for a Two-Factor Analysis of Variance

In addition to reporting the statistical significance of mean differences, it is also recommended that you provide a report of the size of the mean differences. Following a two-factor analysis of variance, the common technique for measuring effect size is to compute the proportion of variance accounted for by the mean differences in both main effects and in the interaction. The resulting values are each called η^2. For a two-factor analysis of variance, it is customary to remove the variance accounted for by other main effects and interactions before computing η^2 for any specific main effect or interaction. With a repeated-measures two-factor design, it is also customary to remove the variance accounted for by the individual differences before computing any η^2 values. In each case, the η^2 values are computed using only the variance for the specific effect being evaluated and the variance for the error term (denominator of the F-ratio).

We demonstrate the calculation of the η^2 values using the data from the previous demonstration of the two-factor analysis of variance. For factor A:

$$\eta^2 = \frac{SS \text{ for factor A}}{SS \text{ for factor A } + SS \text{ for the error term}}$$

For the data from the two-factor demonstration, this value is

$$\eta^2 = \frac{750}{750 + 2,400} = 0.238$$

Similarly, the η^2 for factor B is computed by

$$\eta^2 = \frac{SS \text{ for factor B}}{SS \text{ for factor B} + SS \text{ for the error term}}$$

$$= \frac{500}{500 + 2,400} = 0.17$$

Finally, the η^2 for the interaction is computed by

$$\eta^2 = \frac{SS \text{ for the interaction}}{SS \text{ for the interaction} + SS \text{ for the error term}}$$

$$= \frac{500}{500 + 2,400} = 0.17$$

For a within-subjects analysis, the calculation of the error term changes somewhat, but the equations for the η^2 values are identical to those used for the between-subjects analysis.

In a research report, the results from this two-factor ANOVA (including the df values and α levels) are reported as follows: There was a significant main effect for factor A, $F(1, 24) = 7.50, p < .05, \eta^2 = 0.238$, no significant main effect for factor B, $F(2, 24) = 2.50, p > .05, \eta^2 = 0.17$, and no significant interaction, $F(2, 24) = 2.50, p > .05, \eta^2 = 0.17$.

Instructions for performing this analysis using SPSS are presented in Appendix C.

Significance of a Correlation

The significance test for a correlation is used to determine whether a sample correlation is sufficiently large to justify concluding that there is a real, nonzero correlation in the population. To demonstrate the test for significance of a correlation, we assume that a researcher has obtained a correlation of $r = +0.41$ for a sample of $n = 25$ individuals.

The significance test is based on a t statistic that is computed as follows:

$$t = \frac{r}{\sqrt{\frac{(1 - r^2)}{df}}}$$

where the degrees of freedom are $df = n - 2$.

Note: If all the terms in the t formula are squared, the calculation produces an F-ratio with degrees of freedom determined by $df = 1, n - 2$.

For the sample in this demonstration, $r = 0.41$, $r^2 = 0.17$, and $df = 23$. With these values:

$$t = \frac{0.41}{\sqrt{\frac{(1 - 0.17)}{23}}} = 2.16$$

You must consult a t distribution table to determine whether the obtained t statistic is large enough to indicate a significant correlation. With $df = 23$, the table shows that a minimum value of $t = 2.069$ is needed to be significant with an alpha level of .05. Our sample exceeds this criterion, so we can conclude that there is a significant correlation between the two variables.

Typically a research report simply states that the correlation is significant without specifying the hypothesis test that was used, and it notes the level of significance ($p < .05$ or $p < .01$).

When SPSS is used to compute a correlation, the output includes a report of the significance level (see Appendix C).

Significance of a Regression Equation (Analysis of Regression)

The significance test for regression is used to determine whether the regression equation predicts a significant proportion of the variance for the Y scores. Alternatively, the test determines whether the slope constant (or constants) in the equation is significantly different from zero. To demonstrate the test for significance, we assume that a researcher has computed a regression equation with $k = 2$ predictor variables and obtained $R^2 = 0.30$ for a sample of $n = 25$ individuals.

The analysis of regression is similar to an analysis of variance and produces an F-ratio that compares the predicted variance (numerator) with the unpredicted error variance (denominator). The general structure of the analysis for SS and for df values is as follows:

For the sample in this demonstration, $R^2 = 0.30$, $n = 25$, and $k = 2$. The predicted variance and the error variance are

$$\text{Predicted variance} = \frac{\text{Predicted } SS}{\text{Predicted } df} = \frac{R^2}{k} = \frac{0.30}{2} = 0.15$$

$$\text{Error variance} = \frac{\text{Error } SS}{\text{Error } df} = \frac{(1 - R^2)}{n - (k + 1)} = \frac{0.70}{22} = 0.032$$

With these values:

$$F = \frac{\text{Predicted variance}}{\text{Error variance}} = \frac{0.15}{0.032} = 4.69$$

You must consult an F distribution table to determine whether the obtained F-ratio is large enough to indicate a significant regression equation. With $df = 2, 22$, the table shows that a minimum value of $F = 3.44$ is needed to be significant with an alpha level of .05. Our sample exceeds this criterion, so we can conclude that the regression equation is significant.

Testing the significance of a regression equation with one predictor variable is equivalent to testing the significance of the corresponding correlation. In either case, a typical research report simply states the level of significance ($p < .05$ or $p < .01$) without specifying the hypothesis test that was used. With multiple predictor variables, the F-ratio is usually reported. The F-ratio for this example would be reported as $F(2, 22) = 4.69$, $p < .05$.

Instructions for using SPSS to compute a regression equation, with either one or multiple predictor variables, are presented in Appendix C. The output from the program includes the equation and a test of significance.

Chi-Square Test for Independence

The chi-square test for independence is a hypothesis test that is used to evaluate the relationship between two variables measured on any measurement scale, provided that there are relatively few measurement categories for both variables. The test evaluates the differences in proportions between separate groups of participants. The following data are used to demonstrate the chi-square test for independence. The data represent a frequency distribution for a sample of 200 people. Each person is classified on two different variables: personality (introvert or extrovert) and favorite color (red, yellow, green, or blue). The number in each cell is the number of individuals with the corresponding personality and color preference. For example, 10 people were classified as Introverts and selected Red as their favorite color. The frequency values found in the data are called *observed frequencies*, or f_O values.

	Favorite Color				
	Red	Yellow	Green	Blue	Total
Introvert	10	3	15	22	50
Extrovert	90	17	25	18	150
Total	100	20	40	40	

For these data, the null hypothesis can be stated in two versions:

1. There is no relationship between personality and color preference.
2. The distribution of color preferences (the set of proportions) is the same for introverts and extroverts.

Step 1:

The first step in the chi-square test is to compute a set of hypothetical frequencies that represent how the sample would appear if it were in perfect accord with the null hypothesis. The hypothetical frequencies are called *expected frequencies* or f_E values. For each cell in the matrix, the expected frequency can be computed by

$$f_E = \frac{(\text{row total})(\text{column total})}{\text{total number}}$$

For example, the upper left-hand cell in the matrix is in the first row (with a total of 50) and in the first column (with a total of 100). The total number of participants in the entire study is 200, so this cell would have an expected frequency of

$$f_E = \frac{(50)(100)}{200} = 25$$

The complete set of expected frequencies is shown in the following matrix.

	Favorite Color				
	Red	Yellow	Green	Blue	Total
Introvert	25	5	10	10	50
Extrovert	75	15	30	30	150
Total	100	20	40	40	

Step 2:

The second step in the chi-square test is to compute the value of chi-square (χ^2), which provides a measure of how well the observed frequencies (the data) fit the expected frequencies (the hypothesis). The formula for chi-square is

$$\chi^2 = \Sigma \frac{(f_O - f_E)^2}{f_E}$$

The step-by-step calculation for our data is shown in the following table:

1. For each cell in the matrix, find the difference between the expected and the observed frequency.
2. Square the difference.
3. Divide the squared difference by the expected frequency.
4. Add the resulting values for each category.

f_o	f_E	$(f_o - f_E)$	$(f_o - f_E)^2$	$(f_o - f_E)^2/f_E$
10	25	15	225	9.00
3	5	2	4	0.80
15	10	5	25	2.50
22	10	12	144	14.40
90	75	15	225	3.00
17	15	2	4	0.27
25	30	5	25	0.83
18	30	12	144	4.80

$$35.60 = \chi^2$$

You must consult a chi-square distribution table to determine whether the obtained chi-square value ($\chi^2 = 35.60$) is large enough to be statistically significant. The chi-square statistic has degrees of freedom given by

$$df = (C_1 - 1)(C_2 - 1)$$

where C_1 is the number of categories for the first variable and C_2 is the number of categories for the second variable. For our data:

$$df = (2 - 1)(4 - 1) = 3$$

With $df = 3$, the table shows that a minimum value of $\chi^2 = 11.34$ is needed for significance with an alpha level of .01. Our data exceed this criterion, so, depending on which version of the null hypothesis was used, we can conclude either there is a significant relationship between personality and color preference or the distribution of color preferences for introverts is significantly different from the distribution for extroverts.

Effect Size for the Chi-Square Test for Independence

When there are exactly two categories for each variable, the data can be displayed as a 2 × 2 matrix and the effect size can be measured with a correlation known as a phi-coefficient. The phi-coefficient can be computed directly from the value obtained for chi-square as follows:

$$\Phi = \sqrt{\frac{\chi^2}{n}}$$

With more than two categories for either variable, effect size is measured with a modification of the phi-coefficient known as Cramér's V. Cramér's V uses the same basic formula as the phi-coefficient but incorporates a modified version of the degrees of freedom (df^*), which is the smaller of either the ($C_1 - 1$) or ($C_2 - 1$) values that are used to compute the df value for the chi-square test. For the data in the previous chi-square example, we obtained $\chi^2 = 35.60$ for a sample of $n = 200$ participants with two categories for personality and four categories for color. For these data, Cramér's V is

$$V = \sqrt{\frac{\chi^2}{n(df^*)}} = \sqrt{\frac{35.60}{200(1)}} = \sqrt{0.178} = 0.422$$

In a research report, the results from this chi-square test (including df, sample size, and level of significance) and the measure of effect size would be reported as χ^2 (3, $n = 200$) = 35.60, $p < .01$, $V = 0.422$.

Instructions for performing a chi-square test for independence using SPSS are presented in Appendix C.

STATISTICAL TABLES

TABLE B.1

The *t* Distribution

Table entries are the minimum values of *t* that are necessary for a *t* statistic to be significant at the alpha level specified. To be significant, a calculated *t* statistic must be greater than or equal to the value in the table.

	Alpha Level for a Directional (One-Tailed) Test					
	0.25	0.10	0.05	0.025	0.01	0.005
	Alpha Level for a Nondirectional (Two-Tailed) Test					
df	0.50	0.20	0.10	0.05	0.02	0.01
1	1.000	3.078	6.314	12.706	31.821	63.657
2	0.816	1.886	2.920	4.303	6.965	9.925
3	0.765	1.638	2.353	3.182	4.541	5.841
4	0.741	1.533	2.132	2.776	3.747	4.604
5	0.727	1.476	2.015	2.571	3.365	4.032
6	0.718	1.440	1.943	2.447	3.143	3.707
7	0.711	1.415	1.895	2.365	2.998	3.499
8	0.706	1.397	1.860	2.306	2.896	3.355
9	0.703	1.383	1.833	2.262	2.821	3.250
10	0.700	1.372	1.812	2.228	2.764	3.169
11	0.697	1.363	1.796	2.201	2.718	3.106
12	0.695	1.356	1.782	2.179	2.681	3.055
13	0.694	1.350	1.771	2.160	2.650	3.012
14	0.692	1.345	1.761	2.145	2.624	2.977
15	0.691	1.341	1.753	2.131	2.602	2.947
16	0.690	1.337	1.746	2.120	2.583	2.921
17	0.689	1.333	1.740	2.110	2.567	2.898
18	0.688	1.330	1.734	2.101	2.552	2.878
19	0.688	1.328	1.729	2.093	2.539	2.861
20	0.687	1.325	1.725	2.086	2.528	2.845
21	0.686	1.323	1.721	2.080	2.518	2.831
22	0.686	1.321	1.717	2.074	2.508	2.819
23	0.685	1.319	1.714	2.069	2.500	2.807
24	0.685	1.318	1.711	2.064	2.492	2.797
25	0.684	1.316	1.708	2.060	2.485	2.787
26	0.684	1.315	1.706	2.056	2.479	2.779
27	0.684	1.314	1.703	2.052	2.473	2.771
28	0.683	1.313	1.701	2.048	2.467	2.763
29	0.683	1.311	1.699	2.045	2.462	2.756
30	0.683	1.310	1.697	2.042	2.457	2.750
40	0.681	1.303	1.684	2.021	2.423	2.704
60	0.679	1.296	1.671	2.000	2.390	2.660
120	0.677	1.289	1.658	1.980	2.358	2.617
∞	0.674	1.282	1.645	1.960	2.326	2.576

Table III of R. A. Fisher and F. Yates, *Statistical Tables for Biological, Agricultural and Medical Research*, 6th ed. London: Longman Group Ltd., 1974 (previously published by Oliver and Boyd Ltd., Edinburgh). Copyright © 1963 R. A. Fisher and Pearson Education Ltd.

TABLE B.2
The *F* Distribution

Table entries lightface type are the minimum values that are necessary for a *F*-ratio to be significant at an alpha level of .05. Boldface entries are the minimum vales that are necessary for an *F*-ratio to be significant at an alpha level of .01. To be significant, a calculated *F*-ratio must be greater than or equal to the value in the table.

Degrees of Freedom: Denominator	Degrees of Freedom: Numerator														
	1	2	3	4	5	6	7	8	9	10	11	12	14	16	20
1	161	200	216	225	230	234	237	239	241	242	243	244	245	246	248
	4052	**4999**	**5403**	**5625**	**5764**	**5859**	**5928**	**5981**	**6022**	**6056**	**6082**	**6106**	**6142**	**6169**	**6208**
2	18.51	19.00	19.16	19.25	19.30	19.33	19.36	19.37	19.38	19.39	19.40	19.41	19.42	19.43	19.44
	98.49	**99.00**	**99.17**	**99.25**	**99.30**	**99.33**	**99.34**	**99.36**	**99.38**	**99.40**	**99.41**	**99.42**	**99.43**	**99.44**	**99.45**
3	10.13	9.55	9.28	9.12	9.01	8.94	8.88	8.84	8.81	8.78	8.76	8.74	8.71	8.69	8.66
	34.12	**30.92**	**29.46**	**28.71**	**28.24**	**27.91**	**27.67**	**27.49**	**27.34**	**27.23**	**27.13**	**27.05**	**26.92**	**26.83**	**26.69**
4	7.71	6.94	6.59	6.39	6.26	6.16	6.09	6.04	6.00	5.96	5.93	5.91	5.87	5.84	5.80
	21.20	**18.00**	**16.69**	**15.98**	**15.52**	**15.21**	**14.98**	**14.80**	**14.66**	**14.54**	**14.45**	**14.37**	**14.24**	**14.15**	**14.02**
5	6.61	5.79	5.41	5.19	5.05	4.95	4.88	4.82	4.78	4.74	4.70	4.68	4.64	4.60	4.56
	16.26	**13.27**	**12.06**	**11.39**	**10.97**	**10.67**	**10.45**	**10.27**	**10.15**	**10.05**	**9.96**	**9.89**	**9.77**	**9.68**	**9.55**
6	5.99	5.14	4.76	4.53	4.39	4.28	4.21	4.15	4.10	4.06	4.03	4.00	3.96	3.92	3.87
	13.74	**10.92**	**9.78**	**9.15**	**8.75**	**8.47**	**8.26**	**8.10**	**7.98**	**7.87**	**7.79**	**7.72**	**7.60**	**7.52**	**7.39**
7	5.59	4.47	4.35	4.12	3.97	3.87	3.79	3.73	3.68	3.63	3.60	3.57	3.52	3.49	3.44
	12.25	**9.55**	**8.45**	**7.85**	**7.46**	**7.19**	**7.00**	**6.84**	**6.71**	**6.62**	**6.54**	**6.47**	**6.35**	**6.27**	**6.15**
8	5.32	4.46	4.07	3.84	3.69	3.58	3.50	3.44	3.39	3.34	3.31	3.28	3.23	3.20	3.15
	11.26	**8.65**	**7.59**	**7.01**	**6.63**	**6.37**	**6.19**	**6.03**	**5.91**	**5.82**	**5.74**	**5.67**	**5.56**	**5.48**	**5.36**
9	5.12	4.26	3.86	3.63	3.48	3.37	3.29	3.23	3.18	3.13	3.10	3.07	3.02	2.98	2.93
	10.56	**8.02**	**6.99**	**6.42**	**6.06**	**5.80**	**5.62**	**5.47**	**5.35**	**5.26**	**5.18**	**5.11**	**5.00**	**4.92**	**4.80**
10	4.96	4.10	3.71	3.48	3.33	3.22	3.14	3.07	3.02	2.97	2.94	2.91	2.86	2.82	2.77
	10.04	**7.56**	**6.55**	**5.99**	**5.64**	**5.39**	**5.21**	**5.06**	**4.95**	**4.85**	**4.78**	**4.71**	**4.60**	**4.52**	**4.41**
11	4.84	3.98	3.59	3.36	3.20	3.09	3.01	2.95	2.90	2.86	2.82	2.79	2.74	2.70	2.65
	9.65	**7.20**	**6.22**	**5.67**	**5.32**	**5.07**	**4.88**	**4.74**	**4.63**	**4.54**	**4.46**	**4.40**	**4.29**	**4.21**	**4.10**
12	4.75	3.88	3.49	3.26	3.11	3.00	2.92	2.85	2.80	2.76	2.72	2.69	2.64	2.60	2.54
	9.33	**6.93**	**5.95**	**5.41**	**5.06**	**4.82**	**4.65**	**4.50**	**4.39**	**4.30**	**4.22**	**4.16**	**4.05**	**3.98**	**3.86**
13	4.67	3.80	3.41	3.18	3.02	2.92	2.84	2.77	2.72	2.67	2.63	2.60	2.55	2.51	2.46
	9.07	**6.70**	**5.74**	**5.20**	**4.86**	**4.62**	**4.44**	**4.30**	**4.19**	**4.10**	**4.02**	**3.96**	**3.85**	**3.78**	**3.67**
14	4.60	3.74	3.34	3.11	2.96	2.85	2.77	2.70	2.65	2.60	2.56	2.53	2.48	2.44	2.39
	8.86	**6.51**	**5.56**	**5.03**	**4.69**	**4.46**	**4.28**	**4.14**	**4.03**	**3.94**	**3.86**	**3.80**	**3.70**	**3.62**	**3.51**
15	4.54	3.68	3.29	3.06	2.90	2.79	2.70	2.64	2.59	2.55	2.51	2.48	2.43	2.39	2.33
	8.68	**6.36**	**5.42**	**4.89**	**4.56**	**4.32**	**4.14**	**4.00**	**3.89**	**3.80**	**3.73**	**3.67**	**3.56**	**3.48**	**3.36**
16	4.49	3.63	3.24	3.01	2.85	2.74	2.66	2.59	2.54	2.49	2.45	2.42	2.37	2.33	2.28
	8.53	**6.23**	**5.29**	**4.77**	**4.44**	**4.20**	**4.03**	**3.89**	**3.78**	**3.69**	**3.61**	**3.55**	**3.45**	**3.37**	**3.25**
17	4.45	3.59	3.20	2.96	2.81	2.70	2.62	2.55	2.50	2.45	2.41	2.38	2.33	2.29	2.23
	8.40	**6.11**	**5.18**	**4.67**	**4.34**	**4.10**	**3.93**	**3.79**	**3.68**	**3.59**	**3.52**	**3.45**	**3.35**	**3.27**	**3.16**
18	4.41	3.55	3.16	2.93	2.77	2.66	2.58	2.51	2.46	2.41	2.37	2.34	2.29	2.25	2.19
	8.28	**6.01**	**5.09**	**4.58**	**4.25**	**4.01**	**3.85**	**3.71**	**3.60**	**3.51**	**3.44**	**3.37**	**3.27**	**3.19**	**3.07**
19	4.38	3.52	3.13	2.90	2.74	2.63	2.55	2.48	2.43	2.38	2.34	2.31	2.26	2.21	2.15
	8.18	**5.93**	**5.01**	**4.50**	**4.17**	**3.94**	**3.77**	**3.63**	**3.52**	**3.43**	**3.36**	**3.30**	**3.19**	**3.12**	**3.00**

TABLE B.2

The *F* Distribution—cont'd

Degrees of Freedom: Denominator							Degrees of Freedom: Numerator									
	1	2	3	4	5	6	7	8	9	10	11	12	14	16	20
20	4.35	3.49	3.10	2.87	2.71	2.60	2.52	2.45	2.40	2.35	2.31	2.28	2.23	2.18	2.12
	8.10	**5.85**	**4.94**	**4.43**	**4.10**	**3.87**	**3.71**	**3.56**	**3.45**	**3.37**	**3.30**	**3.23**	**3.13**	**3.05**	**2.94**
21	4.32	3.47	3.07	2.84	2.68	2.57	2.49	2.42	2.37	2.32	2.28	2.25	2.20	2.15	2.09
	8.02	**5.78**	**4.87**	**4.37**	**4.04**	**3.81**	**3.65**	**3.51**	**3.40**	**3.31**	**3.24**	**3.17**	**3.07**	**2.99**	**2.88**
22	4.30	3.44	3.05	2.82	2.66	2.55	2.47	2.40	2.35	2.30	2.26	2.23	2.18	2.13	2.07
	7.94	**5.72**	**4.82**	**4.31**	**3.99**	**3.76**	**3.59**	**3.45**	**3.35**	**3.26**	**3.18**	**3.12**	**3.02**	**2.94**	**2.83**
23	4.28	3.42	3.03	2.80	2.64	2.53	2.45	2.38	2.32	2.28	2.24	2.20	2.14	2.10	2.04
	7.88	**5.66**	**4.76**	**4.26**	**3.94**	**3.71**	**3.54**	**3.41**	**3.30**	**3.21**	**3.14**	**3.07**	**2.97**	**2.89**	**2.78**
24	4.26	3.40	3.01	2.78	2.62	2.51	2.43	2.36	2.30	2.26	2.22	2.18	2.13	2.09	2.02
	7.82	**5.61**	**4.72**	**4.22**	**3.90**	**3.67**	**3.50**	**3.36**	**3.25**	**3.17**	**3.09**	**3.03**	**2.93**	**2.85**	**2.74**
25	4.24	3.38	2.99	2.76	2.60	2.49	2.41	2.34	2.28	2.24	2.20	2.16	2.11	2.06	2.00
	7.77	**5.57**	**4.68**	**4.18**	**3.86**	**3.63**	**3.46**	**3.32**	**3.21**	**3.13**	**3.05**	**2.99**	**2.89**	**2.81**	**2.70**
26	4.22	3.37	2.98	2.74	2.59	2.47	2.39	2.32	2.27	2.22	2.18	2.15	2.10	2.05	1.99
	7.72	**5.53**	**4.64**	**4.14**	**3.82**	**3.59**	**3.42**	**3.29**	**3.17**	**3.09**	**3.02**	**2.96**	**2.86**	**2.77**	**2.66**
27	4.21	3.35	2.96	2.73	2.57	2.46	2.37	2.30	2.25	2.20	2.16	2.13	2.08	2.03	1.97
	7.68	**5.49**	**4.60**	**4.11**	**3.79**	**3.56**	**3.39**	**3.26**	**3.14**	**3.06**	**2.98**	**2.93**	**2.83**	**2.74**	**2.63**
28	4.20	3.34	2.95	2.71	2.56	2.44	2.36	2.29	2.24	2.19	2.15	2.12	2.06	2.02	1.96
	7.64	**5.45**	**4.57**	**4.07**	**3.76**	**3.53**	**3.36**	**3.23**	**3.11**	**3.03**	**2.95**	**2.90**	**2.80**	**2.71**	**2.60**
29	4.18	3.33	2.93	2.70	2.54	2.43	2.35	2.28	2.22	2.18	2.14	2.10	2.05	2.00	1.94
	7.60	**5.42**	**4.54**	**4.04**	**3.73**	**3.50**	**3.33**	**3.20**	**3.08**	**3.00**	**2.92**	**2.87**	**2.77**	**2.68**	**2.57**
30	4.17	3.32	2.92	2.69	2.53	2.42	2.34	2.27	2.21	2.16	2.12	2.09	2.04	1.99	1.93
	7.56	**5.39**	**4.51**	**4.02**	**3.70**	**3.47**	**3.30**	**3.17**	**3.06**	**2.98**	**2.90**	**2.84**	**2.74**	**2.66**	**2.55**
32	4.15	3.30	2.90	2.67	2.51	2.40	2.32	2.25	2.19	2.14	2.10	2.07	2.02	1.97	1.91
	7.50	**5.34**	**4.46**	**3.97**	**3.66**	**3.42**	**3.25**	**3.12**	**3.01**	**2.94**	**2.86**	**2.80**	**2.70**	**2.62**	**2.51**
34	4.13	3.28	2.88	2.65	2.49	2.38	2.30	2.23	2.17	2.12	2.08	2.05	2.00	1.95	1.89
	7.44	**5.29**	**4.42**	**3.93**	**3.61**	**3.38**	**3.21**	**3.08**	**2.97**	**2.89**	**2.82**	**2.76**	**2.66**	**2.58**	**2.47**
36	4.11	3.26	2.86	2.63	2.48	2.36	2.28	2.21	2.15	2.10	2.06	2.03	1.98	1.93	1.87
	7.39	**5.25**	**4.38**	**3.89**	**3.58**	**3.35**	**3.18**	**3.04**	**2.94**	**2.86**	**2.78**	**2.72**	**2.62**	**2.54**	**2.43**
38	4.10	3.25	2.85	2.62	2.46	2.35	2.26	2.19	2.14	2.09	2.05	2.02	1.96	1.92	1.85
	7.35	**5.21**	**4.34**	**3.86**	**3.54**	**3.32**	**3.15**	**3.02**	**2.91**	**2.82**	**2.75**	**2.69**	**2.59**	**2.51**	**2.40**
40	4.08	3.23	2.84	2.61	2.45	2.34	2.25	2.18	2.12	2.07	2.04	2.00	1.95	1.90	1.84
	7.31	**5.18**	**4.31**	**3.83**	**3.51**	**3.29**	**3.12**	**2.99**	**2.88**	**2.80**	**2.73**	**2.66**	**2.56**	**2.49**	**2.37**
42	4.07	3.22	2.83	2.59	2.44	2.32	2.24	2.17	2.11	2.06	2.02	1.99	2.5	1.89	1.82
	7.27	**5.15**	**4.29**	**3.80**	**3.49**	**3.26**	**3.10**	**2.96**	**2.86**	**2.77**	**2.70**	**2.64**	**2.54**	**2.46**	**2.35**
44	4.06	3.21	2.82	2.58	2.43	2.31	2.23	2.16	2.10	2.05	2.01	1.98	1.92	1.88	1.81
	7.24	**5.12**	**4.26**	**3.78**	**3.46**	**3.24**	**3.07**	**2.94**	**2.84**	**2.75**	**2.68**	**2.62**	**2.52**	**2.44**	**2.32**
46	4.05	3.20	2.81	2.57	2.42	2.30	2.22	2.14	2.09	2.04	2.00	1.97	1.91	1.87	1.80
	7.21	**5.10**	**4.24**	**3.76**	**3.44**	**3.22**	**3.05**	**2.92**	**2.82**	**2.73**	**2.66**	**2.60**	**2.50**	**2.42**	**2.30**
48	4.04	3.19	2.80	2.56	2.41	2.30	2.21	2.14	2.08	2.03	1.99	1.96	1.90	1.86	1.79
	7.19	**5.08**	**4.22**	**3.74**	**3.42**	**3.20**	**3.04**	**2.90**	**2.80**	**2.71**	**2.64**	**2.58**	**2.48**	**2.40**	**2.28**

TABLE B.2
The *F* Distribution—cont'd

Degrees of Freedom: Denominator	Degrees of Freedom: Numerator														
	1	2	3	4	5	6	7	8	9	10	11	12	14	16	20
50	4.03	3.18	2.79	2.56	2.40	2.29	2.20	2.13	2.07	2.02	1.98	1.95	1.90	1.85	1.78
	7.17	5.06	4.20	3.72	3.41	3.18	3.02	2.88	2.78	2.70	2.62	2.56	2.46	2.39	2.26
55	4.02	3.17	2.78	2.54	2.38	2.27	2.18	2.11	2.05	2.00	1.97	1.93	1.88	1.83	1.76
	7.12	5.01	4.16	3.68	3.37	3.15	2.98	2.85	2.75	2.66	2.59	2.53	2.43	2.35	2.23
60	4.00	3.15	2.76	2.52	2.37	2.25	2.17	2.10	2.04	1.99	1.95	1.92	1.86	1.81	1.75
	7.08	4.98	4.13	3.65	3.34	3.12	2.95	2.82	2.72	2.63	2.56	250	2.40	2.32	2.20
65	3.99	3.14	2.75	2.51	2.36	2.24	2.15	2.08	2.02	1.98	1.94	1.90	1.85	1.80	1.73
	7.04	4.95	4.10	3.62	3.31	3.09	2.93	2.79	2.70	2.61	2.54	2.47	2.37	2.30	2.18
70	3.98	3.13	2.74	2.50	2.35	2.23	2.14	2.07	2.01	1.97	1.93	1.89	1.84	1.79	1.72
	7.01	4.92	4.08	3.60	3.29	3.07	2.91	2.77	2.67	2.59	2.51	2.45	2.35	2.28	2.15
80	3.96	3.11	2.72	2.48	2.33	2.21	2.12	2.05	1.99	1.95	1.91	1.88	1.82	1.77	1.70
	6.96	4.88	4.04	3.56	3.25	3.04	2.87	2.74	2.64	2.55	2.48	2.41	2.32	2.24	2.11
100	3.94	3.09	2.70	2.46	2.30	2.19	2.10	2.03	1.97	1.92	1.88	1.85	1.79	1.75	1.68
	6.90	4.82	3.98	3.51	3.20	2.99	2.82	2.69	2.59	2.51	2.43	2.36	2.26	2.19	2.06
125	3.92	3.07	2.68	2.44	2.29	2.17	2.08	2.01	1.95	1.90	1.86	1.83	1.77	1.72	1.65
	6.84	4.78	3.94	3.47	3.17	2.95	2.79	2.65	2.56	2.47	2.40	2.33	2.23	2.15	2.03
150	3.91	3.06	2.67	2.43	2.27	2.16	2.07	2.00	1.94	1.89	1.85	1.82	1.76	1.71	1.64
	6.81	4.75	3.91	3.44	3.14	2.92	2.76	2.62	2.53	2.44	2.37	2.30	2.20	2.12	2.00
200	3.89	3.04	2.65	2.41	2.26	2.14	2.05	1.98	1.92	1.87	1.83	1.80	1.74	1.69	1.62
	6.76	4.71	3.88	3.41	3.11	2.90	2.73	2.60	2.50	2.41	2.34	2.28	2.17	2.09	1.97
400	3.86	3.02	2.62	2.39	2.23	2.12	2.03	1.96	1.90	1.85	1.81	1.78	1.72	1.67	1.60
	6.70	4.66	3.83	3.36	3.06	2.85	2.69	2.55	2.46	2.37	2.29	2.23	2.12	2.04	1.92
1000	3.85	3.00	2.61	2.38	2.22	2.10	2.02	1.95	1.89	1.84	1.80	1.76	1.70	1.65	1.58
	6.66	4.62	3.80	3.34	3.04	2.82	2.66	2.53	2.43	2.34	2.26	2.20	2.09	2.01	1.89
∞	3.84	2.99	2.60	2.37	2.21	2.09	2.01	1.94	1.88	1.83	1.79	1.75	1.69	1.64	1.57
	6.64	4.60	3.78	3.32	3.02	2.80	2.64	2.51	2.41	2.32	2.24	2.18	2.07	1.99	1.87

Table A14 of *Statistical Methods*, 7th ed., by George Snedecor and William G. Cochran. Copyright © 1980 by the Iowa State University Press. Used with permission.

TABLE B.3
The Chi-Square Distribution

Table entries are the minimum values of chi-square (χ^2) that are necessary for a chi-square statistic to be significant at the alpha level specified. To be significant, a calculated χ^2 statistic must be greater than or equal to the value in the table.

Df	Proportion in Critical Region				
	0.10	0.05	0.025	0.01	0.005
1	2.71	3.84	5.02	6.63	7.88
2	4.61	5.99	7.38	9.21	10.60
3	6.25	7.81	9.35	11.34	12.84
4	7.78	9.49	11.14	13.28	14.86
5	9.24	11.07	12.83	15.09	16.75
6	10.64	12.59	14.45	16.81	18.55
7	12.02	14.07	16.01	18.48	20.28
8	13.36	15.51	17.53	20.09	21.96
9	14.68	16.92	19.02	21.67	23.59
10	15.99	18.31	20.48	23.21	25.19
11	17.28	19.68	21.92	24.72	26.76
12	18.55	21.03	23.34	26.22	28.30
13	19.81	22.36	24.74	27.69	29.82
14	21.06	23.68	26.12	29.14	31.32
15	22.31	25.00	27.49	30.58	32.80
16	23.54	26.30	28.85	32.00	34.27
17	24.77	27.59	30.19	33.41	35.72
18	25.99	28.87	31.53	34.81	37.16
19	27.20	30.14	32.85	36.19	38.58
20	28.41	31.41	34.17	37.57	40.00
21	29.62	32.67	35.48	38.93	41.40
22	30.81	33.92	36.78	40.29	42.80
23	32.01	35.17	38.08	41.64	44.18
24	33.20	36.42	39.36	42.98	45.56
25	34.38	37.65	40.65	44.31	46.93
26	35.56	38.89	41.92	45.64	48.29
27	36.74	40.11	43.19	46.96	49.64
28	37.92	41.34	44.46	48.28	50.99
29	39.09	42.56	45.72	49.59	52.34
30	40.26	43.77	46.98	50.89	53.67
40	51.81	55.76	59.34	63.69	66.77
50	63.17	67.50	71.42	76.15	79.49
60	74.40	79.08	83.30	88.38	91.95
70	85.53	90.53	95.02	100.42	104.22
80	96.58	101.88	106.63	112.33	116.32
90	107.56	113.14	118.14	124.12	128.30
100	118.50	124.34	129.56	135.81	140.17

Instructions for Using SPSS

The Statistical Package for the Social Sciences (SPSS) is a computer program that performs statistical calculations and is widely available on college campuses. The program is updated regularly and the current version is IBM SPSS Statistics Version 24. SPSS consists of two basic components: a data matrix and a set of statistical commands.

The **data matrix** is a huge matrix of numbered rows and columns. To begin any analysis, you must type your data into the matrix. Typically, the scores are entered into columns of the matrix. Before scores are entered, each of the columns is labeled "var." After scores are entered, the first column becomes var00001, the second column becomes var00002, and so on. To enter data into the matrix, the **Data View** tab must be set at the bottom left of the screen. If you want to assign a name to a column (instead of using var00001), click on the **Variable View** tab at the bottom of the data matrix. You will get a description of each variable in the matrix, including a box for the name. You may type in a new name using up to eight lower-case characters (no spaces, no hyphens). Click the **Data View** tab to go back to the data matrix.

The **statistical commands** are listed in menus that are made available by clicking on the **Analyze** box that is located on the tool bar at the top of the screen. When you select a statistical command, SPSS typically asks you to identify exactly where the scores are located and exactly what other options you want to use. This is accomplished by identifying the column(s) in the data matrix that contain the needed information. Typically, you are presented with a display similar to the following figure. On the left is a box that lists all of the columns in the data matrix that contain information. In this example, we have typed values into columns 1, 2, 3, and 4. On the right is an empty box that is waiting for you to identify the correct column. For example, suppose that you wanted to do a statistical calculation using the scores in column 3. You should highlight var00003 by clicking on it in the left-hand box, then click the arrow to move the column label into the right hand box. (If you make a mistake, you can highlight the variable in the right-hand box, and the arrow will reverse so that you can move the variable back to the left-hand box.)

Variable (s)

var00001
var00002
var00003
var00004

$\rightarrow$

Following is a set of basic statistical operations that can be performed with SPSS. This is only a partial listing of the many statistical computations that SPSS can do, but it should cover most of the statistics that would be needed in an introductory research methods course.

Frequency Distributions

A frequency distribution is an organized tabulation showing how many individuals have scores in each category on the scale of measurement. A frequency distribution can be presented either as a table or a graph.

A Frequency Distribution Table

Data Entry

1. Enter all the scores in one column of the data matrix, probably var00001.

Data Analysis

1. Click **Analyze** on the tool bar.
2. Select **Descriptive Statistics**.
3. Select **Frequencies**.
4. Highlight the column label for the set of scores (var0001) in the left box.
5. Click the arrow to move the column label into the **Variable** box.
6. Be sure that the option to **Display Frequency Table** is selected.
7. Click **OK**.

Output

The frequency distribution table lists the score values in a column from smallest to largest, with the percentage and cumulative percentage also listed for each score. Score values that do not occur (zero frequency) are not included in the table, and the program does not group scores into class intervals (all values are listed).

A Frequency Distribution Histogram or Bar Graph

Data Entry

1. Enter all the scores in one column of the data matrix, probably var00001.

Data Analysis

1. Click **Analyze** on the tool bar.
2. Select **Descriptive Statistics**.
3. Select **Frequencies**.
4. Highlight the column label for the set of scores (var00001) in the left box.
5. Click the arrow to move the column label into the **Variable** box.
6. Click **Charts**.
7. Select either **Bar Graph** or **Histogram**.
8. Click **Continue**.
9. Click **OK**.

Output

SPSS displays a frequency distribution table and a graph (Figure C.1). Note that the program often produces a histogram that groups the scores in unpredictable intervals. A bar graph usually produces a clearer picture of the actual frequency associated with each score.

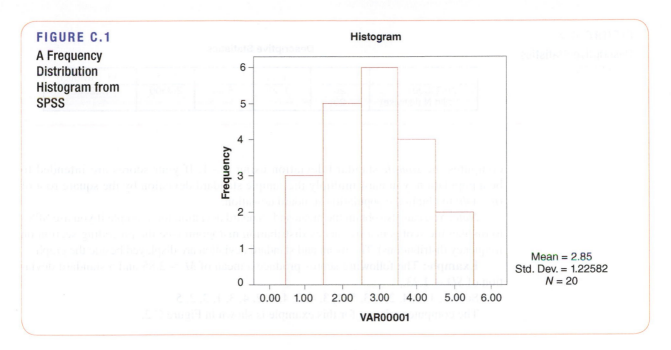

FIGURE C.1

A Frequency Distribution Histogram from SPSS

Example: The following set of scores produce a frequency distribution (either a table or a graph) showing that three people had scores of $X = 1$, five people had $X = 2$, six people had $X = 3$, four had $X = 4$, and two had $X = 5$.

Scores: 1, 2, 4, 2, 3, 3, 5, 1, 3, 4, 2, 4, 3, 2, 4, 3, 1, 3, 2, 5

The histogram from the computer printout for this example is shown in Figure C.1.

Means and Standard Deviations

The mean and standard deviation are probably the two most commonly used statistics for describing a set of scores. The mean describes the center of the set of scores and the standard deviation describes how the scores are scattered around the mean. In simple terms, the standard deviation provides a measure of the average distance from the mean.

Data Entry

1. Enter all of the scores in one column of the data matrix, probably var00001.

Data Analysis

1. Click **Analyze** on the tool bar.
2. Select **Descriptive Statistics**.
3. Select **Descriptives**.
4. Highlight the column label for the set of scores (var00001) in the left box.
5. Click the arrow to move the column label into the **Variable** box.
6. Click **OK**.

Output

SPSS produces a summary table listing the number of scores (N), the minimum score, the maximum score, the mean, and the standard deviation (Figure C.2). Note that SPSS

FIGURE C.2

Descriptive Statistics from SPSS

Descriptive Statistics

	N	Minimum	Maximum	Mean	Std. Deviation
VAR00001	20	1.00	5.00	2.8500	1.22582
Valid N (listwise)	20				

computes the *sample* standard deviation using $n - 1$. If your scores are intended to be a population, you must multiply the sample standard deviation by the square root of $(n - 1)/n$ to obtain the population standard deviation.

Note: You can also obtain the mean and standard deviation for a sample if you use SPSS to display the scores in a frequency distribution histogram (see the preceding section on frequency distributions). The mean and standard deviation are displayed beside the graph.

Example: The following scores produce a mean of $M = 2.85$ and a standard deviation of $SD = 1.23$.

Scores: 1, 2, 4, 2, 3, 3, 5, 1, 3, 4, 2, 4, 3, 2, 4, 3, 1, 3, 2, 5

The computer printout for this example is shown in Figure C.2.

The Independent-Measures *t* Test

The independent-measures *t* test is used to compare two means from a between-subjects research design: That is, the test evaluates the mean difference between two separate samples that represent two separate treatment conditions or two separate populations. A *significant difference* indicates that there appears to be a consistent, systematic difference between the two treatments and that the obtained mean difference is very unlikely ($p < .05$) to have occurred by chance alone. The significance is determined by the p value that is reported as part of the computer output.

Data Entry

1. The scores are entered in what is called a *stacked format,* which means that all the scores from *both samples* are entered in one column of the data matrix (probably var00001).
2. Values are then entered into a second column (var00002) to designate the sample or treatment condition corresponding to each of the scores. For example, enter a 1 beside each score from sample #1 and enter a 2 beside each score from sample #2.

Data Analysis

1. Click **Analyze** on the tool bar.
2. Select **Compare Means**.
3. Click on **Independent-Samples T Test**.
4. Highlight the column label for the set of scores (var00001) in the left box.
5. Click the arrow to move the column label into the **Test Variable** box.
6. Highlight the column label containing the sample numbers (var00002) in the left box.
7. Click the arrow to move the column label into the **Grouping Variable** box.
8. Click on **Define Groups**.
9. Click on the button for **Use Specific Values** and enter a 1 in the box for Group 1 and a 2 in the box for Group 2.

10. Click **Continue**.
11. Click **OK**.

Output

SPSS produces a summary table showing the number of scores, the mean, the standard deviation, and the standard error for each of the two samples (Figure C.3). SPSS also conducts a test for homogeneity of variance, using Levene's test. Homogeneity of variance is an assumption for the t test and requires that the two populations from which the samples were obtained have equal variances. This test should *not* be significant (you do not want the two variances to be different), so you want the reported **Sig.** value to be greater than .05. Next, the results of the hypothesis test are presented using two different assumptions; we focus on the top row, where equal variances are assumed. (If Levene's test is significant [the Sig. value is less than .05], then use the values in the bottom row.) The test results include the calculated t value, the degrees of freedom, the level of significance (probability of a Type I error), and the size of the mean difference. Finally, the output includes a report of the standard error for the mean difference and a 95% confidence interval that provides a range of values estimating how much difference exists between the two treatment conditions.

The output also includes the information necessary to compute measures of effect size. The values for t and df can be used to calculate r^2. The sample mean difference and the two sample standard deviations can be used to compute Cohen's d (see Appendix B, p. 459).

Example: The following two samples produce a t statistic of $t = 3.834$, with degrees of freedom equal to $df = 6$, and a significance level of $p = .009$ with Cohen's $d = 2.71$ and $r^2 = 0.710$. The computer printout for this example is shown in Figure C.3.

Treatment 1 (Sample 1)	Treatment 2 (Sample 2)
3	12
5	10
7	8
1	14

FIGURE C.3

An Independent Samples t Test Printout from SPSS

The portions of the printout showing Levine's test and the confidence interval have been deleted to conserve space.

Group Statistics

	VAR00002	N	Mean	Std. Deviation	Std. Error Mean
VAR00001	1.00	4	4.0000	2.58199	1.29099
	2.00	4	11.0000	2.58199	1.29099

Independent Samples Test

		t	df	Sig. (2-tailed)	Mean Difference	Std. Error Difference
VAR00001	Equal variances assumed	−3.834	6	.009	−7.00000	1.82574
	Equal variances not assumed	−3.834	6.000	.009	−7.00000	1.82574

t-test for Equality of Mean

The Repeated-Measures *t* Test

The repeated-measures *t* test is used to compare two means from a within-subjects research design: that is, the test evaluates the mean difference between two treatment conditions in which the same set of individuals is measured in both treatments. A *significant difference* indicates that there appears to be a consistent, systematic difference between the two treatments and that the obtained mean difference is very unlikely ($p < .05$) to have occurred by chance alone. The significance is determined by the *p* value that is reported as part of the computer output.

Data Entry

1. Enter the data into two columns (var00001 and var00002) in the data matrix with the first score for each participant in the first column and the second score in the second column.

Data Analysis

1. Click **Analyze** on the tool bar.
2. Select **Compare Means**.
3. Click on **Paired-Samples T Test**.
4. Highlight the label for the first data column in the left box and then click on the arrow to move the label into the **Variable 1** area of the **Paired Variables** box.
5. Highlight the label for the second data column in the left box and then click on the arrow to move the label into the **Variable 2** area of the **Paired Variables** box.
6. Click **OK**.

Output

SPSS produces a summary table showing descriptive statistics for each of the two sets of scores, and a table showing the correlation between the first and second scores. Finally, SPSS conducts the *t* test for the difference scores. The output shows the mean difference, the standard deviation, and the standard error for the difference scores, as well as the value for *t*, the value for *df*, and the level of significance (Figure C.4). The output also includes a 95% confidence interval that provides a range of values estimating how much difference exists between the two treatment conditions.

The output includes the information necessary to compute measures of effect size. The values for *t* and *df* can be used to calculate r^2. The mean and the standard deviation for the difference scores can be used to compute Cohen's *d* (see Appendix B, p. 460).

Note: If you have already computed the difference score for each participant (instead of pairs of scores), you can do the repeated-measures *t* test by entering the difference scores in one column and selecting the **One-Sample T Test** option. Click **Analyze** on the tool bar, select **Compare Means**, and click on **One-Sample T Test**. Move the column label for the set of difference scores into the **Test Variable** box, and enter a value of zero in the **Test Value** box.

Example: The following data show a mean difference of five points between the two treatments and produce $t = 2.50$, with $df = 3$, and a significance level of $p = .088$ with Cohen's $d = 1.25$ and $r^2 = 0.676$. The computer printout for this example is shown in Figure C.4.

FIGURE C.4

An SPSS Printout for a Paired Samples *t* Test

The table showing the correlation and a portion of the printout showing the confidence interval have been deleted to conserve space.

Paired Samples Statistics

		Mean	N	Std. Deviation	Std. Error Mean
Pair 1	VAR00001	26.2500	4	7.97392	3.98696
	VAR00002	21.2500	4	11.23610	5.61805

Paired Samples Test

		Paired Differences					
		Mean	Std. Deviation	Std. Error Mean	t	df	Sig. (2-tailed)
Pair 1	VAR00001 - VAR00002	5.00000	4.00000	2.00000	2.500	3	.088

Participant	First Treatment	Second Treatment	Difference
A	19	12	−7
B	35	36	+1
C	20	13	−7
D	31	24	−7

Single-Factor, Independent-Measures Analysis of Variance (Anova)

The single-factor, independent-measures ANOVA is used to compare the means from a between-subjects research study using two or more separate samples to compare two or more separate treatment conditions or populations. A significant difference indicates that there appears to be a consistent, systematic difference between at least two of the treatments and that the obtained mean differences are very unlikely ($p < .05$) to have occurred by chance alone. The significance is determined by the p value that is reported as part of the computer output.

Data Entry

1. The scores are entered in a *stacked format* in the data matrix, which means that all the scores from all of the different treatments are entered in a single column (var00001).
2. In a second column (var00002), enter a number to designate the treatment condition for each score. For example, enter a 1 beside each score from the first treatment, enter a 2 beside each score from the second treatment, and so on.

Data Analysis

1. Click **Analyze** on the tool bar.
2. Select **Compare Means**.
3. Click on **One-Way ANOVA**.

4. Highlight the column label for the scores (var00001) in the left box.
5. Click the arrow to move the column label into the **Dependent List** box.
6. Highlight the column label for the treatment numbers in the left box.
7. Click the arrow to move the column label into the **Factor** box.
8. If you want to conduct post hoc tests to determine exactly which means are different, click on the **Post Hoc** box, select a test, and click **Continue**.
9. Click on the **Options** box and select **Descriptives** if you want descriptive statistics for each sample, then click **Continue**.
10. Click **OK**.

Output

If you select the **Descriptives** Option, SPSS produces a table showing descriptive statistics for each of the samples along with a summary table showing the results from the analysis of variance (Figure C.5). Also note that the Between-Groups and Total Sum of Squares values in the summary table can be used to compute η^2 to measure effect size (see Appendix B, p. 463).

Example: For the following data, the first treatment has $M = 1.00$ with $SD = 1.73$, the second treatment has $M = 5.00$ with $SD = 2.24$, and the third treatment has $M = 6.00$ with $SD = 1.87$. The analysis produces an F-ratio of $F = 9.13$, with $df = 2, 12$, and a significance level of $p = .004$ with $\eta^2 = 0.603$. The computer printout for this example is shown in Figure C.5.

First Treatment	Second Treatment	Third Treatment
0	6	6
4	8	5
0	5	9
1	4	4
0	2	6

FIGURE C.5

An SPSS Printout for a Single-Factor Independent-Measures ANOVA

A portion of the Descriptives table showing the minimum and maximum scores has been omitted to conserve space.

Descriptives

VAR00001

	N	Mean	Std. Deviation	Std. Error	95% Confidence Interval for Mean Lower Bound	Upper Bound
1.00	5	1.0000	1.73205	.77460	−1.1506	3.1506
2.00	5	5.0000	2.23607	1.00000	2.2236	7.7764
3.00	5	6.0000	1.87083	.83666	3.6771	8.3229
Total	15	4.0000	2.87849	.74322	2.4059	5.5941

ANOVA

VAR00001

	Sum of Squares	df	Mean Square	F	Sig.
Between Groups	70.000	2	35.000	9.130	.004
Within Groups	46.000	12	3.833		
Total	116.000	14			

Single-Factor, Repeated-Measures Anova

The single-factor, repeated-measures ANOVA is used to compare the means from a within-subjects research study using one sample to compare two or more separate treatment conditions (each individual is measured in each of the treatment conditions). A *significant difference* indicates that there appears to be a consistent, systematic difference between at least two of the treatments and that the obtained mean differences are very unlikely ($p < .05$) to have occurred by chance alone. The significance is determined by the p value that is reported as part of the computer output.

Data Entry

1. Enter the scores for each treatment condition in a separate column, with the scores for each individual in the same row. All the scores for the first treatment go in var00001, the second treatment scores in var00002, and so on.

Data Analysis

1. Click **Analyze** on the tool bar.
2. Select **General Linear Model**.
3. Click on **Repeated Measures**.
4. SPSS presents a box titled **Repeated-Measures Define Factors**. Within the box, the Within-Subjects Factor Name should already contain **Factor1**. If not, type in Factor 1.
5. Enter the **Number of Levels** (number of different treatment conditions) in the next box.
6. Click on **Add**.
7. Click **Define**.
8. One by one, move the column labels for your treatment conditions into the **Within-Subjects Variables** box. (Highlight the column label on the left and click the arrow to move it into the box.)
9. If you want to conduct post hoc tests to determine exactly which means are different, click on the **Post Hoc** box, select a test, and click **Continue**.
10. Click on the **Options** and select **Descriptives** if you want descriptive statistics for each treatment, then click **Continue**.
11. Click **OK**.

Output

If you select the **Descriptives** Option, SPSS produces a table showing the mean and standard deviation for each treatment condition. The rest of the Output is relatively complex and includes a lot of statistical information that goes well beyond the scope of this book. However, if you focus on the table showing **Test of Within-Subjects Effects**, the top line of the **factor1** box and the top line of the **Error(factor1)** box shows the sum of squares, the degrees of freedom, and the mean square for the numerator and denominator of the F-ratio, as well as the value of the F-ratio and the level of significance (Figure C.6). The two Sum of Squares values that are used in the calculation of the F-ratio are also the values needed to measure effect size (see Appendix B, p. 465).

Example: For the following data, the first treatment has $M = 5.00$ with $SD = 1.87$, the second treatment has $M = 4.00$ with $SD = 1.58$, and the third treatment has $M = 3.00$ with $SD = 1.58$. The analysis produces an F-ratio of $F = 10.00$, with $df = 2, 8$, and a significance level of $p = .007$ with $\eta^2 = 0.714$. Part of the computer printout for this example is shown in Figure C.6.

FIGURE C.6

Part of the SPSS Printout for a Single-Factor Repeated-Measures ANOVA

The top line for "factor1" and the top line for "Error(factor1)" contain the relevant portions of the analysis.

Tests of Within-Subjects Effects

Measure: MEASURE_1

Source		Type III Sum of Squares	df	Mean Square	F	Sig.
factor1	Sphericity Assumed	10.000	2	5.000	10.000	.007
	Greenhouse-Geisser	10.000	1.000	10.000	10.000	.034
	Huynh-Feldt	10.000	1.000	10.000	10.000	.034
	Lower-bound	10.000	1.000	10.000	10.000	.034
Error(factor1)	Sphericity Assumed	4.000	8	.500		
	Greenhouse-Geisser	4.000	4.000	1.000		
	Huynh-Feldt	4.000	4.000	1.000		
	Lower-bound	4.000	4.000	1.000		

Participant	First Treatment	Second Treatment	Third Treatment
A	5	4	3
B	3	2	1
C	4	3	2
D	5	6	4
E	8	5	5

Two-Factor, Independent-Measures Anova

The two-factor, independent-measures ANOVA is used to compare the means from a between-subjects research study using two independent variables (or quasi-independent variables). The structure of a two-factor study can be represented as a matrix, with the levels of one independent variable defining the rows and the levels of the second independent variable defining the columns. Each cell in the matrix corresponds to a unique treatment condition, and there is a separate sample for each cell. The two-factor ANOVA consists of three separate tests for mean differences: (1) the main effect for the first factor consists of the mean differences between the rows of the matrix; (2) the main effect for the second factor consists of the mean differences between the columns of the matrix; and (3) the interaction consists of any additional mean differences that are not accounted for by the two main effects. For each of the three tests, a *significant difference* indicates that there appears to be a consistent, systematic difference between at least two of the treatments and that the obtained mean differences are very unlikely ($p < .05$) to have occurred by chance alone. The significance is determined by the p value that is reported as part of the computer output.

Data Entry

1. The scores are entered into the SPSS data matrix in a *stacked format*, which means that all the scores from all the different treatment conditions are entered in a single column (var00001).
2. In a second column (var00002), enter a number to designate the level of factor A for each score. If factor A defines the rows of the data matrix, enter a 1 beside each score from the first row, enter a 2 beside each score from the second row, and so on.

3. In a third column (var00003), enter a number to designate the level of factor B for each score. If factor B defines the columns of the data matrix, enter a 1 beside each score from the first column, enter a 2 beside each score from the second column, and so on.

Data Analysis

1. Click **Analyze** on the tool bar.
2. Select **General Linear Model**.
3. Click on **Univariant**.
4. Highlight the column label for the scores (var00001) in the left box.
5. Click the arrow to move the column label into the **Dependent Variable** box.
6. One by one, highlight the two column labels for the two factors (var0002 and var003) and click the arrow to move the labels into the **Fixed Factors** box.
7. If you want to conduct post hoc tests to determine exactly which means are different, click on the **Post Hoc** box, select a test, and click **Continue**.
8. Click on **Options** and select **Descriptives** if you want descriptive statistics for each sample, then click **Continue**.
9. Click **OK**.

Output

If you select the **Descriptives** option, SPSS produces a table showing the means and standard deviations for each treatment condition. The results of the ANOVA are shown in a summary table in which each factor is identified by its column label (Figure C.7). Note that the summary table includes some extra values, such as *Corrected Model* and *Intercept,* that are beyond the scope of this text. Effect size for each main effect and for the interaction is measured with an η^2 value that is calculated using the Sum of Squares values in the output (see Appendix B, p. 469).

Example: The following data produce an F-ratio for the main effect of factor A of $F = 8.167$ with $df = 1, 24$ and a significance level of $p = .009$ with $\eta^2 = 0.254$. The F-ratio

Tests of Between-Subjects Effects

Dependent Variable: VAR00001

Source	Type III Sum of Squares	df	Mean Square	F	Sig.
Corrected Model	84.167[a]	5	16.833	3.367	.019
Intercept	300.833	1	300.833	60.167	.000
VAR00002	40.833	1	40.833	8.167	.009
VAR00003	31.667	2	15.833	3.167	.060
VAR00002 * VAR00003	11.667	2	5.833	1.167	.328
Error	120.000	24	5.000		
Total	505.000	30			
Corrected Total	204.167	29			

a. R Squared = .412 (Adjusted R Squared = .290)

FIGURE C.7

Part of the Printout for a Two-Factor Independent-Measures ANOVA

Relevant information about the two main effects, the interaction, and the error term is contained in the middle four lines of the table titled "Tests of Between-Subjects Effects."

for the main effect of factor B is $F = 3.167$ with $df = 2, 24$ and a significance level of $p = .060$ (not significant) with $\eta^2 = 0.209$. The A × B interaction has $F = 1.167$ with $df = 2, 24$ and a significance level of $p = .328$ (not significant) with $\eta^2 = 0.089$. The means and standard deviations are shown with the individual samples. The computer printout for this example is shown in Figure C.7.

Two-Factor Mixed Design Anova (One Between-Subjects Factor and One Within-Subjects Factor)

The mixed design two-factor ANOVA is used to compare the means from a research study using one between-subjects factor (with a different sample for each level) and one within-subjects factor (with the same sample participating in every level). The structure of the mixed design can be represented as a matrix with the levels of the between-subjects factor defining the rows and the levels of the within-subjects factor defining the columns (see the data on p. 494). The two-factor ANOVA consists of three separate tests for mean differences:

1. The main effect for the between-subjects factor consists of the mean differences between the rows of the matrix (note that there is a separate sample for each row).
2. The main effect for the within-subjects factor consists of the mean differences between the columns of the matrix (note that the same individuals are tested in the first column and in the second column, etc.).
3. The interaction consists of any additional mean differences that are not accounted for by the two main effects (note that the interaction is also considered to be a within-subjects test).

For each of the three tests, a significant difference indicates that there appears to be a consistent, systematic difference between at least two of the treatments and that the obtained mean differences are very unlikely ($p < .05$) to have occurred by chance alone. The significance is determined by the p value that is reported as part of the computer output.

Data Entry

1. All of the scores for each level of the within-subjects factor go into a separate column of the data matrix, with the scores for each participant in the same row. For the data in the following example, all the scores from the "quiet" condition are entered in order into one column (var00001), the scores from the "moderate" condition are entered in a second column (var00002), and the scores from the "loud" condition are entered in a third column (var00003).
2. An additional column is then used to identify the levels of the between-subjects factor. For the data in the following example, in a fourth column (var00004) enter a 1 for each of the three males and a 2 for each of the three females.

Data Analysis

1. Click **Analyze** on the tool bar.
2. Select **General Linear Model**.
3. Click on **Repeated Measures**.

4. SPSS presents a box titled **Repeated-Measures Define Factors.** Within the box, the Within-Subjects Factor Name should already contain **Factor1**. If not, type in Factor1.
5. Enter the **Number of Levels** (number of treatment conditions for the within-subjects factor) in the next box.
6. Click on **Add**.
7. Click **Define**.
8. One by one, move the column labels for your within-subjects treatment conditions into the **Within-Subjects Variables** box. (Highlight the column label on the left and click the arrow to move it into the box.)
9. Move the column label for the column containing the levels of your between-subjects factor into the **Between-Subjects Factor(s)** box. (Highlight the column label on the left and click the arrow to move it into the box.)
10. If you want to conduct post hoc tests to determine exactly which means are different, click on the **Post Hoc** box, select a test, and click **Continue**.
11. Click on **Options** and select **Descriptives** if you want descriptive statistics for each treatment combination, then click **Continue**.
12. Click **OK**.

Output

If you select the **Descriptives** option, the output includes a table with the mean and standard deviation for each treatment condition. Near the bottom of the output, you will find a box labeled **Tests of Within-Subjects Effects** (Figure C.8) containing the *F*-ratios, *df* values, and significance levels for the main effect of the within-subjects factor and the

FIGURE C.8

Portions of the SPSS Printout for a Mixed Design Two-Factor ANOVA

The top line in each of the three sections of the within-subjects table shows relevant information for the main effect, interaction, and error term for the within-subjects factor. The between-subjects table shows the main effect and error term for the between-subjects factor.

Tests of Within-Subjects Effects

Measure: MEASURE_1

Source		Type III Sum of Squares	df	Mean Square	F	Sig.
factor1	Sphericity Assumed	52.000	2	26.000	78.000	.000
	Greenhouse-Geisser	52.000	1.000	52.000	78.000	.001
	Huynh-Feldt	52.000	1.333	39.000	78.000	.000
	Lower-bound	52.000	1.000	52.000	78.000	.001
factor 1 * VAR00004	Sphericity Assumed	12.000	2	6.000	18.000	.001
	Greenhouse-Geisser	12.000	1.000	12.000	18.000	.013
	Huynh-Feldt	12.000	1.333	9.000	18.000	.006
	Lower-bound	12.000	1.000	12.000	18.000	.013
Error(factor1)	Sphericity Assumed	2.667	8	.333		
	Greenhouse-Geisser	2.667	4.000	.667		
	Huynh-Feldt	2.667	5.333	.500		
	Lower-bound	2.667	4.000	.667		

Tests of Between-Subjects Effects

Measure: MEASURE_1
Transformed Variable: Average

Source	Type III Sum of Squares	df	Mean Square	F	Sig.
Intercept	242.000	1	242.000	55.846	.002
VAR00004	18.000	1	18.000	4.154	.111
Error	17.333	4	4.333		

interaction (use the top row labeled **Sphericity Assumed** for each). Finally, the box labeled **Tests of Between-Subjects Effects** contains the F-ratio, df values, and significance level for the main effect of the between-subjects factor (use the middle row labeled with the variable name).

Effect size for each main effect and for the interaction is measured with an η^2 value that is calculated using the Sum of Squares values in the output. For each specific treatment effect, the value is computed as

$$\eta^2 \text{ for the treatment effect} = \frac{SS_{treatment}}{SS_{treatment} + SS_{error}}$$

The η^2 value for the main effect for the within-subjects factor and the interaction use the error Sum of Squares from the Tests-of-Within-Subjects Effects box in the output, and η^2 for the main effect of the between-subjects factor uses the error Sum of Squares from the Tests-of-Between-Subjects Effects box.

Example: The following data represent a mixed design, two-factor study. The between-subjects factor is gender (male/female) with two separate samples, a group of three males and a group of three females. The within-subjects factor is the level of background noise (quiet/moderate/loud). Note that each of the two samples is tested in all three of the noise conditions. For the main effect for gender, the ANOVA produces $F = 4.154$ with $df = 1, 4$ and $p = .111$ (not significant) with $\eta^2 = 0.509$. The main effect for background noise produces $F = 78.00$ with $df = 2, 8$ and a significance level of $p = .000$ (reported as $p < .001$) with $\eta^2 = 0.951$. The interaction produces $F = 18.00$ with $df = 2, 8$ and a significance level of $p = .001$ with $\eta^2 = 0.818$. The computer printout for this example is shown in Figure C.8.

			Background Noise	
	Participant	Quiet	Moderate	Loud
Males	A	1	3	1
	B	2	3	2
	C	3	6	3
Females	D	3	7	1
	E	4	7	2
	F	5	10	3

The means and standard deviations for the different treatment conditions are as follows:

	Quiet	Moderate	Loud
Males	$M = 2.00$	$M = 4.00$	$M = 2.00$
	$SD = 1.00$	$SD = 1.73$	$SD = 1.00$
Females	$M = 4.00$	$M = 8.00$	$M = 2.00$
	$SD = 1.00$	$SD = 1.73$	$SD = 1.00$

The Pearson Correlation

The Pearson correlation measures and describes the direction and degree of linear relationship between two variables. The data are numerical scores, with two separate scores, representing two different variables, for each individual. The two scores are identified as X and Y. A positive correlation indicates that X and Y tend to vary in the same direction (as X increases, Y also increases), and a negative correlation indicates that X and Y vary in opposite directions (as X increases, Y decreases). A correlation of 1.00 (or −1.00) indicates that the data points fit perfectly on a straight line. A correlation of 0.00 indicates that there is no linear relationship whatsoever. Values between 0 and 1.00 indicate intermediate degrees of relationship. It is also possible to evaluate the statistical significance of a correlation by determining the probability that the sample correlation was obtained, just by chance, from a population in which there is a zero correlation.

Data Entry

1. The data are entered into two columns in the data matrix, one for the X values (var00001) and one for the Y values (var00002), with the two scores for each individual in the same row.

Data Analysis

1. Click **Analyze** on the tool bar.
2. Select **Correlate**.
3. Click on **Bivariate**.
4. One by one move the labels for the two data columns into the **Variables** box. (Highlight each label and click the arrow to move it into the box.)
5. The **Pearson** box should be checked, but you can click the **Spearman** box if you want to compute a Spearman correlation (SPSS converts the scores to ranks).
6. Click **OK**.

Output

SPSS produces a correlation matrix showing all the possible correlations (Figure C.9). You want the correlation of X and Y, which is contained in the upper right corner (or the lower left). The output includes the significance level (p value) for the correlation. Effect size, r^2, is obtained by simply squaring the correlation.

   Example: The following data produce a Pearson correlation of 0.535 with a significance level of $p = .216$ (not significant) and $r^2 = 0.286$. The computer printout for this example is shown in Figure C.9.

X	Y
3	6
5	9
2	12
1	8
5	13
4	10
6	14

FIGURE C.9

An SPSS Printout for the Pearson Correlation

Correlations

		VAR00001	VAR00002
VAR00001	Pearson Correlation	1	.535
	Sig. (2-tailed)		.216
	N	7	7
VAR00002	Pearson Correlation	.535	1
	Sig. (2-tailed)	.216	
	N	7	7

Regression with One or Two Predictor Variables

With one predictor variable, regression produces the equation for the best fitting straight line for a set of X and Y data points. The data for regression are the same as would be used for a Pearson correlation. It is also possible to evaluate the statistical significance of the regression equation by determining the probability that the equation would be obtained if the sample was selected from a population in which there is no relationship between X and Y (the Pearson correlation is zero).

With two predictor variables, multiple regression produces the best-fitting linear equation of the form: $Y = b_1 X_1 + b_2 X_2 + a$. Again, it is possible to evaluate the statistical significance of the multiple regression equation by determining the probability that the equation would be obtained if the sample were selected from a population in which X_1 and X_2 have no relationship with Y.

Data Entry

1. With one predictor variable (X), you enter the X values in one column (var00001) and the Y values in a second column (var00002) of the SPSS data editor. With two predictors (X_1 and X_2), enter the X_1 values in one column, X_2 in a second column, and Y in a third column.

Data Analysis

1. Click **Analyze** on the tool bar, select **Regression**, and click on **Linear**.
2. In the left-hand box, highlight the column label for the Y values, then click the arrow to move the column label into the **Dependent Variable** box.
3. For one predictor variable, highlight the column label for the X values and click the arrow to move it into the **Independent Variable(s)** box. For two predictor variables, highlight the X_1 and X_2 column labels, one at a time, and click the arrow to move them into the **Independent Variable(s)** box.
4. Click **OK**.

Output

The printout includes a table that simply lists the predictor variables that were entered into the regression equation. A second table (Model Summary) presents the values for R, R^2, and the standard error of estimate. R^2 is the customary measure of effect size, or the strength of the regression equation. Note that for a single predictor, R is simply the Pearson correlation between X and Y (Figure C.10). The third table (ANOVA) presents the analysis of regression evaluating the significance of the regression equation, including the F-ratio and the level of significance. The final table summarizes the unstandardized

FIGURE C.10

An SPSS Printout for
Regression with One
Predictor Variable

Model Summary

Model	R	R Square	Adjusted R Square	Std. Error of the Estimate
1	.535[a]	.286	.143	2.65684

a. Predictors: (Constant), VAR00001

ANOVA[b]

Model		Sum of Squares	df	Mean Square	F	Sig.
1	Regression	14.134	1	14.134	2.002	.216[a]
	Residual	35.294	5	7.059		
	Total	49.429	6			

a. Predictors: (Constant), VAR00001
b. Dependent Variable: VAR00002

Coefficients[a]

Model		Unstandardized Coefficients		Standardized Coefficients		
		B	Std. Error	Beta	t	Sig.
1	(Constant)	7.118	2.454		2.901	.034
	VAR00001	.853	.603	.535	1.415	.216

a. Dependent Variable: VAR00002

and the standardized coefficients for the regression equation. For one predictor, the table shows the values for the constant (a) and the coefficient (b). For two predictors, the table shows the constant a and the two coefficients b_1 and b_2 (Figure C.11). The standardized coefficients are the beta values. For one predictor, beta is simply the Pearson correlation between X and Y. Finally, the table uses a t statistic to evaluate the significance of each predictor variable. For one predictor variable, this is identical to the significance of the regression equation, and you should find that the t value is equal to the square root of the F-ratio from the analysis of regression. For two predictor variables, the t values measure the significance of the contribution of each variable beyond what is already predicted by the other variable.

Example for one predictor: The same data that were used to demonstrate the Pearson correlation produce a regression equation of $Y = 0.853X + 7.118$. The equation is not significant with $p = .216$ (which is identical to the significance level obtained for the correlation) and has $R^2 = 0.286$. The computer printout for this example is shown in Figure C.10.

Example for two predictors: The following data add a second predictor (X_2) to the same X and Y values that were used for the single predictor regression example (the original X values are now labeled X_1). The data produce a multiple regression equation of $Y = 1.288X_1 + 0.445X_2 + 0.168$. The equation is significant with $p = .030$ and has $R^2 = 0.827$. Each of the predictor variables makes a significant contribution (ΔR^2) beyond the prediction of the other variable alone (the additional contribution of X_1 is significant with $p = .022$ and the additional contribution of X_2 is significant with $p = .024$). The computer printout for this example is shown in Figure C.11. The values in the ANOVA table evaluate the significance of the overall equation and the values in the Coefficients table evaluate the significance of the contribution of each predictor.

FIGURE C.11

An SPSS Printout for Regression with Two Predictor Variables

Note that the first table of the printout is not shown.

Model Summary

Model	R	R Square	Adjusted R Square	Std. Error of the Estimate
1	.910[a]	.827	.741	1.46007

a. Predictors: (Constant), VAR00002, VAR00001

ANOVA[b]

Model		Sum of Squares	df	Mean Square	F	Sig.
1	Regression	40.901	2	20.451	9.593	.030[a]
	Residual	8.527	4	2.132		
	Total	49.429	6			

a. Predictors: (Constant), VAR00002, VAR00001
b. Dependent Variable: VAR00003

Coefficients[a]

Model		Unstandardized Coefficients		Standardized Coefficients		
		B	Std. Error	Beta	t	Sig.
1	(Constant)	.168	2.380		.070	.947
	VAR00001	1.288	.353	.807	3.645	.022
	VAR00002	.445	.125	.785	3.543	.024

a. Dependent Variable: VAR00003

X_1	X_2	Y
3	5	6
5	6	9
2	18	12
1	16	8
5	10	13
4	14	10
6	15	14

The Chi-Square Test for Independence

The chi-square test for independence evaluates the relationship between two variables. Instead of measuring numerical scores, each individual is simply classified into a category for each of the two variables; for example, each individual could be classified by gender (male/female) and by personality (introvert/extrovert). The data are usually organized in a matrix with the categories of one variable defining the rows and the categories of the second variable defining the columns. The actual data (called *observed frequencies*) consist of the number of individuals from the sample who are in each cell of the matrix;

for example, how many introverted males, how many introverted females, how many extroverted males, and how many extroverted females.

Suppose, for example, that you are using a chi-square test to examine the relationship between gender and self-esteem for a sample of $n = 50$ students (see the following example). Each student is classified as male or female, and each student is classified as high, medium, or low in terms of self-esteem. Note that the data are organized in a matrix with two rows and three columns.

Data Entry
1. Enter all of the observed frequencies into one column in the data matrix (var00001).
2. In a second column (var00002), enter a number designating the row from which the observed frequency was obtained. For the data in the following example, enter a 1 beside each observed frequency for the males, and enter a 2 beside each frequency for the females.
3. In a third column (var00003), enter a number designating the column from which the observed frequency was obtained. For the data in the example, enter a 1 beside each observed frequency for high self-esteem, enter a 2 beside each frequency for medium self-esteem, and enter a 3 beside each frequency for low self-esteem.
4. Click **Data** on the tool bar.
5. Select the **weigh cases** option.
6. Click the **weigh cases by** option.
7. Move the label for the column containing the observed frequencies (var00001) into the **Frequency Variable** box. (Highlight the column label and click the arrow to move it into the box.)
8. Click **OK**.

Data Analysis
1. Click **Analyze** on the tool bar.
2. Select **Descriptive Statistics**.
3. Click on **Crosstabs**.
4. Move the label for the column containing the rows (var00002) into the **Rows** box. (Highlight the label and click the arrow to move it into the box.)
5. Move the label for the column containing the columns (var00003) into the **Columns** box. (Highlight the label and click the arrow to move it into the box.)
6. Click on **Statistics**.
7. Select **Chi-Square**.
8. Click **Continue**.
9. Click **OK**.

Output
The Output includes a cross-tabulation table showing the matrix of observed frequencies, and a table of chi-square tests in which you should focus on the **Pearson Chi-Square** (Figure C.12). The table includes the calculated chi-square value, the degrees of freedom, and the level of significance (p value). A measure of effect size (either ϕ for a 2×2 data matrix, or Cramér's V) can be calculated using the value obtained for chi-square, the sample size, and the number of rows and columns in the data matrix (see Appendix B, p. 473).

Example: The following data represent the observed frequencies for a sample of 50 students who have been classified by gender (male/female) and by self-esteem (high,

FIGURE C.12

An SPSS Printout for Chi-Square

The top row of the chi-square tests table shows the results of the chi-square test.

VAR00002 * VAR00003 Cross-tabulation

Count

		VAR00003			
		1.00	2.00	3.00	Total
VAR00002	1.00	10	6	4	20
	2.00	8	12	10	30
Total		18	18	14	50

Chi-Square Tests

	Value	df	Asymp. Sig. (2-sided)
Pearson Chi-Square	2.910[a]	2	.233
Likelihood Ratio	2.904	2	.234
Linear-by-Linear Association	2.495	1	.114
N of Valid Cases	50		

[a] 0 cells (.0%) have expected count less than 5. The minimum expected count is 5.60.

medium, low). The data produce a chi-square statistic of 2.91 with $df = 2$ and a significance level of $p = .233$ (no significant relationship) with Cramér's $V = 0.241$. The computer printout for this example is shown in Figure C.12.

Self-Esteem

	High	Medium	Low
Males	10	6	4
Females	8	12	10

Sample APA-Style Research Report Manuscript for Publication

This appendix presents an example of a complete APA-style research report manuscript using the current guidelines presented in the *Publication Manual of the American Psychological Association* (6th edition, 2010). The manuscript is an edited version of a research manuscript prepared by undergraduate student Chad Mazzarella as part of a course requirement at The College at Brockport, State University of New York. The intent of this example is to demonstrate the appearance of manuscript pages as well as the content of each section of an APA-style research report. Portions of the manuscript are presented as figures and discussed in Chapter 16.

Effects of Psychotherapy and Psychotropics on Relapse for Major Depressive Disorder

Chad Mazzarella

The College at Brockport, State University of New York

Author Note

Chad Mazzarella, Department of Psychology, The College at Brockport, State University of New York.

Correspondence concerning this article should be addressed to Chad Mazzarella at the Department of Psychology, The College at Brockport, State University of New York, Brockport, NY 14420.

E-mail: cmaz1@brockport.edu

MAJOR DEPRESSIVE DISORDER TREATMENT AND RELAPSE 2

Abstract

According to the DSM IV a person who suffers from major depressive disorder must have depression symptoms such as either a depressed mood or a loss of interest or pleasure in daily activities consistently for at least a two-week period. Major depressive disorder is a debilitating personality disorder that affects one's everyday life and can be very difficult to treat. Because past research offers conflicting views as to which type of treatment offers the best outcome to people who are diagnosed with the disorder, the purpose of this study is to compare two approaches to treatment and determine which is more effective and results in a lower risk of relapse. Two groups of individuals, all diagnosed with major depressive disorder, participated in the study. One group of 20 participants received only cognitive behavioral therapy and a second group of 20 received cognitive behavioral therapy combined with a 50 mg daily dose of Zoloft. Three years post-treatment, the group receiving only therapy showed significantly higher scores on the Beck Depression Inventory and higher rates of relapse, as measured by inpatient treatments for major depressive disorder after their initial discharge. The results suggest that a combination of psychotherapy and psychotropics is most effective for the long-term treatment of major depressive disorder.

Effects of Psychotherapy and Psychotropics on Relapse for Major Depressive Disorder

Major depressive disorder is a severe condition in which the person affected must meet at least three of the following five symptoms: low mood, loss of interest, guilt or worthlessness, impaired concentration of indecisiveness, and death wishes or suicidal thoughts, one of which is low mood or loss of interest (Zimmerman, Emmeret-Aronson, & Brown, 2011). Major depression is a chronic and ongoing condition that affects the individual for approximately 17–30 years and is a particularly disabling disorder which is associated with greater comorbidity, more significant impairments in functioning, increased health care utilization, and more frequent suicide attempts and hospitalizations than acute major depressive episodes (Schramm et al., 2011). Since hospitalization could be frequent and behavior can be severe, it is imperative that the most effective type of treatment be administered to individuals diagnosed with major depressive disorder. There is debate about which type of treatment will yield the best results since major depressive disorder is so pervasive and relapse can happen without warning. If more clinical trials are done showing that one treatment is more efficacious than the other, it could give individuals diagnosed with major depressive disorder a better chance at remission without relapse.

Inpatients who are suffering from major depressive disorder are treated in a variety of ways. There has yet to be an agreed upon method for treating inpatients with major depressive disorder, but the most widely used methods involve either some form of psychotherapy or psychotherapy combined with psychotropic drugs (Kennard et al., 2008). The goal for individuals diagnosed with major depressive disorder is to achieve remission with minimum relapse, and the question is which treatment will effectively allow this to be attained. Cuijpers, Andersson, Donker, and van Stratten (2011) concluded that psychotherapy is effective in the treatment of major depression and dysthymia but probably less than psychotropic drugs. This type of conclusion tends to make psychotherapy appear to be less effective. In contrast, some individuals diagnosed with major depressive disorder have been known to

MAJOR DEPRESSIVE DISORDER TREATMENT AND RELAPSE   4

not respond to psychotropic medicine and according to Riedel et al. (2011) the longer the search for an effective antidepressant treatment is, the higher the risk for a chronic condition, the higher the overall cost, and the worse the functional outcome. Such conclusions often contradict each other leaving no clear distinction about which form of treatment is the most efficacious for treating individuals diagnosed with major depressive disorder.

Unfortunately, individuals diagnosed with major depressive disorder have a relatively high relapse rate. A study by Richards (2011) reports a relapse rate of 37% within 12 months for primary care patients. Many factors can contribute to the relapse rate and it is important to determine whether one treatment will make patients more prone to relapse than another. In order to establish this, individuals diagnosed with major depressive disorder must be followed after deinstitutionalization to determine their level of depression and rate of relapse.

Previous research has attempted to find ways to lower relapse rate in individuals diagnosed with major depressive disorder by creating two different groups of adults with major depressive disorder. For example, Kennard et al. (2008) compared one group of patients who received medication management (MM) with another that received MM with cognitive behavioral therapy (MM + CBT). The results showed that the hazard of relapse for those who received MM treatment was approximately eight time greater than that for those who received MM + CBT treatment (Kennard et al., 2008). This gives the indication that in order to help reduce relapse there must be a combination of drug therapy and CBT. Studies like this are convincing because they appear to produce a clear distinction between the two treatments. However, Kennard et al. stated that there were many limitations to the study, which included a small sample size and the fact that assessment ceased when a patient relapsed or withdrew from the study. Because there was no follow-up after relapse, it is difficult to assess which treatment has a longer impact and why.

MAJOR DEPRESSIVE DISORDER TREATMENT AND RELAPSE   5

There is general evidence for both types of therapy producing effective results, yet there is little

evidence to show the relationship between the types of therapy and relapse rate. This is significant because

major depressive disorder has such a large risk of relapse. We addressed this issue with a long-term study

comparing individuals diagnosed with major depressive disorder who received only psychotherapy with

patients who received both psychotherapy and psychotropic drugs three years after inpatient discharge. We

hypothesized that patients receiving therapy with medication will have lower depression scores and a lower

relapse rate than those who receive only therapy. This outcome would support and strengthen the results

reported by Kennard et al. (2008).

Method

Participants

The study used a sample of 40 participants whose only diagnosis was Major Depressive Disorder and

who received inpatient treatment at Rochester Psychiatric Center or Rochester General Hospital Psychiatric

Unit three years ago. Half of the participants had received only cognitive behavioral therapy for one hour

daily and the other half had received the same therapy along with a 50 mg daily dose of Zoloft. For both

groups the treatments lasted an average of approximately three weeks before discharge. Potential participants

were contacted, given a brief overview of the study, and asked if they were willing to participate. The final

sample consisted of the first 20 from each treatment condition who agreed to participate. The therapy-only

group consisted of 15 Caucasian males, 3 Caucasian females, and 2 African American males with an average

age of 34.2 years. The therapy-plus-drug group consisted of 14 Caucasian males, 3 Caucasian females, and 3

African American males with an average age of 32.5 years.

MAJOR DEPRESSIVE DISORDER TREATMENT AND RELAPSE   6

Procedure

Individuals who agreed to participate were mailed a packet containing an informed consent form, a copy

of the Beck Depression Inventory II (Beck, Steer, & Brown, 1996) with instructions, a brief questionnaire

that covered their mental health history, including number of readmissions for inpatient treatments for

major depressive disorder, since discharge from inpatient treatment three years earlier, and a pre paid return

envelope. The questionnaires were coded to identify the treatment condition for each participant but no other

identifying information was requested.

Results

Three years post treatment, the group that received only therapy had a mean score of $M = 28.90$ for the

Beck Depression Inventory II with $SD = 9.6$ and the group that received a combination of psychotherapy and

psychotropic drugs had a mean score of $M = 23.05$ with $SD = 8.3$. An independent-measures t test showed a

significant mean difference between the two groups of clients, $t(38) = 2.06, p < .05, d = 0.65$.

Three years post treatment, the group that received only therapy had nine individuals who were

readmitted for inpatient treatments for major depressive disorder and the group that received a combination

of psychotherapy and psychotropic drugs had seven readmissions. A chi-square test showed a significant

difference between the two groups, $\chi^2 = 3.95, p < .05, \varphi = 0.31$.

Discussion

The results support the research hypothesis showing that three years post-treatment, the group that

received only therapy showed significantly higher scores on the Beck Depression Inventory II and higher

number of readmissions for inpatient treatments for major depressive disorder than the group that received

a combination of psychotherapy and psychotropic drugs. These findings are consist with and extend the

research of Kennerd et al. (2008), which illustrates that psychoactive drugs alone results in higher relapse

rates than when given in combination with psychotherapy.

Future research could examine psychotherapy in combination with different psychotropic mediations and different doses. Also, examining the effectiveness of combination treatments in individuals who differ in the severity of their symptoms is warranted. Because of the pervasiveness and dangerousness of this debilitating disorder, as well as the high incidence of relapse after treatment, it is imperative that subsequent research continues to examine the most efficacious treatments.

MAJOR DEPRESSIVE DISORDER TREATMENT AND RELAPSE   8

References

Beck, A. T., Steer, R. A., & Brown, G. K. (1996). *Manual for the Beck Depression Inventory-II*. San Antonio,
TX: Psychological Corporation.

Cuijpers, P., Andersson, G., Donker, T., & van Straten, A. (2011). Psychological treatment of depression:
Results of a series of meta-analyses. *Nordic Journal of Psychiatry, 65,* 354–364. doi:10.3109/08039488
.2011.596570

Kennard, B. D., Emslie, G. J., Mayes, T. L., Nightingale-Teresi, J., Nakonezny, P. A., Hughes, J. L., Jones,
J. M., Tao, R., Steward, S. M., & Jarrett, R. B (2008). Cognitive-behavioral therapy to prevent relapse
in pediatric responders to pharmacotherapy for major depressive disorder. *Journal of the American
Academy of Child and Adolescent Psychology, 47*, 1395–1404.

Richards, D. (2011). Prevalence and clinical course of depression: A review. *Clinical Psychology Review, 31*,
1117–1125.

Schramm, E., Hautzinger, M., Zobel, I., Kriston, L., Berger, M., & Harter, M. (2011). Comparative efficacy
of the cognitive behavioral analysis system of psychotherapy versus supportive psychotherapy for
early onset chronic depression: Design and rationale of a multisite randomized controlled trial. *BMC
Psychiatry*, *11,* 134–142.

Zimmerman, M., Emmert-Aronson, B., & Brown, T. (2011). Concordance between a simpler definition
of major depressive disorder and *Diagnostic and Statistical Manual of Mental Disorders*, Fourth
edition: An independent replication in an outpatient sample. *Journal of Comprehensive Psychology, 52*,
261–264.

ABAB design A single-case experimental design consisting of four phases: a baseline phase, a treatment phase, a return-to-baseline phase, and a second treatment phase. The ABAB design is the most commonly used reversal design.

Abstract A brief summary of a research study, usually totaling no more than 150 to 250 words.

Accessible population The easily available segment of a target population. Researchers typically select their samples from this type of population.

Accuracy (of measurement) The degree to which a measure conforms to the established standard.

Active deception The intentional presentation of misinformation about a study to its participants. The most common form of active deception is misleading participants about the specific purpose of the study. Also known as commission.

Alpha level In a hypothesis test, the criterion for statistical significance that defines the maximum probability that the research result was obtained simply by chance. Also known as level of significance.

Anchors On a rating scale question, the verbal labels that identify the opposite extremes and establish the endpoints of the scale.

Anonymity The practice of ensuring that an individual's name is not directly associated with the information or measurements obtained from that individual. Keeping records anonymous is a

way to preserve the confidentiality of research participants.

APA Ethics Code A common set of principles and standards on which psychologists build their professional and scientific work. This code is intended to provide specific standards that cover most situations encountered by psychologists. Its primary goal is the welfare and protection of the individuals and groups with whom psychologists work.

Apparatus subsection In a research report, the portion of the method section that describes any equipment used in the study.

Appendix The section of a research report that presents detailed information that is useful but would interrupt the flow of information if presented in the body of the paper.

Applied research Research studies that are intended to answer practical questions or solve practical problems.

Apprehensive subject role In a study, a participant's tendency to respond in a socially desirable fashion rather than truthfully.

Archival research Looking at historical records (archives) to measure behaviors or events that occurred in the past.

Argument In the rational method, a set of premise statements that are logically combined to yield a conclusion.

Artifact In the context of a research study, an external factor that could influence or distort measures. Artifacts threaten the validity of the measurement, as well as both internal and external validity.

Assessment sensitization *See* sensitization.

Assignment bias A threat to internal validity that occurs when the process used to assign different participants to different treatments produces groups of individuals with noticeably different characteristics.

Author note The section of a research report that provides details about the authors. It is placed on the title page below the title, byline, and affiliation.

Autonomy *See* principle of respect.

Bar graph A frequency distribution graph in which a vertical bar indicates the frequency of each score from a nominal or ordinal scale of measurement.

Baseline observations In a single-case research study, observations or measurements made while no treatment is being administered.

Baseline phase In a single-case research study, a series of baseline observations identified by the letter A.

Basic research Research studies that are intended to answer theoretical questions or gather knowledge simply for the sake of new knowledge.

Behavior categories Categories of behavior to be observed (such as group play, play alone, aggression, social interaction). A set of behavior categories and a list of exactly which behaviors count as examples of each are developed before observation begins.

Behavioral measure A measurement obtained by the direct observation of an individual's behavior.

511

Behavioral observation Direct observation and systematic recording of behaviors.

Belmont Report A summary of the basic ethical principles for protecting humans in research published in 1979 by the National Commission for the Protection of Human Subjects in Biomedical and Behavioral Research. Today's federal regulations for protecting human participants are based on the Belmont Report.

Between-subjects design A research design in which each of the different groups of scores is obtained from a separate group of participants. Also known as an independent-measures design.

Between-subjects experimental design An experimental design using a separate, independent group of individuals for each treatment condition being compared. Also known as an independent-measures experimental design.

Biased sample A sample with characteristics different from those of the population.

Carryover effects Changes in the scores observed in one treatment condition that are caused by the lingering aftereffects of a specific earlier treatment condition.

Case history A case study that does not include a treatment or intervention.

Case study design An in-depth study and detailed description of a single individual (or a very small group). A case study may involve an intervention or treatment administered by the researcher.

Ceiling effect The clustering of scores at the high end of a measurement scale, allowing little or no possibility of increases in value.

Central tendency A statistical measure that identifies a single score that defines the center of a distribution.

Chi-square test for independence A hypothesis test that evaluates the statistical significance of the differences between proportions for two or more groups of participants.

Citation An identification of the author(s) and year of publication for the source of a specific fact or idea mentioned in a research report.

Clinical equipoise The ethical issue requiring clinicians to provide the best possible treatment for their patients, thus limiting research to studies that compare equally preferred treatments.

Clinical significance See practical significance.

Cluster sampling A probability sampling technique involving random selection of groups instead of individuals from a population.

Coefficient of determination, r^2 The squared value of a correlation that measures the percentage of variability in one variable, which is determined or predicted by its relationship with the other variable.

Cohen's d A standard measure of effect size computed by dividing the sample mean difference by the sample standard deviation.

Cohen's kappa A calculation that corrects for chance agreement when inter-rater reliability is measured.

Cohort effects Differences between age groups that are caused by characteristics or experiences other than age. Also called generation effect.

Cohorts Individuals who were born at roughly the same time and grew up under similar circumstances.

Combined strategy A factorial study that combines two different research strategies, such as experimental and nonexperimental or quasi-experimental, in the same factorial design.

Commission See active deception.

Common Rule The Code of Federal Regulations, Title 45, Part 46 (1991), which is based on the principles of the Belmont Report and provides a common set of federal regulations for protecting human participants. It is used by review boards.

Compensatory equalization A threat to internal validity that occurs when an untreated group demands to receive a treatment that is the same as or equivalent to the treatment received by another group in the research study.

Compensatory rivalry A threat to internal validity that occurs when an untreated group learns about special treatment received by another group, then works extra hard to show they can perform just as well as that group.

Complete counterbalancing In within-subjects designs, using a separate group of participants for every possible order of the treatment conditions. With n different treatment conditions, there are $n!$ (n factorial) different orders.

Component-analysis design A single-case design consisting of a series of phases in which each phase adds or subtracts one component of a complex treatment.

Concurrent validity The type of validity demonstrated when scores obtained from a new measure are directly related to scores obtained from a more established measure of the same variable.

Confederate A person who pretends to be a participant in a research study but actually is working for the researcher to create a false environment.

Confidence interval A range of values, centered around a sample statistic, used to estimate the magnitude of an unknown population value such as a mean difference or a correlation. The width of the interval is directly related to the degree of confidence in its accuracy.

Confidentiality The practice of keeping strictly secret and private the information or measurements obtained from an individual during a research study. APA ethical guidelines require researchers to ensure the confidentiality of their research participants.

Confounding variable An extraneous variable (usually unmonitored) that is allowed to change systematically along with the two variables being studied. In the context of an experiment, an extraneous variable that changes systematically along with the independent variable *and* has the potential to influence the dependent variable. A confounding variable provides an alternative explanation for the observed relationship and, therefore, is a threat to internal validity.

Consent form A written statement by the researcher containing all of the elements of informed consent and a line for the participant's signature. The consent form is provided before the study so that potential participants have all the information they need to make an informed decision regarding participation.

Constructs Hypothetical attributes or mechanisms that help explain and predict behavior in a theory. Also known as hypothetical constructs.

Construct validity The type of validity demonstrated when scores obtained from a measurement behave exactly the same as the variable itself. Construct validity is based on many research studies and grows gradually as each new study contributes more evidence.

Content analysis Using the techniques of behavioral observation to measure the occurrence of specific events in literature, movies, television programs, or similar media that present replicas of behaviors.

Contrast effect An example of a carryover effect in which the perception of a treatment condition is influenced by its contrast with the previous treatment.

Contrived observation Observation in settings arranged specifically to facilitate the occurrence of specific behaviors. Also known as structured observation.

Control condition In a research study, a condition that involves no treatment or a placebo treatment.

Convenience sampling A nonprobability sampling method involving selection of individuals on the basis of their availability and willingness to respond; that is, because they are easy to get. Occasionally called accidental sampling or haphazard sampling.

Convergent validity The type of validity demonstrated by a strong relationship between the scores obtained from two different methods of measuring the same construct.

Correlation A statistical value that measures and describes the direction and degree of relationship between two variables. The sign (+/−) indicates the direction of the relationship. The numerical value (0.0 to 1.0) indicates the strength or consistency of the relationship. The type (Pearson or Spearman) indicates the form of the relationship. Also known as correlation coefficient.

Correlation coefficient *See* correlation.

Correlational research strategy A general approach to research that involves measuring two or more variables for each individual to describe the relationship between the variables. The measurements are reviewed to identify any patterns of relationship that exist between the variables and to measure the strength of the relationship; however, no attempt is made to explain the relationship.

Counterbalancing In a within-subjects design, a procedure to minimize threats from order effects and time-related factors by changing the order in which treatment conditions are administered from one participant to another so that the treatment conditions are matched with respect to time. The goal is to use every possible order of treatments with an equal number of individuals participating in each sequence.

Criterion variable In a correlational study, a researcher often is interested in the relationship between two variables to use knowledge about one variable to help predict or explain the second variable. In this situation, the second variable (being explained or predicted) is called the criterion variable.

Cronbach's alpha A generalization of the Kuder-Richardson formula that estimates the average of all possible split-half reliability correlations when each test item has more than two responses.

Cross-sectional developmental research design A developmental design comparing different groups of individuals, each group representing a different age.

Curvilinear relationship In a graph showing the changing values of two variables, a pattern in which the data points tend to cluster around a curved line.

Database A computerized cross-referencing tool that focuses on an individual topic area (such as psychology); used for searching the literature for articles relevant to a topic.

Debriefing A postexperimental explanation of the purpose of the study. A debriefing is given after a participant completes a study, especially if deception was used.

Deception The purposeful withholding of information or misleading of participants about a study. There are two forms of deception: passive and active.

Deduction The use of a general statement as the basis for reaching a conclusion about specific examples. Also known as deductive reasoning.

Deductive reasoning *See* deduction.

Degrees of freedom The value $n - 1$ when the variance is computed for a sample of n scores. In general, the number of independent elements when a sample statistic is computed.

Demand characteristics Any potential cues or features of a study that (1) suggest to the participants what the purpose and hypothesis are, and (2) influence the participants to respond or behave in a certain way. Demand characteristics are artifacts and can threaten the validity of the measurement, as well as both internal and external validity.

Dependent variable In an experiment, the variable that is observed for changes to assess the effects of manipulating the independent variable. In nonexperiments and quasi-experiments the dependent variable is the variable that is measured to obtain the scores within each group. The dependent variable is typically a behavior or a response measured in each treatment condition.

Descriptive research strategy A general approach to research that involves measuring a variable or set of variables as they exist naturally to produce a description of individual variables as they exist within a specific group, but does not attempt to describe or explain relationships between variables.

Descriptive statistics Statistical methods used to organize, summarize, and simplify the results obtained from research studies.

Developmental research designs Nonexperimental research designs used to examine the relationship between age and other variables.

Differential attrition A threat to internal validity that occurs when attrition in one group is systematically different from the attrition in another group.

Differential effects In a research study, time-related threats to internal validity that affect the groups differently. For example, differential history effects, differential instrumentation effects, differential maturation, differential testing, and differential regression.

Differential research design A nonexperimental research design that compares preexisting groups rather than randomly assigning individuals to groups. Usually, the groups are defined by a participant characteristic such as gender, race, or personality.

Diffusion A threat to internal validity that occurs when a treatment effect spreads from the treatment group to the control group, usually from participants talking to each other.

Directionality problem Demonstrating that changes in one variable tend to be accompanied by changes in another variable simply establishes that the two variables are related. The remaining problem is to determine which variable is the cause and which is the effect.

Discussion section The portion of a research report that restates the hypothesis, summarizes the results, and presents a discussion of the interpretation, implications, and possible applications of the results.

Divergent validity A type of validity demonstrated by using two different methods to measure two different constructs. Convergent validity then must be shown for each of the two constructs. Finally, there should be little or no relationship between the scores obtained for the two different constructs when they are measured by the same method.

Double-blind research A research study in which both the researcher and the participants are unaware of the predicted outcome for any specific participant.

Duration method In behavioral observation, a technique for converting observations into numerical scores; involves recording how much time an individual spends engaged in a specific behavior during a fixed-time observation period.

Effect size The measured magnitude of a treatment effect or relationship that is not influenced by factors such as sample size.

Empirical method A method of acquiring knowledge in which observation and direct sensory experience are used to obtain knowledge. Also known as empiricism.

Empiricism *See* empirical method.

Ethics The study of proper action.

Event sampling A technique of behavioral observation that involves observing and recording one specific event or behavior during the first interval, then shifting to a different event or behavior during the second interval, and so on for the full series of intervals.

Experiment A study that attempts to show that changes in one variable are directly responsible for causing changes in a second variable. Also known as a true experiment.

Experimental condition The treatment condition in an experiment.

Experimental realism In simulation research, the extent to which the psychological aspects of the research environment duplicate the real-world environment that is being simulated.

Experimental research strategy A research strategy that attempts to establish the existence of a cause-and-effect relationship between two variables by manipulating one variable while measuring the second variable and controlling all other variables.

Experimenter bias The influence on the findings of a study from the experimenter's expectations about the study. Experimenter bias is a type of artifact and threatens the validity of the measurement, as well as both internal and external validity.

External validity The extent to which we can generalize the results of a research study to people, settings, times, measures, and characteristics other than those used in that study.

Extraneous variable Any variable that exists within a study other than the variables being studied. In an experiment, any variable other than the independent and dependent variables.

Face validity An unscientific form of validity that concerns whether a measure superficially appears to measure what it claims to measure.

Factor A variable that differentiates a set of groups or conditions being compared in a research study. In an experimental design, a factor is an independent variable.

Factorial design A research design that includes two or more factors.

Faithful subject role In a study, a participant's attempt to follow experimental instructions to the letter and to avoid acting on the basis of any suspicions about the purpose of the experiment.

Fatigue A threat to internal validity that occurs when prior participation in a treatment condition or measurement procedure tires the participants and influences their performance on subsequent measurements; an example of an order effect.

Field Any research setting that the participant or subject perceives as a natural environment.

Field study An experiment conducted in a setting that the participant or subject perceives as a natural environment.

Floor effect The clustering of scores at the low end of a measurement scale, allowing little or no possibility of decreases in value; a type of range effect.

Fraud The explicit efforts of a researcher to falsify and misrepresent data. Fraud is unethical.

Frequency distribution An organized display of a set of scores that shows how many scores are located in each category on the scale of measurement.

Frequency method In behavioral observation, a technique for converting observations into numerical scores that involves counting the instances of each specific behavior that occur during a fixed-time observation period.

Generation effects *See* cohort effects.

Good subject role In a study, a participant's tendency to respond in a way that is expected to corroborate the investigator's hypothesis.

Habituation In behavioral observation, repeated exposure of participants to the observer's presence until it is no longer a novel stimulus.

Higher-order factorial design A factorial research design with more than two factors.

Histogram A frequency distribution graph in which a vertical bar indicates the frequency of each score from an interval or ratio scale of measurement.

History A threat to internal validity from any outside event that influences the participants' scores in one treatment differently than in another treatment.

Hypothesis A statement that provides a tentative description or explanation for the relationship between variables.

Hypothesis test An inferential statistical procedure that uses sample data to evaluate the credibility of a hypothesis about a population. A hypothesis test determines whether research results are statistically significant.

Hypothetical constructs *See* constructs.

IACUC *See* Institutional Animal Care and Use Committee.

Idiographic approach The study of individuals, in contrast to the study of groups.

Independent-measures design *See* between-subjects design.

Independent-measures experimental design *See* between-subjects experimental design.

Independent-measures *t* test In a between-subjects design, a hypothesis test that evaluates the statistical significance of the mean difference between two separate groups of participants.

Independent variable In an experiment, the variable manipulated by the researcher. In behavioral research, the independent variable usually consists of two or more treatment conditions to which participants are exposed.

Individual differences Personal characteristics that differ from one participant to another. Individual differences are part of every study. Individual differences can produce high variability in the scores and can, for studies that use different groups for each treatment condition, if there are consistent differences between the groups, individual differences can become a confound.

Individual sampling A technique of behavioral observation involving identifying one participant to be observed during the first interval, then shifting attention to a different individual for the second interval, and so on.

Induction The use of a relatively small set of specific observations as the basis for forming a general statement about a larger set of possible observations. Also known as inductive reasoning.

Inductive reasoning *See* induction.

Inferential statistics Statistical methods used to determine when it is appropriate to generalize the results from a sample to an entire population.

Informed consent The ethical principle requiring the investigator to provide all available information about a study so that a participant can make a rational, informed decision regarding whether to participate in the study.

Institutional Animal Care and Use Committee (IACUC) A committee that examines all proposed research with respect to its treatment of non-human subjects. IACUC approval must be obtained prior to conducting any research with nonhuman subjects.

Institutional Review Board (IRB) A committee that examines all proposed research with respect to its treatment of human participants. IRB approval must be obtained prior to conducting any research with human participants.

Instrumental bias *See* instrumentation.

Instrumental decay *See* instrumentation.

Instrumentation A threat to internal validity from changes in the measurement instrument that occur during the time a research study is being conducted. Also known as instrumental bias or instrumental decay.

Interaction *See* interaction between factors.

Interaction between factors In a factorial design, whenever one factor modifies the effects of a second factor.

If the mean differences between the treatment conditions are explained by the main effects, then the factors are independent and there is no interaction. Also, when the effects of one factor depend on the different levels of a second factor. Indicated by the existence of nonparallel (converging or crossing) lines in a graph showing the means for a two-factor design. Also known as interaction.

Internal validity The extent to which a research study produces a single, unambiguous explanation for the relationship between two variables.

Inter-rater reliability The degree of agreement between two observers who simultaneously record measurements of a behavior.

Interrupted time-series design A quasi-experimental research design consisting of a series of observations before and after an event. The event is not a treatment or an experience created or manipulated by the researcher.

Interval method In behavioral observation, a technique for converting observations into numerical scores; involves dividing the observation period into a series of intervals, recording whether or not a specific behavior occurs during each interval, and then counting the number of intervals in which the behavior occurred.

Interval scale A scale of measurement in which the categories are organized sequentially and all categories are the same size. The zero point of an interval scale is arbitrary and does not indicate a total absence of the variable being measured.

Interviewer bias The influence of the researcher verbally asking participants questions on the participants' natural responses.

Introduction The first major section of a research report, which presents a logical development of the

research question including a review of the relevant background literature, a statement of the research question or hypothesis, and a brief description of the methods used to answer the question or test the hypothesis.

IRB *see* Institutional Review Board.

K-R 20 *See* Kuder-Richardson formal 20.

Kuder-Richardson formula 20 (K-R 20) A formula for computing split-half reliability that uses one split-half correlation to estimate the average of all possible split-half correlations when each test item has only two responses.

Laboratory A research setting that is obviously devoted to the discipline of science. It can be any room or space that the subject or participant perceives as artificial.

Latin square An $n \times n$ matrix in which each of n different items appears exactly once in each column and exactly once in each row. Used to identify sequences of treatment conditions for partial counterbalancing.

Law of large numbers In the field of statistics, the principle that states that the larger the sample size, the more likely it is that values obtained from the sample are similar to the actual values for the population.

Level In a single-case research study, the overall magnitude for a series of observations. A consistent level occurs when measurements in a series are all approximately the same magnitude.

Level of significance *See* alpha level.

Levels In an experiment, the different values of the independent variable selected to create and define the treatment conditions. In other research studies, the different values of a factor.

Likert scale A rating scale presented as a horizontal line divided into categories so that participants can circle a number or mark an X at the location corresponding to their response.

Linear relationship In a graph showing the changing values of two variables, a pattern in which the data points tend to cluster around a straight line.

Line graph A display in which points connected by straight lines show several different means obtained from different groups or treatment conditions. Also used to show different medians, proportions, or other sample statistics.

Literature search The process of gaining a general familiarity with the current research conducted in a subject area, and finding a small set of journal articles that serve as the basis for a research idea and provide the justification or foundation for new research.

Longitudinal developmental research design A developmental research design that examines development by making a series of observations or measurements over time. Typically, a group of individuals who are all the same age is measured at different points in time.

Main effect In a factorial study, the mean differences among the levels of one factor.

Manipulation In an experiment, identifying the specific values of the independent variable to be examined and then creating treatment conditions corresponding to each of these values. The researcher then manipulates the variable by changing from one condition to another.

Manipulation check In an experiment, an additional measure used to assess how the participants perceived and interpreted the manipulation and/or to assess the direct effect of the manipulation.

Matched-subjects design A research design comparing separate groups of individuals in which each individual in one group is matched with a participant in each of the other groups. The matching is done so that the matched individuals are equivalent with respect to a variable that the researcher considers to be relevant to the study.

Matching The assignment of individuals to groups so that a specific variable is balanced or matched across the groups.

Materials subsection In a research report, the portion of the method section that describes any questionnaires used in the study.

Maturation A threat to internal validity from any physiological or psychological changes that occur in a participant during the time that research study is being conducted and that can influence the participant's scores.

Mean A measure of central tendency obtained by adding the individual scores and dividing the sum by the number of scores.

Median A measure of central tendency that identifies the score that divides the distribution in half so that 50% of the individuals have scores at or below the median.

Method of authority A method of acquiring knowledge in which a person relies on information or answers from an expert in the subject area.

Method of faith A variant of the method of authority in which people have unquestioning trust in the authority figure and, therefore, accept information from the authority without doubt or challenge.

Method of intuition A method of acquiring knowledge in which information is accepted on the basis of a hunch or "gut feeling."

Method of tenacity A method of acquiring knowledge in which information is accepted as true because it has always been believed or because superstition supports it.

Method section The section of a research report that describes how the study was conducted, including information about the subjects or participants and the procedures used.

Methods of acquiring knowledge The variety of ways in which a person can know things or discover answers to questions.

Mixed design A factorial study that combines two different research designs, such as between-subjects and within-subjects, in the same factorial design.

Mode A measure of central tendency that identifies the most frequently occurring score in the distribution.

Monotonic relationship A consistently one-directional relationship between two variables. As one variable increases, the other variable also tends to increase or tends to decrease. The relationship can be either linear or curvilinear.

Multiple-baseline across behaviors A multiple-baseline design in which the initial baseline phases correspond to two separate behaviors for the same participant.

Multiple-baseline across situations A multiple-baseline design in which the initial baseline phases correspond to the same behavior in two separate situations.

Multiple-baseline across subjects A multiple-baseline design in which the initial baseline phases correspond to the same behavior for two separate participants.

Multiple-baseline design A single-case design that begins with two simultaneous baseline phases, then initiates a treatment for one baseline, and, at a later time, initiates the treatment for the second baseline.

Multiple regression A statistical technique used for studying multivariate relationships. The statistical process of finding the linear equation that produces the most accurate predicted values for Y using more than one predictor variable.

Multiple-regression equation The resulting equation from a multiple regression analysis.

Multiple-treatment interference A threat to external validity that occurs when participants are exposed to more than one treatment and their responses are affected by an earlier treatment.

Mundane realism In simulation research, the extent to which the superficial, usually physical, characteristics of the research environment duplicate the real-world environment that is being simulated.

National Research Act A set of regulations for the protection of human participants in research, mandated by Congress in 1974.

Naturalistic observation A type of observation in which a researcher observes behavior in a natural setting as unobtrusively as possible. Also known as nonparticipant observation.

Negative relationship A relationship in which the two variables or measurements tend to change together in opposite directions.

Negativistic subject role In a study, a participant's tendency to respond in a way that is expected to refute the investigator's hypothesis.

Nominal scale A scale of measurement in which the categories represent qualitative differences in the variable being measured. The categories have different names but are not related to each other in any systematic way.

Nomothetic approach The study of groups in contrast to the study of individuals.

Nonequivalent control group design A research design in which the researcher does not randomly assign individuals to groups but rather uses preexisting groups, with one group serving in the treatment condition and another group serving in the control condition.

Nonequivalent group design A research study in which the different groups of participants are formed under circumstances that do not permit the researcher to control the assignment of individuals to groups and the groups of participants are, therefore, considered nonequivalent.

Nonexperimental research strategy A research strategy that attempts to demonstrate a relationship between two variables by comparing different groups of scores, but makes no attempt to minimize threats to internal validity or to explain the relationship.

Nonparticipant observation *See* naturalistic observation.

Nonprobability sampling A method of sampling in which the population is not completely known, individual probabilities cannot be known, and the selection is based on factors such as common sense or ease with an effort to maintain representativeness and avoid bias.

Nonresponse bias In survey research involving mailed surveys, individuals who return the survey are not usually representative of the entire group who received the survey. Nonresponse bias is a threat to external validity.

No-treatment control condition In an experiment, a group or condition in which the participants do not receive the treatment being evaluated.

Novelty effect A threat to external validity that occurs when individuals participating in a research study (a novel situation) perceive and respond differently than they would in the normal, real world.

Null hypothesis In a hypothesis test, a statement about the population(s) or treatments being studied that says there is no change, no effect, no difference, or no relationship.

Nuremberg Code A set of 10 guidelines for the ethical treatment of human participants in research. The Nuremberg Code, developed from the Nuremberg Trials in 1947, laid the groundwork for the current ethical standards for medical and psychological research.

Observational research design Descriptive research in which the researcher observes and systematically records the behavior of individuals to describe the behavior.

Omission *See* passive deception.

One-way ANOVA *See* single-factor analysis of variance.

Operational definition A procedure for indirectly measuring and defining a variable that cannot be observed or measured directly. An operational definition specifies a measurement procedure (a set of operations) for measuring an external, observable behavior and uses the resulting measurements as a definition and a measurement of the hypothetical construct.

Order effects Whenever individuals participate in a series of treatment conditions and experience a series of measurements, their behavior or performance at any point in the series may be influenced by experience that occurred earlier in the sequence. Order effects include carryover effects and progressive error.

Ordinal scale A scale of measurement on which the categories have different names and are organized sequentially (for example, first, second, third).

Parallel-forms reliability The type of reliability established by comparing scores obtained by using two alternate versions of a measuring instrument to measure the same individuals and calculating a correlation between the two sets of scores.

Parameter A summary value that describes a population.

Partial counterbalancing A system of counterbalancing that ensures that each treatment condition occurs first for one group of participants, second for one group, third for one group, and so on, but does not require that every possible order of treatment conditions be used.

Participant attrition The loss of participants that occurs during the course of a research study conducted over time. Attrition can be a threat to internal validity. Also known as participant mortality.

Participant mortality *See* participant attrition.

Participant observation A type of observation in which the researcher engages in the same activities as the people being observed in order to observe and record their behavior.

Participants Humans who take part in a research study.

Participants subsection In a research report, the portion of the method section that describes the humans who participated in the study.

Participant variable Personal characteristics that can differ from one individual to the another, creating individual differences in every study. Individual differences can produce high variability in the scores and can, for studies that use different groups for each treatment condition, if there are consistent differences between the groups,

individual differences can become a confound.

Passive deception The intentional withholding or omitting of information whereby participants are not told some information about the study. Also known as omission.

Pearson correlation A correlation used to evaluate linear (straight-line) relationships.

Peer review The editorial process that many articles undergo when a researcher submits a research report for publication. In a typical peer-review process, the editor of the journal and a few experts in the field of research review the paper in extreme detail. The reviewers critically scrutinize every aspect of the research with the primary purpose of evaluating the quality of the study and its contribution to scientific knowledge. Reviewers are also likely to detect anything suspect about the research or the findings.

Percentage of variance accounted for (r^2 or η^2) The percentage of variance for one variable that can be predicted using the known values for a second variable.

Phase In a single-case research design, a series of observations of the same individual under the same conditions.

Phase change In a single-cases research study, a change in the conditions from one phase to another, usually involving administering or stopping a treatment.

Physiological measure Measurement obtained by recording a physiological activity such as heart rate.

Placebo An ineffective, inert substitute for a treatment or medication.

Placebo control condition A group or condition in which the participants receive a placebo instead of the actual treatment.

Placebo effect A participant's response to an inert medication or treatment that has no real effect on the body; occurs simply because the individual thinks the placebo is effective.

Plagiarism Presenting someone else's ideas or words as one's own. Plagiarism is unethical.

Polygon A frequency distribution graph in which a series of points connected by straight lines indicates the frequency of each score from an interval or ratio scale of measurement.

Population The entire set of individuals of interest to a researcher. Although the entire population usually does not participate in a research study, the results from the study will be generalized to the entire population. Also known as target population.

Positive relationship A relationship in which the two variables or measurements tend to change together in the same direction.

Post hoc tests or post tests Follow-up hypothesis tests done after an analysis of variance to determine exactly which mean differences are significant.

Posttest-only nonequivalent control group design A nonexperimental design in which one group is observed (measured) after receiving a treatment, and a second, nonequivalent group is measured at the same time but receives no treatment.

Practical significance In a research study, a result or treatment effect that is large enough to have value in a practical application. Also known as clinical significance.

Practice A threat to internal validity that occurs when prior participation in a treatment condition or measurement procedure provides participants with additional skills that influence their performance on subsequent measurements. An example of an order effect.

Predictive validity The type of validity demonstrated when scores obtained from a measure accurately predict behavior according to a theory.

Predictor variable In a correlational study, a researcher often is interested in the relationship between two variables to use knowledge about one variable to help predict or explain the second variable. In this situation, the first variable is called the predictor variable.

Premise statements Sentences used in logical reasoning that describe facts or assumptions.

Pre–post designs Quasi-experimental and nonexperimental designs consisting of a series of observations made over time. The goal is to evaluate the effect of an intervening treatment or event by comparing observations made before versus after the treatment.

Pretest-posttest design A nonexperimental design involving one measurement before treatment and one measurement after treatment for a single group of participants.

Pretest–posttest nonequivalent control group design A quasi-experimental research design comparing two nonequivalent groups; one group is measured twice, once before treatment is administered and once after. The other group is measured at the same two times but receives no treatment.

Pretest sensitization *See* sensitization.

Principle of beneficence Belmont Report principle requiring researchers not harm the participants, minimize risks, and maximize possible benefits.

Principle of justice Belmont Report principle requiring fair and

non-exploitative procedures for the selection and treatment of participants so that the costs and benefits of participation are distributed equally, such that participants are representative of the people who may benefit from the research.

Principle of respect for persons Belmont Report principle requiring that individuals should consent to participate in studies (i.e., after learning about the research study, people should be free to decide whether they would like to participate in the study) and those who cannot give their consent, such as children, people with diminished abilities, and prisoners, need special protection. Also known as automomy.

Primary source A firsthand report of observations or research results written by the individual(s) who actually conducted the research and made the observations.

Probability sampling A sampling method in which the entire population is known, each individual in the population has a specifiable probability of selection, and sampling is done using a random process based on the probabilities.

Procedure subsection In a research report, the portion of the method section that describes the step-by-step process used to complete the study.

Progressive error In a research study, changes in the scores observed in one treatment condition that are related to general experience in a research study over time, but not to a specific treatment or treatments. Common kinds of progressive error are practice effects and fatigue.

Proportionate random sampling *See* proportionate stratified random sampling.

Proportionate stratified random sampling A probability sampling

technique that involves identifying specific subgroups to be included, determining what proportion of the population corresponds to each subgroup, and randomly selecting individuals so that the proportion for each subgroup in the sample exactly matches the corresponding proportion in the population. Also known as proportionate random sampling.

Pseudoscience A set of ideas based on nonscientific theory, faith, and belief.

PsycARTICLES A computerized database for searching the psychological literature that contains the full text of the original publication.

PsycINFO A computerized database for searching the psychology literature for articles relevant to a research topic. PsycINFO provides abstracts or summaries for each publication.

Publication Manual of the American Psychological Association A manual that describes conventions for style and structure of written research reports in the behavioral sciences.

Qualitative research Research that is based on observations that are summarized and interpreted in a narrative report.

Quantitative research Research that is based on measuring variables for individual participants or subjects to obtain scores, usually numerical values, that are submitted to statistical analyses for summary and interpretation.

Quasi-experimental research strategy A research strategy that attempts to limit threats to internal validity and produce cause-and-effect conclusions (like an experiment), but lacks one of the critical components—either manipulation or control—that is necessary for a true experiment. Typically compares groups or conditions that are defined with a nonmanipulated variable.

Quasi-independent variable In a quasi-experimental or nonexperimental research study, the variable that differentiates the groups or conditions being compared. Similar to the independent variable in an experiment.

Quota sampling A nonprobability sampling method; a type of convenience sampling involving identifying specific subgroups to be included in the sample and then establishing quotas for individuals to be sampled from each group.

Random assignment A procedure in which a random process is used to assign participants to treatment conditions.

Randomization The use of a random process to help avoid a systematic relationship between two variables. The intent is to disrupt any systematic relationship that might exist between extraneous variables and the independent variable.

Random process A procedure that produces one outcome from a set of possible outcomes. The outcome must be unpredictable each time, and the process must guarantee that each of the possible outcomes is equally likely to occur.

Range effect The clustering of scores at one end of a measurement scale. Ceiling effects and floor effects are types of range effects.

Rationalism *See* rational method.

Rational method A method of acquiring knowledge that involves seeking answers by the use of logical reasoning. Also known as rationalism.

Ratio scale A scale of measurement in which the categories are sequentially organized, all categories are the same size, and the zero point

is absolute or nonarbitrary, and indicates a complete absence of the variable being measured.

Reactivity Participants' modification of their natural behavior in response to the fact that they are participating in a research study or the knowledge that they are being measured. Reactivity is an artifact and can threaten the validity of the measurement, as well as both internal and external validity.

Reference section The section of a research report that lists complete references for all sources of information cited in the report, organized alphabetically by the last name of the first author.

Refutable hypothesis A hypothesis that can be demonstrated to be false. That is, the hypothesis allows the possibility that the outcome will differ from the prediction.

Regression A statistical technique used for predicting one variable from another. The statistical process of finding the linear equation that produces the most accurate predicted values for Y using one predictor variable, X.

Regression equation The equation from a regression analysis.

Regression toward the mean *See* statistical regression.

Reliability The degree of stability or consistency of measurements. If the same individuals are measured under the same conditions, a reliable measurement procedure will produce identical (or nearly identical) measurements.

Repeated-measures design *See* within-subjects design.

Repeated-measures experimental design *See* within-subjects experimental design.

Repeated-measures *t* test In a within-subjects or matched-subjects

design, a hypothesis test that evaluates the statistical significance of the mean difference between two sets of scores obtained from the same group of participants.

Replication Repetition of a research study with the same basic procedures used in the original study. The intent of replication is to test the validity of the original study. Either the replication will support the original study by duplicating the original results, or it will cast doubt on the original study by demonstrating that the original result is not easily repeated.

Representativeness The extent to which the characteristics of the sample accurately reflect the characteristics of the population.

Representative sample A sample with the same characteristics as the population.

Research design A general plan for implementing a research strategy. A research design specifies whether the study will involve groups or individual subjects, will make comparisons within a group or between groups, or specifies how many variables will be included in the study.

Research ethics The responsibility of researchers to be honest and respectful to all individuals who may be affected by their research studies or their reports of the studies' results. Researchers are usually governed by a set of ethical guidelines that assist them to make proper decisions and choose proper actions. In psychological research, the American Psychological Association (APA) maintains a set of ethical principles for research.

Research procedure The exact, step-by-step description of a specific research study.

Research proposal A written report presenting the plan and underlying rationale for a future research study. A proposal includes a review of the relevant background literature, an explanation of how the proposed study is related to other knowledge in the area, a description of how the planned research will be conducted, and a description of the possible results.

Research report A written description of a research study that includes a clear statement of the purpose of the research, a review of the relevant background literature that led to the research study, a description of the methods used to conduct the research, a summary of the research results, and a discussion and interpretation of the results.

Research strategy A general approach to research determined by the kind of question that the research study hopes to answer.

Resentful demoralization A threat to internal validity that occurs when an untreated group learns of special treatment given to another group, and becomes less productive and less motivated because they resent the other group's expected superiority.

Response set On a rating-scale question, a participant's tendency to answer all (or most) of the questions the same way.

Restricted random assignment A random process for assigning individuals to groups that has a limitation to ensure predetermined characteristics (such as equal size) for the separate groups.

Results section The section of a research report that presents a summary of the data and the statistical analysis.

Reversal design A single-case experimental design consisting of a series of phases including a baseline phase followed by a treatment phase

and at least one replication of a baseline followed by a treatment.

Running head The abbreviated title of a research report containing a maximum of 50 characters that appears on the title page and at the top of every page of the manuscript. It also appears at the top of the pages in a published article.

Sample A set of individuals selected from a population, usually intended to represent the population in a research study.

Sampling The process of selecting individuals to participate in a research study.

Sampling bias *See* selection bias.

Sampling error The naturally occurring difference between a sample statistic and the corresponding population parameter.

Sampling methods The variety of ways of selecting individuals to participate in a research study. Also known as sampling techniques or sampling procedures.

Sampling procedures *See* sampling methods.

Sampling techniques *See* sampling methods.

Scale of measurement The set of categories used for classification of individuals. The four types of measurement scales are nominal, ordinal, interval, and ratio.

Scatter plot A graph that shows the data from a correlational study. The two scores for each individual appear as a single point in the graph with the vertical position of the point corresponding to one score and the horizontal position corresponding to the other.

Scientific method A method of acquiring knowledge that uses observations to develop a hypothesis, then uses the hypothesis to make logical predictions that can

be empirically tested by making additional, systematic observations. Typically, the new observations lead to a new hypothesis, and the cycle continues.

Secondary source A description or summary of another person's work, written by someone who did not participate in the research or observations discussed.

Selection bias When participants or subjects are selected in a manner that increases the probability of obtaining a biased sample. A threat to external validity that occurs when the selection process produces a sample with characteristics that are different from those in the population. Also known as sampling bias.

Self-report measure A measurement obtained by asking a participant to describe his or her own attitude, opinion, or behavior.

Sensitization A threat to external validity that occurs when the assessment procedure alters participants so that they react differently to treatment than they would in the real world when the treatment is used without assessment. Also known as assessment sensitization or pretest sensitization.

Significant result *See* statistically significant result.

Simple random sampling A probability sampling technique in which each individual in the population has an equal and independent chance of selection.

Simulation In an experiment, the creation of conditions that simulate or closely duplicate the natural environment in which the behaviors being examined would normally occur.

Single-blind research A research study in which the researcher does not know the predicted outcome for any specific participant.

Single-case designs Experimental research designs that use the results from a single participant or subject to establish the existence of a cause-and-effect relationship. Also known as single-subject designs.

Single-factor analysis of variance A hypothesis test that evaluates the statistical significance of the mean differences among two or more sets of scores obtained from a single-factor multiple-group design. Also known as one-way ANOVA.

Single-factor design A research study with one independent variable or one quasi-independent variable.

Single-factor multiple-group design A research design comparing more than two groups of participants (or groups of scores) representing more than two levels of the same factor.

Single-factor two-group design A research design comparing two groups of participants or two groups of scores representing two levels of a factor. Also known as the two-group design.

Single-subject designs See single-case designs.

Slope constant In the linear equation $Y = bX + a$, b describes the slope of the line (how much Y changes when X is increased by 1 point).

Spearman-Brown formula A formula for computing split-half reliability that corrects for the fact that individual scores are based on only half of the total test items.

Spearman correlation A correlation used with ordinal data or to evaluate monotonic relationships.

Split-half reliability A measure of reliability obtained by splitting the items on a questionnaire or test in half, computing a separate score for each half, and then measuring the degree of consistency between the two scores for a group of participants.

Stability The degree to which a series of observations shows a consistent level or trend.

Standard deviation A measure of variability that describes the average distance from the mean; obtained by taking the square root of the variance.

Standard error A measure of the average or standard distance between a sample statistic and the corresponding population parameter.

Statistic A summary value that describes a sample.

Statistically significant result In a research study, a result that is extremely unlikely (as defined by an alpha level, or level of significance) to have occurred simply by chance. Also known as a significant result.

Statistical regression A statistical phenomenon in which extreme scores (high or low) on a first measurement tend to be less extreme on a second measurement; considered a threat to internal validity because changes in participants' scores could be caused by regression rather than by the treatments. Also known as regression toward the mean.

Statistical significance In a research study, a result or treatment effect that is large enough to be extremely unlikely to have occurred simply by chance.

Statistical significance of a correlation In a correlational study, the correlation in the sample is large enough that it is very unlikely to have been produced by random variation, but rather represents a real relationship in the population.

Stratified random sampling A probability sampling technique that involves identifying specific subgroups to be included in the sample and then selecting equal-sized random samples from each pre-identified subgroup.

Structured observation See contrived observation.

Subject role behavior See subject roles.

Subject roles The different ways that participants respond to experimental cues based on whatever they judge to be appropriate in the situation. Also known as subject role behavior.

Subjects Nonhumans who take part in a research study.

Subjects subsection In a research report, the portion of the method section that describes the nonhumans who participated in the study.

Subject words Terms used to identify and describe the variables in a study. Subject words are used to direct a search in a database.

Survey research design A research study that uses a survey to obtain a description of a particular group of individuals.

Systematic sampling A probability sampling technique in which a sample is obtained by selecting every nth participant from a list containing the total population after a random starting point.

Target population A group defined by a researcher's specific interests; see also population.

Testable hypothesis A hypothesis for which all of the variables, events, and individuals are real and can be defined and observed.

Test-retest reliability The type of reliability established by comparing the scores obtained from two successive measurements of the same individuals and calculating a correlation between the two sets of scores.

Test statistic A summary value computed in a hypothesis test to measure the degree to which the sample data are in accord with the null hypothesis.

Theories In the behavioral sciences, statements about the mechanisms underlying a particular behavior.

Third-variable problem The possibility that two variables appear to be related when, in fact, they are both influenced by a third variable that causes them to vary together.

Threat to external validity Any characteristic of a study that limits the ability to generalize the results.

Threat to internal validity Any factor that allows for an alternative explanation for the results of a study.

Three-factor design A research study involving three independent or quasi-independent variables.

Time-related variables Environmental or participant variables that change over time. A threat to the internal validity of studies that compare measures of the same individuals taken at different times.

Time sampling A technique of behavioral observation that involves observing for one interval, then pausing during the next interval to record all the observations. The sequence of observe–record–observe–record is continued through the series of intervals.

Time-series design A quasi-experimental research design consisting of a series of observations before a treatment or event and a series of observations after the treatment or event. A treatment is a manipulation administered by the researcher and an event is an outside occurrence that is not controlled or manipulated by the researcher.

Title A concise statement of the content of a paper that identifies the main variables being investigated.

Title page The first page of a research report manuscript; contains the running head and page number, the title of the paper, the author names and affiliations, and the author note.

Treatment condition In an experiment, a situation or environment characterized by one specific value of the manipulated variable. An experiment contains two or more treatment conditions that differ according to values of the manipulated variable.

Treatment observations In a single-case research study, observations or measurements made while a treatment is being administered.

Treatment phase In a single-case research study, a series of treatment observations identified by the letter B.

Trend In a single-case research study, a consistent difference in direction and magnitude from one measurement to the next in a series.

True experiment *See* experiment.

Two-factor ANOVA *See* two-way analysis of variance.

Two-factor design A research study involving two independent or quasi-independent variables.

Two-group design *See* single-factor two-group design.

Two-way analysis of variance A hypothesis test that evaluates the statistical significance of the mean differences (both main effects and interaction) obtained in a two-factor research study. Also known as two-factor ANOVA.

Type I error The conclusion, based on a hypothesis test, that a result is statistically significant when, in fact, there is no effect (no relationship) in the population.

Type II error The conclusion, based on a hypothesis test, that a result is not statistically significant when, in fact, a real effect or relationship does exist in the population.

Validity (of a measurement procedure) The degree to which the measurement process measures the variable it claims to measure.

Variables Characteristics or conditions that change or have different values for different individuals.

Variance A measure of variability obtained by computing the average squared distance from the mean.

Variance within groups *See* variance within treatments.

Variance within treatments A measure of the differences between scores for a group of individuals who have all received the same treatment. The intent is to measure naturally occurring differences that have not been caused by a treatment effect. Also known as variance within groups.

Volunteer bias A threat to external validity that occurs because volunteers are not perfectly representative of the general population.

Within-subjects design A research design in which the different groups of scores are all obtained from the same group of participants. Also known as repeated-measures design.

Within-subjects experimental design An experimental design in which the same group of individuals participates in all of the different treatment conditions. Also known as a repeated-measures experimental design.

Y-intercept In the linear equation $Y = bX + a$, a, the Y-intercept is the point at which the line intersects the Y-axis.

REFERENCES

Ackerman, P. L., & Beier, M. E. (2007). Further explorations of perceptual speed abilities in the context of assessment methods, cognitive abilities, and individual differences during skill acquisition. *Journal of Experimental Psychology: Applied, 13,* 249–272.

Ackerman, R., & Goldsmith, M. (2011). Metacognitive regulation of text learning: On screen versus on paper. *Journal of Experimental Psychology: Applied, 17,* 18–32. doi:10.1037/a0022086

Agocha, V. B., & Cooper, M. L. (1999). Risk perceptions and safer-sex intentions: Does a partner's physical attractiveness undermine the use of risk-relevant information? *Personality and Social Psychology Bulletin, 25,* 746–750. doi:10.1177/0146167299025006009

Allport, G. W. (1961). *Pattern and growth in personality.* New York: Holt, Reinhart, and Winston.

American Psychological Association. (1973). Ethical principles in the conduct of research with human participants. *American Psychologist, 28,* 79–80. doi:10.1037/h0038067

American Psychological Association. (2002). Ethical principles of psychologists and code of conduct. *American Psychologist, 57,* 1060–1073. Retrieved from http://www.apa.org/ethics/code2002.html

American Psychological Association (2010). *Ethical principles of psychologists and code of conduct.* Retrieved from http://www.apa.org/ethics/code/principles.pdf

American Psychological Association (2010). *Publication manual of the American Psychological Association* (6th ed.). Washington, DC: Author.

American Psychological Association (2010). 2010 amendments to the 2002 'Ethical principles of psychologists and code of conduct.' *American Psychologist, 65,* 493.

American Psychological Association (2012). *Guidelines for ethical conduct in the care and use of nonhuman animals in research.* Retrieved from http://www.apa.org/science /leadership/care/guidelines.aspx

Anderson, C. A., & Dill, K. E. (2000). Video games and aggressive thoughts, feelings, and behavior in the laboratory and in life. *Journal of Personality and Social Psychology, 78,* 772–790

Anderson, D. R., Huston, A. C., Wright, J. C., & Collins, P. A. (1998). Initial findings on the long term impact of *Sesame Street* and educational television for children: The recontact study. In R. Noll & M. Price (Eds.), *A communication cornucopia: Markle Foundation essays on information policy* (pp. 279–296). Washington, DC: Brookings Institution.

Andison, F. S. (1977). TV violence and viewer aggression: A cumulation of study results. *Public Opinion Quarterly, 41,* 314–331

Aronson, E., & Carlsmith, J. M. (1968). Experimentation in social psychology. In G. Lindzey & E. Aronson (Eds.), *Handbook of social psychology* (2nd ed., Vol. 2, pp. 1–79). Reading, MA: Addison-Wesley.

Asch, S. (1956). Studies of independence and conformity: A minority of one against a unanimous majority. *Psychological Monographs: General and Applied, 76*(9), 1–70.

Babcock, P., & Marks, M. (2010). Leisure college, USA: The decline in student study time. *Education Outlook,* No. 7. Retrieved from http://www.aei.org/article/education /higher-education/leisure-college-usa/

Baker, S. C., & Serdikoff, S. L. (2013). Addressing the role of animal research in psychology. In D. S. Dunn, R. A. R. Gurung, K. Z. Naufel, and J. H. Wilson (Eds.), *Controversy in the psychology classroom. Using hot topics to foster critical thinking* (pp. 105–112). Washington, DC: American Psychological Association.

Baltes, P. B., & Schaie, K. W. (1974). The myth of the twilight years. *Psychology Today, 8,* 35–40.

Barlow, D. H., Nock, M. K., & Hersen, M. (2009). *Single case experimental designs: Strategies for studying\behavior change* (3rd ed.). Boston, MA: Pearson.

Bartholow, B. D., & Anderson, C. A. (2002). Effects of violent video games on aggressive behavior: Potential sex differences. *Journal of Experimental Social Psychology, 38,* 283–290.

Baumrind, D. (1985). Research using intentional deception: Ethical issues revisited. *American Psychologist, 40,* 165–174. doi:10.1037/0003-066X.40.2.165

Bhattacharjee, Y. (Ed.). (2008). Memorable. *Science, 322,* 1765–1765.

Bicard, D. F., Lott, V., Mills, J., Bicard, S., & Baylot-Casey, L. (2012). Effects of text messaged self-monitoring on class attendance and punctuality of at-risk college student athletes. *Journal of Applied Behavior Analysis, 45,* 205–210. doi:10.1901/jaba.2012.45-205

Bornstein, B. H., Golding, J. M., Neuschatz, J. Kimbrough, C., Reed, K., Magyarics, C., & Luecht, K. (2016). *Law and Human Behavior,* Oct. 2016.

Brennan, K. A., & Morris, K. A. (1997). Attachment styles, self-esteem, and patterns of seeking feedback from romantic partners. *Personality and Social Psychology Bulletin, 23,* 23–31. doi:10.1177/0146167297231003

Brooks, M. E., Bichard, S., & Craig, C. (2016). A content analysis of mature adults in super bowl commercials. *Howard Journal of Communications, 27,* 347–366.

Brown, M. V., Flint, M., & Fuqua, J. (2014). The effects of a nutrition education intervention on vending machine sales on a university campus. *Journal of American College Health, 62,* 512–516.

Burke, K. (1974). *The philosophy of literary form: Studies in symbolic action* (3rd ed.). Berkeley, CA: University of California Press.

Burt, C. (1972). Inheritance of general intelligence. *American Psychologist, 27,* 175–190.

Bushman, B. J., & Huesmann, L. R. (2001). Effects of televised violence on aggression. In D. Singer & J. Singer (Eds.), *Handbook for children and the media* (pp. 223–254). Thousand Oaks, CA: Sage.

Camara, W., & Echternacht, G. (2000). *The SAT I and high school grades: Utility in predicting success in college* (College Board Report No. RN-10). New York: College Entrance Examination Board.

Campbell, D. T., & Fiske, D. W. (1959). Convergent and discriminant validation by the multitrait-multimethod matrix. *Psychological Bulletin, 56,* 81–105. doi:10.1037 /h0046016

Campbell, D. T., & Stanley, J. C. (1963). *Experimental and quasi-experimental designs for research.* Chicago: Rand McNally.

Carey, B. (2011, November 3). Fraud case seen as a red flag for psychology research, *New York Times.* Retrieved from http://www.sakkyndig.com/psykologi/artvit/nytimes 2011.pdf

CDC. (1997). Press release: Remarks by the President in apology for study done in Tuskegee. Retrieved from http://www.cdc.gov/tuskegee/clintonp.htm

Cohen, J. (1960). A coefficient of agreement for nominal scales. *Educational and Psychological Measurement, 20,* 37–46. doi:10.1177/001316446002000104

Cohen, J. (1988). *Statistical power analysis for the behavioral sciences* (2nd ed.). New York: Academic Press.

Cohn, E. J., & Rotton, J. (2000). Weather, disorderly conduct, and assaults: From social contact to social avoidance. *Environment and Behavior, 32,* 651–673. doi: 10.1177 /00139160021972720

Collins, R. L., Elliott, M. N., Berry, S. H., Kanouse, D. E., Kunkel, D., Hunter, S. B., & Miu, A. (2004). Watching sex on television predicts adolescent initiation of sexual behavior. *Pediatrics, 114,* e280–289.

Collins, R. L., & Ellickson, P. L. (2004). Integrating four theories of adolescent smoking. *Substance Use & Misuse, 39,* 179–209. doi:10.1081/JA-120028487

Cooper, M. L. (2002). Alcohol use and risky sexual behavior among college students and youth: Evaluating the evidence. *Journal of Studies on Alcohol Supplement, 14,* 101–117.

Craft, M. A., Davis, G. C., & Paulson, R. M. (2013). Expressive writing in early breast cancer survivors. *Journal of Advanced Nursing, 69,* 305–315.

Crafts, L. W., & Gilbert, R. W. (1934). The effect of punishment during learning upon retention. *Journal of Experimental Psychology, 17,* 73–84. doi:10.1037 /h0072744

Craik, F. I. M., & Lockhart, R. S. (1972). Levels of processing: A framework for memory research. *Journal of Verbal Learning and Verbal Behavior, 11,* 671–684. doi:10.1016 /S0022-5371(72)80001-X

Cronbach, L. J. (1951). Coefficient alpha and the internal structure of tests. *Psychometrika, 16,* 297–334. doi:10.1007/BF02310555

DeGoede, K. M., Ashton-Miller, J. A., Liao, J. M., & Alexander, N. B. (2001). How quickly can healthy adults move their hands to intercept an approaching object? Age and gender effects. *Journals of Gerontology: Series A: Biological Sciences and Medical Sciences, 56,* 584–588.

Dillman, D. A., Clark, J. R., & Sinclair, M. A. (1995). How prenotice letters, stamped return envelopes, and reminder postcards affect mailback responses rates for census questionnaires. *Survey Methodology, 21,* 1–7.

Dillman, D. A., Smyth, J. D., & Christian, L. M. (2014). *Internet, mail, and mixed-mode surveys: The tailored design method* (4th ed.). Hoboken, NJ: Wiley.

Dunn, C. M., & Chadwick, G. (1999). *Protecting study volunteers in research: A manual for investigative sites.* Boston, MA: CenterWatch.

Durso, G. R. O., Luttrell, A., & Way, B. M. (2015). Over-the-counter relief from pains and pleasures alike: Acetaminophen blunts evaluation sensitivity to both negative and positive stimuli. *Psychological Science, 26,* 750–758.

Elliot, A. J., Niesta, K., Greitemeyer, T., Lichtenfeld, S., Gramzow, R., Maier, M. A., & Liu, H. (2010). Red, rank, and romance in women viewing men. *Journal of Experimental Psychology: General, 139,* 399–417.

Elstad, J. I., & Bakken, A. (2015). The effects of parental income on Norwegian adolescents' school grades: A sibling analysis. *Acta Sociologica, 58,* 265–283.

Feeney, J. A. (2004). Transfer of attachment from parents to romantic partners: Effects of individual and relationship variables. *Journal of Family Studies, 10,* 220–238.

Feshbach, S., & Singer, R. (1971). *Television and aggression.* San Francisco, CA: Jossey-Bass.

Fisher, C. B., & Fyrberg, D. (1994). Participant partners: College students weigh the costs and benefits of deceptive research. *American Psychologist, 49,* 417–425. doi:10.1037/0003-066X.49.5.417

Fleming, A. P., McMahan, R. J., & King, K. M. (2016). *Prevention Science, 18,* 257–267. doi:10.1007 /s11121-016-0672-1

Fontes, L. A. (2004). Ethics in violence against women research: The sensitive, the dangerous, and the overlooked. *Ethics and Behavior, 14,* 141–174. doi:10.1207/s15327019eb1402

Fossey, D. (1983). *Gorillas in the mist.* Boston, MA: Houghton Mifflin.

Furnes, B., & Dysvik, E. (2012). Therapeutic writing and chronic pain: Experiences of therapeutic writing in a cognitive behavioural programme for people with chronic pain. *Journal of Clinical Nursing, 21,* 3372–3381. doi:10.1111/j.1365-2702.2012.04268.x

Garrett, B. L. (2008). Judging innocence. *Columbia Law Review, 108*, 55–142.

Geiser, S., & Studley, R. (2002). UCX and the SAT: Predictive validity and differential impact of the SAT I and SAT II at the University of California. *Educational Assessment, 8*, 1–26. doi:10.1207/S15326977EA0801_01

Gentile, D. A., Lynch, P. J., Linder, J. R., & Walsh, D. A. (2004). The effects of video game habits on adolescent hostility, aggressive behaviors, and school performance. *Journal of Adolescence, 27*, 5–22. doi:10.1016/j.adolescence.2003.10.002

Gillespie, J. F. (1999). The why, what, how and when of effective faculty use of Institutional Review Boards. In G. Chastain, & R. E. Landrum (Eds.), *Protecting human subjects* (pp. 157–177). Washington, DC: APA.

Glasofer, D. R., Albano, A. M., Simpson, H. B., & Steinglass, J. E. (2016). Overcoming fear of eating: A case study of a novel use of exposure and response prevention. *Psychotherapy, 53*, 223–231.

Goldie, J., Schwartz, L., McConnachie, A., & Morrison, J. (2001). Impact of a new course on students' potential behavior on encountering ethical dilemmas. *Medical Education, 35*(Special Issue), 295–302. doi:10.1046/j.1365-2923.2001.00872.x

Goodall, J. (1971). *In the shadow of man*. Boston, MA: Houghton Mifflin.

Goodall, J. (1986). *The chimpanzees of Gombe: Patterns of behavior*. Cambridge, MA: Harvard University Press.

Greer, B. D., Neidert, P. L., & Dozier, C. L. (2016). A component analysis of toilet training procedures recommended for young children. *Journal of Applied Behavior Analysis, 49*, 69–84.

Guéguen, N., & Jacob, C. (2012, April). Clothing color and tipping: Gentlemen patrons give more tips to waitresses with red clothes. *Journal of Hospitality & Tourism Research*. doi:10.1177/1096348012442546

Hallam, S., Price, J., & Katsarou, G. (2002). The effects of background music on primary school pupils' task performance. *Educational Studies, 28*, 111–122. doi:10.1080/03055690220124551

Haney, C., Banks, C., & Zimbardo, P. (1973). Interpersonal dynamics in a simulated prison. *International Journal of Criminology and Penology, 1*, 69–97.

Harmon, T. M., Nelson, R. O., & Hayes, S. C. (1980). Self-monitoring of mood versus activity by depressed clients. *Journal of Consulting and Clinical Psychology, 48*, 30–38. doi:10.1037/0022-006X.48.1.30

Herbert, J. D., Lilienfeld, S. O., Lohr, J. M., Montgomery, R. W., O'Donohue, W. T., Rosen, G. M., & Tolin, D. F. (2000). Science and pseudoscience in the development of eye movement desensitization and reprocessing: Implications for clinical psychology. *Clinical Psychology Review, 20*, 945–971. doi:10.1016/S0272-7358(99)00017-3

Holmes, D. S. (1976a). Debriefing after psychological experiments I: Effectiveness of post-deception dehoaxing. *American Psychologist, 31*, 858–867. doi:10.1037/0003-066X.31.12.858

Holmes, D. S. (1976b). Debriefing after psychological experiments II: Effectiveness of post-deception desensitizing. *American Psychologist, 31*, 868–875. doi:10.1037/0003-066X.31.12.868

Holmes, T. (2017). Group; healing through sharing, poetry, songs, and stories: Learning through participant observation in rural Victoria. *Journal of Poetry Therapy, 30*, 3–16.

Horn, J. L., & Donaldson, G. (1976). On the myth of intellectual decline in adulthood. *American Psychologist, 31*, 701–719. doi:10.1037/0003-066X.31.10.701

Hornstein, H. A., Fisch, E., & Holmes, M. (1968). Influence of a model's feeling about his behavior and his relevance as a comparison on other observers' helping behavior. *Journal of Personality and Social Psychology, 10*, 222–226. doi:10.1037/h0026568

Huck, S. W., & Sandler, H. M. (1979). *Rival hypotheses: Alternative explanations of data based conclusions*. New York: Harper & Row.

Hunter, J. E. (1997). Needed: A ban on the significance test. *Psychological Science, 8*, 3–7. doi:10.1111/j.1467-9280.1997 .tb00534.x

Ijuin, M., Homma, A., Mimura, M., Kitamura, S., Kawai, Y., Imai, Y., & Gondo, Y. (2008). Validation of the 7-minute screen for the detection of early-stage Alzheimer's disease. *Dementia and Geriatric Cognitive Disorders, 25*, 248–255. doi:10.1159/000115972

James, J. M., & Bolstein, R. (1992). Large monetary incentives and their effect on mail survey response rates. *Public Opinion Quarterly, 56*, 442–453. doi:10.1086/269336

Jones, J. H. (1981). *Bad blood: The Tuskegee syphilis experiment*. New York: Free Press.

Jones, B. T, Jones, B. C. Thomas, A. P., & Piper, J. (2003). Alcohol consumption increases attractiveness ratings of opposite sex faces: A possible third route to risky sex. *Addiction, 98*, 1069–1075. doi:10.1046/j.1360-0443.2003.00426.x

Jones, J. T., Pelham, B. W., Carvallo, M., & Mirenberg, M. C. (2004). How do I love thee, let me count the Js: Implicit egotism and interpersonal attraction. *Journal of Personality and Social Behavior, 87*, 665–683. doi:10.1037/0022-3514.87.5.665

Junco, R. (2015). Student class standing, Facebook use, and academic performance. *Journal of Applied Developmental Psychology, 36*, 18–29. doi:10.1016/j.appdev.2014.11.001

Kamin, L. J. (1974). *The science and politics of IQ*. Potomac, MD: Lawrence Erlbaum.

Kassin, S. M., & Kiechel, K. (1996). The social psychology of false confessions: Compliance, internalization, and confabulation. *Psychological Science, 7*, 125–128. doi:10.1111/j.1467-9280.1996.tb00344.x

Katz, J. (1972). *Experimentation with human beings*. New York: Russell Sage Foundation.

Kazdin, A. E. (2003). *Research design in clinical psychology* (4th ed.). Boston, MA: Allyn and Bacon.

Kazdin, A. E. (2016). Single-case experimental research design. In A. E. Kazdin (Ed.), *Methodological issues and strategies in clinical research* (4th ed., pp. 459–483). Washington DC: American Psychological Association.

Kercood, S., & Grskovic, J. A. (2009). The effects of highlighting on the math computation performance and off-task behavior of students with attention problems. *Education & Treatment of Children, 32,* 231–241.

Killeen, P. R. (2005). An alternative to null-hypothesis significance tests. *Psychological Science, 16,* 345–353. doi:10.1111/j.0956-7976.2005.01538.x

Klohnen, E. C., & Luo, S. (2003). Interpersonal attraction and personality: What is attractive—self similarity, ideal similarity, complementarity, or attachment security? *Journal of Personality and Social Psychology, 83,* 709–722. doi:10.1037/0022-3514.85.4.709

Kuder, G. F., & Richardson, M. W. (1937). The theory of estimation of test reliability. *Psychometrika, 2,* 151–160. doi:10.1007/BF02288391

Kuo, M., Adlaf, E. M., Lee, H., Gliksman, L., Demers, A., & Wechsler, H. (2002). More Canadian students drink but American students drink more: Comparing college alcohol use in two countries. *Addiction, 97,* 1583–1592. doi:10.1046/j.1360-0443.2002.00240.x

La Vaque, T. J., & Rossiter, T. (2001). The ethical use of placebo controls in clinical research: The declaration of Helsinki. *Psychophysiology & Biofeedback, 26,* 23–37. doi: 10.1023/A:1009563504319

Lawrence, E., Barry, R. A., Brock, R. L., Bunde, M., Langer, A., Ro, E., …Dzankovic, S. (2011). The relationship quality interview: Evidence of reliability, convergent and divergent validity, and incremental utility. *Psychological Assessment, 23,* 44–63. doi:10.1037/a0021096

Lederer, A. M., Autry, D. M., Day, C. R. T., & Oswalt, S. B. (2015). The impact of work and volunteer hours on the health of undergraduate students. *Journal of American College Health, 63,* 403–408.

Li, C., Pentz, M. A., & Chou, C. (2002). Parental substance use as a modifier of adolescent substance use risk. *Addiction, 97,* 1537–1550. doi:10.1046/j.1360-0443.2002.00238.x

Liguori, A., & Robinson, J. H. (2001). Caffeine antagonism of alcohol-induced driving impairment. *Drug and Alcohol Dependence, 63,* 123–129. doi:10.1016/S0376-8716(00)00196-4

Likert, R. (1932). A technique for the measurement of attitudes. *Archives of Psychology, 22* (No. 140), 1–55.

Lilienfeld, S. O., Lynn, S. J., & Lohr, J. M. (2003). Science and pseudoscience in clinical psychology: Initial thoughts, reflections, and considerations. In S. O. Lilienfeld, S. J. Lynn, & J. M. Lohr (Eds.), *Science and pseudoscience in clinical psychology* (pp. 1–11). New York: The Guilford Press.

Loftus, G. R. (1996). Psychology will be a much better science when we change the way we analyze data. *Current Directions in Psychological Science, 5,* 161–171. doi:10.1111/1467-8721.ep11512376

Loftus, E. F., & Palmer, J. C. (1974). Reconstruction of automobile destruction: An example of the interaction between language and memory. *Journal of Verbal Learning & Verbal Behavior, 13,* 585–589. doi:10.1016/S0022-5371(74)80011-3

Logue, A. W. (1991). *The psychology of eating and drinking: An introduction* (2nd ed.). New York: W. H. Freeman.

Long, D. M., Uematsu, S., & Kouba, R. B. (1989). Placebo responses to medical device therapy for pain. *Stereotactic & Functional Neurosurgery, 53,* 149–156.

Lord, F. M. (1953). On the statistical treatment of football numbers. *American Psychologist, 8,* 750–751. doi:10.1037/h0063675

McAllister, T. W. Flashman, L. A. Maerlender, A., Greenwald, R. M., Beckwith, J. G., Tosteson, T. D., … Grove, M. R. (2012). Cognitive effects of one season of head impacts in a cohort of collegiate contact sport athletes. *Neurology, 78,* 1777–1784. doi:10.1212 /WNL.0b013e3182582fe7

McHugh, M. B., Tingstrom, D. H., Radley, K. C., Barry, C. T., & Walker, K. M. (2016). Effects of tootling on classwide and individual disruptive and academically engaged behavior of lower-elementary students. *Behavioral Interventions, 31,* 332–354.

McKenna, K. Y., & Bargh, J. A. (2000). Plan 9 from cyberspace: The implications of the Internet for personality and social psychology. *Personality and Social Psychology Review, 4,* 57–75. doi:10.1207/S15327957PSPR0401_6

Melton, G. B., Levine, R. J., Koocher, G. P., Rosenthal, R., & Thompson, W. C. (1988). Community consultation in socially sensitive research: Lessons from clinical trials in treatments for AIDS. *American Psychologist, 43,* 573–581. doi:10.1037/0003-066X.43.7.573

Menzies, H. M., & Lane, K. L. (2012). Validity of the student risk screening scale: Evidence of predictive validity in a diverse, suburban elementary setting. *Journal of Emotional and Behavioral Disorders, 20,* 82–91.

Messerti, F. H. (2012). Chocolate consumption, cognitive function, and Nobel laureates. *The New England Journal of Medicine, 367,* 1562–1564. doi:10.1056/NEJMon1211064

Milgram, S. (1963). Behavioral study of obedience. *Journal of Abnormal and Social Psychology, 67,* 371–378. doi:10.1037/h0040525

Mitchell, K. J., Wolak, J., & Finkelhor, D. (2007). Trends in youth reports of sexual solicitations, harassment and unwanted exposure to pornography on the internet. *Journal of Adolescent Health, 40,* 116–126. doi:10.1016/j.jadohealth.2006.05.021

Mitteer, D. R., Romani, P. W., Greer, B. D., & Fisher, W. W. (2015). Assessment and treatment of pica and destruction of holiday decorations. *Journal of Applied Behavior Analysis, 48,* 912–917. doi:10.1002/jaba.255

Moore, M. J., Barr, E. M., & Johnson, T. M. (2013). Sexual behaviors of middle school students: 2009 youth risk behavior survey results from 16 locations. *Journal of School Health, 83,* 61–68. doi:10.1111/j.1746-1561.2012.00748.x

Mueller, P. A., & Oppenheimer, D. M. (2014). The pen is mightier than the keyboard: Advantages of longhand over laptop note taking. *Psychological Science, 25,* 1159–1168.

Myers, A., & Hansen, C. (2006). *Experimental psychology* (6th ed.). Belmont, CA: Wadsworth.

National Commission for the Protection of Human Subjects of Biomedical and Behavioral Research (1979). *The Belmont Report: Ethical principles and guidelines for the protection of human subjects of research.* Retrieved from http://www. hhs.gov /ohrp/humansubjects/guidance/belmont.htm

National Institute of Health Office of Laboratory Animal Welfare (2015). *Public Health Service policy on humane care and use of laboratory animals.* Retrieved from https://grants.nih.gov/grants/references/phspol.him

National Research Council. (2011). *Guide for the care and use of laboratory animals.* Retrieved from http://grants. nih.gov/grants/OLAW/Guide-for-the-Care-and-Use-of-Laboratory-Animals.pdf

Nicks, S. D., Korn, J. H., & Mainieri, T. (1997). The rise and fall of deception in social psychology and personality research. *Ethics and Behavior, 7,* 69–77. doi:10.1207 /s15327019eb0701

Norman, G. (2010). Likert scales, levels of measurement and the "laws" of statistics. Retrieved from http://www .springerlink.com/content/p111562668125341/

Normand, M. P., & Bailey, J. S. (2006). The effects of celeration lines on visual data analysis. *Behavior Modification, 30,* 295–314. doi:10.1177/0145445503262406

Office of Human Research Protection (1993). *93 Guidebook.* Retrieved from http://www.hhs.gov/ohrp /education-and-outreach/archived-materials/+irb+gui debook&site=OHRP&output=xml_no_dtd&ie=UTF-8&lr=lang_en&client=OHRP&proxystylesheet=ohrp_ drupal&access=p&oe=UTF-8

O'Hara, R., Brooks, J. O., Friedman, L., Schroder, C. M., Morgan, K. S., & Kraemer, H. C. (2007). Long-term effects of mnemonic training in community-dwelling older adults. *Journal of Psychiatric Research, 4,* 585–590. doi:10.1016/j.jpsychires.2006.04.010

Oppenheimer, L. (2006). The belief in a just world and subjective perceptions of society: A developmental perspective. *Journal of Adolescence, 29,* 655–669. doi:10.1016/j.adolescence.2005.08.014

Orne, M. T. (1962). On the social psychology of the psychological experiment: With particular reference to demand characteristics and their implications. *American Psychologist, 17,* 776–783. doi:10.1037/h0043424

Orth, U., Robins, R. W., & Soto, C. J. (2010). Tracking the trajectory of shame, guilt, and pride across the life span. *Journal of Personality and Social Psychology, 99,* 1061–1071.

Paterson, T. S. E., Yeung, S. E., & Thornton, W. L. (2016). Positive affect predicts everyday problem-solving ability in older adults. *Aging and Mental Health, 20,* 871–879.

Perillo, J. T., & Kassin, S. M. (2011). Inside interrogation: The lie, the bluff, and false confessions. *Law and Human Behavior, 35,* 327–337. doi:10.1007/s10979-010-9244-2

Piliavin, I. M., Rodin, J., & Piliavin, J. A. (1969). Good samaritanism: An underground phenomenon. *Journal of Personality and Social Psychology, 13,* 289–299. doi:10.1037/h0028433

Piliavin, J. A., & Piliavin, I. (1972). Effects of blood on reactions to a victim. *Journal of Personality and Social Psychology, 23,* 353–361. doi:10.1037/h0033166

Plomin, R., Corley, R., DeFries, J. C., & Fulker, D. W. (1990). Individual differences in television viewing in early childhood: Nature as well as nurture. *Psychological Science, 1,* 371–377.

Polman, H., de Castro, B. O., & van Aken, M. A. G. (2008). Experimental study of the differential effects of playing versus watching violent video games on children's aggressive behavior. *Aggressive Behavior, 34,* 256–264. doi:10.1002/ab.20245

Pope, H. G., Ionescu-Pioggia, M., & Pope, K. W. (2001). Drug use and life style among college undergraduates: A 30-year longitudinal study. *American Journal of Psychiatry, 158*(Special Issue), 1519–1521. doi:10.1176 /appi.ajp.158.9.1519

Posner, M. I., & Badgaiyan, R. D. (1998). Attention and neural networks. In R. W. Parks & D. S. Levine (Eds.), *Fundamentals of neural network modeling: Neuropsychology and cognitive neuroscience* (pp. 61–76). Cambridge, MA: The MIT Press.

Quirin, M., Kazén, M., & Kuhl, J. (2009). When nonsense sounds happy or helpless: The implicit positive and negative affect test (IPANAT). *Journal of Personality and Social Psychology, 97,* 500–516. doi:10.1037/a0016063

Ray, W. J. (2000). *Methods: Toward a science of behavior and experience* (6th ed.). Bellmont, CA: Wadsworth.

Rea, L. M., & Parker, R. A. (2014). *Designing and conducting survey research: A comprehensive guide* (4th ed.). San Francisco: Jossey-Bass.

Reich, W. T. (Ed.). (1995). *Encyclopedia of bioethics: Revised edition* (vol. 3). New York: Simon & Schuster.

Resenhoeft, A., Villa, J., & Wiseman, D. (2008). Tattoos can harm perceptions: A study and suggestions. *Journal of American College Health, 56,* 593–596.

Ring, K., Wallston, K., & Corey, M. (1970). Mode of debriefing as a factor affecting subjective reaction to a Milgram-type obedience experiment: An ethical inquiry. *Representative Research in Social Psychology (University of North Carolina, Department of Psychology), 1,* 67–88.

Romanov, L. (2006). *Car carma.* Toronto: InsuranceHotline.com.

Rosenhan, D. L. (1973). On being sane in insane places. *Science, 179,* 250–258.

Rosenthal, R., & Fode, K. L. (1963). The effect of experimenter bias on the performance of the albino rat. *Behavioral Science, 8,* 183–189.

Rosenthal, R., & Rosnow, R. (1975). *The volunteer subject.* New York: Wiley.

Rosnow, R., & Rosenthal, R. (1997). *People studying people: Artifacts and ethics in behavioral research.* New York: W. H. Freeman.

Rubin, Z. (1985). Deceiving ourselves about deception. Comment on Smith and Richardson's "Amelioration of deception and harm in psychological research." *Journal of Personality and Social Psychology, 48,* 252–253. doi:10.1037/0022-3514.48.1.252

Rucklidge, J. J. (2009). Successful treatment of OCD with a micronutrient formula following partial response to cognitive behavioral therapy (CBT): A case study. *Journal of Anxiety Disorders, 23,* 836–840. doi:10.1016/j.janxdis.2009.02.012

Sales, B. D., & Folkman, S. (2000). *Ethics in research with human participants.* Washington, DC: APA.

Schmidt, S. R. (1994). Effects of humor on sentence memory. *Journal of Experimental Psychology: Learning, Memory, & Cognition, 20,* 953–967. doi:10.1037/0278-7393.20.4.953

Scoville, W. B., & Milner, B. (1957). Loss of recent memory after bilateral hippocampal lesions. *Journal of Neurology, Neurosurgery, and Psychiatry, 20,* 11–21. doi:10.1136/jnnp.20.1.11

Sears, D. (1986). College sophomores in the laboratory: Influences of a narrow data base on social psychology's view of human nature. *Journal of Personality and Social Psychology, 51,* 515–530. doi:10.1037/0022-3514.51.3.515

Seery, M. D., Holman, E. A., & Silver, R. C. (2010). Whatever does not kill us: Cumulative lifetime adversity, vulnerability, and resilience. *Journal of Personality and Social Psychology, 99,* 1025–1041. doi:10.1037/a0021344

Shrauger, J. S. (1972). Self-esteem and reactions to being observed by others. *Journal of Personality and Social Psychology, 23,* 192–200. doi:10.1037/h0033046

Skjoeveland, O. (2001). Effects of street parks on social interactions among neighbors. *Journal of Architectural and Planning Research, 18(Special Issue),* 131–147.

Smith, S. S., & Richardson, D. (1983). Amelioration of deception and harm in psychological research: The important role of debriefing. *Journal of Personality and Social Psychology, 44,* 1075–1082. doi:10.1037/0022-3514.44.5.1075

Stanley, B., Sieber, J., & Melton, G. (1996). *Research ethics: A psychological approach.* Lincoln, NE: University of Nebraska Press.

Stephens, R., Atkins, J., & Kingston, A. (2009). Swearing as a response to pain. *NeuroReport: For Rapid Communication of Neuroscience Research, 20,* 1056–1060. doi:10.1097/WNR.0b013e32832e64b1

Stewart, K. K., Carr, J. E., Brandt, C. W, & McHenry, M. M. (2007). An evaluation of the conservative dual-criterion method for teaching university students to visually inspect AB-design graphs. *Journal of Applied Behavior Analysis, 40,* 713–718. doi:10.1901/jaba.2007.713-718

Strack, F., Martin, L. L., & Stepper, S. (1988). Inhibiting and facilitating conditions of the human smile: A nonobtrusive test of the facial feedback hypothesis. *Journal of Personality and Social Psychology, 54,* 768–777. doi:10.1037/0022-3514.54.5.768

Sun, Y. (2001). Family environment and adolescents' well-being before and after parents' marital disruption: A longitudinal analysis. *Journal of Marriage and Family, 63,* 697–713. doi:10.1111/j.1741-3737.2001.00697.x

Szuchman, L. T. (2014). *Writing with style: APA style made easy* (6th ed.). Belmont, CA: Thomson Wadsworth.

Thigpen, C. H., & Cleckley, H. M. (1954). A case of multiple personality. *Journal of Abnormal and Social Psychology, 49,* 135–151.

Thigpen, C. H., & Cleckley, H. M. (1957). *Three faces of Eve.* New York: McGraw-Hill.

Thompson, T., Webber, K., & Montgomery, I. (2002). Performance and persistence of worriers and non-worriers following success and failure feedback. *Personality & Individual Differences, 33,* 837–848. doi:10.1016/S0191-8869(01)00076-9

Tilburg University (2011). Interim report regarding the breach of scientific integrity committed by prof. D. A. Stapel. (PDF, 385KB), *Tilburg University,* 1–21.

Trockel, M. T., Barnes, M. D., & Egget, D. L. (2000). Health-related variables and academic performance among first-year college students: Implications for sleep and other behaviors. *Journal of American College Health, 49,* 125–131.

Tversky, A., & Kahneman, D. (1973). Availability: A heuristic for judging frequency and probability. *Cognitive Psychology, 5,* 207–232. doi:10.1016/0010-0285(73)90033-9

United States Department of Agriculture (2013). *Animal Welfare Act.* Retrieved from https://www.nal.usda.gov/awic/animal-welfare-act

Van Emmerik, A. A. P., Kamphuis, J. H., & Emmelkamp, P. M. G. (2008). Treatment of acute stress disorder and posttraumatic stress disorder with cognitive behavioral therapy or structured writing therapy. A randomized controlled trial. *Psychotherapy & Psychosomatics, 77,* 93–100.

Verfaellie, M., & McGwin, J. (2011). The case of Diederik Stapel. *Psychological Science Agenda.* Retrieved from http://www.apa.org/science/about/psa/2011/12/diederik-stapel.aspx

Wager, T. D., & Smith, E. E. (2003). Neuroimaging studies of working memory: A meta-analysis. *Cognitive, Affective & Behavioral Neuroscience, 3,* 255–274. doi:10.3758/CABN.3.4.255

Wager, T. D., Rilling, J. K., Smith, E. E., Sokolik, A., Casey, K. L., Davidson, R. J., … Cohen, J. D. (2004). Placebo-induced changes in fMRI in the anticipation and experience of pain. *Science, 303,* 1162–1167.

Wang, S., & Repetti, R. L. (2016). Who gives to whom? Testing the support gap hypothesis with naturalistic observations of couple interactions. *Journal of Family Psychology, 30,* 492–502.

Weber, S. J., & Cook, T. D. (1972). Subject effects in laboratory research: An examination of subject roles, demand characteristics, and valid inferences. *Psychological Bulletin, 77,* 273–295. doi:10.1037/h0032351

Wilkinson, L., & Task Force on Statistical Inference (1999). Statistical methods in psychology journals. *American Psychologist, 54,* 594–604. doi:10.1037/0003-066X.54. 8.594

Wolak, J., Mitchell, K. J., & Finkelhor, D. (2002). Close online relationships in a national sample of adolescents. *Adolescence, 37,* 441–455.

Wolosin, R., Sherman, S., & Mynat, C. (1972). Perceived social influence in a conformity situation. *Journal of Personality and Social Psychology, 23,* 184–191. doi: 10.1037/h0033041

Wright, K. B. (2005). Researching Internet-based populations: Advantages and disadvantages of online survey research, online questionnaire authoring software packages, and Web survey services. *Journal of Computer-Mediated Communication, 10*(3), article 11. Retrieved from http://jcmc.indiana.edu/vol10/issue3/wright.html

Young, S. N. (2002). The ethics of placebo in clinical psychopharmacology: The urgent need for consistent regulation. *Journal of Psychiatry & Neuroscience, 27,* 319–321.

NAME INDEX

SUBJECT INDEX